HOLT
SCIENCE &
TECHNOLOGY

CALIFORNIA

Earth
Science

HOLT, RINEHART AND WINSTON

A Harcourt Classroom Education Company

Austin • New York • Orlando • Atlanta • San Francisco • Boston • Dallas • Toronto • London

Staff Credits

Editorial

Robert W. Todd, Executive Editor

David F. Bowman, Managing Editor

Robert Tucek, Senior Editor

Leigh Ann Garcia, Timothy Pierce, Clay Walton, Robin Goodman (Feature Articles)

ANNOTATED TEACHER'S EDITION

Jim Ratcliffe, Bill Burnside, Kelly Graham

ANCILLARIES

Jennifer Childers, Senior Editor

Erin Bao, Kristen Karns, Andrew Strickler, Clay Crenshaw, Wayne Duncan, Molly Frohlich, Amy James, Monique Mayer, Traci Maxwell

COPYEDITORS

Steve Oelenberger, Copyediting Supervisor

Suzanne Brooks, Brooke Fugitt, Tania Hannan, Denise Nowotny

EDITORIAL SUPPORT STAFF

Christy Bear, Jeanne Graham, Rose Segrest, Tanu'e White

EDITORIAL PERMISSIONS

Catherine J. Paré, Permissions Manager

Jan Harrington, Permissions Editor

Art, Design, and Photo

BOOK DESIGN

Richard Metzger, Art Director

Marc Cooper, Senior Designer

David Hernandez, Designer

Alicia Sullivan (ATE), **Cristina Bowerman** (ATE), **Eric Rupprath** (Ancillaries)

IMAGE SERVICES

Elaine Tate, Art Buyer Supervisor

Erin Cone, Art Buyer

PHOTO RESEARCH

Jeannie Taylor, Senior Photo Researcher

Andy Christiansen, Photo Researcher

PHOTO STUDIO

Sam Dudgeon, Senior Staff Photographer

Victoria Smith, Photo Specialist

DESIGN NEW MEDIA

Susan Michael, Art Director

DESIGN MEDIA

Joe Melomo, Art Director

Shawn McKinney, Designer

Production

Mimi Stockdell, Senior Production Manager

Beth Sample, Production Coordinator

Suzanne Brooks, Sara Carroll-Downs

Media Production

Kim A. Scott, Senior Production Manager

Nancy Hargis, Production Supervisor

Adriana Bardin, Production Coordinator

New Media

Jim Bruno, Senior Project Manager

Lydia Doty, Senior Project Manager

Jessica Bega, Project Manager

Armin Gutzmer, Manager Training and Technical Support

Cathy Kuhles, Nina Degollado

Design Implementation and Production

Mazer Corporation

X 259117

Printed in the United States of America
ISBN 0-03-055667-8
    4 5 6 7 8 048 05 04 03 02 01

Acknowledgments

Chapter Writers

Kathleen Meehan Berry
Earth Science Teacher
Canon-McMillan Senior
    High School
Canonsburg, Pennsylvania

Robert H. Fronk, Ph.D.
*Chair of Science and
    Mathematics Education
    Department*
Florida Institute of Technology
West Melbourne, Florida

Kathleen Kaska
Life and Earth Science Teacher
Lake Travis Middle School
Austin, Texas

Linda Ruth Berg, Ph.D.
*Adjunct Professor–Natural
    Sciences*
St. Petersburg Junior College
St. Petersburg, Florida

William G. Lamb, Ph.D.
Science Teacher and Dept. Chair
Oregon Episcopal School
Portland, Oregon

Peter E. Malin, Ph.D.
Professor of Geology
Division of Earth and Ocean
    Sciences
Duke University
Durham, North Carolina

Robert J. Sager
*Chair and Professor of Earth
    Sciences*
Pierce College
Tacoma, Washington

Lab Writers

Kenneth Creese
Science Teacher
White Mountain Junior
    High School
Rock Springs, Wyoming

Linda A. Culp
Science Teacher and Dept. Chair
Thorndale High School
Thorndale, Texas

Bruce M. Jones
Science Teacher and Dept. Chair
The Blake School
Minneapolis, Minnesota

Shannon Miller
Science Teacher
Llano Junior High School
Llano, Texas

Robert Stephen Ricks
Special Services Teacher
Alabama State Department
    of Education
Montgomery, Alabama

James J. Secosky
Science Teacher
Bloomfield Central School
Bloomfield, New York

Academic Reviewers

Mead Allison, Ph.D.
*Assistant Professor of
    Oceanography*
Texas A & M University
Galveston, Texas

**David M. Armstrong,
    Ph.D.**
Professor of Biology
Department of EPO Biology
University of Colorado
Boulder, Colorado

Alissa Arp, Ph.D.
*Director and Professor of
    Environmental Studies*
Romberg Tiburon Center
San Francisco State University
Tiburon, California

Paul D. Asimow, Ph.D.
Postdoctoral Research Fellow
Lamont-Doherty Earth
    Observatory
Columbia University
Palisades, New York

**Russell M. Brengelman,
    Ph.D.**
Professor of Physics
Morehead State University
Morehead, Kentucky

John A. Brockhaus, Ph.D.
Associate Professor
Department of Geography and
    Environmental Engineering
United States Military
    Academy
West Point, New York

Peter E. Demmin, Ed.D.
*Former Science Teacher and
    Department Chair*
Amherst Central High School
Amherst, New York

Roy Hann, Ph.D.
Professor of Civil Engineering
Texas A & M University
College Station, Texas

Frederick R. Heck, Ph.D.
Professor of Geology
Ferris State University
Big Rapids, Michigan

Richard N. Hey, Ph.D.
Professor of Geophysics
Hawaii Institute of Geophysics
    and Planetology
University of Hawaii
Honolulu, Hawaii

John E. Hoover, Ph.D.
Associate Professor of Biology
Millersville University
Millersville, Pennsylvania

**Robert W. Houghton,
    Ph.D.**
Professor
Lamont-Doherty Earth
    Observatory
Columbia University
Palisades, New York

John L. Hubisz, Ph.D.
Professor of Physics
North Carolina State
    University
Raleigh, North Carolina

Steven A. Jennings, Ph.D.
Assistant Professor
Department of Geography &
    Environmental Studies
University of Colorado
Colorado Springs, Colorado

Eric Lee Johnson, Ph.D.
Assistant Professor of Geology
Central Michigan University
Mount Pleasant, Michigan

John Kermond, Ph.D.
Visiting Scientist
NOAA–Office of Global
    Programs
Silver Spring, Maryland

Zavareh Kothavala, Ph.D.
Postdoctoral Associate Scientist
Kline Geology Laboratory
Yale University
New Haven, Connecticut

Valerie Lang, Ph.D.
*Project Leader of Environmental
    Programs*
The Aerospace Corporation
Los Angeles, California

Duane F. Marble, Ph.D.
Professor Emeritus
Department of Geography and
    Natural Resources
Ohio State University
Columbus, Ohio

Joseph A. McClure, Ph.D.
Associate Professor
Department of Physics
Georgetown University
Washington, D.C.

Frank K. McKinney, Ph.D.
Professor of Geology
Appalachian State University
Boone, North Carolina

Joann Mossa, Ph.D.
Associate Professor of Geography
University of Florida
Gainesville, Florida

LaMoine L. Motz, Ph.D.
Coordinator of Science Education
Department of Learning
    Services
Oakland County Schools
Waterford, Michigan

Acknowledgments (cont.)

Barbara Murck, Ph.D.
Assistant Professor of Earth Science
Erindale College
University of Toronto
Mississauga, Ontario
CANADA

Hilary C. Olson, Ph.D.
Research Associate
Institute for Geophysics
The University of Texas
Austin, Texas

John R. Reid, Ph.D.
Professor Emeritus
Department of Geology and Geological Engineering
University of North Dakota
Grand Forks, North Dakota

Gary Rottman, Ph.D.
Associate Director
Laboratory for Atmosphere and Space Physics
University of Colorado
Boulder, Colorado

Dork L. Sahagian, Ph.D.
Professor
Institute for the Study of Earth, Oceans, and Space
University of New Hampshire
Durham, New Hampshire

Jack B. Swift, Ph.D.
Professor of Physics
The University of Texas
Austin, Texas

Lynne D. Talley, Ph.D.
Professor and Research Oceanographer
Scripps Institution of Oceanography
University of California, San Diego
La Jolla, California

Glenn Thompson, Ph.D.
Scientist
Geophysical Institute
University of Alaska
Fairbanks, Alaska

Martin VanDyke, Ph.D.
Professor of Chemistry Emeritus
Front Range Community College
Westminister, Colorado

Mollie Walton, Ph.D.
Scientist
U.S. Dept. of Agriculture–ARS
Jornada Experimental Range
Las Cruces, New Mexico

Thad A. Wasklewicz, Ph.D.
Assistant Professor of Geography
Colgate University
Hamilton, New York

Hans Rudolf Wenk, Ph.D.
Professor of Geology and Geophysical Sciences
University of California
Berkeley, California

Lisa D. White, Ph.D.
Associate Professor of Geosciences
San Francisco State University
San Francisco, California

Lorraine W. Wolf, Ph.D.
Associate Professor of Geology
Auburn University
Auburn, Alabama

Charles A. Wood, Ph.D.
Chairman and Professor of Space Studies
University of North Dakota
Grand Forks, North Dakota

Safety Reviewer

Jack Gerlovich, Ph.D.
Associate Professor
School of Education
Drake University
Des Moines, Iowa

Teacher Reviewers

Barry L. Bishop
Science Teacher and Dept. Chair
San Rafael Junior High School
Ferron, Utah

Daniel L. Bugenhagen
Science Teacher and Dept. Co-chair
Yutan Junior & Senior High School
Yutan, Nebraska

Yvonne Brannum
Science Teacher and Dept. Chair
Hine Junior High School
Washington District of Columbia

Kenneth Creese
Science Teacher
White Mountain Junior High School
Rock Springs, Wyoming

Linda A. Culp
Science Teacher and Dept. Chair
Thorndale High School
Thorndale, Texas

Alonda Droege
Science Teacher
Pioneer Middle School
Steilacom, Washington

Rebecca Ferguson
Science Teacher
North Ridge Middle School
North Richland Hills, Texas

Laura Fleet
Science Teacher
Alice B. Landrum Middle School
Ponte Vedra Beach, Florida

Jennifer Ford
Science Teacher and Dept. Chair
North Ridge Middle School
North Richland Hills, Texas

C. John Graves
Science Teacher
Monforton Middle School
Bozeman, Montana

Janel Guse
Science Teacher and Dept. Chair
West Central Middle School
Hartford, South Dakota

Gary Habeeb
Science Teacher
Sierra–Plumas Joint Unified School District
Downieville, California

Dennis Hanson
Science Teacher and Dept. Chair
Big Bear Middle School
Big Bear Lake, California

Norman Holcomb
Science Teacher
Marion Local Schools
Maria Stein, Ohio

Roberta Jacobowitz
Science Teacher
C.W. Otto Middle School
Lansing, Michigan

Tracy Jahn
Science Teacher
Berkshire Junior–Senior High School
Canaan, New York

David D. Jones
Science Teacher
Andrew Jackson Middle School
Cross Lanes, West Virginia

Howard Knodle
Science Teacher
Belvidere High School
Belvidere, Illinois

Michael E. Kral
Science Teacher
West Hardin Middle School
Cecilia, Kentucky

Kathy LaRoe
Science Teacher
East Valley Middle School
East Helena, Montana

Scott Mandel, Ph.D.
Director and Educational Consultant
Teachers Helping Teachers
Los Angeles, California

Jason Marsh
Science Teacher
Montevideo High and Country School
Montevideo, Minnesota

Acknowledgments continue on page 616

Contents in Brief

Contents

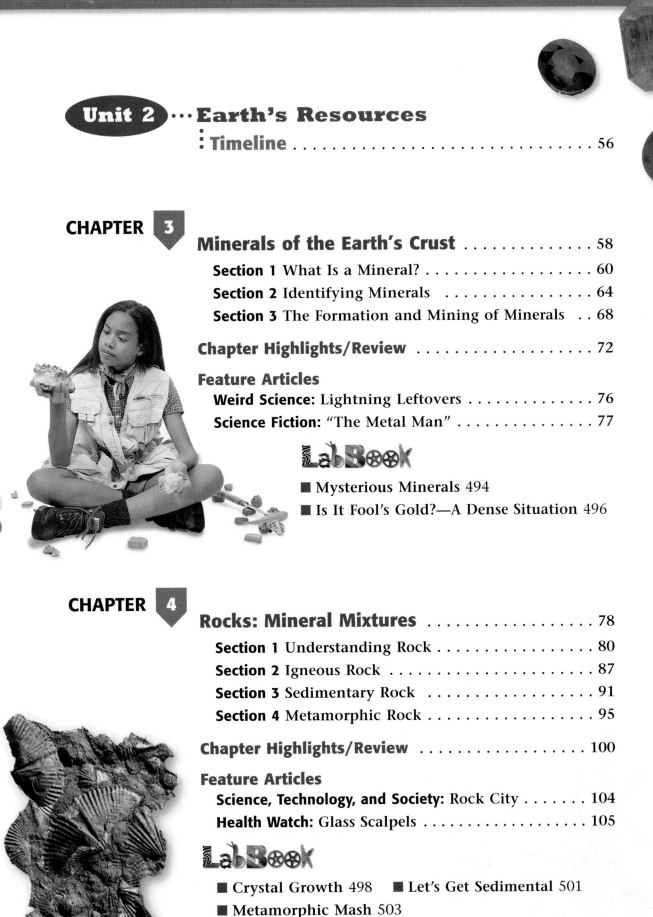

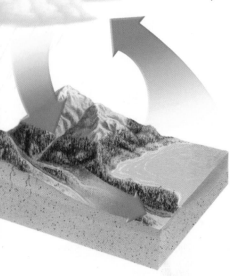

Unit 4 ··· Reshaping the Land

CHAPTER 10

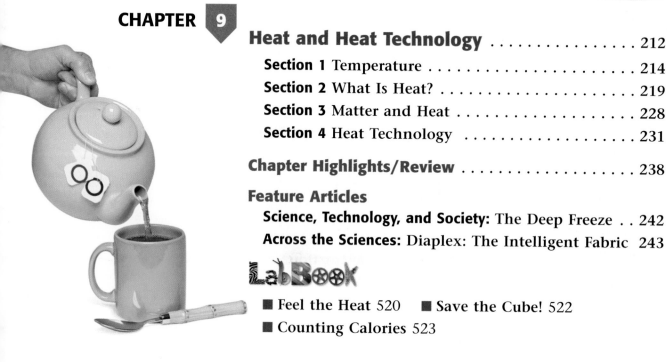

CHAPTER 17

Now is the time to Investigate!

Science is a process in which investigation leads to information and understanding. The **Investigate!** at the beginning of each chapter helps you gain scientific understanding of the topic through hands-on experience.

*Quick*Lab

Not all laboratory investigations have to be long and involved.

The **QuickLabs** found throughout the chapters in this book require only a small amount of time and limited equipment. But just because they are quick, don't skimp on the safety.

$\div \quad 5 \div \quad ^\Omega \quad \leq \infty \quad +_\Omega \quad ^\sqrt{} \quad 9 \quad \infty \quad ^\leq \quad \Sigma \quad 2$
$+$

MATH **BREAK**

Science and math go hand in hand.

The **MathBreaks** in the margins of the chapters show you many ways that math applies directly to science and vice versa.

APPLY

Science can be very useful in the real world.

It is interesting to learn how scientific information is being used in the real world. You can see for yourself in the **Apply** features. You will also be asked to apply your own knowledge. This is a good way to learn!

Connections

astronomy CONNECTION

One science leads to another.

You may not realize it at first, but different areas of science are related to each other in many ways. Each **Connection** explores a topic from the viewpoint of another science discipline. In this way, areas of science merge to improve your understanding of the world around you.

chemistry CONNECTION

oceanography CONNECTION

physics CONNECTION

physical science CONNECTION

environmental science CONNECTION

life science CONNECTION

weather CONNECTION

Feature Articles

ACROSS THE SCIENCES

Science, Technology, and Society

EYE ON THE ENVIRONMENT

Feature articles for any appetite!
Science and technology affect us all in many ways. The following articles will give you an idea of just how interesting, strange, helpful, and action-packed science and technology are. At the end of each chapter, you will find two feature articles. Read them and you will be surprised at what you learn.

Eureka!

Health WATCH

SCIENTIFIC DEBATE

Science Fiction

WEIRD SCIENCE

UNIT

1

Introduction to Earth Science

In this unit, you will start your own investigation of the planet Earth and of the regions of space beyond it. But first you should prepare yourself by learning about the tools and methods used by Earth scientists. As you can imagine, it is not easy to study something as large as the Earth or as far away as Venus. Yet that is what Earth scientists do. The timeline shown here identifies a few of the events that have helped shape our understanding of Earth.

1669

Nicolaus Steno accurately describes the process by which living organisms become fossils.

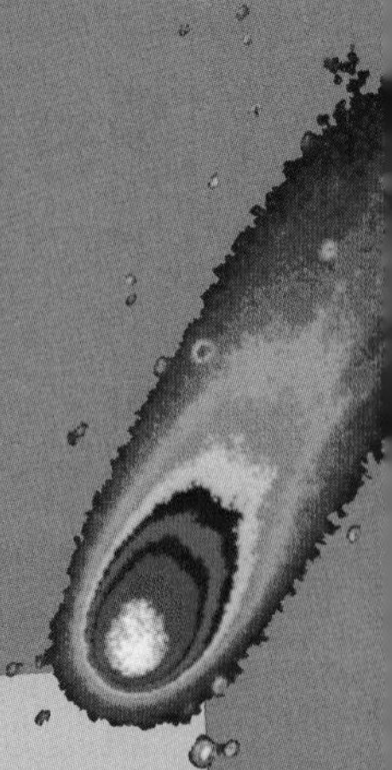

1758

Halley's comet makes a reappearance, confirming Edmond Halley's 1705 prediction. Unfortunately, the comet reappeared 16 years after his death.

1943

The volcano *Paricutín* grows more than 150 m tall during its first six days of eruption.

1960

The first weather satellite, *Tiros I*, is launched by the United States.

1962

By reaching an altitude of 95 km, the *X-15* becomes the first fixed-wing plane to reach outer space.

1896

The first modern Olympic Games are held in Athens, Greece.

1899

The Rosetta stone is discovered in Egypt. It enables scholars to decipher Egyptian hieroglyphics.

1906

Roald Amundsen determines the position of the magnetic north pole.

1922

Roy Chapman Andrews discovers fossilized dinosaur eggs in the Gobi Desert. They are the first such eggs to be found.

1997

China begins construction of Three Gorges Dam, the world's largest dam. Designed to control the Yangtze River, the dam will supply 84 billion kilowatt-hours of hydroelectric power per year.

1970

The United States holds its first Earth Day on April 22. More than 20 million people participate in peaceful demonstrations to show their concern for the environment.

1990

The Hubble Space Telescope is launched into orbit. Three years later, faulty optics are repaired during a space walk.

CHAPTER 1
The World of Earth Science

This Really Happened!

The year was 1979. The place was a hot, wind-swept mesa in northwestern New Mexico. Two hikers were on their way to see some 1,000-year-old American Indian rock carvings on a sandstone cliff. Just before reaching the site, however, the hikers came across a row of several huge half-buried tailbones. What kind of animal could these bones possibly have come from? Judging by the size of the bones, the hikers guessed that they had belonged to some kind of dinosaur. What they didn't realize was just how important that dinosaur would turn out to be.

These hikers happened to stumble on their discovery, but their actions illustrate several qualities of Earth scientists. First, the hikers were observers. They did not simply trek right over the half-hidden bones without paying attention. Instead, they looked at the bones carefully. Earth scientists use observations as a primary tool in their work. The hikers' observations then led them to ask a question—what type of animal did these bones come from? Scientists also ask questions about things in nature they do not understand. Finally, the hikers guessed at what type of animal the bones might have come from. In a similar manner, scientists make educated guesses to answer the questions they ask. A scientist's guess is given a special name—*hypothesis.*

In this chapter you will learn how Earth scientists investigate the world we live in. You too can practice the things Earth scientists do as you begin your adventure through the world of Earth science.

In your ScienceLog, try to answer the following questions based on what you already know:

1. How many kinds of Earth scientists are there?

2. What is the scientific method?

3. What is the difference between a physical model and a mathematical model?

A Little Bit of Science

You are about to take a journey through the world of Earth science. While different scientists study many different things, they each encounter questions and problems that they try to answer and solve. Earth scientists must often rely on indirect measurements using tools to sense things that are beyond the reach of their own five senses. In this activity, you'll discover how limited senses can restrict your ability to learn about the unknown.

Procedure

1. Put on a pair of latex or plastic **gloves.** Make sure they are snug around your fingers.

2. Your teacher will supply you with a **coffee can** to which a **sock** has been attached. Do not look into the can.

3. Reach your gloved hand through the opening in the sock and into the can. You will be able to feel several objects inside the can.

4. Try to determine what the objects are by feeling them, moving them around, shaking the can, etc. Again, do not look into the can.

5. In your ScienceLog, make a list of the items that you think are in the can. State some reasons for your decisions.

6. Finally, pour the contents of the can onto your desk and see what was in the can.

Analysis

7. Were you correct in figuring out what was in the can?

8. Which items confused you? Why?

9. What characteristics of the objects were you not able to identify while they were in the can? Which of your five senses was needed to identify each of these characteristics?

10. What does the glove between your hand and the object represent? Explain.

11. How does this activity compare to the way scientists must study the Earth?

Going Further

Think about the types of things an Earth scientist might study. Would that scientist ever get to "open the can"? Explain.

Branches of Earth Science

OBJECTIVES

- List major branches of Earth science.
- Identify branches of Earth science that are linked to other areas of science.
- Describe careers associated with different branches of Earth science.

Planet Earth! How can anyone study something as large and complicated as our planet? One way is to divide the study of Earth into pieces. It's easier to study something large and complicated if you break it down into smaller, simpler things. Scientists divide the study of the physical planet Earth into three general categories—*geology, oceanography,* and *meteorology. Astronomy* is the study of all physical things beyond planet Earth. Let's take a look at each of these four sciences and at some of the people who work within them. Then we'll look at a few other areas of science that relate to these four.

Geology—Science that Rocks

Geology is the study of the solid Earth. Anything and everything that has to do with the solid Earth is part of geology. Most geologists specialize in a particular aspect of the Earth.

Would you like to put on an insulated suit and walk to the edge of a 1,000°C pool of lava? If so, you could be a *volcanologist,* a geologist who studies volcanoes. Are earthquakes more to your liking? Then you could be a *seismologist,* a geologist who studies earthquakes. How about digging up dinosaurs? You could be a *paleontologist,* a geologist who studies fossils. These are only a few of the careers you could have as a geologist.

Some geologists become highly specialized. For instance, geologist Robert Fronk, at the Florida Institute of Technology, explores the subsurface of Earth by scuba-diving in underwater caves in Florida and the Bahamas. Fronk says, "Bahamians call caves in the ocean floor 'blue holes.' This describes them well. From the surface, they are usually dark blue surrounded by bright white sand." Underwater caves often contain evidence that sea level was once much lower than it is now. They contain *stalagmites* and *stalactites,* as shown in **Figure 1.** These formations develop from minerals in dripping water in air-filled caves. When Fronk sees these kinds of geologic formations in underwater caves, he knows that the caves were once above sea level.

Figure 1 *Stalagmites grow upward from the floors of caves, and stalactites grow downward from the ceilings of caves. Both formations develop over millions of years in air-filled caves.*

Oceanography—Water, Water Everywhere

Oceanography, which is the study of the ocean, is often divided into four areas: physical oceanography, biological oceanography, geological oceanography, and chemical oceanography. Physical oceanographers study things like waves and ocean currents. Biological oceanographers study the plants and animals that live in the ocean. Geological oceanographers study the ocean floor. Chemical oceanographers study natural chemicals and chemicals from pollution in the ocean.

Not long ago, people studied the ocean only from the surface. But as technology has advanced, scientists have worked with engineers to build miniature research submarines. Now oceanographers can go practically anywhere in the oceans. Below, oceanographer John Trefry talks about a trip he took in the minisub *Alvin.*

"We move through the darkness of the Pacific Ocean at a depth of almost one and a half miles [2.2 km] with the lights of the submersible shining on the glassy black rock that is new ocean crust. Then, in a magic moment, we can peer ahead through a small porthole at a 300°C [572°F] black smoker surrounded by an oasis of beautiful and exotic life-forms. The feeling of exhilaration inspires renewed wonderment and makes the many years of study in oceanography seem so satisfying and worthwhile. What a beautiful Earth! What a great career!"

Trefry and other oceanographers have discovered one of the most exciting oceanographic finds of the twentieth century—the world of the black smokers. *Black smokers* are rock chimneys on the ocean floor that spew black clouds of minerals. Black smokers are a type of *hydrothermal vent,* which is a crack in the ocean floor that releases very hot water from beneath the Earth's surface. The minerals and hot water from these vents support a biological community like no other on Earth—one that does not depend on sunlight. Animals that call this community home include blood-red tube worms that are 3.5 m long, clams that are 30 cm in diameter, and blind white crabs.

*Quick*Lab

How Hot Is 300°C?

1. Use a **thermometer** to measure the air's temperature in the room in degrees Celsius. Record your reading.
2. Hold the thermometer near a **heat source** in the room, such as a light bulb or a heating vent. Be careful not to burn yourself. Record your reading.
3. How do the temperatures you recorded compare with the 300°C temperature of the water from a black smoker? Write your answer and observations in your ScienceLog.

Meteorology—It's a Gas!

You might think that meteorology is the study of meteors. Not a bad guess, but not quite right. *Meteors* are the flashes of light seen when objects fall from space into our atmosphere. **Meteorology,** however, is the study of the entire atmosphere.

When you ask, "Is it going to rain today?" you are asking a meteorological question. One of the most common careers in meteorology is weather forecasting. Sometimes knowing what the weather is going to be like makes our lives more comfortable. And occasionally our lives depend on these forecasts.

Figure 2 *This satellite photo of Hurricane Andrew shows the storm at three different positions. You can trace Andrew's path from the Atlantic Ocean (right) to the Gulf of Mexico (left).*

Hurricanes In 1928, a major hurricane hit Florida and killed 1,836 people. In comparison, a hurricane of similar strength—Hurricane Andrew, shown in **Figure 2**—hit Florida in 1992, killing only 48 people. Why were there far fewer deaths in 1992? Two major reasons were hurricane tracking and weather forecasting.

Meteorologists began tracking Hurricane Andrew on Monday, August 17. By the following Sunday morning, most South Floridians had left the coast because the National Hurricane Center had warned them that Andrew was headed their way. Hurricane Andrew hit southern Florida early on Monday morning, August 24. The hurricane caused a lot of damage, but it killed very few people thanks to meteorologists' warnings.

Figure 3 *Too close for comfort? Not for Howard Bluestein and his tornado-chasing team. These meteorologists risk their lives to gather data.*

Tornadoes Another dangerous weather element is tornadoes. An average of 780 tornadoes touch down each year in the United States. What do you think about a meteorologist who chases tornadoes as a career? Howard Bluestein does just that. Bluestein predicts where tornadoes are likely to form and then drives to within a couple of kilometers of the site to gather data, as shown in **Figure 3**. By gathering data this way, scientists like Bluestein hope to understand tornadoes better. The better they understand them, the better they can predict how these violent storms will behave.

Astronomy—Far, Far Away

How do you study things that are far away in space? That's a question that astronomers can answer. **Astronomy** is the study of all physical things beyond Earth. Astronomers study stars, asteroids, planets, and everything else in space.

Because most things in space are too far away to sense directly, astronomers depend on technology to help them study objects in space. Astronomers use a variety of instruments. Optical telescopes have been used for hundreds of years—Galileo built one in 1609. Astronomers still use optical telescopes to look into space, but they also use other types of telescopes. For example, the radio telescopes shown in **Figure 4** allow astronomers to study objects that are too far away to be seen using optical telescopes or that do not give off visible light.

Astronomers spend much of their time studying stars. Astronomers estimate that there are 100 billion billion stars in the sky. That's a lot of stars! Try the MathBreak at right to get an idea of how many stars there are.

The most familiar star in the universe is the sun, which is the closest star to Earth. Astronomers have studied the sun more than any other star. Astronomers have also studied planets that are close to Earth. **Figure 5** illustrates the sun, the Earth, and some nearby planets. Can you name these planets?

Figure 4 *These radio telescopes receive radio waves from space. Researchers use computers to turn the radio waves into visible data that they can study.*

Figure 5 *Astronomers know more about the sun and other nearby objects than they know about objects that are farther away in space.*

MATH BREAK

Lots of Zeros!

Astronomers estimate that there are more than 100 billion billion stars in the sky! One billion written out in numerals looks like this:

1,000,000,000

1. How many zeros do you need in order to write 100 billion billion in numerals? To find out, multiply 1 billion by 1 billion, then multiply your answer by 100. Count the zeros in the final answer.

2. Now time how long it takes you to count to 100. How long would it take you to count to 100 a billion billion times?

Special Branches of Earth Science

In addition to the main branches of Earth science, there are branches that depend more heavily on other areas of science. Earth scientists often find themselves in careers that rely on life science, chemistry, physics, and many other areas of science. Let's take a look at some Earth science careers with strong ties to other sciences.

Ecology It is difficult to understand the behavior of certain organisms without studying the relationships between these organisms and their surroundings. Ecologists study ecosystems, like the one in **Figure 6.** An **ecosystem** is a community of organisms and their nonliving environment. The principles of ecology are useful in many related fields, such as wildlife management, agriculture, forestry, and conservation. The science of ecology requires people trained in many disciplines, such as biology, geology, chemistry, climatology, mathematics, and computer technology.

Geochemistry As the name implies, geochemistry combines the studies of geology and chemistry. Geochemists, like the one in **Figure 7,** specialize in the chemistry of rocks, minerals, and soil. They study the chemistry of these materials to determine their economic value, interpret what the environment was like when they formed, and learn what has happened to them since they first formed.

Figure 6 *Because beavers spend time in water as well as on land, they share their ecosystem with many plants and animals, such as fishes, turtles, birds, reeds, and trees.*

Is there water on Mars? Turn to page 31 to see how one geophysicist is finding out.

Figure 7 *This geochemist is taking rock samples from the field so she can perform chemical analyses of them in her laboratory.*

Environmental Science Humans have recently begun to examine their relationship with their surroundings, or *environment,* more closely. The study of how humans interact with the environment is called *environmental science.* As shown in **Figure 8,** one common task of an environmental scientist is trying to find out whether humans are damaging the environment. Pollution of the air, water, and land can harm natural resources, such as wildlife, drinking water, and soil. Environmental science, which relies on life science, chemistry, physics, and geology, is helping us to preserve Earth's resources and to use them more wisely.

Figure 8 *This environmental scientist is testing the effects of industry on the environment.*

Geography and Cartography Geographers, who are educated in geology, life science, and physics, study the surface features of the Earth. Cartographers make maps of those features. Have you ever wondered why our cities are located where they are? Often, the location of a city is determined by geography. Many cities, such as the one in **Figure 9,** were built near rivers, lakes, or oceans because boats were used for transporting people and items of trade. Rivers and lakes also provide communities with plenty of water for drinking and for raising crops and animals. We make maps to record the geography of our world. Maps help us keep track of natural resources and navigate the surface of the Earth.

Figure 9 *The easily accessible Mississippi River helped St. Louis become the large city it is today.*

REVIEW

1. List three major branches of Earth Science.

2. Name two branches of Earth science that rely heavily on other areas of science. Explain how the branches rely on the other areas of science.

3. List and describe three Earth-science careers.

4. **Inferring Relationships** If you were a *hydrogeologist,* what kind of work would you do?

Explore

Find and cut out a newspaper article about some topic in Earth science. After reading the article, classify it according to one of the following areas—geology, meteorology, oceanography, or astronomy.

The Scientific Method in Earth Science

Seismosaurus hallorum

Imagine that you are standing in a thick forest on the bank of a river. The sun is shining through the needles of the trees. You notice that the vegetation quickly becomes sparse not far from the river and that the land is much more open. Insects are buzzing, but no birds are flying because they don't yet exist. It is the Jurassic period, 150 million years ago.

Wading in the shallow water, several long-necked dinosaurs quietly munch on vegetation. As you peer through the trees, you spot a different type of dinosaur on the prowl for prey. It is about 12 m long and appears to weigh about 4 tons. It is an allosaur, the most common meat-eating predator of this time.

Suddenly you feel the ground begin to shake. The tremors are slight at first, but they grow stronger. You begin to hear a booming noise that accompanies the tremors. The allosaur stops and looks in the direction of the sound. Startled pterosaurs, winged reptiles, fly noisily by. The booming gets louder, and the tremors get stronger.

Suddenly you notice a creature's head looming over the treetops. The creature's head is so high that its neck must be 20 m long! Then the entire animal comes into view. You understand why the ground is shaking. The animal is *Seismosaurus hallorum* (SEIZ moh SAWR uhs hah LOHR uhm), the "earth shaker." You are looking at one of the largest dinosaurs known.

The scene you just witnessed is not based on imagination alone. Scientists have been studying dinosaurs for years. From the bits and pieces of information they gather about dinosaurs and their environment, scientists re-create what the Earth might have been like 150 million years ago. But how do scientists tell one dinosaur species from another? How do they know if they have discovered a new species? The answers to these questions are related to the methods that scientists use.

Steps of the Scientific Method

When scientists make observations about the natural world, they are often presented with a question or problem. But scientists don't just throw out random answers. Instead, they follow a series of steps called the *scientific method*. The **scientific method** is a series of steps that scientists use to answer questions and solve problems. The most basic steps are illustrated in **Figure 10.**

Although the scientific method has several distinct steps, it is not a rigid procedure. Scientists may use all of the steps or just some of the steps of the scientific method. They may even repeat some of the steps or do them in a different order. The goal of the scientific method is to come up with reliable answers and solutions. As long as scientists use the scientific method effectively, the overall result is the same—they gain more insight into the problems they investigate.

BRAIN FOOD

Several species of dinosaurs are claimed to be the largest known. So which is the largest? Good scientists look carefully at the information available and judge for themselves.

Figure 10 *The scientific method is illustrated in this flowchart. Notice that there are several ways to follow the paths.*

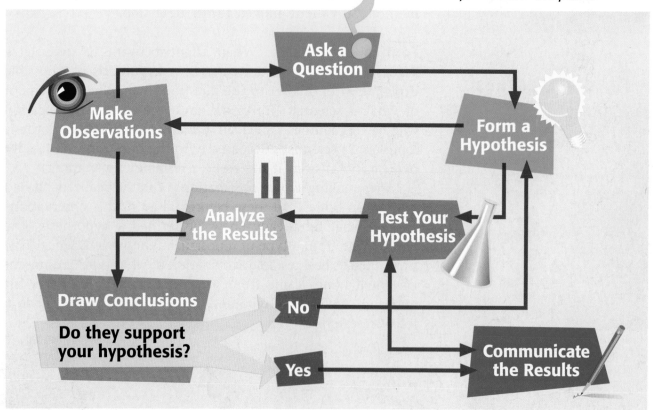

Dino Discovery—A Case for the Scientific Method

One of the first things a scientist does, even before starting an investigation, is make observations. An **observation** is any use of the senses to gather information. While observations can be made at any time, it is observations of objects and events in nature that lead to scientific investigations.

Remember the hikers at the beginning of this chapter and their discovery of dinosaur bones in the desert? Those hikers may have been the first to examine the bones, but they weren't the last. In May 1985, paleontologist David D. Gillette visited the site. Excited by what he saw, Gillette began to wonder what type of dinosaur these huge bones came from. As you will see, this started him on the path to using the scientific method.

Ask a Question

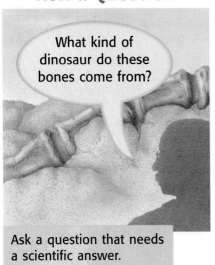

What kind of dinosaur do these bones come from?

Ask a question that needs a scientific answer.

Ask a Question When scientists make observations, they often have questions that they would like answered. Good scientists recognize these questions as the potential beginning of an investigation. When scientists try to answer these questions, they begin to change from passive observer to active investigator.

Gillette may have asked, "What type of dinosaur did these bones come from?" He recognized this question as the beginning of a scientific investigation. Gillette knew that in order to answer this question, he would have to use the scientific method. So Gillette moved to the next step.

Form a Hypothesis

These bones come from a brand-new dinosaur!

Propose a possible answer to the question.

Form a Hypothesis When scientists want to investigate a question, they form a *hypothesis*. A **hypothesis** is a possible explanation or answer to the question. It may be a statement of what a scientist thinks the outcome of an investigation will be. Sometimes called an *educated guess*, the hypothesis represents a scientist's best answer to the question. But it can't be just any answer. It has to be a testable explanation.

After making closer observations, Gillette realized he had never seen bones like these before. Based on his observations and on what he already knew, he formed a hypothesis—the bones came from a type of dinosaur unknown to science. This was Gillette's best testable explanation of what type of dinosaur the fossil bones came from. If correct, it would answer his question. To test his hypothesis, Gillette would have to do a lot of research.

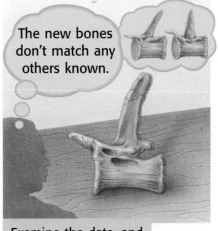

Scientists exploring the Texas Gulf Coast have discovered American Indian artifacts that are thousands of years old. The odd thing about it is that the artifacts were buried in the sea floor several meters below sea level. These artifacts were in-place, meaning that they had not been moved since they were originally buried. The *observation* is that there are American Indian artifacts several meters below sea level, and the *question* is, "Why are they there?" Your job is to *form a hypothesis* that answers this question. Remember, your hypothesis must be stated in such a way that it can be tested using the scientific method.

Test the Hypothesis Once a hypothesis is established, it must be tested. Scientists test hypotheses by gathering data that can help determine whether the hypotheses are valid or not. Often a scientist will run experiments to test a hypothesis.

To test a hypothesis, a scientist may conduct a controlled experiment. *A controlled experiment* is an experiment that tests only one factor at a time. By changing only one factor (the *variable*), scientists can see the results of just that one change. Experiments are often done in laboratories, where conditions are more easily controlled. Earth scientists, however, usually rely more heavily on observations to test their hypotheses. The Earth scientist's laboratory is the Earth itself, where variables cannot be easily controlled. Instead of trying to control nature, Earth scientists more often observe nature and collect large amounts of data to test their hypotheses.

To test his hypothesis, Gillette gathered all the data he could find. He took hundreds of measurements of the bones, carefully documenting their size and shape. He then compared his measurements with those of tailbones from known dinosaurs. He visited museums and talked with other paleontologists. His testing took more than a year to complete.

Analyze the Results Once scientists finish their tests, they must analyze the results. In this step, scientists often create tables and graphs to organize their data. When Gillette analyzed the results of the bone comparisons, he found that the bones of the mystery dinosaur were either too large or shaped too differently to have belonged to any of the dinosaurs he used for comparison.

Test the Hypothesis

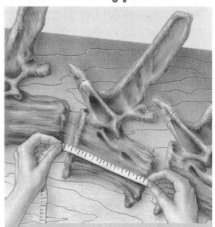

Test the hypothesis with observations or experiments.

Analyze the Results

The new bones don't match any others known.

Examine the data, and look for patterns.

The World of Earth Science **15**

Draw Conclusions

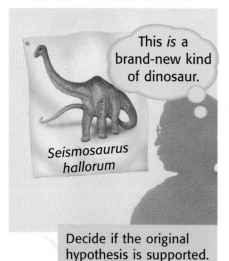

Seismosaurus hallorum

This *is* a brand-new kind of dinosaur.

Decide if the original hypothesis is supported.

Communicate Results

I'd like to introduce *Seismosaurus*!

Share your discoveries with other scientists.

Draw Conclusions Finally, after carefully analyzing the results of their tests, scientists must draw conclusions. Scientists must conclude whether the results supported the hypothesis. If the hypothesis was not supported, scientists may repeat the investigation to check for errors. Or they may ask new questions and form a new hypothesis.

Based on all his analyses, Gillette concluded that the eight bones found in New Mexico were indeed from a newly discovered dinosaur species that was probably 45 m long and weighed at least 100 tons. The creature certainly fit the name Gillette gave it—*Seismosaurus hallorum,* the "earth shaker."

Communicate Results Upon completing an investigation, scientists communicate their results. In this way, scientists share what they have learned with other scientists, who may want to repeat the investigation to see if they get the same results. Science depends on the sharing of information.

Scientists share information by publishing reports in scientific journals or by sharing their information over the Internet. Scientists also give lectures on the results of their scientific investigations at conferences, seminars, or other professional meetings. This method is appealing because it allows other scientists to ask questions directly to the scientist who performed the investigation.

Figure 11 *This reconstruction of the skeleton of* Seismosaurus hallorum *is based on Gillette's research. The bones shown in the darker color are those that have so far been identified.*

Gillette communicated his results by holding a press conference at the New Mexico Museum of Natural History and Science. There he announced his discovery of *Seismosaurus*, carefully answered questions, and defended his investigation. Gillette later submitted a report to the *Journal of Vertebrate Paleontology* that summarized his investigation. After two years of careful checking by other scientists, the journal published Gillette's report.

Case Closed?

All of the *Seismosaurus* bones that Gillette found have been dug up, but the *Seismosaurus* project continues in a laboratory phase as the remains of one of the largest dinosaurs ever discovered are still being studied. Like so many other scientific investigations, Gillette's work led to new problems to be explored using the scientific method.

Figure 12 *David Gillette continues to study the bones of* Seismosaurus *for new insights into the past.*

REVIEW

1. What is the scientific method? How do scientists use it?

2. After observing eight tailbones, Gillette hypothesized that they were from a newly discovered dinosaur species. What was his hypothesis based on?

3. Why do scientists communicate the results of their investigations?

4. **Applying Concepts** Why might two scientists develop different hypotheses based on the same observations?

To try your hand at using the scientific method, turn to page 486 in the LabBook.

Section 3

Life in a Warmer World— An Earth Science Model

NEW TERMS

global warming
model
theory

OBJECTIVES

- Demonstrate how models are used in science.
- Compare mathematical models with physical models.
- Determine limitations of models.

There has been a lot of talk lately about changes in Earth's climate. Some people think the world is getting dangerously warm; others say it is only a natural cycle. But what would happen if Earth's average surface-air temperature rose only a few degrees? Look at **Figure 13;** the answers might surprise you.

A worldwide increase in temperature is called **global warming.** Is global warming really happening? What would cause global warming? To answer these questions, many scientists are studying the concept of global warming. One way they study global warming is by making a model of it.

Figure 13 *A rise in Earth's average surface-air temperature would affect the world in many ways.*

Rotting Remains The rate of decay of plant and animal remains would increase if the Earth's temperature rose. This in turn would increase the amount of carbon dioxide (CO_2) released into the atmosphere. Later in this section, you will see that this is an important concern.

Ice Is Nice Warmer temperatures would mean that much of the sea ice near the North and South Poles would melt. Also, areas of the Earth that now have permanently frozen ground, such as some subpolar and mountainous regions, would thaw.

Rain, Rain, Go Away Overall, there would be more rain. This is because warmer air causes more evaporation from oceans, lakes, and streams. More water vapor in the atmosphere would lead to more rain. Some areas of the world might benefit from the extra water, but other areas might experience flooding and lose fertile soil.

Water, Water Everywhere As temperatures increased, the volume of the oceans would expand, causing sea level to rise. Melting ice would also add water, making sea level rise even more. In states such as Florida and New York, millions of people live in cities near the coast at an elevation of 8 m above sea level or less. If sea level rose only 8 m, these cities would be underwater!

Types of Scientific Models

You are probably familiar with many types of models—models of ships, cars, planes, buildings, and other objects. **Models** are representations of objects or systems. Models are used to represent things that are too small to see, such as atoms, or too large to completely see, like the Earth or the solar system. Models can also be used to explain the past and present as well as to predict the future. Scientific models come in three major types.

across the sciences
CONNECTION

All the Earth's a magnet. Turn to page 30 to learn about Earth's magnetic field.

Physical Models Physical models are models that you can touch. Model airplanes, car kits, and dolls are all physical models. Physical models should look and act just like the real thing. For example, engineers put very accurate models of new airplanes in wind tunnels, as shown in **Figure 14,** to see how aerodynamic they are. It is safer and less expensive to discover problems with models than with real planes.

Mathematical Models Every day, people try to predict the weather. One way they do this is by making climate models, because weather patterns are part of the Earth's climate systems. Climate models, however, are not physical representations of climate. Instead, they are mathematical models. A mathematical model is made up of mathematical equations and data. Some mathematical models are so complex that only supercomputers can handle them. Climate models include information from meteorologists, oceanographers, and ecologists. These models are complicated, but then so is trying to predict the weather!

Conceptual Models The third type of model is a conceptual model, or system of ideas. These take the form of theories. A **theory** is a unifying explanation for a broad range of hypotheses and observations that have been supported by testing. Atomic theory and the big bang theory can be thought of as conceptual models. Conceptual models are composed of many hypotheses, each of which has found support through the scientific method.

Figure 14 *Models of airplanes are tested in models of wind, as shown here by a prototype jet inside a wind tunnel.*

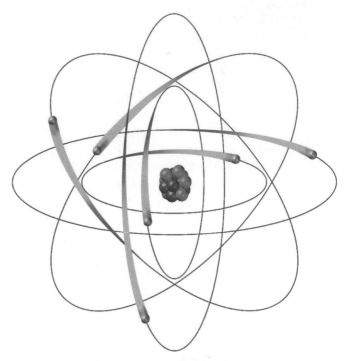

Figure 15 *Atoms are not really made up of tiny colored balls, but using a model like this helps scientists understand atoms.*

The World of Earth Science **19**

The Greenhouse Effect—A Piece of the Global-Warming Model

All models have pieces. A model ship, for example, may contain hundreds of pieces that are glued together. Mathematical models also contain pieces. The pieces are numbers that represent pieces of information that describe real events. Thousands of these pieces may be used in a single model. The global-warming model is a mathematical model that depends on such information. One of the pieces used in the global-warming climate model is the *greenhouse effect.*

A greenhouse is a building made mostly of glass in which plants are grown. If you have been in a greenhouse, you know that it is usually warmer inside than outside. This is because sunlight not only heats the greenhouse directly after passing through the glass, but also reflects off the Earth's surface, producing heat that is trapped inside the greenhouse. The greenhouse effect, shown in **Figure 16,** works a lot like a greenhouse made of glass.

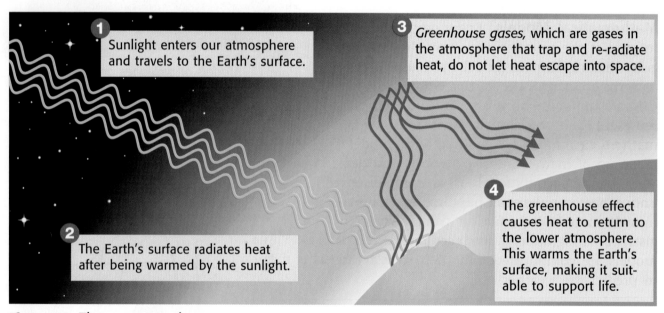

1. Sunlight enters our atmosphere and travels to the Earth's surface.

2. The Earth's surface radiates heat after being warmed by the sunlight.

3. *Greenhouse gases,* which are gases in the atmosphere that trap and re-radiate heat, do not let heat escape into space.

4. The greenhouse effect causes heat to return to the lower atmosphere. This warms the Earth's surface, making it suitable to support life.

Figure 16 *The more greenhouse gases there are in the atmosphere, the greater the greenhouse effect is. When the amount of greenhouse gases increases, so does the temperature on Earth.*

Testing the Global-Warming Model

Models are used to try to explain the present. But how do we know if models are accurate? Physical, mathematical, and conceptual models can be tested. For instance, we can compare the model of a car with the real car. Similarly, we can compare our climate model's prediction of Earth's climate with Earth's actual climate. If the model can accurately explain the present, then we can be more confident that the model will be able to accurately predict the future.

Scientists have estimated the amount of carbon dioxide that has been added to the atmosphere over the last 100 years. The model should therefore be able to predict how much warmer the atmosphere is today than it was 100 years ago. Most climate models tell us that overall global warming due to increased greenhouse gases during the last 100 years should be between 0.5°C and 1.5°C. Now comes the test: How much global warming has actually taken place? The answer is 0.5°C. So far so good!

Using the Global-Warming Model

Models are used to predict the future. Models are good for asking, "What if?"

What will happen if we try to decrease the amount of greenhouse gases by using natural gas instead of coal?

What will happen if people use more-fuel-efficient engines?

Since trees take in CO_2, what will happen if we reduce the number of trees we cut down each year?

What will happen if we cut our CO_2 emissions in half over the next 50 years?

These are the kinds of questions that many nations are asking as they enter the new millennium. The global-warming climate model can give them answers, but will these answers be accurate? The more complicated models are, the more careful scientists must be when using them to make predictions. Climate models are extremely complicated, so scientists often use words like *possible* and *probable* when making climate predictions. The only certain test of these models is the test of time.

REVIEW

1. How might a scientist use a model to test a new airplane design?

2. How are astronomers limited when they design models of the universe?

3. **Analyzing Relationships** Name one advantage of physical models and one advantage of mathematical models.

Measurement and Safety

Hundreds of years ago, different countries used different systems of measurement. These systems were developed from local customs and were often not interchangeable. At one time in England, the standard for an inch was three grains of barley placed end to end. Other standardized units of the modern English system, which is used in the United States, were once based on parts of the body, such as the foot. Such units were not very accurate because they were based on objects that varied in size.

Eventually people recognized that there was a need for a global measurement system that was simple and accurate. In the late 1700s, the French Academy of Sciences set out to develop that system. Over the next 200 years, the metric system, now called the International System of Units (SI), was refined.

Using the Same System

Figure 17 *Prefixes are used with SI units to convert them to larger or smaller units. For example,* kilo *indicates 1,000 times, and* milli *indicates 1/1,000 times. The prefix used depends on the size of the object being measured.*

Today most scientists and almost all countries use the International System of Units. One advantage of using SI measurements is that it helps all scientists to share and compare their observations and results. Another advantage of SI is that all units are based on the number 10, which is a number that is easy to use in calculations. The table in **Figure 17** contains the commonly used SI units for length, volume, mass, and temperature.

Common SI Units		
Length 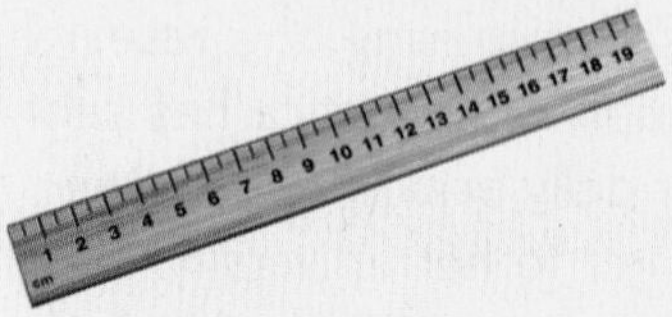	**meter (m)**	
	kilometer (km)	1 km = 1,000 m
	decimeter (dm)	1 dm = 0.1 m
	centimeter (cm)	1 cm = 0.01 m
	millimeter (mm)	1 mm = 0.001 m
	micrometer (µm)	1 µm = 0.000001 m
	nanometer (nm)	1 nm = 0.000000001 m
Volume 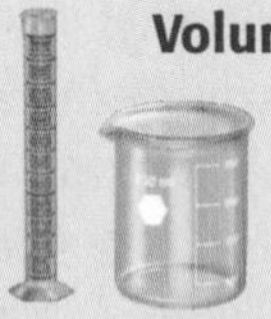	**cubic meter (m^3)**	
	cubic centimeter (cm^3)	$1\ cm^3 = 0.000001\ m^3$
	liter (L)	$1\ L = 1\ dm^3 = 0.001\ m^3$
	milliliter (mL)	$1\ mL = 0.001\ L = 1\ cm^3$
Mass 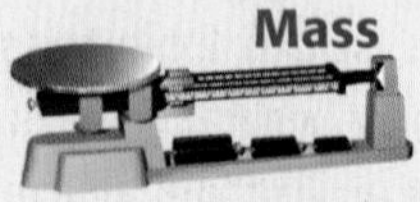	**kilogram (kg)**	
	gram (g)	1 g = 0.001 kg
	milligram (mg)	1 mg = 0.000001 kg
Temperature 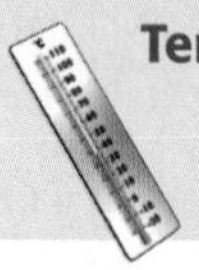	**Kelvin (K)**	
	Celsius (°C)	0°C = 273 K
		100°C = 373 K

Length How thick is the ice sheet in **Figure 18?** To describe this length, an Earth scientist would probably use meters (m). A **meter** is the basic unit of length in the SI system. A meter is divided or multiplied by powers of 10 to produce the other SI units of length. If you divide 1 m into 100 parts, each part equals 1 cm. In other words, 1 cm is one-hundredth of a meter. If you divide 1 m into 1,000 parts, each part equals 1 mm. This means that 1 mm is one-thousandth of a meter. Although that seems pretty small, some objects are so tiny that even smaller units must be used. To describe the length of microscopic objects, micrometers (µm) or nanometers (nm) are used. Going the other way, 1,000 m is equal to one kilometer. **Figure 19** shows how the units of length relate to various objects.

Figure 18 *This scientist is measuring the thickness of an ice sheet. Which unit of length would best describe this length?*

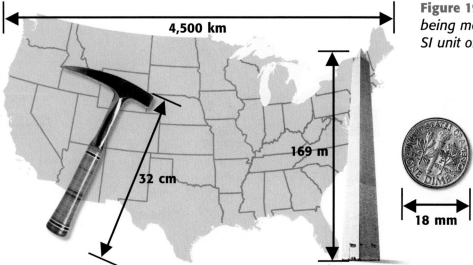

Figure 19 *The size of the object being measured determines which SI unit of length is used.*

4,500 km

169 m

32 cm

18 mm

Volume Imagine that you're a scientist who needs to move some fossils to a museum. How many fossils will fit into a crate? That depends on the volume of the crate and the volume of each fossil. **Volume** is the amount of space that something occupies, or, as in the case of the crate, the amount of space that something contains.

The volume of a liquid is often given in liters (L). Liters are based on the meter. A cubic meter (m^3) is equal to 1,000 L. In other words, 1,000 L of liquid will fit into a box 1 m on each side. You're probably more familiar with a 2 L soda bottle. Just like the meter, the liter can be divided into smaller units. A milliliter (mL) is one-thousandth of a liter and is equal to one cubic centimeter (1 cm^3). A microliter (µL) is one-millionth of a liter. Graduated cylinders are used to measure the volume of liquids.

Explore

Measure the width of your desk, but do not use a ruler or a tape measure. Pick an object to use as your unit of measurement. It could be a pencil, your hand, or anything else. Find how many units wide your desk is, and compare your measurement with those of your classmates. In your ScienceLog, explain why it is important to use standard units of measurement.

Figure 20 *The volume of the crate chosen by this scientist is just right for storing the fossil she is holding.*

The volume of a large solid object is given in cubic meters (m³). The volumes of smaller objects, such as the crate in **Figure 20,** can be given in cubic centimeters (cm³) or cubic millimeters (mm³). To calculate the volume of a box-shaped object, multiply the object's length by its width by its height.

Objects like fossils and rocks have irregular shapes. If you multiplied only their length, width, and height, you would not get a very accurate measure of their volume. One way to determine the volume of an irregularly shaped object is to measure how much liquid the object displaces. The student in **Figure 21** is measuring the volume of a rock by placing it in a graduated cylinder that contains a known quantity of water. The rock causes the level of the water to rise. The student can find the volume of the rock by subtracting the volume of the water alone from the volume of the water and the rock.

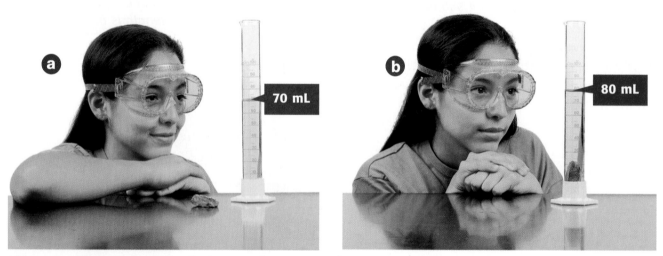

Figure 21 *This graduated cylinder contains 70 mL of water. After the rock was added, the water level moved to 80 mL. Because the rock displaced 10 mL of water, and because 1 mL = 1 cm³, the volume of the rock is 10 cm³.*

Mass How large of a boulder can a rushing stream move? That depends on the energy of the stream and the mass of the boulder. **Mass** is the amount of matter that something is made of. The kilogram (kg) is the basic unit for mass and is used to describe the mass of things like boulders. Many common objects are not so large, however. Grams (one-thousandth of a kilogram) are used to describe the mass of smaller objects. A medium-sized apple, for example, has a mass of about 100 g. The mass of very large objects is given in metric tons. A metric ton equals 1,000 kg.

Temperature How hot is a lava flow? To answer this question, an Earth scientist would need to measure the temperature of the lava. **Temperature** is a measure of how hot (or cold) something is. You are probably used to describing temperature with degrees Fahrenheit (°F). Scientists use degrees Celsius (°C) and kelvins, which is the SI unit for temperature. The thermometer at right shows the relationship between °F and °C, the unit you will most often see in this book.

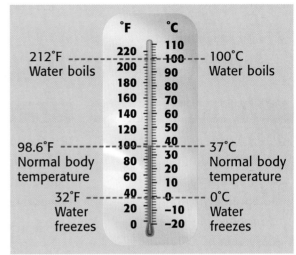

Safety Rules!

Earth science is exciting and fun, but it can also be dangerous. So don't take any chances! Always follow your teacher's instructions, and don't take short-cuts—even when you think there is little or no danger.

Before starting any science investigation, get your teacher's permission and read the lab procedures carefully. Pay particular attention to safety information and caution statements. The table below shows the safety symbols used in this book. Get to know these symbols and what they mean. Do this by reading the safety information starting on page 482. **This is important!** If you are still unsure about what a safety symbol means, ask your teacher.

Stay on the safe side by reading the safety information on page 482. **This is a must before doing any science activity!**

Safety Symbols		
Eye protection	Clothing protection	Hand safety
Heating safety	Electric safety	Sharp object
Chemical safety	Animal safety	Plant safety

REVIEW

1. What are two benefits of using the International System of Units?

2. Which SI unit best describes the volume of gasoline in a car?

3. **Doing Calculations** What is the minimum length and width (in meters) of a box that can contain an object 56 cm wide and 843 mm long?

Chapter Highlights

SECTION 1

Vocabulary

geology *(p. 6)*
oceanography *(p. 7)*
meteorology *(p. 8)*
astronomy *(p. 9)*
ecosystem *(p. 10)*

Section Notes

- Earth science can be divided into three general categories: geology, oceanography, and meteorology.

- Astronomy is the study of physical things beyond planet Earth.

- Careers in Earth science often require knowledge of more than one science.

SECTION 2

Vocabulary

scientific method *(p. 13)*
observation *(p. 14)*
hypothesis *(p. 14)*

Section Notes

- The scientific method is essential for proper scientific investigation.

- Different scientists may use the scientific method differently.

- The discovery of *Seismosaurus hallorum* as a new kind of dinosaur was made using the scientific method.

- When scientists finish investigations, it is important that they communicate the results to other scientists.

Labs

Using the Scientific Method *(p. 486)*

☑ Skills Check

Math Concepts

CONVERTING SI UNITS Take another look at the SI chart on page 22. The SI units for most categories of measurement, such as length and mass, are all expressed in terms of a single unit. For example, the unit *centimeter* is expressed in terms of the unit *meter*. To write 50 cm in terms of meters, divide 50 by 100 (there are 100 cm in 1 m).

$$50 \text{ cm} \times \frac{1 \text{ m}}{100 \text{ cm}} = 0.5 \text{ m}$$

Visual Understanding

WHICH PATH SHOULD YOU FOLLOW? Review the flowchart on page 13. The scientific method can follow many paths. For example, a scientist may make observations before asking a question or after forming a hypothesis.

Make Observations

Vocabulary

global warming *(p. 18)*

model *(p. 19)*

theory *(p. 19)*

Section Notes

- Models are used in science to represent physical things and systems.

- Typically, physical models represent objects, and mathematical models represent systems.

- Climate models are very complicated mathematical models.

- The global-warming model is a mathematical climate model.

- The greenhouse effect is an important part of the global-warming model.

- Scientists use models to explain the past and present as well as to predict the future.

- The only way to measure the accuracy of a climate model is to compare predictions based on the model with what actually occurs.

Vocabulary

meter *(p. 23)*

volume *(p. 23)*

mass *(p. 24)*

temperature *(p. 25)*

Section Notes

- The International System of Units (SI) helps all scientists share and compare their work.

- The basic SI units of measurement for length, volume, and mass are the meter, cubic meter, and kilogram, respectively.

- To describe temperature, scientists use degrees Celsius (°C) and kelvins (K), which is the SI unit for temperature.

---

  internetconnect

GO TO: go.hrw.com

Visit the **HRW** Web site for a variety of learning tools related to this chapter. Just type in the keyword:

KEYWORD: HSTWES

 GO TO: www.scilinks.org

Visit the **National Science Teachers Association** on-line Web site for Internet resources related to this chapter. Just type in the *sci*LINKS number for more information about the topic:

TOPIC: Branches of Earth Science	*sci*LINKS NUMBER: HSTE005
TOPIC: Careers in Earth Science	*sci*LINKS NUMBER: HSTE010
TOPIC: Using Models in Earth Science	*sci*LINKS NUMBER: HSTE015
TOPIC: Systems of Measurement	*sci*LINKS NUMBER: HSTE020

Chapter Review

Use the following terms in a sentence to show that you know what they mean:

1. hypothesis, scientific method

2. meteorology, model

3. geology, ecosystem

4. global warming, oceanography

UNDERSTANDING CONCEPTS

Multiple Choice

5. Earth science can be divided into three general categories: meteorology, oceanography, and
   a. geography.
   b. geology.
   c. geochemistry.
   d. ecology.

6. The science that deals with fossils is
   a. paleontology.
   b. ecology.
   c. seismology.
   d. volcanology.

7. Meteorology is the study of
   a. meteors.
   b. meteorites.
   c. the atmosphere.
   d. maps.

8. Gillette's hypothesis was
   a. supported by his results.
   b. not supported by his results.
   c. based only on observations.
   d. based only on what he already knew.

9. Two of the most common greenhouse gases are water vapor (H_2O) and
   a. carbon dioxide (CO_2).
   b. krypton (Kr).
   c. radon (Rn).
   d. neon (Ne).

10. Over the past 100 years, the average temperature of Earth's atmosphere has risen about
    a. 10°C.   c. 1°C.
    b. 5°C.   d. 0.5°C.

11. The greenhouse effect is used to explain
    a. volcanoes.
    b. earthquakes.
    c. fossilization.
    d. global warming.

12. Global warming would cause
    a. some polar ice to melt.
    b. more rain.
    c. overall rise in sea level.
    d. All of the above

13. An ecosystem can include
    a. plants and animals.
    b. weather and climate.
    c. humans.
    d. All of the above

Short Answer

14. How did Gillette determine that the dinosaur he found was new to science?

15. How and why do scientists use models?

16. Why is the temperature inside a greenhouse usually warmer than the temperature outside?

Concept Mapping

17. Use the following terms to create a concept map: Earth science, model, the scientific method, geology, hypothesis, meteorology, oceanography, observation, International System of Units.

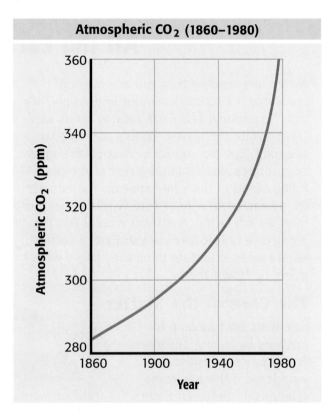

CRITICAL THINKING AND PROBLEM SOLVING

Write one or two sentences to answer the following questions:

18. A rock that contains fossil seashells might be studied by scientists in at least two branches of Earth science. Name those branches. Why did you choose those two?

19. Why might two scientists working on the same problem draw different conclusions?

20. The scientific method often begins with observation. How does observation limit what scientists can study?

21. Why are scientists so careful about making predictions from certain models, such as climate models?

MATH IN SCIENCE

22. Scientists often use scientific laws when constructing models. According to Boyle's law, for example, if you increase the pressure outside a balloon, the balloon will get smaller. This law is expressed as the following formula:

$$P_1 \times V_1 = P_2 \times V_2$$

If the pressure on a balloon (P_1) is one atmosphere (1 atm) and the volume of air in the balloon (V_1) is one liter (1 L), what will the volume be (in liters) if the pressure is increased to 3 atm?

INTERPRETING GRAPHICS

Examine the graph below, and answer the questions that follow.

Atmospheric CO$_2$ (1860–1980)

23. Has the amount of CO$_2$ in the atmosphere increased or decreased since 1860?

24. The line on the graph is curved. What does this mean?

25. Was the rate of change in the level of CO$_2$ between 1940 and 1960 higher or lower than it was between 1880 and 1900? How can you tell?

NOW What Do You Think?

Take a minute to review your answers to the ScienceLog questions on page 5. Have your answers changed? If necessary, revise your answers based on what you have learned since you began this chapter.

All the Earth's a Magnet

As you are reading this, you are moving around at 1,670 km/h. Sound impossible? It's true. That's how fast Earth rotates on its axis. Deep inside the planet, Earth's core is also spinning. But did you know that Earth's inner core rotates *faster* than the rest of the planet? If you stood in the same spot on the equator for a year, Earth's inner core would travel more than 20 km farther than you would! But the inner core is 5,150 km below Earth's surface. What makes scientists think they know what's going on down there?

The Core of the Matter

Scientists start looking for answers by asking questions. For instance, scientists have wondered if there is some relationship between Earth's core and Earth's magnetic field. To build their hypothesis, scientists started with what they knew: Earth has a dense, solid inner core and a molten outer core. They then created a computer model to simulate how Earth's magnetic field is generated. The model predicted that Earth's inner core spins in the same direction as the rest of the Earth but slightly faster than the surface. If that theory is correct, it might explain how Earth's magnetic field is generated. But how could the researchers test the theory?

Because scientists couldn't drill down to the core, they had to get their information indirectly. They decided to track seismic waves created by earthquakes.

Upper mantle

Crust

Lower mantle

Outer core

Inner core

Catch the Waves

Scientists analyzed 30 years' worth of earthquake seismic data. They knew that seismic waves traveling through the inner core along a north-south path travel faster than waves passing through it along an east-west line. Scientists searched seismic data records to see if the orientation of the "fast path" for seismic waves changed over time. They found that in the last 30 years, the direction of the "fast path" for seismic waves had indeed shifted. This is strong evidence that Earth's core does travel faster than the surface, and it strengthens the theory that the spinning core creates Earth's magnetic field.

Now That We Know . . .

This discovery will lead to more research into how Earth's magnetic field changes and how the north and south poles "wander" and even occasionally reverse. The new information may also lead to a better understanding of the flow of planetary heat that moves the tectonic plates on Earth's surface.

Write About It

▶ Imagine what would happen if the magnetic poles were suddenly reversed or if magnetism disappeared completely. How would you be affected personally? How would it affect our civilization? Write a funny story describing a world with no magnetism.

CAREERS

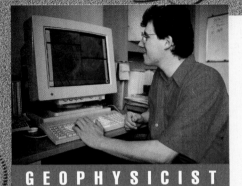

Bob Grimm is looking for water on Mars. Grimm is a geophysicist, a scientist who uses the science of physics to study Earth, its structure, and its atmosphere. Some geophysicists try to answer questions about the origin and history of Earth, while others use their knowledge of Earth to answer questions about other planets. One of those questions is whether there is water on Mars.

It isn't likely that humans will be living on Mars anytime soon, so why try to find water there? Bob Grimm explains the importance of his work this way: "The search for water on Mars really is the search for life. Are there microorganisms, algae, or other primitive life-forms beneath the surface? By finding liquid water, we will know where to look for life."

Probing Mars

Grimm isn't going to Mars in person. Instead, he and others are developing instruments to send to Mars to try to locate water beneath that planet's surface. These instruments work by reading patterns of electromagnetic waves reflected by formations beneath the surface. When electromagnetic waves hit something under the surface that conducts electricity, the pattern of the waves changes. By looking at the patterns in the waves as they are reflected back to the equipment, Grimm and others will be able to "see" what lies beneath Mars's surface. If there is underground water on Mars, it should show up as a change in the wave patterns.

Meanwhile, Back on Earth

The same procedures Grimm is using to find water on Mars can be used to locate objects, such as land mines, buried beneath the ground here on Earth. Standard metal detectors are useful, but they can't tell the difference between a mine and a piece of scrap metal. Along with electromagnetic pulses, Grimm uses imaging technologies similar to medical scanners to create images of objects buried beneath the ground. Once their location is pinpointed, mines can be safely removed or detonated.

An Interesting Career

Being a geophysicist has been rewarding for Grimm. "The sense of exploration really appeals to me," he explains. "It's like a hunt—I try to figure something out to bring some relationships together, and soon I have a story to tell!"

Think It Over

▶ Think of ways to locate objects buried more than 2 m below the surface. Could you use sound, light, X rays, or something else? What problems would you have to solve to make a useful detector to send to Mars?

▲ *The Surface of Mars*

2 Maps as Models of the Earth

Imagine...

Imagine that friends from school are coming to visit you at home. You don't want them to get lost, so you decide to make a map. How would you make a map of where you live? Would you include everything in your neighborhood? What materials would you use to make your map?

The first mapmakers probably used sticks to scratch maps in the dirt. One of the oldest surviving maps is of an ancient city in Mesopotamia, which is in present-day Iraq. The nearly 5,000-year-old map was etched onto a clay tablet. The first paper map was printed in China in about A.D. 1155.

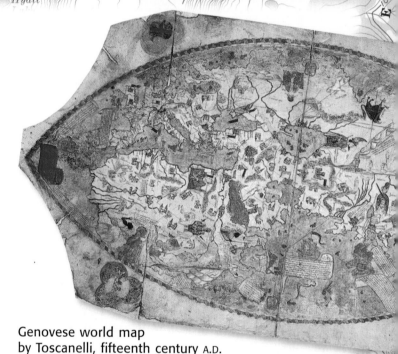

Genovese world map by Toscanelli, fifteenth century A.D.

Babylonian plan of the world, seventh century B.C.

During medieval times, maps of the known world produced by Europeans were often based on imagination, guesswork, and travelers' tales. At the center of the Earth was Europe. Areas that had not yet been visited and explored were sometimes filled in with scenes of mythical places and monsters.

Today computer technology and satellite images allow us to make maps that are extremely accurate. In this chapter you will learn about different types of maps, how these maps are represented, and what goes into making a map.

What Do You Think?

In your ScienceLog, try to answer the following questions based on what you already know:

1. Do all maps represent the world accurately?

2. How is information shown on maps?

3. What information must every map contain?

Follow the Yellow Brick Road

Have you ever been lost? Would a map have helped? Maps are the basic tools for visually presenting locations. Maps are necessary parts of your everyday life. They range from your teacher's seating chart of the class to the map of the United States hanging on your classroom wall. In this activity, you will draw and exchange maps with a partner. In doing so, you not only will learn how to read a map but also will make a map that someone else can read.

Procedure

1. With **colored pencils** and **paper,** draw a map illustrating how to get from your classroom to another location in your school, such as the restroom or the gym. Make sure you include enough information for someone unfamiliar with your school to find his or her way.

2. After you finish drawing your map, exchange maps with a partner. Study your classmate's map, and try to figure out where the map is leading you. Note what aspects of the map make it easy or difficult to read.

Analysis

3. Is your map an accurate representation of your school? Explain.

4. How do you think your map could be made better? What do you think is missing?

5. Compare your map with your partner's map. How are your maps alike? How are they different? What symbols does your map have in common with your partner's map?

Going Further

Perform the same activity, but this time walk the route before making the map, and make a mental note of landmarks and the distance between locations on the way. How does this improve your map? What additions would make your map easier to read?

You Are Here

NEW TERMS

map	equator
reference point	latitude
cardinal directions	longitude
true north	prime meridian
magnetic declination	

OBJECTIVES

- Describe directions on a globe.
- Explain how a magnetic compass can be used to find directions on the Earth.
- Distinguish between true north and magnetic north.
- Distinguish between lines of latitude and lines of longitude on a globe or map.
- Explain how latitude and longitude can be used to locate places on Earth.

When you walk across the Earth's surface, the Earth does not appear to be curved. It looks flat. In the past, beliefs about the Earth's shape changed. Maps reflected the time's knowledge and views of the world as well as the current technology. A **map** is a model or representation of the Earth's surface. If you look at Ptolemy's world map from the second century, as shown in **Figure 1,** you probably will not recognize what you are looking at. Today satellites in space provide us with true images of what the Earth looks like. There is no guesswork involved. In this section you will learn how early scientists knew the Earth was round long before pictures from space were taken. You will also learn how to determine location and direction on the Earth's surface.

What Does the Earth Really Look Like?

The Greeks thought of the Earth as a sphere almost 2,000 years before Christopher Columbus made his voyage in 1492. The Greeks thought that the sphere was the most perfect form and that the Earth therefore had to be a sphere. Evidence based on observations supported the assumption. For example, the observation that a ship sinks below the horizon as it sails into the distance supported the idea of a round Earth. If the Earth were flat the ship would appear smaller as it moved away. Today we know the Earth is not a perfect sphere.

Figure 1 *This map shows what people thought the world looked like in the second century* A.D. *Can you recognize any continents or oceans?*

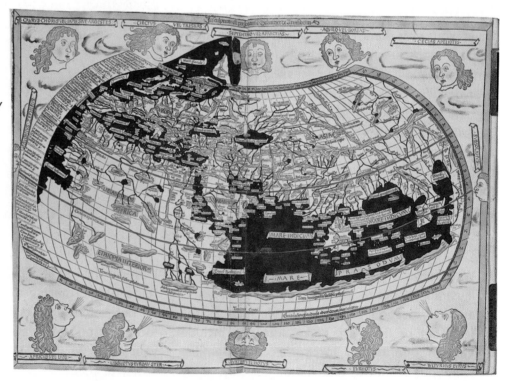

Eratosthenes (ER uh TAHS thuh neez), a Greek mathematician, wanted to know how big the Earth was. In about 240 B.C., he calculated the Earth's circumference using geometry and observations of the sun. We now know his estimation was off by only 6,250 km, an error of 15 percent. That's not bad for someone who lived more than 2,000 years ago, in a time when computer and satellite technology did not exist!

Finding Direction on Earth

How would you give a friend from school directions to your home? You might mention a landmark, such as a grocery store or a restaurant, as a reference point. A **reference point** is a fixed place on the Earth's surface from which direction and location can be described.

Because the Earth is round, it has no top, bottom, or sides for people to use as reference points for determining locations on its surface. The Earth does, however, turn on its axis. The Earth's axis is an imaginary line that runs through the Earth. At either end of the axis is a geographic pole. The North and South Poles, as shown in **Figure 2,** are used as reference points when describing direction and location on Earth.

Cardinal Directions North, south, east, and west are called **cardinal directions. Figure 3** shows these basic cardinal directions and various combinations of these directions. Using these directions is much more precise than using directions such as turn left, go straight, and turn right. Unfortunately for most of us, using cardinal directions requires the use of a compass.

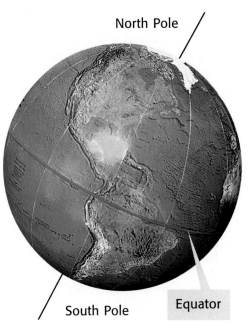

Figure 2 *Like the poles, the equator can be used as a reference. The equator is a circle halfway between the poles that divides the Earth into the Northern and Southern Hemispheres.*

Figure 3 *A compass rose helps you orient yourself on a map.*

Using a Compass   One way to determine north is by using a magnetic compass. The compass uses the natural magnetism of the Earth to indicate direction. A compass needle points to the magnetic north pole. The Earth has two different sets of poles—the geographic poles, which you learned about on the previous page, and the magnetic poles. As you can see in **Figure 4,** the magnetic poles have a slightly different location than the geographic poles.

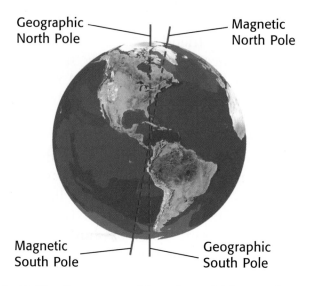

Geographic North Pole — Magnetic North Pole

Magnetic South Pole — Geographic South Pole

Figure 4 *Unlike the geographic poles, which are always in the same place, the magnetic poles have changed location throughout the history of the Earth.*

Self-Check

Does the Earth rotate around the geographic poles or the magnetic poles? *(See page 564 to check your answer.)*

True North and Magnetic Declination   Because the geographic North Pole never changes, it is called **true north.** The difference between the location of true north and the magnetic north pole requires that one more step be added to using a compass. Remember, a compass points to magnetic north, not geographic north. So when using a compass to map or explore the Earth's surface, you need to make a correction for the difference between geographic north and magnetic north. This angle of correction is called **magnetic declination.** Magnetic declination is measured in degrees east or west of true north.

Magnetic declination has been determined for different points on the Earth's surface. Once you know the declination for your area, you can use a compass to determine true north.

It's better than a scavenger hunt! Interested? Turn to page 490 of your LabBook.

This adjustment is like the adjustment you would make to the handlebars of a bike with a bent front wheel. You know how much you have to turn the handlebars to make the bike go straight.

As **Figure 5** shows, a compass needle at Pittsburgh, Pennsylvania, points 5° west of true north. At Savannah, Georgia, the compass needle lines up with true north, so the declination is 0°. At San Diego, California, the needle points 15° east of true north.

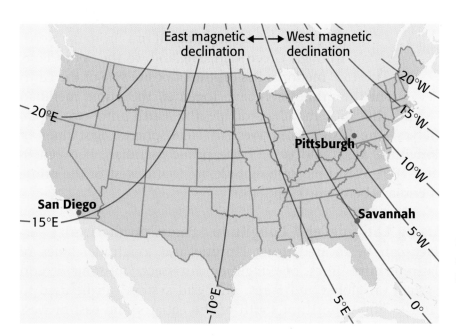

Figure 5 *The red lines on the map connect points with the same magnetic declination.*

Finding Locations on the Earth

The houses and buildings in your neighborhood all have addresses that identify their location. But how would you find the location of something on the Earth's surface that is much bigger, like a city or an island? These things can be given an "address" using *latitude* and *longitude*. Latitude and longitude are intersecting lines on a globe or map that allow you to find exact locations. They are used in combination to create global addresses. Read on to see how this system works.

Latitude Imaginary lines drawn around the Earth parallel to the equator are called lines of latitude, or *parallels*. The **equator** is a circle halfway between the poles that divides the Earth into the Northern and Southern Hemispheres. It represents 0° latitude. **Latitude** is the distance north or south, measured in degrees, from the equator, as shown in **Figure 6.** The North Pole is 90° north latitude, and the South Pole is 90° south latitude.

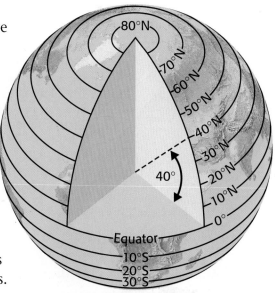

Figure 6 *The degree measure of latitude is the angle created by the equator, the center of the Earth, and the location on the Earth's surface.*

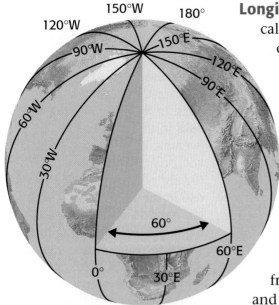

Figure 7 *The degree measure of longitude is the angle created by the prime meridian, the center of the Earth, and the location on the Earth's surface.*

Longitude Imaginary lines that pass through the poles are called lines of longitude, or *meridians.* **Longitude** is the distance east and west, measured in degrees, from the prime meridian, as shown in **Figure 7.** By international agreement, one meridian was selected to be 0°. The **prime meridian,** which passes through Greenwich, England, is the line that represents 0° longitude. Unlike lines of latitude, lines of longitude are not parallel. They touch at the poles and are farthest apart at the equator.

The prime meridian does not completely circle the globe like the equator does. It runs from the North Pole through Greenwich, England, to the South Pole. The 180° meridian lies on the opposite side of the Earth from the prime meridian. Together, the prime meridian and the 180° meridian divide the Earth into two equal halves—the Eastern and Western Hemispheres. East lines of longitude are found east of the prime meridian, between 0° and 180°. West lines of longitude are found west of the prime meridian, between 0° and 180°.

Using Latitude and Longitude Points on the Earth's surface can be located using latitude and longitude. Lines of latitude and lines of longitude intersect, forming a grid system on globes and maps. This grid system can be used to find locations north or south of the equator and east or west of the prime meridian.

Finding Your Way

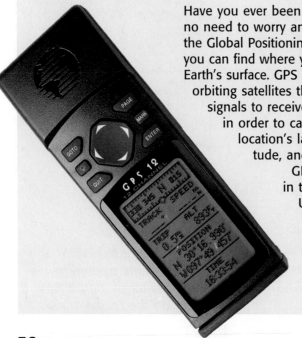

Have you ever been lost? There's no need to worry anymore. With the Global Positioning System (GPS), you can find where you are on the Earth's surface. GPS consists of 25 orbiting satellites that send radio signals to receivers on Earth in order to calculate a given location's latitude, longitude, and elevation.

GPS was invented in the 1970s by the United States Department of Defense for military purposes. During the last 20 years, this technology has made its way into many people's daily lives. Today, GPS is used in a variety of ways. Airplane and boat pilots use it for navigation, and industry uses include mining and resource mapping as well as environmental planning. Even some cars are equipped with a GPS unit that can display the vehicle's specific location on a computer screen on the dashboard.

Figure 8 shows you how latitude and longitude can be used to find the location of your state capital. First locate the star symbol representing your state capital on the appropriate map. Find the lines of latitude and longitude closest to your state capital. From here you can estimate your capital's approximate latitude and longitude.

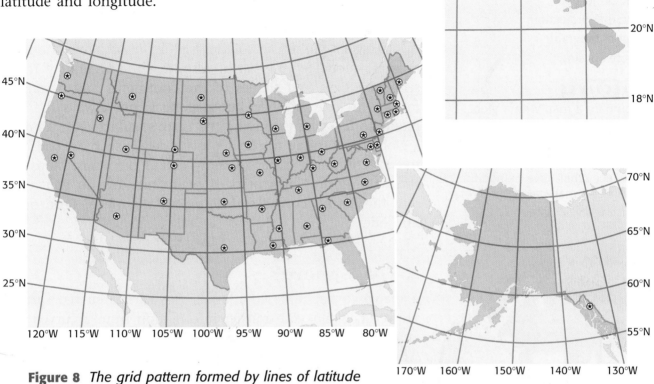

Figure 8 *The grid pattern formed by lines of latitude and longitude allows you to pinpoint any location on the Earth's surface.*

REVIEW

1. Explain the difference between true north and magnetic north.

2. When using a compass to map an area, why is it important to know an area's magnetic declination?

3. In what three ways is the equator different from the prime meridian?

4. How do lines of latitude and longitude help you find locations on the Earth's surface?

5. **Applying Concepts** While digging through an old trunk, you find a treasure map. The map shows that the treasure is buried at 97° north and 188° east. Explain why this is impossible.

Explore

Use an atlas or globe to find the latitude and longitude of the following cities:
New York, New York
Sao Paulo, Brazil
Rome, Italy
Sydney, Australia
Madrid, Spain
Reykjavik, Iceland
Cairo, Egypt

Mapping the Earth's Surface

OBJECTIVES

- Compare a map with a globe.
- Describe the three types of map projections.
- Describe recent technological advances that have helped the science of mapmaking progress.
- List the parts of a map.

Models are often used to represent real objects. For example, architects use models of buildings to give their clients an idea of what a building will look like before it is completed. Likewise, Earth scientists often make models of the Earth. These models are globes and maps.

Because a globe is a sphere, a globe is probably the most accurate model of the Earth. Also, a globe accurately represents the sizes and shapes of the continents and oceans in relation to one another. But a globe is not always the best model to use when studying the Earth's surface. For example, a globe is too small to show a lot of detail, such as roads and rivers. It is much easier to show details on maps. Maps can show the entire Earth or parts of it. But how do you represent the Earth's curved surface on a flat surface? Read on to find out.

A Flat Sphere?

A map is a flat representation of the Earth's curved surface. However, when you transfer information from a curved surface to a flat surface, you lose some accuracy. Changes called distortions occur in the shapes and sizes of landmasses and oceans. These distortions make some landmasses appear larger than they really are. Direction and distance can also be distorted. Consider the example of the orange peel shown in **Figure 9.**

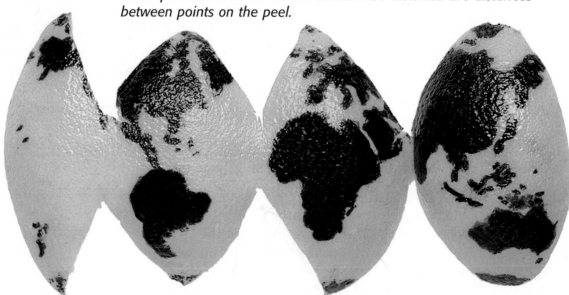

Figure 9 *If you remove the peel from an orange and flatten the peel, it will stretch and tear. The larger the piece of peel, the more its shape is distorted as it is flattened. Also distorted are distances between points on the peel.*

Mapmakers use map projections to transfer the image of Earth's curved surface onto a flat surface. No map projection of the Earth can represent the surface of a sphere exactly. All flat maps have some amount of distortion. A map showing a smaller area, such as a city, has much less distortion than a map showing a larger area, such as the entire world.

To understand how map projections are made, imagine the Earth as a transparent globe with a light inside. If you hold a piece of paper up against the globe, shadows appear on the paper that show markings on the globe, such as continents, oceans, lines of latitude, and lines of longitude. The way the paper is held against the globe determines the kind of projection that is made. The most common projections are based on three geometric shapes—cylinders, cones, and planes.

Mercator Projection A **Mercator projection** is a map projection that results when the contents of the globe are transferred onto a cylinder of paper, as shown in **Figure 10.**

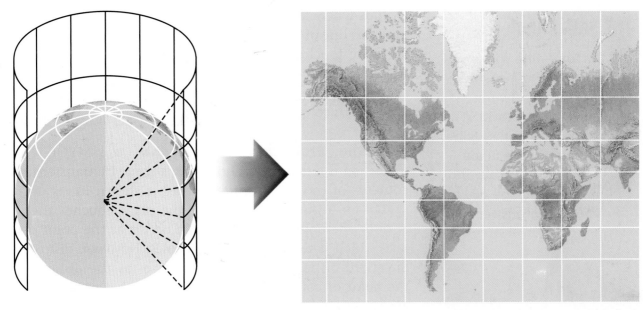

Figure 10 *A Mercator projection, though accurate near the equator, distorts distances between regions of land and distorts the sizes of areas near the poles.*

The Mercator projection shows the Earth's latitude and longitude as straight, parallel lines. Lines of longitude are plotted with an equal amount of space between each line. Lines of latitude are spaced farther apart north and south of the equator. This makes it easy to determine direction and measure latitude and longitude with a ruler. But remember, on a globe, lines of longitude are not parallel. They meet at the poles. Making the lines parallel widens and lengthens the size of areas near the poles. For example, on the Mercator projection in the map shown above, Greenland appears almost as large as Africa. Actually, Africa is 15 times larger than Greenland.

Conic Projection A **conic projection** is a map projection that is made by transferring the contents of the globe onto a cone, as shown in **Figure 11.** This cone is then unrolled to form a flat plane.

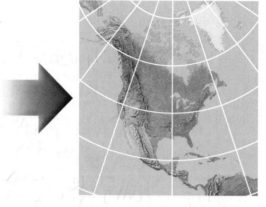

Figure 11 *A series of conic projections can be used to map a large area. Because each cone touches the globe at a different latitude, it reduces distortion.*

The cone touches the globe at each line of longitude but only one line of latitude. There is no distortion along the line of latitude where the globe comes in contact with the cone. Areas near this line of latitude are distorted the least amount. Because the cone touches many lines of longitude and only one line of latitude, conic projections are best for mapping landmasses that have more area east to west, such as the United States, than north to south, such as South America.

Azimuthal Projection An **azimuthal** (AZ i MYOOTH uhl) **projection** is a map projection that is made by transferring the contents of the globe onto a plane, as shown in **Figure 12.**

On an azimuthal projection, the plane touches the globe at only one point. Little distortion occurs at the point of contact, which is usually one of the poles. However, distortion of direction, distance, and shape increases as the distance from the point of contact increases. On azimuthal projections, true directions are shown from one central point to all other points.

✔ **Self-Check**

Imagine that you are assigned to measure distances between cities of the world. Will your measurements be more accurate if you use a globe or a world map? *(See page 564 to check your answer.)*

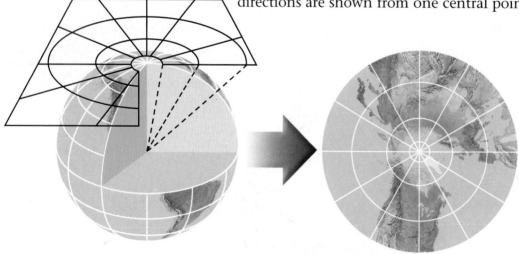

Figure 12 *This azimuthal projection is produced when points on the globe are projected onto a sheet of paper in contact with the North Pole.*

Modern Mapmaking

The science of mapmaking has changed more since the beginning of the 1900s than during any other time in history. This has been due to many technological advances in the twentieth century, such as the airplane, photography, computers, and space exploration.

Airplanes and Cameras The development of the airplane and advancements in photography have had the biggest effect on modern mapmaking. Airplanes give people a bird's-eye view of the Earth's surface. Improvements on the camera made it possible to take photographs of the land below. Photographs from the air are called **aerial photographs.** These photographs are important in helping mapmakers make accurate maps. **Figure 13** shows an example of an aerial photograph.

Figure 13 *What is this aerial photograph showing?*

Remote Sensing The combined use of airplanes and photography led to the science of remote sensing. **Remote sensing** is gathering information about something without actually being there. Remote sensing can be as basic as cameras in planes or as sophisticated as satellites with sensors that can sense and record what our eyes cannot see. Remotely-sensed images allow a mapmaker to map the surface of the Earth more accurately.

To learn more about current advances in mapmaking, turn to page 55.

We see only a small part of the sun's radiation. Radiation travels in waves of different lengths. The part of radiation we see is called visible light. Remote sensors on satellites can detect wavelengths that are longer and shorter than those of visible light. Satellites do not take photographs with film like cameras do. A satellite collects information about energy coming from the Earth's surface and sends it back to receiving stations on Earth. A computer is then used to process the information to create an image we can see, like the one shown in **Figure 14.**

Figure 14 *Satellites can detect objects the size of a baseball stadium. The satellite that took this picture was 220 km above the Earth's surface!*

Information Shown on Maps

As you have already learned, there are many different ways of making maps. It is also true that there are many types of maps. You might already be familiar with some, such as road maps or political maps of the United States. But regardless of its type, each map should contain the information shown in **Figure 15.**

Figure 15 Road Map of Connecticut

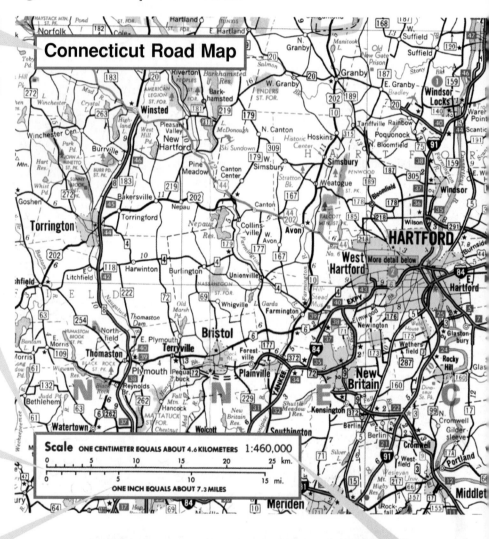

The **title** tells you what the map is about. The title will tell you what area is being shown on the map or give you information about the subject of the map.

A **map's scale** shows the relationship between the distance on the Earth's surface and the distance on the map. There are three ways a scale is shown on the map–verbal scale, graphic scale, and representative fraction.

A **graphic scale** is like a ruler. The distance on the Earth's surface is represented by a bar graph that shows units of distance.

A **verbal scale** is stated in words. It is a phrase that describes the measure of distance on the map relative to the distance on the Earth's surface.

A **representative fraction** is a fraction that shows the relationship between the distance on the map and the distance on the Earth's surface. It is unitless, meaning it stays the same no matter what units of measurement you are using. For example, say you are using a map with a representative fraction scale that is 1:24,000. If you are measuring distance on the map in centimeters, 1 cm on the map represents 24,000 cm on the Earth's surface. If the unit of measurement is an inch, then 1 in. on the map would represent 24,000 in. on the Earth's surface.

Imagine that you are a trip planner for an automobile club. A couple of people come in who want to travel from Torrington, Connecticut, to Bristol, Connecticut. Using the map in Figure 15, describe the shortest travel route you would suggest they take between the two cities. List the roads they would take, the direction they would travel, and the towns they would pass through. Use the map scale to determine approximately how many miles there are between Torrington and Bristol.

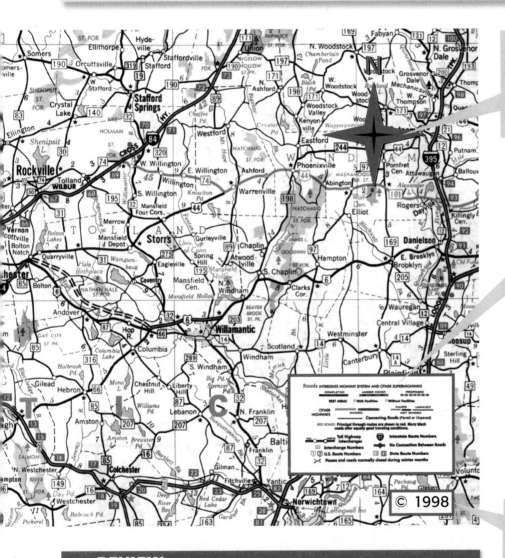

It is important to know direction on the map. One way to figure this out is to look at the compass rose. The **north arrow** shows you how the map is positioned in relation to true north.

Maps often use symbols for features such as highways and rivers. A **legend** is a list of the symbols used in the map and their explanations.

The **date** of a map is important because it gives the time at which the information was accurate. Features such as roads or buildings are frequently added or changed.

REVIEW

1. A globe is a fairly accurate model of the Earth, yet it has some weaknesses. What is one weakness?

2. What is distortion on a map, and why does it occur?

3. What is remote sensing? How has it changed mapmaking?

4. **Summarizing Data**   List five items found on maps. Explain how each item is important to reading a map.

Topographic Maps

OBJECTIVES

- Describe how contour lines show elevation and landforms on a map.
- List the rules of contour lines.
- Interpret a topographic map.

Imagine that you are on an outdoor adventure trip. The trip's purpose is to improve your survival skills by having you travel across undeveloped territory with only a compass and a map. What kind of map will you be using? Well, it's not a road map—you won't be seeing a lot of roads where you are going. You will need a topographic map. A **topographic map** is a map that shows surface features, or topography, of the Earth. Topographic maps show both natural features, such as rivers, lakes and mountains, and features made by humans, such as cities, roads, and bridges. Topographic maps also show elevation. **Elevation** is the height of an object above sea level. The elevation at sea level is 0. In this section you will learn how to interpret a topographic map.

Elements of Elevation

The United States Geological Survey (USGS), a federal government agency, has made topographic maps for all of the United States. Each of these maps is a detailed description of a small area of the Earth's surface. Because the topographic maps produced by the USGS use feet as their unit of measure rather than meters, we will follow their example.

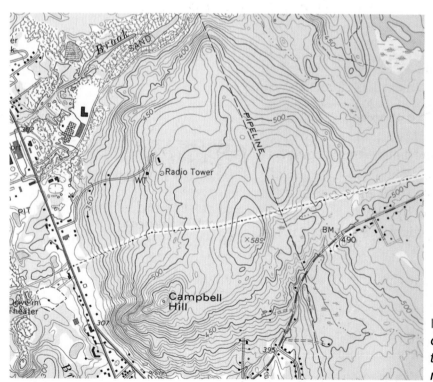

Contour Lines On a topographic map, contour lines are used to show elevation. **Contour lines** are lines that connect points of equal elevation. For example, one contour line would connect points on a map that have an elevation of 100 ft. Another line would connect points on a map that have an elevation of 200 ft. **Figure 16** illustrates how contour lines appear on a map.

Figure 16 *Because contour lines connect points of equal elevation, the shape of the contour lines reflects the shape of the land.*

Contour Interval The difference in elevation between one contour line and the next is called the **contour interval.** For example, a map with a contour interval of 20 ft would have contour lines every 20 ft of elevation change, such as 0 ft, 20 ft, 40 ft, 60 ft, and so on. A mapmaker chooses a contour interval based on the area's relief. **Relief** is the difference in elevation between the highest and lowest points of the area being mapped. Because the relief of a mountainous area is high, it might be shown on a map using a large contour interval, such as 100 ft. However, a flat area has low relief and might be shown on a map using a small contour interval, such as 10 ft.

The spacing of contour lines also indicates slope, as shown in **Figure 17.** Contour lines that are close together, with little space between them, usually show a steep slope. Contour lines that are spaced far apart generally represent a gentle slope.

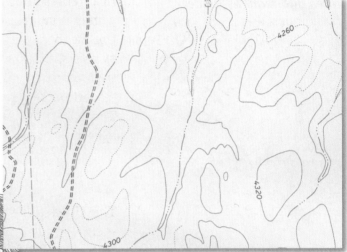

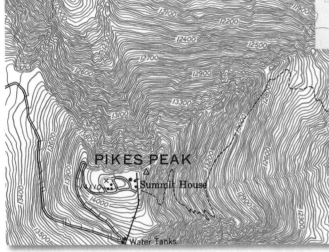

Figure 17 *The portion of the topographic map on the left shows Pikes Peak, in Colorado. Notice how close together the contour lines are. The map above shows a valley in Big Bend Ranch State Park, in Texas. Notice the widely spaced contour lines.*

Index Contour On many topographic maps, the mapmaker uses an index contour to make reading the map a little easier. An **index contour** is a darker, heavier contour line that is usually every fifth line and that is labeled by elevation. Find an index contour on both of the topographic maps shown above.

MATH BREAK

Counting Contours

Calculate the contour interval for the map shown in Figure 16 on the previous page. (Hint: Find the difference between two bold lines found next to each other. Subtract the lower marked elevation from the higher marked elevation. Divide by 5.)

✓ **Self-Check**

If elevation is not labeled on a map, how can you determine if the mapped area is steep or not? *(See page 564 to check your answer.)*

Reading a Topographic Map

Topographic maps, like other maps, use symbols to represent parts of the Earth's surface. The legend from the USGS topographic map in **Figure 18** shows some of the common symbols used to represent certain features in topographic maps.

Different colors are also used to represent different features of the Earth's surface. In general, buildings, roads, bridges, and railroads are black. Contour lines are brown. Major highways are red. Cities and towns are pink. Bodies of water, such as rivers, lakes, and oceans, are shown in blue, and wooded areas are represented by the color green.

Figure 18 *All USGS topographic maps use the same legend to represent natural features and features made by humans.*

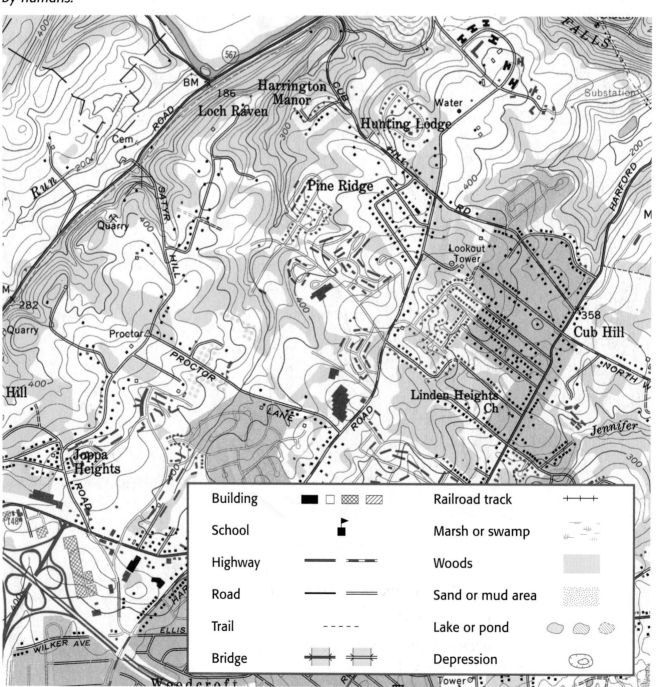

The Golden Rules of Contour Lines Contour lines are the key to interpreting the size and shape of landforms on a topographic map. When you first look at a topographic map, it might seem confusing. Accurately reading a topographic map requires training and practice. The following rules will help you understand how to read topographic maps:

1. Contour lines never cross. All points along a contour line represent a single elevation.

2. The spacing of contour lines depends on slope characteristics. Closely spaced contour lines represent a steep slope. Widely spaced contour lines represent a gentle slope.

3. Contour lines that cross a valley or stream are V-shaped. The V points toward the area of higher elevation. If a stream or river flows through the valley, the V points upstream.

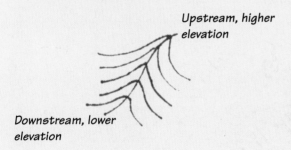

Upstream, higher elevation

Downstream, lower elevation

4. Contour lines form closed circles around the tops of hills, mountains, and depressions. One way to tell hills and depressions apart is that depressions are marked with short, straight lines inside the circle, pointing downslope toward the center of the depression.

 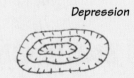

Hill   Depression

REVIEW

1. How do topographic maps represent the Earth's surface?

2. If a contour map contains streams, can you tell where the higher ground is even if all of the numbers are removed?

3. Why can't contour lines cross?

4. **Inferring Conclusions** Why isn't the highest point on a hill or a mountain represented by a contour line?

Chapter Highlights

Vocabulary

map *(p. 34)*

reference point *(p. 35)*

cardinal directions *(p. 35)*

true north *(p. 36)*

magnetic declination *(p. 36)*

equator *(p. 37)*

latitude *(p. 37)*

longitude *(p. 38)*

prime meridian *(p. 38)*

Section Notes

- The North and South Poles are used as reference points for describing direction and location on the Earth.

- The cardinal directions—north, south, east, and west—are used for describing direction.

- Magnetic compasses are used to determine direction on the Earth's surface. The north needle on the compass points to the magnetic north pole.

- Because the geographic North Pole never changes location, it is called true north. The magnetic poles are different from the Earth's geographic poles and have changed location throughout the Earth's history.

- The magnetic declination is the adjustment or difference between magnetic north and geographic north.

- Latitude and longitude are intersecting lines that help you find locations on a map or a globe. Lines of latitude run east-west. Lines of longitude run north-south through the poles.

Labs

Round or Flat? *(p. 488)*

Orient Yourself! *(p. 490)*

Vocabulary

Mercator projection *(p. 41)*

conic projection *(p. 42)*

azimuthal projection *(p. 42)*

aerial photograph *(p. 43)*

remote sensing *(p. 43)*

Section Notes

- A globe is the most accurate representation of the Earth's surface.

- Maps have built-in distortion because some information is lost when mapmakers transfer images from a curved surface to a flat surface.

☑ Skills Check

Math Concepts

REPRESENTATIVE FRACTION One type of map scale is a representative fraction. A representative fraction is a fraction or ratio that shows the relationship between the distance on the map and the distance on the Earth's surface. It is unitless, meaning it stays the same no matter what units of measurement you are using. For example, say you are using a map with a representative fraction scale that is 1:12,000. If you are measuring distance on the map in centimeters, 1 cm on the map represents 12,000 cm on the Earth's surface. A measure of 3 cm on the map represents $12,000 \times 3$ cm = 36,000 cm on the Earth's surface.

Visual Understanding

THE POLES The Earth has two different sets of poles—the geographic poles and the magnetic poles. See Figure 4 on page 36 to review how the geographic poles and the magnetic poles differ.

INFORMATION SHOWN ON MAPS Study Figure 15 on pages 44 and 45 to review the necessary information each map should contain.

- Mapmakers use map projections to transfer images of the Earth's curved surface to a flat surface.

- The most common map projections are based on three geometric shapes—cylinders, cones, and planes.

- Remote sensing has allowed mapmakers to make more accurate maps.

- All maps should have a title, date, scale, legend, and north arrow.

Vocabulary

topographic map *(p. 46)*

elevation *(p. 46)*

contour lines *(p. 46)*

contour interval *(p. 47)*

relief *(p. 47)*

index contour *(p. 47)*

Section Notes

- Topographic maps use contour lines to show a mapped area's elevation and the shape and size of landforms.

- The shape of contour lines reflects the shape of the land.

- The contour interval and the spacing of contour lines indicate the slope of the land.

- Like all maps, topographic maps use a set of symbols to represent features of the Earth's surface.

- Contour lines never cross. Contour lines that cross a valley or stream are V-shaped. Contour lines form closed circles around the tops of hills, mountains, and depressions.

Labs

Topographic Tuber *(p. 492)*

---

internetconnect

 GO TO: go.hrw.com

Visit the **HRW** Web site for a variety of learning tools related to this chapter. Just type in the keyword:

KEYWORD: HSTMAP

 GO TO: www.scilinks.org

Visit the **National Science Teachers Association** on-line Web site for Internet resources related to this chapter. Just type in the *sci*LINKS number for more information about the topic:

TOPIC: Finding Locations on the Earth   *sci*LINKS NUMBER: HSTE030

TOPIC: Latitude and Longitude   *sci*LINKS NUMBER: HSTE035

TOPIC: Mapmaking   *sci*LINKS NUMBER: HSTE040

TOPIC: Topographic Maps   *sci*LINKS NUMBER: HSTE045

Chapter Review

Explain the difference between the following sets of words:

1. true north/magnetic north

2. latitude/longitude

3. equator/prime meridian

4. Mercator projection/azimuthal projection

5. contour interval/index contour

6. elevation/relief

UNDERSTANDING CONCEPTS

Multiple Choice

7. A point whose latitude is 0° is located on the
   a. North Pole.
   b. equator.
   c. South Pole.
   d. prime meridian.

8. The distance in degrees east or west of the prime meridian is
   a. latitude.
   b. declination.
   c. longitude.
   d. projection.

9. The needle of a magnetic compass points toward the
   a. meridians.
   b. parallels.
   c. geographic North Pole.
   d. magnetic north pole.

10. The most common map projections are based on three geometric shapes. Which of the following geometric shapes is not one of them?
    a. cylinder
    b. square
    c. cone
    d. plane

11. A Mercator projection is distorted near the
    a. equator.
    b. poles.
    c. prime meridian.
    d. date line.

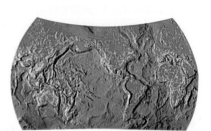

12. What kind of map scale is represented by a bar graph that shows units of distance?
    a. graphic
    b. verbal
    c. representative fraction
    d. ratio

13. What is the relationship between the distance on a map and the actual distance on the Earth called?
    a. legend
    b. elevation
    c. relief
    d. scale

14. The latitude of the North Pole is
    a. 100° north.
    b. 90° north.
    c. 180° north.
    d. 90° south.

15. Widely spaced contour lines indicate a
    a. steep slope.
    b. gentle slope.
    c. hill.
    d. river.

16. __?__ is the height of an object above sea level.
    a. Contour interval
    b. Elevation
    c. Declination
    d. Index contour

Short Answer

17. How can a magnetic compass be used to find direction on the Earth's surface?

18. Why is a map legend important?

19. Why does Greenland appear so large in relation to other landmasses on a map with a Mercator projection?

20. What is the function of contour lines on a topographic map?

Concept Mapping

21. Use the following terms to create a concept map: maps, legend, map projection, map parts, scale, cylinder, title, cone, plane, date, north arrow.

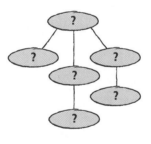

CRITICAL THINKING AND PROBLEM SOLVING

Write one or two sentences to answer the following questions:

22. One of the important parts of a map is its date. Why is this so important?

23. A mapmaker has to draw one map for three different countries that do not share a common unit of measure. What type of scale would this mapmaker use? Why?

24. How would a topographic map of the Rocky Mountains differ from a topographic map of the Great Plains?

MATH IN SCIENCE

25. A map has a verbal scale of 1 cm equals 200 m. If the actual distance between two points is 12,000 m, how far apart will they appear on the map?

26. On a topographic map, the contour interval is 50 ft. The bottom of a mountain begins on a contour line marked with a value of 1050 ft. The top of the mountain is within a contour line that is 12 lines higher than the bottom of the mountain. What is the elevation of the top of the mountain?

INTERPRETING GRAPHICS

Use the topographic map below to answer the questions that follow.

27. What is the elevation change between two adjacent lines on this map?

28. What type of relief does this area have?

29. What surface features are shown on this map?

30. What is the elevation at the top of Ore Hill?

NOW What Do You Think?

Take a minute to review your answers to the ScienceLog questions on page 33. Have your answers changed? If necessary, revise your answers based on what you have learned since you began this chapter.

Science, Technology, and Society

The Lost City of Ubar

Can you imagine tree sap being more valuable than gold? Well, about 2,000 years ago, a tree sap called frankincense was just that! Frankincense was used to treat illnesses and to disguise body odor. Ancient civilizations from Rome to India treasured it. While the name of the city that was the center of frankincense production and export had been known for generations—Ubar—there was just one problem: No one knew where it was! The name Ubar comes from Arab tradition, but the city's location had remained a mystery for more than 1,500 years. But now the mystery is solved. Using remote sensing, scientists have found clues hidden beneath desert sand dunes.

▲ *Trails and roads appear as purple lines on this computer-generated remote-sensing image.*

Using Eyes in the Sky

The process of remote sensing uses satellites to take pictures of large areas of land. The satellite records images as sets of data and sends these data to a receiver on Earth. A computer processes the data and displays the images. These remote sensing images can then be used to reveal differences unseen by the naked eye.

Remote-sensing images reveal modern roads as well as ancient caravan routes hidden beneath sand dunes in the Sahara Desert. But how could researchers tell the difference between the two? Everything on Earth reflects or radiates energy. Soil, vegetation, cities, and roads all emit a unique wavelength of energy. The problem is, sometimes modern roads and ancient roads are difficult to distinguish. The differences between similar objects can be enhanced by assigning color to an area and then displaying the area on a computer screen. Researchers used differences in color to distinguish between the roads of Ubar and modern roads. Decades of rubber tires cannot grind dirt and rock as fine as the hooves of camels can over hundreds of years. When researchers found ancient caravan routes and discovered that all the routes met at one location, they knew they had discovered the lost city of Ubar!

Continuing Discovery

Archaeologists continue to investigate the region around Ubar. They believe the great city may have collapsed into a limestone cavern beneath its foundation. Researchers are continuing to use remote sensing to study more images for clues to aid their investigation.

Think About It!

▶ Do modern civilizations value certain products or resources enough to establish elaborate trade routes for their transport? If so, what makes these products so valuable? Record your thoughts in your ScienceLog.

CAREERS

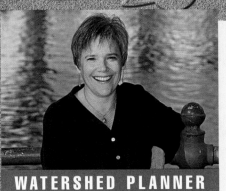

WATERSHED PLANNER

Have you ever wondered if the water you drink is safe, or what you could do to make sure it stays safe? As a watershed planner, **Nancy Charbeneau** identifies and solves land-use problems that may affect water quality.

Nancy Charbeneau enjoys using her teaching, biology, and landscape architecture background in her current career as a watershed planner. A watershed is any area of land where water drains into a stream, river, lake, or ocean. Charbeneau spends a lot of time writing publications and developing programs that explain the effects of land use on the quality of water.

Land is used in hundreds of ways. In urban areas, land is used for buildings and transportation. In rural areas, land is used for farming, ranching, and drilling. These land uses can have negative effects on water resources. Charbeneau produces educational materials to inform the public about threats to water quality.

Mapping the Problems

Charbeneau uses Geographic Information System (GIS) maps to determine types of vegetation and the functions of different sections of land. GIS is a computer-based tool that allows people to store, access, and display geographic information collected through remote-sensing field work, global positioning systems, and other sources. Maps and mapping systems play an important role in identifying land areas with water problems. Aerial photography as well as satellite and infrared imaging provide important information about topography, soil conditions, vegetation, and pollution.

Maps tell Charbeneau whether an area has problems with soil erosion that could threaten water quality. Often the type of soil plays an important role in erosion. Thin or sandy soil does not hold water well, allowing for faster runoff and erosion. Flat land with heavy vegetation holds more water and is less prone to erosion.

Understanding the Importance

Charbeneau's biggest challenge is raising awareness and increasing understanding of the link between land use and water quality. Many people who own land don't realize they could be using it in ways that damage their own drinking water. If a harmful substance is introduced into a watershed, it may contaminate an aquifer or a well. As Charbeneau puts it, "Most people want to do the right thing, but they need help identifying and implementing land management practices that will protect water quality but still allow them to earn a decent living off their land."

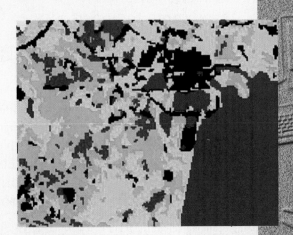

▲ *This GIS map shows the location of water in blue.*

Reading the Possibilities

▶ Map out your nearest watershed. Can you find any potential sources of contamination?

UNIT 2

Earth's Resources

In this unit, you will learn about the basic components of the solid Earth—rocks and the minerals from which they are made. The ground beneath your feet is a treasure-trove of interesting materials, some of which are very valuable. Secrets of the past are also hidden within its depths. This timeline shows some of the events that have occurred through history as scientists have come to understand more about our planet.

1533

Nicolaus Copernicus argues that the sun is the center of the universe rather than the Earth, as was commonly believed, but does not publish his findings for another 10 years.

1680

The dodo, a flightless bird, is driven to extinction by hunters. It is the first extinction of a species in recorded history.

1955

Using 1 million pounds of pressure and temperatures of more than 3,000°F, General Electric creates the first artificial diamonds from graphite.

1969

Apollo 11 astronauts Neil Armstrong and Edwin "Buzz" Aldrin bring 20 kg of moon rocks back to Earth.

1975

Junko Tabei becomes the first woman to successfully climb Mount Everest, 22 years after Edmund Hillary and Tenzing Norgay first conquered the mountain in 1953.

1848

Gold is discovered in California. Prospectors during the gold rush of the following year are referred to as "forty-niners."

1735

George Brandt identifies a new element and names it cobalt. This is the first metal to be discovered since ancient times.

1861

Fossil remains of *Archaeopteryx*, a possible link between reptiles and birds, are discovered in Germany.

1936

Hoover Dam is completed. This massive hydroelectric dam, standing more than 72 stories high, required 450,000 cement-truck loads of concrete to build.

1946

Willard F. Libby develops a method of dating prehistoric objects by using radioactive carbon.

1997

Sojourner, a roving probe on Mars, investigates a Martian boulder nicknamed Yogi.

1984

Russian engineers drill a borehole 12 km into the Earth's crust, three times deeper than the deepest mine shaft.

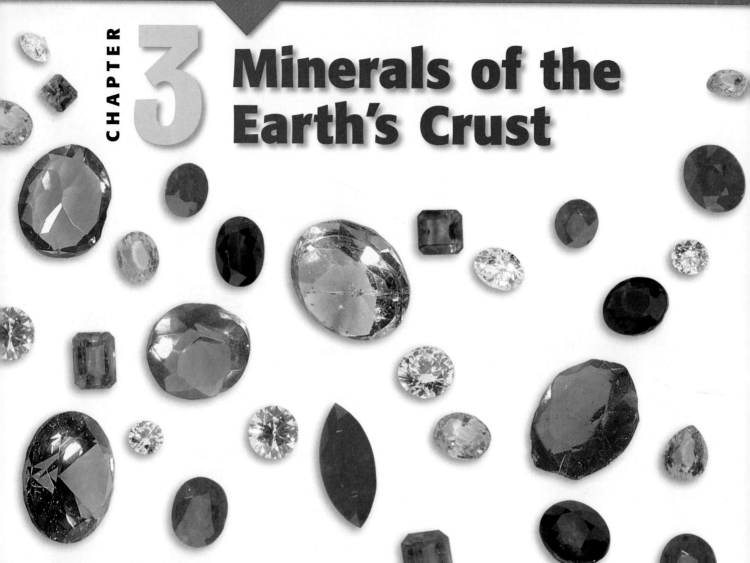

CHAPTER

3 Minerals of the Earth's Crust

Imagine...

If you owned all of the jewels shown on this page, you would be a millionaire. These precious gems—diamonds, rubies, sapphires, and emeralds—are valued at anywhere from $1,000 to $50,000 per carat (1 carat = 200 mg).

You may not be surprised that precious gems are so expensive. But did you know that the value of these gems has little to do with what they're made of? For example, rubies and sapphires are two varieties of the same mineral that is used to make sandpaper. And diamonds are made of the same material as the graphite in your pencil. Unlike gems, however, a few handfuls of pencils will not make you rich.

Gems are valuable not because of the elements they contain but because of how their atoms are arranged. Under certain conditions, common atoms can be arranged into rare crystal forms. Gems are rare because the conditions that produce them exist in only a few places in the world. The crystals that form gems are prized for their durability, subtle colors, and translucent quality. When properly cut and polished, like the examples shown above, gems sparkle brilliantly.

58 Chapter 3

Investigate!

Animal, Vegetable, or Mineral?

All the gems shown on the previous page are *minerals.* More than 3,000 different minerals occur naturally on Earth, and gems make up a very small number of them. What is a mineral? Do the following investigation, and see if you can figure it out.

Procedure

1. In your ScienceLog, make two columns—one for minerals and one for nonminerals. Based on what you already know about minerals, classify *all* of the materials you see on this page into things that come from minerals and things that come from nonminerals.

2. Ask your classmates what ideas they have about the materials that make up the motorcycle. Take notes as you gather information. You can add the information to your list later.

Analysis

3. Based on your list, what kinds of materials made up most of the motorcycle—minerals or nonminerals?

4. Where do you think the minerals that make the metallic parts of the motorcycle come from?

Minerals of the Earth's Crust   **59**

What Is a Mineral?

NEW TERMS

mineral	crystal
element	silicate mineral
atom	nonsilicate mineral
compound	

OBJECTIVES

- Explain the four characteristics of a mineral.
- Classify minerals according to the two major compositional groups.

Not all minerals look like gems. In fact, most of them look more like rocks. But are minerals the same as rocks? Well, not really. So what's the difference? For one thing, rocks are made of minerals, but minerals are not made of rocks. Then what exactly is a mineral? By asking the following four questions, you can tell whether something is a mineral:

Is it a solid? Minerals can't be gases or liquids.

Is it formed in nature? Crystalline materials made by people aren't classified as minerals.

Does it have a crystalline structure? Minerals are crystals, which have a repeating inner structure that is often reflected in the shape of the crystal. Minerals generally have the same chemical composition throughout.

Is it nonliving material? A mineral is inorganic, meaning it isn't made of living things.

A **mineral** is a naturally formed, inorganic solid with a crystalline structure. If you cannot answer "yes" to all four questions above, you don't have a mineral.

Minerals: From the Inside Out

Three of the four questions might be easy to answer. The one about crystalline structure may be more difficult. In order to understand what crystalline structure is, you need to know a little about the elements that make up a mineral. **Elements** are substances that cannot be broken down into simpler forms by ordinary chemical means. All minerals contain one or more of the 92 elements present in the Earth's crust.

How many elements does it take to "set" the periodic table? Find out by turning to page 582.

Each element is made of only one kind of atom. An **atom,** as you may recall, is the smallest part of an element that has all the properties of that element. Like all other substances, minerals are made up of atoms of one or more elements.

Most minerals are made of compounds of several different elements. A **compound** is a substance made of two or more elements that have been chemically joined, or bonded together. Halite, for example, is a compound of sodium and chlorine, as shown in **Figure 1.** A few minerals, such as gold and silver, are composed of only one element. For example, pure gold is made up of only one kind of atom—gold.

Atoms within a mineral are arranged in specific patterns, as shown in **Figure 2.** When atoms are arranged in a pattern, they form crystals.

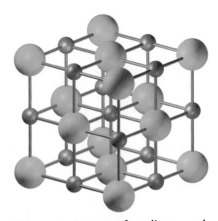

Figure 1 *Atoms of sodium and chlorine are joined together in a compound commonly known as rock salt, or the mineral halite.*

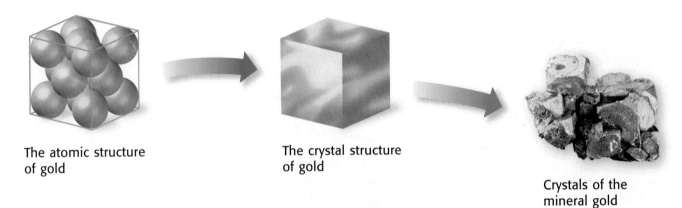

The atomic structure of gold

The crystal structure of gold

Crystals of the mineral gold

A mineral is made up of one or more crystals. **Crystals** are solid, geometric forms of minerals produced by a repeating pattern of atoms that is present throughout the mineral. A crystal's shape is determined by the arrangement of the atoms within the crystal. The arrangement of atoms in turn is determined by the kinds of atoms that make up the mineral. Each mineral has a definite crystalline structure. All of these structures can be grouped into six major classes according to the kinds of crystals they form. A chart of these six major crystal classes is shown below.

Figure 2 *The mineral gold is composed of gold atoms arranged in a crystalline structure.*

Crystal Classes

Isometric	Hexagonal	Tetragonal	Orthorhombic	Monoclinic	Triclinic

Types of Minerals

Minerals can be classified by a number of different characteristics. The most common classification of minerals is based on chemical composition. Minerals are divided into two groups based on the elements they are composed of. These groups are the silicate minerals and the nonsilicate minerals.

Silicate minerals   Silicon and oxygen are the two most common elements in the Earth's crust. Minerals that contain a combination of these two elements are called **silicate minerals.** Silicate minerals make up more than 90 percent of the Earth's crust—the rest is made up of nonsilicate minerals. Silicon and oxygen usually combine with other elements, such as aluminum, iron, magnesium, and potassium, to make up silicate minerals. Some of the more common silicate minerals are shown in **Figure 3.**

Feldspar The most common silicate mineral group in the crust is the feldspars. Feldspar minerals make up about half the Earth's crust, and they are the main component of most rocks on the Earth's surface. They contain the elements silicon and oxygen along with aluminum, potassium, sodium, and calcium. The pinkish crystals in the sample of granite shown below are feldspar.

Mica Mica minerals are shiny and soft, and they separate easily into sheets when they break. You can see one variety of mica in the granite sample. The two most common minerals of the mica group are *muscovite* and *biotite*. Muscovite is usually pale green, pale red, or clear, and biotite is brown or black.

Quartz Quartz (silicon dioxide, SiO_2) is the basic building block of many rocks. If you look closely at the piece of granite, you can see the quartz crystals. Even though there are many different forms of quartz, they all have the same chemical composition.

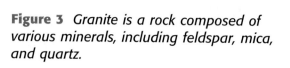

Figure 3 *Granite is a rock composed of various minerals, including feldspar, mica, and quartz.*

Nonsilicate Minerals Minerals that do not contain a combination of the elements silicon and oxygen form a group called the **nonsilicate minerals.** Some of these minerals are made up of elements such as carbon, oxygen, iron, and sulfur. Below are several categories of nonsilicate minerals.

Native elements are minerals that are composed of only one element. About 20 minerals are native elements. Some examples are gold (Au), platinum (Pt), diamond (C), copper (Cu), sulfur (S), and silver (Ag).	Native copper
Carbonates are minerals that contain combinations of carbon and oxygen in their chemical structure. Calcite ($CaCO_3$) is an example of a carbonate mineral. We use carbonate minerals in cement, building stones, and fireworks.	Calcite
Halides are compounds that form when atoms of the elements fluorine (F), chlorine (Cl), iodine (I), or bromine (Br) combine with sodium (Na), potassium (K), or calcium (Ca). Halite (NaCl) is better known as rock salt. Fluorite (CaF_2) can have many different colors. Halide minerals are often used to make fertilizer.	Fluorite
Oxides are compounds that form when an element, such as aluminum or iron, combines chemically with oxygen. Corundum (Al_2O_3) is an oxide mineral. Magnetite (Fe_3O_4) is an important iron ore. Oxide minerals are used to make abrasives and aircraft parts. They are also used to give false teeth a natural color.	Corundum
Sulfates contain sulfur and oxygen (SO_4). The mineral gypsum ($CaSO_4 \cdot 2H_2O$) is a common sulfate. It makes up the white sand at White Sands National Monument, in New Mexico. Sulfates are used in cosmetics, toothpaste, and paint.	Gypsum
Sulfides are minerals that contain one or more elements, such as lead, iron, or nickel, combined with sulfur. Galena (PbS) is a sulfide. Sulfide minerals are used to make batteries, medicines, and electronic parts.	Galena

REVIEW

1. What are the differences between atoms, compounds, and minerals?

2. Which two elements are most commonly found in minerals?

3. How are silicate minerals different from nonsilicate minerals?

4. **Making Inferences** Explain why each of the following is not considered a mineral: a cupcake, water, teeth, oxygen.

Identifying Minerals

If you found the two mineral samples below, how would you know if they were the same mineral?

By looking at these photographs, you can easily see physical similarities in the two mineral crystals. But how can you tell whether they are the same mineral? Moreover, how can you determine the identity of a mineral? In this section you will learn about the different properties that can help you identify minerals.

Luster Chart

Metallic

Submetallic

Nonmetallic

Vitreous
glassy, brilliant

Silky
swirly, fibrous

Resinous
plastic

Waxy
greasy, oily

Pearly
creamy

Earthy
rough, dull

Color

When you see a mineral, its *color* is probably the first thing you notice. Minerals come in many different colors and shades. The same mineral can come in a variety of colors. For example, in its purest state quartz is colorless. Quartz that contains small amounts of impurities, however, can be a variety of colors. Rose quartz gets its color from certain kinds of impurities. Amethyst, another variety of quartz, is purple because it contains other kinds of impurities.

Besides impurities, other factors can change the appearance of minerals. The mineral pyrite, often called fool's gold, normally has a golden color. But if pyrite is exposed to weather for a long period, it turns black. Because of factors such as weathering and impurities, color usually is not a reliable indicator of a mineral's identity. Although color can be helpful, other properties should be used to identify minerals.

Luster

The way a surface reflects light is called **luster.** When you say an object is shiny or dull, you are describing its luster. Minerals have metallic, submetallic, or nonmetallic luster. If a mineral is shiny, it may have either a glassy or a metallic luster. If the mineral is dull, its luster is either submetallic or nonmetallic. The different types of lusters are shown in the chart at left.

Streak

The color of a mineral in powdered form is called the mineral's **streak.** To find a mineral's streak, the mineral is rubbed against a piece of unglazed porcelain called a streak plate. The mark left on the streak plate by the mineral is the streak. The color of a mineral's streak is not always the same as the color of the mineral sample, as shown in **Figure 4.** Unlike the surface of the mineral sample, the streak is not affected by weathering. For this reason, streak is more reliable than color as an indicator of a mineral's identity.

Figure 4 *The color of the mineral hematite may vary, but the streak is always red-brown.*

Cleavage and Fracture

Different types of minerals break in different ways. The way a mineral breaks is determined by the arrangement of its atoms. **Cleavage** is the tendency of some minerals to break along flat surfaces. Gem cutters take advantage of natural cleavage to remove flaws from certain minerals, such as diamonds and rubies, and to shape them into beautiful gemstones. **Figure 5** shows minerals with different cleavage patterns.

Fracture is the tendency of some minerals to break unevenly along curved or irregular surfaces. Minerals that display fracture are shown in the chart below.

Figure 5 *Cleavage varies with mineral type. Mica breaks easily into distinct sheets. Halite breaks at 90° angles in three directions. Diamond breaks in four different directions.*

Mica

Halite

Diamond

Fracture

Conchoidal

Hackly

Splintery/uneven

Irregular/uneven

Once you've learned about the properties of minerals, put your knowledge to the test! To find out how, turn to page 494 in your LabBook.

Hardness

Hardness refers to a mineral's resistance to being scratched. If you try to scratch a diamond, you will have a tough time because diamond is the hardest mineral. Talc, on the other hand, is one of the softest minerals. You can scratch it with your fingernail. To determine the hardness of minerals, scientists use *Mohs' hardness scale,* shown below. Notice that talc has a rating of 1 and diamond has a rating of 10. Between these two extremes are other minerals with progressively greater hardness. For example, calcite is harder than gypsum, and fluorite is harder than calcite.

To identify a mineral using Mohs' scale, try to scratch the surface of a mineral with the edge of one of the 10 reference minerals. If the reference mineral scratches your mineral, it is harder than your mineral. Continue trying to scratch the mineral until you find a reference mineral that cannot scratch your mineral. If the two minerals do not scratch each other, they have the same hardness.

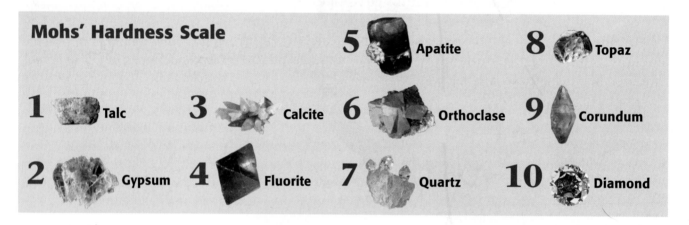

Mohs' Hardness Scale

1 Talc
2 Gypsum
3 Calcite
4 Fluorite
5 Apatite
6 Orthoclase
7 Quartz
8 Topaz
9 Corundum
10 Diamond

Density

If you pick up a golf ball and a table-tennis ball, which will feel heavier? Although the balls are of similar size, the golf ball will feel heavier because it is denser, as shown in **Figure 6**. **Density** is the measure of how much matter there is in a given amount of space. In other words, density is a ratio of an object's mass to its volume. Density is usually measured in grams per cubic centimeter. Because water has a density of 1 g/cm^3, it is used as a reference point for other substances. The ratio of an object's density to the density of water is called the object's *specific gravity.* The specific gravity of gold, for example, is 19. This means that gold has a density of 19 g/cm^3. In other words, there is 19 times more matter in 1 cm^3 of gold than in 1 cm^3 of water. Most nonmetallic minerals have a specific gravity between 2.5 and 4. Specific gravity can be used to help determine a mineral's identity.

Figure 6 *Because a golf ball has a greater density than a table-tennis ball, more table-tennis balls are needed to balance the scale.*

Special Properties

Some properties are particular to only a few types of minerals. The properties below can quickly help you identify the minerals shown. To identify some properties, however, you will need specialized equipment.

Fluorescence—Calcite and fluorite glow under ultraviolet light. The same fluorite sample below is shown in ultraviolet light and in white light.

Chemical reaction—Calcite will effervesce, or "fizz," when a drop of weak acid is placed on it.

Optical properties—A thin, clear piece of calcite placed over an image will cause a double image.

Special Properties of Some Minerals

Radioactivity—Minerals that contain radium or uranium can be detected by a Geiger counter.

Taste—Halite has a salty taste.

Magnetism—Magnetite and pyrrhotite are both natural magnets that attract iron.

REVIEW

1. How do you determine a mineral's streak?

2. What is the difference between cleavage and fracture?

3. How would you determine the hardness of an unidentified mineral sample?

4. **Applying Concepts** Suppose you have two minerals that have the same hardness. Which other mineral properties would you use to determine whether the samples are the same mineral?

For a list of minerals and their properties, see page 588.

The Formation and Mining of Minerals

NEW TERMS

ore
reclamation

OBJECTIVES

■ Describe the environments in which minerals are formed.
■ Compare and contrast the different types of mining.

Almost all known minerals can be found in the Earth's crust. They form in a large variety of environments under a variety of physical and chemical conditions. The environment in which a mineral forms determines the mineral's properties. Minerals form both deep beneath the Earth's surface and on or near the Earth's surface.

When a body of salt water, such as a lake or sea, dries up, minerals such as gypsum, anhydrite, and halite are left behind. As the salt water evaporates, these minerals crystallize, indicating where a body of salt water once existed.

Water that exists under ground is called ground water. Surface water and ground water carry dissolved materials into lakes and seas, where they crystallize. Minerals that may form in these environments include calcite and aragonite.

Changing conditions beneath the Earth's surface can alter the mineral composition of a preexisting rock. When changes in pressure, temperature, or chemical makeup alter a rock, *metamorphism* takes place. Minerals that form in metamorphic rock include calcite, garnet, graphite, hematite, magnetite, mica, and talc.

Heat and Pressure

Self-Check

Where do minerals such as gypsum, anhydrite, and halite form? *(See page 564 to check your answer.)*

Ground water that works its way down through cracks in the overlying rock is heated by magma. It then reacts with minerals in the walls of the cracks to form a hot liquid solution. Dissolved metals and other elements crystallize out of the hot fluid to form new minerals. Gold, copper, sulfur, pyrite, and galena form in such hot-water environments.

As magma moves upward it fills in pockets in preexisting rock, forming teardrop-shaped formations called *pegmatites.* Minerals crystallize from this magma as it cools. The presence of hot fluids causes the mineral crystals to become extremely large, sometimes growing to several meters across! Many gems and rare minerals, such as topaz and tourmaline, form in pegmatites.

As magma rises upward through the crust, it sometimes stops moving before it reaches the surface and cools slowly, forming millions of mineral crystals. The crystals that form are relatively large because they have a long time to grow as the magma cools. Eventually, the entire magma body solidifies to form a *pluton.* Mica, feldspar, magnetite, and quartz are some of the minerals that form from magma.

Magma

÷ 5 ÷ Ω ≤ ∞ +Ω √ 9 ∞ ≤ Σ 2
+

MATH BREAK

How Pure Is Pure?

Gold classified as 24-karat is 100 percent gold. Gold classified as 18-karat is 18 parts gold and 6 parts another, similar metal. It is therefore 18/24 or 3/4 pure. What is the percentage of pure gold in 18-karat gold?

Mining

Many kinds of rocks and minerals must be mined in order to extract the valuable elements they contain. Geologists use the term **ore** to describe a mineral deposit large enough and pure enough to be mined for a profit. Rocks and minerals are removed from the ground by one of two methods—surface mining or deep mining. The method miners choose depends on how far down in the Earth the mineral is located and how valuable the ore is. The two types of mining are illustrated below.

Surface mining is the removal of minerals or other materials at or near the Earth's surface. Types of surface mines include open pits, strip mines, and quarries. Materials mined in this way include copper ores and bauxite, a mixture of minerals rich in aluminum.

Deep mining is the removal of minerals or other materials from deep within the Earth. Shafts, tunnels, and other passageways must be dug underground to reach the ore. The retrieval of diamonds and coal commonly requires deep mining.

The Value of Minerals

Many of the metals you are familiar with originally came from mineral ores. You may not be familiar with the minerals, but you will probably recognize the metals extracted from the minerals. The table at right lists some mineral ores and some of the familiar metals that come from them.

As you have seen, some minerals are highly valued for their beauty rather than for their usefulness. Mineral crystals that are attractive and rare are called gems, or gemstones. An example of a gem is shown in **Figure 7.** Gems must be hard enough to be cut and polished.

Common Uses of Minerals		
Mineral	**Metal**	**Uses**
Chalcopyrite	copper	coins, electrical wire
Galena	lead	batteries, paints
Beryl	beryllium	bicycle frames, airplanes
Chromite	chromium	stainless steel, cast iron, leather tanners

Figure 7 *The Cullinan diamond is the largest diamond ever found. Before the largest piece of it was placed in the royal scepter of the British crown jewels, it had a mass of 3,106 carats.*

Responsible Mining

Mining gives us the minerals we need, but it also creates problems. Mining can destroy or disturb the habitats of plants and animals. The waste products from a mine can get into water sources, polluting both surface water and ground water.

One way to reduce the harmful effects of mining is to return the land to its original state after the mining is completed. This process is called **reclamation.** Reclamation of mined public land has been required by law since the mid-1970s. But reclamation is an expensive and time-consuming process. Another way to reduce the effects of mining is to reduce our need for minerals. We do this by recycling many of the mineral products we currently use, such as aluminum and iron. Mineral ores are *nonrenewable resources;* therefore, the more we recycle, the more we will have in the future.

Both sapphires and rubies are forms of the mineral *corundum.* The difference in the color of the gems is caused by trace amounts of metals within the crystal structure of corundum. Sapphires are blue due to the presence of iron and titanium. Rubies are red due to the presence of chromium.

REVIEW

1. Describe how minerals form underground.

2. What are the two main types of mining?

3. **Analyzing Ideas** How does reclamation protect the environment around a mine?

Chapter Highlights

SECTION 1

Vocabulary

mineral *(p. 60)*

element *(p. 60)*

atom *(p. 61)*

compound *(p. 61)*

crystal *(p. 61)*

silicate mineral *(p. 62)*

nonsilicate mineral *(p. 63)*

Section Notes

- A mineral is a naturally formed, inorganic solid with a definite crystalline structure.

- An atom is the smallest unit of an element that retains the properties of the element.

- A compound forms when atoms of two or more elements bond together chemically.

- Every mineral has a unique crystalline structure. The crystal class a mineral belongs to is directly related to the mineral's chemical composition.

- Minerals are classified as either silicates or nonsilicates. Each group includes different types of minerals.

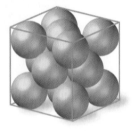  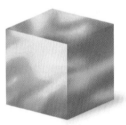

SECTION 2

Vocabulary

luster *(p. 64)*

streak *(p. 65)*

cleavage *(p. 65)*

fracture *(p. 65)*

hardness *(p. 66)*

density *(p. 66)*

Section Notes

- Color is not a reliable indicator for identifying minerals.

- The luster of a mineral can be metallic, submetallic, or nonmetallic.

- A mineral's streak does not necessarily match its surface color.

- The way a mineral breaks can be used to determine its identity. Cleavage and fracture are two ways that minerals break.

☑ Skills Check

Math Concepts

THE PURITY OF GOLD The karat is a measure of the purity of gold. Gold that is 24 karats is 100 percent gold. But gold that is less than 24 karats is mixed with other elements, so it is less than 100 percent gold. If you have a gold nugget that is 16 karats, then 16 parts out of 24 are pure gold—the other 8 parts are composed of other elements.

> 24 karats = 100% gold
> 16 karats = 24 karats − 8 karats
> $\frac{16}{24} = \frac{2}{3} = 0.67 = 67\%$ gold

Visual Understanding

ATOMIC STRUCTURE This illustration of the atomic structure of the mineral halite shows that halite is made of two elements—sodium and chlorine. The large spheres represent atoms of chlorine, and the small spheres represent atoms of sodium. The bars between the atoms represent the chemical bonds that hold them together.

- Mohs' hardness scale provides a numerical rating for the hardness of minerals.

- The density of a mineral can be used to identify it.

- Some minerals have special properties that can be used to quickly identify them.

Labs

Mysterious Minerals *(p. 494)*

Is It Fools Gold?—A Dense Situation *(p. 496)*

Vocabulary

ore *(p. 70)*

reclamation *(p. 71)*

Section Notes

- Minerals form in both underground environments and surface environments.

- Two main types of mining are surface mining and deep mining.

- Reclamation is the process of returning mined land to its original state.

Chapter Review

USING VOCABULARY

For each pair of terms, explain the difference in their meaning.

1. fracture/cleavage

2. element/compound

3. color/streak

4. density/hardness

5. silicate mineral/nonsilicate mineral

6. mineral/atom

UNDERSTANDING CONCEPTS

Multiple Choice

7. On Mohs' hardness scale, which of the following minerals is harder than quartz?
   a. talc
   b. apatite
   c. gypsum
   d. topaz

8. A mineral's streak
   a. is more reliable than color in identifying a mineral.
   b. reveals the mineral's specific gravity.
   c. is the same as a luster test.
   d. reveals the mineral's crystal structure.

9. Which of the following factors is **not** important in the formation of minerals?
   a. heat
   b. volcanic activity
   c. presence of ground water
   d. wind

10. Which of the following terms is **not** used to describe a mineral's luster?
    a. pearly
    b. waxy
    c. dull
    d. hexagonal

11. Which of the following is considered a special property that applies to only a few minerals?
    a. color
    b. luster
    c. streak
    d. magnetism

12. Which of the following physical properties can be expressed in numbers?
    a. luster
    b. hardness
    c. color
    d. reaction to acid

13. How many basic crystal classes are there?
    a. 3
    b. 10
    c. 5
    d. 6

14. Which of the following minerals would scratch fluorite?
    a. talc
    b. quartz
    c. gypsum
    d. calcite

Short Answer

15. Using no more than 25 words, define the term *mineral*.

16. In one sentence, describe how density is used to identify a mineral.

17. What methods of mineral identification are the most reliable? Explain.

Concept Mapping

18. Use the following terms to create a concept map: minerals, oxides, nonsilicates, carbonates, silicates, hematite, calcite, quartz.

Write one or two sentences to answer the following questions:

19. Suppose you have three rings, each with a different gem. One has a diamond, one has an amethyst (purple quartz), and one has a topaz. You mail the rings in a small box to your friend who lives five states away. When the box arrives at its destination, two of the gems are damaged. One gem, however, is damaged much worse than the other. What scientific reason can you give for the difference in damage?

20. While trying to determine the identity of a mineral, you decide to do a streak test. You rub the mineral across the plate, but it does not leave a streak. Does this mean your test failed? Explain your answer.

21. Imagine that you work at a jeweler's shop and someone brings in some "gold nuggets" that they want to sell. The person claims that an old prospector found the gold nuggets during the California gold rush. You are not sure if the nuggets are real gold. How would you decide whether to buy the nuggets? Which identification tests would help you decide the nuggets' identity?

22. Suppose that you find a mineral crystal that is as tall as you are. What kinds of environmental factors would cause such a crystal to form?

23. Gold has a specific gravity of 19. Pyrite's specific gravity is 5. How much denser is gold than pyrite?

24. In a quartz crystal there is one silicon atom for every two oxygen atoms. That means that the ratio of silicon atoms to oxygen atoms is 1:2. If there were 8 million oxygen atoms in a sample of quartz, how many silicon atoms would there be?

Imagine that you had a sample of feldspar and you analyzed it to find out what it is made of. The results of your analysis are shown below.

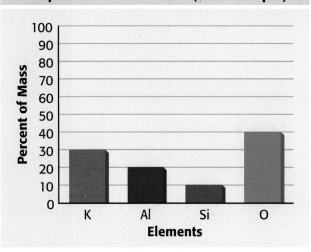

Composition of Orthoclase (Pink Feldspar)

25. Your sample consists of four elements. What percentage of each one is your sample made of?

26. If your mineral sample has a mass of 10 g, how many grams of oxygen does it contain?

27. Make a circle graph showing how much of each of the four elements the feldspar contains? (You will find help on making graphs in the Appendix of this book.)

NOW What Do You Think?

Take a minute to review your answers to the ScienceLog questions on page 59. Have your answers changed? If necessary, revise your answers based on what you have learned since you began this chapter.

WEIRD SCIENCE

LIGHTNING LEFTOVERS

Without warning, a bolt of lightning lashes out from a storm cloud and strikes a sandy shoreline with a crash. Almost instantly, the sky is dark again—the lightning has disappeared without a trace. Or has it?

Nature's Glass Factory

Fulgurites are a rare type of natural glass formed when lightning strikes silica-rich minerals that occur commonly in sand, soil, and some rocks. *Tubular fulgurites* are found in areas with a lot of silica, such as beaches or deserts. Lightning creates a tubular fulgurite when a bolt penetrates the sand and melts silica into a liquid. The liquid silica cools and hardens quickly, leaving behind a thin glassy tube, usually with a rough outer surface and a smooth inner surface. Underground, a fulgurite may be shaped like the roots of a tree. It branches out with many arms that trace the zigzag path of the lightning bolt. Some fulgurites are as short as your little finger, while others stretch 20 m into the ground.

Underground Puzzles

So should you expect to run across a fulgurite on your next trip to the beach? Don't count on it. Scientists and collectors search long and hard for the dark glass formations, which often form with little or no surface evidence pointing to their underground location. Even when a fulgurite is located, removing it in one piece is difficult. They are quite delicate, with walls no thicker than 1–2 mm. Some of the largest fulgurites are removed from the ground in many pieces then glued back into their original shape.

Rock Fulgurites

Rock fulgurites are extremely rare, usually occurring only on high mountains. These oddities are created when lightning strikes the surface of a silica-rich rock. A rock fulgurite often looks like a bubbly glass case 1–3 mm thick around the rock. Lightning travels around the outside of the rock, fusing silica-rich minerals on its surface. Depending on which minerals melt, a rock fulgurite's color can range from glassy black to light gray or even bright yellow.

Find Out More

► Investigate how scientists studying the formation of fulgurites try to make lightning bolts strike a precise location to create a new fulgurite. You may also want to do some research to find out about companies that will *create* a fulgurite just for you!

◄ *A Tubular Fulgurite*

Science Fiction

"The Metal Man"

by Jack Williamson

In a dark, dusty corner of Tyburn College Museum stands a life-sized statue of a man. Except for its strange greenish color, the statue looks pretty ordinary. But if you look closely, you will marvel at the perfect detail of the hair and skin. You will also see a strange mark on the statue's chest, a dark crimson shape with six sides.

No one knows how the statue ended up in the dark corner. Everyone believes that the Metal Man is, or once was, Professor Thomas Kelvin of the Geology Department. Professor Kelvin had for many years spent his summer vacations along the Pacific coast of Mexico, prospecting for radium. Then at the end of one summer, Kelvin did not return to Tyburn. He had been more successful than he ever dreamed, and he had become very rich. But high in the mountains, he had also found something else . . .

Now there is only one person who knows what really happened to Professor Kelvin, and he tells the professor's story in "The Metal Man," by Jack Williamson. The tale involves Kelvin's expedition to search for the source of El Rio de la Sangre, the River of Blood, and the radium that makes the river radioactive. Did he find it? Is that what made Kelvin so rich? And what else did Professor Kelvin find there in the remote mountain valley?

Read for yourself the strange story of Professor Kelvin and the Metal Man in the *Holt Anthology of Science Fiction.*

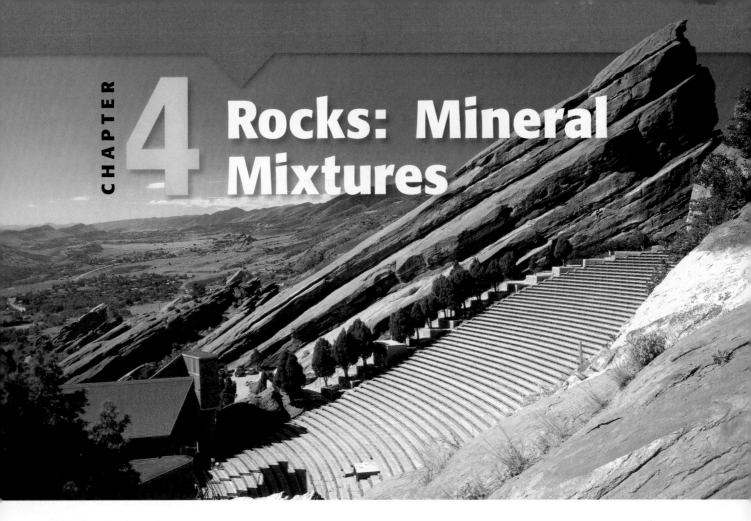

CHAPTER

4 Rocks: Mineral Mixtures

Imagine...

Imagine that you are an architect who has just been hired to design an amphitheater. The client wants the amphitheater to be big enough to host large concerts. In fact, she wants the amphitheater to seat an audience of 9,200. The client also wants excellent acoustics (sound qualities), and she wants it without a roof so the guests can enjoy the open air. She also wants the audience to be awed by two red sandstone formations that will tower 122 m above the stage.

You think about the design and come back with a plan that requires a minimum of 400 trillion metric tons of red sandstone for the walls and floor. You also estimate that it will take about 12 million years to form that much red sandstone. Sound ridiculous? Well, such an amphitheater actually exists.

Welcome to the Red Rocks Amphitheater just outside of Denver, Colorado. As you can

see, this amphitheater was created by the forces of nature rather than by human hands. The amphitheater is a perfect place for a rock concert, and it is also a good place to start thinking about rocks. Exploring rocks will help you better understand the natural world. For example, what exactly is a rock? And how are rocks important to the study of Earth science? You will be able to answer these questions as you read this chapter.

What Do You Think?

In your ScienceLog, try to answer the following questions based on what you already know:

1. What is the difference between a rock and a mineral?

2. What are some modern uses of rock?

3. How does rock form?

Investigate!

Round and Round in Circles

The type of rock you can see at Red Rocks Amphitheater is one of three major types of rock found on Earth. In the pages that follow, you will learn the names of these rock types and how they actually form. But first do this activity to demonstrate one of the most important ideas about rock.

Procedure

1. Using several pieces of **modeling clay** of different colors, form as many tiny balls as you can from each piece. These will represent tiny pieces of rock or sand.

2. Gather all the tiny balls of clay together in one pile. With your hand, gently press down on the clay until the balls stick together. This mixture of minerals will represent *sedimentary rock.* In your ScienceLog, describe the properties of your new "rock." How is it different from the tiny balls of clay you started with?

3. Now press down on the clay a little harder, flattening the tiny balls. Fold the clay in half and press down some more. This is your second type of rock. This new "rock" will represent *metamorphic rock.* Describe how it was formed in your ScienceLog.

4. Now press the clay and roll it around your desktop. Knead it like dough until the clay becomes one large mass of only one color. If you work the clay enough, it should start to feel a little warm. In this state, the clay represents hot, liquid rock material.

5. After your clay is warm and soft, form it into a rounded shape and let it cool and harden. This time the clay represents *igneous rock.* Describe how this "rock" is different from the first two you made.

6. Finally, break off bits of the "rock" and form tiny balls of clay. If you have time, go back to step 2.

Analysis

7. Review your descriptions of each type of "rock" in your ScienceLog. Which "rock" do you think resembles the rock that forms from erupting volcanoes?

8. In step 6 you were asked to go back to step 2. Explain how this activity can be described as a rock cycle.

Section 1

Understanding Rock

NEW TERMS

rock
rock cycle
magma
sedimentary rock
metamorphic rock
igneous rock
lava
composition
texture

OBJECTIVES

- Describe two ways rocks were used by early humans, and describe two ways they are used today.
- Describe how each type of rock changes into another as it moves through the rock cycle.
- List two characteristics of rock that are used to help classify it.

The Earth's crust is made up mostly of rock. But what exactly is rock? **Rock** is simply a solid mixture of crystals of one or more minerals. However, some types of rock, such as coal, are made of organic materials. Rocks come in all sizes—from pebbles to formations thousands of kilometers long!

The Value of Rock

Rock has been an important natural resource as long as humans have existed. Early humans used rocks as hammers to make other tools. They discovered that they could make arrowheads, spear points, knives, and scrapers by carefully hammering flint, chert, and obsidian rocks. See **Figure 1.** These rocks were shaped to form extremely sharp edges and points. Even today, obsidian is used to form special scalpels, as shown in **Figure 2.**

Rock has also been used for centuries to make buildings, roads, and monuments. **Figure 3** shows some inventive uses of rock by both ancient and modern civilizations. Buildings have been made out of marble, granite, sandstone, limestone, and slate. Modern buildings also use concrete, in which rock is an important ingredient. Concrete is one of the most common building materials used today.

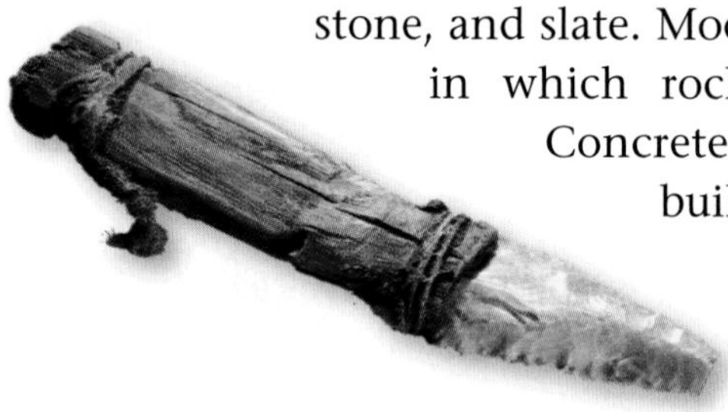

Figure 1 *This stone tool was made and used more than 5,000 years ago.*

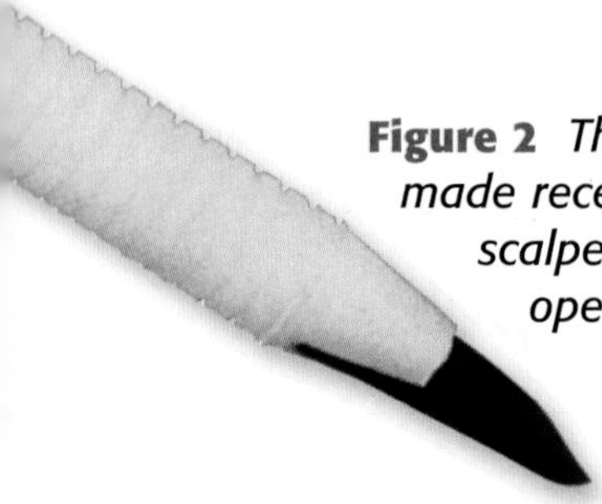

Figure 2 *This stone tool was made recently. It is an obsidian scalpel used in delicate operations.*

Figure 3 *These photos show a few samples of structures built with rock. On this page are structures built by ancient civilizations. On the facing page are some more-modern examples.*

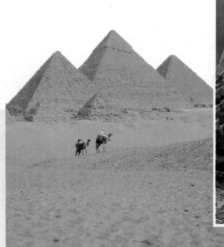

Pyramids at Giza, Egypt (3000 B.C.)

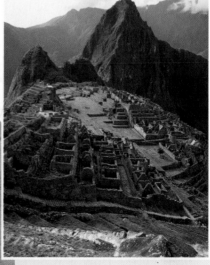

Machu Picchu, Peru (A.D. 600)

Humans have a long history with rock. Certain types of rock have helped us to survive and to develop both our ancient and modern civilizations. Rock is also very important to scientists. The study of rocks helps answer questions about the history of the Earth and our solar system. Rocks provide a record of what the Earth and other planets were like before recorded history.

The fossils some rocks contain also provide clues about life-forms that lived billions of years ago, long before dinosaurs walked the Earth. **Figure 4** shows how rocks can capture evidence of life that became extinct long ago. Without such fossils, scientists would know very little about the history of life on Earth. The answers we get from studying rocks often cause us to ask even more questions!

Is it possible to carve an entire city out of stone? Turn to page 104 to find out more.

Figure 4 *These fossilized remains of brachiopods were found on a mountaintop. Their presence indicates that what is now a mountaintop was once the bottom of a shallow sea.*

BRAIN FOOD

Some meteorites are actually rocks that come from other planets. Below is a microscopic view of a meteorite that came from Mars. The tiny structures may indicate that microscopic life once existed on Mars.

Exeter Cathedral, Exeter, England (A.D. 1120–1520)

LBJ Library, Austin, Texas (1972)

The Rock Cycle

The rocks in the Earth's crust are constantly changing. Rock changes its shape and composition in a variety of ways. The way rock forms determines what type of rock it is. The three main types of rock are *igneous, sedimentary,* and *metamorphic.* Each type of rock is a part of the *rock cycle.* The **rock cycle** is the process by which one rock type changes into another. Follow this diagram to see one way sand grains can change as they travel through the rock cycle.

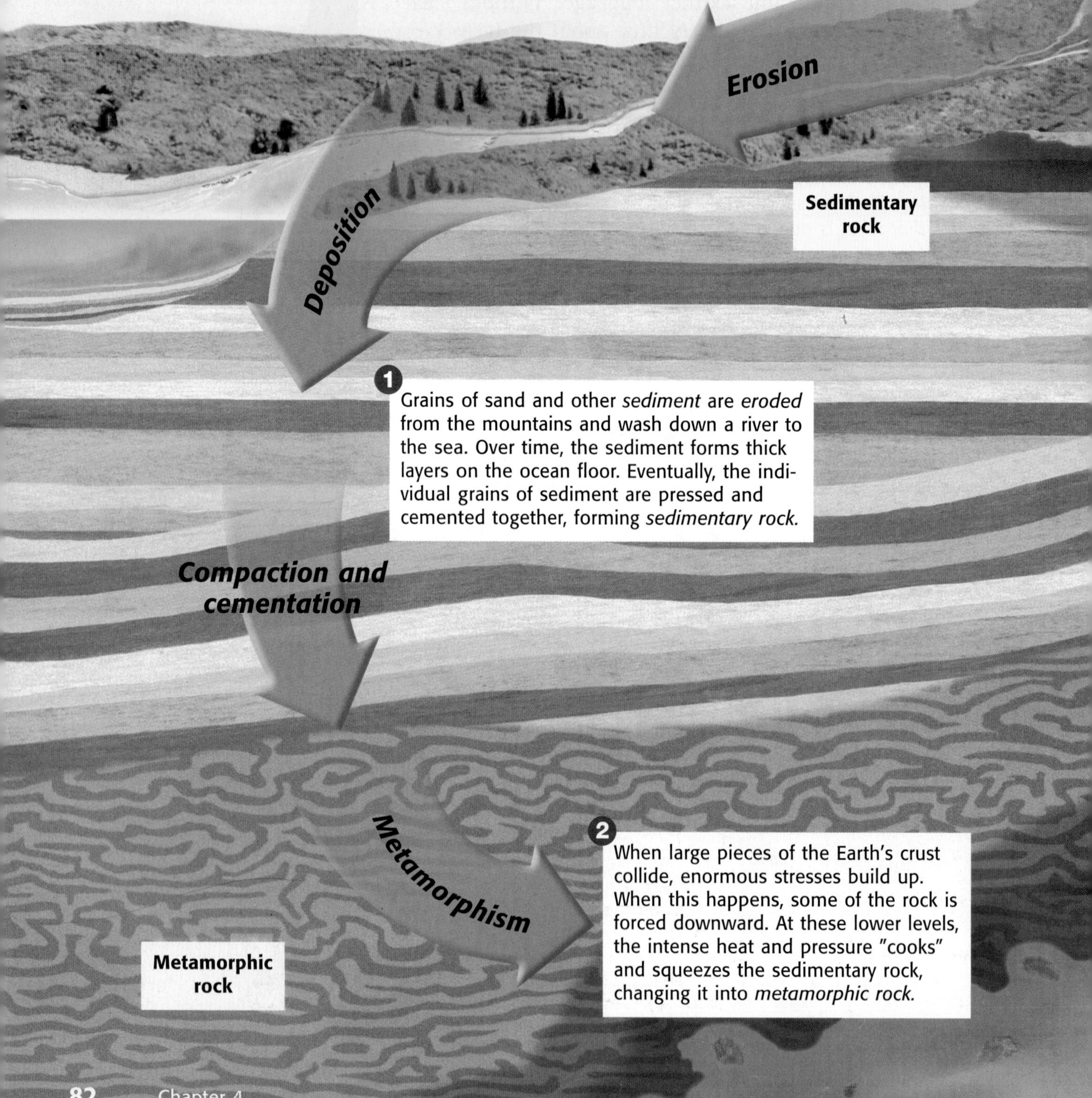

Erosion

Deposition

Sedimentary rock

1 Grains of sand and other *sediment* are *eroded* from the mountains and wash down a river to the sea. Over time, the sediment forms thick layers on the ocean floor. Eventually, the individual grains of sediment are pressed and cemented together, forming *sedimentary rock.*

Compaction and cementation

Metamorphism

2 When large pieces of the Earth's crust collide, enormous stresses build up. When this happens, some of the rock is forced downward. At these lower levels, the intense heat and pressure "cooks" and squeezes the sedimentary rock, changing it into *metamorphic rock.*

Metamorphic rock

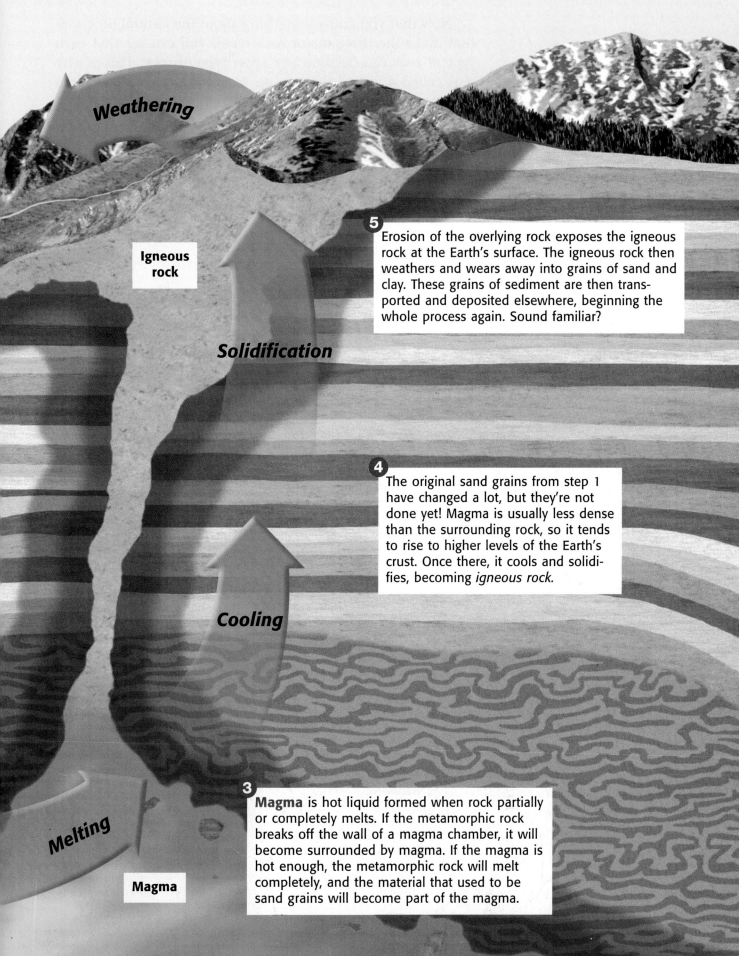

Weathering

Igneous
rock

5 Erosion of the overlying rock exposes the igneous rock at the Earth's surface. The igneous rock then weathers and wears away into grains of sand and clay. These grains of sediment are then transported and deposited elsewhere, beginning the whole process again. Sound familiar?

Solidification

4 The original sand grains from step 1 have changed a lot, but they're not done yet! Magma is usually less dense than the surrounding rock, so it tends to rise to higher levels of the Earth's crust. Once there, it cools and solidifies, becoming *igneous rock.*

Cooling

3 **Magma** is hot liquid formed when rock partially or completely melts. If the metamorphic rock breaks off the wall of a magma chamber, it will become surrounded by magma. If the magma is hot enough, the metamorphic rock will melt completely, and the material that used to be sand grains will become part of the magma.

Melting

Magma

Rocks: Mineral Mixtures   **83**

Now that you know something about the natural processes that make the three major rock types, you can see that each type of rock can become any other type of rock. This is why it is called a cycle—there is no beginning or end. All rocks are at some stage of the rock cycle and can change into a different rock type. **Figure 5** shows how the three types of rock change form.

Figure 5 The Rock Cycle

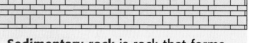

Sedimentary rock is rock that forms when sediments are compacted and cemented together. The sediments that form sedimentary rock come from the weathering and erosion of igneous, metamorphic, or even other sedimentary rock.

Weathering and erosion

Heat and pressure

Weathering and erosion

Weathering and erosion

Melting and cooling

Weathering and erosion

Metamorphic rock is rock that forms when the texture and composition of a preexisting rock is changed by heat or pressure deep underground. Igneous and sedimentary rock can change into metamorphic rock, and metamorphic rock can even change into another metamorphic rock.

Melting and cooling

Heat and pressure

Igneous rock is rock that forms from the cooling of *magma.* When magma cools and solidifies, it forms igneous rock. Magma forms in Earth's lower crust and upper mantle. When magma flows out onto the Earth's surface, it is called **lava.**

Heat and pressure

Melting and cooling

APPLY

Suppose you have an apple, a tomato, a peach, a kiwi fruit, a pineapple, a banana, a lemon, a cactus, a blue ball, a coconut, a brick, a sugar cube, a pair of sunglasses, and a garden hose. Use your imagination to invent three different ways to classify these objects into groups with similar characteristics. You may have as few as one group or as many as fourteen. What criteria did you use for each of your classification schemes? Which criteria would you use to classify rocks?

The Nitty-Gritty on Rock Classification

You now know that scientists classify all rock into three main types based on how they formed. But did you know that each type of rock is divided into even smaller groups? These smaller groups are also based on differences in the way rocks form. For example, all igneous rock forms when hot liquid cools and solidifies. But some igneous rocks form when lava cools on the Earth's surface, while others form when magma cools deep beneath the surface. Therefore, igneous rock is divided into two smaller groups, depending on how and where it forms. In the same way, sedimentary and metamorphic rocks are also divided into smaller groups. How do Earth scientists know how to classify different rocks? They study them in detail using two important criteria—*composition* and *texture*.

Composition The minerals a rock is made of determine the **composition** of the rock. For example, a rock that is made up mostly of the mineral quartz will have a composition very similar to quartz. A rock that is made of 50 percent quartz and 50 percent feldspar will have a very different overall composition. Use this idea to compare the examples given in **Figure 6**.

Figure 6 *The overall composition of a rock depends on the minerals it contains.*

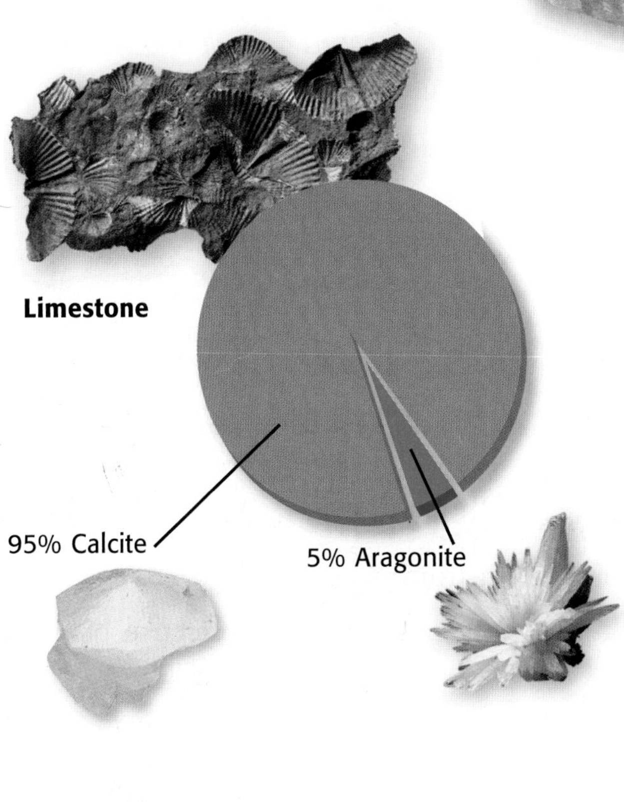

MATH BREAK

What's in It?

Assume that a granite rock you are studying is made of 30 percent quartz, 55 percent feldspar, and the rest biotite mica. What percentage of the rock is biotite mica?

Quartzite

100% Quartz

Limestone

95% Calcite

5% Aragonite

Granite

10% Biotite mica

35% Quartz

55% Feldspar

Texture The **texture** of a rock is determined by the sizes, shapes, and positions of the grains of which it is made. Rocks that are made entirely of small grains, such as silt or clay particles, are said to have a *fine-grained* texture. Rocks that are made of large grains, such as pebbles, are said to have a *coarse-grained* texture. Rocks that have a texture between fine- and coarse-grained are said to have a *medium-grained* texture. Examples of these textures are shown in **Figure 7.**

Figure 7 *These three sedimentary rocks are made up of grains of different sizes. Can you see the differences in their textures?*

Fine-grained	**Medium-grained**	**Coarse-grained**

Siltstone	Sandstone	Conglomerate

Each rock type has a different kind of texture. The texture of a rock is a good clue to how and where the rock formed. For example, the two rocks shown in **Figure 8** have textures that reflect how they formed. Both texture and composition are important characteristics that scientists use to understand the origin and history of rocks. Keep these characteristics in mind as you continue reading through this chapter.

Figure 8 *History is recorded in the texture of rock.*

This layered sandstone formed at the bottom of a river. You can see that the sediments from which it is made were deposited in layers.

This volcanic rock formed as a result of a violent eruption. The angular rock fragments were broken off a volcano during the eruption.

REVIEW

1. List two ways rock is important to humans today.

2. What are the three major rock types, and how can they change from one type to another type?

3. How is lava different from magma?

4. **Comparing Concepts** Explain the difference between texture and composition.

Igneous Rock

The word *igneous* comes from the Latin word for "fire." Magma cools into various types of igneous rock depending on the composition of the magma and the amount of time it takes the magma to cool and solidify. Like all other rock, igneous rock is classified according to its composition and texture.

Origins of Igneous Rock

Magma and lava solidify in the same way that water freezes. When magma or lava cools down enough, it solidifies, or "freezes," to form igneous rock. One major difference between water freezing and magma freezing is that water freezes at 0°C and magma and lava freeze at between 700°C and 1,250°C.

There are three ways magma can form: when rock is heated, when pressure is released, or when rock changes composition. To see how this can happen, follow along with **Figure 9.**

Figure 9 *There are three ways a rock can melt.*

Temperature An increase in temperature deep within the Earth's crust can cause the minerals in a rock to melt. Different minerals melt at different temperatures. So depending on how hot a rock gets, some of the minerals can melt while other minerals remain solid.

Pressure The high pressure deep within the Earth forces minerals to stay in the solid state, when otherwise they would melt from the intense heat. When hot rocks rise to shallow depths, the pressure is finally released and the minerals can melt.

Composition Sometimes fluids like water and carbon dioxide enter a rock that is close to its melting point. When these fluids combine with the rock, they can lower the melting point of the rock enough for it to melt and form magma.

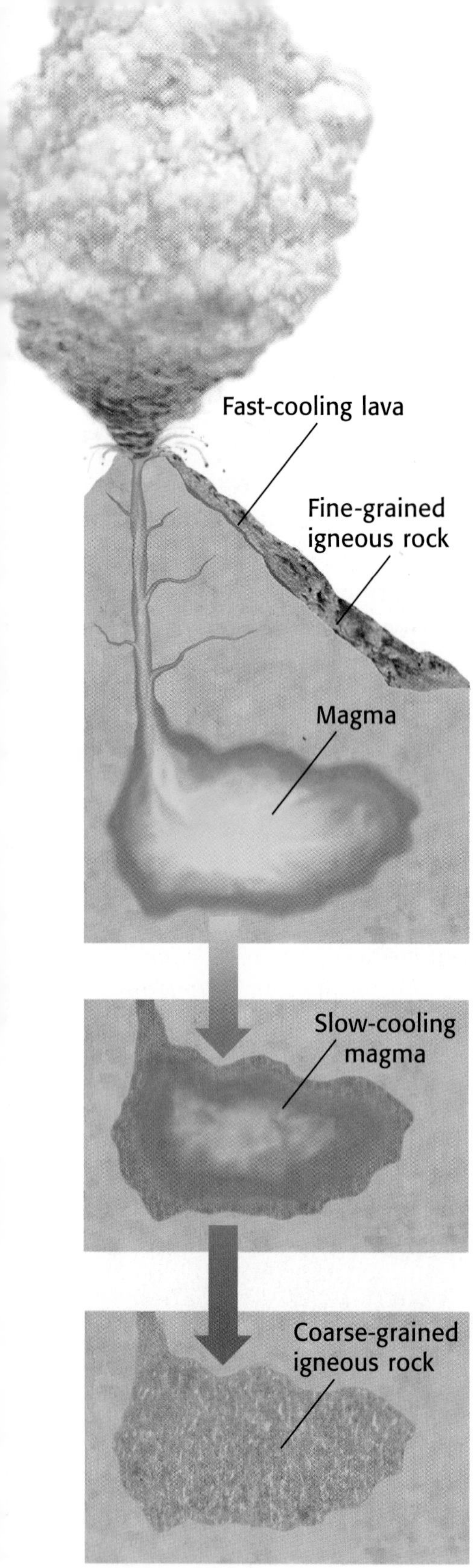

Composition and Texture of Igneous Rock

Look at the rocks in **Figure 10.** All of these are igneous rocks, even though they look very different from one another. These rocks differ from one another in what they are made of and how fast they cooled. Remember that igneous rocks are simply rocks that form as magma or lava cools. They are made of a variety of common minerals.

The light-colored rocks are not only lighter in color but also lighter in weight. These rocks are rich in elements such as silicon, aluminum, sodium, and potassium. These lightweight rocks are called *felsic*. The darker rocks are heavier than the felsic rocks. These rocks are rich in iron, magnesium, and calcium and are called *mafic*.

Figure 10 *Light-colored igneous rock generally has a felsic composition. Dark-colored igneous rock generally has a mafic composition.*

	Coarse-grained	Fine-grained
Felsic	 Granite	 Rhyolite
Mafic	 Gabbro	 Basalt

Now look at **Figure 11.** This illustration shows what happens to magma when it cools at different rates. The longer it takes for the magma or lava to cool, the more time mineral crystals have to grow. And the more time the crystals have to grow, the coarser the texture of the resulting igneous rock.

Figure 11 *The amount of time it takes for magma or lava to cool determines the texture of igneous rock.*

Fast-cooling lava

Fine-grained igneous rock

Magma

Slow-cooling magma

Coarse-grained igneous rock

✓ Self-Check

Rank the rocks shown in Figure 10 by how fast they cooled. Hint: Pay attention to their texture. (See page 564 to check your answer.)

Igneous Rock Formations

You have probably seen igneous rock formations that were caused by lava cooling on the Earth's surface. But not all magma reaches the surface. Some magma cools and solidifies deep within the Earth's crust.

Intrusive Igneous Rock When magma cools beneath the Earth's surface, the resulting rock is called **intrusive.** Intrusive rock usually has a coarse-grained texture. This is because it is well insulated by the surrounding rock and thus cools very slowly.

Intrusive rock formations are named for their size and the way in which they intrude, or push into, the surrounding rock. *Plutons* are large, balloon-shaped intrusive formations that result when magma cools at great depths. Intrusive rocks are also called *plutonic rocks,* after Pluto, the Roman god of the underworld. **Figure 12** shows an example of an intrusive formation that has been exposed on the Earth's surface. Some common intrusive rock formations are shown in **Figure 13.**

Figure 12 *Enchanted Rock, near Llano, Texas, is an exposed pluton made of granite.*

Figure 13 *Intrusive igneous rock formations occur in many different shapes and sizes. Dikes, plutons, and batholiths cut through existing rock formations. Sills and laccoliths intrude between layers of existing rock formations. Batholiths are the largest igneous formations of all.*

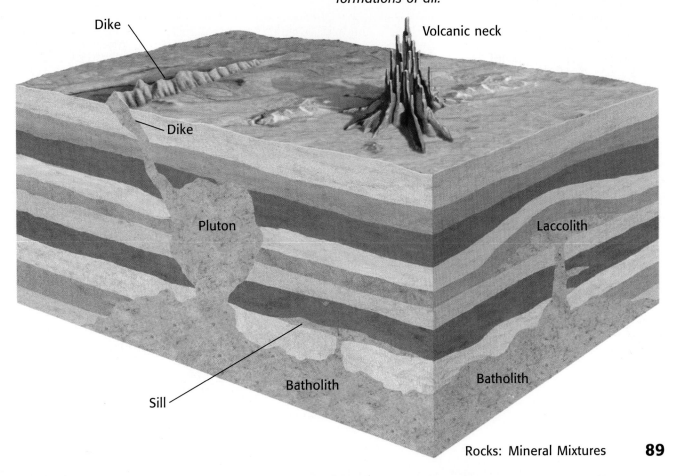

Dike

Volcanic neck

Dike

Pluton

Laccolith

Sill

Batholith

Batholith

Extrusive Igneous Rock Igneous rock that forms on the Earth's surface is called **extrusive.** Most volcanic rock is extrusive. Extrusive rock cools quickly on the surface and contains either very small crystals or none at all. Look at **Figure 14** to see samples of some common extrusive rocks.

When lava erupts from a volcano, a formation called a *lava flow* is made. You can see an active lava flow in **Figure 15.** But lava does not always come from volcanoes. Sometimes lava erupts from long cracks in the Earth's surface called *fissures.* When a large amount of lava flows out of a fissure, it can cover a vast area, forming a plain called a *lava plateau.* Preexisting landforms are often buried by extrusive igneous rock formations.

Figure 15 *Below is an active basalt flow. When exposed to surface conditions, lava quickly cools and solidifies.*

Pumice

Obsidian

Basalt

Figure 14 *These are some common extrusive igneous rocks. All three formed from volcanic eruptions.*

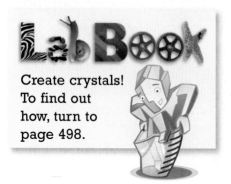

Create crystals! To find out how, turn to page 498.

REVIEW

1. What two properties are used to classify igneous rock?

2. How does the cooling rate of lava or magma affect the texture of an igneous rock?

3. **Interpreting Illustrations** Use the diagram in Figure 13 to compare a sill with a dike. What makes them different from each other?

Sedimentary Rock

Wind, water, ice, sunlight, and gravity all cause rock to *weather* into fragments. **Figure 16** shows how some sedimentary rocks form. Through the process of erosion, rock fragments, called sediment, are transported from one place to another. Eventually the sediment is deposited in layers. Sedimentary rock then forms as sediments become compacted and cemented together.

NEW TERMS
strata
stratification

OBJECTIVES

■ Describe how the two types of sedimentary rock form.
■ Explain how sedimentary rocks record Earth's history.

Origins of Sedimentary Rock

As new layers of sediment are deposited, the layers eventually become compressed, or compacted. Dissolved minerals separate out of the water to form a natural glue that binds the sediments together into sedimentary rock. Sedimentary rock forms at or near the Earth's surface, without the heat and pressure involved in the formation of igneous and metamorphic rocks. The physical features of sedimentary rock tell part of its history. The most noticeable feature of sedimentary rock is its layers, or **strata.** Road cuts and construction zones are good places to observe sedimentary rock formations, and as you can see in **Figure 17,** canyons carved by rivers provide some spectacular views.

Figure 16 **A Sedimentary Rock Cycle**

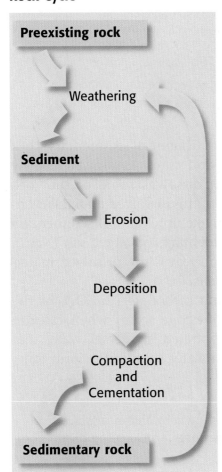

Preexisting rock

Weathering

Sediment

Erosion

Deposition

Compaction and Cementation

Sedimentary rock

Figure 17 *Millions of years of erosion by the Colorado River have revealed the rock strata in the walls of the Grand Canyon. In some parts of the canyon, the river has cut to a depth of 1.6 km below the rim.*

Rocks: Mineral Mixtures   **91**

Composition of Sedimentary Rock

Sedimentary rock is also classified by the way it forms. There are two main categories of sedimentary rock—clastic and chemical. *Clastic* rock forms when rock or mineral fragments, called clasts, stick together. *Chemical* rock forms when minerals crystallize out of a solution, such as sea water, to become rock.

Clastic Sedimentary Rock Clastic sedimentary rock is made of fragments of other rocks and minerals. As you can see in **Figure 18,** the size and shape of the rock fragments that make up clastic sedimentary rock influence their names.

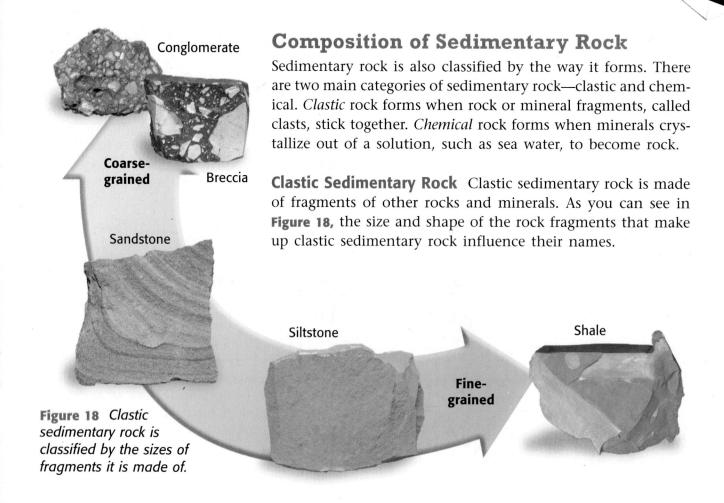

Conglomerate

Breccia

Coarse-grained

Sandstone

Siltstone

Shale

Fine-grained

Figure 18 *Clastic sedimentary rock is classified by the sizes of fragments it is made of.*

Chemical Sedimentary Rock Chemical sedimentary rock forms from *solutions* of minerals and water. As rainwater slowly makes its way to the ocean, it dissolves some of the rock material it passes through. Some of this dissolved material eventually forms the minerals that make up chemical sedimentary rock. One type of chemical sedimentary rock, rock salt (NaCl), forms when water evaporates and leaves the dissolved material behind in the form of minerals.

Limestone is made of calcium carbonate ($CaCO_3$), or the mineral calcite. One kind of limestone forms when calcium and carbonate become so concentrated in the sea water that calcite crystallizes out of the sea water solution to form limestone, as shown in **Figure 19.**

Figure 19 *Both salt water and fresh water contain dissolved calcium and carbonate. Chemical limestone forms on the ocean floor.*

Ca^{2+}

CO_3^{2-} → $CaCO_3$

Limestone

Most limestone forms from the remains of organisms, such as the shells of clams and the skeletons of tiny organisms called coral, that lived at the bottom of shallow seas. The shells or skeletons of these organisms are made of calcium carbonate, which comes from the sea water. This type of chemical sedimentary rock is forming even today. The remains of these sea animals are continuously accumulating on the ocean floor. Over time, these animal remains become cemented together to form *fossiliferous limestone.*

Figure 20 *One member of a coral colony is very small (left), but a colony of coral (center) is huge! Colonies of coral produced the Great Barrier Reef, which can be seen from orbiting satellites as a thin blue band (right).*

Fossils are the remains or traces of plants and animals that have been preserved in sedimentary rock. Fossils have given us enormous amounts of information about ancient life-forms and how they lived. Most fossils come from animals that lived in the oceans. Another type of organic limestone, shown in **Figure 21,** forms from organisms that leave their shells in the mud on the ocean floor.

Figure 21 *Shellfish, such as clams (left), get the calcium for their shells from sea water. When these organisms die, their shells collect on the ocean floor, eventually becoming rock (center). In time, huge rock formations result (right).*

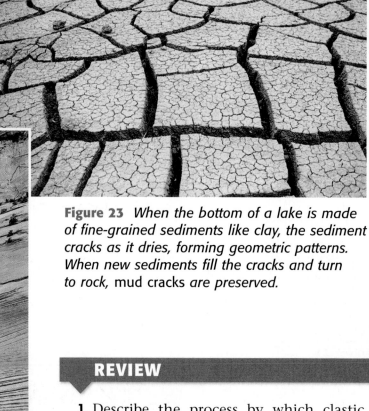

Sedimentary Rock Structures

Many sedimentary rock features can tell you about the way the rock formed. The most characteristic feature of sedimentary rock is **stratification,** or layering. Strata differ from one another depending on the kind, size, and color of their sediment. The rate of deposition can also affect the thickness of the layers. Sedimentary rocks sometimes record the motion of wind and water waves on lakes, seas, rivers, and sand dunes. Some of these features are shown in **Figures 22** through **24.**

Figure 22 *When water and wind transport and deposit sediments, some unique patterns develop.* Ripple marks *are made by flowing water and are preserved when the sediments become sedimentary rock.*

Figure 23 *When the bottom of a lake is made of fine-grained sediments like clay, the sediment cracks as it dries, forming geometric patterns. When new sediments fill the cracks and turn to rock,* mud cracks *are preserved.*

Figure 24 *Strata are not always parallel like the layers in a cake. Some strata are slanted. Wind caused these slanted deposits, called* cross-beds, *but water can also cause them.*

REVIEW

1. Describe the process by which clastic sedimentary rock forms.

2. List three sedimentary rock structures, and explain how they record geologic processes.

3. **Analyzing Relationships** Both clastic and chemical sedimentary rocks are classified according to texture and composition. Which property is more important for each sedimentary rock type? Explain.

Metamorphic Rock

The word *metamorphic* comes from *meta*, meaning "changed," and *morphos*, meaning "shape." Remember, metamorphic rocks are those in which the structure, texture, or composition of the rock has changed. Rock can undergo metamorphism by heat or pressure acting alone, or by a combination of the two. All three types of rock—igneous, sedimentary, and even metamorphic—can change into metamorphic rock.

How, you may ask, can a metamorphic rock change into another metamorphic rock? The answer is that there are different kinds of metamorphism. A metamorphic rock can be changed again when even more heat and pressure are applied to it. You will learn more about this as you read on.

NEW TERMS
foliated
nonfoliated

OBJECTIVES

- Describe two ways a rock can undergo metamorphism.
- Explain how the mineral composition of rocks changes as they undergo metamorphism.
- Describe the difference between foliated and nonfoliated metamorphic rock.

Origins of Metamorphic Rock

The texture or mineral composition of a rock can change when its surroundings change. If the temperature or pressure of the new environment is different from the one the rock formed in, the rock will undergo metamorphism.

Most metamorphic change is caused by increased pressure that takes place at depths greater than 2 km. At depths greater than 16 km, the pressure can be more than 4,000 times the pressure of the atmosphere! Look at **Figure 25.** This rock, called garnet schist, formed at a depth of about 30 km. Other types of schist form at much shallower depths.

The temperature at which metamorphism occurs ranges from 50°C to 1,000°C. At temperatures higher than 1,000°C, most rocks will melt. Metamorphism does not melt rock—when rock melts, it becomes magma and then igneous rock. In **Figure 26** you can see that this rock was deformed by intense pressure.

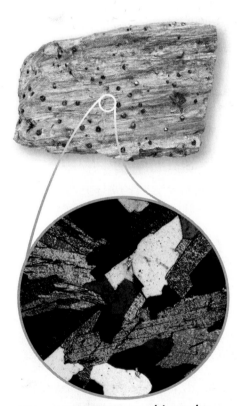

Figure 25 *Metamorphic rocks generally look as if they have been cooked and squeezed. At top is a metamorphic rock called garnet schist. At bottom is a microscopic view of a thin slice of a garnet schist.*

Figure 26 *In this outcrop, you can see an example of how sedimentary rock was deformed as it underwent metamorphism.*

One way rock can undergo metamorphism is by coming into contact with magma. When magma moves through the crust, its heat flows into the surrounding rock and "cooks" it. The heat and fluids from the magma change some of the minerals in the surrounding rock into other minerals. The greatest change takes place where magma comes into direct contact with the surrounding rock. The effect of heat gradually lessens with distance from the magma. As you can see in **Figure 27,** *contact metamorphism* only happens next to igneous intrusions, so it affects small amounts of rock.

Rock can also undergo *regional metamorphism* when enormous pressure builds up in rock that is deeply buried under other rock formations, or when large pieces of the Earth's crust collide with each other. The pressure and increased temperature that exist under these conditions cause rock to become deformed and chemically changed. This kind of metamorphic rock is underneath most continental rock formations, as shown below.

✓ Self-Check

How could a rock undergo both contact and regional metamorphism? *(See page 564 to check your answer.)*

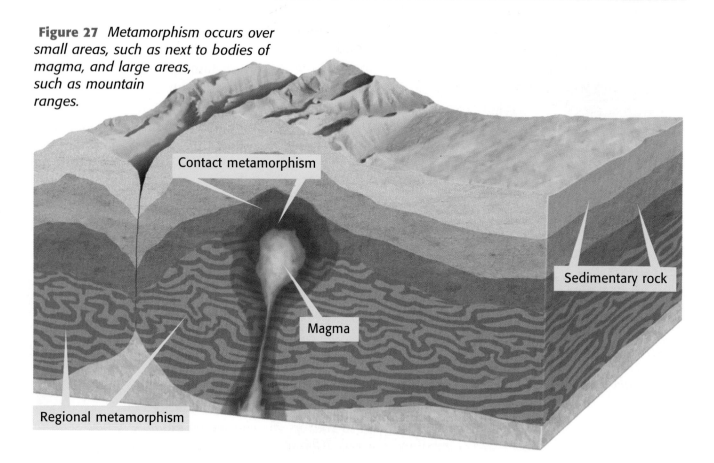

Figure 27 *Metamorphism occurs over small areas, such as next to bodies of magma, and large areas, such as mountain ranges.*

Contact metamorphism

Magma

Sedimentary rock

Regional metamorphism

Composition of Metamorphic Rock

When conditions within the Earth's crust change because of collisions between continents or the intrusion of magma, the temperature and pressure of the existing rock change. Minerals that were present in the rock when it formed may no longer be stable in the new environment. The original minerals change into minerals that are more stable in the new temperature and pressure conditions. Look at **Figure 28** to see an example of how this happens.

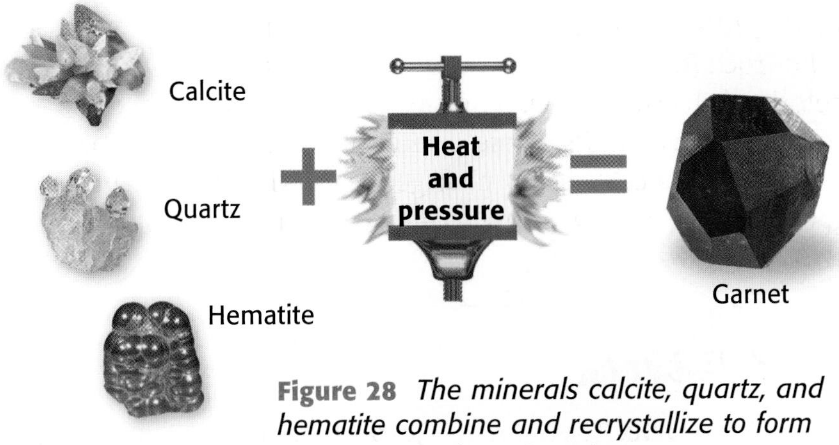

Calcite

Quartz

Heat and pressure

Hematite

Garnet

Figure 28 *The minerals calcite, quartz, and hematite combine and recrystallize to form the metamorphic mineral garnet.*

Explore

Did you know that you have a birthstone? Birthstones are gemstones, or mineral crystals. For each month of the year, there are one or two different birthstones. Find out which birthstone or birthstones you have by doing research in your school library or on the Internet. The names of birthstones are not usually the same as their actual mineral names. Find out which mineral is your birthstone. In what kind of rock would you likely find your birthstone? Why?

Many of these new minerals occur only in metamorphic rock. As shown in **Figure 29,** different metamorphic minerals reflect the different temperature and pressure conditions that existed when they formed. By knowing the temperature and pressure at which metamorphic minerals form, scientists can determine the depth and temperature at which recently exposed rock underwent metamorphism.

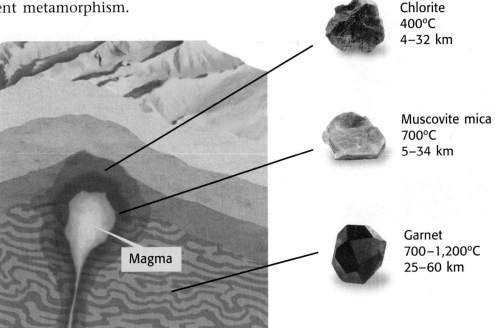

Figure 29
Metamorphism can occur in many different environments. Temperature and pressure conditions, as well as the composition of the rock, determine which metamorphic minerals will form.

Magma

Chlorite
400°C
4–32 km

Muscovite mica
700°C
5–34 km

Garnet
700–1,200°C
25–60 km

Textures of Metamorphic Rock

As you know, texture helps to classify igneous and sedimentary rock. The same is true of metamorphic rock. All metamorphic rock has one of two textures—*foliated* or *nonfoliated*. **Foliated** metamorphic rock consists of minerals that are aligned and look almost like pages in a book. **Nonfoliated** metamorphic rock does not appear to have any regular pattern. Let's take a closer look at each of these types of metamorphic rock to find out how they form.

Sedimentary shale

Slate

Phyllite

Figure 30 *The effects of metamorphism depend on the amount of heat and pressure applied to the rock. The more heat and pressure applied, the more intense the effects of metamorphism. Here you can see what happens to shale when it is exposed to more and more heat and pressure.*

Schist

Gneiss

Foliated Metamorphic Rock Foliated metamorphic rock contains mineral grains that are aligned by pressure. Strongly foliated rocks usually contain flat minerals, like biotite mica. Look at the foliated metamorphic rock slate and the original sedimentary rock shale, shown in **Figure 30.** Shale consists of layers of clay minerals. When subjected to a small degree of heat and pressure, the clay minerals change into mica minerals and the shale becomes a fine-grained, foliated metamorphic rock called slate. What happens if the slate is then put under more heat and pressure?

Metamorphic rocks can become other metamorphic rocks if the environment changes again. With additional heat and pressure, slate can change into phyllite, another metamorphic rock. When phyllite is exposed to additional heat and pressure, it can change into a metamorphic rock called schist.

As the degree of metamorphism increases, the arrangement of minerals in the rock changes. With additional heat and pressure, coarse-grained minerals separate into bands in a metamorphic rock called *gneiss* (pronounced "nice").

LabBook

Wouldn't it be "gneiss" to make your own foliated rock? Turn to page 503 in your LabBook to find out how.

Nonfoliated Metamorphic Rock Nonfoliated metamorphic rocks are shown in **Figure 31.** Do you notice anything missing? The lack of aligned mineral grains makes them nonfoliated. They are rocks commonly made of only one, or just a few, minerals.

Sandstone is a sedimentary rock made of distinct quartz sand grains. But when sandstone is subjected to the heat and pressure of metamorphism, the spaces between the sand grains disappear as they recrystallize, forming quartzite. Quartzite has a shiny, glittery appearance. It is still made of quartz, but the mineral grains are larger. When limestone undergoes metamorphism, the same process happens to the mineral calcite, and the limestone becomes marble. Marble has larger calcite crystals than limestone. You have probably seen marble in buildings and statues.

The term *metamorphosis* means "change in form." When certain animals undergo a dramatic change in the shape of their body, they are said to have undergone a metamorphosis. As part of their natural life cycle, moths and butterflies go through four stages of life. The first stage is when they are in the egg. After they hatch from an egg, they are in the larval stage, the form of a caterpillar. In the next stage they build a cocoon or become a chrysalis in response to chemical changes in their body. This is called the pupal stage. They finally emerge from the pupal stage and enter the adult stage of their life, complete with wings, antennae, and legs!

Marble

Quartzite

Figure 31 *Marble and quartzite are nonfoliated metamorphic rocks. As you can see in the microscopic views, none of the mineral crystals are aligned.*

REVIEW

1. What environmental factors cause rock to undergo metamorphism?

2. What is the difference between foliated and nonfoliated metamorphic rock?

3. **Making Inferences** If you had two metamorphic rocks, one with garnet crystals and the other with chlorite crystals, which one would have formed at a deeper level in the Earth's crust? Explain.

Chapter Highlights

SECTION 1

Vocabulary

rock (*p. 80*)

rock cycle (*p. 82*)

magma (*p. 83*)

sedimentary rock (*p. 84*)

metamorphic rock (*p. 84*)

igneous rock (*p. 84*)

lava (*p. 84*)

composition (*p. 85*)

texture (*p. 86*)

Section Notes

• Rocks have been used by humans for thousands of years, and they are just as valuable today.

• Rocks are classified into three main types—igneous, sedimentary, and metamorphic—depending on how they formed.

• The rock cycle describes the process by which a rock can change from one rock type to another.

• Scientists further classify rocks according to two criteria—composition and texture.

• Molten igneous material creates rock formations both below and above ground.

SECTION 2

Vocabulary

intrusive (*p. 89*)

extrusive (*p. 90*)

Section Notes

• The texture of igneous rock is determined by the rate at which it cools. The slower magma cools, the larger the crystals are.

• Felsic igneous rock is light-colored and lightweight, while mafic igneous rock is dark-colored and heavy.

• Igneous material that solidifies at the Earth's surface is called extrusive, while igneous material that solidifies within the crust is called intrusive.

Lab

Crystal Growth (*p. 498*)

☑ Skills Check

Math Concepts

MINERAL COMPOSITION Rocks are classified not only by the minerals they contain but also by the amounts of those minerals. Suppose a particular kind of granite is made of feldspar, biotite mica, and quartz. If you know that feldspar makes up 55 percent of the rock and biotite mica makes up 15 percent of the rock, the remaining 30 percent must be made of quartz.

55% feldspar	100% of granite
+ 15% biotite mica .or	– 55% feldspar
+ 30% quartz	– 15% biotite mica
= 100% of granite	= 30% quartz

Visual Understanding

PIE CHARTS The pie charts on page 85 help you visualize the relative amounts of minerals in different types of rock. The circle represents the whole rock, or 100%. Each part, or "slice," of the circle represents a fraction of the rock.

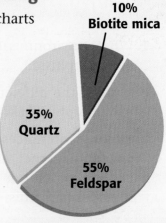

10%
Biotite mica

35%
Quartz

55%
Feldspar

SECTION 3

SECTION 3

Vocabulary

strata *(p. 91)*

stratification *(p. 94)*

Section Notes

- Clastic sedimentary rock is made of rock and mineral fragments that are compacted and cemented together. Chemical sedimentary rock forms when dissolved minerals crystallize out of a solution such as sea water.

- Sedimentary rocks record the history of their formation in their features. Some common features are strata, ripple marks, mud cracks, and fossils.

Lab

Let's Get Sedimental *(p. 501)*

SECTION 4

Vocabulary

foliated *(p. 98)*

nonfoliated *(p. 98)*

Section Notes

- One kind of metamorphism is the result of magma heating small areas of surrounding rock, changing its texture and composition.

- Most metamorphism is the product of heat and pressure acting on large regions of the Earth's crust.

- The mineral composition of a rock changes when the minerals it is made of recrystallize to form new minerals. These new minerals are more stable under increased temperature and pressure.

- Metamorphic rock that contains aligned mineral grains is called foliated, and metamorphic rock that does not contain aligned mineral grains is called nonfoliated.

Lab

Metamorphic Mash *(p. 503)*

 internet**connect**

 GO TO: go.hrw.com

GO TO: www.scilinks.org

Visit the **HRW** Web site for a variety of learning tools related to this chapter. Just type in the keyword:

KEYWORD: HSTRCK

Visit the **National Science Teachers Association** on-line Web site for Internet resources related to this chapter. Just type in the *sci*LINKS number for more information about the topic:

TOPIC: Rocks and Human History	*sci*LINKS NUMBER: HSTE080
TOPIC: Rock in Architecture	*sci*LINKS NUMBER: HSTE085
TOPIC: Composition of Rock	*sci*LINKS NUMBER: HSTE090
TOPIC: Rock Formations	*sci*LINKS NUMBER: HSTE095
TOPIC: Petra: The Rock City	*sci*LINKS NUMBER: HSTE100

Chapter Review

To complete the following sentences, choose the correct term from each pair of terms listed below:

1. ___?___ igneous rock is more likely to have coarse-grained texture than ___?___ igneous rock. (*Extrusive/intrusive* or *Intrusive/extrusive*)

2. ___?___ metamorphic rock texture consists of parallel alignment of mineral grains. (*Foliated* or *Nonfoliated*)

3. ___?___ sedimentary rock forms when grains of sand become cemented together. (*Clastic* or *Chemical*)

4. ___?___ cools quickly on the Earth's surface. (*Lava* or *Magma*)

5. Strata are found in ___?___ rock. (*igneous* or *sedimentary*)

UNDERSTANDING CONCEPTS

Multiple Choice

6. A type of rock that forms deep within the Earth when magma solidifies is called
   a. sedimentary.
   b. metamorphic.
   c. organic.
   d. igneous.

7. A type of rock that forms under high temperature and pressure but is not exposed to enough heat to melt the rock is
   a. sedimentary.
   b. metamorphic.
   c. organic.
   d. igneous.

8. After they are deposited, sediments, such as sand, are turned into sedimentary rock when they are compacted and
   a. cemented.
   b. metamorphosed.
   c. melted.
   d. weathered.

9. An igneous rock with a coarse-grained texture forms when
   a. magma cools very slowly.
   b. magma cools very quickly.
   c. magma cools quickly, then slowly.
   d. magma cools slowly, then quickly.

10. The layering that occurs in sedimentary rock is called
    a. foliation.
    b. ripple marks.
    c. stratification.
    d. compaction.

11. An example of a clastic sedimentary rock is
    a. obsidian.
    b. sandstone.
    c. limestone.
    d. marble.

12. A common sedimentary rock structure is
    a. a sill.
    b. a pluton.
    c. cross-bedding.
    d. a lava flow.

13. An example of mafic igneous rock is
    a. granite.
    b. basalt.
    c. quartzite.
    d. pumice.

14. Chemical sedimentary rock forms when
    a. magma cools and solidifies.
    b. minerals are twisted into a new arrangement.
    c. minerals crystallize from a solution.
    d. sand grains are cemented together.

15. Which of the following is a foliated metamorphic rock?
    a. sandstone
    b. gneiss
    c. shale
    d. basalt

Short Answer

16. In no more than three sentences, explain the rock cycle.

17. How are sandstone and siltstone different from one another? How are they the same?

18. In one or two sentences, explain how the cooling rate of magma affects the texture of the igneous rock that is formed.

Concept Mapping

19. Use the following terms to create a concept map: rocks, clastic, metamorphic, nonfoliated, igneous, intrusive, chemical, foliated, extrusive, sedimentary.

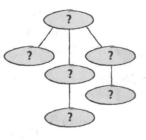

CRITICAL THINKING AND PROBLEM SOLVING

Write one or two sentences to answer the following questions:

20. The sedimentary rock coquina is made up of pieces of seashells. Which of the two kinds of sedimentary rock could it be? Explain.

21. If you were looking for fossils in the rocks around your home and the rock type that was closest to your home was metamorphic, would you find many fossils? Why or why not?

22. Suppose you are writing a book about another planet. In your book, you mention that the planet has no atmosphere or weather. Which type of rock will you not find on the planet? Explain.

23. Imagine that you want to quarry or mine granite. You have all of the equipment, but you need a place to quarry. You have two pieces of land to choose from. One piece is described as having a granite batholith under it, and the other has a granite sill. If both plutonic bodies were at the same depth, which one would be a better buy for you? Explain your answer.

MATH IN SCIENCE

24. If a 60 kg granite boulder were broken down into sand grains and if quartz made up 35 percent of the boulder's mass, how many kilograms of the resulting sand would be quartz grains?

INTERPRETING GRAPHICS

The red curve on the graph below shows how the melting point of a particular rock changes with increasing temperature and pressure. Use the graph to answer the questions below.

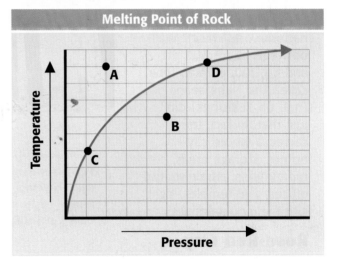

25. What type of material, liquid or solid, would you find at point **A**? Why?

26. What would you find at point **B**?

27. Points **C** and **D** represent different temperature and pressure conditions for a single, solid rock. Why does this rock have a higher melting temperature at point **D** than it does at point **C**?

NOW What Do You Think?

Take a minute to review your answers to the ScienceLog questions on page 79. Have your answers changed? If necessary, revise the answers based on what you have learned since you began this chapter.

Science, Technology, and Society

Rock City

Today when we dig into a mountainside to build a highway or make room for a building, we use heavy machinery and explosives. Can you imagine doing the same job with just a hammer and chisel? Well, between about 300 B.C. and A.D. 200, an Arab tribe called the Nabataeans (nab uh TEE uhns) did just that. In fact, they carved a whole city—homes, storage areas, monuments, administrative offices, and temples—right into the mountainsides!

▲ Petra's most famous building, the Treasury, was shown in the movie Indiana Jones and the Last Crusade.

Rose-Red City

This amazing city in southern Jordan is Petra (named by the Roman emperor Hadrian Petra during a visit in A.D. 131). A poet once described Petra as "the rose-red city" because all the buildings and monuments were carved from the pink sandstone mountains surrounding Petra.

Using this reddish stone, the Nabataeans lined the main street in the center of the city with tall stone columns. The street ends at what was once the foot of a mountain but is now known as the Great Temple—a two-story stone religious complex larger than a football field!

The High Place of Sacrifice, another site near the center of the city, was a mountaintop. The Nabataeans leveled the top and created a place of worship more than 1,000 m above the valley floor. Today visitors climb stairs to the top. Along the way, they pass dozens of tombs carved into the pink rock walls.

Tombs and More Tombs

There are more than 800 other tombs dug into the mountainsides in and around Petra. One of them, the Treasury (created for a Nabataean ruler), stands more than 40 m high! It is a magnificent building with an elaborate facade. Behind the massive stone front, the Nabataeans carved one large room and two smaller rooms deeper into the mountain.

Petra Declines

The Nabataeans once ruled an area extending from Petra to Damascus. They grew wealthy and powerful by controlling important trade routes near Petra. But their wealth attracted the Roman Empire, and in A.D. 106, Petra became a Roman province. Though the city prospered under Roman rule for almost another century, a gradual decline in Nabataean power began. The trade routes by land that the Nabataeans controlled for hundreds of years were abandoned in favor of a route by the Red Sea. People moved and the city faded. By the seventh century, nothing was left of Petra but empty stone structures.

Think About It!

▶ Petra is sometimes referred to as a city "from the rock as if by magic grown." Why might such a city seem "magic" to us today? What might have encouraged the Nabataeans to create this city? Share your thoughts with a classmate.

Glass Scalpels

Would you want your surgeon to use a scalpel that was thousands of years old? Probably not, unless it was a razor-sharp knife blade made of obsidian, a natural volcanic glass. Such blades and arrowheads were used for nearly 18,000 years by our ancestors. Recently, physicians have found a new use for these Stone Age tools. Obsidian blades, once used to hunt woolly mammoths, are now being used as scalpels in the operating room!

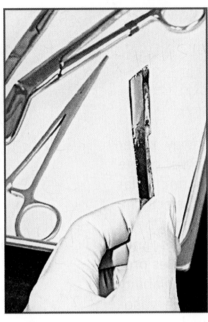

▲ *An obsidian scalpel can have an edge as fine as a single molecule.*

Obsidian or Stainless Steel?

Traditionally, physicians have used inexpensive stainless-steel scalpel blades for surgical procedures. Steel scalpels cost about $2 each, and surgeons use them just once and throw them away. Obsidian scalpels are more expensive—about $20 each—but they can be used many times before they lose their keen edge. And obsidian scalpel blades can be 100 times sharper than traditional scalpel blades!

During surgery, steel scalpels actually tear the skin apart. Obsidian scalpels divide the skin and cause much less damage. Some plastic surgeons use obsidian blades to make extremely fine incisions that leave almost no scarring. An obsidian-scalpel incision heals more quickly because the blade causes less damage to the skin and other tissues.

Many patients have allergic reactions to mineral components in steel blades. These patients often do not have an allergic reaction when obsidian scalpels are used. Given all of these advantages, it is not surprising that some physicians have made the change to obsidian scalpels.

A Long Tradition

Early Native Americans were among the first people to recognize that chipped obsidian has extremely sharp edges. Native Americans made obsidian arrowheads and knife blades by flaking away chips of rock by hand. Today obsidian scalpels are fashioned in much the same way by a *knapper,* a person who makes stone tools by hand. Knappers use the same basic technique that people have used for thousands of years to make obsidian blades and other stone tools.

Find Out for Yourself!

► Making obsidian blades and other stone tools requires a great deal of skill. Find out about the steps a knapper follows to create a stone tool. Find a piece of rock, and see if you can follow the steps to create a stone tool of your own. Be careful not to hit your fingers, and wear safety goggles.

5 Energy Resources

Imagine . . .

Imagine cruising down the highway faster than 100 km/h using only the power of the sun! Sound impossible? Well, it's not. Solar cars—cars that run exclusively on electricity converted from the sun's energy—have been around for years. Unlike driving gasoline-powered vehicles, driving these vehicles produces no air pollution, and the availability of the sun's energy isn't limited like gasoline. Scientists expect the sun to keep giving off energy for billions of years! Gasoline, on the other hand, comes from oil that we pump out of the Earth's crust. And most scientists think that oil will become scarce sometime in the twenty-first century.

So why don't you see solar cars zipping down the roads in your town every day after school? The main reason is that the technology still has a long way to go before solar cars will be practical. But the technology is becoming more advanced, and perhaps one day soon solar cars will be an option for motorists. Take a look at the variety of solar cars shown here, and prepare to learn how solar energy fits in with our wide assortment of energy resources.

All over the world, car companies, universities, and experimental technologists are continuing to develop more-efficient solar cars.

What Do You Think?

In your ScienceLog, try to answer the following questions based on what you already know:

1. List four nonrenewable resources.

2. On which energy resources do humans currently depend the most?

3. What is the difference between a solar cell and a solar panel?

What Is the Sun's Favorite Color?

Are some colors better than others at absorbing the sun's energy? If so, how might this relate to collecting solar energy? Try the following activity to answer these questions.

Procedure

1. Obtain at least five **balloons** that are the same size and shape. One balloon should be white, and one should be black. The others can be whatever colors you can find.

2. Use **scissors** to cut at least half the stem off each of the balloons.

3. Place one large **ice cube** or several small cubes in each balloon. Each balloon should contain the same amount of ice.

4. Line the balloons up on a flat, uniformly colored surface that receives direct sunlight. Make sure that all the balloons receive the same amount of sunlight and that the openings in the balloons are not facing directly toward the sun.

5. Keep track of how much time it takes for the ice to melt completely in each of the balloons. You can tell how much ice has melted in each balloon by pinching the balloon's opening and then gently squeezing the balloon.

Analysis

6. In which balloon did the ice melt first? Why?

7. What color would you paint a device used to collect solar energy?

Natural Resources

NEW TERMS
natural resource
renewable resource
nonrenewable resource
recycling

OBJECTIVES
- Determine how humans use natural resources.
- Contrast renewable resources with nonrenewable resources.
- Explain how humans can conserve natural resources.

Think of the Earth as a giant life-support system for all of humanity. The Earth's atmosphere, waters, and solid crust provide almost everything we need to survive. The atmosphere provides the air we need to breathe, distributes heat to maintain air temperatures, and produces rain. The oceans and other waters of the Earth provide food and needed fluids. The solid part of the Earth provides nutrients and minerals.

Interactions between the Earth's systems can cause changes in the Earth's environments. Organisms must adapt to these changes if they are to survive. Humans have found ways to survive by using natural resources to change their immediate surroundings. A **natural resource** is any natural substance, organism, or energy form that living things use. Few of the Earth's natural resources are used in their unaltered state. Most resources are made into products that make people's lives more comfortable and convenient, as shown in **Figure 1.**

Figure 1 *Lumber, gasoline, and electricity are all products that come from natural resources.*

This pile of lumber is made of wood, which comes from trees.

The gasoline in this can is made from oil pumped from the Earth's crust.

Electricity generated by these wind turbines ultimately comes from the sun's energy.

Renewable Resources

Some natural resources are renewable. A **renewable resource** is a natural resource that can be used and replaced over a relatively short time. **Figure 2** shows several examples of renewable resources. Although many resources are renewable, humans often use them more quickly than they can be replaced. Trees, for example, are renewable, but humans are currently cutting trees down more quickly than other trees can grow to replace them.

Figure 2 *Fresh water, fish, and trees are just a few of the renewable resources available on Earth.*

Nonrenewable Resources

Not all of Earth's natural resources are renewable. A **nonrenewable resource** is a natural resource that cannot be replaced or that can be replaced only over thousands or millions of years. Examples of nonrenewable resources are shown in **Figure 3.** The amounts of nonrenewable resources on Earth are fixed with respect to their availability for human use. Once nonrenewable resources are used up, they are no longer available. Oil and natural gas, for example, exist in limited quantities. When these resources become scarce, humans will have to find other resources to replace them.

Figure 3 *Nonrenewable resources, such as coal, natural gas, and iron ore, can be replaced only over thousands or millions of years once they are used up.*

APPLY

Find five products in your home that were made from natural resources. List the resource or resources from which each product was made. Label each resource as renewable or nonrenewable.

Are the products made from mostly renewable or nonrenewable resources? Are those renewable resources plentiful on Earth? Do humans use those renewable resources more quickly than the resources can be replaced? What can you do to help conserve nonrenewable resources and renewable resources that are becoming more scarce?

Figure 4 *You can recycle many household items to help conserve natural resources.*

Sit on your trash! Turn to page 130 to find out how today's garbage becomes tomorrow's park benches.

Conserving Natural Resources

Whether the natural resources we use are renewable or nonrenewable, we should be careful how we use them. To conserve natural resources, we should try to use them only when necessary. For example, leaving the faucet running while brushing your teeth wastes clean water. Turning the faucet on only to rinse your brush saves a lot of water that you or others need for other uses.

Another way to conserve natural resources is to recycle, as shown in **Figure 4. Recycling** is the use of used or discarded materials that have been reprocessed into new products. Recycling allows manufacturers to reuse natural resources when making new products. This in turn reduces the amount of natural resources that must be obtained from the Earth. For example, recycling aluminum cans reduces the amount of aluminum that must be mined from the Earth's crust to make new cans.

> **REVIEW**

1. How do humans use most natural resources?

2. What is the difference between renewable and nonrenewable resources?

3. Name two ways to conserve natural resources.

4. **Applying Concepts** List three renewable resources not mentioned in this section.

Fossil Fuels

OBJECTIVES

- Classify the different forms of fossil fuels.
- Determine how fossil fuels form.
- Identify where fossil fuels are found in the United States.
- Explain how fossil fuels are obtained.
- Identify problems with fossil fuels.
- List ways to deal with fossil-fuel problems.

Energy resources are natural resources that humans use to produce energy. There are many types of renewable and nonrenewable energy resources, and all of the energy released from these resources ultimately comes from the sun. The energy resources on which humans currently depend the most are fossil fuels. **Fossil fuels** are nonrenewable energy resources that form in the Earth's crust over millions of years from the buried remains of once-living organisms. Energy is released from fossil fuels when they are burned. There are many types of fossil fuels, which exist as liquids, gases, and solids, and humans use a variety of methods to obtain and process them. These methods depend on the type of fossil fuel, where the fossil fuel is located, and how the fossil fuel formed. Unfortunately, the methods of obtaining and using fossil fuels can have negative effects on the environment. Read on to learn about fossil fuels and the role they play in our lives.

Liquid Fossil Fuels—Petroleum

Petroleum, or crude oil, is an oily mixture of flammable organic compounds from which liquid fossil fuels and other products, such as asphalt, are separated. Petroleum is separated into several types of fossil fuels and other products in refineries, such as the one shown in **Figure 5.** Among the types of fossil fuels separated from petroleum are gasoline, jet fuel, kerosene, diesel fuel, and fuel oil.

Figure 5 *Fossil fuels and other products are separated from petroleum in a process called* fractionation. *In this process, petroleum is gradually heated in a tower so that different components boil and vaporize at different temperatures. Lighter components vaporize first and collect at the top of the tower, while heavier components vaporize last and collect at the bottom of the tower.*

Gaseous Fossil Fuels—Natural Gas

Gaseous fossil fuels are classified as **natural gas.** Most natural gas is used for heating and for generating electricity. The stove in your kitchen may be powered by natural gas. Many motor vehicles, such as the van in **Figure 6,** are fueled by liquefied natural gas. Vehicles like these produce less air pollution than vehicles powered by gasoline.

Methane is the main component of natural gas. But other natural-gas components, such as butane and propane, can be separated and used by humans. Butane is often used as fuel for camp stoves. Propane is often used as a heating fuel and as a cooking fuel, especially for outdoor grills.

chemistry
CONNECTION

Petroleum and natural gas are both made of compounds called hydrocarbons. A *hydrocarbon* is an organic compound containing only carbon and hydrogen.

Figure 6 *Vehicles powered by liquefied natural gas are becoming more common.*

Figure 7 *This coal is being gathered so that it may be burned in the power plant shown in the background. Burning coal provides energy that can be converted to electricity.*

Solid Fossil Fuels—Coal

The solid fossil fuel that humans use most is coal. **Coal** is a solid fossil fuel formed underground from buried, decomposed plant material. Coal, the only fossil fuel that is a rock, was once the leading source of energy in the United States. People burned coal for heating and transportation. Many trains in the 1800s and early 1900s were powered by coal-burning steam locomotives.

People began to use coal less because burning coal often produces large amounts of air pollution and because better energy resources were discovered. Coal is no longer used much as a fuel for heating or transportation in the United States. However, many power plants, like the one shown in **Figure 7,** burn coal to produce electricity.

How Do Fossil Fuels Form?

All fossil fuels form from the buried remains of ancient organisms. But different types of fossil fuels form in different ways and from different types of organisms. Petroleum and natural gas form mainly from the remains of microscopic sea life. When these organisms die, their remains settle on the ocean floor, where they decay and become part of the ocean sediment. Over time, the sediment slowly becomes rock, trapping the decayed remains. Through physical and chemical changes over millions of years, the remains become petroleum and gas. Gradually, more rocks form above the rocks that contain the fossil fuels. Under the pressure of overlying rocks and sediments, the fossil fuels are squeezed out of their source rocks and into permeable rocks. As shown in **Figure 8,** these permeable rocks become reservoirs for petroleum and natural gas. The formation of petroleum and natural gas is an ongoing process. Part of the remains of today's sea life will probably become petroleum and natural gas millions of years from now.

Turn to page 131 to read about the nineteenth-century "oil rush" in the United States.

To obtain petroleum and gas, engineers must drill wells into the reservoir rock.

After fuels are successfully tapped, pumps must sometimes be installed to remove them.

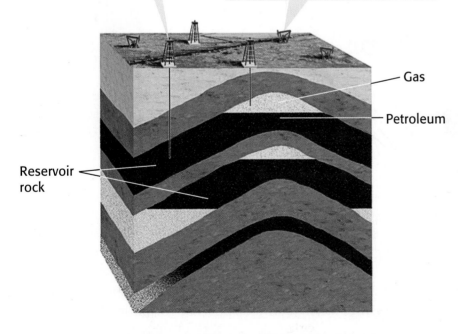

Gas

Petroleum

Reservoir rock

Figure 8 *Petroleum and gas rise from source rock into reservoir rock. Sometimes the fuels are trapped by overlying rock that is impermeable. Rocks that are folded upward are excellent fossil-fuel traps.*

Quick Lab

Rock Sponge

What properties of reservoir rock allow oil and gas to be easily pumped from it? Investigate this question by trying the following activity:

1. Place samples of **sandstone, limestone,** and **shale** in separate **Petri dishes.**

2. Place 5 drops of light **machine oil** on each rock sample.

3. Observe and record the time required for the oil to be absorbed by each of the rock samples.

4. Which rock sample absorbed the oil fastest? Why?

5. Based on your findings, describe a property that allows for easy removal of fossil fuels from reservoir rock. Write your answers and observations in your ScienceLog.

Coal forms differently from petroleum and natural gas. Coal forms underground over millions of years from decayed swamp plants. When swamp plants die, they sink to the bottom of the swamps. This begins the process of coal formation, which is illustrated below. Notice that the percentage of carbon increases with each stage. The higher the carbon content, the cleaner the material burns. However, all grades of coal will pollute the air when burned.

The Process of Coal Formation

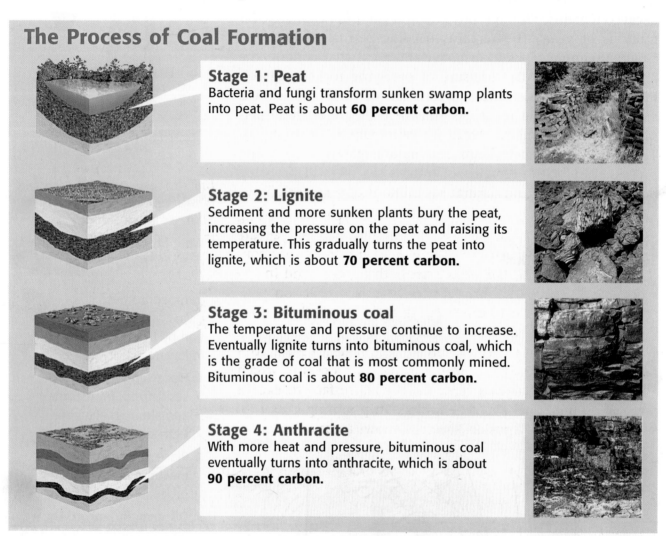

Stage 1: Peat
Bacteria and fungi transform sunken swamp plants into peat. Peat is about **60 percent carbon.**

Stage 2: Lignite
Sediment and more sunken plants bury the peat, increasing the pressure on the peat and raising its temperature. This gradually turns the peat into lignite, which is about **70 percent carbon.**

Stage 3: Bituminous coal
The temperature and pressure continue to increase. Eventually lignite turns into bituminous coal, which is the grade of coal that is most commonly mined. Bituminous coal is about **80 percent carbon.**

Stage 4: Anthracite
With more heat and pressure, bituminous coal eventually turns into anthracite, which is about **90 percent carbon.**

REVIEW

1. Name a solid, liquid, and gaseous fossil fuel.

2. What component of coal-forming organic material increases with each step in coal formation?

3. **Comparing Concepts** What is the difference between the organic material from which coal forms and the organic material from which petroleum and natural gas mainly form?

Where Are Fossil Fuels Found?

Fossil fuels are found in many parts of the world, both on land and beneath the ocean. As shown in **Figure 9,** the United States has large reserves of petroleum, natural gas, and coal. In spite of all our petroleum reserves, we import about one-half of our petroleum and petroleum products from the Middle East, South America, and Africa.

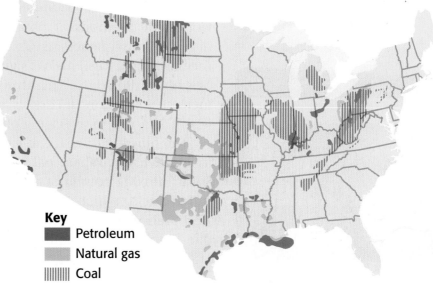

Key

■ Petroleum

░ Natural gas

||||||| Coal

How Do Humans Obtain Fossil Fuels?

Humans use different methods to remove fossil fuels from the Earth's crust. These methods depend on the type of fuel being obtained and its location. Petroleum and natural gas are removed from the Earth by drilling wells into rock that contains these resources. Oil wells exist both on land and in the ocean. For offshore drilling, engineers mount drills on platforms that are secured to the ocean floor or float at the ocean's surface. **Figure 10** shows an offshore oil rig.

Coal is obtained either by mining deep beneath the Earth's surface or by strip mining. **Strip mining** is a process in which rock and soil are stripped from the Earth's surface to expose the underlying materials to be mined. Strip mining is used to mine shallow coal deposits. **Figure 11** shows a coal strip mine.

Figure 9 *Coal beds in the United States range in thickness from a few centimeters to nearly 50 m. Most oil and gas produced in the continental United States comes from California, Louisiana, and Texas. There are also large volumes of oil and gas in Alaska and offshore in the Gulf of Mexico.*

Figure 10 *Large oil rigs, some more than 300 m tall, operate offshore in many places, such as the Gulf of Mexico and the North Sea.*

Figure 11 *Strip miners use explosives to blast away rock and soil and to expose the material to be mined.*

Problems with Fossil Fuels

Although fossil fuels provide energy for our technological world, the methods of obtaining and using them can have negative consequences. For example, some scientists think that the burning of fossil fuels is significantly increasing the amount of carbon dioxide in the atmosphere. It is possible that this increase in carbon dioxide is contributing to *global warming,* which is a rise in average global temperatures.

The burning of coal can cause damage to the environment in another way. When coal is burned, sulfur dioxide is released. Sulfur dioxide combines with moisture in the air to produce sulfuric acid, which is one of the acids in acid precipitation. **Acid precipitation** is rain or snow that has a high acid content due mainly to air pollutants. Acid precipitation negatively affects wildlife, plants, buildings, and statues, as shown in **Figure 12.**

The mining of coal can also create environmental problems. Strip mining removes soil, which plants need for growth and some animals need for shelter. If land is not properly repaired afterward, strip mining can destroy wildlife habitats. Coal mines that are deep underground, such as the one shown in **Figure 13,** can be hazardous to the men and women working in them. Coal mining can also lower local water tables, pollute water supplies, and cause the overlying earth to collapse.

Figure 12 *Acid precipitation can exist as rain, snow, mist, or any other form of precipitation. Acid precipitation can dissolve parts of statues (top) and kill trees (bottom).*

Figure 13 *Coal dust can damage the human respiratory system. And because coal dust is flammable, it increases the danger of fire and explosion in coal mines.*

Obtaining petroleum can also cause environmental problems. In 1989, the supertanker *Exxon Valdez* spilled about 257,000 barrels of crude oil into the water when it ran aground off the coast of Alaska. The oil killed hundreds of thousands of animals and damaged the local fishing industry.

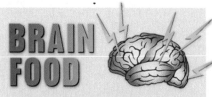

Although some countries have reduced their use of coal, the known coal reserves will last no more than 250 years at the present rates of coal consumption.

In addition to possibly contributing to global warming, burning petroleum products causes a big environmental problem called smog. **Smog** is a photochemical fog produced by the reaction of sunlight and air pollutants. Smog is particularly serious in places such as Denver and Los Angeles. In these cities, the sun shines most of the time, there are millions of automobiles, and surrounding mountains prevent the wind from blowing pollutants away. **Figure 14** shows a city with a smog problem. Smog levels in some cities, including Denver and Los Angeles, have begun to decrease in recent years.

Figure 14 *Smog reduces visibility and is dangerous to the human respiratory system.*

Dealing with Fossil-Fuel Problems

So what can be done to solve fossil-fuel problems? Obviously we can't stop using fossil fuels any time soon—we are too dependent on them. But there are things we can do to minimize the negative effects of fossil fuels. By traveling in automobiles only when absolutely necessary, people can cut down on car exhaust in the air. Carpooling, riding a bike, walking, and using mass-transit systems also help by reducing the number of cars on the road. These measures help reduce the negative effects of using fossil fuels, but they do not eliminate the problems. Only by using certain alternative energy resources, which you will learn about in the next section, can we eliminate them.

REVIEW

1. Name a state with petroleum, natural-gas, and coal reserves.

2. How do we obtain petroleum and natural gas? How do we obtain coal?

3. Name three problems with fossil fuels. Name three ways to minimize the negative effects of fossil fuels.

4. **Making Inferences** Why does the United States import petroleum from other regions even though the United States has its own petroleum reserves?

Figure 15 *Using mass transit or modes of transportation other than automobiles can help reduce air pollution due to burning fossil fuels.*

Alternative Resources

The energy needs of industry, transportation, and housing are increasingly met by electricity. However, most electricity is currently produced from fossil fuels, which are nonrenewable and cause pollution when burned. In the past, geologists have been able to find new fossil-fuel reserves to balance those being consumed. But this cannot go on forever. For people to continue their present lifestyles, new sources of energy must become available.

Splitting the Atom

Nuclear energy is an alternative source of energy that is derived from the nuclei of atoms. Most often it is produced by a process called *fission*. Fission is a process in which the nuclei of radioactive atoms are split and energy is released, as shown in **Figure 16.** Nuclear power plants use radioactive atoms, such as uranium-235, as fuel. When fission takes place, a large amount of energy is released. The energy is used to produce steam to run electric generators in the power plant.

There are more than 400 nuclear power plants in operation around the world. About 75 percent of France's electricity comes from nuclear energy, while less than 10 percent of the energy used in the United States comes from nuclear energy.

OBJECTIVES

■ Describe alternatives to the use of fossil fuels.

■ List advantages and disadvantages of using alternative energy resources.

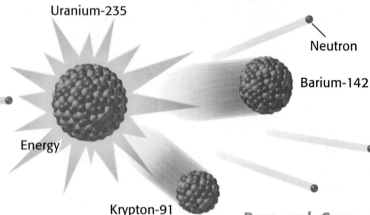

Uranium-235

Neutron

Barium-142

Energy

Krypton-91

Figure 16 *The process of fission generates a tremendous amount of energy.*

Pros and Cons Nuclear power plants provide alternative sources of energy without the problems that come with fossil fuels. So why don't we use nuclear energy instead of fossil fuels? Nuclear power plants produce dangerous wastes. The wastes are unsafe because they are radioactive. Radioactive wastes, such as the ones shown in **Figure 17,** must be removed from the plant and stored until they lose their radioactivity. But nuclear wastes can remain dangerously radioactive for thousands of years. A safe place must be found to store these wastes so that radiation cannot escape into the environment.

Figure 17 *The symbol on these barrels of nuclear waste represents radioactivity. Areas or objects marked with this symbol should be approached only after taking proper precautions.*

Because nuclear power plants generate a lot of heat, large amounts of water are used in cooling towers, like the ones shown in **Figure 18,** to cool the plants. If a plant's cooling system were to stop working, the plant would overheat, and its reactor could possibly melt. Then a large amount of radiation could escape into the environment, as it did at Chernobyl, Ukraine, in 1986.

There is another type of nuclear energy that is potentially so abundant as to be considered inexhaustible. This energy is produced by *fusion.* Fusion is the joining of nuclei of small atoms to form larger atoms. This is the same process that is thought to produce energy in the sun.

The main advantage of fusion compared with fission is that fusion produces few dangerous wastes. The main disadvantage of fusion is that very high temperatures are required for the reaction to take place. No known material can withstand temperatures that high, so the reaction must occur within a special environment, such as a magnetic field. So far, fusion reactions have been limited to laboratory experiments.

Figure 18 *Cooling towers are one of many safety mechanisms used in nuclear power plants. Their purpose is to prevent the plant from overheating.*

Sitting in the Sun

When sunlight falls on your skin, the warmth you feel is part of solar energy. **Solar energy** is energy from the sun. Every day, the Earth receives more than enough solar energy to meet all of our energy needs. And since the Earth continuously receives solar energy, the energy is a renewable resource.

There are two common ways that we use solar energy. The use you are probably most familiar with is changing it directly into electricity. Sunlight can be changed into electricity by the use of solar cells. You may have used a calculator, like the one shown in **Figure 19,** that was powered by solar cells.

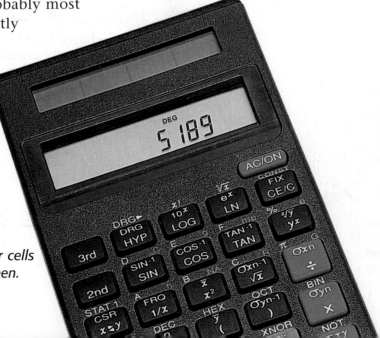

Figure 19 *This solar calculator receives all the energy it needs through the four solar cells located above its screen.*

Did you know that the energy from petroleum, coal, and natural gas is really a form of stored solar energy? All organisms ultimately get their energy from sunlight and store it in their cells. When ancient organisms died and became trapped in sediment, some of their energy was stored in the fossil fuel that formed in the sediment. So the gasoline that powers today's cars contains energy from sunlight that fell on the Earth millions of years ago!

A single solar cell produces only a tiny amount of electricity. For small electronic devices, such as calculators, this is not a problem because enough energy can be obtained with only a few cells. But in order to provide enough electricity for larger objects, such as a house, thousands of cells are needed. Has anyone tried this? They sure have. Many homes and businesses use solar panels mounted on their roof to provide much of their needed electricity. Solar panels are large panels made up of many solar cells wired together. **Figure 20** shows a building with solar panels.

Figure 20 *Although they are expensive to install, solar panels are good investments in the long run.*

Solar cells are reliable and quiet, have no moving parts, and can last for years with little maintenance. They produce no pollution during use, and pollution created by their manufacturing process is very low.

So why doesn't everyone use solar cells? The answer is cost. While solar energy itself is free, solar cells are relatively expensive to make. In a house built with enough solar panels to provide all needed electricity, the cost of the solar power system could account for one-third of the cost of the entire house. But in remote areas where it is difficult and costly to run electric wires, solar power systems can be a realistic option. In the United States today, tens of thousands of homes use solar panels to produce electricity.

Can you think of other places that you have seen solar panels? Take a look at **Figure 21.** There are even experimental solar-powered airplanes and cars, such as the cars you read about at the beginning of this chapter.

Figure 21 *Perhaps you have seen solar panels used in this manner in your town.*

Another use of solar energy is direct heating through solar collectors. Solar collectors are dark-colored boxes with glass or plastic tops. Sun shines into the boxes, making the temperature inside very hot. Running through the boxes are liquid-filled tubes. As the liquid moves through the box, the liquid increases in temperature. A common use of solar collectors is heating water, as shown in **Figure 22.** Over 1 million solar water heaters have been installed in the United States. They are especially common in Florida, California, and some southwestern states.

As with solar cells, the problem with solar collectors is cost. But solar collectors quickly pay for themselves—heating water is one of the major uses of electricity in American homes. Also, solar collectors can be used to generate electricity.

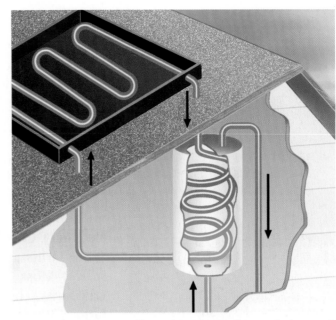

Figure 22 *After the liquid in the collector is heated by the sun, it is pumped through tubes that run through a water heater, causing the temperature of the water to rise.*

Large-Scale Solar Power So far you have seen how solar cells and solar panels can be used to generate electricity for a building or other solitary object. But what about providing solar energy for multiple objects? Experimental solar-power facilities, such as the one shown in **Figure 23,** have shown that this is a possibility. Facilities like this one are designed to use mirrors to focus sunlight onto coated steel pipes filled with synthetic oil. The oil is heated by the sunlight and is then used to heat water. The heated liquid water turns to steam, which is used to drive electric generators.

Turn to page 506 to calculate the power of the sun.

An alternative design for solar power facilities is one that uses mirrors to reflect sunlight onto a receiver on a central tower. The receiver captures the sunlight's energy and stores it in tanks of molten salt. The stored energy is then used to create steam, which drives a turbine in an electric generator. *Solar Two,* a solar-power facility designed in this manner, was capable of generating enough energy to power 10,000 homes in southern California.

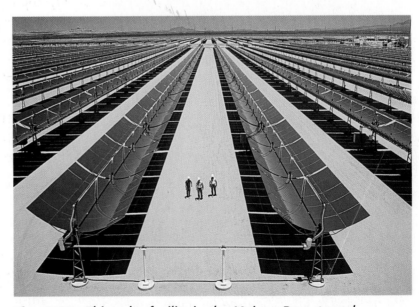

Figure 23 *This solar facility in the Mojave Desert used sun-tracking mirrors called* heliostats.

Capture the Wind

Wind is created indirectly by solar energy through the uneven heating of air. There is a tremendous amount of energy in wind, called **wind energy.** You can see the effects of this energy unleashed in a hurricane or tornado. Wind energy can also be used productively by humans. Wind energy can turn a windmill, like the one shown in **Figure 24,** pumping water or producing electricity. Small windmills have been generating electricity in the United States since the 1920s.

Today, fields of modern wind turbines—technological updates of the old windmills—generate significant amounts of electricity. Clusters of these turbines are often called wind farms. Wind farms are located in areas where winds are strong and steady. Most of the wind farms in the United States are in California. The amount of energy produced by California wind farms could power all of the homes in San Francisco. Scientists have determined that portions of 37 states in the United States have enough wind to support commercial wind farms.

There are many benefits of using wind energy. Wind energy is renewable. Wind farms can be built in only 3–6 months. Wind turbines produce no carbon dioxide or other air pollutants during operation. The land used for wind farms can also be used for other purposes, such as cattle grazing, as shown in **Figure 25.** However, the wind blows strongly and steadily enough to produce electricity on a large scale only in certain places. Currently, wind energy accounts for only a small percentage of the energy used in the United States.

Figure 24 *Windmills like this one are still common in rural areas of the United States.*

Figure 25 *Wind turbines take up only a small portion of the ground's surface. This allows the land on wind farms to be used for more than one purpose.*

REVIEW

1. Briefly describe two ways of using solar energy.

2. In addition to multiple turbines, what is needed to produce electricity from wind energy on a large scale?

3. **Analyzing Methods** Nuclear power plants are found in many places in the United States. But they are rarely found in the middle of deserts or other extremely dry areas. If you were going to build a nuclear plant, why would you not build it in the middle of a desert?

Hydroelectric Energy

The energy of falling water has been used by humans for thousands of years. Water wheels, such as the one shown in **Figure 26,** have been around since ancient times. In the early years of the Industrial Revolution, water wheels provided energy for many factories. More recently, the energy of falling water has been used to generate electricity. Electricity produced by falling water is called **hydroelectric energy.**

Hydroelectric energy is inexpensive and produces little pollution, and it is renewable because water constantly cycles from the ocean to the air, to the land, and back to the ocean. But like wind energy, hydroelectric energy is not available everywhere. Hydroelectric energy can be produced only where large volumes of falling water can be harnessed. Huge dams, like the one in **Figure 27,** must be built on major rivers to capture enough water to generate significant amounts of electricity. There are many hydroelectric dams around the world, but the production of hydroelectric energy can be greatly increased. There are many places in the world where large volumes of falling water are not currently being used to generate electricity.

Figure 26 *Falling water turns water wheels, which turn giant millstones used to grind grain into flour.*

Turn to page 504 to make your own water wheel.

Figure 27 *Falling water turns huge turbines inside hydroelectric dams, generating electricity for millions of people.*

Increased use of hydroelectric energy could reduce the demand for fossil fuels, but there are trade-offs. Construction of the large dams necessary for hydroelectric power plants often destroys other resources, such as forests and wildlife habitats. For example, hydroelectric dams on the Lower Snake and Columbia Rivers in Washington disrupt the migratory paths of local populations of salmon and steelhead. Large numbers of these fish die each year because their life cycle is disrupted. Dams can also decrease water quality and create erosion problems.

Self-Check

How are ancient water wheels like modern hydroelectric dams? *(See page 564 to check your answer.)*

Powerful Plants

Plants are similar to solar collectors, absorbing energy from the sun and storing it for later use. Leaves, wood, and other parts of plants contain the stored energy. Even the dung of plant-grazing animals is high in stored energy. These sources of energy are called biomass. **Biomass** is organic matter that contains stored energy.

Biomass energy can be released in several ways. The most common is the burning of biomass. Approximately 70 percent of people living in developing countries heat their homes and cook their food by burning wood or charcoal. In the United States this number is about 5 percent. United Nations scientists estimate that the burning of wood and animal dung accounts for approximately 14 percent of the world's total energy use.

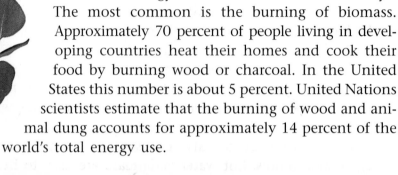

Figure 28 *In many parts of the world where firewood is scarce, people burn animal dung for energy. This woman is preparing cow dung that will be dried and used as fuel.*

÷ 5 ÷ Ω ≤ ∞ +Ω √ 9 ∞ ≤ Σ 2

MATH BREAK

Miles per Acre

Imagine that you own a car that runs on alcohol made from corn that you grow. You drive your car about 15,000 miles in a year, and you get 240 gallons of alcohol from each acre of corn that you process. If your car gets 25 mi/gal, how many acres of corn would you have to grow to fuel your car for a year?

Plant material can also be changed into liquid fuel. Plants containing sugar or starch, for example, can be made into alcohol. The alcohol is burned as a fuel or mixed with gasoline to make a fuel mixture called **gasohol.** An acre of corn can produce more than 1,000 L of alcohol. But in the United States we use a lot of fuel for our cars. It would take about 40 percent of the entire United States corn harvest to make enough alcohol to make just 10 percent of the fuel we use in our cars!

Biomass is obviously a renewable source of energy, but producing biomass requires land that could be used for growing food. And it takes about 10 times as much land to grow biomass fuel as land required by solar cells to produce the same amount of electricity.

Deep Heat

Imagine being able to tap into the energy of the Earth. In a few places this is possible. This type of energy is called geothermal energy. **Geothermal energy** is energy produced by heat within the Earth's crust.

In some locations, rainwater penetrates porous rock near a source of magma. The heat from the magma heats the water, often turning it to steam. The steam and hot water escape through natural vents, like the one in **Figure 29,** or through wells drilled into the rock. The steam and water contain geothermal energy. Some geothermal power plants, such as The Geysers, in northern California, use primarily steam to generate electricity. This process is illustrated in **Figure 30.** In recent years, geothermal power plants that use primarily hot water instead of steam have become more common.

Geothermal energy can also be used as a direct source of heat. In this process, hot water and steam are used to heat a fluid that is pumped through a building in order to heat it. Buildings in Iceland are heated in this way from the country's many geothermal sites.

Figure 29 *Natural holes in the Earth's surface allow hot water and steam to escape from the Earth's crust.*

Figure 30 How a Geothermal Power Plant Works

❹ The steam escapes the power plant through vents.

❺ Leftover liquid water is injected back into the hot rock.

❸ The generators produce electricity.

❷ The steam drives turbines, which in turn drive electric generators.

❶ Steam rises through a well.

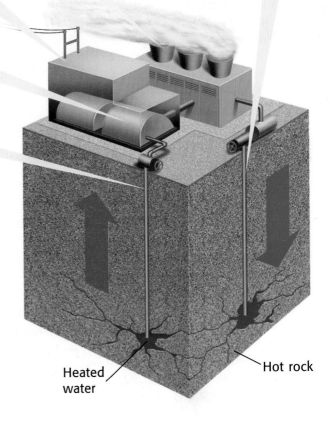

Heated water

Hot rock

REVIEW

1. Where is the production of hydroelectric energy practical?

2. Name two ways to release biomass energy.

3. Describe two ways to use geothermal energy.

4. **Summarizing Data** List four energy alternatives to fossil fuels, and give one advantage and one disadvantage of each alternative.

Chapter Highlights

SECTION 1

Vocabulary

natural resource (*p. 108*)
renewable resource (*p. 109*)
nonrenewable resource (*p. 109*)
recycling (*p. 110*)

Section Notes

- Natural resources include everything that is not made by humans and that can be used by organisms.

- Renewable resources, like trees and water, can be replaced in a relatively short period of time.

- Nonrenewable resources cannot be replaced, or they take a very long time to replace.

- Recycling reduces the amount of natural resources that must be obtained from the Earth.

SECTION 2

Vocabulary

energy resource (*p. 111*)
fossil fuel (*p. 111*)
petroleum (*p. 111*)
natural gas (*p. 112*)
coal (*p. 112*)
strip mining (*p. 115*)
acid precipitation (*p. 116*)
smog (*p. 117*)

Section Notes

- Fossil fuels, including petroleum, natural gas, and coal, form from the buried remains of once-living organisms.

- Petroleum and natural gas form mainly from the remains of microscopic sea life.

- Coal forms from decayed swamp plants and varies in quality based on its percentage of carbon.

- Petroleum and natural gas are obtained through drilling, while coal is obtained through mining.

- Obtaining and using fossil fuels can cause many environmental problems, including acid precipitation, water pollution, smog, and the release of excess carbon dioxide.

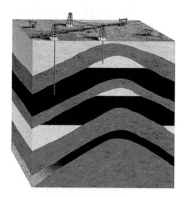

☑ Skills Check

Math Concepts

THE CARBON CONTENT OF COAL Turn back to page 114 to study the process of coal formation. Notice that at each stage, 10% more of the organic material becomes carbon. To calculate the percentage of carbon present at the next stage, just add 10%, or 0.10. For example:

peat → lignite
60% → 70%
$0.60 + 0.10 = 0.70$, or 70%

Visual Understanding

NO DIRECT CONTACT Take another look at Figure 22 on page 121. It is important to realize that the heated liquid inside the solar collector's tubes never comes in direct contact with the water in the tank. Cold water enters the tank, receives heat from the hot, coiled tube, and leaves the tank when someone turns on the hot-water tap.

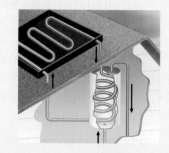

Vocabulary

nuclear energy *(p. 118)*

solar energy *(p. 119)*

wind energy *(p. 122)*

hydroelectric energy *(p. 123)*

biomass *(p. 124)*

gasohol *(p. 124)*

geothermal energy *(p. 125)*

Section Notes

- Nuclear energy is most often produced by fission.

- Radioactive wastes and the threat of overheating in nuclear power plants are among the major problems associated with using nuclear energy.

- Solar energy can be converted to electricity by using solar cells.

- Solar energy can be used for direct heating by using solar collectors.

- Solar energy can be converted to electricity on both a small and large scale.

- Although harnessing wind energy is practical only in certain areas, the process produces no air pollutants, and land on wind farms can be used for more than one purpose.

- Hydroelectric energy is inexpensive, renewable, and produces little pollution. However, hydroelectric dams can damage wildlife habitats, create erosion problems, and decrease water quality.

- Plant material and animal dung that contains plant material can be burned to release energy.

- Some plant material can be converted to alcohol. This alcohol can be mixed with gasoline to make a fuel mixture called gasohol.

- Geothermal energy can be harnessed from hot, liquid water and steam that escape through natural vents or through wells drilled into the Earth's crust. This energy can be used for direct heating or can be converted to electricity.

Labs

Make a Water Wheel *(p. 504)*

Power of the Sun *(p. 506)*

---

 internet**connect**

 GO TO: go.hrw.com

SCi**LINKS** **GO TO:** www.scilinks.org

Visit the **HRW** Web site for a variety of learning tools related to this chapter. Just type in the keyword:

KEYWORD: HSTENR

Visit the **National Science Teachers Association** on-line Web site for Internet resources related to this chapter. Just type in the *sci*LINKS number for more information about the topic:

TOPIC: Natural Resources	*sci*LINKS NUMBER: HSTE105
TOPIC: Renewable Resources	*sci*LINKS NUMBER: HSTE110
TOPIC: Nonrenewable Resources	*sci*LINKS NUMBER: HSTE115
TOPIC: Fossil Fuels	*sci*LINKS NUMBER: HSTE120

Chapter Review

For each pair of terms, explain the difference in their meanings.

1. natural resource/energy resource

2. acid precipitation/smog

3. biomass/gasohol

4. hydroelectric energy/ geothermal energy

UNDERSTANDING CONCEPTS

Multiple Choice

5. Of the following, the one that is a renewable resource is
   a. coal.   c. oil.
   b. trees.   d. natural gas.

6. All of the following are separated from petroleum except
   a. jet fuel.   c. kerosene.
   b. lignite.   d. fuel oil.

7. Which of the following is a component of natural gas?
   a. gasohol   c. kerosene
   b. methane   d. gasoline

8. Peat, lignite, and anthracite are all stages in the formation of
   a. petroleum.   c. coal.
   b. natural gas.   d. gasohol.

9. Which of the following factors contribute to smog problems?
   a. high numbers of automobiles
   b. lots of sunlight
   c. mountains surrounding urban areas
   d. all of the above

10. Which of the following resources produces the least pollution?
    a. solar energy
    b. natural gas
    c. nuclear energy
    d. petroleum

11. Nuclear power plants use a process called _____?_____ to produce energy.
    a. fission
    b. fusion
    c. fractionation
    d. None of the above

12. A solar-powered calculator uses
    a. solar collectors.
    b. solar panels.
    c. solar mirrors.
    d. solar cells.

13. Which of the following is a problem with using wind energy?
    a. air pollution
    b. amount of land required for wind turbines
    c. limited locations for wind farms
    d. none of the above

14. Dung is a type of
    a. geothermal energy.
    b. gasohol.
    c. biomass.
    d. None of the above

Short Answer

15. Since renewable resources can be replaced, why do we need to conserve them?

16. How does acid precipitation form?

17. If sunlight is free, why is electricity from solar cells expensive?

Concept Mapping

18. Use the following terms to create a concept map: fossil fuels, wind energy, energy resources, biomass, renewable resources, solar energy, nonrenewable resources, natural gas, gasohol, coal, oil.

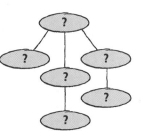

CRITICAL THINKING AND PROBLEM SOLVING

Write one or two sentences to answer the following questions:

19. How would your life be different if all fossil fuels suddenly disappeared?

20. Are fossil fuels really nonrenewable? Explain.

21. What solutions are there for the problems associated with nuclear waste?

22. How could the problems associated with the dams in Washington and local fish populations be solved?

23. What limits might there be on the productivity of a geothermal power plant?

MATH IN SCIENCE

24. Imagine that you are designing a solar car. If you mount solar cells on the underside of the car as well as on the top in direct sunlight, and it takes five times as many cells underneath to generate the same amount of electricity generated by the cells on top, what percentage of the sunlight is reflected back off the pavement?

INTERPRETING GRAPHICS

The chart below shows how various energy resources meet the world's energy needs. Use the chart to answer the following questions:

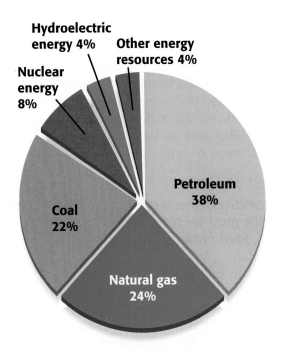

25. What percentage of the world's total energy needs is met by coal? by natural gas? by hydroelectric energy?

26. What percentage of the world's total energy needs is met by fossil fuels?

27. How much more of the world's total energy needs is met by petroleum than by natural gas?

NOW What Do You Think?

Take a minute to review your answers to the ScienceLog questions on page 107. Have your answers changed? If necessary, revise your answers based on what you have learned since you began this chapter.

EYE ON THE ENVIRONMENT

Sitting on Your Trash

Did you know that the average person creates about 2 kg of waste every day? About 7 percent of this waste is composed of plastic products that can be recycled. Instead of adding to the landfill problem, why not recycle your plastic trash so you can sit on it? Well you can, you know! Today plastic is recycled into products like picnic tables, park benches, and even highchairs! But how on Earth does the plastic you throw away become a park bench?

Sort It Out

Once collected and taken to a recycling center, plastic must be sorted. This process involves the coded symbols that are printed on every recyclable plastic product we use. Each product falls into one of two types of plastic—*polyethylene* or *polymer*. The plastic mainly used to make furniture includes the polyethylene plastics called *high density polyethylene,* or HDPE, and *low density polyethylene,* or LDPE. These are items such as milk jugs, detergent bottles, plastic bags, and grocery bags.

Grind It and Wash It

The recycling processes for HDPE and LDPE are fairly simple. Once it reaches the processing facility, HDPE plastic is ground into small flakes about 1 cm in diameter. In the case of LDPE plastic, which are thin films, a special grinder is used to break it down. From that point on, the recycling process is pretty much the same for LDPE and HDPE. The pieces are then washed with hot water and detergent. In this step, dirt and things like labels are removed. After the wash, the flakes are dried with blasts of hot air.

Recycle It!

Some recycling plants sell the recycled flakes. But others may reheat the flakes, change the color by adding a pigment, and then put the material in a *pelletizer.* The little pellets that result are then purchased by a company that molds the pellets into pieces of plastic lumber. This plastic lumber is used to create flowerpots, trash cans, pipes, picnic tables, park benches, toys, mats, and many other products!

From waste...

to plastic lumber...

to a park bench!

Can You Recycle It?

▶ The coded symbol on a plastic container tells you what type of plastic the item is made from, but it doesn't mean that you can recycle it in your area. Find out which plastics can be recycled in your state.

Eureka!

Oil Rush!

You may have heard of the great California gold rush. In 1849, thousands of people moved to the West hoping to strike gold. But you may not have heard about another rush that followed 10 years later. What lured people to northwestern Pennsylvania in 1859? The thrill of striking oil!

Demand for Petroleum

People began using oil as early as 3000 B.C., and oil has been a valuable substance ever since. In Mesopotamia, people used oil to waterproof their ships. The Egyptians and Chinese used oil as a medicine. It was not until the late 1700s and early 1800s that people began to use oil as a fuel. Oil was used to light homes and factories.

Petroleum Collection

But what about the oil in northwestern Pennsylvania? Did people use the oil in Pennsylvania before the rush of 1859? Native Americans were the first to dig pits to collect oil near Titusville, Pennsylvania. Early settlers used the oil as a medicine and as a fuel to light their homes. But their methods for collecting the oil were very inefficient.

The First Oil Well

In 1859, "Colonel" Edwin L. Drake came up with a better method of collecting oil from the ground. Drilling for oil! Drake hired salt-well drillers to burrow to the bedrock where oil deposits lay. But each effort was unsuccessful because water seeped into the wells, causing them to cave in. Then Drake came up with a unique idea that would make him a very wealthy man. Drake suggested that the drillers drive an iron pipe down to the bedrock 21.2 m below the surface. Then they could drill through the inner diameter of the pipe. The morning after the iron pipe was drilled, Drake woke to find that the pipe had filled with oil!

Oil City

Within 3 months, nearly 10,000 people rushed to Oil City, Pennsylvania, in search of the wealth that oil promised. Within 2 years, the small village became a bustling oil town of 50,000 people! In 1861, the first gusher well was drilled nearby, and some 3,000 barrels of oil spouted out daily. Four years later, the first oil pipeline carried crude oil a distance of 8 km.

▲ *Edwin Drake (right) and his friend Peter Wilson (left) in front of Drake Oil Well, near Titusville, Pennsylvania*

Find Out for Yourself!

▶ Drake's oil well was the first well used to collect oil from the ground. Research the oil wells today. How are they similar to Drake's well?

UNIT 3

The Restless Earth

In this unit, you will learn about the Earth's internal structure. Many mysteries remain because we cannot see very far inside the Earth. The deepest holes we can dig barely scratch the planet's surface. If the Earth were an orange, our attempts to dig into it would not even break through the peel. One way scientists can learn about the Earth's interior is by studying earthquakes and volcanoes. This timeline shows some of the events that have occurred as scientists have tried to understand our dynamic Earth.

1864

Jules Verne's *A Journey to the Center of the Earth* is published. In this fictional story, the heroes enter and exit the Earth through volcanoes.

1883

Krakatau erupts, killing 36,000 people.

1966

A worldwide network of seismographs is established.

1979

Volcanoes are discovered on Io, one of Jupiter's moons.

1980

Mount St. Helens erupts.

1896
Henry Ford builds his first car.

1906
San Francisco burns in the aftermath of an earthquake.

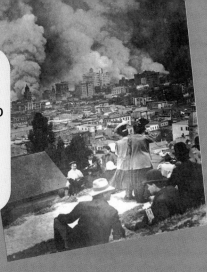

1935
Charles Richter devises a system of measuring the strength of earthquakes.

1912
Alfred Wegener proposes his continental-drift theory.

1951
Color television is introduced in the United States.

1994
An eight-legged robot named *Dante II* descends into the crater of an active volcano in Alaska.

1997
The population of the Caribbean island of Montserrat dwindles to less than half its original size as frequent eruptions of the Soufriere Hills volcano force evacuations.

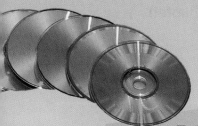

1982
Compact discs (CDs) and compact-disc players are made available to the public.

6 Plate Tectonics

This Really Happened!

It was a grueling climb to the top of Mount Everest. The temperature was well below freezing, and the blinding snow made it difficult to see. These harsh conditions and the extreme altitude are what make Mount Everest one of the most difficult mountains to climb. But these conditions did not stop a professional mountain climber by the name of Wally Berg. He was on a mission—a scientific mission that had been years in the planning.

Once at the top of the world's highest mountain, some 8,848 m high, Wally began drilling a hole in the rock. At this altitude the air is so thin that even easy tasks are difficult to accomplish. Wally brought bottles of oxygen with him to make his breathing easier.

Why did Wally drill a hole in Mount Everest? He needed the hole in order to secure a special device that receives and records signals from a network of satellites called the Global Positioning System (GPS).

GPS can pinpoint the exact location of these special receivers over long periods of time. In analyzing GPS data, scientists found out that Mount Everest not only is moving but also is growing taller every year. Over a year's time, the mountain moves northeast about 27 mm and grows from 3 to 5 mm taller!

Why is Mount Everest moving and growing? The answer is *plate tectonics.* Plate tectonics is also the reason why California has so many earthquakes and why volcanoes are found all around the rim of the Pacific Ocean. Get ready to learn much more about plate tectonics in this chapter.

What Do You Think?

In your ScienceLog, try to answer the following questions based on what you already know:

1. Why do entire mountain ranges move?

2. How do mountains form?

Investigate!

Continental Collisions

Believe it or not, continents not only move but also sometimes crash into each other. For the past 40 to 60 million years, the Indian subcontinent has been colliding with the Eurasian continent. As these continents push against each other, they buckle and bend. As a result, the Himalaya Mountains, where Mount Everest is located, are still forming today. In this investigation you will create a model to help explain how the Himalaya Mountains formed.

Procedure

1. Cut a 7 cm long slit in a large piece of **cardboard** about 6 cm from one edge of the cardboard. Cut the slit wide enough so that a 50 cm long strip of **adding-machine paper** will feed through it.

2. Use **tape** to secure a small **wood block** next to the slit, between the slit and the edge of the cardboard. Tape another small **wood block** to one end of the adding-machine paper. Both blocks should be parallel to each other.

3. Cut eight identical strips about 8 cm wide and 15 to 20 cm long from several **paper napkins.**

4. Stack the napkin strips on top of each other.

5. Place the napkin strips on the adding-machine paper next to the wood block.

6. Attach the napkin strips to the adding-machine paper using two **bobby pins,** one at each end of the strips.

7. Push the end of the adding-machine paper through the slit in the cardboard until the napkin strips rest against the wood block you attached to the cardboard. Hold the cardboard at about eye level, and pull gently and slowly downward on the paper strip.

Analysis

8. What happens as the paper napkin strips come in contact with the block of wood?

9. What happens as you continue to pull downward on the strip of paper?

10. How does this model represent what is happening between India and Eurasia?

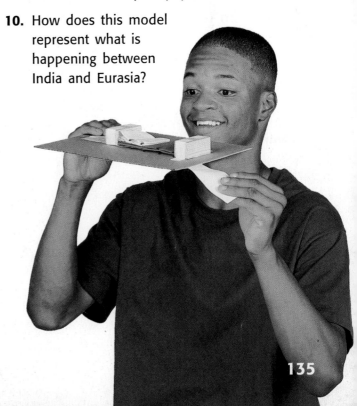

135

Inside the Earth

NEW TERMS

crust   asthenosphere

mantle   mesosphere

core   outer core

lithosphere   inner core

tectonic plates

OBJECTIVES

- Identify and describe the layers of the Earth by what they are made of.
- Identify and describe the layers of the Earth by their physical properties.
- Define *tectonic plate.*
- Explain how scientists know about the structure of Earth's interior.

The Earth is not just a ball of solid rock. It is made of several layers with different physical properties and compositions. As you will discover, there are two ways scientists think about the Earth's layers—by their *composition* and by their *physical properties.*

The layers of the Earth are made of different mixtures of elements. This is what is meant by differences in composition. Many of the Earth's layers also have different physical properties. Physical properties include temperature, density, and ability to flow. Let's first take a look at the composition of the Earth.

The Composition of the Earth

The Earth is divided into three layers—the *crust, mantle,* and *core*—based on what each one is made of. The lightest materials make up the outermost layer, and the densest materials make up the inner layers. This is because lighter materials tend to float up, while heavier materials sink. First let's take a look at the outer layer, the Earth's crust.

The Crust The **crust** is the outermost layer of the Earth. Ranging from 5 to 100 km thick, it is also the thinnest layer of the Earth. And because it is the layer we live on, we know more about this layer than we know about the other two.

There are two types of crust—continental and oceanic. *Continental crust* has a composition similar to granite. It has an average thickness of 30 km. In some mountainous areas continental crust is as much as 100 km thick. *Oceanic crust* has a composition similar to basalt. It is generally between 5 and 8 km thick. Because basalt is denser than granite, oceanic crust is denser than continental crust.

Figure 1 *Oceanic crust is thinner but denser than continental crust.*

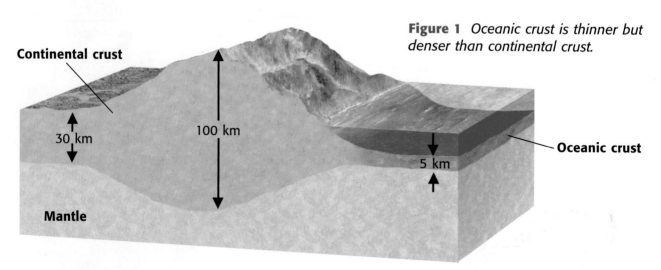

Continental crust

30 km

100 km

Mantle

Oceanic crust

5 km

The Mantle The **mantle** is the layer of the Earth between the crust and the core. Compared with the crust, the mantle is extremely thick. The mantle is about 2,900 km thick and contains most of the Earth's mass.

No one has ever seen what the mantle really looks like. It is just too far down to drill for a sample. Scientists must infer what the composition and other characteristics of the mantle are from observations they make on the Earth's surface. In some places mantle rock has been pushed up to the surface by tectonic forces, allowing scientists to observe the rock directly.

As you can see in **Figure 2,** one place scientists look is on the ocean floor, where molten rock from the mantle flows out of active volcanoes. These underwater volcanoes are like windows through the crust into the mantle. The "windows" have given us strong clues about the composition of the mantle. Scientists have learned that the mantle's composition is similar to that of the mineral olivine, which has large amounts of iron and magnesium compared with other common minerals.

Figure 2 *Volcanic vents on the ocean floor, such as this one off the coast of Hawaii, allow magma to escape from the mantle beneath oceanic crust.*

The Core By studying the different layers that make up the Earth, geologists can get an idea of which elements each is made of. They think that the Earth's *core* is made mostly of iron, with smaller amounts of nickel and possibly some sulfur and oxygen. The **core** extends from the bottom of the mantle to the center of the Earth. The diameter of the core is about 6,856 km. As you can see in **Figure 3,** at 6,787 km, the diameter of the planet Mars is slightly smaller than that of the Earth's core.

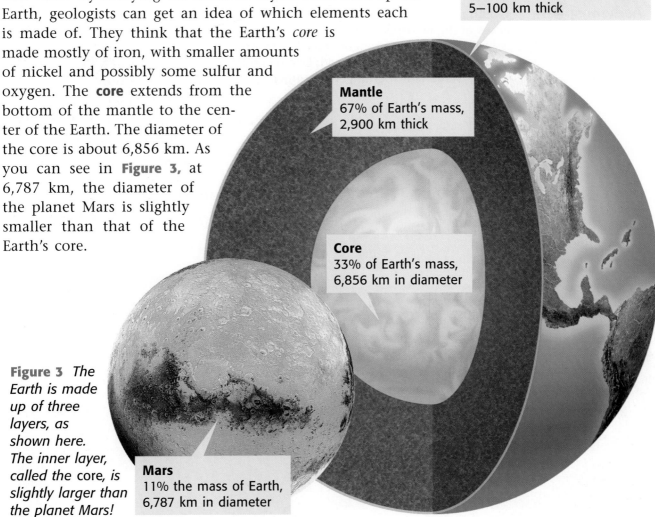

Crust
less than 1% of Earth's mass, 5–100 km thick

Mantle
67% of Earth's mass, 2,900 km thick

Core
33% of Earth's mass, 6,856 km in diameter

Mars
11% the mass of Earth, 6,787 km in diameter

Figure 3 *The Earth is made up of three layers, as shown here. The inner layer, called the* core, *is slightly larger than the planet Mars!*

The Structure of the Earth

So far we have talked about the composition of the Earth. Another way to look at how the Earth is made is to examine the physical properties of its layers. The Earth is divided into five main physical layers—the *lithosphere, asthenosphere, mesosphere, outer core,* and *inner core.* As shown below, each layer has its own set of physical properties.

÷ 5 ÷ Ω ≤ ∞ +Ω √ 9 ∞ ≤ Σ 2
+

MATH BREAK

Using Models

Imagine that you are building a model of the Earth that is going to have a radius of 1 m in diameter. You find out that the average radius of the Earth is 6,378 km and that the thickness of the lithosphere is about 150 km. What percentage of the Earth's radius is the lithosphere? How thick (in centimeters) would you make the lithosphere in your model?

Lithosphere The outermost, rigid layer of the Earth is called the **lithosphere** ("rock sphere"). The lithosphere is made of two parts—the crust and the rigid upper part of the mantle. Unlike the other physical layers of the Earth, the lithosphere is not a single, solid layer. Instead, it is made up of pieces called *tectonic plates.*

Asthenosphere The **asthenosphere** ("weak sphere") is a soft layer of the mantle on which pieces of the lithosphere move. It is made of solid rock that flows very slowly, like putty. Low-strength rocks like those in the asthenosphere tend to lose their shape when stressed. Like warm tar, they flow very slowly—at about the same rate your fingernails grow.

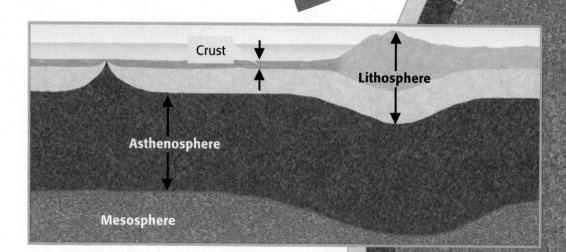

Crust

Lithosphere

Asthenosphere

Mesosphere

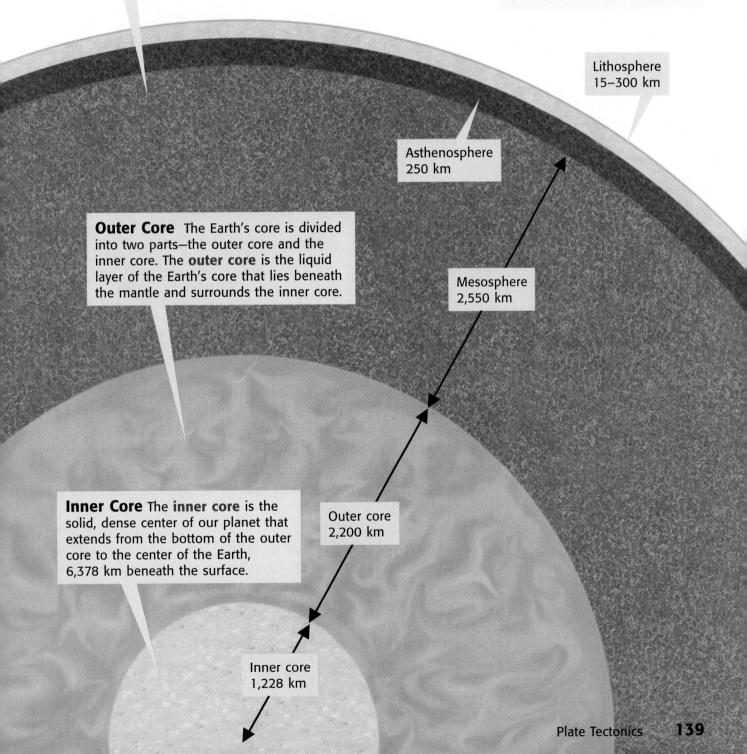

Mesosphere Beneath the asthenosphere is the strong, lower part of the mantle called the **mesosphere** ("middle sphere"). The mesosphere extends from the bottom of the asthenosphere down to the Earth's core.

life science
CONNECTION

Scientists call the part of the Earth where life is possible the *biosphere.* The biosphere is the layer of the Earth above the crust and below the uppermost part of the atmosphere. It includes the oceans, the land surface, and the lower part of the atmosphere.

Lithosphere
15–300 km

Asthenosphere
250 km

Outer Core The Earth's core is divided into two parts—the outer core and the inner core. The **outer core** is the liquid layer of the Earth's core that lies beneath the mantle and surrounds the inner core.

Mesosphere
2,550 km

Inner Core The **inner core** is the solid, dense center of our planet that extends from the bottom of the outer core to the center of the Earth, 6,378 km beneath the surface.

Outer core
2,200 km

Inner core
1,228 km

Tectonic Plates

Tectonic plates are pieces of the lithosphere that move around on top of the asthenosphere. But what exactly does a tectonic plate look like? How big are tectonic plates? How and why do they move around? To answer these questions, start by thinking of the lithosphere as a giant jigsaw puzzle.

Figure 4 *Tectonic plates fit together like the pieces of a jigsaw puzzle. On this map, the relative motions of some of the major tectonic plates are shown with arrows.*

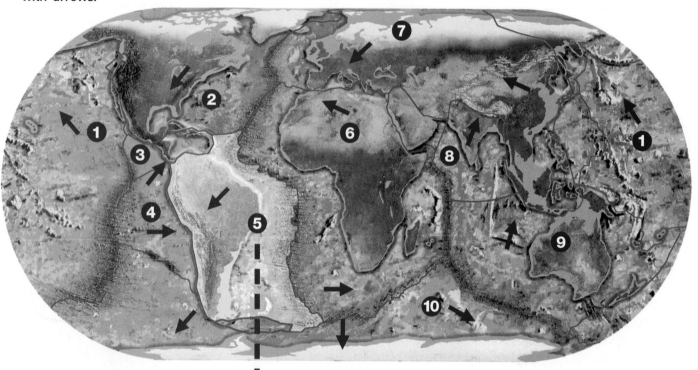

Major Tectonic Plates

1. Pacific plate
2. North American plate
3. Cocos plate
4. Nazca plate
5. South American plate
6. African plate
7. Eurasian plate
8. Indian plate
9. Australian plate
10. Antarctic plate

A Giant Jigsaw Puzzle Look at the world map above. All of the plates have names, some of which you may already be familiar with. Some of the major tectonic plates are listed in the key at left. Notice that each tectonic plate fits the other tectonic plates that surround it. The lithosphere is like a jigsaw puzzle, and the tectonic plates are like the pieces of a jigsaw puzzle.

You will also notice that not all tectonic plates are the same. Compare the size of the North American plate with that of the Cocos plate. But tectonic plates are different in other ways too. For example, the North American plate has an entire continent on it, while the Cocos plate only has oceanic crust. Like the North American plate, some tectonic plates include both continental *and* oceanic crust.

A Tectonic Plate Close Up What would a tectonic plate look like if you could lift it out of its place? **Figure 5** shows what the South American plate might look like if you could. Notice that this tectonic plate consists of both oceanic and continental crust, just like the North American plate.

The thickest part of this tectonic plate is on the South American continent, under the Andes mountain range. The thinnest part of the South American plate is at the Mid-Atlantic Ridge.

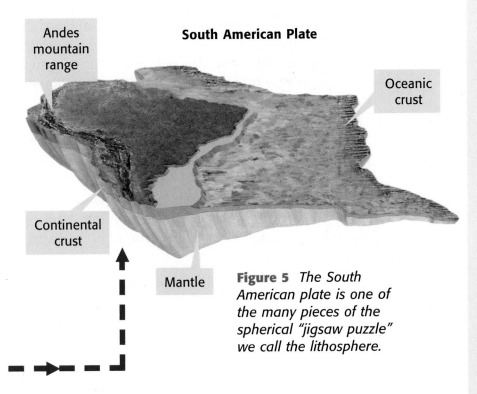

South American Plate

Andes mountain range

Oceanic crust

Continental crust

Mantle

Figure 5 *The South American plate is one of the many pieces of the spherical "jigsaw puzzle" we call the lithosphere.*

Tip of the Iceberg If you could look at a tectonic plate from the side, you would see that mountain ranges are like the tips of icebergs—there is much more material below the surface than above. Mountain ranges that occur in continental crust have very deep roots relative to their height. For example, the Rocky Mountains rise less than 5 km above sea level, but their roots go down to about 60 km *below* sea level.

But if continental crust is so much thicker than oceanic crust, why doesn't it sink down below the oceanic crust? Think back to the difference between continental and oceanic crust. Continental crust stands much higher than oceanic crust because it is both thicker and less dense. Both kinds of crust are less dense than the mantle and "float" on top of the asthenosphere, similar to the way ice floats on top of water.

QuickLab

Floating Mountains

1. Take a large **block** of wood and place it in a clear plastic **container.** The block of wood represents the mantle part of the lithosphere.

2. Fill the container with **water** at least 10 cm deep. The water represents the asthenosphere. Use a ruler to measure how far the top of the wood block sits above the surface of the water.

3. Now try loading the block of wood with several different **wooden objects,** each with a different weight. These objects represent different amounts of crustal material loaded onto the lithosphere during mountain building. Measure how far the block sinks under each different weight.

4. What can you conclude about how the tectonic plate reacts to increasing weight of crustal material?

5. What happens to a tectonic plate when the crustal material is removed?

Mapping the Earth's Interior

How do we know all these things about the deepest parts of the Earth, where no one has ever been? Scientists have never even drilled through the crust, which is only a thin skin on the surface of the Earth. So how do we know so much about the mantle and the core?

Would you be surprised to know that the answers come from earthquakes? When an earthquake occurs, vibrations called seismic waves are produced. *Seismic waves* are vibrations that travel through the Earth. Depending on the density and strength of material they pass through, seismic waves travel at different speeds. For example, a seismic wave traveling through solid rock will go faster than a seismic wave traveling through a liquid.

When an earthquake occurs, *seismographs* measure the difference in the arrival times of seismic waves and record them. Seismologists can then use these measurements to calculate the density and thickness of each physical layer of the Earth. **Figure 6** shows how one kind of seismic wave travels through the Earth.

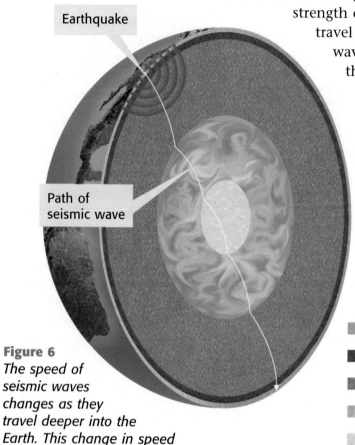

Earthquake

Path of seismic wave

Figure 6
The speed of seismic waves changes as they travel deeper into the Earth. This change in speed causes their travel paths to bend, particularly when passing from one layer of the Earth to another.

Lithosphere 7–8 km/second

Asthenosphere 7–11 km/second

Mesosphere 11–13 km/second

Outer core 7–10 km/second

Inner core 11–12 km/second

REVIEW

1. What is the difference between continental and oceanic crust?

2. How is the lithosphere different from the asthenosphere?

3. How do scientists know about the structure of the Earth's interior? Explain.

4. **Analyzing Relationships** Explain the difference between the crust and the lithosphere.

Restless Continents

Take a look at **Figure 7.** It shows how continents would fit together if you removed the Atlantic Ocean and moved the land together. Is it just coincidence that the coastlines fit together so well? Is it possible that the continents were actually together sometime in the past?

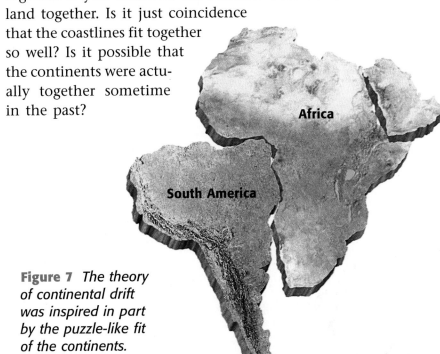

Figure 7 *The theory of continental drift was inspired in part by the puzzle-like fit of the continents.*

Wegener's Theory of Continental Drift

One scientist who looked at the pieces of this puzzle was Alfred Wegener. In the early 1900s he wrote about his theory of *continental drift.* **Continental drift** is the theory that continents can drift apart from one another and have done so in the past.

This theory seemed to explain a lot of puzzling observations, including the very good fit of some of the continents.

Continental drift also explained why fossils of the same plant and animal species are found on both sides of the Atlantic Ocean. Many of these ancient species could not have made it across the Atlantic Ocean. As you can see in **Figure 8,** without continental drift, this pattern of fossil findings would be hard to explain. In addition to fossils, similar types of rock and evidence of the same ancient climatic conditions were found on several continents.

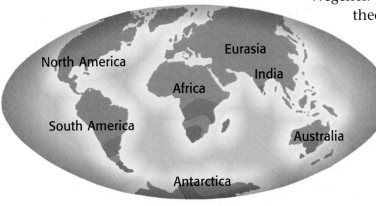

Mesosaurus Glossopteris

Figure 8 *Fossils of* Mesosaurus, *a small, aquatic reptile, and* Glossopteris, *an ancient plant species, have been found on several continents.*

Figure 9 *The arrows show the direction ancient glaciers traveled when the continents were joined together.*

Continental drift also explained puzzling evidence left by ancient glaciers. Glaciers cut grooves in the ground that indicate the direction they traveled. When you look at the placement of today's continents, these glacial activities do not seem to be related. But when you bring all of these continental pieces back to their original arrangement, the glacial grooves fit together! **Figure 9** shows how they would look. You can imagine a huge ice sheet expanding in all directions from the center of this giant landmass.

The Breakup of Pangaea

Wegener studied many observations before establishing his theory of continental drift. He thought that all the separate continents of today were once joined in a single landmass that he called *Pangaea*, which is Greek for "all earth." As shown in **Figure 10,** almost all of Earth's landmasses were joined together in one huge continent 245 million years ago.

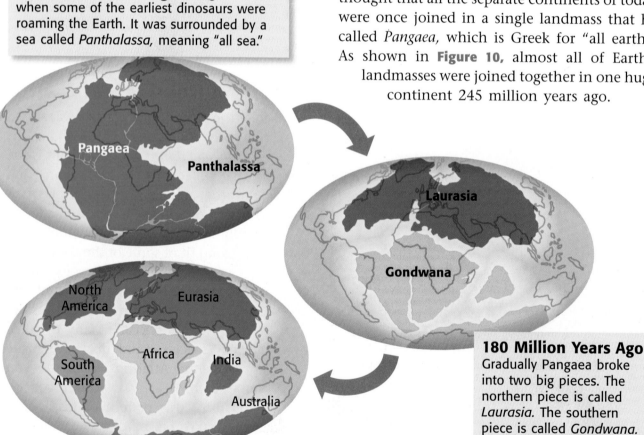

245 Million Years Ago Pangaea existed when some of the earliest dinosaurs were roaming the Earth. It was surrounded by a sea called *Panthalassa,* meaning "all sea."

180 Million Years Ago Gradually Pangaea broke into two big pieces. The northern piece is called *Laurasia.* The southern piece is called *Gondwana.*

65 Million Years Ago By the time the dinosaurs became extinct, Laurasia and Gondwana had split into smaller pieces.

Figure 10 *Over time, Earth's continents have changed shape and traveled great distances.*

Sea-Floor Spreading

When Wegener put forth his theory of continental drift, many scientists would not accept his theory. What force of nature, they wondered, could move entire continents? In Wegener's day, no one could answer that question. It wasn't until many years later that new evidence provided some clues.

In **Figure 11** you will notice that there is a chain of submerged mountains running through the center of the Atlantic Ocean. The chain is called the Mid-Atlantic Ridge, part of a worldwide system of ocean ridges. Mid-ocean ridges are underwater mountain chains that run through Earth's ocean basins.

Mid-ocean ridges are places where sea-floor spreading takes place. **Sea-floor spreading** is the process by which new oceanic lithosphere is created as older materials are pulled away. As tectonic plates move away from each other, the sea floor spreads apart and magma rises to fill in the gap. Notice in **Figure 12** that the crust increases in age the farther it is from the mid-ocean ridge. This is because new crust continually forms from molten material at the ridge. The oldest crust in the Atlantic Ocean is found along the edges of the continents. It dates back to the time of the dinosaurs. The newest crust is in the center of the ocean. This crust has just formed!

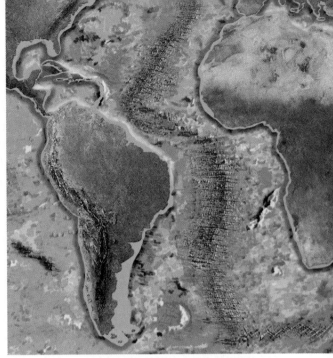

Figure 11 *The Mid-Atlantic Ridge is part of the longest mountain chain in the world.*

Figure 12 *Sea-floor spreading creates new oceanic lithosphere at mid-ocean ridges.*

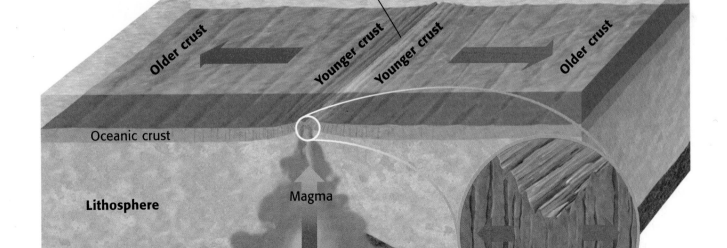

New lithosphere forms

Mid-ocean ridge

Older crust

Younger crust

Younger crust

Older crust

Oceanic crust

Lithosphere

Magma

Asthenosphere

Magnetic Reversals

Some of the most important evidence of sea-floor spreading comes from magnetic reversals recorded in the ocean floor. Throughout Earth's history, the north and south magnetic poles have changed places many times. When Earth's magnetic poles change place, this is called a *magnetic reversal.*

The molten rocks at the mid-ocean ridges contain tiny grains of magnetic minerals. These mineral grains act like compasses. They align with the magnetic field of the Earth. Once the molten rock cools, the record of these tiny compasses is literally set in stone. This record is then carried slowly away from the spreading center as sea-floor spreading occurs. As you can see in **Figure 13,** when the Earth's magnetic field reverses, a new band is started, and this time the magnetic mineral grains point in the opposite direction. The new rock records the direction of the Earth's magnetic field. This record of magnetic reversals was the final proof that sea-floor spreading does occur.

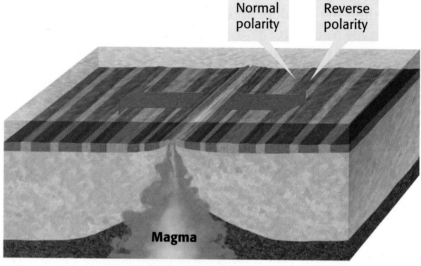

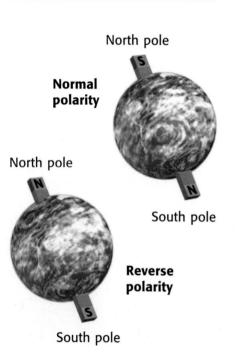

Figure 13 *Magnetic reversals in oceanic crust are shown here in light and dark blue. The dark blue stripes represent periods when magnetic north was true north. The light blue stripes represent periods when magnetic north was at the South Pole.*

REVIEW

1. List three puzzling occurrences that the theory of continental drift helped to explain, and describe how it explained them.

2. Explain why Wegener's theory of continental drift was not accepted at first.

3. **Identifying Relationships** Explain how the processes of sea-floor spreading and magnetic reversal produce bands of oceanic crust that have different magnetic polarities.

The Theory of Plate Tectonics

NEW TERMS

NEW TERMS
plate tectonics
convergent boundary
subduction zone
divergent boundary
transform boundary

OBJECTIVES

- Describe the three forces thought to move tectonic plates.
- Describe the three types of tectonic plate boundaries.
- Explain how scientists measure the rate at which tectonic plates move.

The proof of sea-floor spreading supported Wegener's original idea that the continents move. But because both oceanic and continental crust appear to move, a new theory was devised to explain both continental drift and sea-floor spreading—the theory of *plate tectonics*. **Plate tectonics** is the theory that the Earth's lithosphere is divided into tectonic plates that move around on top of the asthenosphere. So what causes tectonic plates to move?

Possible Causes of Tectonic Plate Motion

An incredible amount of energy is needed to move something as massive as a tectonic plate! We still don't know exactly why tectonic plates move as they do, but recently scientists have come up with some possible answers, as shown in **Figure 14**. Notice how all three are affected by the force of gravity.

Figure 14 Three Possible Driving Forces of Plate Tectonics

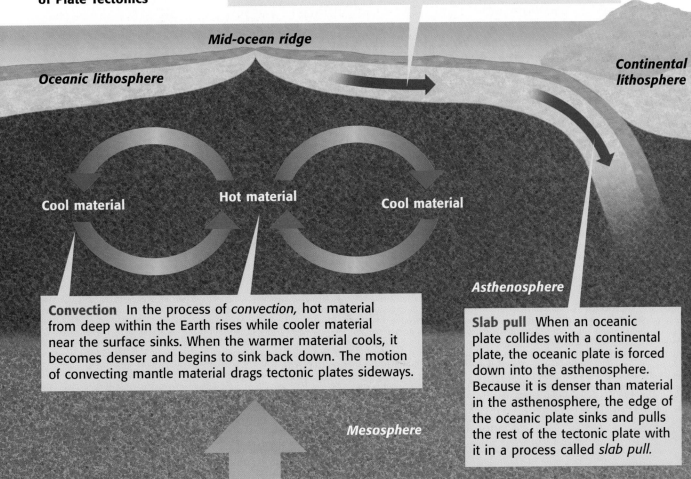

Ridge push At mid-ocean ridges, the oceanic lithosphere is higher than it is where it sinks beneath continental lithosphere. *Ridge push* is the process by which an oceanic plate slides down the slope of the lithosphere-asthenosphere boundary.

Mid-ocean ridge

Oceanic lithosphere

Continental lithosphere

Cool material   Hot material   Cool material

Asthenosphere

Convection In the process of *convection,* hot material from deep within the Earth rises while cooler material near the surface sinks. When the warmer material cools, it becomes denser and begins to sink back down. The motion of convecting mantle material drags tectonic plates sideways.

Slab pull When an oceanic plate collides with a continental plate, the oceanic plate is forced down into the asthenosphere. Because it is denser than material in the asthenosphere, the edge of the oceanic plate sinks and pulls the rest of the tectonic plate with it in a process called *slab pull.*

Mesosphere

Tectonic Plate Boundaries

All tectonic plates have boundaries with other tectonic plates. These boundaries are divided into three main types depending on how the tectonic plates move relative to one another. Tectonic plates can collide, separate, or slide past each other. **Figure 15** shows some examples of tectonic plate boundaries.

Convergent Boundaries When two tectonic plates push into one another, the boundary where they meet is called a **convergent boundary.** What happens at a convergent boundary depends on what kind of crust—continental or oceanic—the leading edge of each tectonic plate has. As you can see below, there are three types of convergent boundaries—continental/continental, continental/oceanic, and oceanic/oceanic.

Figure 15 *This diagram shows five tectonic plate boundaries. Each pair of arrows shows the relative movement of the tectonic plates. Notice that there are three types of convergent boundaries.*

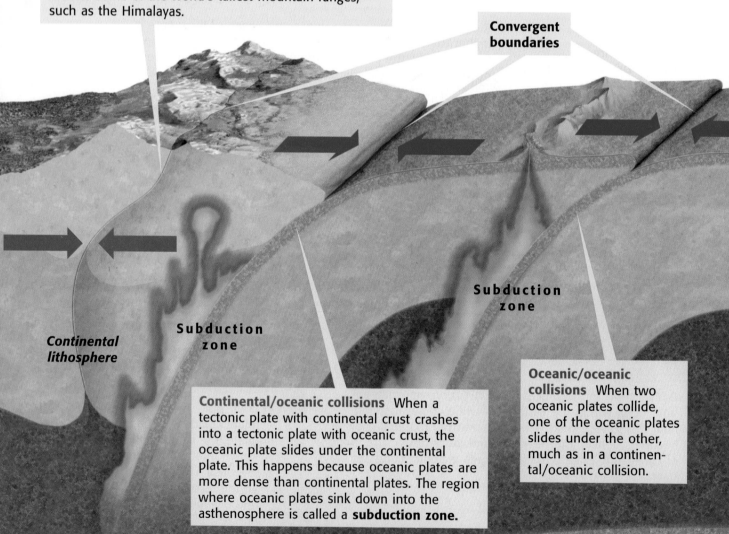

Continental/continental collisions When two tectonic plates with continental crust collide, they buckle and thicken, pushing the continental crust upward. This creates some of the world's tallest mountain ranges, such as the Himalayas.

Convergent boundaries

Continental lithosphere

Subduction zone

Subduction zone

Continental/oceanic collisions When a tectonic plate with continental crust crashes into a tectonic plate with oceanic crust, the oceanic plate slides under the continental plate. This happens because oceanic plates are more dense than continental plates. The region where oceanic plates sink down into the asthenosphere is called a **subduction zone.**

Oceanic/oceanic collisions When two oceanic plates collide, one of the oceanic plates slides under the other, much as in a continental/oceanic collision.

Divergent Boundaries When two tectonic plates move away from one another, the boundary between them is called a **divergent boundary.** Remember sea-floor spreading? The mid-ocean ridges that mark the spreading centers are the most common type of divergent boundary. Remember, divergent boundaries are where new oceanic lithosphere forms.

Transform Boundaries When two tectonic plates slide past each other horizontally, the boundary between them is called a **transform boundary.** The San Andreas Fault, in southern California, is a good example of a *transform boundary.* This fault marks the place where the Pacific plate and the North American plate slide past each other.

What is it like living on top of a mid-ocean spreading center? To find out how plate tectonics affects Icelanders, turn to page 162.

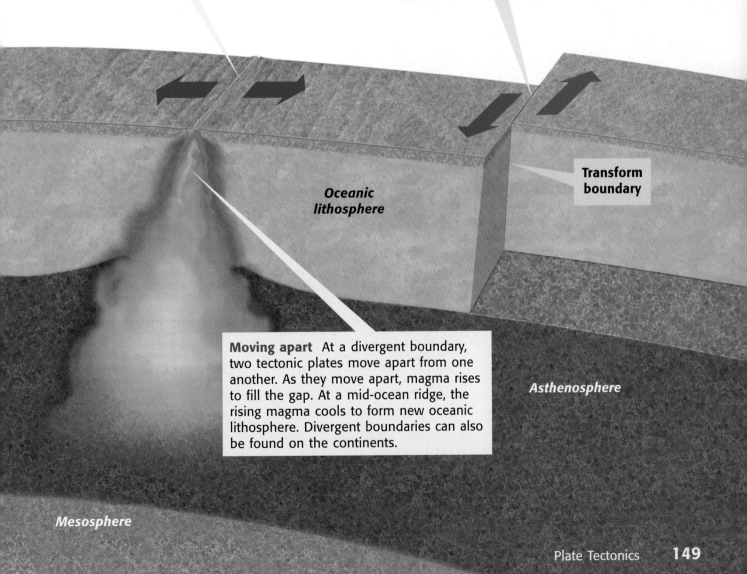

Divergent boundary

Sliding past At a transform boundary, two tectonic plates slide past one another. Because tectonic plates are not smooth, they grind and jerk as they slide. People who live in southern California can feel these frequent jerks. They call them earthquakes!

Oceanic lithosphere

Transform boundary

Moving apart At a divergent boundary, two tectonic plates move apart from one another. As they move apart, magma rises to fill the gap. At a mid-ocean ridge, the rising magma cools to form new oceanic lithosphere. Divergent boundaries can also be found on the continents.

Asthenosphere

Mesosphere

Tracking Tectonic Plate Motion

Just how fast do tectonic plates move? The answer to this question depends on many factors, such as the type of tectonic plate, the shape of the tectonic plate, and the way it interacts with the tectonic plates that surround it. Tectonic movements are generally so slow and gradual that you can't see or feel them—they are measured in centimeters per year.

As you have seen, one exception to this rule is the San Andreas Fault, in California. The San Andreas Fault is a part of the transform boundary between the Pacific plate and the North American plate. The two tectonic plates do not slide past each other smoothly or continuously. Instead, this movement happens in jerks and jolts. Sections of the San Andreas fault remain stationary for years and then suddenly shift several meters, causing an earthquake.

Large shifts that occur at the San Andreas fault can be measured right on the surface. Unfortunately for scientists, most movements of tectonic plates are very difficult to measure.

Scientists use a network of satellites called the *Global Positioning System* (GPS), shown in **Figure 16,** to measure the rate of tectonic plate movement. Radio signals are continuously beamed from satellites to GPS ground stations, which record the exact distance between the satellites and the ground station. Over time, these distances change slightly. By recording the time it takes for the GPS ground stations to move a given distance, scientists can measure the rate of motion of each tectonic plate.

GPS satellite

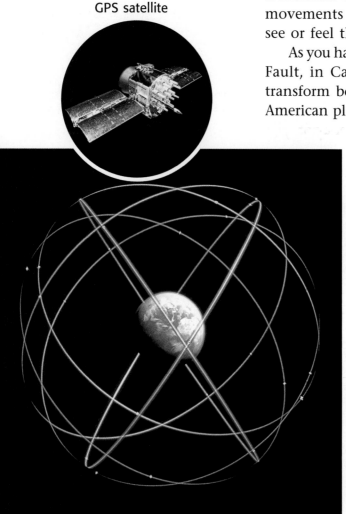

Figure 16 *The image above shows the orbits of the GPS satellites. Known as a "constellation," this group of satellites helps to measure the movement of tectonic plates on Earth.*

REVIEW

1. List and describe three possible driving forces of tectonic plate motion.

2. How do the three types of convergent boundaries differ from one another?

3. Explain how scientists measure the rate at which tectonic plates move.

4. **Identifying Relationships** When convection takes place in the mantle, why does cooler material sink, while warmer material rises?

Deforming the Earth's Crust

NEW TERMS

stress   folding
compression   normal fault
tension   reverse fault
fault   strike-slip fault

OBJECTIVES

- Describe major types of folds.
- Explain how the three major types of faults differ.
- Name and describe the most common types of mountains.
- Explain how various types of mountains form.

Have you ever tried to bend something, only to have it break? Try this: take a long, uncooked piece of spaghetti, and bend it very slowly, and only a little. Now bend it again, but this time much farther and faster. What happened to it the second time? How can the same material bend at one time and break at another? The answer is that the *stress* you put on it was different. **Stress** is the amount of force per unit area that is put on a given material. The same principle works on the rocks in the Earth's crust. The conditions under which a rock is stressed determine its behavior.

Rocks Get Stressed

When rock changes its shape due to stress, this reaction is called *deformation*. In the example above, you saw the spaghetti

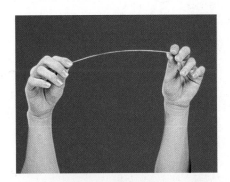
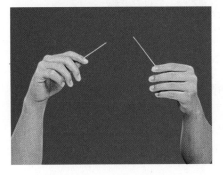

Figure 17 Materials react to different types of stress in different ways.

deform in two different ways—by bending and by breaking. The same thing happens in rock layers. Rock layers can bend when certain types of stress are placed on them. But when other kinds of stress are placed on them, they break. Rocks can deform due to the forces of plate tectonics.

The type of stress that occurs when an object is squeezed, as when two tectonic plates collide, is called **compression.** Compression can have some spectacular results. The Rocky Mountains and the Cascade Range are two examples of compression at a convergent plate boundary.

Another form of stress is *tension*. **Tension** is stress that occurs when forces act to stretch an object. As you might guess, tension occurs at divergent plate boundaries, when two tectonic plates pull away from each other. In the following pages you will learn how these two tectonic forces—compression and tension—bend and break rock to form some of the common landforms you already know.

After you've read about how tectonic forces cause rocks to bend and break, you may want to create some stress of your own. To find out how, turn to page 509 in your LabBook.

Folding

Folding occurs when rock layers bend due to stress in the Earth's crust. We assume that all sedimentary rock layers started out as horizontal layers. So when you see a fold, you know that deformation has taken place. Depending on how the rock layers deform, different types of folds are made. **Figure 18** shows the two most common types—*anticlines* and *synclines.*

Another type of fold is a *monocline.* In a monocline, rock layers are folded so that both ends of the fold are still horizontal. Imagine taking a stack of paper and laying it on a table top. Think of all the sheets of paper as different rock layers. Now put a book under one end of the stack. You can see that both ends of the sheets are still horizontal, but all the sheets are bent in the middle.

Folds can be large or small. Take a look at **Figure 19.** The largest folds are measured in kilometers. They can make up the entire side of a mountain. Other folds are still obvious but much smaller. Note the size of the pocket knife in the smaller photo. Now look at the smallest folds. You would measure these folds in centimeters.

Undeformed Rock Layers

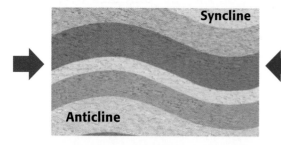
Syncline

Anticline

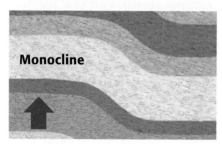
Monocline

Figure 18 *When two tectonic forces compress rock layers, they can cause the layers to bend and fold. Anticlines and* synclines *form when horizontal stress acts on rock. Monoclines form when vertical stress acts on rock.*

Figure 19 *Folds vary greatly in size. The larger photo at left shows mountain-sized folds in the Rocky Mountains.*

Faulting

While some rock layers bend and fold when stress is applied, under other conditions rock layers break. At first the rocks will only bend slightly. But if the stress is great enough, the rocks can eventually break. The surface along which rocks break and slide past each other is called a **fault.** The blocks of crust on each side of the fault are called *fault blocks.*

If a fault is not vertical, it is useful to distinguish between its two sides—the *hanging wall* and the *footwall.* **Figure 20** shows the difference between a hanging wall and a footwall. Depending on how the hanging wall and footwall move relative to each other, one of two main types of faults can form.

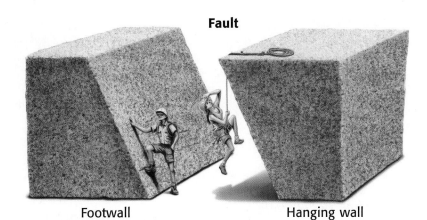

Fault

Footwall   Hanging wall

Figure 20 *The position of a fault block determines whether it is a hanging wall or a footwall.*

Normal Faults A *normal fault* is shown in **Figure 21.** The movement of a **normal fault** causes the hanging wall to move down relative to the footwall. Normal faults usually occur when tectonic forces cause tension that pulls rocks apart.

Reverse Faults A *reverse fault* is shown in **Figure 22.** The movement of a **reverse fault** causes the hanging wall to move up relative to the footwall—the "reverse" of a normal fault. Reverse faults usually happen when tectonic forces cause compression that pushes rocks together.

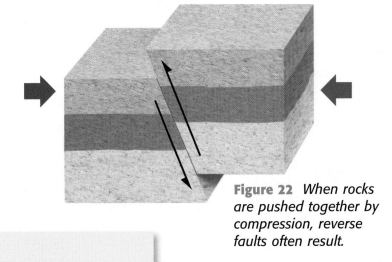

Normal Fault

Figure 21 *When rocks are pulled apart due to tension, normal faults often result.*

Reverse Fault

Figure 22 *When rocks are pushed together by compression, reverse faults often result.*

✓ Self-Check

How is folding different from faulting? *(See page 564 to check your answer.)*

Figure 23 *The photo at left is a normal fault. The photo at right is a reverse fault. Can you tell which kind of tectonic stress—compression or tension—must have acted on the rocks in each photo?*

Telling the Difference It's easy to tell the difference between a normal fault and a reverse fault in diagrams with arrows. But what about the faults in **Figure 23**? You can certainly see the faults, but which one is a normal fault, and which one is a reverse fault? In the top left photo, one side has obviously moved relative to the other. You can tell this is a normal fault by looking at the sequence of sedimentary rock layers. You can see by the relative positions of the two dark layers that the hanging wall has moved down relative to the footwall.

Figure 24 *In this photo of the San Andreas fault, you can see how the course of two river channels changed when the fault moved. The land at the top moved to the right relative to the land at the bottom.*

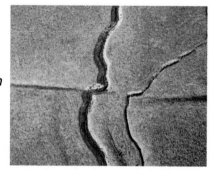

Strike-Slip Faults A third major type of fault is shown in **Figure 24**. **Strike-slip faults** occur when opposing forces cause rock to break and move horizontally. If you were standing on one side of a strike-slip fault looking across the fault when it moved, the ground on the other side would appear to move to your left or right.

Natural gas is used in many homes and factories as a source of energy. Some companies explore for sources of natural gas just as other companies explore for oil and coal. Like oil, natural gas travels upward through rock layers until it hits a layer through which it cannot travel and becomes trapped. Imagine that you are searching for pockets of trapped natural gas. Would you expect to find these pockets associated with anticlines, synclines, or faults? Explain your answer in your ScienceLog. Include drawings to help in your explanation.

Plate Tectonics and Mountain Building

You have just learned about several ways the Earth's crust changes due to the forces of plate tectonics. When tectonic plates collide, land features that start out as small folds and faults can eventually become great mountain ranges. The reason mountains exist is that tectonic plates are continually moving around and bumping into one another. As you can see in **Figure 25,** most major mountain ranges form at the edges of tectonic plates.

When tectonic plates undergo compression or tension, they can form mountains in several different ways. Let's take a look at three of the most common types of mountains—*folded mountains, fault-block mountains,* and *volcanic mountains.*

Folded Mountains *Folded mountains* form when rock layers are squeezed together and pushed upward. If you take a pile of paper on a table top and push on opposite edges of the pile, you will see how a folded mountain forms. You saw how these layers crunched together in Figure 18. **Figure 26** shows an example of a folded mountain range that formed at a convergent boundary.

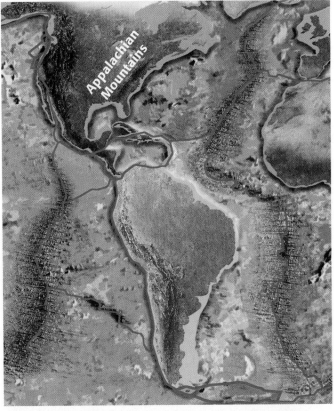

Figure 25 *Most of the world's major mountain ranges form at tectonic plate boundaries. Notice that the Appalachian Mountains, however, are located in the middle of the North American plate.*

Figure 26 *Once as mighty as the Himalayas, the Appalachians have been worn down by hundreds of millions of years of weathering and erosion.*

BRAIN FOOD

By now you know that plate tectonics is the force that creates the world's highest mountains, but did you know that plate tectonics is also responsible for creating some of the lowest places on Earth? It's true. When one tectonic plate is subducted beneath another, a deep valley called a *trench* forms at the boundary. The Mariana Trench is the deepest point in the oceans—11,033 m below sea level!

Formation of the Appalachian Mountains

Look back at Figure 25. The Appalachians are in the middle of the North American plate. How can this be? Shouldn't they be at the edge of a tectonic plate? Follow along in this diagram to find the answer.

1 About 500 million years ago, the landmasses that would become North America and Africa were on a collision course.

500 million years ago

North America · Europe · Africa

390 million years ago
Appalachian Mountains

2 About 390 million years ago, these tectonic plates collided, and the crust between them buckled and folded, forming the Appalachian Mountains.

65 million years ago

North America · Atlantic Ocean · Africa

3 About 208 million years ago, North America and Africa began to break apart, and a mid-ocean ridge formed between them. By 65 million years ago, so much new oceanic lithosphere had formed between the two tectonic plates that the Appalachian Mountains were no longer at a tectonic plate boundary at all—they were in the middle of the North American plate!

Figure 27 *When the crust is subjected to tension, the rock can break along a series of normal faults, resulting in fault-block mountains.*

Fault-Block Mountains Where tectonic forces put enough tension on the Earth's crust, a large number of normal faults can result. *Fault-block mountains* form when this faulting causes large blocks of the Earth's crust to drop down relative to other blocks. **Figure 27** shows one way this can happen.

When sedimentary rock layers are tilted up by faulting, they can produce mountains with sharp, jagged peaks. As you can see in **Figure 28,** the Tetons of western Wyoming are a spectacular example of this type of mountain.

Figure 28 *The Tetons formed as a result of tectonic forces that stretched the Earth's crust, causing it to break in a series of normal faults. Compare this photo with the illustration in Figure 27.*

Volcanic Mountains Most of the world's major volcanic mountains are located at convergent boundaries. Most volcanic mountains tend to form over the type of convergent boundaries that include subduction zones. There are so many volcanic mountains around the rim of the Pacific Ocean that early explorers named it the *Ring of Fire*. **Figure 29** shows an active volcano of the Ring of Fire.

Volcanic mountains form when molten rock erupts onto the Earth's surface. Unlike folded and fault-block mountains, volcanic mountains form from new material being added to the Earth's surface.

Figure 29 *A recent flow of mud and ash shows up starkly against the snow on Mount St. Helens, a mountain that formed from volcanic activity. Many of the mountains in the Cascade Range formed in this way.*

REVIEW

1. What is the difference between an anticline and a syncline?

2. What is the difference between a normal fault and a reverse fault?

3. Name and describe the type of tectonic stress that forms folded mountains.

4. Name and describe the type of tectonic stress that forms fault-block mountains.

5. **Making Predictions** If a fault occurs in an area where rock layers have been folded, which type of fault is it likely to be? Why?

Chapter Highlights

SECTION 1

Vocabulary

crust *(p. 136)*

mantle *(p. 137)*

core *(p. 137)*

lithosphere *(p. 138)*

asthenosphere *(p. 138)*

mesosphere *(p. 139)*

outer core *(p. 139)*

inner core *(p. 139)*

tectonic plates *(p. 140)*

Section Notes

• The Earth is made of three basic compositional layers—the crust, the mantle, and the core.

• The Earth is made of five main structural layers—lithosphere, asthenosphere, mesosphere, outer core, and inner core.

• Tectonic plates are large pieces of the lithosphere that move around on the Earth's surface.

• Knowledge about the structure of the Earth comes from the study of seismic waves caused by earthquakes.

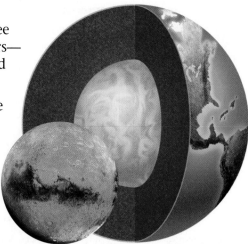

SECTION 2

Vocabulary

continental drift *(p. 143)*

sea-floor spreading *(p. 145)*

Section Notes

• Wegener's theory of continental drift explained many puzzling facts, including the fit of the Atlantic coastlines of South America and Africa.

• Today's continents were originally joined together in the ancient continent Pangaea.

• Some of the most important evidence for sea-floor spreading comes from magnetic reversals recorded in the ocean floor.

☑ Skills Check

Math Concepts

MAKING MODELS Suppose you built a model of the Earth that had a radius of 100 cm (diameter of 200 cm). The radius of the real Earth is 6,378 km, and the thickness of its outer core is 2,200 km. What percentage of the Earth's radius is the outer core? How thick would the outer core be in your model?

$$\frac{2{,}200 \text{ km}}{6{,}378 \text{ km}} = 0.34 = 34\%$$

34% of 100 cm = 0.34 × 100 cm = 34 cm

Visual Understanding

SEA-FLOOR SPREADING This close-up view of a mid-ocean ridge shows how new oceanic lithosphere forms. As the two tectonic plates pull away from each other, magma fills in the cracks that open between them. When this magma solidifies, it becomes the newest part of the oceanic plate.

SECTION 3

Vocabulary

plate tectonics *(p. 147)*
convergent boundary *(p. 148)*
subduction zone *(p. 148)*
divergent boundary *(p. 149)*
transform boundary *(p. 149)*

Section Notes

- The processes of ridge push, convection, and slab pull provide some possible driving forces for plate tectonics.

- Tectonic plate boundaries are classified as convergent, divergent, or transform.

- Data from satellite tracking indicate that some tectonic plates move an average of 3 cm a year.

Labs

Convection Connection *(p. 508)*

SECTION 4

Vocabulary

stress *(p. 151)*
compression *(p. 151)*
tension *(p. 151)*
folding *(p. 152)*
fault *(p. 153)*
normal fault *(p. 153)*
reverse fault *(p. 153)*
strike-slip fault *(p. 154)*

Section Notes

- As tectonic plates move next to and into each other, a great amount of stress is placed on the rocks at the boundary.

- Folding occurs when rock layers bend due to stress.

- Faulting occurs when rock layers break due to stress and then move on either side of the break.

- Mountains are classified as either folded, fault-block, or volcanic, depending on how they form.

- Mountain building is caused by the movement of tectonic plates. Different types of movement cause different types of mountains.

Labs

Oh, the Pressure! *(p. 509)*

---

 internetconnect

 GO TO: go.hrw.com

Visit the **HRW** Web site for a variety of learning tools related to this chapter. Just type in the keyword:

KEYWORD: HSTTEC

SCiLINKS. **GO TO:** www.scilinks.org

N S T A

Visit the **National Science Teachers Association** on-line Web site for Internet resources related to this chapter. Just type in the *sci*LINKS number for more information about the topic:

TOPIC: Composition of the Earth   *sci*LINKS NUMBER: HSTE155
TOPIC: Structure of the Earth   *sci*LINKS NUMBER: HSTE160
TOPIC: Tectonic Plates   *sci*LINKS NUMBER: HSTE165
TOPIC: Faults   *sci*LINKS NUMBER: HSTE170
TOPIC: Mountain Building   *sci*LINKS NUMBER: HSTE175

Chapter Review

For each pair of terms, explain the difference in their meanings.

1. oceanic crust/continental crust

2. lithosphere/asthenosphere

3. convergent boundary/divergent boundary

4. folding/faulting

5. oceanic crust/oceanic lithosphere

6. normal fault/reverse fault

UNDERSTANDING CONCEPTS

Multiple Choice

7. The part of the Earth that is a liquid is the
   a. crust.
   b. mantle.
   c. outer core.
   d. inner core.

8. The part of the Earth on which the tectonic plates are able to move is the
   a. lithosphere.
   b. asthenosphere.
   c. mesosphere.
   d. subduction zone.

9. The ancient continent that contained all the landmasses is called
   a. Pangaea.
   b. Gondwana.
   c. Laurasia.
   d. Panthalassa.

10. The type of tectonic plate boundary involving a collision between two tectonic plates is
    a. divergent.
    b. transform.
    c. convergent.
    d. normal.

11. The type of tectonic plate boundary that sometimes has a subduction zone is
    a. divergent.
    b. transform.
    c. convergent.
    d. normal.

12. The San Andreas fault is an example of a
    a. divergent boundary.
    b. transform boundary.
    c. convergent boundary.
    d. normal boundary.

13. When a fold is shaped like an arch, with the fold in an upward direction, it is called a(n)
    a. monocline.
    b. anticline.
    c. syncline.
    d. decline.

14. The type of fault in which the hanging wall moves down relative to the footwall is called
    a. strike-slip.
    b. reverse.
    c. normal.
    d. fault block.

15. The type of mountain involving huge sections of the Earth's crust being pushed up into anticlines and synclines is the
    a. folded mountain.
    b. fault-block mountain.
    c. volcanic mountain.
    d. strike-slip mountain.

16. Continental mountain ranges are usually associated with
    a. divergent boundaries.
    b. transform boundaries.
    c. convergent boundaries.
    d. normal boundaries.

17. Mid-ocean ridges are associated with
    a. divergent boundaries.
    b. transform boundaries.
    c. convergent boundaries.
    d. normal boundaries.

Short Answer

18. What is a tectonic plate?

19. What was the major problem with Wegener's theory of continental drift?

20. Why is there stress on the Earth's crust?

Concept Mapping

21. Use the following terms to create a concept map: sea-floor spreading, convergent boundary, divergent boundary, subduction zone, transform boundary, tectonic plates.

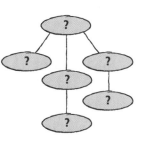

CRITICAL THINKING AND PROBLEM SOLVING

Write one or two sentences to answer each of the following questions:

22. Why is it necessary to think about the different layers of the Earth in terms of both their composition and their physical properties?

23. Folded mountains usually form at the edge of a tectonic plate. How can you explain old folded mountain ranges located in the middle of a tectonic plate?

24. New tectonic plate material continually forms at divergent boundaries. Tectonic plate material is also continually destroyed in subduction zones at convergent boundaries. Do you think the total amount of lithosphere formed on Earth is about equal to the amount destroyed? Why?

MATH IN SCIENCE

25. Assume that a very small oceanic plate is between a mid-ocean ridge to the west and a subduction zone to the east. At the ridge, the oceanic plate is growing at a rate of 5 km every million years. At the subduction zone, the oceanic plate is being destroyed at a rate of 10 km every million years. If the oceanic plate is 100 km across, in how many million years will the oceanic plate disappear?

INTERPRETING GRAPHICS

Imagine that you could travel to the center of the Earth. Use the diagram below to answer the questions that follow.

Composition	Structure
Crust (50 km)	Lithosphere (150 km)
Mantle (2,900 km)	Asthenosphere (250 km)
	Mesosphere (2,550 km)
Core (3,428 km)	Outer core (2,200 km)
	Inner core (1,228 km)

26. How far beneath Earth's surface would you have to go to find the liquid material in the Earth's core?

27. At what range of depth would you find mantle material but still be within the lithosphere?

NOW What Do You Think?

Take a minute to review your answers to the ScienceLog questions on page 135. Have your answers changed? If necessary, revise your answers based on what you have learned since you began this chapter.

Science, Technology, and Society

Living on the Mid-Atlantic Ridge

Imagine living hundreds of miles from other people on an icy outcrop of volcanic rock surrounded by the cold North Atlantic Ocean. How would you stay warm? For the people of Iceland, this is an important question that affects their daily life. Iceland is a volcanic island situated on the Mid-Atlantic Ridge, just south of the Arctic Circle. Sea-floor spreading produces active volcanoes, earthquakes, hot springs, and geysers that make life on this island seem a little unstable. However, the same volcanic force that threatens civilization provides the heat necessary for daily life. Icelanders use the geothermal energy supplied by their surroundings in ways that might surprise you.

▲ *The Blue Lagoon in Iceland is the result of producing energy from water power.*

Let's Go Geothermal!

Geothermal literally means "earth heat," *geo* meaning "earth" and *therme* meaning "heat." Around the ninth century A.D., Iceland's earliest settlers took advantage of the Earth's heat by planting crops in naturally heated ground. This encouraged rapid plant growth and an early harvest of food. In 1928, Iceland built its first public geothermal utility project—a hole drilled into the Earth in order to pump water from a hot spring. After the oil crisis of the 1970s,

geothermal-energy projects were built on a grand scale in Iceland. Today 85 percent of all houses in Iceland are heated by geothermal energy. Hot water from underground pools is pumped directly to houses, where it is routed through radiators to provide heat.

Geothermal water is also pumped to homes to provide hot tap water. This natural source meets all the hot-water needs for the city of Reykjavik, with a population of about 150,000 people!

There are still other uses for this hot water. For example, it is used to heat 120 public swimming pools. Picture yourself swimming outside in naturally hot water during the dead of winter! Greenhouses, where fruits and vegetables are grown, are also warmed by this water. Even fish farming on Iceland's exposed coastline wouldn't be possible without geothermal heat to adjust the water temperature. In other industries, geothermal energy is used to dry timber, wool, and seaweed.

Power Production

Although hydropower (producing energy from water power) is the principal source of electricity in Iceland, geothermal energy is also used. Water ranging in temperature from 300–700°C is pumped into a reservoir, where the water turns into steam that forces turbines to turn. The spinning motion of these turbines generates electricity. Power generation from geothermal sources is only about 5–15 percent efficient and results in a very large amount of water runoff. At the Svartsengi power plant, this water runoff has created a beautiful pool that swimmers call the Blue Lagoon.

Going Further

▶ Can you think of other abundant clean-energy resources? How could we harness such sources?

Continental Drift

When Alfred Wegener proposed his theory of continental drift in the early 1900s, many scientists laughed at the idea of continents plowing across the ocean. In fact, many people found his theory so ridiculous that Wegener, a university professor, had difficulty getting a job! Wegener's theory jolted the very foundation of geology.

Wegener's Theory

Wegener used geologic, fossil, and glacial evidence gathered on opposite sides of the Atlantic Ocean to support his theory of continental drift. For example, Wegener recognized geologic similarities between the Appalachian Mountains, in eastern North America, and the Scottish Highlands, as well as similarities between rock strata in South Africa and Brazil. He believed that these striking similarities could be explained only if these geologic features were once part of the same continent.

Wegener proposed that because they are less dense, continents float on top of the denser rock of the ocean floor. Although continental drift explained many of Wegener's observations, he could not find scientific evidence to develop a complete explanation of how continents move.

Alfred Wegener (1880–1930)

The Critics

Most scientists were skeptical of Wegener's theory and dismissed it as foolishness. Some critics held fast to old theories that giant land bridges could explain similarities among fossils in South America and Africa. Others argued that Wegener's theory could not account for the tremendous forces that would have been required to move continents such great distances. Wegener, however, believed that these forces could be the same forces responsible for earthquakes and volcanic eruptions.

The Evidence

During the 1950s and 1960s, discoveries of sea-floor spreading and magnetic reversal provided the evidence that Wegener's theory needed and led to the theory of plate tectonics. The theory of plate tectonics describes how the continents move. Today geolo-gists recognize that continents are actually parts of moving tectonic plates that float on the asthenosphere, a layer of partially molten rock.

Like the accomplishments of so many scientists, Wegener's accomplishments went unrecognized until years after his death. The next time you hear a scientific theory that sounds far out, don't underestimate it. It may be proven true!

Also an Astronomer and Meteorologist

Wegener had a very diverse background in the sciences. He earned a Ph.D. in astronomy from the University of Berlin. But he was always very interested in geophysics and meteorology. His interest in geophysics led to his theory on continental drift. His interest in meteorology eventually led to his death. He froze to death in Greenland while returning from a rescue mission to bring food to meteorologists camped on a glacier.

On Your Own

▶ Photocopy a world map. Carefully cut out the continents from the map. Be sure to cut along the line where the land meets the water. Slide the continents together like a jigsaw puzzle. How does this relate to the tectonic plates and continental drift?

7 Earthquakes

Tokyo

Kobe

Brace Yourself!

Imagine visiting Kobe, Japan. The date is January 17, 1995. It's early in the morning—5:46 A.M. to be exact—and you're in a taxi on the Hanshin Expressway. The expressway is elevated, supported by a long row of large columns. All of a sudden, you feel the taxi start to shake. The driver slows down. You watch a truck pass you. It looks like it is out of control. Suddenly the truck disappears! The taxi stops. You look out the window to see what is going on. The superhighway is twisting like a giant snake. The shaking lasts for less than a minute. The part of the highway that you are on seems to be in one piece, but for nearly half a mile in front of you, the expressway has collapsed. It looks as if something jerked the ground right out from under it, snapping the support columns like twigs. You now know why the truck disappeared, and you feel very lucky the taxi stopped in time.

The event you just imagined witnessing was the Great Hanshin earthquake. It killed 5,500 people and left 300,000 others homeless. Nearly 200,000 buildings were destroyed. While the earthquake tremor lasted less than a minute, terrible disasters continued afterward. Natural gas lines that ruptured and kerosene stoves that were crushed started huge fires. Pipes carrying the water that would have been used to put out the fires were broken, so the fires burned for days. Kobe was devastated, with damage totaling more than $100 billion.

In this chapter, you will learn what causes earthquakes and how earthquakes work. You will also learn how they affect our lives. There is much that we can do with the knowledge we gain from studying earthquakes. Think about what you could do with this knowledge as you learn about one of the most powerful parts of nature.

What Do You Think?

In your ScienceLog, try to answer the following questions based on what you already know:

1. What causes earthquakes?

2. Why are some earthquakes stronger than others?

3. Why do some buildings remain standing during earthquakes while others fall down?

Bend, Break, or Shake

If you were in a building during an earthquake, how would you want the building to respond to the ground's movement? What would you want the building to be made of? How would you want it to be constructed?

To answer these questions, you need to know how building materials behave during earthquakes. Do different materials react differently to the ground's movement? Try this activity to find out.

Procedure

1. Gather all (or most) of the following items: a piece of **rope** or **cord** about 30 cm long, a **wooden stick** about the size of a pencil, a large **paper clip**, a **plastic spoon**, a **wire clothes hanger**, a **plastic clothes hanger**, and a **spring.**

2. Using the straight edge of a **protractor,** draw a straight line on a sheet of **paper.** Measure the following angles from the line, and draw them on the paper: 20°, 45°, and 90°.

3. Put on your goggles and gloves. Using the angles that you drew as a guide, try bending each item 20° and then releasing it (you should still hold the item in your hands as you stop bending it). What happens? Does it break? If it bends, what happens when you stop bending it? Does it stay bent? Does it return to its original shape? Write your observations in your ScienceLog.

4. Repeat step 3, but this time bend each item 45°. Now repeat the test, this time bending each item 90°.

5. In your ScienceLog, make three lists: one for materials that broke, one for materials that stayed bent, and one for materials that bent and then returned to their original shape.

Analysis

6. How do the materials' responses to bending compare?

7. In earthquake-prone areas, engineers use building materials that move with the ground as it shakes but that do not break or bend permanently. Based on this knowledge, which materials from this experiment would you want building materials to behave like? Which materials would you not want building materials to behave like? Explain.

Going Further

Name some building materials that might behave like each of the lab materials. For example, wooden beams might behave like the stick.

What Are Earthquakes?

The word *earthquake* defines itself fairly well. But there is more to an earthquake than just ground shaking. In fact, there is a branch of Earth science devoted to earthquakes called seismology (siez MAHL uh jee). **Seismology** is the study of earthquakes. Earthquakes are complex, and they present many questions for *seismologists,* the scientists who study earthquakes. Although much about earthquakes is unknown, seismologists have found some answers to the following questions.

Where Do Earthquakes Occur?

Most earthquakes take place near the edges of tectonic plates. *Tectonic plates* are giant masses of solid rock that make up the outermost part of the Earth. **Figure 1** shows the Earth's tectonic plates and the locations of recent major earthquakes recorded by scientists. Note the high number of earthquakes near plate boundaries.

Tectonic plates move in different directions and at different speeds. Two plates can push toward each other or pull away from each other. They can also slip past each other like slow-moving trains traveling in opposite directions.

As a result of these movements, numerous features called faults exist in the Earth's crust. A **fault** is a break in the Earth's crust along which blocks of the crust slide relative to one another. Earthquakes occur along faults due to this sliding.

Faults occur in many places, but they are especially common near the edges of tectonic plates where they form the boundaries along which the plates move. This is why earthquakes are so common near plate boundaries.

NEW TERMS

seismology
fault
deformation
elastic rebound

seismic waves
P waves
S waves

OBJECTIVES

- Determine where earthquakes come from and what causes them.
- Identify different types of earthquakes.
- Describe how earthquakes travel through the Earth.

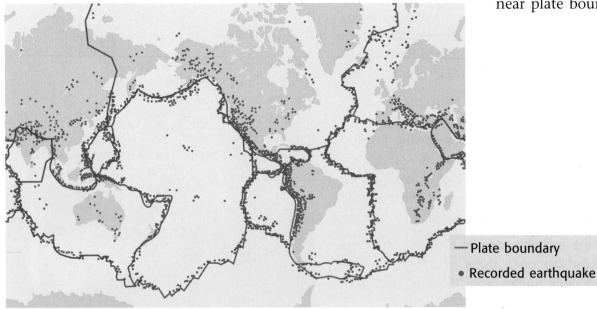

Figure 1 *The largest and most active earthquake zone lies along the plate boundaries surrounding the Pacific Ocean.*

— Plate boundary
• Recorded earthquake

What Causes Earthquakes?

As tectonic plates push, pull, or scrape against each other, stress builds up along faults near the plates' edges. In response to this stress, rock in the plates deforms. **Deformation** is the change in the shape of rock in response to stress. Rock along a fault deforms in mainly two ways—in a plastic manner, like a piece of molded clay, or in an elastic manner, like a rubber band. Plastic deformation, which is shown in **Figure 2,** does not lead to earthquakes.

Elastic deformation, however, does lead to earthquakes. While rock can stretch farther than steel without breaking, it will break at some point. Think of elastically deformed rock as a stretched rubber band. You can stretch a rubber band only so far before it breaks. When the rubber band breaks, it releases energy, and the broken pieces return to their unstretched shape.

Like the return of the broken rubber-band pieces to their unstretched shape, **elastic rebound** is the sudden return of elastically deformed rock to its undeformed shape. Elastic rebound occurs when more stress is applied to rock than the rock can withstand. During elastic rebound, rock releases energy that causes an earthquake, as shown in **Figure 3.**

Figure 2 *This photograph, taken in Hollister, California, shows how plastic deformation along the Calaveras Fault permanently bent a wall. No major earthquakes have occurred since the wall was built.*

Figure 3 *Elastic rebound releases energy that causes earthquakes.*

1 The rock along the fault has no stress acting on it.

Fault

2 Tectonic forces push rock on either side of the fault in opposite directions, but the rock is locked together and does not move. The rock deforms in an elastic manner.

3 When enough stress is applied, the rock slips along the fault and releases energy, which travels as seismic waves.

Are All Earthquakes the Same?

Earthquakes differ in strength and in the depth at which they begin. These differences depend on the type of tectonic plate motion that produces the earthquake. Examine the chart and the diagram below to learn how earthquakes differ.

Plate motion	Prominent fault type	Earthquake characteristics
Transform	strike-slip fault	moderate, shallow
Convergent	reverse fault	strong, deep
Divergent	normal fault	weak, shallow

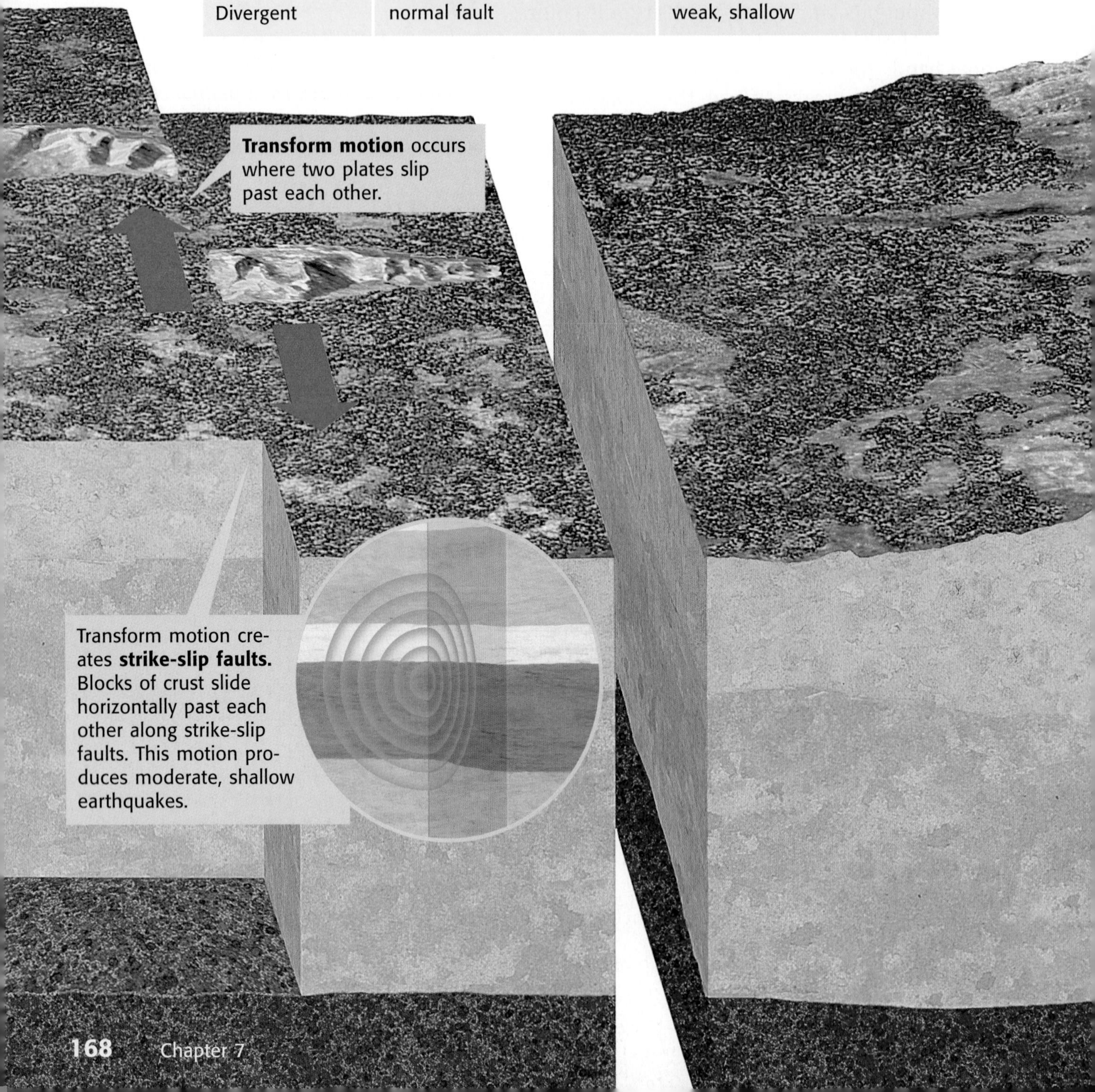

Transform motion occurs where two plates slip past each other.

Transform motion creates **strike-slip faults.** Blocks of crust slide horizontally past each other along strike-slip faults. This motion produces moderate, shallow earthquakes.

Self-Check

Name two differences between the results of convergent motion and the results of divergent motion.
(See page 564 to check your answer.)

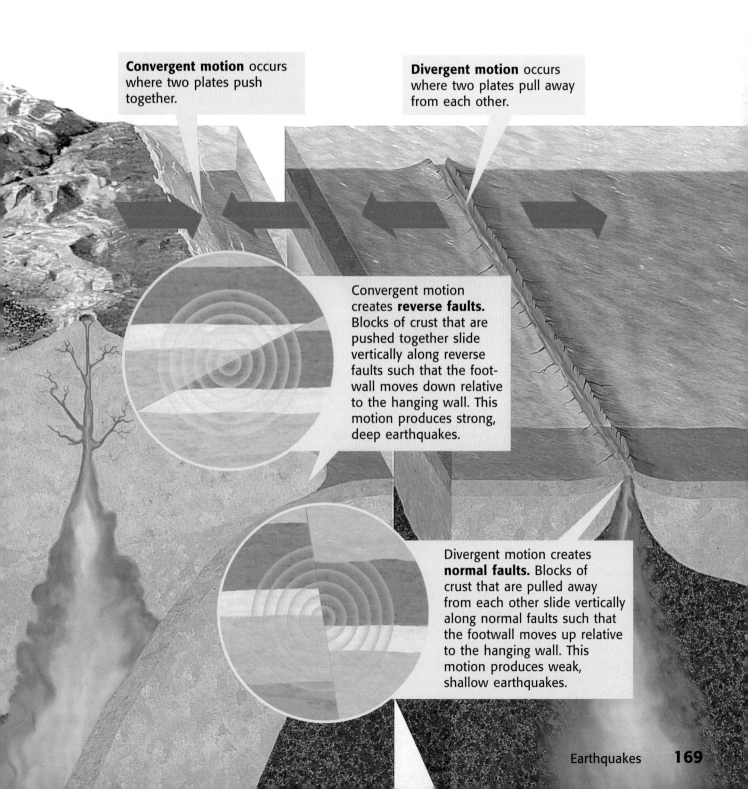

Convergent motion occurs where two plates push together.

Divergent motion occurs where two plates pull away from each other.

Convergent motion creates **reverse faults.** Blocks of crust that are pushed together slide vertically along reverse faults such that the footwall moves down relative to the hanging wall. This motion produces strong, deep earthquakes.

Divergent motion creates **normal faults.** Blocks of crust that are pulled away from each other slide vertically along normal faults such that the footwall moves up relative to the hanging wall. This motion produces weak, shallow earthquakes.

How Do Earthquakes Travel?

Remember that rock releases energy when it springs back after being deformed. This energy travels in the form of seismic waves. **Seismic waves** are waves of energy that travel through the Earth. Seismic waves that travel through the Earth's interior are called *body waves*. There are two types of body waves: P waves and S waves. Seismic waves that travel along the Earth's surface are called *surface waves*. Different types of seismic waves travel at different speeds and move the materials that they travel through differently.

physics
CONNECTION

All types of waves share basic features. Understanding one type, such as seismic waves, can help you understand many other types. Other types of waves include light waves, sound waves, and water waves.

P Is for Primary If you squeeze an elastic material into a smaller volume or stretch it into a larger volume, the pressure inside the material changes. When you suddenly stop squeezing or stretching the material, it springs briefly back and forth before returning to its original shape. This is how P waves (pressure waves) affect rock, as shown in **Figure 4**. **P waves,** which travel through solids, liquids, and gases, are the fastest seismic waves. Because they are the fastest seismic waves and because they can move through all parts of the Earth, P waves always travel ahead of other seismic waves. Because P waves are always the first seismic waves to be detected, they are also called *primary* waves.

S Is for Secondary Rock can also be deformed from side to side. When the rock springs back to its original position after being deformed, S waves are created. **S waves,** or shear waves, are the second-fastest seismic wave. S waves shear rock back and forth, as shown in **Figure 5**. *Shearing* stretches parts of rock sideways from other parts.

Direction of wave travel

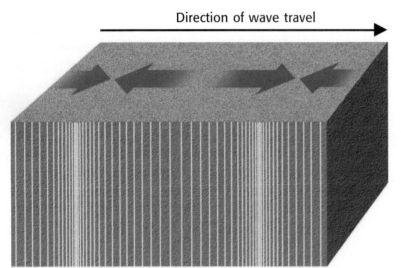

Figure 4 *P waves move rock back and forth between a squeezed position and a stretched position as they travel through it.*

Direction of wave travel

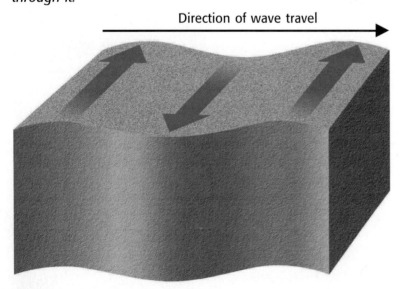

Figure 5 *S waves shear rock back and forth as they travel through it.*

Unlike P waves, S waves cannot travel through parts of the Earth that are completely liquid. Also, S waves are slower than P waves and always arrive second; thus, they are also called *secondary* waves. The graph in **Figure 6,** which is called a *time-distance graph,* compares the speeds of P waves and S waves.

Surface Waves Surface waves move the ground up and down in circles as the waves travel along the surface. This is shown in **Figure 7.** Many people have reported feeling like they were on a roller coaster during an earthquake. This feeling comes from surface waves passing along the Earth's surface. Surface waves travel more slowly than body waves but are more destructive. Most damage during an earthquake comes from surface waves, which can literally shake the ground out from under a building.

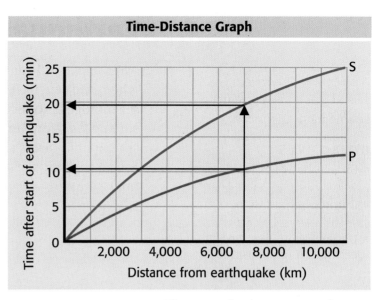

Time-Distance Graph

Figure 6 *As you can see, it takes S waves nearly 20 minutes to travel 7,000 km, while it takes P waves less than 11 minutes to travel the same distance.*

Direction of wave travel

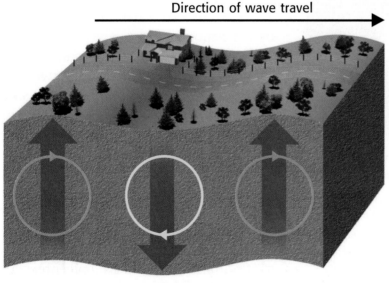

Figure 7 *Surface waves move the ground much like ocean waves move water particles.*

REVIEW

1. Where do earthquakes occur?

2. What directly causes earthquakes?

3. Arrange the types of earthquakes caused by the three plate-motion types from weakest to strongest.

4. **Using Graphics** Refer to Figure 6. How long does it take S waves to travel 1,500 km?

Earthquake Measurement

NEW TERMS

seismograph   epicenter
seismogram   focus

OBJECTIVES

- Explain how earthquakes are detected.
- Demonstrate how to locate earthquakes.
- Describe how the strength of an earthquake is measured.

After an earthquake occurs, seismologists try to find out when and where it started. Earthquake-sensing devices enable seismologists to record and measure seismic waves. These measurements show how far the seismic waves traveled. The measurements also show how much the ground moved. Seismologists use this information to pinpoint where the earthquake started and to find out how strong the earthquake was.

Locating Earthquakes

How do seismologists know when and where earthquakes begin? They depend on earthquake-sensing instruments called seismographs. **Seismographs** are instruments located at or near the surface of the Earth that record seismic waves. When the waves reach a seismograph, the seismograph creates a seismogram, such as the one in **Figure 8.** A **seismogram** is a tracing of earthquake motion created by a seismograph.

Seismologists use seismograms to calculate when an earthquake started. An earthquake starts when rock slips suddenly enough along a fault to create seismic waves. Remember the time-distance graph in Figure 6? Seismologists find an earthquake's start time by comparing seismograms to the time-distance graph and noting the difference in arrival times of P waves and S waves.

Seismologists also use seismograms to find an earthquake's epicenter. An **epicenter** is the point on the Earth's surface directly above an earthquake's starting point. A **focus** is the point inside the Earth where an earthquake begins. **Figure 9** shows the relationship between an earthquake's epicenter and its focus.

Figure 8 *The line in a seismogram traces the movement of the ground as it shakes. The more the ground moves, the farther back and forth the line traces.*

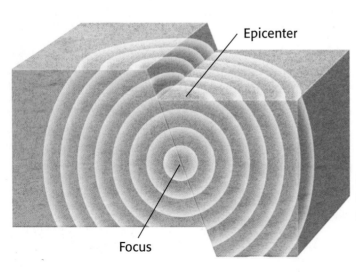

Epicenter

Focus

Figure 9 *An earthquake's epicenter is on the Earth's surface directly above the earthquake's focus.*

Perhaps the most common method by which seismologists find an earthquake's epicenter is the *S-P-time method*. When using the S-P-time method, seismologists begin by collecting several seismograms of the same earthquake from different locations. Seismologists then place the seismograms on the time-distance graph so the first P waves line up with the P-wave curve and the first S waves line up with the S-wave curve. This is shown in **Figure 10.**

After the seismograms are placed on the graph, seismologists can see how far away from each station the earthquake was by reading the distance axis. After seismologists find out the distances, they can find the earthquake's epicenter as shown below.

Plotting Seismograms on a Time-Distance Graph

Figure 10 *Seismograms are lined up so that the first P wave and the first S wave line up with the correct curves. Seismologists subtract a wave's travel time (read from the vertical axis) from the time that the wave was recorded. This determines when the earthquake started. The distance of the stations from the epicenter is read from the horizontal axis.*

Finding an Earthquake's Epicenter

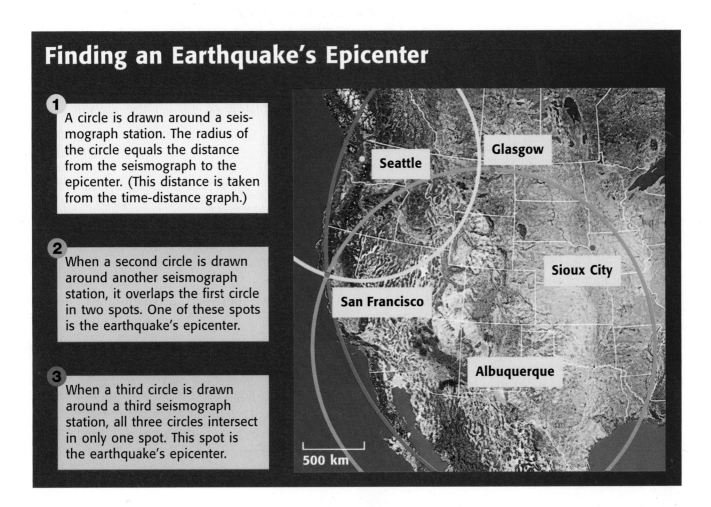

1 A circle is drawn around a seismograph station. The radius of the circle equals the distance from the seismograph to the epicenter. (This distance is taken from the time-distance graph.)

2 When a second circle is drawn around another seismograph station, it overlaps the first circle in two spots. One of these spots is the earthquake's epicenter.

3 When a third circle is drawn around a third seismograph station, all three circles intersect in only one spot. This spot is the earthquake's epicenter.

500 km

Measuring Earthquake Strength

"How strong was the earthquake?" is a common question asked of seismologists. This is not an easy question to answer. But it is an important question for public officials, safety organizations, and businesses as well as seismologists. Fortunately, seismograms can be used not only to determine an earthquake's epicenter and its start time but also to find out an earthquake's strength.

The *Richter scale* is a commonly used tool for measuring earthquake strength. It is named after Charles Richter, an American seismologist who developed the scale in the 1930s. Richter used the same type of seismograph to record seismograms from numerous earthquakes. He then plotted the maximum height of each seismogram and found that the heights varied dramatically. The smallest height that he could measure was between 0.1 mm and 0.3 mm, and the greatest height that he could measure was more than 100 mm. After some trial and error, Richter created the scale that was later named after him. A modified version of the Richter scale is shown at left.

There is a pattern in the Richter scale relating an earthquake's magnitude and the amount of energy released by the earthquake. Each time the magnitude increases by 1 unit, the amount of energy released becomes 31.7 times larger. For example, an earthquake with a magnitude of 5.0 on the Richter scale will release 31.7 times as much energy as an earthquake with a magnitude of 4.0 on the Richter scale. An earthquake with a magnitude of 6.0 releases 31.7×31.7— or about 1,000 times—as much energy as an earthquake with a magnitude of 4.0 does. Try the MathBreak at left to see if you understand the relationship between strength and magnitude on the Richter scale.

Modified Richter Scale	
Magnitude	**Estimated Effects**
2.0	can be detected only by seismograph
3.0	can be felt at epicenter
4.0	felt by most in area
5.0	causes damage at epicenter
6.0	causes widespread damage
7.0	causes great, widespread damage

MATH BREAK

Moving Up the Scale

If the amount of energy released by an earthquake with a magnitude of 2.0 on the Richter scale is *n*, what are the amounts of energy released by earthquakes with the following magnitudes in terms of *n*: 3.0, 4.0, 5.0, and 6.0? (Hint: The energy released by an earthquake with a magnitude of 3.0 is 31.7*n*.)

REVIEW

1. What is the difference between a seismogram and a seismograph?

2. How many seismograph stations are needed to use the S-P-time method? Why?

3. **Doing Calculations** If the amount of energy released by an earthquake with a magnitude of 7.0 on the Richter scale is *x*, what is the amount of energy released by an earthquake with a magnitude of 6.0 in terms of *x*?

Earthquakes and Society

Earthquakes are a fascinating part of Earth science, but they are very dangerous. Seismologists have had some success in predicting earthquakes, but simply being aware of earthquakes is not enough. It is important for people in earthquake-prone areas to be prepared.

NEW TERMS

gap hypothesis
seismic gap

OBJECTIVES

- Explain earthquake hazard.
- Compare methods of earthquake forecasting.
- List ways to safeguard buildings against earthquakes.
- Outline earthquake safety procedures.

Earthquake Hazard

Earthquake hazard measures how prone an area is to experiencing earthquakes in the future. An area's earthquake-hazard level is determined by past and present seismic activity. Look carefully at the map in **Figure 11.** As you can see, some areas of the United States have a higher earthquake-hazard level than others. This is because some areas have more seismic activity than others. The West Coast, for example, has a very high earthquake-hazard level because it has a lot of seismic activity. Areas such as the Gulf Coast or the Midwest have much lower earthquake-hazard levels because they do not have as much seismic activity.

Can you find the area where you live on the map? What level or levels of earthquake hazard are shown for your area? Look at the hazard levels in nearby areas. How do their hazard levels compare with your area's hazard level? What could explain the earthquake-hazard levels in your area and nearby areas?

Figure 11 *This is an earthquake-hazard map of the continental United States. It shows various levels of earthquake hazard for different areas of the country.*

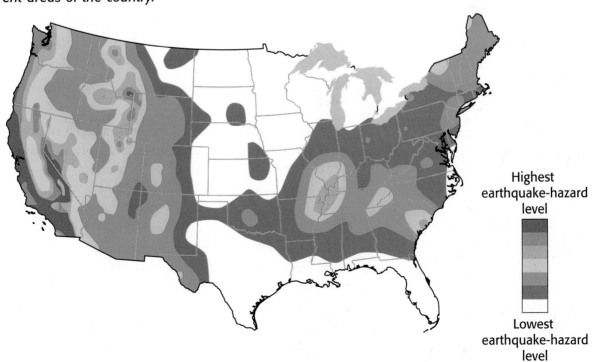

Highest earthquake-hazard level

Lowest earthquake-hazard level

Earthquake Forecasting

Predicting when and where earthquakes will occur and how strong they will be is a very difficult task. Earthquakes are perhaps the most unpredictable part of Earth science. However, by closely monitoring active faults and other areas of seismic activity, seismologists have discovered some patterns in earthquakes that allow them to make some broad predictions.

Worldwide Earthquake Frequency (Based on Observations Since 1900)		
Descriptor	**Magnitude**	**Average occurring annually**
Great	8.0 and higher	1
Major	7.0–7.9	18
Strong	6.0–6.9	120
Moderate	5.0–5.9	800
Light	4.0–4.9	about 6,200
Minor	3.0–3.9	about 49,000
Very minor	2.0–2.9	about 365,000

Figure 12 *Generally, with each step down in earthquake magnitude, the number of earthquakes per year is about 10 times greater.*

Strength and Frequency As you learned earlier, earthquakes vary in strength. And you can probably guess that earthquakes don't occur on a set schedule. But what you may not know is that the strength of earthquakes is related to how often they occur. The chart in **Figure 12** provides more detail on this relationship.

This relationship between earthquake strength and frequency is also observed on a local scale. For example, each year approximately 10 earthquakes occur in the Puget Sound area of Washington with a magnitude of 4 on the Richter scale. Over this same time period, approximately 100 earthquakes occur in the same area with a magnitude of 3. This means that 10 times as many earthquakes with a magnitude of 3 occur in this area as earthquakes with a magnitude of 4. Scientists use these statistics to make predictions about the strength, location, and frequency of future earthquakes.

Can animals predict earthquakes? To decide for yourself, turn to page 188 to read about links between animal behavior and earthquakes.

Self-Check

According to the chart above, about how many earthquakes with a magnitude between 6.0 and 6.9 occur annually? *(See page 564 to check your answer.)*

The Gap Hypothesis Another method of predicting an earthquake's strength, location, and frequency is based on the gap hypothesis. The **gap hypothesis** states that sections of active faults that have had relatively few earthquakes are likely to be the sites of strong earthquakes in the future. The areas along a fault where relatively few earthquakes have occurred are called **seismic gaps.**

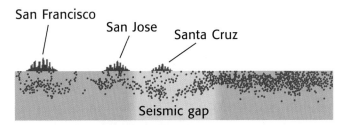

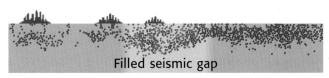

Before 1989 Earthquake

After 1989 Earthquake

The gap hypothesis helped seismologists forecast the approximate time, strength, and location of the 1989 Loma Prieta earthquake in the San Francisco Bay area. The seismic gap that they identified is illustrated in **Figure 13.** In 1988, seismologists predicted that over the next 30 years there was a 30 percent chance that an earthquake with a magnitude of at least 6.5 would fill this seismic gap. Were they correct? The Loma Prieta earthquake, which filled in the seismic gap in 1989, measured 7.1 on the Richter scale. That's very close, considering how complicated the forecasting of earthquakes is.

Figure 13 *This diagram shows a cross section of the San Andreas Fault. Notice the highlighted seismic gap before the 1989 earthquake. Note how the gap was filled by the 1989 earthquake and its* aftershocks, *which are weaker earthquakes that follow a stronger earthquake.*

Earthquakes and Buildings

Much like a judo master knocks the feet out from under his or her opponent, earthquakes shake the ground out from under buildings and bridges. Once the center of gravity of a structure has been displaced far enough off the structure's supporting base, most structures simply collapse.

Figure 14 shows what can happen to buildings during an earthquake. These buildings were not designed or constructed to withstand the forces of an earthquake. Similar collapses can occur on bridges, highway overpasses, gas and water pipelines, and dams.

Figure 14 *These cars are pinned under the second story of the apartment buildings that they were parked beside. An earthquake shook the ground floor out from under the second story, which then collapsed.*

Explore

Research a tall building to find out how its structure is reinforced. Would any of the building's reinforcements safeguard it against earthquakes? Has an earthquake occurred in the building's area since the building was constructed? If so, how well did the building withstand the shaking?

People have learned a lot from building failure during earthquakes. Architects and engineers use the newest technology to design and construct buildings and bridges to better withstand earthquakes. Study this diagram carefully to learn about some of this modern technology.

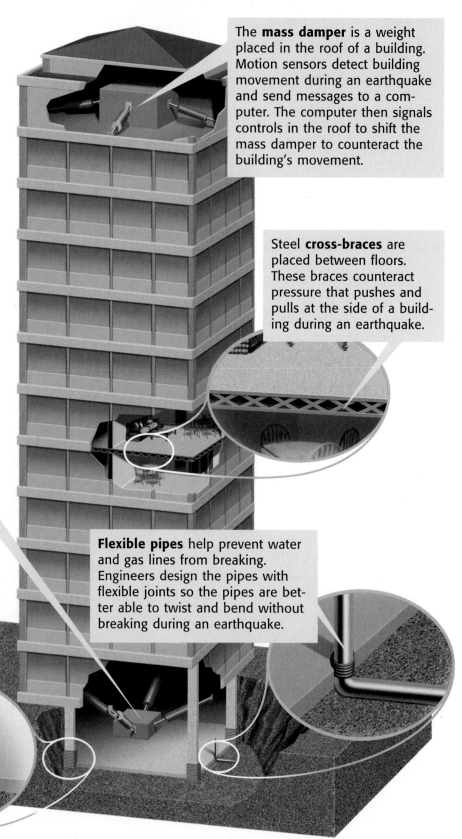

The **mass damper** is a weight placed in the roof of a building. Motion sensors detect building movement during an earthquake and send messages to a computer. The computer then signals controls in the roof to shift the mass damper to counteract the building's movement.

Steel **cross-braces** are placed between floors. These braces counteract pressure that pushes and pulls at the side of a building during an earthquake.

The **active tendon system** works much like the mass damper system in the roof. Sensors notify a computer that the building is moving. Then the computer activates devices to shift a large weight to counteract the movement.

Base isolators act as shock absorbers during an earthquake. They are made of layers of rubber and steel wrapped around a lead core. Base isolators absorb seismic waves, preventing them from traveling through the building.

Flexible pipes help prevent water and gas lines from breaking. Engineers design the pipes with flexible joints so the pipes are better able to twist and bend without breaking during an earthquake.

178   Chapter 7

Are You Prepared for an Earthquake?

If you live in an earthquake-prone area or ever plan to visit one, there are many things you can do to protect yourself and your property from earthquakes. Plan ahead so you will know what to do before, during, and after an earthquake. Stick to your plan as closely as possible.

Turn to page 512 to build your own earthquake-safe building.

Before the Shaking Starts The first thing you should do is safeguard your house against earthquakes. For example, put heavier objects on lower shelves so they do not fall on anyone during the earthquake. You can also talk to adults about having your home reinforced. Make a plan with others (your family, neighbors, or friends) to meet somewhere after the earthquake is over. This way someone will know you are safe. During the earthquake, waterlines, power lines, and roadways may be damaged. Therefore, you should store nonperishable food, water, a fire extinguisher, a flashlight with batteries, and a first-aid kit in a place you can access after the earthquake.

When the Shaking Starts The best thing to do if you are indoors is to crouch or lie face down under a table or desk in the center of a room, as shown in **Figure 16**. If you are outside, lie face down away from buildings, power lines, and trees, and cover your head with your hands. If you are in a car on an open road, you should stop the car and remain inside.

Figure 15 *Simple precautions, such as storing heavy objects on lower shelves instead of higher ones, can greatly reduce the chance of injury during an earthquake.*

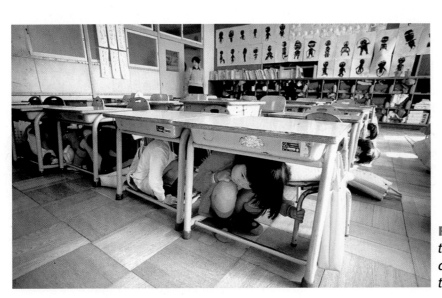

You finally make it to a World Series game, but the game is called halfway through. Is it rain? Hardly. Turn to page 189 to find out what happens.

Figure 16 *These students are participating in an earthquake drill. If an earthquake occurs during class, these students will know what to do.*

After the Shaking Stops Being in an earthquake is a startling experience. Afterward, you should not be surprised to find yourself and others puzzled about what happened. You should try to calm down, get your bearings, and remove yourself from immediate danger, such as downed power lines, broken glass, and fire hazards. Be aware that there may be aftershocks. Recall your earthquake plan, and follow it through.

REVIEW

1. How is an area's earthquake hazard determined?

2. Which earthquake forecast predicts a more precise location—a forecast based on the relationship between strength and frequency or a forecast based on the gap hypothesis?

3. Describe two ways that buildings are reinforced against earthquakes.

4. Name four items that you should store in case of an earthquake.

5. **Using Graphics** Would the street shown in the photo at left be a safe place during an earthquake? Why or why not?

##

Y ou are at home reading the evening news. On the front page you read a report from the local seismology station. Scientists predict an earthquake in your area sometime in the near future. You realize that you are not prepared.

Make a detailed outline of how you would prepare yourself and your home for an earthquake. Then write a list of safety procedures to follow during an earthquake. When you are done, exchange your work with a classmate. How do your plans differ from your classmate's? How might you work together to improve your earthquake safety plans?

Earthquake Discoveries Near and Far

NEW TERMS

Moho

shadow zone

OBJECTIVES

- Describe how seismic studies reveal Earth's interior.
- Summarize seismic discoveries on other cosmic bodies.

The study of earthquakes has led to many important discoveries about the Earth's interior. Seismologists learn about the Earth's interior by observing how seismic waves travel through the Earth. Likewise, seismic waves on other cosmic bodies allow seismologists to study the interiors of those bodies.

Discoveries in Earth's Interior

Have you ever noticed how light bends in water? If you poke part of a pencil into water and look at it from a certain angle, the pencil looks bent. This is because the light waves that bounce off the pencil bend as they pass through the water's surface toward your eye. Seismic waves bend in much the same way as they travel through rock. Seismologists have learned a lot about the Earth's interior by studying how seismic waves bend.

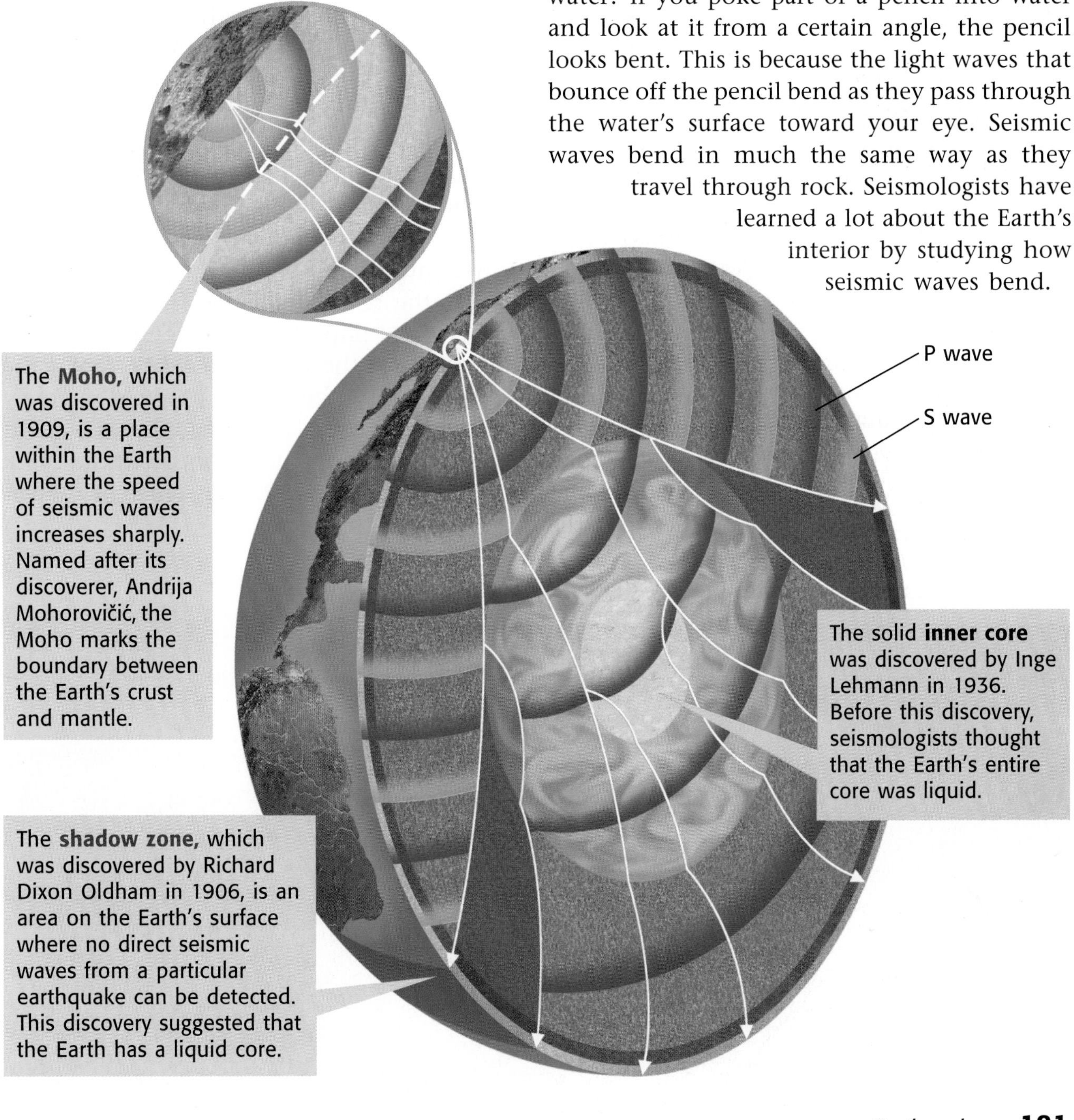

P wave

S wave

The **Moho,** which was discovered in 1909, is a place within the Earth where the speed of seismic waves increases sharply. Named after its discoverer, Andrija Mohorovičić, the Moho marks the boundary between the Earth's crust and mantle.

The solid **inner core** was discovered by Inge Lehmann in 1936. Before this discovery, seismologists thought that the Earth's entire core was liquid.

The **shadow zone,** which was discovered by Richard Dixon Oldham in 1906, is an area on the Earth's surface where no direct seismic waves from a particular earthquake can be detected. This discovery suggested that the Earth has a liquid core.

Quakes and Shakes on Other Cosmic Bodies

Seismologists have taken what they have learned from earthquakes and applied it to studies of other cosmic bodies, such as planets and moons. They have been able to learn about the interiors of these cosmic bodies by studying how seismic waves behave within them. The first and perhaps most successful seismic test on another cosmic body was on Earth's moon. Other studies have taken place on Mars, and even the sun's seismicity has been studied via satellite.

The Moon In July 1969, humans set foot on the moon for the first time. They brought with them a seismograph. Not knowing if the moon was seismically active, they left nothing to chance—they purposely crashed their landing vehicle back into the moon's surface after they left to create artificial seismic waves. What happened after that left seismologists astonished.

If the lander had crashed into the Earth, the equivalent seismograms would have lasted 20–30 seconds at most. The surface of the moon, however, vibrated for more than an hour and a half! At first scientists thought the equipment was not working properly. But the seismograph recorded similar signals produced by meteoroid impacts and "moonquakes" long after the astronauts had left the moon. **Figure 17** shows the nature of these seismic events, which were observed remotely from Earth. Based on these long-lasting seismic events and other studies of seismic waves on the moon, scientists think that the material in the moon's interior has different properties than the moon's surface material.

Figure 17 *These seismograms show that seismic waves in the moon last longer than they do in the Earth. Seismic waves from a shallow "moonquake" last 50 minutes. Seismic waves from a meteoroid impact last an hour and a half. Similar disturbances on Earth last less than a minute.*

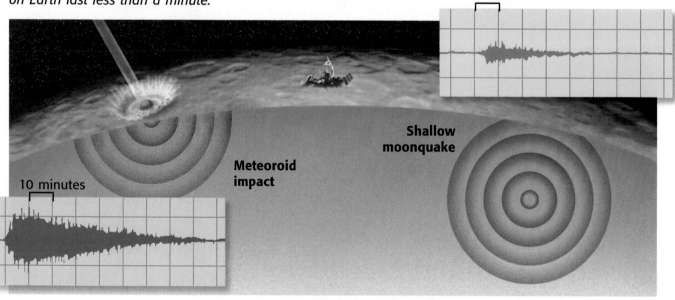

10 minutes

Meteoroid impact

Shallow moonquake

10 minutes

Mars In 1976, a space probe called *Viking 1* allowed seismologists to learn about seismic activity on Mars. The probe, which was controlled remotely from Earth, landed on Mars and conducted several experiments. A seismograph was placed on top of the spacecraft, a model of which is shown in **Figure 18,** to measure seismic waves on Mars. However, as soon as the craft landed, the seismograph began to shake. Scientists immediately discovered that Mars is a very windy planet, and the seismograph worked mainly as a wind gauge!

Although the wind on Mars interfered with the seismograph, the seismograph recorded seismograms for months. During that time, only one possible "marsquake" shook the seismograph harder than the wind did. Seismic activity is just one of several aspects of Mars that scientists study. Several projects are currently underway to study Mars's water supply, wind, soil, atmosphere and climate, and many other aspects of the planet.

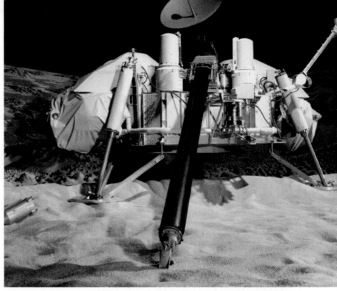

Figure 18 *Scientists attempted to obtain Martian seismic data with a seismograph on top of Viking I.*

The Sun Seismologists have also studied seismic waves on the sun. Because humans cannot directly access the sun, scientists study it remotely by using a satellite called *SOHO.* Information gathered by *SOHO* has shown that solar flares produce seismic waves. *Solar flares* are powerful magnetic disturbances in the sun. The seismic waves that result cause "sunquakes," which are similar to earthquakes but are generally much stronger. For example, a moderate sunquake detected by *SOHO* in 1996 was equivalent to an earthquake with a magnitude of 11.3. This sunquake, which is shown in **Figure 19** beneath an image of *SOHO,* released more than 1 million times as much energy as the Great Hanshin earthquake mentioned at the beginning of this chapter!

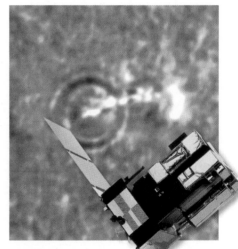

Figure 19 SOHO *detects "sunquakes" that dwarf the greatest earthquakes in history.*

REVIEW

1. What observation of seismic-wave travel led to the discovery of the Moho?

2. Briefly describe one discovery seismologists have made about each of the following cosmic bodies: the moon, Mars, and the sun.

3. **Interpreting Graphics** Take another look at the figure on the first page of Section 4. Why don't S waves enter the Earth's outer core?

Chapter Highlights

SECTION 1

Vocabulary

seismology *(p. 166)*
fault *(p. 166)*
deformation *(p. 167)*
elastic rebound *(p. 167)*
seismic waves *(p. 170)*
P waves *(p. 170)*
S waves *(p. 170)*

Section Notes

- Earthquakes mainly occur along faults near the edges of tectonic plates.

- Elastic rebound is the direct cause of earthquakes.

- Earthquakes differ depending on what type of plate motion causes them.

- Seismic waves are classified as body waves or surface waves.

- Body waves travel through the Earth's interior, while surface waves travel along the surface.

- There are two types of body waves: P waves and S waves.

SECTION 2

Vocabulary

seismograph *(p. 172)*
seismogram *(p. 172)*
epicenter *(p. 172)*
focus *(p. 172)*

Section Notes

- Seismographs detect seismic waves and record them as seismograms.

- An earthquake's focus is the underground location where seismic waves begin. The earthquake's epicenter is on the surface directly above the focus.

- Seismologists use the S-P-time method to find an earthquake's epicenter.

- Seismologists use the Richter scale to measure an earthquake's strength.

Labs

Earthquake Waves *(p. 514)*

☑ Skills Check

Math Concepts

EARTHQUAKE STRENGTH The energy released by an earthquake increases by a factor of 31.7 with each increase in magnitude. The energy released decreases by a factor of 31.7 with each decrease in magnitude. All you have to do is multiply or divide.

If magnitude 4 releases energy y, then:

- magnitude 5 releases energy $31.7y$

- magnitude 3 releases energy $\dfrac{y}{31.7}$

Visual Understanding

TIME-DISTANCE GRAPH Note on the time-distance graph in Figure 10 that the difference in arrival times between P waves and S waves increases with distance from the epicenter.

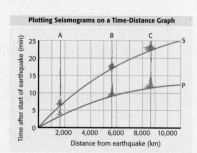

Plotting Seismograms on a Time-Distance Graph

SECTION 3

Vocabulary

gap hypothesis (*p. 176*)

seismic gap (*p. 176*)

Section Notes

- Earthquake hazard measures how prone an area is to experiencing earthquakes in the future.

- Some earthquake predictions are based on the relationship between earthquake strength and earthquake frequency. As earthquake frequency decreases, earthquake strength increases.

- Predictions based on the gap hypothesis target seismically inactive areas along faults for strong earthquakes in the future.

- An earthquake usually collapses a structure by displacing the structure's center of gravity off the structure's supporting base.

- Buildings and bridges can be reinforced to minimize earthquake damage.

- People in earthquake-prone areas should plan ahead for earthquakes.

Labs

Quake Challenge (*p. 512*)

SECTION 4

Vocabulary

Moho (*p. 181*)

shadow zone (*p. 181*)

Section Notes

- The Moho, shadow zone, and inner core are features discovered on and inside Earth by observing seismic waves.

- Seismology has been used to study other cosmic bodies.

- Seismic waves last much longer on the moon than they do on Earth.

- Based on early seismic studies, Mars appears much less active seismically than the Earth.

- "Sunquakes" produce energy far greater than any earthquakes we know of.

Chapter Review

To complete the following sentences, choose the correct term from each pair of terms listed below:

1. Energy is released as __?__ occurs. (*deformation* or *elastic rebound*)

2. __?__ cannot travel through parts of the Earth that are completely liquid. (*S waves* or *P waves*)

3. Seismic waves are recorded by a __?__. (*seismograph* or *seismogram*)

4. Seismologists use the S-P-time method to find an earthquake's __?__. (*shadow zone* or *epicenter*)

5. The __?__ is a place that marks a sharp increase in seismic wave speed. (*seismic gap* or *Moho*)

UNDERSTANDING CONCEPTS

Multiple Choice

6. When rock is __?__, energy builds up in it. Seismic waves occur as this energy is __?__.
   a. elastically deformed; released
   b. plastically deformed; released
   c. elastically deformed; increased
   d. plastically deformed; increased

7. The strongest earthquakes usually occur
   a. near divergent boundaries.
   b. near convergent boundaries.
   c. near transform boundaries.
   d. along normal faults.

8. The last seismic waves to arrive are
   a. P waves.
   b. S waves.
   c. surface waves.
   d. body waves.

9. If an earthquake begins while you are in a building, the safest thing to do first is
   a. get under the strongest table, chair, or other piece of furniture.
   b. run out into the street.
   c. crouch near a wall.
   d. call home.

10. Studying earthquake waves currently allows seismologists to do all of the following *except*
    a. determine when an earthquake started.
    b. learn about the Earth's interior.
    c. decrease an earthquake's strength.
    d. determine where an earthquake started.

11. If a planet has a liquid core, then S waves
    a. speed up as they travel through the core.
    b. maintain their speed as they travel through the core.
    c. change direction as they travel through the core.
    d. cannot pass through the core.

Short Answer

12. What is the relationship between the strength of earthquakes and earthquake frequency?

13. You learned earlier that if you are in a car during an earthquake and are out in the open, it is best to stay in the car. Briefly describe a situation in which you might want to leave a car during an earthquake.

14. How did Richard Oldham discover that the outer core of the Earth was liquid?

Concept Mapping

15. Use the following terms to create a concept map: focus, epicenter, earthquake start time, seismic waves, P waves, S waves.

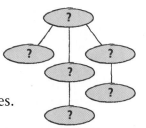

Write one or two sentences to answer the following questions:

16. How might the wall in Figure 2 appear if it had deformed elastically instead of plastically?

17. Why do strong earthquakes occur where there have not been many recent earthquakes? (**Hint:** Think about what gradually happens to rock before an earthquake occurs.)

18. What could be done to solve the wind problem with the seismograph on Mars? Explain how you would set up the seismograph.

19. Based on the relationship between earthquake magnitude and frequency, if 150 earthquakes with a magnitude of 2 occur in your area this year, about how many earthquakes with a magnitude of 4 should occur in your area this year?

The graph below illustrates the relationship between earthquake magnitude and the height of the tracings on a seismogram. Charles Richter initially formed his magnitude scale by comparing the heights of seismogram readings for different earthquakes. Study the graph, and then answer the questions that follow.

Seismogram Height vs. Earthquake Magnitude

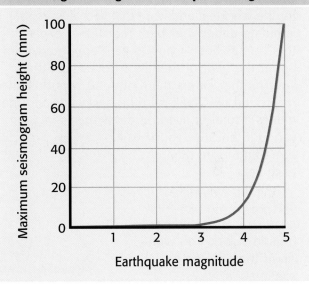

20. What would the magnitude of an earthquake be if the height of its seismogram readings were 10 mm?

21. Look at the shape of the curve on the graph. What does this tell you about the relationship between seismogram heights and earthquake magnitudes? Explain.

NOW What Do You Think?

Take a minute to review your answers to the ScienceLog questions on page 165. Have your answers changed? If necessary, revise your answers based on what you have learned since you began this chapter.

WEIRD SCIENCE

CAN ANIMALS PREDICT EARTHQUAKES?

It Could Happen to You!

One day you come home from visiting a friend for the weekend and learn that your dog Pepper is hiding under your bed. Your father explains that he has been trying to get Pepper out from under the bed for the last 6 hours. Just then your mother enters the room and says that she has found two snakes in the backyard—and that makes a total of five in 2 days! This is very odd because you usually don't find more than one each year.

All the animals seem to be acting very strange. Your goldfish is even hiding behind a rock. You wonder if there is some explanation.

What's Going On?

So what's your guess? What do you think is happening? Did you guess that an earthquake is about to occur?

Publications from as far back as 1784 record unusual animal behavior prior to earthquakes. Some examples included zoo animals refusing to go into their shelters at night and domestic cattle seeking high ground. Other animals, like lizards, snakes, and small mammals, evacuate their underground burrows, and wild birds leave their usual habitats. All of these events occurred a few days, several hours, or a few minutes before the earthquakes happened.

Animals on Call?

Today the majority of scientists look to physical instruments in order to help them predict earthquakes. Yet the fact remains that none of the geophysical instruments we have allow scientists to predict exactly when an earthquake will occur. Could animals know the answer?

◄ *Goldfish or earthquake sensor?*

There are changes in the Earth's crust that occur prior to an earthquake, such as magnetic field changes, subsidence (sinking), tilting, and bulging of the surface. These things can be monitored by modern instruments. Many studies have shown that electromagnetic fields affect the behavior of living organisms. Is it possible that animals close to the epicenter of an earthquake are able to sense changes in their environment? Should we pay attention?

You Decide

► Currently, the United States government does not fund research that investigates whether animals can predict earthquakes. Have a debate with your classmates about whether the government should fund such research.

EYE ON THE ENVIRONMENT

What Causes Such Destruction?

At 5:04 P.M. on October 14, 1989, life in California's San Francisco Bay Area seemed as normal as ever. The third game of the World Series was underway in Candlestick Park, now called 3Com Park. While 62,000 fans filled the park, other people were rushing home from a day's work. By 5:05 P.M., however, things had changed drastically. The fact sheet of destruction looks like this:

Injuries:	3,757
Deaths:	68
Damaged homes:	23,408
Destroyed homes:	1,018
Damaged businesses:	3,530
Destroyed businesses:	366
Financial loss:	over $6 billion

The Culprit

The cause of such destruction was a 7.1 magnitude earthquake that lasted for 20 seconds. Its epicenter was 97 km south of San Francisco in an area called Loma Prieta. The earthquake was so strong that people in San Diego and western Nevada (740 km away) felt it too. Considering the earthquake's high magnitude and the fact that it occurred during rush hour, it is amazing that more people did not die. However, the damage to buildings was widespread—it covered an area of 7,770 km². And by October 1, 1990, there had been more than 7,000 aftershocks of this quake.

Take Heed

Engineers and seismologists had expected a major earthquake, so the amount of damage they saw from this earthquake was no surprise. But experts agree that if the earthquake were of a higher magnitude or centered closer to Oakland, San Jose, or San Francisco, the damage would have been much worse. They are concerned that people who live in these areas aren't paying attention to the warning this earthquake represents.

Many people have a false sense of security because their buildings withstood the quake with little or no damage. But engineers and seismologists agree that the only reason the buildings survived was because the ground motion in those areas was fairly low.

Tomorrow May Be Too Late

Many buildings that withstood this earthquake were poorly constructed and would not withstand another earthquake. Experts say there is a 50 percent chance that one or more 7.0 magnitude earthquakes will occur in the San Francisco Bay Area in the next 30 years. And the results of the next quake could be much more devastating if people don't reinforce their buildings before it's too late.

▲ *Notice the different levels of destruction for various buildings on the same street.*

On Your Own

▶ Research the engineering innovations for constructing bridges and buildings in areas with seismic activity. Share your information with the class.

8 Volcanoes

"All of a sudden there was a terrible noise. Everybody was screaming 'Help! Help! I'm burning! I'm dying!!' Five minutes later, nobody was crying out anymore—except me."

Auguste Ciparis   May 11, 1902

This Really Happened!

Auguste Ciparis was a condemned man. He was sentenced to be executed for murder in the town of St. Pierre, on Martinique, a small volcanic island in the Caribbean Sea. On the morning of May 8, 1902, Ciparis sat in jail waiting for his breakfast. As he waited, disaster struck the town—a disaster that killed thousands of people.

That morning, one of the island's volcanoes, Mount Pelée, erupted in a series of explosions. The eruption sent a fiery cloud of volcanic debris, superheated steam, and toxic gases through the town. Everyone in St. Pierre, nearly 30,000 people, died. Everyone, that is, except Auguste.

Auguste had survived the deadliest volcanic eruption of the century. Underground in his dungeon, Auguste had been sheltered from the worst of the fiery fallout. Auguste cried out for help for four days before rescuers found him. He was exhausted and badly burned, but alive.

Spared from execution, Auguste joined the Barnum & Bailey circus as a sideshow attraction. Known as the Prisoner of St. Pierre, Auguste was hired to tell his tale and show off his burns in a replica of the dungeon that had saved his life.

Anticipation

Imagine the thousands of lives that might have been saved if the people of St. Pierre could have predicted the eruption of Mount Pelée in 1902. Unfortunately, because volcanic eruptions are caused by processes deep within the Earth, they are very difficult to predict. See for yourself by creating your own volcano and then predicting its eruption.

Procedure

1. Tear off a sheet of **bathroom tissue,** and place 10 mL (2 tsp) of **baking soda** in the center of the tissue. Fold the corners of the tissue over the baking soda, and press the edges until the ends stay in place. Place the tissue packet in the middle of a large **plate** or **pan.**

2. Put some **modeling clay** around the top edge of a **funnel.** Turn the funnel upside down over the tissue packet in the bottom of the pan. The clay should form a watertight seal between the base of the funnel and the plate or pan. Press down to make a tight seal.

3. Add 50 mL ($1/4$ cup) of **vinegar,** two drops of **red food coloring**, and several drops of **liquid dish soap** to a 200 mL **beaker** or **measuring cup,** and stir.

4. Carefully pour the liquid into the spout of the upturned funnel. In your ScienceLog, record the time you began to pour.

5. Now predict how much time will elapse before your volcano erupts. Write your prediction in your ScienceLog.

6. When the volcano finally erupts, record the time again. How long did it take for your volcano to erupt? How close was your prediction?

Analysis

7. In what ways is your model volcano similar to a real one? In what ways is it different?

8. Based on the predictions of the entire class, what can you conclude about the accuracy of predicting volcanic eruptions?

Volcanic Eruptions

OBJECTIVES

- Distinguish between nonexplosive and explosive volcanic eruptions.
- Explain how the composition of magma determines the type of volcanic eruption that will occur.
- Classify the main types of lava and volcanic debris.

Think about the force of the explosion produced by the first atomic bomb used in World War II. Now imagine an explosion 10,000 times stronger, and you get an idea of how powerful a volcanic eruption can be. This was the size of the explosion that occurred in Indonesia when the Krakatau volcano erupted in 1883. The eruption of Krakatau was so powerful that it was heard 4,000 km away.

Fortunately, few volcanoes give rise to explosive eruptions like that of Krakatau, which killed 36,000 people. Most eruptions are of a nonexplosive variety. You can compare these two types of eruptions for yourself by looking at the photographs on this and the next page.

Nonexplosive Eruptions

When people think of volcanic eruptions, they often imagine rivers of red-hot lava, called *lava flows*. Lava flows come from nonexplosive eruptions. Relatively calm outpourings of lava, like the ones shown below, can release a huge amount of molten rock. Some of the largest mountains on Earth grew from repeated lava flows over hundreds of thousands of years.

In this nonexplosive eruption, a continuous stream of lava pours quietly from the crater of Kilauea, in Hawaii.

Sometimes nonexplosive eruptions can spray lava into the air. Lava fountains, such as this one, rarely exceed a few hundred meters in height. Most of the lava falls back to the ground while still molten.

Lava can flow many kilometers before it finally cools and hardens. As you can see in this photograph, lava flows often pose a greater threat to property than to human life.

Explosive Eruptions

In an explosive volcanic eruption, clouds of hot debris and gases shoot out from the volcano, often at supersonic speeds. Instead of producing lava flows, molten rock is blown into millions of pieces that harden in the air, as shown in **Figure 1**. The dust-sized particles can circle the globe for years in the upper atmosphere, while larger pieces of debris fall closer to the volcano.

In addition to shooting molten rock into the air, an explosive eruption can blast millions of tons of solid rock from a volcano. In a matter of minutes, an explosive eruption can demolish rock formations that took thousands of years to accumulate. Thus, a volcano may actually shrink in size rather than grow from repeated eruptions.

Figure 1 *In what resembles a nuclear explosion, volcanic debris rockets skyward during an eruption of Mount Redoubt, in Alaska.*

After an explosive eruption, thick, gooey lava slowly oozes from the Soufriere Hills volcano, in Montserrat, hardening to form a dome-shaped mass. Molten rock rising up from below causes the dome to expand. If enough lava hardens to plug the volcano, the molten rock below has nowhere to go. Pressure then mounts until it is great enough to cause another explosive eruption.

This photograph shows part of the blast area from the 1980 eruption of Mount St. Helens, in Washington. In minutes, the explosive eruption flattened and scorched 600 km² of forest. Notice how the downed trees clearly show the direction of the blast (from left to right).

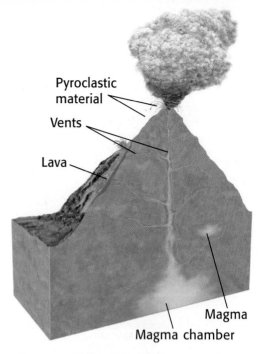

Pyroclastic material

Vents

Lava

Magma

Magma chamber

Figure 2 *Volcanoes form around vents that release magma onto the Earth's surface.*

Cross Section of a Volcano

Whether they produce explosive or nonexplosive eruptions, all volcanoes share the same basic features. **Figure 2** shows some of the features that you might see if you could look inside an erupting volcano. Deep underground, the driving force that creates volcanoes is hot, liquid material known as **magma.** Magma collects in *magma chambers* as deep as 160 km below the surface. From there, the magma rises through holes in the Earth's crust called **vents.** Magma that erupts and flows onto the Earth's surface is called **lava.** Magma that erupts as fragments of molten material that solidify in the air is called *pyroclastic material.* **Pyroclastic material** includes magma and fragments of rock that are blasted into the air during violent volcanic eruptions. A vent or a group of vents combined with the buildup of lava or pyroclastic material on the Earth's surface is a **volcano.**

Magma

By comparing the composition of magma from different types of eruptions, scientists have made an important discovery—the composition of the magma determines whether a volcanic eruption is nonexplosive, explosive, or somewhere in between.

Water A volcano is more likely to erupt explosively if its magma has a high water content. The effect water has on magma is similar to the effect carbon dioxide gas has in a can of soda. When you shake the can up, the carbon dioxide that was dissolved in the soda is released, and because gases need much more room than liquids, a great amount of pressure builds up. When you open the can, soda comes shooting out. The same phenomenon occurs with explosive volcanic eruptions. The more water magma contains, the greater the pressure is and the greater the chances are that a violent explosion will occur.

Silica Explosive eruptions are also caused by magma that contains a large percentage of silica (a basic building block of most minerals). Silica-rich magma has a thick, stiff consistency. It flows slowly and tends to harden in the volcano's vent. This plugs the vent, resulting in a buildup of pressure as magma pushes up from below. If enough pressure builds up, an explosive eruption results. Thick magma also prevents water vapor and other gases from easily escaping. Magma that contains a smaller percentage of silica has a thinner, runnier consistency. Gases escape this type of magma more easily, making it less likely that explosive pressure will build up.

Quick Lab

Bubble, Bubble, Toil and Trouble

With a few simple items, you can easily discover how the consistency of a liquid affects the flow of gases. You will need **water, honey,** two small **drinking cups,** and two **straws.**

1. Fill one cup halfway with water and the other cup halfway with honey.
2. Using one of the straws, blow into the water and observe the bubbles.
3. Take the other straw and blow into the honey. What happens?
4. How does the honey behave differently from the water?
5. How do you think this difference relates to volcanic eruptions?

What Erupts from a Volcano?

Depending on how explosive a volcanic eruption is, magma erupts as either lava or pyroclastic material. The composition of both lava and pyroclastic material differs from that of magma because much of the magma's gases is released in an eruption. Nonexplosive eruptions produce mostly lava. Explosive eruptions produce mostly pyroclastic material. Over many years, a volcano may alternate between eruptions of lava and eruptions of pyroclastic material. Eruptions of lava and pyroclastic material may also occur as separate stages of a single eruption event.

across the sciences
CONNECTION

Fire and ice! A phrase to describe volcanoes? That depends on where they are. Turn to page 211 to find out more.

Lava Lava is magma that flows onto the Earth's surface. Like magma, lava ranges in consistency from thick to thin. Blocky lava is so thick in consistency that it barely creeps along the ground. Other types of lava, such as *pahoehoe* (pah HOY HOY), *aa* (AH ah), and *pillow lava,* are thinner in consistency and produce faster lava flows. These types of lava are shown in the photographs below.

Blocky lava *is cool, stiff lava that cannot travel far from the erupting vent. Blocky lava usually oozes from a volcano only after an explosive eruption has released much of the gas pressure from the magma chamber. As shown here, blocky lava forms jumbled heaps of sharp-edged chunks.*

Pahoehoe *lava flows slowly, like wax dripping from a candle, forming a glassy surface with rounded wrinkles. This lava gets its name from the Hawaiian word for "ropy" because its surface resembles coils of rope.*

Aa *is a Hawaiian word that refers to a type of lava that has a jagged surface. This slightly stiffer lava pours out quickly and forms a brittle crust. The crust is torn into jagged pieces as the molten lava underneath continues to move. Aa is named after the sound you would make if you were to walk across this type of lava barefoot.*

Pillow lava *forms when lava erupts underwater. As you can see here, it forms rounded lumps that are the size and shape of pillows. Pillow lava has a rounded shape because contact with water causes rapid cooling of the lava's surface.*

Pyroclastic material Pyroclastic material refers to the rock fragments created by explosive volcanic eruptions. Pyroclastic material is produced when magma explodes from a volcano and solidifies in the air. It is also produced when existing rock is shattered by powerful eruptions. It comes in a variety of sizes, from boulders the size of houses to particles so small they can remain suspended in the atmosphere for years. The photographs on this page show four major kinds of pyroclastic material: volcanic bombs, volcanic blocks, lapilli (luh PILL ee), and volcanic ash.

Volcanic blocks are the largest pieces of pyroclastic material. They consist of solid rock blasted out of the volcano.

Volcanic bombs are large blobs of magma that harden in the air. The flattened, elongated shape of the bomb shown here resulted from the magma's spinning through the air as it cooled. Volcanic bombs are more than 64 mm in diameter.

Lapilli, which means "little stones" in Italian, are pebble-like bits of pyroclastic material between 2 and 64 mm in diameter. Both lapilli and volcanic bombs are solid when they hit the ground, although they may still be red hot.

Volcanic ash consists of particles that are less than 2 mm in diameter. Volcanic ash forms when the gases in stiff magma expand rapidly and the walls of the gas bubbles explode into tiny glasslike slivers.

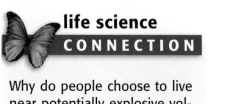

life science
CONNECTION

Why do people choose to live near potentially explosive volcanoes? One reason is that these volcanoes provide some of the most productive farmland in the world. Volcanic rocks contain almost all of the elements plants need to grow, though it may take hundreds or even thousands of years for volcanic rock to break down into usable soil nutrients. On the other hand, the ash from a single explosive eruption can greatly increase the fertility of soil in only a few years and can keep the soil fertile for centuries.

REVIEW

1. Is a nonexplosive volcanic eruption more likely to produce lava or pyroclastic material? Explain.

2. If a volcano contained magma with small proportions of water and silica, would you predict a nonexplosive eruption or an explosive one? Why?

3. **Making Inferences** Pyroclastic material is classified primarily by the size of the particles. What is the basis for classifying lava?

Volcanoes' Effects on Earth

NEW TERMS

shield volcano

cinder cone volcano

composite volcano

crater

caldera

OBJECTIVES

- Describe the effects that volcanoes have on Earth.
- Compare the different types of volcanoes.

The effects of volcanic eruptions can be seen both on land and in the air. Heavier pyroclastic materials fall to the ground, causing great destruction, while ash and escaping gases affect global climatic patterns. Volcanoes also build mountains and plateaus that become lasting additions to the landscape.

An Explosive Impact

Because it is thrown high into the air, ash ejected during explosive volcanic eruptions can have widespread effects. The ash can block out the sun for days over thousands of square kilometers. Volcanic ash can blow down trees and buildings and can blanket nearby towns with a fine powder.

Figure 3 *During the 1991 eruption of Mount Pinatubo, in the Philippines, clouds of volcanic gases and ash sped downhill at up to 250 km/h.*

Flows As shown in **Figure 3,** clouds of hot ash can flow rapidly downhill like an avalanche, choking and searing every living thing in their path, as happened at Mount Pelée in 1902. Sometimes large deposits of ash mix with rainwater or the water from melted glaciers during an eruption. With the consistency of wet cement, the mixture flows downhill, picking up boulders, trees, and buildings along the way. More powerful than ordinary rivers, these mudflows move swiftly and cause immense damage.

Fallout As volcanic ash falls to the ground, the effects can be devastating. Buildings may collapse under the weight of so much ash. Ash can also dam up river valleys, resulting in massive floods. And although ash is an effective plant fertilizer, too much ash can smother crops, causing food shortages and loss of livestock.

Climatic Fluctuation In large-scale eruptions, volcanic ash, along with sulfur-rich gases, can reach the upper atmosphere. As the ash and gases spread around the globe, they can block out enough sunlight to cause the average global surface temperature to drop noticeably. The eruption of Mount Pinatubo in 1991 caused average global temperatures to drop by as much as 0.5°C. Although this may not seem like a large change in temperature, such a shift can disrupt climates all over the world. The lower average temperatures may last for several years, bringing wetter, milder summers and longer, harsher winters. Such changes in climate can cause worldwide food shortages that result in starvation and disease.

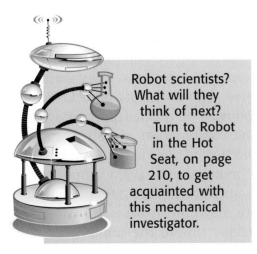

Robot scientists? What will they think of next? Turn to Robot in the Hot Seat, on page 210, to get acquainted with this mechanical investigator.

Different Types of Volcanoes

The lava and pyroclastic material that erupt from volcanoes create a variety of landforms. Perhaps the best known of all volcanic landforms are the volcanoes themselves. Volcanoes result from the buildup of rock around a vent. Three basic types of volcanoes are illustrated in **Figure 4.**

To find out more about the types of volcanoes, turn to page 516 in the LabBook.

Shield volcanoes are built out of layers of lava from repeated nonexplosive eruptions. Because the lava is very runny, it spreads out over a wide area. Over time, the layers of lava create a volcano with gently sloping sides. Although their sides are not very steep, shield volcanoes can be enormous. Hawaii's Mauna Kea, the shield volcano shown here, is the largest mountain on Earth. Measured from its base on the sea floor, Mauna Kea is taller than Mount Everest, the tallest mountain on land.

Cinder cone volcanoes are small volcanic cones made entirely of pyroclastic material from moderately explosive eruptions. The pyroclastic material forms steeper slopes with a narrower base than the lava flows of shield volcanoes, as you can see in this photo of the volcano Paricutín, in Mexico. Cinder cone volcanoes usually erupt for only a short time and often occur in clusters, commonly on the sides of shield and composite volcanoes. They erode quickly because the pyroclastic particles are not cemented together by lava.

Composite volcanoes, sometimes referred to as *stratovolcanoes,* are one of the most common types of volcanoes. They form by explosive eruptions of pyroclastic material followed by quieter outpourings of lava. The combination of both types of eruptions forms alternating layers of pyroclastic material and lava. Composite volcanoes, such as Japan's Mount Fuji, shown here, have broad bases and sides that get steeper toward the summit.

Figure 4 Three Types of Volcanoes

Shield volcano

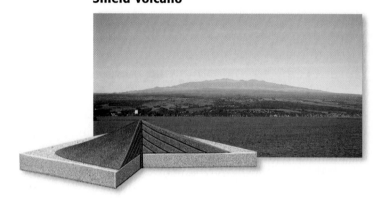

Cinder cone volcano

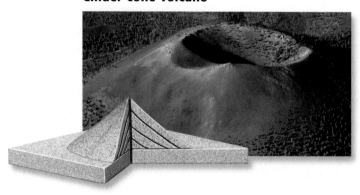

Composite volcano

Craters and Calderas

At the top of the central vent in most volcanoes is a funnel-shaped pit called a **crater.** (Craters are also the circular pits made by meteorite impacts.) The photograph of the cinder cone on the previous page shows a well-defined crater. A crater's funnel shape results from explosions of material out of the vent as well as the collapse of material from the crater's rim back into the vent. A **caldera** forms when a magma chamber that supplies material to a volcano empties and its roof collapses. This causes the ground to sink, leaving a large, circular depression.

Volcano

Caldera

Vent

Magma chamber

Figure 5 *A caldera forms when enough magma is ejected from a magma chamber that the ground above collapses to fill the empty space. Calderas are generally much larger than volcanic craters.*

Lava Plateaus

The most massive outpourings of lava do not come from individual volcanoes. Most of the lava on Earth's continents erupts from long cracks, or *fissures,* in the crust. In this nonexplosive type of eruption, runny lava pours from a series of fissures and may spread evenly over thousands of square kilometers. The resulting landform is known as a *lava plateau.* **Figure 6** shows a portion of the Columbia River Plateau, a lava plateau that formed about 15 million years ago in what is now the northwestern United States.

Figure 6 *This formation in the Columbia River Plateau reveals rock layers that were created by a series of large lava flows.*

REVIEW

1. Briefly explain why the ash from a volcanic eruption can be hazardous.

2. Why do cinder cone volcanoes have narrower bases and steeper sides than shield volcanoes?

3. **Comparing Concepts** Briefly describe the difference between a crater and a caldera.

astronomy CONNECTION

Have you ever noticed the dark patches on the moon? Early astronomers thought these areas were bodies of water. Astronomers now know that these areas are basins filled with dark solidified lava. They formed in much the same way as Earth's lava plateaus.

What Causes Volcanoes?

NEW TERMS

rift   hot spot

OBJECTIVES

■ Describe the formation and movement of magma.

■ Identify the places where magma forms.

■ Explain the relationship between volcanoes and plate tectonics.

■ Summarize the methods scientists use to predict volcanic eruptions.

Scientists have learned a great deal over the years about what happens when a volcano erupts. Many of the results are dramatic and immediately visible. Unfortunately, understanding what causes a volcano to erupt in the first place is much more difficult. Scientists have no way of seeing firsthand what is going on deep within the Earth. They must rely on models based on rock samples and other data that provide insight into volcanic processes. Because it is so difficult to "see" what is going on deep inside the Earth, there are many uncertainties about why volcanoes form.

The Formation of Magma

You learned in the previous section that volcanoes form by the eruption of lava and pyroclastic material onto the Earth's surface. But the key to understanding why volcanoes erupt is understanding how magma forms. As you can see in **Figure 7,** all volcanoes begin when magma collects in pockets in the deeper regions of the Earth's crust and in the uppermost layers of the mantle, the zone of intensely hot and pliable rock between the Earth's crust and the core. This zone of magma formation is between 25 and 160 km below the surface.

Although hot and pliable, the rock of the mantle is considered a solid. But the temperature of the mantle is high enough to melt almost any rock, so why doesn't it melt? The answer has to do with pressure. The weight of the rock above the mantle exerts a tremendous amount of pressure. This pressure keeps the atoms of mantle rock tightly packed, preventing the rock from changing into a liquid state. An increase in pressure raises the melting point of most materials.

Quick **Lab**

Reaction to Stress

1. Make a pliable "rock" by pouring 60 mL (¹/4 cup) of **water** into a **plastic cup** and adding 150 mL of **cornstarch,** 15 mL (1 tbsp) at a time. Stir well after each addition. (The mixture should be hard to stir, but not powdery.)

2. Pour half of the cornstarch mixture into a **clear bowl.** Carefully observe how the "rock" flows. Be patient—this is a slow process!

3. Scrape the rest of the "rock" out of the cup with a **spoon.** Observe the behavior of the "rock" as you scrape.

4. What happened to the "rock" when you let it flow by itself? What happened when you put stress on the "rock"?

5. How is this pliable "rock" similar to the rock of the upper part of the mantle?

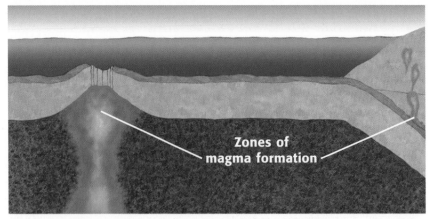

Zones of magma formation

Figure 7 *Magma forms below the Earth's surface in a region that includes the lower crust and part of the upper mantle.*

As you can see in **Figure 8,** rock melts and forms magma when the temperature of the rock increases or when the pressure on the rock decreases. Because the temperature of the mantle is relatively constant, a decrease in pressure is usually what causes magma to form. In some cases, the magma melts the solid rock above it to make its way upward. In other cases, the magma rises through existing cracks and fissures in the overlying rock.

Once formed, the magma rises toward the surface of the Earth because it is less dense than the surrounding rock. Magma is commonly a mixture of liquid and solid mineral crystals and is therefore normally less dense than the completely solid rock that surrounds it. Like air bubbles that form on the bottom of a pan of boiling water, magma will rise toward the surface.

Not all magma makes it all the way to the Earth's surface to form a volcano. Stiff magma often cools and solidifies while still in the Earth's crust.

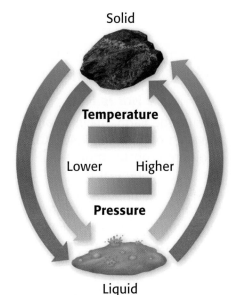

Figure 8 *This diagram shows how both pressure and temperature affect the formation of magma within the mantle.*

✔ Self-Check

1. What two factors may cause solid rock to become magma?

2. Where does magma form?

(See page 564 to check your answers.)

Where Volcanoes Form

The locations of volcanoes around the globe provide clues to how volcanoes form. The world map in **Figure 9** shows the location of the world's active volcanoes on land. It also shows tectonic plate boundaries. As you can see, a large number of the volcanoes lie directly on tectonic plate boundaries. In fact, the plate boundaries surrounding the Pacific Ocean have so many volcanoes that these boundaries together are called the *Ring of Fire.*

Why are most volcanoes on tectonic plate boundaries? These boundaries are where the plates either collide with one another or separate from one another. At these boundaries, it is easier for magma to travel upward through the crust. In other words, the boundaries are where the action is!

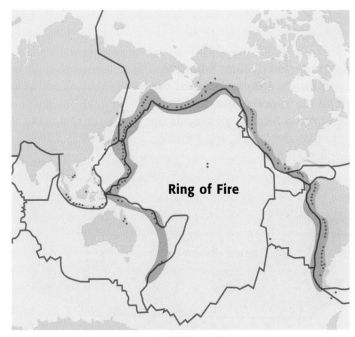

Figure 9 *Tectonic plate boundaries are likely places for volcanoes to form. The Ring of Fire contains nearly 75 percent of the world's active volcanoes on land.*

MATH**BREAK**

How Hot Is Hot?

Inside the Earth, magma can reach a burning-hot 1,400°C! You are probably more familiar with Fahrenheit temperatures, so convert 1,400° Celsius to degrees Fahrenheit by using the formula below.

$$°F = \frac{9}{5}°C + 32$$

What is the magma's temperature in degrees Fahrenheit?

When Tectonic Plates Separate When two tectonic plates separate and move away from each other, a *divergent boundary* forms. As the tectonic plates separate, a deep crack, or **rift,** forms between the plates. Mantle material then rises to fill in the gap. Because the mantle material is closer to the surface, the pressure on it becomes less. This decrease in pressure causes the mantle rock below the rift to partially melt and become magma.

Because magma is less dense than the surrounding rock, it rises up through the rift. As the magma rises, it cools down, and the pressure on it decreases. So even though it becomes cooler as it rises, it remains molten because of the reduced pressure. By the time the magma spills out onto the Earth's surface as lava, it may have decreased in temperature by as much as 800°C.

Magma continuously rises up through the rift between the separating plates and creates new crust. Although a few divergent boundaries exist on land, most are located on the ocean floor, where they produce long mountain chains called mid-ocean spreading centers, or mid-ocean ridges. **Figure 10** shows the process of forming such an underwater mountain range at a divergent boundary.

Figure 10 How Magma Forms at a Divergent Boundary

As the tectonic plates separate, a rift forms. Mantle material rises to fill the space opened by the separating tectonic plates. As the pressure decreases, the mantle begins to melt.

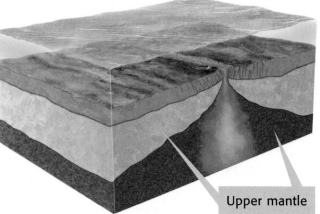

Upper mantle

Because magma is less dense than the surrounding rock, it rises toward the surface, where it forms new crust on the ocean floor.

Oceanic crust

Formation of magma

When Tectonic Plates Collide If you slide two pieces of notebook paper into one another on a flat desktop, the papers will either buckle upward or one piece of paper will move under the other. This gives you an idea of what happens when tectonic plates collide. The place where two tectonic plates collide is called a *convergent boundary.* The movement of one tectonic plate under another is called *subduction,* shown in **Figure 11.** Convergent boundaries are commonly located where oceanic plates collide with continental plates. The oceanic crust is denser and thinner and therefore is subducted underneath the continental crust.

Oceanic crust contains water, which lowers the melting point of rocks it comes in contact with. As the descending oceanic crust scrapes past the continental crust, it sinks deeper and deeper into the mantle, getting hotter and hotter. As it does so, the pressure on the oceanic crust increases as well. The combination of increased heat and pressure causes the water contained in the oceanic crust to be released. The water then mixes with the mantle rock, causing it to melt.

On its way to the surface, heat from rising magma may cause some of the overlying continental crust (rich in silica) to melt and become part of the magma. The silica from the continental crust then becomes part of a gooey, silica-rich lava that is likely to cause an explosive eruption when it finally reaches the surface.

Figure 11 How Magma Forms at a Convergent Boundary

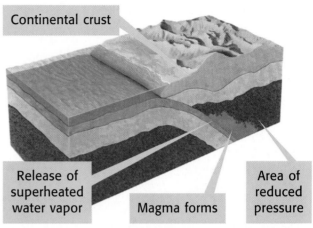

Continental crust

Release of superheated water vapor

Magma forms

Area of reduced pressure

When an oceanic plate and a continental plate converge, the denser oceanic plate is subducted. As the subducted plate moves downward, the rock melts and forms magma.

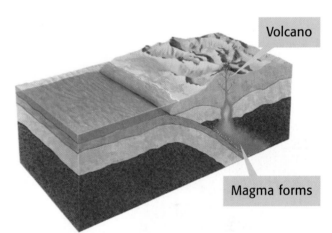

Volcano

Magma forms

When magma is less dense than the surrounding rock, it rises toward the surface.

Hot Spots

Not all magma develops along tectonic plate boundaries. For example, the Hawaiian Islands, some of the most well-known volcanoes on Earth, are nowhere near a plate boundary. The volcanoes of Hawaii and several other places on Earth are caused by **hot spots.** Hot spots are places within tectonic plates that are directly above columns of rising magma, called *mantle plumes,* that begin deep in the Earth, possibly at the boundary between the mantle and the core. Scientists are not sure what causes these plumes, but some think that a combination of heat conducted upward from the core and heat from radioactive elements keeps the plumes rising.

BRAIN FOOD

There are 10 times as many active volcanoes at the bottom of the ocean as there are on land. The ocean floor, roughly three-fourths of the Earth's surface, was produced primarily by volcanic activity.

Figure 12 *A plume of hot mantle rock flows slowly upward through the mantle. As the tectonic plate moves slowly over the hot spot, a chain of volcanic islands forms.*

A hot spot often produces a long chain of volcanoes. This is because the mantle plume stays in the same spot, while the tectonic plate above moves over it. The Hawaiian Islands, for example, are riding on the Pacific plate, which is moving slowly to the northwest. **Figure 12** shows how a hot spot creates a volcano in an island chain. Each of the islands was once an erupting volcano situated directly over the hot spot.

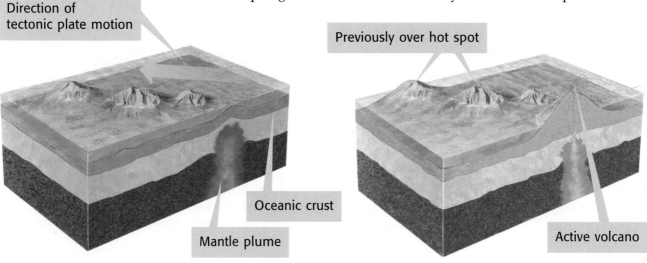

Direction of tectonic plate motion

Previously over hot spot

Oceanic crust

Mantle plume

Active volcano

Figure 13 *Seismographs help scientists determine when magma is moving beneath a volcano.*

How do poisonous gases help scientists predict eruptions? Turn to page 518 in the LabBook to find out.

Predicting Volcanic Eruptions

It is one thing to know where volcanoes occur, but it is quite another thing to predict when they might erupt. To help predict volcanic eruptions, scientists classify volcanoes based on their eruption histories and on how likely it is that they will erupt again. *Extinct* volcanoes are those that have not erupted in recorded history and probably never will again. *Dormant* volcanoes are those that are not currently erupting but have erupted at some time in recorded history. *Active* volcanoes are those that are in the process of erupting or that show signs of erupting in the very near future.

When it comes to predicting eruptions, the dormant and active volcanoes keep scientists guessing. However, scientists have found certain clues that reveal when a volcano is likely to erupt. For example, most active volcanoes produce small earthquakes as the magma within them moves upward and causes the surrounding rock to shift. Just before an eruption, the number and intensity of the small earthquakes increase, and the occurrence of quakes may be continuous. These earthquakes are measured with a *seismograph,* as shown in **Figure 13.**

Measurements of a volcano's slope also give scientists clues with which to predict eruptions. For example, bulges in the volcano's slope may form as magma pushes against the inside of the volcano. By attaching an instrument called a *tiltmeter* to the surface of the volcano, scientists can detect small changes in the angle of the slope.

The outflow of volcanic gases from a volcano can also help scientists predict eruptions. As magma rises, the pressure from trapped volcanic gases builds. The pressure may reach a point where it breaks small holes in the rock, allowing the gases to escape through the sides of the volcano. Some scientists think that the ratio of certain gases, especially that of sulfur dioxide (SO_2) to carbon dioxide (CO_2), is important in predicting eruptions. They know that when this ratio changes, it is an indication that things are changing in the magma chamber down below, which means an eruption may not be far away! As you can see in **Figure 14,** collecting this type of data is often dangerous.

Figure 14 *As if getting this close to an active volcano is not dangerous enough, the gases that are being collected here are extremely poisonous.*

Some of the newest methods scientists are using to predict volcanic eruptions rely on satellite images. Many of these images record infrared radiation, which allows scientists to measure changes in temperature over time. They are taken from satellites orbiting more than 700 km above the Earth. By analyzing images taken at different times, scientists can determine if the site is getting hotter as magma pushes closer to the surface.

chemistry
CONNECTION

Ground water can seep through cracks and pores in the rocks of an active volcano, where it is heated by the underlying magma and reacts with volcanic gases to form sulfuric acid. The acid turns solid rock into soft clay and weakens the sides of a volcano. This can cause parts of the volcano to collapse, producing avalanches, mudflows, or even eruptions.

REVIEW

1. How does pressure determine whether the mantle is solid or liquid?

2. Describe a technology scientists use to predict volcanic eruptions.

3. **Interpreting Illustrations** Figure 9, shown earlier in this chapter, shows the locations of active volcanoes on land. Describe where on the map you would plot the location of underwater volcanoes and why. (Do not write in this book.)

Although scientists have learned a lot about volcanoes, they cannot predict eruptions with total accuracy. Sometimes there are warning signs before an eruption, but often there are none. Imagine that you are the mayor of a town near a large volcano, and a geologist warns you that an eruption is probable. You realize that ordering an evacuation of your town could be an expensive embarrassment if the volcano doesn't erupt. But if you decide to keep quiet, people could be in serious danger if the volcano does erupt. Considering the social and economic consequences of your decision, your job is perhaps even more difficult. What would you do?

Chapter Highlights

Vocabulary

magma *(p. 194)*

vent *(p. 194)*

lava *(p. 194)*

pyroclastic material *(p. 194)*

volcano *(p. 194)*

Section Notes

- Volcanoes erupt both explosively and nonexplosively.

- The characteristics of a volcanic eruption are largely determined by the type of magma within the volcano.

- The amount of silica in magma determines whether it is thin and fluid or thick and stiff.

- Lava hardens into characteristic features that range from smooth to jagged, depending on how thick the lava is and how quickly it flows.

- Pyroclastic material, or volcanic debris, consists of solid pieces of the volcano as well as magma that solidifies as it travels through the air.

Vocabulary

shield volcano *(p. 198)*

cinder cone volcano *(p. 198)*

composite volcano *(p. 198)*

crater *(p. 199)*

caldera *(p. 199)*

Section Notes

- The effects of volcanic eruptions are felt both locally and around the world.

- Volcanic mountains can be classified according to their composition and overall shape.

- Craters are funnel-shaped pits that form around the central vent of a volcano. Calderas are large bowl-shaped depressions formed by a collapsed magma chamber.

☑ Skills Check

Math Concepts

CONVERTING TEMPERATURE SCALES So-called low-temperature magmas can be 1,100°C. Just how hot is such a magma? If you are used to measuring temperature in degrees Fahrenheit, you can use a simple formula to find out.

$$°F = \frac{9}{5}°C + 32$$

$$°F = \frac{9}{5}(1,100) + 32$$

$$°F = 1,980 + 32 = 2,012$$

$$2,012°F = 1,100°C$$

Visual Understanding

CALDERAS Calderas are caused by the release of massive amounts of magma from beneath the Earth's surface. When the volume of magma decreases, it no longer exerts pressure to hold the ground up. As a result, the ground sinks, forming a caldera.

SECTION 2

- In the largest type of volcanic eruption, lava simply pours from long fissures in the Earth's crust to form lava plateaus.

Labs

Some Go "Pop," Some Do Not *(p. 516)*

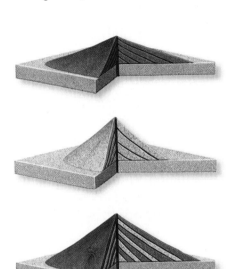

SECTION 3

Vocabulary

rift *(p. 202)*

hot spot *(p. 203)*

Section Notes

- Volcanoes result from magma formed in the mantle.

- When pressure is reduced, some of the solid rock of the already hot mantle melts to form magma.

- Because it is less dense than the surrounding rock, magma rises to the Earth's surface. It either erupts as lava or solidifies in the crust.

- Most volcanic activity takes place along tectonic plate boundaries, where plates either separate or collide.

- Volcanoes also occur above hot spots in the mantle. As a tectonic plate moves over the hot spot, a chain of volcanic islands forms.

- Volcanic eruptions cannot be predicted with complete accuracy. But scientists now have several methods of forecasting future eruptions.

Labs

Volcano Verdict *(p. 518)*

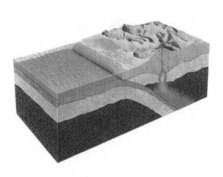

Chapter Review

For each pair of terms listed below, explain the difference in their meanings.

1. caldera/crater

2. lava/magma

3. lava/pyroclastic material

4. vent/rift

5. cinder cone volcano/shield volcano

UNDERSTANDING CONCEPTS

Multiple Choice

6. The type of magma that often produces a violent eruption can be described as
   a. thin due to high silica content.
   b. thick due to high silica content.
   c. thin due to low silica content.
   d. thick due to low silica content.

7. When lava hardens quickly to form ropy formations, it is called

   a. aa lava.
   b. pahoehoe lava.
   c. pillow lava.
   d. blocky lava.

8. Volcanic dust and ash can remain in the atmosphere for months or years, causing
   a. decreased solar reflection and higher temperatures.
   b. increased solar reflection and lower temperatures.
   c. decreased solar reflection and lower temperatures.
   d. increased solar reflection and higher temperatures.

9. Mount St. Helens, in Washington, covered the city of Spokane with tons of ash. Its eruption would most likely be described as
   a. nonexplosive, producing lava.
   b. explosive, producing lava.
   c. nonexplosive, producing pyroclastic material.
   d. explosive, producing pyroclastic material.

10. Magma forms within the mantle most often as a result of
    a. high temperature and high pressure.
    b. high temperature and low pressure.
    c. low temperature and high pressure.
    d. low temperature and low pressure.

11. At divergent plate boundaries,
    a. heat from the Earth's core produces mantle plumes.
    b. plates are subducted, causing magma to form.
    c. tectonic plates move apart.
    d. hot spots produce volcanoes.

12. A theory that helps to explain the causes of both earthquakes and volcanoes is the theory of
    a. subduction.
    b. plate tectonics.
    c. climatic fluctuation.
    d. mantle plumes.

Short Answer

13. Briefly describe two methods that scientists use to predict volcanic eruptions.

14. Describe how differences in magma affect volcanic eruptions.

15. Along what types of tectonic plate boundaries are volcanoes generally found? Why?

16. Describe the characteristics of the three types of volcanic mountains.

Concept Mapping

17. Use any of the terms from the vocabulary lists in Chapter Highlights to construct a concept map that illustrates the relationship between types of magma, the eruptions they produce, and the shapes of the volcanoes that result.

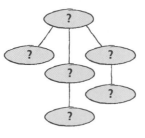

The following graph illustrates the average change in temperature above or below normal for a community over several years.

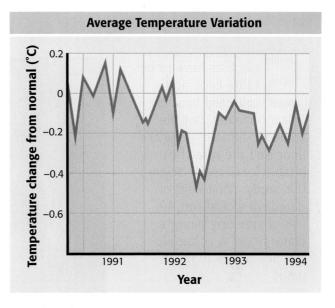

CRITICAL THINKING AND PROBLEM SOLVING

Write one or two sentences to answer the following questions:

18. Imagine that you are exploring a volcano that has been dormant for some time. You begin to keep notes on the types of volcanic debris you encounter as you walk. Your first notes describe volcanic ash, and later your notes describe lapilli. In what direction would you most likely be traveling—toward or away from the crater? Explain.

19. Loihi is a future Hawaiian island in the process of forming on the ocean floor. Considering how this island chain formed, tell where you think the new volcanic island will be located and why.

20. What do you think would happen to the Earth's climate if volcanic activity increased to 10 times its current level?

MATH IN SCIENCE

21. Midway Island is 1,935 km northwest of Hawaii. If the Pacific plate is moving to the northwest at 9 cm/yr, how long ago was Midway Island located over the hot spot that formed it?

22. If the variation in temperature over the years was influenced by a major volcanic eruption, when did the eruption most likely take place? Explain.

23. If the temperature were measured only once each year (at the beginning of the year), how would your interpretation be different?

NOW What Do You Think?

Take a minute to review your answers to the ScienceLog questions on page 191. Have your answers changed? If necessary, revise your answers based on what you have learned since you began this chapter.

Science, Technology, and Society

Robot in the Hot Seat

Scientists have to be calm, cool, and collected to study volcano craters. But the cooled magma of a crater's floor isn't the most hospitable location for scientific study. What kind of daredevil would run the risk of creeping along a crater floor? A volcanologist like *Dante II*, that's who!

Hot Stuff

A volcano crater may seem empty after a volcano erupts, but it is in no way devoid of volcanic information. Gases hissing up through the crater floor give scientists clues about the molten rock underneath, which may help them understand how and why volcanoes erupt repeatedly. But these gases may be poisonous or scalding hot, and the crater's floor can crack or shift at any time. Over the years, dozens of scientists have been seriously injured or killed while trying to explore volcano craters. Obviously, volcanologists needed some help studying the steamy abyss.

Getting a Robot to Take the Heat

Enter *Dante II*, an eight-legged robot with cameras for eyes and computers for a brain. In 1994, led by a team of scientists from NASA, Carnegie Mellon University, and the Alaskan Volcano Observatory, *Dante II* embarked on its first mission. It climbed into a breach called Crater Peak on the side of Mount Spurr, an active volcano in Alaska. Anchored at the crater's rim by a strong cable, *Dante II* was

▲ *Dante II*

controlled partly by internal computers and partly by a team of scientists. The team communicated with the robot through a satellite link and Internet connections. *Dante II* moved very slowly, taking pictures and collecting scientific data. It was equipped with gas sensors that provided continuous readings of the crater gases. It performed the tasks human scientists could not, letting the humans keep their cool.

Mission Accomplished?

During its expedition, *Dante II* encountered large rocks, some of which were as big as the robot itself. In addition, *Dante II* slipped and fell, damaging one of its legs, while climbing out of the volcano. Its support cable broke, and it eventually had to be rescued by a helicopter. Despite these obstacles, *Dante II* was able to gather valuable data from the volcano's crater.

Dante II's mission also met one of NASA's objectives: to prove that robots could be used successfully to explore extreme terrain, such as that found on planetary surfaces. *Dante II* paved the way for later robotic projects, such as the exploration of the surface of Mars by the *Sojourner* rover in 1997.

Write About It

▶ Write a proposal for a project in which a robot is used to explore a dangerous place. Don't forget to include what types of data the robot would be collecting.

EARTH   SCIENCE   •   LIFE   SCIENCE

Europa: Life on a Moon?

Smooth and brownish white, one of Jupiter's moons, Europa, has fascinated scientists and science-fiction writers for decades. More recently, scientists were excited by tantalizing images from the Galileo Europa Mission. Could it be that life is lurking (or sloshing) beneath Europa's surface?

An Active History

Slightly smaller than Earth's moon, Europa is the fourth largest of Jupiter's moons. It is unusual among other bodies in the solar system because of its extraordinarily smooth surface. But the ridges and brownish channels that crisscross Europa's smooth surface may tell a unique story—the surface appears to be a slushy combination of ice and water. Some scientists think that the icy ridges and channels are ice floes left over from ancient volcanoes that erupted water! The water flowed over Europa's surface and froze, like lava flows and cools on Earth's surface.

A Slushy Situation

Scientists speculate that Europa's surface consists of thin tectonic plates of ice floating on a layer of slush or water. These plates, which would look like icy rafts floating in an ocean of slush, have been compared to giant glaciers floating in polar regions on Earth.

Where plates push together, the material of the plates may crumple, forming an icy ridge. Where plates pull apart, warmer liquid mixed with darker silicates may erupt toward the surface and freeze, forming the brownish icy channels that create Europa's cracked cue-ball appearance.

Life on Europa?

These discoveries have led scientists to consider an exciting possibility: Does Europa have an environment that could support primitive life-forms? In general, at least three things are necessary for life as we know it to develop—water, organic compounds (substances that contain carbon), and heat. Europa has water, and organic compounds are fairly common in the solar system. But does it have heat? Europa's slushy nature suggests a warm interior. One theory is that the warmth is the result of Jupiter's strong gravitational pull on Europa. Another theory is that warmth is brought to Europa's surface by convection heating.

So does Europa truly satisfy the three requirements for life? The answer is still unknown, but the sloshing beneath Europa's surface has sure heightened some scientists' curiosity!

If You Were in Charge . . .

▶ If you were in charge of NASA's space-exploration program, would you send a space-craft to look for life on Europa? (Remember that this would cost millions of dollars and would mean sacrificing other important projects!) Explain your answer.

◀ *Europa looks like a cracked cue ball.*

9 Heat and Heat Technology

Strange but True!

Would you want to live in a house without a heating system? You could if you lived in an Earthship! Earthships are the brainchild of Michael Reynolds, an architect in Taos, New Mexico. These ultra-modern housing structures are designed to make the most of our planet's most abundant source of energy, the sun.

Each Earthship is custom-built to take full advantage of passive solar heating opportunities. For example, large windows face south in order to maximize the amount of radiant energy—energy from the sun—the house receives. Each home is partially buried in the ground, with the excavated soil piled almost to the roof. The energy-absorbing soil helps to keep the energy that comes in through the windows inside the house.

In many traditional houses, the outer walls are too thin and lightweight to absorb radiant energy. But Reynolds designs the outer walls of Earthships to be massive and thick. The walls are sometimes filled with crushed aluminum cans packed tightly together. For especially large projects, Reynolds uses stacks of old automobile tires filled with dirt. These materials absorb the sun's energy during daylight hours and naturally heat the house from the walls inward. Air pockets between the packed cans and the dirt filling the tires provide extra insulation. As a result, a lot of energy is prevented from leaving the house, even as the sun goes down and the outside air grows cold. Because an Earthship can maintain a steady temperature around 15°C (about 60°F), it can keep its occupants comfortable through all but the coldest winter nights.

Technology that keeps you warm or cool can be very important. In this chapter, you'll learn about temperature and heat, how different materials transfer energy, and how heat technology is used in everyday life.

What Do You Think?

In your ScienceLog, try to answer the following questions based on what you already know:

1. How do you measure how hot or cold an object is?

2. What makes an object hot or cold?

3. How can heat be used in your home?

Some Like It Hot

Sometimes you can tell the relative temperature of something by touching it with your hand. But how well does your hand work as a thermometer? In this activity, you will find out!

Procedure

1. Gather small pieces of the following materials from your teacher: **metal, wood, plastic foam, rock, plastic,** and **cardboard.**

2. Allow the materials to sit untouched on a table for several minutes.

3. Put your hands palms down on each of the various materials. Compare how warm or cool the materials feel.

4. In your ScienceLog, list the materials in order from coolest to warmest. Compare your results with those of your classmates.

5. Based on your discussion, arrange the materials in order from coolest to warmest.

6. Place a **thermometer strip** on the surface of each material. In your ScienceLog, record the temperature of each material.

Analysis

7. Which material felt the warmest?

8. Which material had the highest temperature?

9. Why do you think some materials felt warmer than others?

10. Was your hand a good thermometer? Why or why not?

Temperature

You probably put on a sweater or a jacket when it's cold outside. Likewise, you probably wear shorts in the summer when it gets hot. But how hot is hot, and how cold is cold? Think about how the knobs on a water faucet are labeled *H* for hot and *C* for cold. But does only hot water come out when the hot-water knob is on? You may have noticed that when you first turn on the water it is warm or even cool. Are you being misled by the label on the knob? The terms *hot* and *cold* are not very scientific terms. If you really want to specify how hot or cold something is, you must use temperature.

What Is Temperature?

You probably think of temperature as a measure of how hot or cold something is. But scientifically, **temperature** is a measure of the average kinetic energy of the particles in an object. Using temperature instead of words like *hot* or *cold* reduces confusion. The scenario below emphasizes the importance of communicating about temperature. You can learn more about hot and cold comparisons by doing the QuickLab on the next page.

Temperature Depends on the Kinetic Energy of Particles

All matter is made of particles—atoms or molecules—that are in constant motion. Because the particles are in motion, they have kinetic energy. The faster particles move, the more kinetic energy they have. What does temperature have to do with kinetic energy? Well, as described in **Figure 1,** the more kinetic energy the particles of an object have, the higher the temperature of the object.

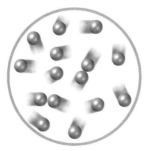

Figure 1 *The gas particles on the right have more kinetic energy than those on the left. So the gas on the right is at a higher temperature.*

Temperature Is an Average Measure Particles of matter are constantly moving, but they don't all move at the same speed and in the same direction all the time. Look back at Figure 1. As you can see, the motion of the particles is random. The particles of matter in an object move in different directions, and some particles move faster than others. As a result, some particles have more kinetic energy than others. So what determines an object's temperature? An object's temperature is the best approximation of the kinetic energy of the particles. When you measure an object's temperature, you measure the average kinetic energy of the particles in the object.

The temperature of a substance is not determined by how much of the substance you have. As shown in **Figure 2,** different amounts of the same substance can have the same temperature. However, the total kinetic energy of the particles in each amount is different. You will learn more about that kind of total kinetic energy in the next section.

Figure 2 *Even though there is more tea in the teapot than in the mug, the average kinetic energy, and therefore the temperature, of the tea in the mug is the same as that of the tea in the teapot.*

Measuring Temperature

How would you measure the temperature of a steaming cup of hot chocolate? Would you take a sip of it or stick your finger into it? Probably not—you would use a thermometer.

Using a Thermometer Many thermometers are thin glass tubes filled with a liquid. Mercury and alcohol are often used in thermometers because they remain liquids over a large temperature range. Thermometers can measure temperature because of thermal expansion. **Thermal expansion** is the increase in volume of a substance due to an increase in temperature. As a substance gets hotter, its particles move faster. The particles themselves do not expand; they just spread out so that the entire substance expands. Different substances expand by different amounts for a given temperature change. When you insert a thermometer into a hot substance, the liquid inside the thermometer expands and rises. You measure the temperature of a substance by measuring the expansion of the liquid in the thermometer.

Temperature Scales Temperature can be expressed according to different scales. Notice how the same temperatures have different readings on the three temperature scales shown below.

Three Temperature Scales

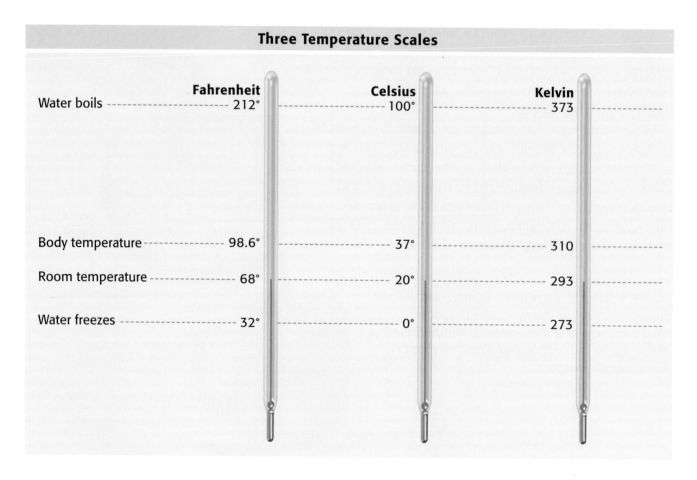

	Fahrenheit	Celsius	Kelvin
Water boils	212°	100°	373
Body temperature	98.6°	37°	310
Room temperature	68°	20°	293
Water freezes	32°	0°	273

When you hear a weather report that gives the current temperature as 65°, chances are you are given the temperature in degrees Fahrenheit (°F). In science, the Celsius scale is used more often than the Fahrenheit scale. The Celsius scale is divided into 100 equal parts called degrees Celsius (°C) between the freezing point and boiling point of water. A third scale, called the Kelvin (or absolute) scale, is the official SI temperature scale. The Kelvin scale is divided into units called kelvins (K)—not degrees kelvin. The lowest temperature on the Kelvin scale is 0 K, which is called **absolute zero.** It is not possible to reach a temperature lower than absolute zero. In fact, temperatures within millionths of a kelvin above absolute zero have been achieved in laboratories, but absolute zero itself has never been reached.

As shown by the thermometers illustrated on the previous page, a given temperature is represented by different numbers on the three temperature scales. For example, the freezing point of water is 32°F, 0°C, or 273 K. As you can see, 0°C is actually a much higher temperature than 0 K, but a change of 1 K is equal to a change of 1 Celsius degree. In addition, 0°C is a higher temperature than 0°F, but a change of 1 Fahrenheit degree is *not* equal to a change of 1 Celsius degree. You can convert from one scale to another using the simple equations shown below. After reading the examples given, try the MathBreak on this page.

What can you do at temperatures near absolute zero? Turn to page 242 and find out!

To convert	Use this equation:	Example
Celsius to Fahrenheit °C ⟶ °F	$°F = \left(\dfrac{9}{5} \times °C\right) + 32$	Convert 45°C to °F. $°F = \left(\dfrac{9}{5} \times 45°C\right) + 32 = 113°F$
Fahrenheit to Celsius °F ⟶ °C	$°C = \dfrac{5}{9} \times (°F - 32)$	Convert 68°F to °C. $°C = \dfrac{5}{9} \times (68°F - 32) = 20°C$
Celsius to Kelvin °C ⟶ K	$K = °C + 273$	Convert 45°C to K. $K = 45°C + 273 = 318$ K
Kelvin to Celsius K ⟶ °C	$°C = K - 273$	Convert 32 K to °C. $°C = 32$ K $- 273 = -241°C$

MATH BREAK

Converting Temperatures

Use the equations at left to answer the following questions:

1. What temperature on the Celsius scale is equivalent to 373 K?

2. Absolute zero is 0 K. What is the equivalent temperature on the Celsius scale? on the Fahrenheit scale?

3. Which temperature is colder, 0°F or 200 K?

Figure 3 *The concrete segments of a bridge can expand on hot days. When the temperature drops, the segments contract.*

More About Thermal Expansion

Have you ever gone across a highway bridge in a car? You probably heard and felt a *"Thuh-thunk"* every couple of seconds as you went over the bridge. That sound occurs when the car goes over small gaps called expansion joints, shown in **Figure 3.** These joints keep the bridge from buckling as a result of thermal expansion. Recall that thermal expansion is the increase in volume of a substance due to an increase in temperature.

Thermal expansion also occurs in a thermostat, the device that controls the heater in your home. Inside a thermostat is a bimetallic strip. A *bimetallic strip* is made of two different metals stacked in a thin strip. Because different materials expand at different rates, one of the metals expands more than the other when the strip gets hot. This makes the strip coil and uncoil in response to changes in temperature. This coiling and uncoiling closes and opens an electric circuit that turns the heater on and off in your home, as shown in **Figure 4.**

Figure 4 How a Thermostat Works

a As the room temperature drops below the desired level, the bimetallic strip coils up, and the glass tube tilts. A drop of mercury closes an electric circuit that turns the heater on.

Electrical contacts

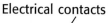

b As the room temperature rises above the desired level, the bimetallic strip uncoils. The drop of mercury rolls back in the tube, opening the electric circuit, and the heater turns off.

Explore

Stand in a huddle with three or four classmates. Have another classmate lay down a piece of string in a circle around you. Without holding on to each other, start moving around inside the circle. Gradually increase your kinetic energy. Did you have to move outside the string as you started to move faster? How is this like thermal expansion?

REVIEW

1. What is temperature?

2. What is the coldest temperature possible?

3. Convert 35°C to degrees Fahrenheit.

4. **Inferring Conclusions** Why do you think heating a full pot of soup on the stove could cause the soup to overflow?

What Is Heat?

It's time for your annual physical. The doctor comes in and begins her exam by looking down your throat using a wooden tongue depressor. Next she listens to your heart and lungs. But when she places a metal stethoscope on your back, as shown in **Figure 5,** you jump a little and say, "Whoa! That's cold!" The doctor apologizes and continues with your checkup.

Why did the metal stethoscope feel cold? After all, it was at the same temperature as the tongue depressor, which didn't make you jump. What is it about the stethoscope that made it feel cold? The answer has to do with how energy is transferred between the metal and your skin. In this section, you'll learn about this kind of energy transfer.

Heat Is a Transfer of Energy

You might think of the word *heat* as having to do with things that feel hot. But heat also has to do with things that feel cold—like the stethoscope. In fact, heat is what causes objects to feel hot or cold or to get hot or cold under the right conditions. You probably use the word *heat* every day to mean different things. However, in this chapter, you will learn a specific meaning for it. **Heat** is the transfer of energy between objects that are at different temperatures.

Why do some things feel hot, while others feel cold? When two objects at different temperatures come in contact, energy is always transferred from the object with the higher temperature to the object with the lower temperature. When the doctor's stethoscope touches your back, energy is transferred from your back to the stethoscope because your back has a higher temperature (37°C) than the stethoscope (probably room temperature, 20°C). So to you, the stethoscope is cold, but compared with the stethoscope, you are hot! You'll learn about why the tongue depressor didn't feel cold a little later in this section.

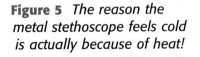

Figure 5 *The reason the metal stethoscope feels cold is actually because of heat!*

Heat and Thermal Energy If heat is a transfer of energy, what form of energy is being transferred? The answer is thermal energy. **Thermal energy** is the total kinetic energy of the particles that make up a substance. Thermal energy, which is expressed in joules (J), depends partly on temperature. An object at a high temperature has more thermal energy than it would at a lower temperature. Thermal energy also depends on how much of a substance you have. As described by **Figure 6,** the more moving particles there are in a substance at a given temperature, the greater the thermal energy of the substance.

When you hold an ice cube, thermal energy is transferred from your hand to the ice cube. The ice cube's thermal energy increases, and it starts to melt. But your hand's thermal energy decreases. The particles in the surface of your skin start moving slower, and the surface temperature of your skin drops slightly. So your hand feels cold!

Reaching the Same Temperature Take a look at **Figure 7.** When objects at different temperatures come in contact, energy will always be transferred from the higher-temperature object to the lower-temperature object until both objects reach the same temperature. This point is called *thermal equilibrium* (EE kwi LIB ree uhm). When objects are at thermal equilibrium, no net change in either object's thermal energy occurs. Although one object may have more thermal energy, both objects have the same temperature.

Figure 6 *Although both soups are at the same temperature, the soup in the pan has more thermal energy than the soup in the bowl.*

Figure 7
Reaching Thermal Equilibrium

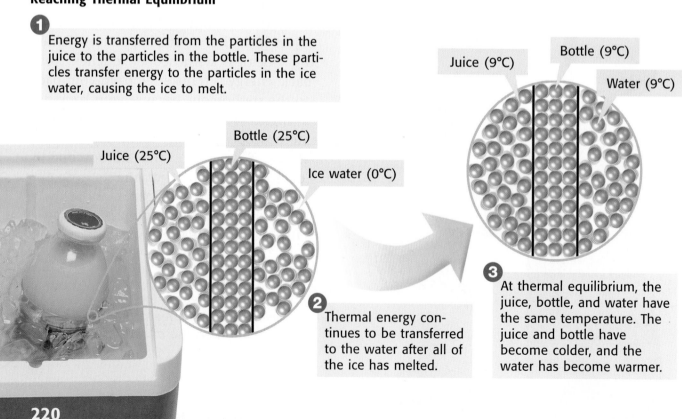

1 Energy is transferred from the particles in the juice to the particles in the bottle. These particles transfer energy to the particles in the ice water, causing the ice to melt.

Juice (25°C)

Bottle (25°C)

Ice water (0°C)

Juice (9°C)

Bottle (9°C)

Water (9°C)

2 Thermal energy continues to be transferred to the water after all of the ice has melted.

3 At thermal equilibrium, the juice, bottle, and water have the same temperature. The juice and bottle have become colder, and the water has become warmer.

Conduction, Convection, and Radiation

So far you've read about several examples of energy transfer: stoves transfer energy to substances in pots and pans, you can adjust the temperature of your bath water by adding cold or hot water to the tub, and the sun warms your skin. In the next couple of pages you'll learn about three processes involving this type of energy transfer: *conduction, convection,* and *radiation.*

Conduction Imagine that you put a cold metal spoon in a bowl of hot soup, as shown in **Figure 8.** Soon the handle of the spoon warms up—even though it is not in the soup! The entire spoon gets warm due to conduction. **Conduction** is the transfer of thermal energy from one substance to another through direct contact. Conduction can also occur within a substance, such as the spoon in Figure 8.

How does conduction work? As substances come in contact, particles collide, and thermal energy is transferred from the higher-temperature substance to the lower-temperature substance. Remember that particles of substances at different temperatures have different average kinetic energy. So when particles collide, higher-kinetic-energy particles transfer kinetic energy to lower-kinetic-energy particles. This makes some particles slow down and other particles speed up until all particles have the same average kinetic energy. As a result, the substances have the same temperature.

Quick **Lab**

Heat Exchange

1. Fill a **film canister** with **hot water.** Insert the **thermometer apparatus** prepared by your teacher. Record the temperature of the water.

2. Fill a **250 mL beaker** two-thirds full with **cool water.** Insert **another thermometer** in the cool water, and record its temperature.

3. Place the canister in the cool water. Record the temperature measured by each thermometer every 30 seconds.

4. When the thermometers read nearly the same temperature, stop and graph your data. Plot temperature (*y*-axis) versus time (*x*-axis).

5. In your ScienceLog, describe what happens to the rate of energy transfer as the two samples of water get closer in temperature.

Figure 8 *The end of this spoon will warm up because conduction, the transfer of energy through direct contact, occurs all the way up the handle.*

Conductors	Insulators
Curling iron	Flannel shirt
Iron skillet	Oven mitt
Cookie sheet	Plastic spatula
Copper pipes	Fiberglass insulation
Stove coils	Ceramic bowl

Substances that conduct thermal energy very well are called **conductors.** For example, a metal spoon in a bowl of hot soup is a conductor, as is the metal in a doctor's stethoscope. Energy is transferred rapidly from your higher-temperature skin to the room-temperature stethoscope. That's why the stethoscope feels cold. Substances that do not conduct thermal energy very well are called **insulators.** For example, the wooden tongue depressor in the doctor's office is an insulator. It has the same temperature as the doctor's stethoscope, but the tongue depressor doesn't feel cold. That's because thermal energy is transferred very slowly from your tongue to the wood. You can compare some typical conductors and insulators in the chart at left.

APPLY

The drink holder shown here is made from a foamlike material that helps keep your can of soda cold. How is this drink holder an insulator?

Figure 9 *The repeated rising and sinking of water during boiling is due to convection.*

Convection When you boil a pot of water, like the one shown in **Figure 9,** the water moves in roughly circular patterns due to convection. **Convection** is the transfer of thermal energy by the movement of a liquid or a gas. The water at the bottom of a pot on a stove burner becomes hot due to contact with the pot itself (conduction). As a result, the hot water becomes less dense because its higher-energy particles have spread apart. The warmer water rises through the denser, cooler water above it. At the surface, the warm water begins to cool, and the lower-energy particles move closer together, making the water denser. The denser, cooler water sinks back to the bottom, where it will be heated again. This circular motion of liquids or gases due to density differences that result from temperature differences is called a *convection current.*

Radiation Unlike conduction and convection, radiation can involve either an energy transfer between particles of matter or an energy transfer across empty space. **Radiation** is the transfer of energy through matter or space as electromagnetic waves, such as visible light or infrared waves. All objects, including the heater in **Figure 10,** radiate electromagnetic waves. The sun emits mostly visible light, which you can see and your body can absorb, making you feel warmer. The Earth emits mostly infrared waves, which you cannot see but can still make you feel warmer.

Figure 10 *The coils of this portable heater warm a room by radiating visible light and infrared waves.*

You might be surprised to learn that the Earth is such a livable place because of radiation and the *greenhouse effect,* illustrated in **Figure 11.** Earth's atmosphere, like the windows of a greenhouse, allows the sun's visible light to pass through it. The Earth radiates infrared waves, but like the windows of a greenhouse keep energy inside the greenhouse, the atmosphere traps some reradiated energy. Some scientists are concerned that high levels of greenhouse gases (water vapor, carbon dioxide, and methane) in the atmosphere may trap too much energy and make Earth too warm. However, if not for the greenhouse effect, the Earth would be a cold, lifeless planet.

Figure 11 The Greenhouse Effect

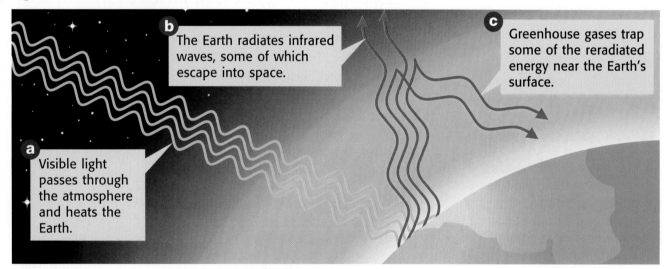

b The Earth radiates infrared waves, some of which escape into space.

c Greenhouse gases trap some of the reradiated energy near the Earth's surface.

a Visible light passes through the atmosphere and heats the Earth.

REVIEW

1. What is heat?

2. Explain how radiation is different from conduction and convection.

3. **Applying Concepts** Why do many metal cooking utensils have wooden handles?

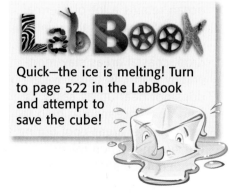

Quick—the ice is melting! Turn to page 522 in the LabBook and attempt to save the cube!

Heat and Temperature Change

On a hot summer day, have you ever fastened your seat belt in a car, as shown in **Figure 12**? If so, you may have noticed that the metal buckle felt hotter than the cloth belt. Why? Keep reading to learn more.

Figure 12 *On a hot summer day, the metal part of a seat belt feels hotter than the cloth part.*

Thermal Conductivity Different substances have different thermal conductivities. *Thermal conductivity* is the rate at which a substance conducts thermal energy. Conductors, such as the metal buckle, have higher thermal conductivities than do insulators, such as the cloth belt. Because of the metal's higher thermal conductivity, it transfers energy more rapidly to your hand when you touch it than the cloth does. So even when the cloth and metal are the same temperature, the metal feels hotter.

Specific Heat Capacity Another difference between the metal and the cloth is how easily they change temperature when they absorb or lose energy. When equal amounts of energy are transferred to or from equal masses of different substances, the change in temperature for each substance will differ. **Specific heat capacity** is the amount of energy needed to change the temperature of 1 kg of a substance by 1°C.

Look at the table below. Notice that the specific heat capacity of the cloth of a seat belt is more than twice that of the metal seat belt buckle. This means that for equal masses of metal and cloth, less energy is required to change the temperature of the metal. So the metal buckle gets hot (and cools off) more quickly than an equal mass of the cloth belt.

Different substances have different specific heat capacities. Check out the specific heat capacities for various substances in the table below.

Specific Heat Capacities of Some Common Substances			
Substance	Specific heat capacity (J/kg•°C)	Substance	Specific heat capacity (J/kg•°C)
Lead	128	Glass	837
Gold	129	Cloth of seat belt	1,340
Silver	234	Wood	1,760
Copper	387	Steam	2,010
Iron	448	Ice	2,090
Metal of seat belt	500	Water	4,184

Calculating Heat Unlike temperature, energy transferred between objects cannot be measured directly—it must be calculated. When calculating energy transferred between objects, it is helpful to define *heat* as the amount of energy that is transferred between two objects that are at different temperatures. With this meaning, heat can be expressed in joules (J).

How much energy is required to heat a cup of water to make tea? To answer this question, you have to consider the water's mass, its change in temperature, and its specific heat capacity. In general, if you know an object's mass, its change in temperature, and its specific heat capacity, you can use the equation below to calculate heat (the amount of energy transferred).

$$\text{Heat (J)} = \text{specific heat capacity (J/kg} \bullet \text{°C)} \times \text{mass (kg)} \times \text{change in temperature (°C)}$$

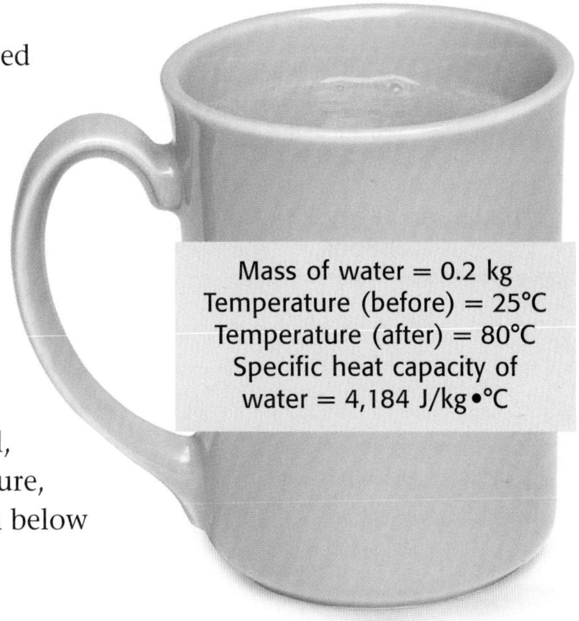

Using this equation and the data shown in **Figure 13,** you can follow the steps below to calculate the amount of thermal energy that was added to the water. Because the water's temperature increases, the value of heat is positive. You can also use this equation to find out the amount of thermal energy that is removed from an object when it cools down. In this case, the value for heat would be negative because the temperature decreases. You can practice using this equation in the MathBreak at right.

Mass of water = 0.2 kg
Temperature (before) = 25°C
Temperature (after) = 80°C
Specific heat capacity of
water = 4,184 J/kg•°C

Figure 13 *Information used to calculate heat, the amount of energy transferred to the water, is shown above.*

÷ 5 ÷ Ω ≤ ∞ +Ω √ 9 ∞ ≤ Σ 2
+

MATH BREAK

Calculating Energy Transfer
Use the equation at left to solve the following problems:

1. Imagine that you heat 2 L of water to make pasta. The temperature of the water before is 40°C, and the temperature after is 100°C. What is the heat involved? (Hint: 1 L of water = 1 kg of water.)

2. Suppose you put a glass filled with 180 mL of water into the refrigerator. The temperature of the water before going into the refrigerator is 25°C, and the temperature after is 10°C. How much energy was transferred away from the water as it became colder?

❶ Write down what you know.
Specific heat capacity of water = 4,184 J/kg•°C
Mass of water = 0.2 kg
Change in temperature = (80°C − 25°C) = 55°C

❷ Substitute the values into the equation.
Heat = specific heat capacity × mass × change in temperature
= 4,184 J/kg•°C × 0.2 kg × 55°C

❸ Solve and cancel units.
Heat = 4,184 J/kg•°C × 0.2 kg × 55°C
= 4,184 J × 0.2 × 55
= 46,024 J

Build your own calorimeter! Try the lab on page 523 of the LabBook.

Calorimeters When one object transfers thermal energy to another object, the energy lost by one object is gained by the other object. This phenomenon is the key to how a *calorimeter* (KAL uh RIM uh ter) works. Inside a calorimeter, shown in **Figure 14,** thermal energy is transferred from a known mass of a test substance to a known mass of another substance, usually water. Water is used in calorimeters because its specific heat capacity is well known. If a hot test substance is placed inside the calorimeter's inner container of water, the substance transfers energy to the water until thermal equilibrium is reached. By measuring the temperature change of the water and using water's specific heat capacity, you can determine the exact amount of energy transferred by the test substance to the water. You can then use this amount of energy (heat), the change in the test substance's temperature, and the mass of the test substance to calculate the specific heat capacity of the substance.

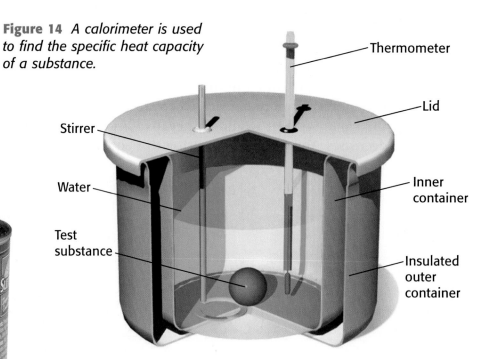

Figure 14 *A calorimeter is used to find the specific heat capacity of a substance.*

Thermometer

Lid

Stirrer

Water

Test substance

Inner container

Insulated outer container

Figure 15 *A serving of this fruit contains 120 Cal (502,080 J) of energy that becomes available when it is eaten and digested.*

Calories and Kilocalories Heat can also be expressed in units called calories. A *calorie (cal)* is the amount of energy needed to change the temperature of 0.001 kg of water by 1°C. Therefore, 1,000 calories are required to change the temperature of 1 kg of water by 1°C. One calorie is equivalent to 4.184 J. Another unit used to express heat is the *kilocalorie (kcal)*, which is equivalent to 1,000 calories. The kilocalorie can also be referred to as the *Calorie* (with a capital C). Calories are the units listed on food labels, such as the label shown in **Figure 15.**

The Differences Between Temperature, Thermal Energy, and Heat

So far in this chapter, you have been learning about some concepts that are closely related: temperature, heat, and thermal energy. But the differences between these concepts are very important.

Temperature Versus Thermal Energy Both temperature and thermal energy involve kinetic energy. Temperature is a measure of the average kinetic energy of an object's particles, and thermal energy is the total kinetic energy of an object's particles. While thermal energy varies with the mass of an object, temperature does not. A drop of boiling water has the same temperature as a pot of boiling water, but the pot has more thermal energy because there are more particles.

Thermal Energy Versus Heat Heat and thermal energy are not the same thing; heat is a transfer of thermal energy. In addition, heat can refer to the amount of energy transferred from one object to another. Objects contain thermal energy, but they do not contain heat. The table below summarizes the differences between temperature, thermal energy, and heat.

Self-Check

How can two substances have the same temperature but different amounts of thermal energy? *(See page 564 to check your answer.)*

Temperature	Thermal energy	Heat
A measure of the average kinetic energy of the particles in a substance	The total kinetic energy of the particles in a substance	The transfer of energy between objects that are at different temperatures
Expressed in degrees Fahrenheit, degrees Celsius, or kelvins	Expressed in joules	Amount of energy transferred expressed in joules or calories
Does not vary with the mass of a substance	Varies with the mass and temperature of a substance	Varies with the mass, specific heat capacity, and temperature change of a substance

REVIEW

1. Why do some substances get hotter faster than others?

2. How are temperature and heat different?

3. **Applying Concepts** Examine the photo at right. How do you think the specific heat capacities for water and air influence the temperature of a swimming pool and the area around it?

Matter and Heat

NEW TERMS
states of matter
change of state

OBJECTIVES

- Identify three states of matter.
- Explain how heat affects matter during a change of state.
- Describe how heat affects matter during a chemical change.

Have you ever eaten a frozen juice bar outside on a hot summer day? It's pretty hard to finish the entire thing before it starts to drip and make a big mess! The juice bar melts because the sun radiates energy to the air, which transfers energy to the frozen juice bar. The energy absorbed by the juice bar increases the kinetic energy of the molecules in the juice bar, which starts to turn to a liquid. In this section, you'll learn more about how heat affects matter.

States of Matter

The matter that makes up a frozen juice bar has the same identity whether the juice bar is frozen or has melted. The matter is just in a different form, or state. The **states of matter** are the physical forms in which a substance can exist. Recall that matter consists of particles—atoms or molecules—that can move around at different speeds. The state a substance is in depends on the speed of its particles and the attraction between them. Three familiar states of matter are solid, liquid, and gas, represented in **Figure 16.** You may recall that thermal energy is the total kinetic energy of the particles that make up a substance. Suppose you have equal masses of a substance in its three states, each at a different temperature. The substance will have the most thermal energy as a gas and the least thermal energy as a solid. That's because the particles move around fastest in the gas.

Figure 16 Models of a Solid, a Liquid, and a Gas

Particles of a solid do not move fast enough to overcome the strong attraction between them, so they are held tightly together. The particles vibrate in place.

Particles of a liquid move fast enough to overcome some of the attraction between them. The particles are able to slide past one another.

Particles of a gas move fast enough to overcome nearly all of the attraction between them. The particles move independently of one another.

Changes of State

When you melt cheese to make a cheese dip, like that shown in **Figure 17,** the cheese changes from a solid to a thick, gooey liquid. A **change of state** is the conversion of a substance from one physical form to another. A change of state is a *physical change,* a change that affects one or more physical properties of a substance without changing the identity of the substance. Common changes of state include *freezing* (liquid to solid), *melting* (solid to liquid), *boiling* (liquid to gas), and *condensing* (gas to liquid).

Figure 17 *When you melt cheese, you change the state of the cheese but not its identity.*

Heat During Changes of State Suppose you put an ice cube in a pan and set the pan on a stove burner. Soon the ice will turn to water and then to steam. If you made a graph of the heat involved versus the temperature of the ice during this process, it would look something like the graph below.

As the ice is heated, its temperature increases from −25°C to 0°C. At 0°C, the ice begins to melt. Notice, however, that the temperature of the ice remains 0°C even when energy is still being added. The energy added at this point is used to change the arrangement of the particles, or molecules, in the ice. The temperature of the ice remains constant until all of its particles have dislodged from their positions in the solid. When all of the ice has become liquid water, the water's temperature will start to increase from 0°C to 100°C. At 100°C, the water will begin to turn into steam. Again, the temperature remains constant, and the energy added at the boiling point is used to change the arrangement of the particles of water. The temperature stays at 100°C until the water has entirely changed to a gaseous state. When all of the water has become steam, the temperature will again increase as it continues to be heated.

> ✔ **Self-Check**
>
> Why do you think you can get a more severe burn from steam than from boiling water?
> *(See page 564 to check your answer.)*

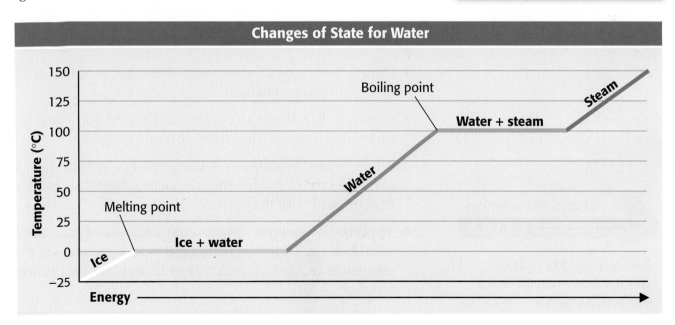

Changes of State for Water

Temperature (°C) vs. Energy

150, 125, 100, 75, 50, 25, 0, −25

Ice — Melting point — Ice + water — Water — Boiling point — Water + steam — Steam

Heat and Chemical Changes

Heat is involved not only in changes of state, which are physical changes, but also in *chemical changes*, changes that occur when one or more substances are changed into entirely new substances with different properties. During a chemical change, new substances are formed. For a new substance to form, old bonds between particles must be broken and new bonds created. The breaking and creating of bonds between particles involves energy. Sometimes a chemical change requires thermal energy to be absorbed. For example, photosynthesis is a chemical change in which carbon dioxide and water combine to form sugar and oxygen. In order for this change to occur, energy must be absorbed. That energy is radiated by the sun. Other times, a chemical change, such as the one shown in **Figure 18,** will result in energy being released.

Figure 18 In a natural-gas fireplace, the methane in natural gas and the oxygen in air change into carbon dioxide and water. As a result of the change, energy is given off, making a room feel warmer.

REVIEW

1. During a change of state, why doesn't the temperature of the substance change?

2. Compare the thermal energy of 10 g of ice with the thermal energy of the same amount of water.

3. When water evaporates (changes from a liquid to a gas), the air near the water's surface becomes cooler. Explain why this happens.

4. **Applying Concepts** Many cold packs used for sports injuries are activated by bending the package, causing the substances inside to interact. How is heat involved in this process?

Section 4

Heat Technology

NEW TERMS

insulation
heat engine
thermal pollution

OBJECTIVES

- Analyze several kinds of heating systems.
- Describe how a heat engine works.
- Explain how a refrigerator keeps food cold.
- Give examples of some effects of heat technology on the environment.

You probably wouldn't be surprised to learn that the heater in your home is an example of heat technology. But did you know that automobiles, refrigerators, and air conditioners are also examples of heat technology? It's true! You can travel long distances, food can stay cold, and you can feel comfortable indoors during the summer—all because of heat technology.

Heating Systems

Many homes and buildings have a central heating system that controls the temperature in every room. On the next few pages, you will see some different central heating systems.

Hot-Water Heating Water's high specific heat capacity makes it a good candidate for heating systems. In a hot-water heating system, shown in **Figure 19,** water is heated by the burning of fuel (usually natural gas or fuel oil) in a hot-water heater. The hot water is then pumped through a pipe network that leads to radiators in each room. The hot water heats the radiators, and the radiators then heat the colder air surrounding them. The water returns to the hot-water heater to be heated again. A *steam-heating system* is similar to a hot-water heating system, except that steam is used. An advantage of using steam instead of water is that steam has a higher temperature than hot water. However, it is more difficult to regulate room temperature with a steam-heating system than with a hot-water heating system.

Figure 19
A Hot-Water Heating System

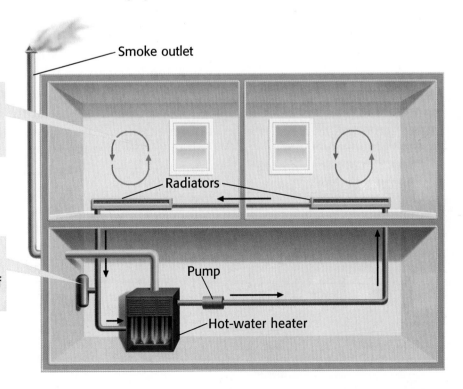

Smoke outlet

Air heated by the radiators circulates in the room by convection currents.

Radiators

An expansion tank handles the increased volume of the heated water.

Pump

Hot-water heater

Warm-Air Heating Although air has a lower specific heat capacity than water, warm-air heating systems are commonly used in homes and offices in the United States. In a warm-air heating system, shown in **Figure 20,** air is heated in a separate chamber by the burning of fuel (usually natural gas) in a furnace. The warm air travels through a network of ducts to different rooms, which it enters through vents. After transferring its thermal energy to the rooms, the air is cooler, so it sinks and enters a vent near the floor. A fan forces cooled air into the furnace, where it will be heated and returned to the ducts. An air filter allows the air to be cleaned as it gets recirculated throughout the system.

Figure 20
A Warm-Air Heating System

Warm air is circulated in the rooms by convection currents.

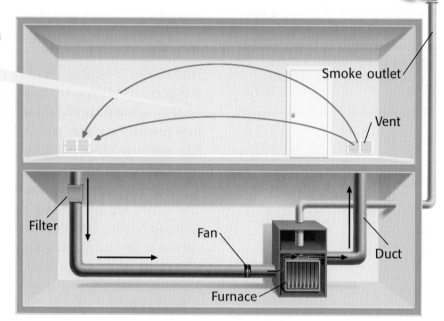

Smoke outlet

Vent

Filter

Fan

Duct

Furnace

Heating and Insulation Because heat is a transfer of energy from high temperatures to low temperatures, thermal energy has a tendency to be transferred out of a house during cold weather and into a house during hot weather. To keep the house comfortable, a heating system must run almost continuously during the winter, and air conditioners often do the same during the summer. This can be wasteful. That's where insulation comes in. **Insulation** is a substance that reduces the transfer of thermal energy. Insulation, such as the fiberglass insulation shown in **Figure 21,** is made of insulators, materials that do not conduct thermal energy very well. Insulation that is used in walls, ceilings, and floors helps a house stay warm in the winter and cool in the summer.

Do you remember the Earthships described at the beginning of this chapter? The tightly packed aluminum cans in the walls of an Earthship have spaces between them. Air filling these spaces insulates the Earthship. These homes also rely on a solar heating system, which you will learn about on the next page.

Figure 21 *Inside the fibers in this insulation are millions of tiny air pockets. Because air is a good insulator, these air pockets help to prevent thermal energy from flowing into or out of a building.*

Solar Heating The sun radiates an enormous amount of energy that can be used by solar heating systems to heat houses and buildings. *Passive solar heating* systems do not have moving parts. They rely on a building's structural design and materials to use energy from the sun as a means of heating. *Active solar heating* systems do have moving parts. They use pumps and fans to distribute energy from the sun throughout a building. The house shown in **Figure 22** uses both forms of solar heating systems. The large windows on the south side of the house are part of the passive solar heating system. These windows receive maximum sunlight, and energy is radiated through the windows into the rooms. Thick, well-insulated concrete walls absorb energy and heat the house at night or when it is cloudy. In the active solar heating system, water is pumped toward the solar collector, where it is heated. The hot water is then pumped through a pathway of pipes, transferring its energy to the pipes. A fan blowing over the pipes helps the pipes transfer their thermal energy to the air. Warm air is then sent into rooms through vents. Cooler water returns to the water storage tank to be pumped back through the solar collector.

Figure 22 *Passive and active solar heating systems work together to use the sun's energy to heat an entire house.*

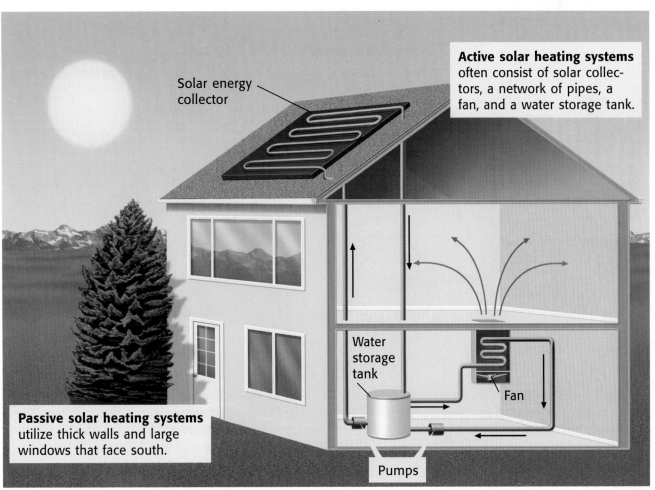

Solar energy collector

Active solar heating systems often consist of solar collectors, a network of pipes, a fan, and a water storage tank.

Water storage tank

Fan

Passive solar heating systems utilize thick walls and large windows that face south.

Pumps

Heat Engines

Did you know cars work because of heat? A car has a **heat engine,** a machine that uses heat to do work. In a heat engine, fuel combines with oxygen in a chemical change that produces thermal energy. This process, called *combustion,* is how engines burn fuel. Heat engines that burn fuel outside the engine are called *external combustion engines.* Heat engines that burn fuel inside the engine are called *internal combustion engines.* In both types of engines, fuel is burned to produce thermal energy that can be used to do work.

External Combustion Engine A simple steam engine, shown in **Figure 23,** is an example of an external combustion engine. Coal is burned to heat water in a boiler and change it to steam. When water changes to steam, it expands. The steam is used to drive a piston, which can be attached to other mechanisms that do work, such as a flywheel. Modern steam engines, such as those used to generate electrical energy at a power plant, drive turbines instead of pistons.

Figure 23 An External Combustion Engine

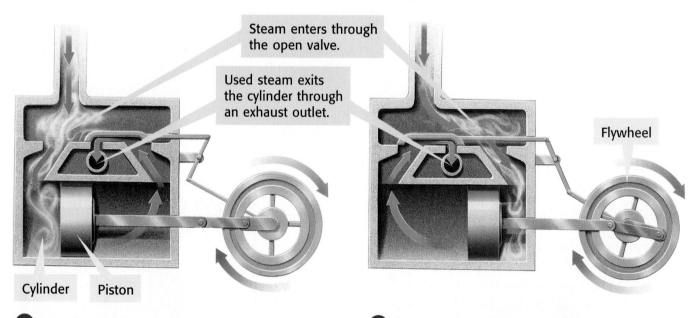

Steam enters through the open valve.

Used steam exits the cylinder through an exhaust outlet.

Flywheel

Cylinder   Piston

a The expanding steam enters the cylinder from one side. The steam does work on the piston, forcing the piston to move.

b As the piston moves to the other side, a second valve opens, and steam enters. The steam does work on the piston and moves it back. The motion of the piston turns a flywheel.

Internal Combustion Engine In the six-cylinder car engine shown in **Figure 24,** fuel is burned inside the engine. During the intake stroke, a mixture of gasoline and air enters each cylinder as the piston moves down. Next the crankshaft turns and pushes the piston up, compressing the fuel mixture. This is called the compression stroke. Next comes the power stroke, in which the spark plug uses electrical energy to ignite the compressed fuel mixture, causing the mixture to expand and force the piston down. Finally, during the exhaust stroke, the crankshaft turns and the piston is forced back up, pushing exhaust gases out of the cylinder.

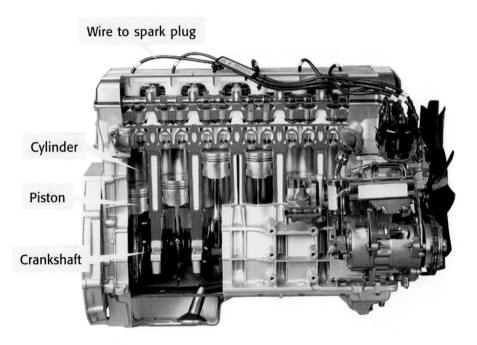

Wire to spark plug

Cylinder

Piston

Crankshaft

Figure 24 *The continuous cycling of the four strokes in the cylinders converts thermal energy into the kinetic energy required to make the car move.*

Cooling Systems

When it gets hot in the summer, an air-conditioned room can sure feel refreshing. Cooling systems are used to transfer thermal energy out of a particular area so that it feels cooler. An air conditioner, shown in **Figure 25,** is a cooling system that transfers thermal energy from a warm area inside a building or car to an area outside, where it is often even warmer. But wait a minute—doesn't that go against the natural direction of heat—from higher temperatures to lower temperatures? Well, yes. A cooling system moves thermal energy from colder temperatures to warmer temperatures. But in order to do that, the cooling system must do work.

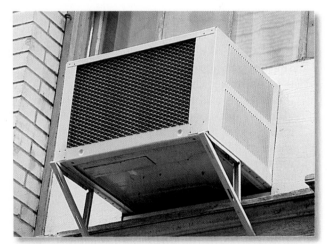

Figure 25 *This air conditioning unit keeps a building cool by moving thermal energy inside the building to the outside.*

If you had a refrigerator in Antarctica, you would actually have to heat it to keep it running at its normal temperature. Otherwise, it would transfer energy to its surroundings until the refrigerator reached the same temperature as its surroundings. So it would freeze!

Electrical energy is required to do the work of cooling. Electrical energy enters a cooling system through a device called a compressor. The compressor does the work of compressing the refrigerant, a gas that has a boiling point below room temperature. This property of the refrigerant allows it to condense easily.

To keep many foods fresh, you store them in a refrigerator. A refrigerator is another example of a cooling system. **Figure 26** shows how a refrigerator continuously transfers thermal energy from inside the refrigerator to the condenser coils on the outside of the refrigerator. That's why the area near the back of a refrigerator feels warm.

Figure 26 How a Refrigerator Works

c When the liquid passes through the expansion valve, it goes from a high-pressure area to a low-pressure area. As a result, the temperature of the liquid decreases.

Low pressure

High pressure

d As the cold liquid refrigerant moves through the evaporating coils, it absorbs thermal energy from the refrigerator compartment, making the inside of the refrigerator cold. As a result, the temperature of the refrigerant increases, and it changes into a gas.

e The gas is then returned to the compressor, and the cycle repeats.

b The hot gas flows through the condenser coils on the outside of the refrigerator. The gas condenses into a liquid, transferring some of its thermal energy to the coils.

a The compressor uses electrical energy to compress the refrigerant gas; this compression increases the pressure and temperature of the gas.

Heat Technology and Thermal Pollution

Heating systems, car engines, and cooling systems all transfer thermal energy to the environment. Unfortunately, too much thermal energy can negatively affect the environment.

One of the negative effects of excess thermal energy is **thermal pollution,** the excessive heating of a body of water. Thermal pollution can occur near large power plants, which are often located near a body of water. Electric power plants burn fuel to produce thermal energy that is used to do the work of generating electrical energy. Unfortunately, it is not possible for all that thermal energy to do work, so some waste thermal energy results. **Figure 27** shows how a cooling tower helps remove this waste thermal energy in order to keep the power plants operating smoothly. In extreme cases, the increase in temperature downstream from a power plant can adversely affect the ecosystem of the river or lake. Some power plants reduce thermal pollution by reducing the temperature of the water before it is returned to the river.

environmental science
CONNECTION

Large cities can exhibit something called a heat island effect when excessive amounts of waste thermal energy are added to the urban environment. This thermal energy comes from automobiles, factories, home heating and cooling, lighting, and even just the number of people living in a relatively small area. The heat island effect can make the temperature of the air in a city higher than that of the air in the surrounding countryside.

Figure 27 *Cool water is circulated through a power plant to absorb waste thermal energy.*

Cool water

Warm water

REVIEW

1. Compare a hot-water heating system with a warm-air heating system.

2. What is the difference between an external combustion engine and an internal combustion engine?

3. **Analyzing Relationships** How are changes of state an important part of the way a refrigerator works?

Chapter Highlights

SECTION 1

Vocabulary

temperature (*p. 214*)
thermal expansion (*p. 216*)
absolute zero (*p. 217*)

Section Notes

- Temperature is a measure of the average kinetic energy of the particles of a substance. It is a specific measurement of how hot or cold a substance is.

- Thermal expansion is the increase in volume of a substance due to an increase in temperature. Temperature is measured according to the expansion of the liquid in a thermometer.

- Fahrenheit, Celsius, and Kelvin are three temperature scales.

- Absolute zero—0 K, or –273°C— is the lowest possible temperature.

- A thermostat works according to the thermal expansion of a bimetallic strip.

SECTION 2

Vocabulary

heat (*p. 219*)
thermal energy (*p. 220*)
conduction (*p. 221*)
conductor (*p. 222*)
insulator (*p. 222*)
convection (*p. 222*)
radiation (*p. 223*)
specific heat capacity (*p. 224*)

Section Notes

- Heat is the transfer of energy between objects that are at different temperatures.

- Thermal energy is the total kinetic energy of the particles that make up a substance.

- Energy transfer will always occur from higher temperatures to lower temperatures until thermal equilibrium is reached.

☑ Skills Check

Math Concepts

TEMPERATURE CONVERSION To convert between different temperature scales, you can use the equations found on page 217. The example below shows you how to convert a Fahrenheit temperature to a Celsius temperature.

Convert 41°F to °C.

$$°C = \frac{5}{9} \times (°F - 32)$$

$$°C = \frac{5}{9} \times (41°F - 32)$$

$$°C = \frac{5}{9} \times 9 = 5°C$$

Visual Understanding

HEAT—A TRANSFER OF ENERGY
Remember that thermal energy is transferred between objects at different temperatures until both objects reach the same temperature. Look back at Figure 7, on page 220, to review what you've learned about heat.

- Conduction, convection, and radiation are three methods of heating.

- Specific heat capacity is the amount of energy needed to change the temperature of 1 kg of a substance by 1°C. Different substances have different specific heat capacities.

- Energy transferred by heat cannot be measured directly. It must be calculated using specific heat capacity, mass, and change in temperature.

- A calorimeter is used to determine the specific heat capacity of a substance.

Labs

Feel the Heat (*p. 520*)
Save the Cube! (*p. 522*)
Counting Calories (*p. 523*)

Vocabulary

states of matter (*p. 228*)
change of state (*p. 229*)

Section Notes

- A substance's state is determined by the speed of its particles and the attraction between them.

- Thermal energy transferred during a change of state does not change a substance's temperature. Rather, it causes a substance's particles to be rearranged.

- Chemical changes can cause thermal energy to be absorbed or released.

Vocabulary

insulation (*p. 232*)
heat engine (*p. 234*)
thermal pollution (*p. 237*)

Section Notes

- Central heating systems include hot-water heating systems and warm-air heating systems.

- Solar heating systems can be passive or active.

- Heat engines use heat to do work. External combustion engines burn fuel outside the engine. Internal combustion engines burn fuel inside the engine.

- A cooling system transfers thermal energy from cooler temperatures to warmer temperatures by doing work.

- Transferring excess thermal energy to lakes and rivers can result in thermal pollution.

 internet**connect**

 GO TO: go.hrw.com

Visit the **HRW** Web site for a variety of learning tools related to this chapter. Just type in the keyword:

KEYWORD: HSTHOT

 GO TO: www.scilinks.org

Visit the **National Science Teachers Association** on-line Web site for Internet resources related to this chapter. Just type in the *sci***LINKS** number for more information about the topic:

TOPIC: What Is Temperature?	*sci*LINKS NUMBER: HSTE555
TOPIC: Thermal Expansion	*sci*LINKS NUMBER: HSTE560
TOPIC: What Is Heat?	*sci*LINKS NUMBER: HSTE565
TOPIC: Methods of Heating	*sci*LINKS NUMBER: HSTE570
TOPIC: Changes of State	*sci*LINKS NUMBER: HSTE575

Chapter Review

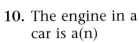

USING VOCABULARY

For each pair of terms, explain the difference in their meanings.

1. temperature/thermal energy

2. heat/thermal energy

3. conductor/insulator

4. conduction/convection

5. states of matter/change of state

UNDERSTANDING CONCEPTS

Multiple Choice

6. Which of the following temperatures is the lowest?
   a. 100°C
   b. 100°F
   c. 100 K
   d. They are the same.

7. Compared with the Pacific Ocean, a cup of hot chocolate has
   a. more thermal energy and a higher temperature.
   b. less thermal energy and a higher temperature.
   c. more thermal energy and a lower temperature.
   d. less thermal energy and a lower temperature.

8. The energy units on a food label are
   a. degrees
   b. Calories
   c. calories
   d. joules

9. Which of the following materials would not be a good insulator?
   a. wood
   b. cloth
   c. metal
   d. rubber

10. The engine in a car is a(n)
    a. heat engine.
    b. external combustion engine.
    c. internal combustion engine.
    d. Both (a) and (c)

11. Materials that warm up or cool down very quickly have a
    a. low specific heat capacity.
    b. high specific heat capacity.
    c. low temperature.
    d. high temperature.

12. In an air conditioner, thermal energy is
    a. transferred from higher to lower temperatures.
    b. transferred from lower to higher temperatures.
    c. used to do work.
    d. taken from air outside a building and transferred to air inside the building.

Short Answer

13. How does temperature relate to kinetic energy?

14. What is specific heat capacity?

15. Explain how heat affects matter during a change of state.

16. Describe how a bimetallic strip works in a thermostat.

Concept Mapping

17. Use the following terms to create a concept map: thermal energy, temperature, radiation, heat, conduction, convection.

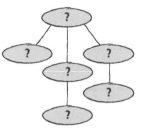

CRITICAL THINKING AND PROBLEM SOLVING

18. Why does placing a jar under warm running water help to loosen the lid on the jar?

19. Why do you think a down-filled jacket keeps you so warm? (Hint: Think about what insulation does.)

20. Would opening the refrigerator cool a room in a house? Why or why not?

21. In a hot-air balloon, air is heated by a flame. Explain how this enables the balloon to float in the air.

MATH IN SCIENCE

22. The weather forecast calls for a temperature of 86°F. What is the corresponding temperature in degrees Celsius? in kelvins?

23. Suppose 1,300 mL of water are heated from 20°C to 100°C. How much energy was transferred to the water? (Hint: Water's specific heat capacity is 4,184 J/kg•°C.)

INTERPRETING GRAPHICS

Examine the graph below, and then answer the questions that follow.

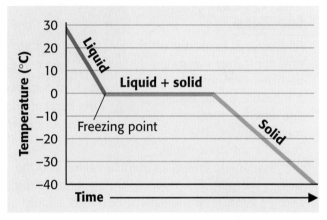

24. What physical change does this graph illustrate?

25. What is the freezing point of this liquid?

26. What is happening at the point where the line is horizontal?

NOW What Do You Think?

Take a minute to review your answers to the ScienceLog questions on page 213. Have your answers changed? If necessary, revise your answers based on what you have learned since you began this chapter.

Science, Technology, and Society

The Deep Freeze

In the dark reaches of outer space, temperatures can drop below −270°C. Perhaps the only place colder is a laboratory here on Earth!

The Quest for Zero

All matter is made up of tiny, constantly vibrating particles. Temperature is a measure of the average kinetic energy of these particles. The colder a substance gets, the less kinetic energy its particles have and the slower the particles move. In theory, at absolute zero (−273°C), all movement of matter should stop. Scientists are working in laboratories to slow down matter so much that the temperature approaches absolute zero.

How Low Can They Go?

Using lasers, along with magnets, mirrors, and supercold chemicals, scientists have cooled matter to within a millionth of a degree of absolute zero. In one method, scientists aim lasers at tiny gas particles inside a special chamber. The lasers hold the particles so still that their temperature approaches −272.999998°C.

To get an idea of what takes place, imagine turning on several garden hoses as high as they can go. Then direct the streams of water at a soccer ball so that each stream pushes the ball from a different angle. If the hoses are aimed properly, the ball won't roll in any direction. That's similar to what happens to the particles in the scientists' experiment.

▲ *This laser device is used to cool matter to nearly absolute zero.*

Cryogenics—Cold Temperature Technology

Supercold temperatures have led to some super-cool technology. Cryosurgery, which is surgery that uses extremely low temperatures, allows doctors to seal off tiny blood vessels during an operation or to freeze diseased cells and destroy them.

Cooling materials to near absolute zero has also led to the discovery of superconductors. Superconductors are materials that lose all of their electrical resistance when they are cooled to a low enough temperature. Imagine the possibilities for materials that could conduct electricity indefinitely without any energy loss. Unfortunately, it takes a great deal of energy to cool such materials. Right now, applications for superconductors are still just the stuff of dreams.

Freezing Fun on Your Own

▶ You can try your hand at cryo-investigation. In three separate plastic containers, place 50 mL of tap water, 50 mL of salt water (50 mL of water plus 15 g salt), and 50 mL of rubbing alcohol (isopropanol). Then put all three containers in your freezer at the same time. Check the containers every 5 minutes for 40 minutes. Which liquid freezes first? How can you explain any differences?

Diaplex: The Intelligent Fabric

Wouldn't it be great if you had a winter coat that could automatically adjust to keep you cozy regardless of the outside temperature? Well, scientists have developed a new fabric, called Diaplex, that can be used to make such a coat!

With Pores or Without?

Winter adventurers usually wear nylon fabrics to keep warm. These nylon fabrics are laminated with a thin coating that contains thousands of tiny pores, or openings. The pores allow moisture, such as sweat from your body, and excess thermal energy to escape. You might think the pores would let moisture and cold air into the fabric, but that's not the case. Because the pores are so small, the nylon fabric is windproof and waterproof.

Diaplex is also made from laminated nylon, but the coating is different. Diaplex doesn't have pores; it is a solid film. This film makes Diaplex even more waterproof and breathable than other laminated nylon fabrics. So how does it work?

Moving Particles

Diaplex keeps you warm by taking advantage of how particles move. When the air outside is cold, the particles of Diaplex arrange themselves into a solid sheet, forming an insulator and preventing the transfer of thermal energy from your body to colder surroundings. As your body gets warm, such as after exercising, the fabric's particles respond to your body's increased thermal energy. Their kinetic energy increases, and they rearrange to create millions of tiny openings that allow excess thermal energy and moisture to escape.

Donning Diaplex

Diaplex has a number of important advantages over traditional nylon fabrics. Salts in perspiration and ice can clog the pores of traditional nylon fabrics, decreasing their ability to keep you warm and dry. But Diaplex does not have this problem because it contains no pores. Since Diaplex is unaffected by UV light and is machine washable, it is also a durable fabric that is easy to care for.

Anatomy Connection

▶ Do some research to find out how your skin lets thermal energy and moisture escape.

▶ *When your body is cold, the Diaplex garment adjusts to prevent the transfer of thermal energy from your body to its surroundings, and you feel warmer.*

▶ *When your body gets too warm, the Diaplex garment adjusts to allow your body to transfer excess thermal energy and moisture to your surroundings, and you feel cooler.*

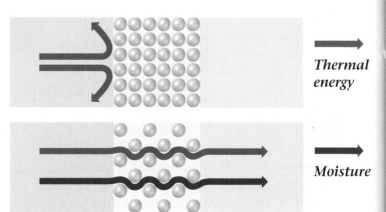

Thermal energy

Moisture

UNIT 4

Reshaping the Land

In this unit, you will learn about the way the surface of the Earth changes. There is a constant struggle between the forces that build up Earth's land features and those that break them down. The mountains built by Earth's internal forces are torn down by the actions of weathering and erosion. This timeline shows some of the events that have occurred in this struggle as natural changes in the Earth's features continue to take place.

320
Million years ago
Vast swamps along the western edge of the Appalachian Mountains are buried by sediment and form the largest coal fields in the world.

280
Million years ago
The shallow inland sea that covered much of what is now the midwestern United States fills with sediment and disappears.

1880
Cleopatra's Needle, a granite obelisk, is moved from Egypt to New York City. Within the next 100 years, the weather and pollution severely damage the 3,000-year-old monument.

1930
Carlsbad Caverns National Park is established. It features the nation's deepest limestone cave and one of the largest underground chambers in the world.

1941
Mount Rushmore is completed—an example of purposeful human erosion.

140
Million years ago

The mouth of the Mississippi River is near present-day Cairo, Illinois.

Chicago

Cairo

65
Million years ago

Dinosaurs become extinct.

6
Million years ago

The Colorado River begins to carve the Grand Canyon, which today is roughly 2 km deep.

1775

The Battle of Bunker Hill, a victory for the Colonials, takes place on a drumlin, a tear-shaped mound of sediment that was formed by an ice-age glacier 10,000 years earlier.

12,000
Years ago

The Great Lakes form at the end of the last ice age.

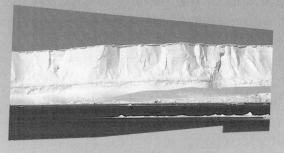

1998

Hong Kong opens a new airport on an artificial island. Almost 150 million metric tons of rock and soil were deposited in the South China Sea to form the 3,000-acre island.

1987

An iceberg twice the size of Rhode Island breaks off the edge of Antarctica's continental glacier.

Reshaping the Land **245**

10 The Flow of Fresh Water

Imagine...

Picture yourself canoeing down a gentle stream on a beautiful sunny afternoon. You can see the gravelly stream bottom through the crystal blue water.

All of a sudden, the silence is broken by the sound of rushing water. You notice that the current has picked up and the water is moving much faster. In the distance you see some large boulders and a waterfall. Unexpectedly, the canoe hits a rock and nearly topples over. You are safe, but your gear is now on a journey of its own. Rather than brave the rapids, you pull your canoe onto shore. You turn around just in time to see your cooler crash against the rocks and tumble over the falls. You think to yourself, "I didn't want tuna for lunch anyway!"

Tired, you walk downstream along the shore, the sound of the rushing falls growing fainter with each step. The stream begins to widen and slow again. Suddenly, you see your cooler washed up on a gravel bar. You run toward it, hoping the canned meat survived. Although badly scraped and empty, the cooler is still usable.

You put your cooler into your canoe and continue your journey downstream, only to again hear the sound of rushing water.

What forces of nature could cause the stream to change so drastically? In this chapter you will learn about river and stream development. You will also learn about how surface water and underground water change the face of our planet.

What Do You Think?

In your ScienceLog, try to answer the following questions based on what you already know:

1. What role does water play in shaping the surface of the Earth?

2. What is the difference between erosion and deposition?

Investigate!

Gently Down the Stream

How do streams and river systems develop? Believe it or not, the process is almost as simple as turning on a garden hose and letting the water run on the ground. How is this possible? Do the following investigation to find out.

Procedure

1. Obtain a bucket of **sand** and enough **gravel** to fill the bottom of a rectangular **plastic washtub.**

2. Spread the gravel in a layer at the bottom of the washtub. Place 4–6 cm of sand on top of the gravel. Create a slope by adding more sand to one end of the washtub.

3. Make a small hole in the bottom of a **plastic-foam cup.** Attach the cup to the inside of the tub with a **clothespin.** The cup should be placed at the end that has more sand. Fill the cup with **water,** and observe the water's movement over the sand.

4. Record your observations in your ScienceLog.

Analysis

5. At the start of your experiment, how did the moving water affect the sand?

6. As time passed, how did the moving water affect the sand?

7. How do you think your results might relate to stream development?

Going Further

Perform the same activity, but this time increase the slope of the washtub by tilting one end of the tub. You can do this by placing an ordinary object, such as a block of wood, under one end of the washtub. How does the increase in slope affect the development of the "stream"?

The Active River

You are probably familiar with the Grand Canyon, shown in **Figure 1.** But did you know that about 6 million years ago, the area now known as the Grand Canyon was nearly as flat as a pancake? The Colorado River cut down into the rock and formed the Grand Canyon over millions of years by washing billions of tons of soil and rock from its riverbed. This process is a type of *erosion*. **Erosion** is the removal and transport of surface material, such as rock and soil. Rivers are not the only agents of erosion. Wind, rain, ice, and snow can cause erosion as well.

Because of erosion caused by water, the Grand Canyon is now about 1.6 km deep and 446 km long. In this section, you will learn about stream development, river systems, and the different factors that affect the rate of stream erosion.

Figure 1 *The Grand Canyon is located in northwestern Arizona. It formed over millions of years as running water eroded rock and soil. In some places the canyon is 29 km wide.*

Have you ever wondered how rivers keep flowing and where rivers get their water? The water cycle answers these and other questions. The **water cycle,** shown on the next page, is the continuous movement of water from water sources, such as lakes or oceans, into the air, onto land, into the ground, and back to the water sources. Running-water sources, such as rivers, depend on the water cycle to maintain a constant flow of water.

The Water Cycle

Condensation occurs when water vapor cools and changes into liquid water droplets that form clouds in the atmosphere.

Precipitation is rain, snow, sleet, or hail that falls from clouds onto the Earth's surface.

Runoff is water that flows across land and collects in rivers, streams, and eventually the ocean.

Evaporation occurs when liquid water from the Earth's surface and from living organisms changes into water vapor.

Infiltration is the movement of water into the ground due to the pull of gravity.

Percolation is the downward movement of water through pores and other spaces in soil due to gravity.

Imagine that you are planning a rafting trip down the Missouri River to the Mississippi River. On a map of the United States, trace the route of your trip from the Rocky Mountains in Montana to the mouth of the Mississippi River, in Louisiana. What major tributaries would you travel past? What cities would you pass through? Mark them on the map. How many kilometers would you travel on this trip?

The Amazon River basin, in South America, is the world's largest drainage basin. It has an area of about 6 million square kilometers. That's almost twice as big as the United States' largest drainage basin, the Mississippi River basin!

River Systems

A river system is a network of streams that drains an area of its runoff. River systems begin to form when an area's precipitation is greater than its evaporation and infiltration. After the ground has soaked up all the water it can hold, the remaining water moves downslope as runoff. Sometimes runoff moving across the land will start to erode a narrow gully. With each passing rain, the water moving through the gully will make the gully wider and deeper.

River systems are divided into regions known as drainage basins, or watersheds. A **drainage basin** is the land drained by a river system, which includes the main river and all of its tributaries. **Tributaries** are smaller streams or rivers that flow into larger ones. The largest drainage basin in the United States is the Mississippi River basin. It has hundreds of tributaries that extend from the Rocky Mountains, in the West, to the Appalachian Mountains, in the East. The Ohio and Missouri Rivers are just two of the main tributaries of the Mississippi River.

A drainage basin is not simply water moving downhill in streams; it is also a system of moving energy and materials. The map in **Figure 2** shows that the Mississippi River drainage basin covers more than one-third of the United States. Other major drainage basins in the United States are the Columbia, Rio Grande, and Colorado River basins.

Drainage basins are separated from each other by an area called a **divide.** A divide is generally an area of higher ground than the basins it separates. On the map below, you can see that the Continental Divide is a major divide in the United States. On which side do you live?

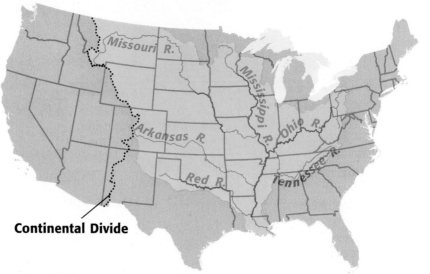

Continental Divide

Figure 2 *The Continental Divide runs through the Rocky Mountains. It separates the drainage basins that flow into the Atlantic Ocean and the Gulf of Mexico from those that flow into the Pacific Ocean.*

Stream Erosion

When a stream first forms, the water cuts downward, eroding soil and rock to create a channel. A **channel** is the path that a stream follows. At first, stream channels are small and steep. As more rock and soil are transported downstream, the channels become wider and deeper, forming broad valleys. When streams become longer, they are referred to as rivers. Have you ever wondered why some streams are fast, while others are slow? In this section, you will find answers to this and other questions.

Rates of Stream Erosion The rate of stream erosion is determined by various factors, including the stream's speed, discharge, and load. One factor that can affect the speed of a river is its gradient. **Gradient** is a measure of the change in elevation over a certain distance. Gradients are usually measured in meters per kilometer or in feet per mile. The steeper a stream's slope is, or the higher its gradient, the faster the stream will flow. A higher gradient gives a stream more energy to erode rock and soil. For example, a mountain stream has a high gradient, as shown in **Figure 3.** It flows rapidly and has more erosive energy. A stream or river on a flat plain has a low gradient, as shown in **Figure 4.** These rivers tend to flow slowly and have less erosive energy.

Discharge is the volume of water transported by a stream in a given amount of time. The discharge of a stream increases when a major storm occurs or when warm weather rapidly melts snow. As the stream's discharge increases, its erosive energy, speed, and load increase. During a drought or a dry season, the stream's discharge can become a mere trickle. When this occurs, the erosive energy, speed, and load drop dramatically.

MATH BREAK

Calculating a Stream's Gradient

If a river starts at an elevation of 4,900 m and travels 450 km downstream to a lake that is at an elevation of 400 m, what is the stream's gradient?

Figure 3 *A mountain stream has a high gradient.*

Figure 4 *A river on a flat plain has a low gradient.*

A Stream's Load The materials carried in a stream's water are collectively called the stream's **load.** The size of the particles in the stream's load is affected by the stream's speed. Fast-moving streams can carry large particles. The load also affects the stream's rate of erosion. Rocks and pebbles bounce and scrape along the bottom and sides of the bed. The illustration below shows the three ways a stream can carry its load.

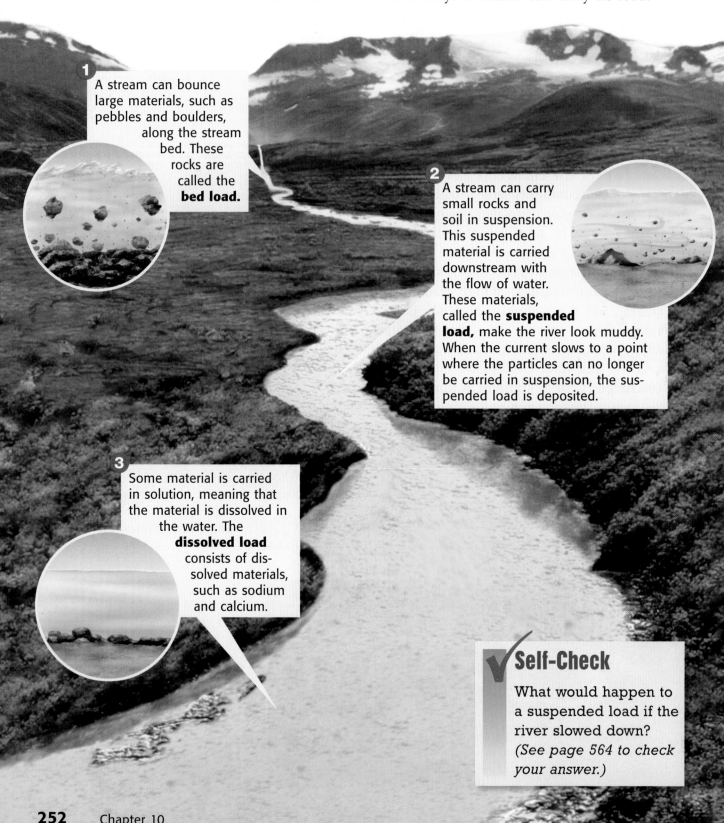

1 A stream can bounce large materials, such as pebbles and boulders, along the stream bed. These rocks are called the **bed load.**

2 A stream can carry small rocks and soil in suspension. This suspended material is carried downstream with the flow of water. These materials, called the **suspended load,** make the river look muddy. When the current slows to a point where the particles can no longer be carried in suspension, the suspended load is deposited.

3 Some material is carried in solution, meaning that the material is dissolved in the water. The **dissolved load** consists of dissolved materials, such as sodium and calcium.

✔ **Self-Check**

What would happen to a suspended load if the river slowed down? *(See page 564 to check your answer.)*

The Stages of a River

In the early 1900s, William Morris Davis developed a model that identified the stages of river development. According to this model, rivers evolve from a youthful stage to an old-age stage. Davis believed that all rivers erode in the same way and at the same rate. Today, however, scientists support a different model that considers the effects of a river's environment on stream development. For example, because different material erodes at different rates, one river may develop more quickly than another river. Many factors, including climate, gradient, and load, influence the development of a river. Although scientists no longer use Davis's model to explain river development, they still use many of his terms to describe a river. Remember, these terms do not tell the actual age of a river. Instead, they are used to describe the general characteristics of the river.

Figure 5 *This youthful river is located in Yellowstone National Park, Wyoming. The rapids and falls are located where the river flows over hard, resistant rock.*

Youthful Rivers A youthful river, like the one shown in **Figure 5,** erodes its channel deeper rather than wider. The river flows quickly because of its steep gradient. Its sides and channel are steep and straight. The river tumbles over rocks in rapids and waterfalls. Youthful rivers have few tributaries.

Mature Rivers A mature river, as shown in **Figure 6,** erodes its channel wider rather than deeper. The gradient of a mature river is not as steep as that of a youthful river, and there are fewer falls and rapids. A mature river is fed by many tributaries, and because of its good drainage, it has more discharge than a younger river.

Figure 6 *A mature river begins to curve back and forth. The bends in the river's channel are called* meanders.

Figure 7 *This old river is located in New Zealand.*

Old Rivers An old river has a low gradient and extremely low erosive power. Instead of widening and deepening its banks, the river deposits sediment in its channel and along its banks. Old rivers, like the one in **Figure 7,** are characterized by wide, flat *flood plains*, or valleys, and more meanders. Also, an older river has fewer tributaries than a mature river because the smaller tributaries have merged.

Rejuvenated Rivers Rejuvenated rivers occur where the land is raised by the Earth's tectonic forces. When land rises, the river's gradient becomes steeper. The increased gradient of a rejuvenated river allows the river to cut more deeply into the valley floor, as shown in **Figure 8.** Steplike *terraces* often form on both sides of a stream valley as a result of rejuvenation. Terraces are nearly flat portions of the landscape that end at a steep cliff.

Figure 8 *This rejuvenated river is located in Canyonlands National Park, Utah.*

REVIEW

1. How does the water cycle help to develop river systems?

2. Describe a drainage basin.

3. What are three factors that affect the rate of stream erosion?

4. **Summarizing Data** How do youthful, mature, and old rivers differ?

Stream and River Deposits

NEW TERMS

deposition   alluvial fan

alluvium   flood plain

delta

OBJECTIVES

- Describe the different types of stream deposits.
- Explain the relationship between rich agricultural regions and river flood plains.

You have learned that flowing rivers can pick up and move soil and rock. Sooner or later, this material must be deposited somewhere. **Deposition** is the process by which material is dropped, or settles. Imagine a mud puddle after a rainy day. If the water is not disturbed, the soil particles will eventually settle and the muddy water will become clear again. Deposition also forms and renews some of the world's most productive soils. People who live in the lower Mississippi River valley depend on the river to bring them new, fertile soil. Before the Aswan Dam was built on the Nile River, the lower Nile River valley, shown in **Figure 9,** was the site of an important agricultural civilization. Every year, the Nile River deposited rich soil in the valley during floods.

Figure 9 *This photograph shows the agricultural communities that lined the Nile River before the Aswan Dam was completed, in 1970. The dam interrupted the annual flooding, altering the landscape and people's livelihood.*

Deposition in Water

After rivers erode rock and soil, they deposit the rock and soil downstream. Rock and soil deposited by streams is called **alluvium.** Alluvium is dropped at places in a river where the speed of the current decreases. Take a look at **Figure 10** to see how this type of deposition occurs.

Figure 10 *Deposition occurs along the inside turns of meanders, often producing sandbars. On the outside turns, where the current flows faster, the meander's banks are eroded and the channel is deepened.*

Heavy minerals are sometimes deposited at places in a river where the current slows down. This kind of alluvium is called a *placer deposit.* Some placer deposits contain gold, as **Figure 11** shows. During the California gold rush, which began in 1849, many miners panned for gold in the placer deposits of rivers.

The current also slows when a river empties into a large body of water, such as a lake or an ocean. Much of the river's load may be deposited where the river reaches the large body of water, forming a fan-shaped deposit called a **delta.** In **Figure 12** you can see an astronaut's view of the Nile Delta. A delta usually forms on a flat surface and consists mostly of mud. These mud deposits form new land, causing the coastline to grow.

Figure 11 *Miners rushed to California in the 1850s to find gold. They often found it in the bends of rivers in placer deposits.*

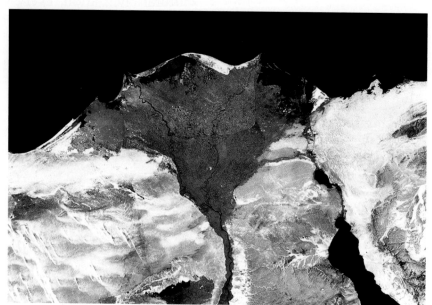

Figure 12 *Sediment is dropped at the mouth of the Nile River, forming a delta.*

If you look back at the map of the Mississippi River drainage basin in Figure 2, you can see where the Mississippi River flows into the Gulf of Mexico. This is where the Mississippi Delta has formed. Each of the fine mud particles in the delta began its journey far upstream. Parts of Louisiana are made up of particles that were transported from as far away as Montana, Minnesota, Ohio, and Illinois.

astronomy
CONNECTION

The remains of an ancient riverbed have been discovered on Mars. Satellite images show the deposits of stream channels, which indicate that liquid water once existed on the surface of this now dry and frozen planet.

Self-Check

What might cause the current of a river to slow?
(See page 564 to check your answer.)

Deposition on Land

When a fast-moving mountain stream flows onto a flat plain, the stream's speed is greatly reduced due to a decrease in the stream's gradient. As the stream slows down, it deposits alluvium where the mountain meets the flat plain, forming an alluvial fan, such as the one shown in **Figure 13. Alluvial fans** are fan-shaped deposits that form on dry land.

During periods of high rainfall or rapid snowmelt, a sudden increase in the volume of water flowing into a stream can cause the stream to overflow its banks, flooding the surrounding land. This land is called a **flood plain.** When a stream floods, a layer of alluvium is deposited across the flood plain. Each flood adds another layer of alluvium.

Flood plains are very rich farming areas because periodic flooding brings new soil to the land. However, flooding can cause extensive property damage. Much farming activity takes place in the Mississippi River valley, a large flood plain with very rich soil. When the Mississippi River flooded in 1993, however, farms were abandoned and whole towns had to be evacuated. The flood was so huge that it caused damage in nine Midwestern states. **Figure 14** shows an area that was flooded just north of St. Louis, Missouri.

Figure 13 *An alluvial fan, such as this one from the Sierra Nevada, in California, forms when a steep-gradient eroding stream changes rapidly into a low-gradient depositing stream.*

Figure 14 *The normal flow of the Mississippi River (top) and Missouri River (bottom) is shown in black. The area that was flooded when both rivers spilled over their banks in 1993 is shaded red.*

REVIEW

1. What happens to a river's flow that causes alluvium to be deposited?

2. How are alluvial fans and deltas similar? How are they different?

3. Explain why flood plains are good farming areas.

4. **Identifying Relationships** What factors increase the likelihood that alluvium will be deposited?

Water Underground

Although we can see surface water in streams and lakes, there is a lot of water flowing underground that we cannot see. The water located within the rocks below the Earth's surface is called **ground water.** Ground water not only is an important resource but also plays an important role in erosion and deposition. In order to understand erosion and deposition by ground water, you must understand where and how ground water collects.

Location of Ground Water

Surface water seeps underground into the soil and rock. Earth scientists divide this underground area into two zones. The upper zone, called the *zone of aeration,* usually is not completely filled with water. The rock and soil that make up the zone of aeration contain air spaces. These air spaces are filled with water only immediately after a rain. Farther down, the water accumulates in an area called the *zone of saturation.* Here the spaces between the rock particles are filled with water.

The zone of aeration and the zone of saturation meet at an underground boundary known as the **water table,** as shown in **Figure 15.** The water table changes with the seasons. It rises during wet seasons and drops during dry seasons. In wet regions the water table can be just beneath the soil's surface or at the surface. But in deserts the water table may be hundreds of meters underground.

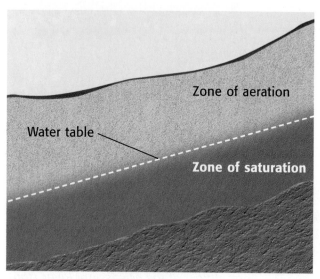

Figure 15 *The water table is the upper surface of the zone of saturation.*

Labels in figure: Zone of aeration, Water table, Zone of saturation

Aquifers

Some types of rock can hold large quantities of water, while other types can hold little or no water. A rock layer that stores and allows the flow of ground water is called an **aquifer.**

A rock layer must have two characteristics to qualify as an aquifer. First the rock layer must be *porous,* or contain open spaces. A rock's **porosity** is the amount of open space between individual rock particles. Second the rock layer must allow water to pass freely through it, from one pore to another. If the pores are connected, ground water can flow through the rock layer. A rock's ability to let water pass through it is called **permeability.** A rock that tends to stop the flow of water is impermeable.

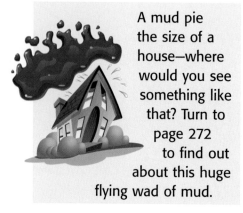

A mud pie the size of a house—where would you see something like that? Turn to page 272 to find out about this huge flying wad of mud.

The best aquifers are usually formed of sandstone, limestone, or layers of sand and gravel. Some aquifers cover large underground areas and are an important source of water for cities and agriculture. The map in **Figure 16** shows the location of aquifers in the United States. Can you locate one that your town might use?

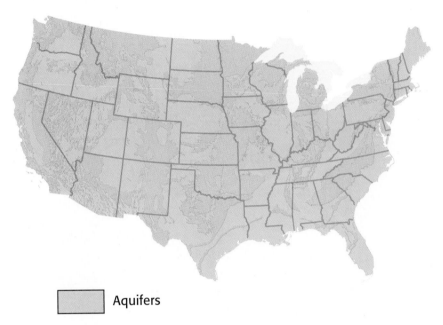

Aquifers

Figure 16 Potential Ground-Water Sources for the Continental United States

Like rivers, aquifers are dependent on the water cycle to maintain a constant flow of water. The ground surface where water enters an aquifer is called the *recharge zone*. The size of the recharge zone varies depending on how permeable rock is at the surface. In an area that contains a permeable rock layer, the water can seep down into the aquifer. In areas where the aquifer is confined on top by an impermeable rock layer, the recharge zone is restricted to areas where there is a permeable rock layer.

Springs and Wells

Ground-water movement is determined by the slope of the water table. Just like surface water, ground water tends to move downslope, toward lower elevations. If the water table reaches the Earth's surface, water will flow out from the ground, forming a *spring*. Springs are an important source of drinking water. Lakes form in low areas, where the water table is higher than the Earth's surface.

Quick **Lab**

Degree of Permeability

1. Obtain five **plastic-foam cups.**

2. Fill one cup halfway with **soil,** such as garden soil. Pack the soil.

3. Fill a second cup halfway with **sand.** Pack the sand.

4. Poke 5 to 7 holes in the bottom of each cup with a sharpened **pencil.**

5. Fill a third cup with **water.** Hold one of the remaining empty cups under the cup filled with soil. Pour the water into the top cup.

6. Allow the cup to drain for 45 seconds, and then put the cup aside (even if it is still draining). Put the cup filled with water aside.

7. Repeat steps 5 and 6 with the cup of sand. Compare the volumes of the two cups of water. The cup that allowed the most water to pass holds the more permeable sediment.

A sloping layer of permeable rock sandwiched between two layers of impermeable rock is called an *artesian formation*. The permeable rock is an aquifer, and the top layer of the impermeable rock is called a *cap rock*, as shown in **Figure 17.** Artesian formations are the source of water for **artesian springs.** Artesian springs are springs that form where cracks occur naturally in the cap rock and the pressurized water in the aquifer flows through the cracks to the surface. Artesian springs are sometimes found in deserts, where they are often the only source of water.

Figure 17 *Artesian springs form when water from an aquifer flows through cracks in the cap rock of an artesian formation.*

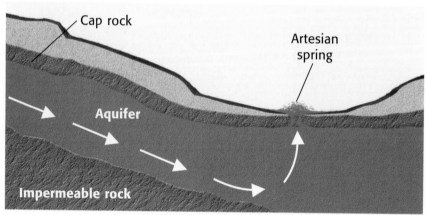

A *well* is a human-made hole that is deeper than the level of the water table; wells therefore fill with ground water, as shown in **Figure 18.** If a well is not deep enough, it will dry up when the water table falls below the bottom of the well. Also, if too many wells in an area remove ground water too rapidly, the water table will drop and all the wells will run dry.

Figure 18 *A good well is drilled deep enough so that when the water table drops, the well still contains water.*

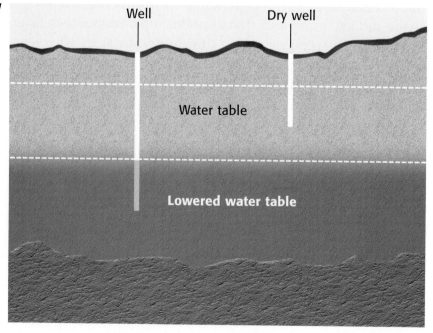

Self-Check

Why is it important that there is a layer of impermeable rock in an artesian formation?

(See page 564 to check your answer.)

Underground Erosion and Deposition

Although most ground water moves slowly, its movement still causes erosion and deposition. Unlike a river, which erodes its banks when water moves over rock and soil, ground water erodes certain types of rock by dissolving the rock. Most of the world's caves formed over thousands of years as ground water dissolved limestone. Limestone, made of calcium carbonate, dissolves easily in water, leaving behind spectacular underground features when the water drains. You can see some of these features in **Figure 19**.

Figure 19 *At Carlsbad Caverns, in New Mexico, underground passages and enormous "rooms" have been eroded below the surface of the Earth.*

While caves are formed by erosion, they are often decorated by deposition. Water that drips from a crack in a cave's ceiling leaves behind deposits of calcium carbonate. These deposits of calcium carbonate are a type of limestone called *dripstone*. Water and dissolved limestone can drip downward into a sharp, icicle-shaped dripstone feature known as a stalactite. At the same time, water drops that fall to the cave's floor add to cone-shaped dripstone features known as stalagmites. **Figure 20** shows some dripstone features formed by deposition. Can you name them?

Figure 20 *If water drips long enough, the stalactites and stalagmites can reach each other and join, forming a dripstone column.*

environmental science CONNECTION

Most bat species live in caves. These night-flying mammals navigate by sound and can reach speeds of 95 km/h. Today scientists know that bats play an extremely important role in the environment. Bats are great consumers of insects, and many bat species pollinate plants and distribute seeds.

Areas where the effects of ground-water erosion are noticeable at the surface are said to have **karst topography.** This landscape is decorated by unusual formations associated with ground-water erosion and underground caves. When the water table is lower than the level of a cave, the cave is no longer supported by the water underneath. The roof of the cave can then collapse, leaving a circular depression called a *sinkhole.* Surface streams can "disappear" into sinkholes and then flow through underground caves. Sinkholes often form lakes in areas where the water table is high. Central Florida is covered with hundreds of round sinkhole lakes. Karst valleys form where many sinkholes have grown together, leaving sharp-edged ridges. Spectacular limestone cliffs sometimes form on the edges of large sinkholes and karst valleys. After thousands of years of ground-water erosion, the level of the whole landscape is lowered. **Figure 21** shows how karst topography can affect a landscape.

Figure 21 *Karst topography is found in various regions, including the Mediterranean coast, southern China, and the United States. The photo above shows the effect of ground-water erosion in China. The photo at right shows the effects of a sinkhole in Winter Park, Florida.*

REVIEW

1. What is the water table?

2. What is an aquifer?

3. What are some of the features formed by underground erosion and deposition?

4. **Analyzing Relationships** What is the relationship between the zone of aeration, the zone of saturation, and the water table?

Using Water Wisely

All living things need water to survive. But there is a limited amount of fresh water available on Earth. Only 3 percent of Earth's water is drinkable. And of the 3 percent that is drinkable, 75 percent is frozen in the polar icecaps. That's more than 100 times the volume of water found in lakes and streams! This frozen water is not readily available for our use. Therefore, it is important that we use our water resources wisely.

Water Pollution

Surface water, such as rivers and lakes, and ground water are often polluted by waste from cities, factories, and farms. One type of pollution is called **point-source pollution** because it comes from one particular point, such as a sewer pipe or a factory drain. Fortunately, laws prohibit much of this type of pollution.

There is growing concern, however, about another type of pollution, called **nonpoint-source pollution**. This type of pollution, as shown in **Figure 22,** is much more difficult to control because it does not come from a single source. Most nonpoint-source pollution contaminates rivers and lakes by runoff. The main sources of nonpoint-source pollution are street gutters, fertilizers, eroded soils and silt from farming and logging, drainage from mines, and salts from irrigation. Some airborne acid pollutants are introduced into freshwater sources through falling rain.

As you know, ground water is an important source of fresh water. In fact, more than half of all household water in the United States comes from ground water. Farms use ground water for irrigation. Because ground water is supplied by water from the Earth's surface, ground water can become contaminated when surface water is polluted. And once polluted, ground water is very difficult and expensive to clean up.

Figure 22 *Ninety-six percent of all pollution is nonpoint-source pollution. This farm irrigator is a potential source of nonpoint-source pollution.*

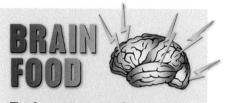
Renewing Polluted Water

When you flush the toilet or watch water go down the shower drain, do you ever wonder where this water goes? If you live in a city or large town, the water flows through sewer pipes to a sewage treatment plant. **Sewage treatment plants** are factories that clean the waste materials out of water that comes from the sewer or drains. These plants help protect the environment from water pollution. They also protect us from diseases that are easily transmitted through dirty water.

Cleaning Up Water When water reaches a sewage treatment plant, it is cleaned in two different ways. First it goes through a series of steps known as *primary treatment*. In primary treatment, dirty water is passed through a large screen to catch solid objects, such as paper, rags, and bottle caps. The water is then placed in a large tank, where smaller particles can sink and be filtered out. These particles include things such as food, coffee grounds, and soil. Any floating oils and scum are skimmed off the surface.

At this point, the water is ready for *secondary treatment*. In secondary treatment, the water is sent to an aeration tank, where it is mixed with oxygen and bacteria. The bacteria feed on the wastes and use the oxygen. The water is then sent to another settling tank, where chlorine is added to disinfect the water. The water is finally released into a water source—a stream, a lake, or the ocean. The treated water is sometimes cleaner than the water into which it is released. **Figure 23** shows the major components of a sewage treatment plant.

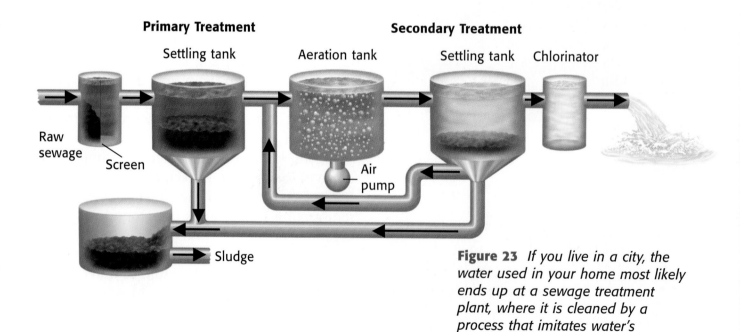

Figure 23 *If you live in a city, the water used in your home most likely ends up at a sewage treatment plant, where it is cleaned by a process that imitates water's natural cleaning cycle.*

If you live in an area without a sewage treatment plant, your house probably has a septic tank, such as the one shown in **Figure 24.** A **septic tank** is a large underground tank that collects and cleans waste water from a household. Waste water flows from the house into the tank, where the solids sink to the bottom. Bacteria consume these wastes on the bottom of the tank. The water flows from the tank into a group of buried pipes. The buried pipes distribute the water, enabling it to soak into the ground. This group of pipes is called a *drain field*.

Get your hands dirty and learn about some of the methods used to clean up water. Check out page 526 of the LabBook.

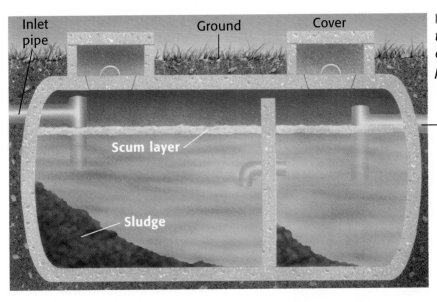

Figure 24 *Most septic tanks must be cleaned out every few years to work properly.*

Inlet pipe · Ground · Cover · Scum layer · Sludge · Outlet pipe

Where the Water Goes

The chart in **Figure 25** shows how an average household in the United States uses water. Notice that less than 8 percent of the water we use in our homes is used for drinking. The rest is used for flushing toilets, doing laundry, bathing, and watering lawns and plants.

Understanding the value of fresh water is the first step to conserving this limited resource.

Explore

After studying the chart at left and determining where the majority of water is used, think of some ways that you can decrease the amount of water that you use in your home.

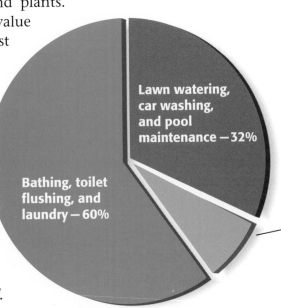

Lawn watering, car washing, and pool maintenance — 32%

Bathing, toilet flushing, and laundry — 60%

Drinking, cooking, washing dishes, running a garbage disposal — 8%

Figure 25 *The average household in the United States uses about 100 gal of water per day. This pie chart shows some common uses of this 100 gal.*

Water in Industry The chart on the previous page shows how fresh water is used in homes. Even more water is required for industry, as shown in **Figure 26.** Water is used to cool power stations, to clean industrial products, to extract minerals, and to create power for factories. Many industries are trying to conserve water by reusing it in their production processes. In the United States, most of the water used in factories is recycled at least once. At least 90 percent of this water can be treated and returned to surface water.

Ground-water supplies also need to be monitored. Although ground water is considered to be a *renewable resource,* a resource that can be replenished, recycling ground water can be a lengthy process. When overused, ground water can sometimes be categorized as a *nonrenewable resource,* a substance that cannot be replaced once it is used. Ground water collects and moves slowly, and water taken from some aquifers might not be replenished for many years. Aquifers are often overused and therefore do not have time to replenish themselves. Like surface water, ground water must be conserved.

Figure 26 **(a)** *The core of a nuclear reactor is cooled by water.* **(b)** *Highly pressurized water is used to dig in mining.* **(c)** *A dam containing water is used to generate hydroelectric power.*

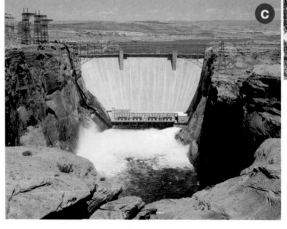

APPLY

How much water do you use when you brush your teeth? Picture yourself at home brushing your teeth. Time how long it takes you to go through the procedure. In your ScienceLog, write down the steps you take, making sure to include how many times you turn on and turn off the faucet. During what percentage of the time spent brushing your teeth is the water running? How do you think you might be wasting water? What are some ways that you could conserve water while brushing your teeth?

Water in Agriculture The Ogallala aquifer is the largest known aquifer in North America. The map in **Figure 27** shows that the Ogallala aquifer runs beneath the ground through eight states, from South Dakota to Texas. For the last 100 years, the aquifer has been used heavily for farming. The Ogallala aquifer provides water for approximately one-fifth of the cropland in the United States. Recently, the water table in the aquifer has dropped so low that some scientists say that it would take at least 1,000 years to replenish the aquifer if it were no longer used.

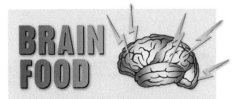

BRAIN FOOD

The Ogallala aquifer can hold enough water to fill Lake Huron. At this time, however, the aquifer is being used 25 times as fast as it is being replenished.

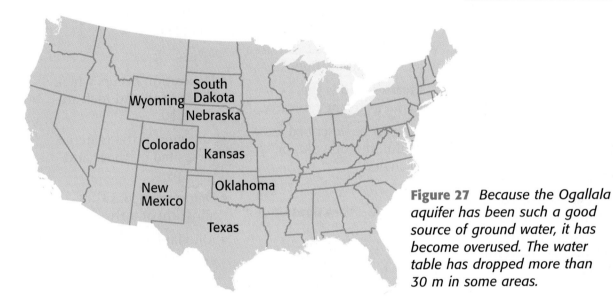

Figure 27 *Because the Ogallala aquifer has been such a good source of ground water, it has become overused. The water table has dropped more than 30 m in some areas.*

Water resources are different from other resources. Because water is necessary for life, there is no alternative resource. To protect supplies of ground water, some communities are regulating its use. These communities monitor water levels and discourage use when levels fall below a certain point.

REVIEW

1. What is the difference between point-source and non-point-source pollution?

2. Summarize the process of water treatment in a sewage treatment plant.

3. What is the difference between a renewable resource and a nonrenewable resource?

4. **Summarizing Data** How does a septic tank work?

Chapter Highlights

Vocabulary

erosion (*p. 248*)

water cycle (*p. 248*)

drainage basin (*p. 250*)

tributary (*p. 250*)

divide (*p. 250*)

channel (*p. 251*)

gradient (*p. 251*)

discharge (*p. 251*)

load (*p. 252*)

Section Notes

• Erosion is the removal and transport of soil and rock.

• The water cycle is the continuous movement of water from water sources into the air, onto land, and back into water sources.

• A drainage basin, or watershed, includes a main river and all of its tributaries.

• The rate of stream erosion is affected by many factors, including the stream's gradient, discharge, speed, and load.

• Gradient is the change in elevation over distance.

• Discharge is the volume of water moved by a stream in a given amount of time.

• A stream's load is the material a stream can carry.

• Rivers can be described as youthful, mature, old, or rejuvenated.

Labs

Water Cycle—What Goes Up . . .
(*p. 524*)

Vocabulary

deposition (*p. 255*)

alluvium (*p. 255*)

delta (*p. 256*)

alluvial fan (*p. 257*)

flood plain (*p. 257*)

Section Notes

• Deposition occurs when eroded soil and rock are dropped.

• Alluvium is the material deposited by rivers and streams.

• Deltas are deposits of alluvium at a river's mouth.

• Alluvial fans are deposits of alluvium at the base of a mountain.

• Flood plains are rich farming areas because flooding brings new soils to the area.

☑ Skills Check

Math Concepts

A STREAM'S GRADIENT One factor that can affect the speed of a river is its gradient. The gradient is a measure of the change in elevation over a certain distance. You can use the following equation to calculate a stream's gradient:

$$\text{gradient} = \frac{\text{change in elevation}}{\text{distance}}$$

For example, consider a river that starts at an elevation of 5,500 m and travels 350 km downstream to a lake, which is at an elevation of 2,000 m. By using the formula above, you would find the stream's gradient to be 10 m/km.

$$10 \text{ m/km} = \frac{(5,500 \text{ m} - 2,000 \text{ m})}{350 \text{ km}}$$

Visual Understanding

A STREAM'S LOAD Look back at the diagram on page 252 to review the different types of loads a stream can carry.

A SEWAGE TREATMENT PLANT Study Figure 23 on page 264 to review the two processes used to clean water in a sewage treatment plant.

SECTION 3

Vocabulary

ground water *(p. 258)*

water table *(p. 258)*

aquifer *(p. 258)*

porosity *(p. 258)*

permeability *(p. 258)*

artesian spring *(p. 260)*

karst topography *(p. 262)*

Section Notes

- Ground water is located below the Earth's surface. Ground water can dissolve rock, especially limestone.

- The zone of aeration and the zone of saturation meet at a boundary called the water table.

- An aquifer is a porous and permeable rock layer through which ground water flows.

- Karst topography forms when ground water erodes certain types of rock, such as limestone, by dissolving the rock.

SECTION 4

Vocabulary

point-source pollution *(p. 263)*

nonpoint-source pollution *(p. 263)*

sewage treatment plant *(p. 264)*

septic tank *(p. 265)*

Section Notes

- Sewage is treated in sewage treatment plants and in septic tanks.

- In a sewage treatment plant, water is cleaned in two different ways—primary treatment and secondary treatment.

- While water is generally considered to be a renewable resource, when overused it can sometimes be categorized as a nonrenewable resource.

Labs

Clean Up Your Act *(p. 526)*

---

 internetconnect

GO TO: go.hrw.com

Visit the **HRW** Web site for a variety of learning tools related to this chapter. Just type in the keyword:

KEYWORD: HSTDEP

 GO TO: www.scilinks.org

Visit the **National Science Teachers Association** on-line Web site for Internet resources related to this chapter. Just type in the *sci*LINKS number for more information about the topic:

TOPIC: The Grand Canyon	*sci*LINKS NUMBER: HSTE255
TOPIC: Rivers and Streams	*sci*LINKS NUMBER: HSTE260
TOPIC: Water Underground	*sci*LINKS NUMBER: HSTE265
TOPIC: Water Pollution and Conservation	*sci*LINKS NUMBER: HSTE270

Chapter Review

USING VOCABULARY

For each set of terms, identify the term that doesn't belong, and explain why.

1. tributary/river/water table

2. load/discharge/aquifer

3. delta/alluvial fan/karst topography

4. porosity/permeability/gradient

5. point-source pollution/nonpoint-source pollution/septic tank

6. primary treatment/secondary treatment/drainage basin

UNDERSTANDING CONCEPTS

Multiple Choice

7. Which of the following processes is not part of the water cycle?
   a. evaporation
   b. infiltration
   c. condensation
   d. deposition

8. Which type of stream load makes a river look muddy?
   a. bed load
   b. dissolved load
   c. suspended load
   d. gravelly load

9. What features are common in youthful river channels?
   a. meanders
   b. flood plains
   c. rapids
   d. sandbars

10. Which depositional feature is found at the coast?
    a. delta
    b. flood plain
    c. alluvial fan
    d. placer deposit

11. Karst topography is mainly a product of
    a. erosion by rivers.
    b. river deposition.
    c. water pollution.
    d. erosion by ground water.

12. The largest drainage basin in the United States is the
    a. Amazon.
    b. Columbia.
    c. Colorado.
    d. Mississippi.

13. An aquifer must be
    a. nonporous and nonpermeable.
    b. nonporous and permeable.
    c. porous and nonpermeable.
    d. porous and permeable.

14. Which of the following is a point source of water pollution?
    a. fertilizer from a farming area
    b. runoff from city streets
    c. a waste-water pipe
    d. leaking septic tanks

15. During primary treatment at a sewage treatment plant,
    a. water is sent to an aeration tank.
    b. water is mixed with bacteria and oxygen.
    c. dirty water is passed through a large screen.
    d. water is sent to a settling tank where chlorine is added.

Short Answer

16. What is the relationship between tributaries and rivers?

17. How are aquifers replenished?

18. Why are caves usually found in limestone-rich regions?

Concept Mapping

19. Use the following terms to create a concept map: zone of aeration, zone of saturation, water table, gravity, porosity, permeability.

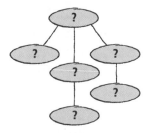

CRITICAL THINKING AND PROBLEM SOLVING

Write one or two sentences to answer the following questions:

20. What role does water play in erosion and deposition?

21. What are the features of a river channel that has a steep gradient?

22. Why is ground water hard to clean up?

23. Imagine you are hiking beside a mature stream. What would the stream be like?

24. How can water be considered both a renewable and a nonrenewable resource? Give an example of each case.

MATH IN SCIENCE

25. A sinkhole has formed in a town with a population of 5,000. The town is declared a disaster area, and $2 million is given to the town by the federal government. The local government uses 60 percent of the money for repairs to city property, and the rest is given to the townspeople.
    a. How much would each person receive?
    b. If there are 2,000 families in the town, how much would each family receive?
    c. Would each family receive enough money to help them rebuild a home? If not, how could the money be distributed more fairly?

INTERPRETING GRAPHICS

The hydrograph below illustrates river flow over a period of 1 year. The discharge readings are from the Yakima River, in Washington. The Yakima River flows eastward from the Cascade Mountains to the Columbia River.

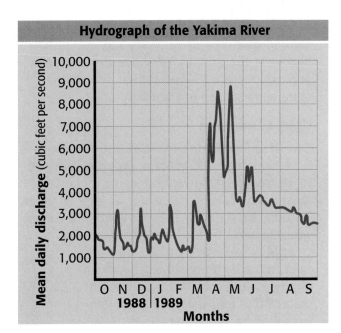

26. In which months is there the highest river discharge?

27. Why is there such a high river discharge during these months?

28. What might cause the peaks in river discharge between November and March?

NOW What Do You Think?

Take a minute to review the answers to the ScienceLog questions on page 247. Have your answers changed? If necessary, revise your answers based on what you have learned since you began this chapter.

WEIRD SCIENCE

BUBBLE, BOIL, & SQUIRT

In parts of Yellowstone National Park boiling water blasts into the sky, lakes of strange-colored mud boil and gurgle, and hot gases hiss from the ground. What are these strange geologic features? What causes them? The story begins deep in the Earth.

Old Geysers

One of Yellowstone's main tourist attractions is a *geyser* called Old Faithful. Erupting every 60 to 70 minutes, Old Faithful sends a plume of steam and scalding-hot water as high as 60 m into the air. A geyser is formed when a narrow vent connects one or more underground chambers to Earth's surface. These underground chambers are heated by nearly molten rock. As underground water flows into the vent and chambers, it is heated above 100°C. The superheated water quickly turns to steam and explodes first toward the surface and then into the air. And Old Faithful erupts right on schedule!

Nature's Hot Tub

A *hot spring* is a geyser without pressure. Its vents are wider than a geyser's, and they let the underground water cool a little and flow to the surface rather than erupt in a big fountain. To be called a hot spring, the water must be at least as warm as human body temperature (37°C). Some underground springs are several hundred degrees Celsius.

Flying Mud Pies

Mud pots form when steam or hot underground water trickles to the surface and chemically weathers and dissolves surface features, such as rocks. The mixture of dissolved rock and water creates a boiling, bubbling pool of sticky liquid clay. But don't get too close! Occasionally, the steam will rise quickly and forcefully enough to make the mud pot behave like a volcano. When it does, a mud pot can toss car-sized gobs of mud high into the air!

Some mud pots become *paint pots* when microorganisms or brightly colored minerals are mixed in. For instance, if there is a lot of iron in the mud, the paint pot will turn reddish brown or yellowish brown. Other minerals and bacteria can make the mud white or bluish in color. Some paint pots may even gurgle up blobs in several different colors.

▲ *Mud Pot in Yellowstone National Park*

What Do You Think?

▶ Some people believe that tapping geothermal energy sources such as geysers could harm the delicate ecology of those sources. Find out about the benefits and the risks of using geothermal energy. What is your opinion?

EYE ON THE ENVIRONMENT

Disaster Along the Delta

As the sun rises over the delta wetlands of the Mississippi River, fishermen test their skills. Long-legged birds step lightly through the marsh, hunting fish or frogs for breakfast. And hundreds of species of plants and animals start another day in this fragile ecosystem. But the delta ecosystem is in danger of being destroyed.

The threat comes from efforts to make the Mississippi more useful. Large portions of the river bottom were dredged to make the river deeper for ship traffic. Underwater channels were built to control flooding. What no one realized was that sediments that were once deposited to form new land now pass through the deep channels and flow out into the ocean.

Those river sediments replaced the land that was lost every year to erosion. Without the sediments, the river can't replace the land lost to erosion. And so the Mississippi River delta is disappearing. By 1995, more than half the wetlands were already gone, swept out to sea by waves along the Louisiana coast.

▲ *The Mississippi River flows from Minnesota through the Midwest to the Gulf of Mexico in the southern United States.*

Sedimental Journey

The Mississippi River journeys 3,766 km to empty 232 million metric tons of sediment into the Gulf of Mexico each year. The end of the Mississippi River delta forms the largest area of wetlands in North America. A *delta* forms when sediments settle at the mouth of a river. At the Mississippi River delta, the sediments build up and form new land along the Louisiana coastline. The area around the delta is called *wetlands.* It has fertile soil, which produces many crops, and a variety of habitats—marsh, freshwater, and saltwater—that support many species of plants and animals.

Taking Action to Preserve the Delta

Since the mid-1980s, local, state, and federal governments, along with Louisiana citizens and businesses, have been working together to monitor and restore the Mississippi River delta. Some projects to protect the delta include filling in canals that divert the sediments and even using old Christmas trees as fences to trap the sediments! With the continued efforts of scientists, government leaders, and concerned citizens, the Mississippi River delta stands a good chance of recovering.

Explore the Delta

▶ Find out more about the industries and organisms that depend on the Mississippi River delta for survival. What will happen to them if we don't take care of the ecosystem?

This Really Happened!

The waves struck at the ocean cliffs, releasing their energy as they do every day. But on this day the waves seemed different—larger and more explosive, cutting away at the rock with each crash.

On February 8, 1998, unusually large waves crashed against the cliffs along Broad Beach Road in Malibu, California. Eventually the ocean-eroded cliffs buckled, causing a landslide. One house collapsed into the ocean, while two more dangled on the edge of the cliff's newly eroded face. How did this happen? What made these waves stronger than usual?

This is all part of the ongoing natural process of coastal erosion along the California shoreline and similar shorelines throughout the world. Winter storms create powerful waves that crash into the cliffs, breaking off pieces of rock that fall into the ocean. Sometimes these natural processes are underestimated, and lives and property are put at risk.

In this chapter, you will study the force of waves on coastlines and how this force changes the landscape. You will also study the effects of wind, moving ice, and the pull of gravity on the landscape.

In your ScienceLog, try to answer the following questions based on what you already know:

1. What do waves and wind have in common?

2. How do waves, wind, and ice erode and deposit rock materials?

Investigate!

Making Waves

Waves move onto the shore continuously. But have you ever thought about how they affect the shoreline? See for yourself by creating waves of your own.

Procedure

1. Fill a **washtub** with **water** to a depth of 5 cm.

2. Make a beach by adding **sand** to one end of the washtub.

3. In your ScienceLog, sketch the beach profile (side view), and label it "A."

4. Place a **block** at the end of the washtub opposite the beach. Move the block up and down very slowly to create small waves for 2 minutes. Sketch the new beach profile in your ScienceLog, and label it "B."

5. Again place a block at the end of the washtub opposite the beach. Move the block up and down more rapidly to create large waves for 2 minutes. Sketch the new beach profile in your ScienceLog, and label it "C."

Analysis

6. Compare beach profiles A, B, and C. What is happening to the beach?

7. How do small waves and large waves erode the beach differently?

8. What other factors might contribute to beach erosion?

Going Further

On the Internet, explore how coastal erosion affects personal property along the West Coast. Learn about the methods used to slow down coastal erosion.

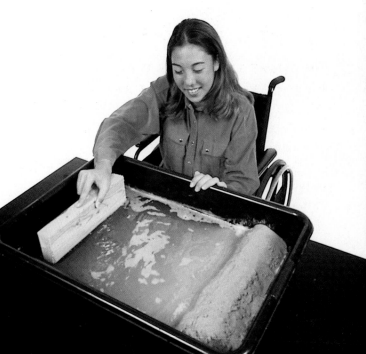

Section 1

Shoreline Erosion and Deposition

NEW TERMS

shoreline
beach
longshore current

OBJECTIVES

- Explain the connection between storms and wave erosion.
- Explain how waves break in shallow water.
- Describe how beaches form.
- Describe types of coastal landforms created by wave action.

What images pop into your head when you hear the word *beach*? You probably picture sand, blue ocean as far as the eye can see, balmy breezes, and waves. In this section you will learn how all those things relate to erosion and deposition along the shoreline. A **shoreline** is where land and a body of water meet. *Erosion,* as you may recall, is the breakdown and movement of materials. *Deposition* takes place when these materials are dropped. Waves can be powerful agents of erosion and deposition, as you will soon learn.

Wave Energy

Have you ever noticed the tiny ripples created by your breath when you blow on a cup of hot chocolate to cool it? Similarly, the wind moves over the ocean surface, producing ripples called *waves.* The size of a wave depends on how hard the wind is blowing and the length of time the wind blows. The harder and longer the wind blows, the bigger the wave is. Try it the next time you drink cocoa.

The wind that comes from severe winter storms and summer hurricanes generally produces the large waves that cause shoreline erosion. Waves may travel hundreds or even thousands of kilometers from a storm before reaching the shoreline. Some of the largest waves to reach the California coast are produced by storms as far away as Alaska and Australia. Thus, the California surfer in **Figure 1** can ride a wave produced by a storm on the other side of the Pacific Ocean.

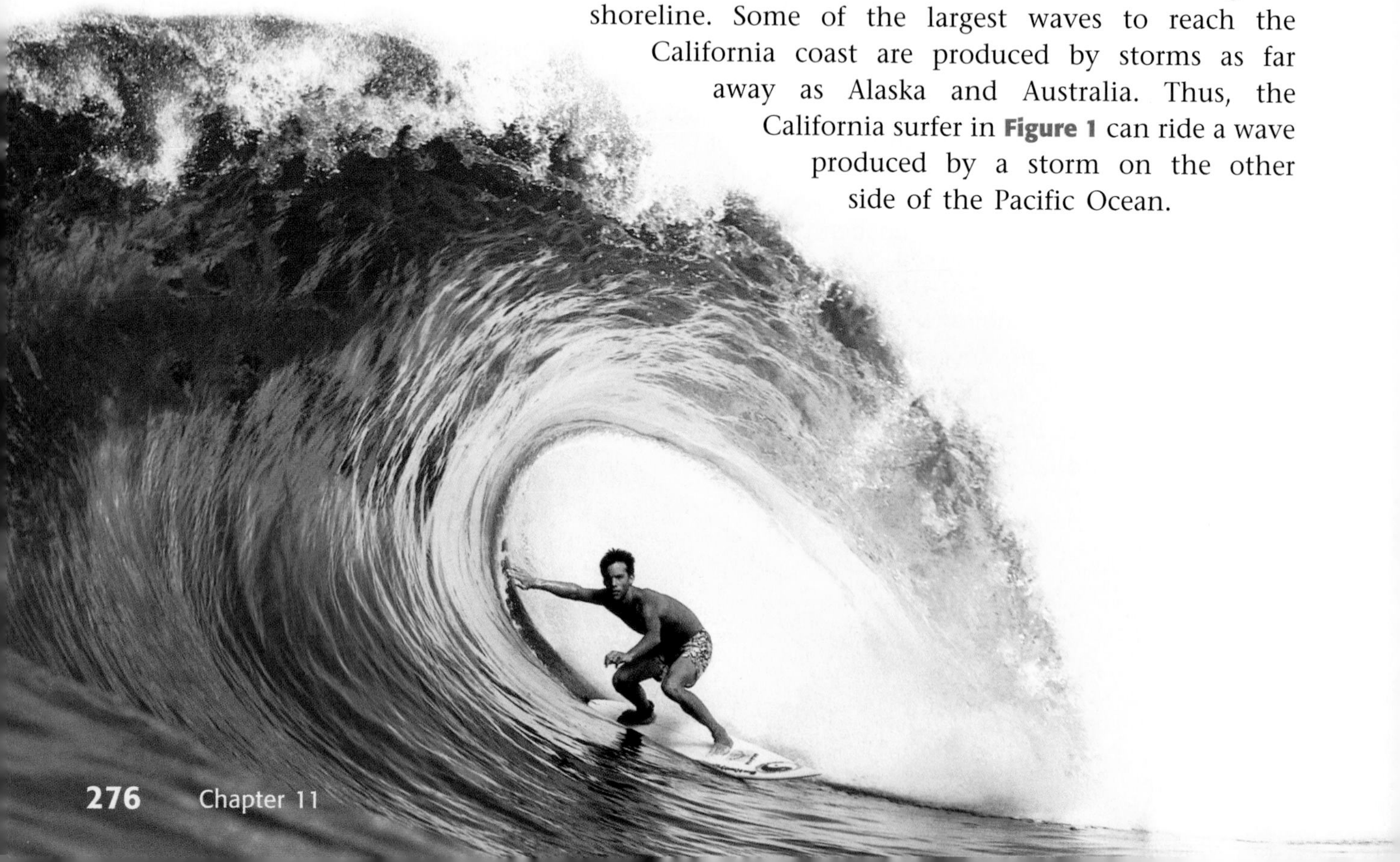

Figure 1 *Waves produced by storms on the other side of the Pacific Ocean propel this surfer toward a California shore.*

Wave Trains On your imaginary visit to the beach, do you remember seeing just one wave? Of course not; waves don't move alone. They travel in groups called *wave trains*. As wave trains move away from their source, they travel through the ocean water without interruption. When they reach shallow water, they change form and begin to break. The ocean floor crowds the lower part of the wave, shortening the wave length and increasing the wave height. This results in taller, more closely spaced waves. When the top of the wave becomes so tall that it cannot support itself, it begins to curl and break. These breaking waves are known as *surf*. Now you know how surfers got their name.

If you've ever heard a surf report, it might have sounded like this: "10- to 12-foot waves from the southwest at 12-second intervals." This type of report gives the wave height, the direction the wave is moving, and the wave period. The *wave period*, as shown in **Figure 2,** is the time interval between breaking waves. Wave periods are usually 10 to 20 seconds long.

The Pounding Surf One reason waves are so effective at picking up, transporting, and depositing material is that they are continually breaking. Another reason is that a tremendous amount of energy is released when waves break, as shown in **Figure 3.** A crashing wave can break solid rock or throw broken rocks back against the shore. The rushing water in breaking waves can easily wash into cracks in rock, helping to break off large boulders or fine grains of sand. The loose sand picked up by the waves polishes and wears down coastal rocks. Waves can also move sand and small rocks and deposit them in other locations, forming beaches.

Figure 2 *Because waves travel in wave trains, they break at regular intervals, such as every 10 to 20 seconds.*

MATH BREAK

Counting Waves

How many waves do you think reach a shoreline in a day if the wave period is 10 seconds?
(Hint: Calculate how many waves occur in a minute, in an hour, and in a day.)

Figure 3 *Breaking waves crash against the rocky shore, releasing their energy.*

✓ Self-Check

Would a large wave or a small wave have more erosive energy? Why? *(See page 564 to check your answer.)*

Agents of Erosion and Deposition   **277**

Wave Deposits

Waves carry an assortment of materials, including sand, rock fragments, and shells. Often this material is deposited on the shore. But as you will learn, this is not always the case.

England

U.S. Virgin Islands

Hawaii

California

Figure 4 *Beaches are made of different types of material deposited by waves.*

Beaches You would probably recognize a beach if you saw one. But technically, a **beach** is any area of the shoreline made up of material deposited by waves. Some beach material arrives on the shoreline by way of rivers. Rivers erode mountains, hills, and higher ground. Some of the eroded material is then carried by the river to the ocean and deposited where the river enters the sea. Later, ocean waves interacting with currents move and redeposit the material along the shoreline. Other beach material is eroded from areas located near the shoreline.

Not all beaches are the same. Compare the beaches shown in **Figure 4.** Notice that the colors and textures vary. This is because the type of material found on a beach depends on its source. Light-colored sand is the most common beach material. Much of this sand comes from the quartz in continental rock. But not all beaches are made of light-colored sand. For instance, on many tropical islands, beaches are made of fine white coral material, and some Florida beaches are made of tiny pieces of broken seashells. In Hawaii, there are black sand beaches made of eroded volcanic lava. In areas where stormy seas are common, beaches are made of pebbles and larger rocks.

Wave Angle Makes a Difference The movement of sand along a beach depends on the angle at which the waves strike the shore. Most waves approach the beach at a slight angle and retreat in a direction more perpendicular to the shore. This moves the sand in a zigzag pattern along the beach, as you can see in **Figure 5.**

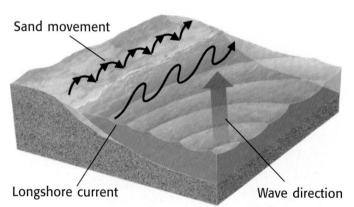

Sand movement

Longshore current

Wave direction

Figure 5 *When waves strike the shoreline at an angle, sand migrates along the beach in a zigzag path.*

Offshore Deposits Waves moving at an angle to the shoreline push water along the shore, creating longshore currents. A **longshore current** is a movement of water parallel to and near the shoreline. Sometimes waves erode material from the shoreline, and a longshore current transports and deposits it offshore, creating landforms in open water. Some of these landforms are shown in **Figure 6.**

Figure 6 Three Common Types of Offshore Deposits

A **sandbar** is an underwater or exposed ridge of sand, gravel, or shell material.

A **barrier spit,** like Cape Cod, Massachusetts, occurs when an exposed sandbar is connected to the shoreline.

A **tombolo** is an offshore island connected to the shore by deposited material. Morro Rock is an old piece of sea floor that has been raised and has resisted erosion better than surrounding rocks. It is now connected to the shore by a ridge of beach sand.

Wave Erosion

Wave erosion produces a variety of features along a shoreline. *Sea cliffs,* like the ones in **Figure 7,** are formed when waves erode and undercut rock, producing steep slopes. Waves strike the base of the cliff, wearing away the soil and rock and making the cliff steeper. The rate at which the sea cliffs erode depends on the hardness of the rock and the energy delivered by the wave. Sea cliffs made of hard rock, such as granite, erode very slowly. Other sea cliffs, such as those made of soft sedimentary rock, erode rapidly, especially during storms.

Figure 7 *Ocean-view homes built on sedimentary rock are often threatened as cliffs erode.*

Much of the erosion responsible for landforms you might see along the shoreline takes place during storms. Large waves generated by storms release far more energy on the shoreline than normal waves. This energy is so powerful that it is capable of removing huge chunks of rock. The following illustrations show some of the major landscape features that result from wave erosion.

Coastal Landforms Created by Wave Erosion

Sea stacks are offshore columns of resistant rock that were once connected to a sea cliff or headland. In these instances, waves have eroded the sea cliffs and headland, leaving behind isolated columns of rock.

Sea arches form when wave action continues to erode a sea cave, cutting completely through the headland.

Sea caves form when waves cut large holes into fractured or weak rock along the base of sea cliffs. Sea caves are common in limestone cliffs, where the rock is usually quite soft.

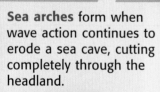

A **headland** is a finger-shaped projection that occurs when cliffs formed of hard rock erode more slowly than surrounding rock. On many shorelines, hard rock will form headlands, and the softer rock will form beaches or bays. Thus, the coastline will alternate between small, pocket-shaped beaches and rocky headlands. This type of shoreline is very common on the West Coast of the United States.

The state of Louisiana is shrinking! Find out why on page 303.

A **wave-cut terrace** forms when a sea cliff is worn back, producing a nearly level platform beneath the water at the base of the cliff. Here the waves break down the materials eroded from the sea cliffs. As the waves cause the cliff to retreat, rocks eroded from the base of the cliff scrape the wave-cut terrace until it is almost flat.

REVIEW

1. What is the source of energy for waves?

2. What are some ways that waves shape the shoreline?

3. Explain how beaches form and why all beaches are not the same.

4. **Summarizing Data** Describe the way beach sand is moved along the shoreline.

Wind Erosion and Deposition

Have you ever tried to track a moving rock? Sounds silly, but people are keeping tabs on some rocks that keep sneaking around behind their backs. To find out more, turn to page 302.

Most of us at one time or another have been frustrated by a gusty wind that blew an important stack of papers all over the place. Remember how fast and far the papers traveled, and how it took forever to pick them up because every time you caught up with them they were on the move again? If you are familiar with this scene, then you already know how wind erosion works. Certain locations are more vulnerable to wind erosion than others. Areas with fine, loose rock material that have little protective plant cover can be significantly affected by the wind. Plant roots anchor sand and soil in place, reducing the amount of wind erosion. The landscapes most commonly shaped by wind processes are deserts and coastlines.

Process of Wind Erosion

Wind moves material in different ways. In areas where strong winds occur, material is moved by saltation. **Saltation** is the movement of sand-sized particles by a skipping and bouncing action in the direction the wind is blowing. As you can see in **Figure 8,** the wind causes the particles to bounce. When bouncing sand particles knock into one another, some particles bounce up in the air and fall forward, striking other sand particles. The impact may in turn cause these particles to roll forward or bounce up in the air.

Figure 8 *The wind causes sand grains to move by saltation.*

Wind

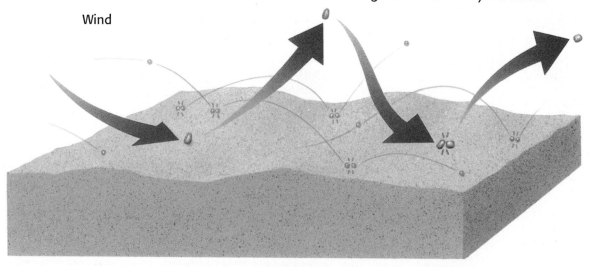

Two other major processes of wind erosion are *deflation* and *abrasion*. **Deflation** is the lifting and removal of fine sediment by wind. During deflation, wind removes the top layer of fine sediment or soil, leaving behind rock fragments that are too heavy to be lifted by the wind. This hard, rocky surface, consisting of pebbles and small broken rocks, is known as *desert pavement*. An example is shown in **Figure 9.**

Figure 9 *Desert pavement, such as that found in the Painted Desert, in Arizona, forms when wind removes all the fine materials.*

Have you ever blown on a layer of dust while cleaning off a dresser? If you have, you might have noticed that in addition to your face getting dirty, a little scooped-out depression formed in the dust. Similarly, where there is little vegetation, wind may scoop out depressions in the sand. These depressions, like the one shown in **Figure 10,** are known as *deflation hollows.*

Figure 10 *Deflation hollows may begin as depressions less than 1 m across. But continued wind erosion can cause them to become hundreds of meters wide and many meters deep.*

Quick Lab

Making Desert Pavement

1. Spread out a mixture of sediments across a **board** or **table** outdoors. Make sure you have a combination of **dust, sand,** and **gravel.**

2. Place an **electric fan** at one end of the board or table.

3. Put on **safety goggles** and a **filter mask.** Aim the fan across the sediment. Start the fan on its lowest speed. Record your observations in your ScienceLog.

4. Turn the fan to a medium speed and then to the highest speed to imitate a wind storm in the desert. Again record your observations.

5. What is the relationship between the wind speed and the sediment size that is moved?

6. Does the remaining sediment fit the definition of desert pavement?

Self-Check

Why do deflation hollows form in areas where there is little vegetation? *(See page 564 to check your answer.)*

When a long period without rain, known as a *drought,* occurs, areas that are farmed or overgrazed can suffer extensive soil loss and dense dust storms. The removal of plants exposes the soil, making it more vulnerable to wind erosion. Dust storms occur when strong winds lift large amounts of dust into the atmosphere. During the 1930s, a section of the Great Plains suffered severe wind erosion and dust storms. This area became known as the *Dust Bowl.* The dust darkened the skies so much that street lights were left on during the day in Midwestern cities. In areas where the conditions were even worse, people had to string ropes from their houses to their barns so they wouldn't get lost in the dense dust. The dust was so bad that people slept with damp cloths over their face to keep from choking. Describe the major erosional process that caused the Dust Bowl.

Turn on a hair dryer—no, not to style your hair, but to find out how dunes migrate. Check out page 530 of the LabBook.

Abrasion is the grinding and wearing down of rock surfaces by other rock or sand particles. Abrasion commonly occurs in areas where there are strong winds, loose sand, and soft rocks. The blowing of millions of sharp sand grains creates a sandblasting effect that helps to erode, smooth, and polish rocks. These wind-polished rocks are called *ventifacts.* The polished side of a ventifact faces the wind.

Wind-Deposited Materials

Like a stack of papers blowing in the wind, all the material carried by the wind is eventually deposited downwind. The amount and size of particles the wind can carry depend on wind speed. The faster the wind blows, the more material and the heavier the particles it can carry. As wind speed slows, heavier particles are deposited first.

Dunes When the wind hits an obstacle, such as a plant or a rock, it slows down. As the wind slows, it deposits, or drops, the heavier material. As the material collects, it creates an additional obstacle. This obstacle causes even more material to be deposited, forming a mound. Eventually even the original obstacle becomes buried. The mounds of wind-deposited sand are called **dunes.** Dunes are common in deserts and along the shores of lakes and oceans.

Dunes tend to move in the direction of strong prevailing winds. Different wind conditions produce dunes in various shapes and sizes. A dune usually has a gently sloped side and a steeply sloped side, or *slip face,* as shown in **Figure 11.** In most cases, the gently sloped side faces the wind. The wind is constantly transporting material up this side of the dune. As sand moves over the crest, or peak, of the dune, it slides down the slip face, creating a steep slope.

The largest sand dunes ever recorded were found in east-central Algeria in the Sahara. These dunes measured about 4.8 km long and 430 m high.

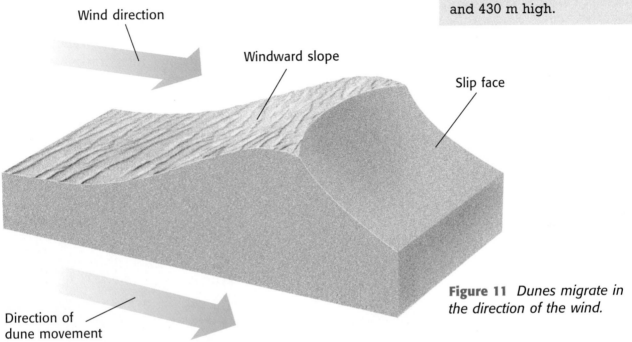

Wind direction

Windward slope

Slip face

Direction of dune movement

Figure 11 *Dunes migrate in the direction of the wind.*

Disappearing Dunes

Dunes provide homes for hundreds of plant and animal species, including the desert tortoise. This tortoise, found in the Mojave and Sonoran Deserts of the southwestern United States, is able to live where ground temperatures are very hot. It escapes the heat by digging burrows in the sand dunes. The desert tortoise has a problem, though. Dune buggies and other motorized vehicles are destroying the dunes. Dunes are easily disturbed and are vulnerable to erosion. Motorized off-road vehicles break down dunes, destroying habitat for the tortoise as well as many other animal and plant species. For this reason, state and federal wildlife and land-management agencies have taken an active role in helping protect habitat for the desert tortoise and other sensitive desert species by making some areas off-limits to off-road vehicles.

The sidewinder adder is a poisonous snake that lives in the dunes of the Namib Desert, in southwestern Africa. It is called a sidewinder because of the way it rolls its body to one side as it moves across the sand. This motion allows the snake to move above the loose, sliding sand. Its close cousin, the sidewinder rattlesnake, found in the deserts of the southwestern United States, uses a similar motion to move. The sidewinder adder's scales look like sand grains. When hiding and waiting for prey, it buries itself in the sand with only its eyes showing above the surface like two dark sand grains.

Loess Wind can deposit material much finer than sand. Thick deposits of this windblown, fine-grained sediment are known as **loess** (LOH es). Loess is very fine and feels much like the talcum powder you use after a shower.

Because wind carries fine-grained material much higher and farther than it carries sand, loess deposits are sometimes found far away from their source. A large area of China is covered completely with loess. This windblown sediment is thought to have originated in the Gobi Desert of Mongolia.

Many loess deposits came from glacial sources during the last ice age. Loess is present in much of the midwestern United States, along the eastern edge of the Mississippi Valley, and in eastern Oregon and Washington. Huge bluffs of loess are found in Mississippi, as shown in **Figure 12.**

Loess deposits can easily be prepared for growing crops and are responsible for the success of many of the grain-growing areas of the world. Outside the United States, these "breadbaskets" are found in Argentina, Ukraine, central Europe, New Zealand, and China.

Figure 12 *The thick loess deposits found in Mississippi contribute to the state's fertile soil.*

REVIEW

1. What areas have the greatest amount of wind erosion and deposition? Why?

2. Explain the process of saltation.

3. What is the difference between a dune and a loess deposit?

4. **Analyzing Relationships** Explain the relationship between deflation and dune movement.

Erosion and Deposition by Ice

OBJECTIVES

- Summarize why glaciers are important agents of erosion and deposition.
- Explain how ice in a glacier flows.
- Describe some of the landforms eroded by glaciers.
- Describe some of the landforms deposited by glaciers.

Can you imagine an ice cube the size of a football stadium? Well, glaciers can be even bigger than that. A **glacier** is an enormous mass of moving ice. Because glaciers are very heavy and have the ability to move across the Earth's surface, they are capable of eroding, moving, and depositing large amounts of rock materials. And while you will never see a glacier chilling a punch bowl, you might one day visit some of the spectacular landscapes carved by glacial activity.

Glaciers—Rivers of Ice

Glaciers form in areas so cold that snow stays on the ground year-round. Areas like these, where you can chill a can of juice by simply carrying it outside, are found at high elevations and in polar regions. Because the average temperature is freezing or near freezing, snow piles up year after year. Eventually, the weight of the snow on top causes the deep-packed snow to become ice crystals, forming a giant ice mass. These ice packs then become slow-moving "rivers of ice" as they are set in motion by the pull of gravity on their extraordinary mass.

Types of Glaciers There are two main types of glaciers, *alpine* and *continental*. **Figure 13** shows an alpine glacier. As you can see, this type of glacier forms in mountainous areas. One common type of alpine glacier is a *valley glacier*. Valley glaciers form in valleys originally created by stream erosion. These glaciers flow slowly downhill, widening and straightening the valleys into broad U-shapes as they travel downward. *Piedmont glaciers*, another type of alpine glacier, form at the base of mountain ranges.

Figure 13 *Alpine glaciers start as snowfields in mountainous areas.*

How far do you think the iceberg that struck the *Titanic* drifted before the two met that fateful night in 1912? Plot on a map of the North Atlantic Ocean the route of the *Titanic* from Southampton, England, to New York. Then plot a possible route of the drifting iceberg from Greenland to where the ship sank, just south of the Canadian island province of Newfoundland.

Not all glaciers are true "rivers of ice." In fact, some glaciers continue to get larger, spreading across entire continents. These glaciers, called continental glaciers, are huge continuous masses of ice. **Figure 14** shows the largest type of this glacier, a *continental ice sheet*. Ice sheets can cover millions of square kilometers with ice. The continent of Antarctica is almost completely covered by one of the largest ice sheets in the world, as you can see below. This ice sheet is approximately one and a half times the size of the United States. It is so thick—more than 4,000 m in places—that it buries everything but the highest mountain peaks.

Antarctica 91%

Figure 14 *Antarctica contains approximately 91 percent of all the glacial ice on the planet.*

A continental ice sheet usually has a dome-shaped center of snow and ice accumulation. Ice flows from the center to the outer edges of the ice sheet and beyond. An area where the ice is attached to the ice sheet but is resting on open water is called an *ice shelf.* The largest ice shelf is the Ross Ice Shelf, shown in **Figure 15,** which is attached to the ice sheet that covers Antarctica. This ice shelf covers an area of ocean about the size of Texas.

Figure 15 *Icebergs break off the Ross Ice Shelf into the Ross Sea.*

Large pieces of ice that break off an ice shelf and drift into the ocean are called **icebergs.** The process by which an iceberg forms is called *calving.* Calving can be a spectacular event, with huge pieces of ice falling into the sea producing giant splashes and waves. Because most of an iceberg is below the surface of the water, it can be a hazard for ships that cannot see how far the iceberg extends. In the North Atlantic Ocean near Newfoundland, the *Titanic* struck an iceberg that calved off the Greenland ice sheet.

Movement of Glaciers When enough ice builds up on a slope, the ice begins to move downhill. The thickness of the ice and the steepness of the slope determine how fast a glacier will move. Thick glaciers move faster than thin glaciers, and the steeper the slope is, the faster the glacier will move. Glaciers move by two different methods. Glaciers move when the weight of the ice causes the ice at the bottom to melt. The water from the melted ice allows the glacier to move forward, like a partially melted ice cube moving across your kitchen counter. Glaciers also move when solid ice crystals within the glacier slip over each other, causing a slow forward motion. However, scientists have found that the rate of movement is not the same for all parts of the glacier. This process is similar to placing a deck of cards on a table and then tilting the table. The top cards will slide farther than the lower cards. Like the cards, the upper part, or surface, of the glacier flows faster than the glacier's base. Also, the center of the glacier flows faster than its sides and base. This is because friction caused by contact of the glacier's sides and base with the rock surface slows the flow rate.

As a glacier flows forward, sometimes crevasses occur. A **crevasse,** as shown in **Figure 16,** is a large crack that forms where the glacier picks up speed or flows over a high point. Crevasses form because the ice cannot stretch quickly, and it cracks. Crevasses can be dangerous for people who are traveling across glaciers because a bridge layer of snow can hide them from view.

Many icebergs now being calved by Alaskan glaciers are made of millions of snowflakes that fell at about the time Columbus arrived in the Americas.

MATH BREAK

Speed of a Glacier

An alpine glacier is estimated to be moving forward at 5 m per day. Calculate how long it will take for the ice to reach a road and campground located 0.5 km from the front of the advancing glacier.

1 km = 1,000 m

Figure 16 *Crevasses can be dangerous for mountain climbers who must cross glaciers.*

Self-Check

How are ice crevasses related to glacier flow? *(See page 564 to check your answer.)*

Landforms Carved by Glaciers

Alpine glaciers and continental glaciers produce landscapes that are very different from one another. Alpine glaciers carve out rugged features in the mountain rocks through which they flow. Continental glaciers smooth the landscape by scraping and removing features that existed before the ice appeared, flattening even some of the highest mountains. **Figure 17** and **Figure 18** show the very different landscapes that each glacial type produces.

Figure 17 *Continental glaciers smooth and flatten the landscape.*

Figure 18 *The hard ice of alpine glaciers carved out this rugged landscape.*

Alpine glaciers carve out large amounts of rock material, creating spectacular landforms. These glaciers are responsible for landscapes such as the Rocky Mountains and the Alps. **Figure 19** shows the kind of landscape that is sculpted by alpine glacial erosion and revealed after the ice melts back.

Figure 19 Landscape Features Carved by Alpine Glaciers

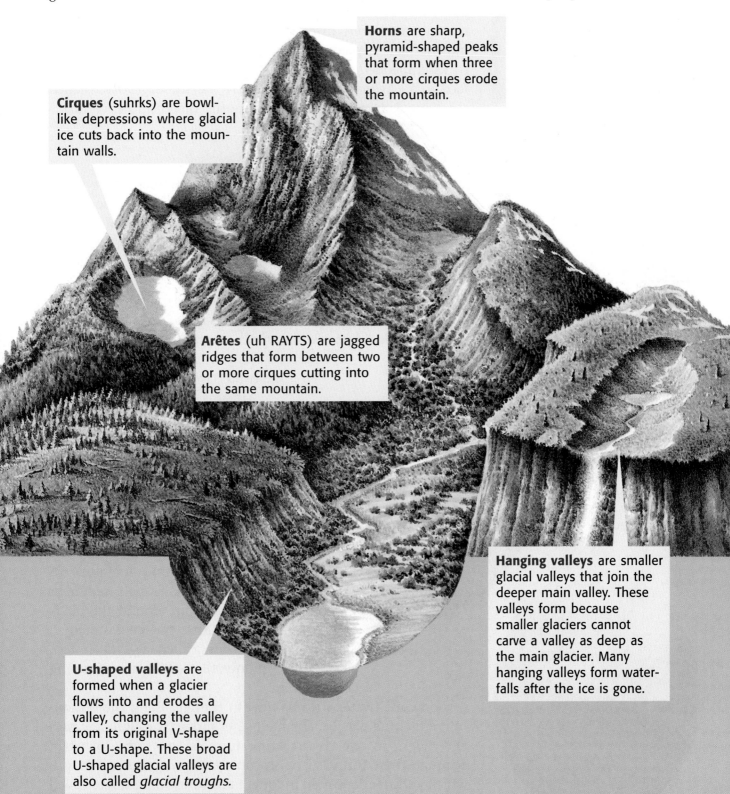

Horns are sharp, pyramid-shaped peaks that form when three or more cirques erode the mountain.

Cirques (suhrks) are bowl-like depressions where glacial ice cuts back into the mountain walls.

Arêtes (uh RAYTS) are jagged ridges that form between two or more cirques cutting into the same mountain.

Hanging valleys are smaller glacial valleys that join the deeper main valley. These valleys form because smaller glaciers cannot carve a valley as deep as the main glacier. Many hanging valleys form waterfalls after the ice is gone.

U-shaped valleys are formed when a glacier flows into and erodes a valley, changing the valley from its original V-shape to a U-shape. These broad U-shaped glacial valleys are also called *glacial troughs*.

Figure 20 *Striations, such as these seen in Central Park, in New York City, are evidence of glacial erosion.*

While many of the erosional features created by glaciers are unique to alpine glaciers, alpine and continental glaciers share some common features. For example, when a glacier erodes the landscape, the glacier picks up rock material and carries it away. This debris is transported on the glacier's surface as well as beneath and within the glacier. Many times, rock material is frozen into the glacier's bottom. As the glacier moves, the rock pieces scrape and polish the surface rock. Larger rocks embedded in the glacier gouge out grooves in the surface rock. As you can see in **Figure 20,** these grooves, called *striations,* help scientists determine the direction of ice flow.

Types of Glacial Deposits

When a glacier melts, all the material it has been carrying is dropped. **Glacial drift** is the general term used to describe all material carried and deposited by glaciers. Glacial drift is divided into two main types, based on whether the material is sorted or unsorted.

Stratified Drift   Rock material that has been sorted and deposited in layers by water flowing from the melted ice is called **stratified drift.** Various types of stratified drift are shown in **Figure 21.** Many streams are created by the meltwater from the glacier. These streams carry an abundance of sorted material, which is deposited in front of the glacier in a broad area called an *outwash plain.* Sometimes a block of ice is left in the outwash plain when the glacier retreats. During the time it takes for the ice to melt, sediment builds up around the block of ice. After the ice has melted, a depression called a *kettle* is left. Kettles commonly fill with water, forming a lake or pond.

Outwash plain

Kettle

Esker

Figure 21 *Stratified drift is deposited to form various types of landscape features.*

Some meltwater streams flow in tunnels along the bottom of the melting glacier. The meltwater moves through crevasses and cracks in the ice, creating tunnels that run downhill. Through these tunnels, the streams transport sand and gravel, which are later deposited in long, narrow, winding ridges called *eskers.* When the glacier melts back, the esker is revealed.

Till Deposits The second type of glacial drift, **till,** is unsorted rock material that is deposited directly by the ice when it melts. *Unsorted* means that the till is made up of different sizes of rock material, ranging from large boulders to fine glacial silt. As a glacier flows, it carries different sizes of rock fragments. When the glacier melts, the unsorted material is deposited on the ground surface. The most common till deposits are *moraines.* Moraines generally form ridges along the edges of glaciers. They are produced when glaciers carry material to the front of the ice and along the sides of the ice. As the ice melts away, the sediment and rock it was carrying are dropped, forming the different types of moraines. The various types of moraines are shown in **Figure 22.**

Figure 22 *Moraines provide clues to where glaciers once were located.*

Medial moraines form when two different valley glaciers with lateral moraines meet.

Lateral moraines form along each side of a glacier.

Ground moraines are the unsorted material left beneath a glacier.

Terminal moraines form when eroded rock material is dropped at the front of the glacier.

REVIEW

1. How does glaciation change the appearance of mountains?

2. Explain why continental glaciers smooth the landscape and alpine glaciers create a rugged landscape.

3. What do moraines indicate?

4. **Applying Concepts** How can a glacier deposit both sorted and unsorted material?

How did this glacier get into my classroom? To find out more about glaciers and erosion, turn to page 531 of the LabBook.

Gravity's Effect on Erosion and Deposition

Waves, wind, and ice are all agents of erosion and deposition that you can see. And though you can't see it and might not be aware of it, gravity is also an agent of erosion and deposition constantly at work on the Earth's surface. Gravity not only influences the movement of water, such as waves, streams, and ice, but also causes rocks and soil to move downslope. **Mass movement** is the movement of any material, such as rock, soil, or snow, downslope. Mass movement is controlled by the force of gravity and can occur rapidly or slowly.

The Forces in Mass Movement

All mass movement occurs on slopes as a result of gravitational pull. If dry sand is piled up, it will move downhill until the slope becomes stable. The *angle of repose* is the steepest angle, or slope, at which loose material will not slide downslope. This is demonstrated in **Figure 23.** The angle of repose is different for each type of sediment. As with any material, loose rock and sediment will not move unless the angle of the material is steeper than the angle of repose.

The effect of gravity on the surface material depends on many of the surface material's characteristics, such as its size, weight, shape, and moisture level. Another factor that influences mass movement is the slope on which the surface material rests. The steeper the slope is, the more likely it is that mass movement will occur.

NEW TERMS

mass movement   mudflow
rock fall   creep
landslide

OBJECTIVES

- Explain how slope is related to mass movement.
- State how gravity affects mass movement.
- Describe different types of mass movement.

Quick Lab

Angle of Repose

1. Pour a **container** of **dry sand** onto a lab table.
2. With a **protractor,** measure the slope of the sand, or the *angle of repose.*
3. Pour another beaker of sand on top of the first pile.
4. Measure the angle of repose again for the new pile.
5. Which pile is more likely to collapse? Why?

Figure 23 *If the angle of a slope on which material rests is less than the angle of repose, the material will stay in place. If the angle is greater than the angle of repose, the material will move downslope.*

Rapid Mass Movement The most destructive mass movements occur suddenly and rapidly. Rapid mass movement occurs when material, such as rock and soil, moves downslope quickly. A rapid mass movement can be very dangerous, destroying everything in its path. While driving along a mountain road, you might have noticed signs that warn of falling rock. A **rock fall** happens when a group of loose rocks falls down a steep slope, as seen in **Figure 24.** Steep slopes are sometimes created to make room for a road in mountainous areas. Loosened and exposed rocks above the road tend to fall as a result of gravity. The rocks in a rock fall can range in size from small fragments to large boulders.

Another type of rapid mass movement is a *landslide*. A **landslide** is the sudden and rapid movement of a large amount of material downslope. A *slump* is an example of one kind of landslide. Slumping occurs when a block of material moves downslope over a curved surface, as seen in **Figure 25.**

physical science
CONNECTION

Gravity is one of the major forces that cause rocks and soil to move from one place to another. Gravity is the force of attraction between objects. The more mass an object has, the more attraction there is between it and other objects.

Figure 24 *If enough rock falls from a mountain, a pile forms at the base of the slope. This pile of rock debris is called a* talus slope.

Figure 25 *A slump is a type of landslide that occurs when a small block of land becomes detached and slides downhill.*

A **mudflow** is a rapid movement of a large mass of mud. Mudflows, which are like giant moving mud pies, occur when a large amount of water mixes with soil and rock. The water causes the slippery mass of mud to flow rapidly downslope. Mudflows most commonly occur in mountainous regions when a long dry season is followed by heavy rains. As you can see in **Figure 26,** a mudflow can carry trees, houses, cars, and other objects that lie in its path.

Figure 26 *When heavy rains saturate mountain slopes, mudflows occur. This photo shows one of the many mudflows that have occurred in California during rainy winters.*

The most dangerous mudflows occur as a result of volcanic eruptions. Mudflows of volcanic origin are called *lahars.* Lahars can move at speeds of more than 80 km/h and are as thick as concrete. In mountains with snowy peaks, a volcanic eruption can suddenly melt a great amount of ice, causing a massive and rapid lahar, as shown in **Figure 27.** The water from the ice liquefies the soil and volcanic ash, sending a hot mudflow downslope. Other lahars are caused by heavy rains on volcanic ash.

Figure 27 *Lahars are extremely dangerous due to their size and speed. This lahar overtook the city of Kyushu, in Japan.*

Slow Mass Movement Sometimes you don't even notice mass movement occurring. While rapid mass movements are visible and dramatic, slow mass movements happen a little at a time. However, because slow mass movements occur more frequently, more material is moved collectively over time.

Although most slopes appear to be stable, they are actually undergoing slow mass movement, as shown in **Figure 28.** The extremely slow movement of material downslope is called **creep.** Many factors contribute to creep. Water breaks up rock particles, allowing them to move freely. The roots of growing plants act as a wedge, forcing rocks and soil particles apart. Burrowing animals, such as gophers and groundhogs, loosen rock and soil particles.

life science
CONNECTION

Since trees need light to grow, they usually grow straight upward, toward the sun. However, if the soil on a slope is creeping downhill, the trees will develop bent trunks. The trunks bend because the trees continue to grow upward even as their roots and trunks are tilted downhill. Trees with a "pistol butt" shape show that mass movement is happening on a slope.

Figure 28 *Tilted fence posts and bent tree trunks are evidence that creep is occurring.*

Another kind of slow mass movement, called *solifluction*, occurs in arctic and alpine climates where the subsoil is permanently frozen. In the spring and summer, only the upper layer of soil thaws, while the ground below remains frozen. The moisture from the thawing soil layer cannot move into the frozen soil below; therefore, the surface layer becomes saturated with water. As a result, the surface layer of soil becomes muddy and moves downslope. This type of mass movement can also occur in warmer regions where the subsoil consists of clay. Clay acts like the permanently frozen layer, preventing water from moving into the subsurface layer.

REVIEW

1. In your own words, explain why slump occurs.

2. What factors increase the potential for mass movement?

3. How do slope and gravity affect mass movement?

4. **Analyzing Relationships** Some types of mass movement are considered dangerous to humans. Which types are most dangerous? Why?

Chapter Highlights

SECTION 1

Vocabulary

shoreline *(p. 276)*

beach *(p. 278)*

longshore current *(p. 279)*

Section Notes

- The wind from storms usually produces the large waves that cause shoreline erosion.

- Waves break when they enter shallow water, becoming surf.

- Beaches are made of any material deposited by waves.

- Sandbars, spits, and tombolos are depositional features caused by longshore currents.

- Sea cliffs, sea caves, sea arches, and sea stacks are coastal formations caused by wave erosion.

SECTION 2

Vocabulary

saltation *(p. 282)*

deflation *(p. 283)*

abrasion *(p. 284)*

dune *(p. 284)*

loess *(p. 286)*

Section Notes

- Wind is an important agent of erosion and deposition in deserts and along coastlines.

- Saltation is the process of the wind bouncing sand grains downwind along the ground.

- Deflation is the removal of materials by wind. If deflation removes all fine rock materials, a barren surface called desert pavement is formed.

- Abrasion is the grinding and wearing down of rock surfaces by other rock or sand particles.

- Dunes are formations caused by wind-deposited sand.

- Loess is wind-deposited silt, and it forms soil material good for farming.

Labs

Dune Movement *(p. 530)*

☑ Skills Check

Math Concepts

WAVE PERIOD Waves travel in intervals that are usually between 10 and 20 seconds apart. Use the following equation to calculate how many waves reach the shore in 1 minute:

$$\frac{\text{number of waves}}{\text{per minute}} = \frac{60 \text{ seconds}}{\text{waves period (seconds)}}$$

After you find out how many waves reach the shore in 1 minute, you can figure out how many waves occur in an hour or even a day. For example, consider a wave period of 15 seconds. Using the formula above, you find that 4 waves occur in 1 minute. To find out how many waves occur in 1 hour, multiply 4 by 60. To find out how many waves occur in 1 day, multiply 240 by 24.

$$\frac{\text{number of waves}}{\text{per day}} = \frac{60}{15} \times 60 \times 24 = 5{,}760$$

Visual Understanding

U-SHAPED VALLEYS AND MORE Look back at the illustration on page 291 to review the different types of landscape features carved by alpine glaciers.

Vocabulary

glacier *(p. 287)*

iceberg *(p. 288)*

crevasse *(p. 289)*

horn *(p. 291)*

cirque *(p. 291)*

arête *(p. 291)*

hanging valley *(p. 291)*

U-shaped valley *(p. 291)*

glacial drift *(p. 292)*

stratified drift *(p. 292)*

till *(p. 293)*

Section Notes

- Masses of moving ice are called glaciers.

- There are two main types of glaciers—alpine glaciers and continental glaciers.

- Glaciers move when the ice that comes into contact with the ground melts and when ice crystals slip over one another.

- Alpine glaciers produce rugged landscape features, such as cirques, arêtes, and horns.

- Continental glaciers smooth the landscape.

- There are two main types of glacial deposits—stratified drift and till.

- Some of the landforms deposited by glaciers include outwash plains, eskers, and moraines.

Labs

Gliding Glaciers *(p. 531)*

Creating a Kettle *(p. 533)*

Vocabulary

mass movement *(p. 294)*

rock fall *(p. 295)*

landslide *(p. 295)*

mudflow *(p. 296)*

creep *(p. 297)*

Section Notes

- Mass movement is the movement of material downhill due to the force of gravity.

- The angle of repose is the steepest slope at which loose material will remain at rest.

- Rock falls, landslides, and mudflows are all types of rapid mass movement.

- Creep and solifluction are types of slow mass movement.

---

 internetconnect

GO TO: go.hrw.com

Visit the **HRW** Web site for a variety of learning tools related to this chapter. Just type in the keyword:

KEYWORD: HSTICE

 GO TO: www.scilinks.org

Visit the **National Science Teachers Association** on-line Web site for Internet resources related to this chapter. Just type in the *sci*LINKS number for more information about the topic:

TOPIC: Wave Erosion	*sci*LINKS NUMBER: HSTE280
TOPIC: Wind Erosion	*sci*LINKS NUMBER: HSTE285
TOPIC: Glaciers	*sci*LINKS NUMBER: HSTE290
TOPIC: Mass Movement	*sci*LINKS NUMBER: HSTE295
TOPIC: Wetlands	*sci*LINKS NUMBER: HSTE300

Chapter Review

Explain the difference between the words in the following pairs:

1. shoreline/longshore current

2. beaches/dunes

3. deflation/saltation

4. horn/arête

5. stratified drift/till

6. mudflow/creep

Multiple Choice

7. *Surf* refers to
   a. large storm waves in the open ocean.
   b. giant waves produced by hurricanes.
   c. breaking waves.
   d. small waves on a calm sea.

8. When waves cut completely through a headland, a ___?___ is formed.
   a. sea cave   c. sea stack
   b. sea cliff   d. sea arch

9. A narrow strip of sand that is formed by wave deposition and is connected to the shore is called a ___?___
   a. marine terrace.   c. spit.
   b. sandbar.   d. headland.

10. A wind-eroded rock is called a
    a. deflation hollow.   c. ventifact.
    b. desert pavement.   d. dust bowl.

11. Where is the world's largest ice sheet located?
    a. Greenland
    b. Canada
    c. Alaska
    d. Antarctica

12. The process of calving forms ___?___
    a. continental ice sheets.
    b. icebergs.
    c. U-shaped valleys.
    d. moraines.

13. What term describes all types of glacial deposits?
    a. drift   c. till
    b. loess   d. outwash

14. Which of the following is not a landform created by an alpine glacier?
    a. cirque   c. horn
    b. deflation hollow   d. arête

15. What is the term for a mass movement that occurs in climates where the subsoil is permanently frozen?
    a. solifluction   c. creep
    b. slump   d. lahar

16. Which of the following is a slow mass movement?
    a. mudflow   c. creep
    b. landslide   d. rock fall

Short Answer

17. Why do waves break when they get near the shore?

18. What role do storms play in coastal erosion?

19. How do humans increase the erosion caused by dust storms?

20. In what direction do sand dunes move?

21. Why are glaciers such effective agents of erosion and deposition?

22. List some evidence for creep.

Concept Mapping

23. Use the following terms to create a concept map: deflation, dust storm, saltation, dune, loess.

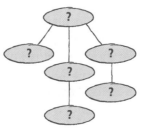

CRITICAL THINKING AND PROBLEM SOLVING

Write one or two sentences to answer the following questions:

24. What role does wind play in the processes of erosion and deposition?

25. What are the main differences between alpine glaciers and continental glaciers?

26. Describe the different types of moraines.

27. What kind of mass movement occurs continuously, day after day? Why can't you see it?

MATH IN SCIENCE

28. While standing on a beach, you can estimate a wave's speed in kilometers per hour. This is done by counting the seconds between each arriving wave crest to determine the wave period and then multiplying the wave period by 3.5. Calculate the speed of a wave with a 10-second period.

INTERPRETING GRAPHICS

The following graph illustrates coastal erosion and deposition occurring at an imaginary beach over a period of 8 years.

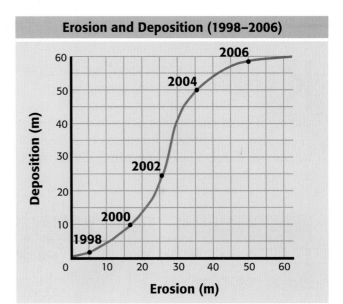

29. What is happening to the beach over time?

30. In what year does the amount of erosion that has occurred along the shoreline equal the amount of deposition?

31. Based on the erosion and deposition data for 2000, what might happen to the beach in the years to follow?

NOW What Do You Think?

Take a minute to review your answers to the ScienceLog questions on page 275. Have your answers changed? If necessary, revise your answers based on what you have learned since you began this chapter.

Science, Technology, and Society

Boulder Boogie

Karen weighs 320 kg. When no one's looking, she slides around, leaving lots of tracks. But Karen's not a person. In fact, she's not even alive—she's a boulder! Over the years, Karen has moved hundreds of meters across the desert floor. How can a 320 kg rock slide around by itself?

California. The Racetrack is very flat and has almost no plants or wildlife. Several times a year, powerful storms rip across the lake bed, bringing plenty of rain, wind, and sometimes snow. The Racetrack's clay surface becomes slippery, and that's apparently when the rocks dance.

▲ *A mystery in Death Valley: What moved this rock across the desert floor?*

▲ *New technology is helping Paula Messina study the paths of the "dancing rocks."*

Slipping and Sliding

Karen is one of the mysterious dancing rocks of Death Valley. These rocks slide around—sometimes together, sometimes alone. There are nearly 200 of them, and they range in size from small to very large. No one has seen them move, but their trails show where they've been.

The rocks are scattered across a dry lake bed, called the Racetrack, in Death Valley,

Puzzles and Clues

What could push a 320 kg boulder hundreds of yards across the mud? With the help of technology, scientists like Paula Messina are finally getting some answers. Messina uses a global positioning system (GPS) receiver and a geographic information system (GIS) to study the rocks. Using GPS satellites, Messina is able to map the movements of the rocks. Her measurements are more accurate than ever before. This new device measures the locations within centimeters! A computer equipped with GIS software constructs maps that allow her to study how the rock movement relates to the terrain. Messina's investigations with this equipment have led her to conclude that wind is probably pushing the rocks.

But how does the wind push such massive rocks? Messina thinks the gaps in the mountains at one end of the valley funnel high-speed winds down onto the slippery clay surface, pushing the rocks along. And why do some rocks move while others nearby do not? This mystery will keep Messina returning to Death Valley for years.

Search and Find

▶ Go to the library or the Internet, and research the many uses for GPS devices. Make a list in your ScienceLog of all the uses for GPS devices you find.

EYE ON THE ENVIRONMENT

Beach Today, Gone Tomorrow

Beaches are fun, right? But what if you went to the coast and found that the road along the beach had washed away? It could happen. In fact, erosion is stripping away beaches from islands and coastlines around the world.

An Island's Beaches

The beaches of Anguilla, a small Caribbean island, are important to the social, economic, and environmental well-being of the island and its inhabitants. Anguilla's sandy shores protect coastal areas from wave action and provide habitats for coastal plants and animals. The shores also provide important recreational areas for tourists and local residents. When Hurricane Luis hit Anguilla in 1995, Barney Bay was completely stripped of sand. But Anguilla's erosion problems started long before Luis hit the island. Normal ocean wave action had already washed away some beaches.

Back in the United States

Louisiana provides a good example of coastal problems in the United States. Louisiana has 40 percent of the nation's coastal wetlands. As important as these wetlands are, parts of the Louisiana coast were disappearing at a rate of 65 to 90 km^2 per year. That's a football field every 15 minutes! At that rate of erosion, Louisiana's new coastline would be 48 km inland by the year 2040!

Save the Sand

The people of Louisiana and Anguilla have acted to stop the loss of their coastlines. But many of their solutions are only temporary. Waves, storms, and human activity continue to erode coastlines. What can be done about beach erosion?

Scientists know that beaches and wetlands come and go to a certain extent. Erosion is part of a natural cycle. Scientists must first determine how much erosion is normal for

Before

After

▲ *This is what Barney Bay looked like in 1995 before and after Hurricane Luis.*

a particular area and how much is the result of human activities or some unusual process. The next step is to preserve or stabilize existing sand dunes, preserve coastal vegetation, and plant more shrubs, vines, grasses, and trees. The people of Louisiana and Anguilla have learned a lot from their problems and are taking many of these steps to slow further erosion. If steps are taken to protect valuable coastal areas, beaches will be there when you go on vacation.

Extending Your Knowledge

▶ What are barrier islands? How are they related to coastal erosion? On your own, find out more about barrier islands and why it is important to preserve them.

12 Interactions of Living Things

Strange but True!

A small fish swims through the darkest part of the ocean in search of its next meal. Food is scarce at this depth, but suddenly a glowing morsel comes into view. The tiny fish swims quickly to it, but just as the little fish is about to nab its meal, large jaws rimmed with needle-sharp teeth appear out of nowhere. Before the fish can escape, it is swallowed whole.

This is how the deep-sea anglerfish—the one with the needle-sharp teeth—catches its food. The anglerfish has a unique way of fooling unsuspecting prey. The anglerfish is equipped with its own "fishing pole," a special branchlike body part that hangs over its head, and bait. The bait is a small mass of bacteria

attached to the tip of the "fishing pole" that glow in the dark. The anglerfish is only about 7 cm long and is hard to see in the murky depths of the ocean. Fish attracted to the bright bait do not notice the lurking anglerfish until it is too late.

The anglerfish and the glowing bacteria are involved in a relationship that benefits both of them. In exchange for providing the anglerfish with a lure to catch fish, the bacteria get to live in a protected and mobile home. In this chapter you will learn more about the diverse ways living things interact with each other and with their environment. Some of these relationships are almost too strange to believe!

What Do You Think?

In your ScienceLog, try to answer the following questions based on what you already know:

1. Imagine a deer living in a meadow. What does the deer eat? What eats the deer? When the deer dies, what happens to its remains?

2. What is the source of energy for plants?

Who Eats Whom?

In this activity, you will learn how certain organisms interact when finding (or becoming) the next meal. You will need **five index cards,** which you can obtain from your teacher.

Procedure

1. On each index card, print the name of one of the organisms shown at right. All these organisms live in the cold ocean water near Antarctica.

2. Arrange the cards on your desk to show who eats whom. (Hint: Algae are small organisms that use the sun's energy to make food. Therefore, the algae card belongs at the bottom of your arrangement.)

3. Draw your card arrangement in your ScienceLog, beginning with the algae card.

4. In its natural habitat, which organism exists in the greatest number? Arrange the cards in order of most to fewest individuals.

Analysis

5. How does the arrangement of who eats whom compare with the arrangement of the number of individuals?

6. What might happen to the other organisms if the algae were removed from this group? What might happen if the killer whales were removed?

7. Are there any organisms in this group that eat more than one kind of food? How would you change the order of your cards to reflect this information?

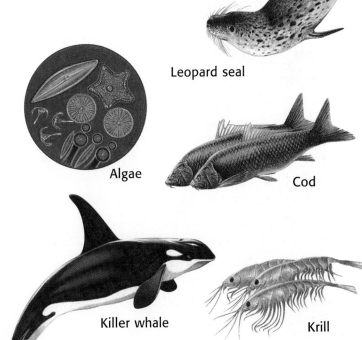

Leopard seal

Algae

Cod

Killer whale

Krill

Everything Is Connected

NEW TERMS

ecology   community
biotic   ecosystem
abiotic   biosphere
population

OBJECTIVES

- Distinguish between the biotic and abiotic environment.
- Explain how populations, communities, ecosystems, and the biosphere are related.
- Explain how the abiotic environment relates to communities.

Look at **Figure 1** below. An alligator drifts in a weedy Florida river, watching a long, thin fish called a gar. The gar swims too close to the alligator. Suddenly, in a rush of snapping jaws and splashing water, the gar becomes a meal for the alligator.

It is clear that these two organisms have just interacted with one another. But organisms have many interactions other than simply "who eats whom." For example, alligators dig underwater holes to escape from the heat. Later, after the alligators abandon these holes, fish and other aquatic organisms live in them when the water level gets low during a drought. Alligators also build nest mounds in which to lay their eggs, and they enlarge these mounds each year. Eventually, the mounds become small islands where trees and other plants grow. Herons, egrets, and other birds build their nests in the trees. It is easy to see that alligators affect many organisms, not just the gars that they eat.

Studying the Web of Life

All living things are connected in a web of life. Scientists who study the connections among living things specialize in the science of ecology. **Ecology** is the study of the interactions between organisms and their environment.

Figure 1 *The alligator affects, and is affected by, many organisms in its environment.*

An Environment Has Two Parts An organism's environment is anything that affects the organism. An environment consists of two parts. The **biotic** part of the environment is all of the organisms that live together and interact with one another. The **abiotic** part of the environment includes all of the physical factors—such as water, soil, light, and temperature—that affect organisms living in a particular area. Take another look at **Figure 1**. How many biotic parts can you see? How many abiotic parts?

Organization in the Environment At first glance, the environment may seem disorganized. To ecologists, however, the environment can be arranged into different levels, as shown in **Figure 2**. The first level contains the individual organism. The second level contains similar organisms, forming a population. The third contains different populations, forming a community. The fourth contains a community and its abiotic environment, forming an ecosystem. Finally, the fifth level contains all ecosystems, forming the biosphere. Turn the page and examine **Figure 3** to see these levels in a salt marsh.

Figure 2 The Five Levels of Environmental Organization

Organism

Population

Community

Ecosystem

Biosphere

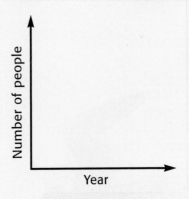

Populations A salt marsh is a coastal area where grasslike plants grow. A **population** is a group of individuals of the same species that live together in the same area at the same time. For example, all of the seaside sparrows that live together in a salt marsh are members of a population. The individuals in the population compete with one another for food, nesting space, and mates.

Communities A **community** consists of all the populations of different species that live and interact in an area. The various animals and plants you see below form a salt-marsh community. The different populations in a community depend on each other for food, shelter, and many other things.

Ecosystems An **ecosystem** is made up of a community of organisms and its abiotic environment. An ecologist studying the salt-marsh ecosystem would examine how the ecosystem's organisms interact with each other and how temperature, precipitation, and soil characteristics affect the organisms. For example, the rivers and streams that empty into the salt marsh carry nutrients, such as nitrogen, from the land. These nutrients influence how the cordgrass and algae grow.

Figure 3 *Examine the picture of a salt marsh below. See if you can find examples of each level of organization in this environment.*

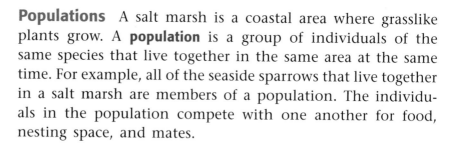

Laughing gull

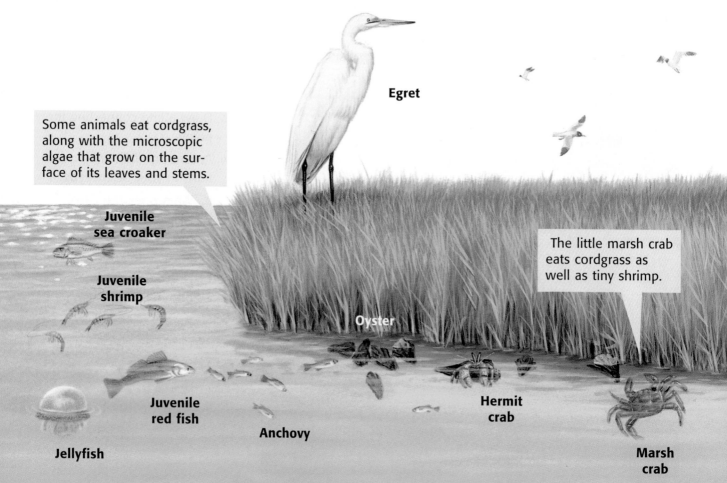

Some animals eat cordgrass, along with the microscopic algae that grow on the surface of its leaves and stems.

Egret

The little marsh crab eats cordgrass as well as tiny shrimp.

Juvenile sea croaker

Juvenile shrimp

Oyster

Juvenile red fish

Anchovy

Jellyfish

Hermit crab

Marsh crab

The Biosphere The **biosphere** is the part of Earth where life exists. It extends from the deepest parts of the ocean to very high in the atmosphere, where tiny insects and plant spores drift, and it includes every ecosystem. Ecologists study the biosphere to learn how organisms interact with the abiotic environment—Earth's gaseous atmosphere, water, soil, and rock. The water in the abiotic environment includes both fresh water and salt water as well as water that is frozen in polar icecaps and glaciers.

REVIEW

1. What is ecology?

2. Give two examples each of biotic and abiotic factors in the salt-marsh ecosystem.

3. Using the salt-marsh example, distinguish between populations, communities, ecosystems, and the biosphere.

4. **Analyzing Relationships** What do you think would happen to the other organisms in the salt-marsh ecosystem if the cordgrass were to suddenly die?

Heron

Laughing gull

Seaside sparrows eat insects, spiders, and small crabs. A male and his mate weave a nest out of cordgrass stalks.

The periwinkle snail eats the algae that grows on the cordgrass. The periwinkle snail also uses the cordgrass as a place to hide from predators.

Clapper rail

Seaside sparrow

Periwinkle snail

Diamondback terrapin

Oyster

Living Things Need Energy

All living things need energy to survive. For example, black-tailed prairie dogs, which live in the grasslands of North America, eat grass and seeds to get the energy they need. They use this energy to grow, move, heal injuries, and reproduce. In fact, everything a prairie dog does requires energy. The same is true for the plants that grow in the grasslands where the prairie dogs live. Coyotes that stalk prairie dogs, as well as the bacteria and fungi that live in the soil, all need energy.

The Energy Connection

Organisms in a prairie or any community can be divided into three groups based on how they obtain energy. These groups are producers, consumers, and decomposers. Examine **Figure 4** to see how energy passes through these groups in an ecosystem.

Producers Organisms that use sunlight directly to make food are called **producers.** They do this using a process called photosynthesis. Most producers are plants, but algae and some bacteria are also producers. Grasses are the main producers in a prairie ecosystem. Examples of producers in other ecosystems include cordgrass and algae in a salt marsh and trees in a forest. Algae are the main producers in the ocean.

Figure 4 *Follow the pathway of energy as it moves from the sun through the ecosystem.*

Energy
Sunlight is the source of energy for almost all living things.

Producer
Plants use the energy in sunlight to make food.

Consumer
The black-tailed prairie dog eats seeds and grass in the grasslands of western North America.

Consumer
All of the prairie dogs in a colony watch for enemies, such as coyotes, hawks, and badgers. Occasionally, a prairie dog is killed and eaten by a coyote.

Herbivore

Carnivore

Consumers Organisms that eat producers or other organisms for energy are called **consumers.** They cannot use the sun's energy directly like producers can. Instead, consumers must eat producers or other animals to obtain energy. There are several kinds of consumers. A **herbivore** is a consumer that eats plants. Herbivores in the prairie ecosystem include grasshoppers, gophers, prairie dogs, bison, and pronghorn antelope. A **carnivore** is a consumer that eats animals. Carnivores in the prairie ecosystem include coyotes, hawks, badgers, and owls. Consumers known as **omnivores** eat a variety of organisms, both plants and animals. The grasshopper mouse is an example of an omnivore in the prairie ecosystem. It eats insects, scorpions, lizards, and grass seeds. **Scavengers** are animals that feed on the bodies of dead animals. The turkey vulture is a scavenger in the prairie ecosystem. Examples of scavengers in aquatic ecosystems include crayfish, snails, clams, worms, and crabs.

Decomposers Organisms that get energy by breaking down the remains of dead organisms are called **decomposers.** Bacteria and fungi are examples of decomposers. These organisms extract the last bit of energy from dead organisms and produce simpler materials, such as water and carbon dioxide. These materials can then be reused by plants and other living things. Decomposers are an essential part of any ecosystem because they are nature's recyclers.

BRAIN FOOD

Prairie dogs are not really dogs. They are rodents. They are called dogs because their warning calls sound like the barking of dogs.

Self-Check

Are you a herbivore, a carnivore, or an omnivore? Explain. *(See page 564 to check your answer.)*

Consumer
A turkey vulture may eat some of the coyote's leftovers. A scavenger can pick bones completely clean.

Decomposer
Any prairie dog remains not eaten by the coyote or the turkey vulture are broken down by bacteria and fungi that live in the soil.

Scavenger

Recycler

Food Chains and Food Webs

Figure 4, on pages 310–311, shows a **food chain,** which represents how the energy in food molecules flows from one organism to the next. But because few organisms eat just one kind of organism, simple food chains rarely occur in nature. The many energy pathways possible are more accurately shown by a **food web.** **Figure 5** shows a simple food web for a forest ecosystem.

Find the fox and the rabbit in the figure below. Notice that the arrow goes from the rabbit to the fox, showing that the rabbit is food for the fox. The rabbit is also food for the owl. Neither the fox nor the owl is ever food for the rabbit. Energy moves from one organism to the next in a one-way direction even in a food web. Any energy not immediately used by an organism is stored in its tissues. Only the energy stored in an organism's tissues can be used by the next consumer.

Figure 5 *Energy moves through an ecosystem in complex ways. Most consumers eat a variety of foods and can be eaten by a variety of other consumers.*

Energy Pyramids

A grass plant uses most of the energy it obtains from the sun for its own life processes. Only a very small amount of energy stored in the tissues of the grass plant is left over for prairie dogs and other animals that eat the grass. Therefore, prairie dogs have to eat a lot of grass to get the energy they need. Likewise, each prairie dog uses most of the energy it obtains from eating grass and stores only a little of it in its tissues. Because of this, a coyote must eat many prairie dogs to survive. There must be many more prairie dogs in the community than there are coyotes that eat prairie dogs. Likewise, the coyote uses most of the energy it obtains from its diet of insects, gophers, and prairie dogs.

The loss of energy at each level of the food chain can be represented by an **energy pyramid,** as shown in **Figure 6.** You can see that the energy pyramid has a large base and becomes smaller at the top. The amount of available energy is reduced at higher levels because most of the energy is either used by the organism or given off as heat. Only energy stored in the tissues of an organism can be transferred to the next level.

MATH BREAK

Energy Pyramids

In your ScienceLog, draw an energy pyramid for a river ecosystem that contains four levels—aquatic plants, insect larvae, bluegill fish, and a largemouth bass. The aquatic plants obtain 10,000 units of energy from the sun. If each level uses 90 percent of the energy it receives from the previous level, how many units of energy are available to the largemouth bass?

Figure 6 *The pyramid represents energy. As you can see, more energy is available at the base of the pyramid than at its top.*

Decreasing number of organisms

Increasing amount of energy

Wolves and the Energy Pyramid

A single species can be very important to the flow of energy in an environment. Gray wolves, for example, are a consumer species that can control the populations of many of the other species in their environment. The diet of gray wolves can include anything from a lizard to an elk.

Gray wolves were once common throughout much of the United States. However, as the wilderness was settled, populations of gray wolves declined until they were almost wiped out. Once the wolves were gone, certain other species, such as elk, were no longer controlled. The overpopulation of elk in some areas led to overgrazing and starvation.

Gray wolves were recently restored to the United States at Yellowstone National Park as shown in **Figure 7.** The U.S. Fish and Wildlife Service hopes this action will restore the natural energy flow in this wilderness area. Not everyone approves of this program, however. Ranchers near Yellowstone are concerned about the safety of their livestock.

Figure 7 *Members of the U.S. Fish and Wildlife Service are moving a caged wolf to a location in Yellowstone National Park.*

Habitat and Niche

An organism's **habitat** is the environment in which it lives. The wolf's habitat was originally very extensive. It included forests, grasslands, deserts, and the northern tundra. Today the wolf's habitat in North America is much smaller. It includes wilderness areas in portions of Montana, Washington, Minnesota, Michigan, and Wisconsin, and parts of Canada. Gray wolves are able to find food and survive best in these wilderness areas.

An organism's way of life within an ecosystem is its **niche.** An organism's niche includes its habitat, its food, its predators, and the organisms it competes with. An organism's niche also includes how the organism affects and is affected by abiotic factors in its environment, such as temperature, light, and moisture.

The Niche of the Gray Wolf

A complete description of a species' niche is very complex. To help you distinguish between habitat and niche, the following is a short description of parts of the niche of the gray wolf.

Gray Wolves Are Consumers Wolves are carnivores. Their diet includes large animals, such as deer, moose (shown in **Figure 8**), reindeer, sheep, and elk, as well as small animals, such as birds, lizards, snakes, and fish.

Figure 8 *Wolves feed mainly on large herbivores, such as elk, moose, and deer.*

Gray Wolves Have a Social Structure

Wolves live and hunt in packs, which are groups of about six animals that are usually members of the same family. Each member of the pack has a particular rank within the pack. The pack has two leaders, as shown in **Figure 9,** that help defend the pack against enemies, such as other wolf packs or bears.

Gray Wolves Nurture and Teach Their Young

A female wolf, shown in **Figure 10,** has five to seven pups and nurses her babies for about two months. The entire pack help bring the pups food and baby-sit when the parents are away from the den. It takes about 2 years for the young wolves to learn to hunt. At that time, some young wolves leave the pack to find mates and start their own pack.

Gray Wolves Are Needed in the Food Web

If wolves become reestablished at Yellowstone National Park, they will reduce the elk population by killing the old, injured, and diseased elk. This in turn will allow more plants to grow, which will allow animals that eat the plants, such as snowshoe hares, and the animals that eat the hares, such as foxes, to increase in number.

Figure 9 *A pack of gray wolves is led by a pair called the alpha male and the alpha female.*

Figure 10 *In small wolf packs, only the alpha female has pups. They are well cared for, however, by all the males and females in the pack.*

REVIEW

1. How are producers, consumers (herbivores, carnivores, and scavengers), and decomposers linked in a food chain?

2. How do food chains link together to form a food web?

3. Distinguish between an organism's habitat and its niche using the prairie dog as an example.

4. **Applying Concepts** Is it possible for an inverted energy pyramid to exist, as shown in the figure at right? Explain why or why not.

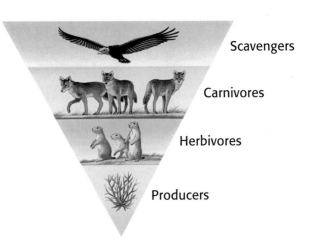

Scavengers

Carnivores

Herbivores

Producers

Types of Interactions

Look at the seaweed forest shown in **Figure 11** below. Notice that some types of organisms are more numerous than others. In natural communities, populations of different organisms vary greatly. The interactions between these populations affect the size of each population.

Figure 11 *This seaweed forest is home to a large number of interacting species.*

Where on Earth could this bird live? Find out on page 536 of your LabBook.

Interactions with the Environment

Most living things produce more offspring than will survive. A female frog, for example, might lay hundreds of eggs in a small pond. In a few months, the population of frogs in that pond will be about the same as it was the year before. Why won't the pond become overrun with frogs? An organism, such as a frog, interacts with biotic or abiotic factors in its environment that can control the size of its population.

Limiting Factors Populations cannot grow indefinitely because the environment contains only so much food, water, living space, and other needed resources. When one or more of those resources becomes scarce, it is said to be a **limiting factor.** For example, food becomes a limiting factor when a population becomes too large for the amount of food available. Any single resource can be a limiting factor to population size.

Carrying Capacity The largest population that a given environment can support over a long period of time is known as the environment's **carrying capacity.** When a population grows larger than its carrying capacity, limiting factors in the environment cause the population to get smaller. For example, after a very rainy growing season in an environment, plants may produce a large crop of leaves and seeds. This may cause a herbivore population to grow large because of the unlimited food supply. If the next year has less rainfall than usual, there won't be enough food to support the large herbivore population. In this way, a population may temporarily exceed the carrying capacity. But a limiting factor will cause the population to die back. The population will return to a size that the environment can support over a long period of time.

Interactions Among Organisms

Populations contain interacting individuals of a single species, such as a group of rabbits feeding in the same area. Communities contain interacting populations of several species, such as a coral reef community with many species trying to find living space. Ecologists have described four main ways species and individuals affect each other: competition, predators and prey, certain symbiotic relationships, and coevolution.

Competition

When two or more individuals or populations try to use the same limited resource, such as food, water, shelter, space, or sunlight, it is called **competition.** Because resources are in limited supply in the environment, their use by one individual or population decreases the amount available to other organisms.

Competition can occur among individuals *within* a population. The elk population in Yellowstone National Park are herbivores that compete with each other for the same food plants in the park. This is a big problem for this species in winter. Competition can also occur *between* populations of different species. The different species of trees in **Figure 12** are competing with each other for sunlight and space.

Figure 12 *Some of the trees in this forest grow tall in order to reach sunlight, reducing the amount of sunlight available to shorter trees nearby.*

Predators and Prey

Many interactions among species occur because one organism eats another. The organism that is eaten is called the **prey.** The organism that eats the prey is called the **predator.** When a bird eats a worm, the worm is the prey and the bird is the predator.

Figure 13 *The goldenrod spider is difficult for its insect prey to see. Can you see it?*

Predator Adaptations In order to survive, predators must be able to catch their prey. Predators have a wide variety of methods and abilities for doing this. The cheetah, for example, is able to run at great speed to catch its prey. Other predators, such as the goldenrod spider, shown in **Figure 13,** ambush their prey. This spider blends in so well with the goldenrod flower that all it has to do is wait for its next insect meal to arrive.

Prey Adaptations Prey organisms have their own methods and abilities to keep from being eaten. Prey are able to run away, stay in groups, or camouflage themselves. Some prey organisms are poisonous to predators. They may advertise their poison with bright colors to warn predators to stay away. The fire salamander, shown in **Figure 14,** sprays a poison that burns. Predators quickly learn to recognize its warning coloration.

Figure 14 *Experienced predators know better than to eat the fire salamander! This colorful animal will make an unlucky predator very sick.*

Many animals run away from predators. Prairie dogs run to their underground burrows when a predator approaches. Many small fishes, such as anchovies, swim in groups called schools. Antelopes and buffaloes stay in herds. All the eyes, ears, and noses of the individuals in the group are watching, listening, and smelling for predators. This behavior increases the likelihood of spotting a potential predator.

Some prey species hide from predators by using camouflage. Certain insects resemble leaves so closely that you would never guess they are animals. Can you find the mantis in **Figure 15?**

Figure 15 *This mantis goes out on a limb to hide from predators.*

Symbiosis

Some species have very close interactions with other species. **Symbiosis** is a close, long-term association between two or more species. The individuals in a symbiotic relationship can benefit from, be unaffected by, or be harmed by the relationship. Often, one species lives in or on the other species. The thousands of symbiotic relationships that occur in nature are often classified into three groups: mutualism, commensalism, and parasitism.

Mutualism A symbiotic relationship in which both organisms benefit is called **mutualism.** For example, you and a species of bacteria that lives in your intestines benefit each other! The bacteria get a plentiful food supply from you, and in return you get vitamins that the bacteria produce.

Another example of mutualism occurs between coral and algae. The living corals near the surface of the water provide a home for the algae. The algae produce food through photosynthesis that is used by the corals. When a coral animal dies, its skeleton serves as a foundation for other corals. Over a long period of time these skeletons build up large, rock-like formations that lie just beneath the surface of warm, sunny seas, as shown in **Figure 16.**

Figure 16 *Coral animals and certain algae are an example of mutualism. In the smaller photo above, you can see the gold-colored algae inside the coral animal.*

Commensalism A symbiotic relationship in which one organism benefits and the other is unaffected is called **commensalism.** One example of commensalism is the relationship between sharks and remoras. **Figure 17** shows a shark with a remora attached to its body. Remoras "hitch a ride" and feed on scraps of food left by sharks. The remoras benefit from this relationship, while sharks are unaffected.

Figure 17 *The remora attached to the shark benefits from the relationship. The shark is neither benefited nor harmed.*

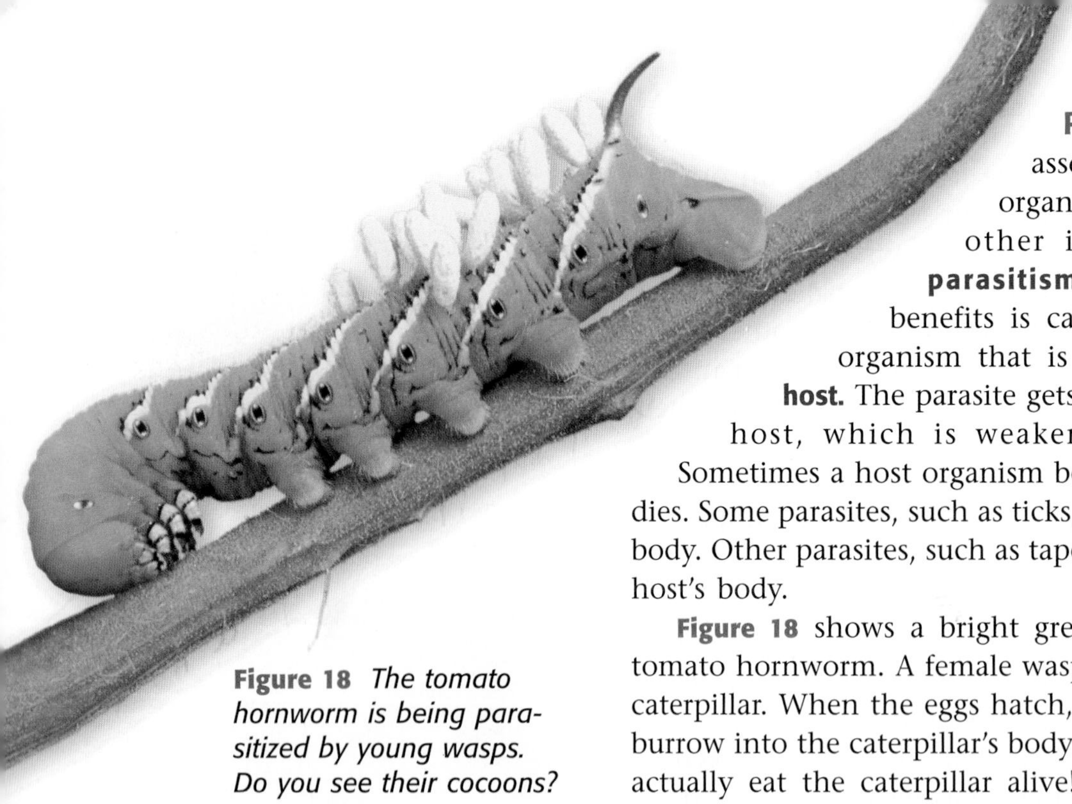

Parasitism A symbiotic association in which one organism benefits while the other is harmed is called **parasitism.** The organism that benefits is called the **parasite.** The organism that is harmed is called the **host.** The parasite gets nourishment from its host, which is weakened in the process. Sometimes a host organism becomes so weak that it dies. Some parasites, such as ticks, live outside the host's body. Other parasites, such as tapeworms, live inside the host's body.

Figure 18 shows a bright green caterpillar called a tomato hornworm. A female wasp laid tiny eggs on the caterpillar. When the eggs hatch, each young wasp will burrow into the caterpillar's body. The young wasps will actually eat the caterpillar alive! In a short time, the caterpillar will be almost completely consumed and die. When that occurs, the mature wasps will fly away.

In this example of parasitism, the host dies. Most parasites, however, do not kill their hosts. Can you think of reasons why?

Figure 18 *The tomato hornworm is being parasitized by young wasps. Do you see their cocoons?*

Coevolution

Symbiotic relationships and other interactions among organisms in an ecosystem may cause coevolution. **Coevolution** is a long-term change that takes place in two species because of their close interactions with one another.

Coevolution sometimes occurs between herbivores and the plants on which they feed. For example, the ants shown in **Figure 19** have coevolved with a tropical tree called the acacia. The ants protect the tree on which they live by attacking any other herbivore that approaches the tree. The plant has coevolved special structures on its stems that produce food for the ants. The ants live in other structures also made by the tree.

Figure 19 *This tropical tree and these ants have coevolved. The ants are shown collecting food made by the tree and storing the food in the ant's shelter, also made by the tree.*

In 1859, settlers released 12 rabbits in Australia. There were no predators or parasites to control the rabbit population, and there was plenty of food. The rabbit population increased so fast that the country was soon overrun by rabbits. To control the rabbit population, the Australian government introduced a virus that makes rabbits sick. The first time the virus was used, more than 99 percent of the rabbits died. The survivors reproduced, and the rabbit population grew large again. The second time the virus was used, about 90 percent of the rabbits died. Once again, the rabbit population increased. The third time the virus was used, only about 50 percent of the rabbits died. Suggest what changes might have occurred in the rabbits and the virus.

Coevolution and Flowers Some of the most amazing examples of coevolution are between flowers and their pollinators. (An organism that carries pollen from flower to flower is called a *pollinator.*) When the pollinator travels to the next flower to feed, some of the pollen is left behind on the female part of the flower, and more pollen is picked up. Because of pollination, reproduction can take place in the plant. Organisms such as bees, bats, and hummingbirds are attracted to a flower because of its colors, odors, and nectar.

During the course of evolution, hummingbird-pollinated flowers, for example, developed nectar with just the right amount of sugar for their pollinators. The hummingbird's long, thin tongue and beak coevolved to fit into the flowers so they could reach the nectar. As the hummingbird, like the one shown in **Figure 20,** feeds on the nectar, its head and body become smeared with pollen.

Figure 20 *The bird is attracted to the flower's nectar and picks up the flower's pollen as it feeds.*

REVIEW

1. Briefly describe one example of a predator-prey relationship. Identify the predator and the prey.

2. Name and define the three kinds of symbiosis.

3. **Analyzing Relationships** Explain the probable relationship between the giant *Rafflesia* flower, shown at right, which smells like rotting meat, and the carrion flies that buzz around it. HINT: *carrion* means "rotting flesh."

Chapter Highlights

SECTION 1

Vocabulary

ecology (p. 306)

biotic (p. 306)

abiotic (p. 306)

population (p. 308)

community (p. 308)

ecosystem (p. 308)

biosphere (p. 309)

Section Notes

• Ecology is the study of the interactions between organisms and their environment.

The environment consists of both biotic (living) and abiotic (nonliving) parts.

• Ecologists study organisms, populations, communities, ecosystems, and the biosphere. A population is a group of the same species living in the same place at the same time. A community is all the populations of different species living together. An ecosystem is a community and its abiotic environment. The biosphere consists of all of Earth's ecosystems.

Labs

Capturing the Wild Bean (p. 534)

SECTION 2

Vocabulary

producer (p. 310)

consumer (p. 311)

herbivore (p. 311)

carnivore (p. 311)

omnivore (p. 311)

scavenger (p. 311)

decomposer (p. 311)

food chain (p. 312)

food web (p. 312)

energy pyramid (p. 313)

habitat (p. 314)

niche (p. 314)

Section Notes

• Producers are organisms that obtain their energy directly from sunlight. Consumers are organisms that eat other organisms to obtain energy. Decomposers are bacteria and fungi that break down the remains of dead organisms to obtain energy.

☑ Skills Check

Math Concepts

ENERGY PYRAMIDS Try calculating the MathBreak on page 313 as if each unit of energy were $1.00. If you have $10,000.00, but you spend 90 percent, how much do you have left to leave in your will? ($1,000.00) If your heir spends 90 percent of that, how much can your heir leave? ($100.00) After four generations, how much will the inheritance be? ($1.00) Not much, huh? That's why there are very few large organisms at the top of the energy pyramid.

Visual Understanding

FOOD WEBS Several food pathways are shown in the food web in Figure 5 on page 312. However, an actual food web in a forest ecosystem is much more complex because hundreds of species live there. Find the mouse in Figure 5. How many organisms feed on the mouse? How many organisms feed on the butterfly? What might happen to this ecosystem if these animals were eliminated?

SECTION 2

- A food chain shows how energy flows from one organism to the next.

- Because most organisms eat more than one kind of food, there are many energy pathways possible; these are represented by a food web.

- Energy pyramids demonstrate that most of the energy at each level of the food chain is used up at that level and is unavailable for organisms higher on the food chain.

- An organism's habitat is the environment in which it lives. An organism's niche is its role in the ecosystem.

SECTION 3

Vocabulary

limiting factor (*p. 316*)

carrying capacity (*p. 317*)

competition (*p. 317*)

prey (*p. 318*)

predator (*p. 318*)

symbiosis (*p. 319*)

mutualism (*p. 319*)

commensalism (*p. 319*)

parasitism (*p. 320*)

parasite (*p. 320*)

host (*p. 320*)

coevolution (*p. 320*)

Section Notes

- Population size changes over time.

- Limiting factors slow the growth of a population. The largest population that an environment can support over a long period of time is called the carrying capacity.

- When one organism eats another, the organism that is eaten is the prey, and the organism that eats the prey is the predator.

- Symbiosis is a close, long-term association between two or more species. There are three general types of symbiosis: mutualism, commensalism, and parasitism.

- Coevolution involves the long-term changes that take place in two species because of their close interactions with one another.

Labs

Adaptation: It's a Way of Life (*p. 536*)

---

internet**connect**

GO TO: go.hrw.com

Visit the **HRW** Web site for a variety of learning tools related to this chapter. Just type in the keyword:

KEYWORD: HSTINT

GO TO: www.scilinks.org

Visit the **National Science Teachers Association** on-line Web site for Internet resources related to this chapter. Just type in the *sci***LINKS** number for more information about the topic:

TOPIC: Biotic and Abiotic Factors	*sci***LINKS NUMBER:** HSTE580
TOPIC: Organization in the Environment	*sci***LINKS NUMBER:** HSTE585
TOPIC: Producers, Consumers, and Decomposers	*sci***LINKS NUMBER:** HSTE590
TOPIC: Food Chains and Food Webs	*sci***LINKS NUMBER:** HSTE595
TOPIC: Habitats and Niches	*sci***LINKS NUMBER:** HSTE600

Chapter Review

To complete the following sentences, choose the correct term from each pair of terms listed below:

1. An organism's environment has two parts, the __?__, or living, and the __?__, or nonliving. *(biotic or abiotic)*

2. A __?__ is a group of individuals of the same species that live in the same area at the same time. *(community or population)*

3. A community and its abiotic environment make up a(an) __?__. *(ecosystem or food web)*

4. Organisms that use photosynthesis to obtain energy are called __?__. *(producers or decomposers)*

5. The environment in which an organism lives is its __?__, and the role the organism plays in an ecosystem is its __?__. *(niche or habitat)*

UNDERSTANDING CONCEPTS

Multiple Choice

6. A tick sucks blood from a dog. In this relationship, the tick is the __?__, and the dog is the __?__.
   a. parasite, prey
   b. predator, host
   c. parasite, host
   d. host, parasite

7. Resources such as water, food, or sunlight are more likely to be limiting factors
   a. when population size is decreasing.
   b. when predators eat their prey.
   c. when the population is small.
   d. when a population is approaching the carrying capacity.

8. "Nature's recyclers" are
   a. predators.
   b. decomposers.
   c. producers.
   d. omnivores.

9. A beneficial association between coral and algae is an example of
   a. commensalism.
   b. parasitism.
   c. mutualism.
   d. predation.

10. How energy moves through an ecosystem can be represented by
    a. food chains.
    b. energy pyramids.
    c. food webs.
    d. All of the above

11. The base of an energy pyramid represents which organisms in an ecosystem?
    a. producers
    b. carnivores
    c. herbivores
    d. scavengers

12. Which of the following is the correct order in a food chain?
    a. sun → producers → herbivores → scavengers → carnivores
    b. sun → consumers → predators → parasites → hosts
    c. sun → producers → decomposers → consumers → omnivores
    d. sun → producers → herbivores → carnivores → scavengers

13. Remoras and sharks have a relationship best described as
    a. mutualism.
    b. commensalism.
    c. predator and prey.
    d. parasitism.

Short Answer

14. Briefly describe the habitat and niche of the gray wolf.

15. What might different species of trees in a forest compete for?

16. How do limiting factors affect the carrying capacity of an environment?

17. What is coevolution?

Concept Mapping

18. Use the following terms to create a concept map: individual organisms, producers, populations, ecosystems, consumers, herbivores, communities, carnivores, the biosphere.

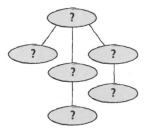

Write one or two sentences to answer the following questions:

19. Could a balanced ecosystem contain producers and consumers but no decomposers? Why or why not?

20. Some biologists think that certain species, such as alligators and wolves, help maintain biological diversity in their ecosystems. Predict what might happen to other species, such as gar fish or herons, if alligators were to become extinct in the Florida Everglades.

21. Does the Earth have a carrying capacity for humans? Explain your answer.

22. Explain why it is important to have a variety of organisms in a community of interacting species. Give an example.

MATH IN SCIENCE

23. The plants in each square meter of an ecosystem obtained 20,810 Calories of the sun's energy by photosynthesis per year. The herbivores in that ecosystem ate all of the plants, but they only obtained 3,370 Calories of energy. How much energy did the plants use for their own life processes?

INTERPRETING GRAPHICS

Examine the following graph, which shows the population growth of a species of *Paramecium*, a slipper-shaped, single-celled microorganism, over a period of 18 days. Food was occasionally added to the test tube in which the paramecia were grown. Answer the following questions:

24. What is the carrying capacity of the test tube as long as food is added?

25. Predict what will happen to the population if the researcher stops adding food to the test tube.

26. What keeps the number of *Paramecium* at a steady level?

27. Predict what might happen if the amount of water is doubled and the food supply stays the same.

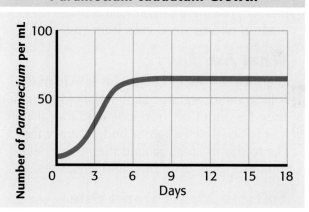

Paramecium caudatum Growth

NOW What Do You Think?

Take a minute to review your answers to the ScienceLog questions on page 305. Have your answers changed? If necessary, revise your answers based on what you have learned since you began this chapter.

Health

An Unusual Guest

What has a tiny tubelike body and short stumpy legs and lives upside down in your eyebrows and eyelashes? Would you believe a small animal? It's called a follicle mite, and humans are its host organism. Like all large animals, human beings are hosts to an interesting variety of smaller creatures. They live in or on our bodies and share our bodies' resources. But none of our guests is stranger than *D. folliculorum*—the follicle mite. They feed on oil and dead cells from your skin.

▲ *A follicle mite is smaller than the period at the end of this sentence.*

What Are They?

There are a couple of types of follicle mites. Follicle mites are arachnids—relatives of spiders. They are about 0.4 mm long, and they live in hair follicles all over your body. Usually they like to live in areas around the nose, cheek, forehead, chin, eyebrows, and eyelashes.

Follicle Mites Don't Bite

Are follicle mites harmful? These tiny guests are almost always harmless and they seldom live on children and adolescents. You probably wouldn't even know they were there. Studies reveal that between 97% and 100% of all adults have one or both kinds of mites. Except in rare cases, follicle mites in adults are also pretty harmless.

Some Health Concerns

Although follicle mites rarely cause problems, they are sometimes responsible for an acnelike condition around the nose, eyebrows, and eyelashes. A large number of mites (up to 25) may live in the same follicle. This can cause an inflammation of the follicle. The follicle does not swell like acne; instead it becomes red and itchy.

Mites living in eyelashes and on eyelids can irritate those areas. The inflammation causes itchy eyelids or eyebrows. But such inflammations are rare, and the condition clears up very quickly when suitable medication is applied. So while follicle mites may be one of the strangest guests living on human skin, they are almost never a problem.

Other Companions

Many tiny organisms make their home in humans' bodies. Bacteria within the body may help maintain proper pH levels. Even *E. coli,* a type of bacteria that can cause severe health problems, lives in the human colon. Without *E. coli,* a person would be unable to produce enough vitamin K or folic acid.

On Your Own

▶ Do some more research on follicle mites. Search for *Demodex folliculorum* or *Demodex brevis.* Find out more about some of the other strange organisms that rely on humans' bodies for food and shelter. Report on your findings, or write a story from the organism's point of view.

EYE ON THE ENVIRONMENT

Alien Invasion

A group of tiny aliens left their ship in Mobile, Alabama. Their bodies were red and shiny, and they walked on six legs. The aliens looked around and then quietly crawled off to make homes in the new land.

Westward Ho!

In 1918, fire ants were accidentally imported into the United States by a freighter ship from South America. In the United States, fire ants have no natural predators or competitors. In addition, these ants are extremely aggressive, and their colonies can harbor many queens, instead of just one queen, like many other ant species. With all these advantages, it is not surprising that the ants have spread like wildfire. By 1965, fire-ant mounds were popping up on the southeastern coast and as far west as Texas. Today they are found in at least 10 southern states and may soon reach as far west as California.

▲ *Three types of fire ants are found in a colony: the queen, workers, and males. Notice how the queen ant dwarfs the worker ants.*

Jaws of Destruction

Imported fire ants have done a lot of damage as they have spread across the United States. Because they are attracted to electrical currents, they chew through wire insulation, causing shorts in electrical circuits. The invaders have also managed to disturb the natural balance of native ecosystems. In some areas, they have killed off 70 percent of the native ant species and 40 percent of other native insect species. Each year, about 25,000 people seek medical attention for painful fire-ant bites.

Fighting Fire

Eighty years after the fire ants' introduction into the United States, the destructive ants continue to multiply. About 157 chemical products, including ammonia, gasoline, extracts from manure, and harsh pesticides, are registered for use against fire ants, but most have little or no success. Unfortunately, many of these remedies also harm the environment. By 1995, the government had approved only one fire-ant bait for large-scale use.

An Ant-Farm Census

▶ How many total offspring does a single fire-ant queen produce if she lives for 5 years and produces 1,000 eggs a day? If a mound contains 300,000 ants, how many mounds is this?

UNIT 5

Oceanography

In this unit, you will learn about the Earth's oceans and the vast landscapes they cover. Together, the oceans form the largest single feature on the planet. In fact, they cover approximately 70 percent of the Earth's surface. Now that's a lot of water! Not only do the oceans serve as home for countless living organisms, but they also affect life on land. You will learn more about the oceans in this unit as well as in the timeline presented here. Take a deep breath, and dive in!

1851
Herman Melville's novel *Moby-Dick* is published.

1872
The HMS *Challenger* begins its four-year voyage. Its discoveries lay the foundation for the science of oceanography.

1977
Thermal vent communities of creatures that exist without sunlight are discovered on the ocean floor.

1978
Louise Brown, the first "test-tube baby," is born in England.

1986
Commercial whaling is officially banned by the International Whaling Commission, but some whaling continues.

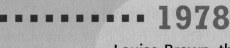
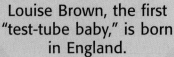

1927
Charles Lindbergh completes the first nonstop solo airplane flight over the Atlantic Ocean.

1914
The Panama Canal is completed, linking the Atlantic Ocean with the Pacific Ocean.

1938
A coelacanth is discovered in the Indian Ocean near South Africa. Called a fossil fish, the coelacanth was thought to have been extinct for 60 million years.

1960
Jacques Piccard and Don Walsh dive to a record 10,910 m below sea level in their bathyscaph *Trieste.*

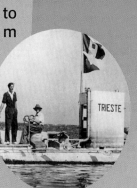

1943
Jacques Cousteau and Émile Gagnon invent the Aqualung, a breathing device that allows divers to freely explore the silent world of the oceans.

1990
The tunnel under the English Channel is completed, making train and auto travel between Great Britain and France possible.

1998
Ben Lecomte of Austin, Texas, successfully swims across the Atlantic Ocean from Massachusetts to France, a distance of 6,015 km. His record-breaking feat took 74 days.

13 Exploring the Oceans

*A glimpse of the future in
the next frontier—the ocean floor*

Imagine . . .

You are living at the bottom of the ocean, surrounded by colorful creatures swimming gracefully around you. Inside glass domes are entire cities of people who mine rich mineral deposits, farm fish and other aquatic life, and study the mysteries of Earth's vast, unexplored oceans.

Scientists are bringing that vision one step closer to reality inside an undersea home off the coast of Key Largo, Florida. There, at a depth of 19 m, scientists called *aquanauts* live and work inside *Aquarius,* an underwater laboratory and living facility.

Inside *Aquarius,* which is about as big as a bus, research teams conduct missions that can last up to 7 days. The purpose of the missions is to study North America's largest living coral-reef system. The scientists' only lifeline is a buoy on the surface of the water. The buoy enables air to be pumped into *Aquarius* and data, such as video images, to be transmitted back to shore.

The aquanauts have made some important discoveries. They have found evidence that ultraviolet rays from the sun are damaging the sensitive coral that live on the ocean floor.

Aquanauts are taking the next step toward underwater living. Aquarius *may not be a high-rise, but it lays the foundation for human colonization of the ocean floor.*

Some people think that these ultraviolet rays are able to reach the coral because air pollution is destroying the atmosphere's protective ozone layer. Water pollution also appears to be harming marine organisms. This concerns the aquanauts, who are extracting natural chemicals from these organisms that may provide cures for certain human diseases.

In this chapter you'll learn more about the Earth's oceans. You'll find out how scientists are exploring Earth's final frontier, uncovering its secrets, and protecting its valuable resources for the next generation.

What Do You Think?

In your ScienceLog, try to answer the following questions based on what you already know:

1. How have Earth's oceans changed over time?

2. Name two ways scientists study the ocean without going underwater.

3. Name two valuable resources that are taken from the ocean.

Investigate!

Exit Only?

How do aquanauts enter and leave *Aquarius*? Believe it or not, the simplest way is through a hole in the lab's floor. You might think water would come in through the hole, but it doesn't. People inside *Aquarius* can breathe freely and can come and go through the hole at any time. How is this possible? Do the following investigation to find out.

Procedure

1. Fill a large **bowl** about two-thirds full of **water.**

2. Turn a clear plastic **cup** upside down.

3. Slowly guide the cup straight down into the water, being careful not to tip the cup.

4. Record your observations in your ScienceLog.

Analysis

5. How far into the cup does the water go?

6. How does the air inside the cup affect the water below the cup?

7. Relate your findings to the hole in the bottom of the underwater research lab.

Going Further

Perform the same experiment, but this time tip the cup slightly to one side after you have submerged it. What does this demonstrate about the limits of the hole-in-the-floor design?

Earth's Oceans

Earth stands out from the other planets in our solar system primarily for one reason—71 percent of the Earth's surface is covered with water. Most of Earth's water is found in the global ocean, which is divided by the continents into four main oceans. This is shown in the figure below. The ocean is a unique body of water that plays many roles in regulating Earth's environment. Read on to learn more about one of our most important resources—the ocean.

Divisions of the Global Ocean

NEW TERMS

salinity
thermocline
water cycle

OBJECTIVES

- Name the major divisions of the global ocean.
- Describe the history of Earth's oceans.
- Summarize the properties and other aspects of ocean water.
- Summarize the interaction between the ocean and the atmosphere.

Indian Ocean The Indian Ocean is the third largest ocean, covering an area about eight times as large as the United States. Part of the longest mountain range in the world, the mid-ocean ridge, runs along the floor of the Indian Ocean.

Arctic Ocean The Arctic Ocean is the smallest ocean. This ocean is unique because much of it is covered by ice. Scientists are just beginning to successfully explore the frozen world of the Arctic Ocean.

Atlantic Ocean The volume of the Atlantic Ocean is about half that of the Pacific. Oceanographers are very knowledgeable about the winds and currents in the Atlantic because sailors have charted its waters for centuries.

Pacific Ocean The largest ocean is the Pacific Ocean. It is a vast body of water that has a volume of about 724 million cubic kilometers. That's enough water to fill 1,200,000,000,000,000,000 bathtubs!

How Did the Oceans Form?

About four and a half billion years ago, the Earth was a very different place. There were no oceans. Volcanoes spewed lava, ash, and gases all over the planet, which was much hotter than it is today. The volcanic gases, including water vapor, began to form Earth's atmosphere. While the atmosphere developed, the Earth was cooling. Sometime before 4 billion years ago, the Earth cooled enough for water vapor to condense and fall as rain. The rain began filling the lower levels of Earth's surface, and the first oceans began to form.

Earth's oceans have changed a lot throughout history. Scientists who study oceans have learned much about the oceans' history, as shown in the diagram below.

Self-Check

Examine the diagram below. If North America and South America continue to drift westward and Asia continues to drift eastward, what will eventually happen? *(See page 564 to check your answer.)*

The Recent History of Earth's Oceans

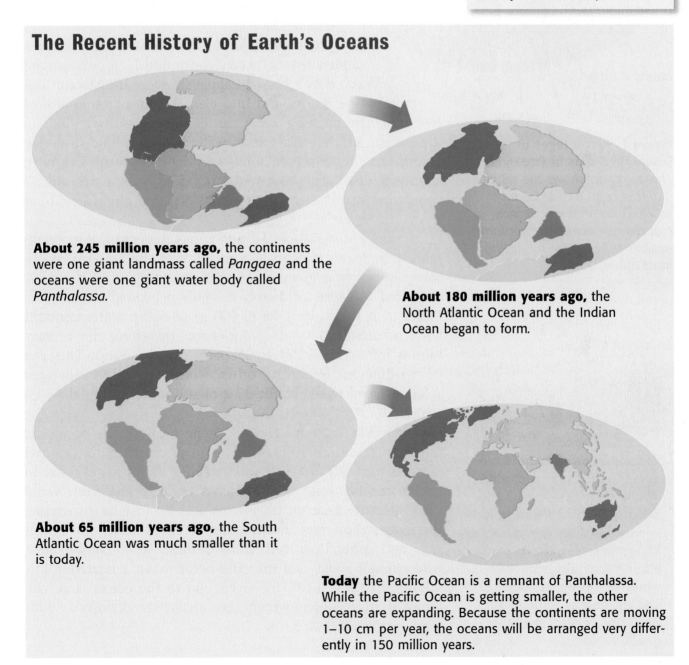

About 245 million years ago, the continents were one giant landmass called *Pangaea* and the oceans were one giant water body called *Panthalassa.*

About 180 million years ago, the North Atlantic Ocean and the Indian Ocean began to form.

About 65 million years ago, the South Atlantic Ocean was much smaller than it is today.

Today the Pacific Ocean is a remnant of Panthalassa. While the Pacific Ocean is getting smaller, the other oceans are expanding. Because the continents are moving 1–10 cm per year, the oceans will be arranged very differently in 150 million years.

Characteristics of Ocean Water

You know that ocean water is different from the water that flows from the faucet of your kitchen sink. For one thing, ocean water is not safe to drink. But there are other characteristics that make ocean water special. Read on to learn about ocean water's characteristics.

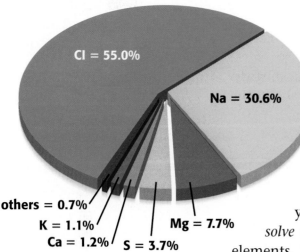

Figure 1 Percentages of Dissolved Solids in Ocean Water
This pie chart shows the relative abundance of the dissolved solids in ocean water. Notice that the two elements that form sodium chloride are by far the most abundant.

Cl = 55.0%
Na = 30.6%
others = 0.7%
K = 1.1%
Ca = 1.2%
S = 3.7%
Mg = 7.7%

Ocean Water Is Salty Have you ever swallowed a mouthful of water while swimming in the ocean? It sure had a nasty taste, didn't it? You know the ocean is salty, but tasting it firsthand can be a shock. Most of the salt in the ocean is the same kind of salt that we sprinkle on our food. Scientists call this salt *sodium chloride.*

The ocean is so salty because salt has been added to the ocean continuously for billions of years. Here's how it happens. Rivers and streams *dissolve* minerals on land into elements and compounds of elements. The running water carries these dissolved solids to the ocean. At the same time, water is *evaporating* from the ocean, but the dissolved solids stay in the ocean. The most abundant dissolved solid in the ocean is sodium chloride, a compound of the elements sodium (Na) and chlorine (Cl), as shown in **Figure 1.**

If more water evaporates than enters the ocean, the ocean's salinity increases. **Salinity** is a measure of the amount of dissolved solids in a given amount of liquid. Salinity is usually measured as grams of dissolved solids per kilogram of water. Think of it this way: 1 kg (1,000 g) of ocean water contains 35 g of dissolved solids on average; therefore, the average salinity of ocean water is 35 parts per thousand. This can be written as 35‰. In other words, if you evaporated 1 kg of ocean water, about 35 g of solids would remain.

Factors That Affect Salinity Some areas of the ocean are saltier than others. Coastal water in areas with hotter, drier climates typically have a higher salinity than coastal water in cooler, more humid areas. This is because less fresh water runs into the ocean in drier areas and because heat increases the evaporation rate. Evaporation removes water but leaves salts and other dissolved solids behind. Also, coastal areas where major rivers run into the ocean have a relatively low salinity. In these areas, the rivers add to the ocean large volumes of fresh water, which contains fewer dissolved solids than sea water.

Another factor that affects ocean salinity is water movement. Surface water in some areas of the ocean, such as bays, gulfs, and seas, circulates less than surface water in other parts. Areas in the open ocean that have no currents running through them can also be slow moving. **Figure 2** shows how salinity variations relate to many factors.

Temperature Zones The temperature of ocean water decreases as the depth of the water increases. However, this does not occur gradually from the ocean's surface to its bottom. Water in the ocean can be divided into three layers according to temperature. As you can see in the graph below, the water at the top is much warmer than the average temperature of the ocean.

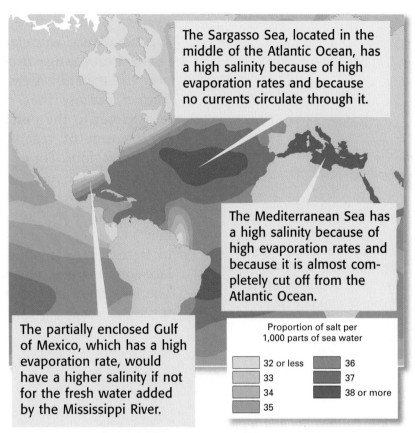

The Sargasso Sea, located in the middle of the Atlantic Ocean, has a high salinity because of high evaporation rates and because no currents circulate through it.

The Mediterranean Sea has a high salinity because of high evaporation rates and because it is almost completely cut off from the Atlantic Ocean.

The partially enclosed Gulf of Mexico, which has a high evaporation rate, would have a higher salinity if not for the fresh water added by the Mississippi River.

Proportion of salt per 1,000 parts of sea water

32 or less	36
33	37
34	38 or more
35	

Figure 2 *Salinity varies in different parts of the ocean because of variations in evaporation, circulation, and freshwater inflow.*

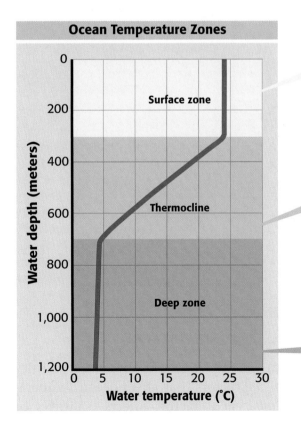

Surface zone
The surface zone is the warm, top layer of ocean water. Sunlight penetrates the top 100 m of the surface zone, heating it with solar energy. Surface currents mix the heated water with cooler water below, which causes the surface zone to extend to 300 m below sea level.

Thermocline
The **thermocline** is a layer of water extending from 300 m below sea level to about 700 m below sea level. In this zone, water temperature drops with increased depth faster than it does in the other two zones. The water in the thermocline is colder and denser than the water in the surface zone.

Deep zone
This bottom layer extends from the base of the thermocline to the bottom of the ocean. The temperature in this zone averages a chilling 2°C, which is 4°C above the freezing point of salt water.

Surface Temperature Changes Temperatures in the surface zone vary with latitude and the time of year. Surface temperatures range from 1°C near the poles to about 24°C near the equator. Areas of the ocean along the equator are warmer because they receive more sunlight per year than areas closer to the poles.

The time of year also affects surface-zone temperatures in most regions. For example, the sun's rays in the Northern Hemisphere are more direct during the summer than during the winter. Therefore, the surface zone absorbs more heat energy during the summer. If you live near the coast, you may know firsthand how different a dip in the ocean feels in December than it feels in July. **Figure 3** shows how surface-zone temperatures vary depending on the time of year. The left image shows the region's winter temperatures, and the right image shows the region's summer temperatures.

Figure 3 *These satellite images show that the surface temperatures in this part of the northern Pacific Ocean are colder during the winter (left) than during the summer (right).*

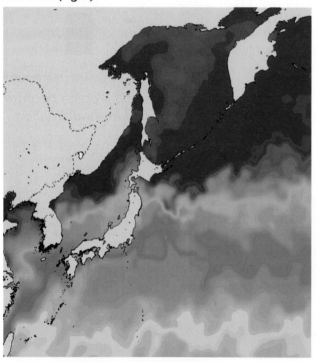

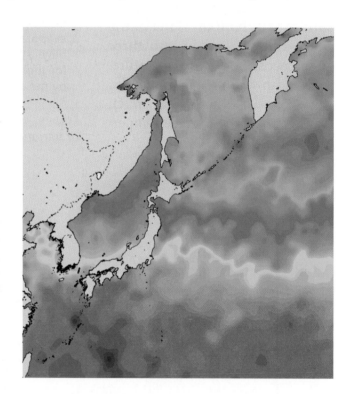

Cool   Warm

REVIEW

1. Name the major divisions of the global ocean.

2. Explain how Earth's first oceans formed.

3. **Summarizing Data** List three factors that affect salinity in the ocean and three factors that affect ocean temperatures. Explain how each factor affects salinity or temperature.

The Ocean and the Water Cycle

If you could sit on the moon and look down at Earth, what would you see? You would notice that Earth's surface is made up of three basic components—water, land, and air. All three are involved in an ongoing process called the water cycle, as shown below. The **water cycle** is a cycle that links all of Earth's solid, liquid, and gaseous water together. The ocean is an important part of the water cycle because nearly all of Earth's water is found in the ocean.

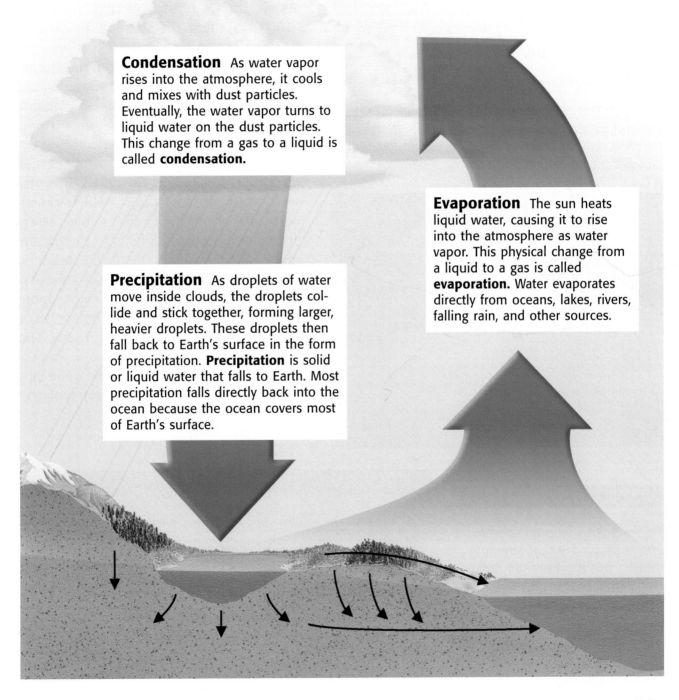

Condensation As water vapor rises into the atmosphere, it cools and mixes with dust particles. Eventually, the water vapor turns to liquid water on the dust particles. This change from a gas to a liquid is called **condensation.**

Evaporation The sun heats liquid water, causing it to rise into the atmosphere as water vapor. This physical change from a liquid to a gas is called **evaporation.** Water evaporates directly from oceans, lakes, rivers, falling rain, and other sources.

Precipitation As droplets of water move inside clouds, the droplets collide and stick together, forming larger, heavier droplets. These droplets then fall back to Earth's surface in the form of precipitation. **Precipitation** is solid or liquid water that falls to Earth. Most precipitation falls directly back into the ocean because the ocean covers most of Earth's surface.

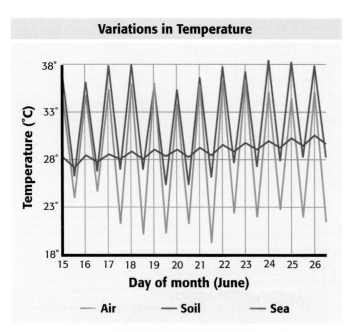

Variations in Temperature

Temperature (°C)

Day of month (June)

— Air   — Soil   — Sea

Figure 4 *This chart compares the fluctuation of the soil and air temperatures in Castle Hayne, North Carolina, with the fluctuation of the ocean temperature just off North Carolina's coast.*

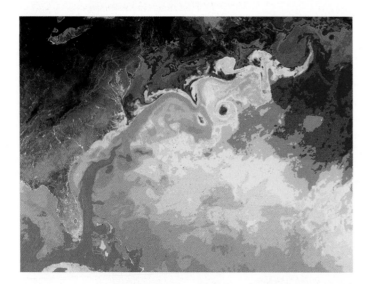

Cool   Warm

Figure 5 *This infrared satellite image shows the Gulf Stream moving warm water from lower latitudes to higher latitudes.*

A Global Thermostat

The ocean plays a vital role in maintaining conditions favorable for life on Earth. Perhaps the most important function of the ocean is to absorb and retain heat from sunlight. This function regulates temperatures in the atmosphere.

As you can see in **Figure 4,** the ocean absorbs and releases heat much more slowly than dry land does. If it were not for this function of the ocean, the average air temperature on Earth would vary from above 100°C during the day to below –100°C at night. In addition to causing this major temperature fluctuation, the rapid exchange of heat between the atmosphere and the Earth's surface would cause sudden changes in weather and violent weather patterns. Life as we know it could not exist with these unstable conditions.

The ocean also regulates temperatures on a more local scale. At the equator, the sun's rays are more direct, which causes equatorial waters to be warmer than waters at higher latitudes. Currents in the oceans move water, as well as the heat it contains, around the Earth, as shown in **Figure 5.** This circulation of warm water causes some coastal lands to have warmer climates than they would have without the currents. The British Isles, for example, have a warmer climate than most regions at the same latitude because of the warm water of the Gulf Stream.

REVIEW

1. Why is the ocean an important part of the water cycle?

2. Between which two steps of the water cycle does the ocean fit?

3. **Making Inferences** Explain why St. Louis, Missouri, has colder winters and warmer summers than San Francisco, California, even though the two cities are at about the same latitude.

The Ocean Floor

NEW TERMS

continental shelf   mid-ocean ridge
continental slope   rift valley
continental rise   seamount
abyssal plain   ocean trench

OBJECTIVES

- Identify the two major regions of the ocean floor.
- Classify subdivisions and features of the two major regions of the ocean floor.
- Describe technologies for studying the ocean floor.

across the sciences
CONNECTION

Turn to page 362 to meet the most famous underwater explorer who ever lived.

What lies at the bottom of the ocean? How deep is the ocean? These are questions that were once unanswerable. But humans have learned a lot about the ocean floor, especially in the last few decades. Using state-of-the-art technology, scientists have discovered a wide variety of landforms on the ocean floor. Scientists have also determined accurate depths for almost the entire ocean floor.

Exploring the Ocean Floor

One of the ways scientists are learning more about the ocean floor is by exploring it. You probably already know that most humans who explore the subsurface ocean do so in submarines. But some parts of the ocean are so deep that humans must use special underwater vessels to travel there.

Perhaps the most familiar underwater vessel used by scientists is a minisub called *Alvin*. *Alvin* is a 7 m long vessel that can reach some of the deepest parts of the ocean. Scientists have used *Alvin* for many underwater missions, including searches for sunken ships, the recovery of a lost hydrogen bomb, and explorations of landforms on the sea floor.

Although the use of *Alvin* has enabled scientists to make some amazing discoveries, scientists are developing new vessels for exploration of the deep ocean. One modern vessel in ocean technology is an underwater airplane called *Deep Flight,* shown in **Figure 6.** This vessel moves through the water much like an airplane moves through the air. Future models of *Deep Flight* will be designed to transport pilots to the deepest part of the ocean, which is more than 11,000 m deep.

Figure 6 *Like the Wright brothers' first successful airplane,* Deep Flight *sets the stage for a bright future— this time in underwater "flight."*

Revealing the Ocean Floor

Want to survey the ocean floor? Turn to page 538 in the LabBook to bring the ocean floor to your desktop.

What if you were an explorer assigned to map uncharted areas on the planet? You might think there were not many uncharted areas left because most of the land had already been explored. But what about the bottom of the ocean? Most of the Earth's surface is hidden by water. What if you could operate *Deep Flight*? You would have a fish's eye view of the land under the ocean. What would it look like? You might think you would see a huge empty bowl, but in fact you would see the world's longest mountain chain and canyons deeper than the Grand Canyon.

As you began your descent into the underwater realm, you would notice that the land under the ocean is divided into two major regions—the *continental margin*, which is made of continental crust, and the *deep-ocean basin*, which is made of oceanic crust. It may help to imagine the ocean as a giant swimming pool; the continental margin is the shallow end and slope of the pool, and the deep-ocean basin is the deep end of the pool. **Figure 7** shows how these two regions are subdivided.

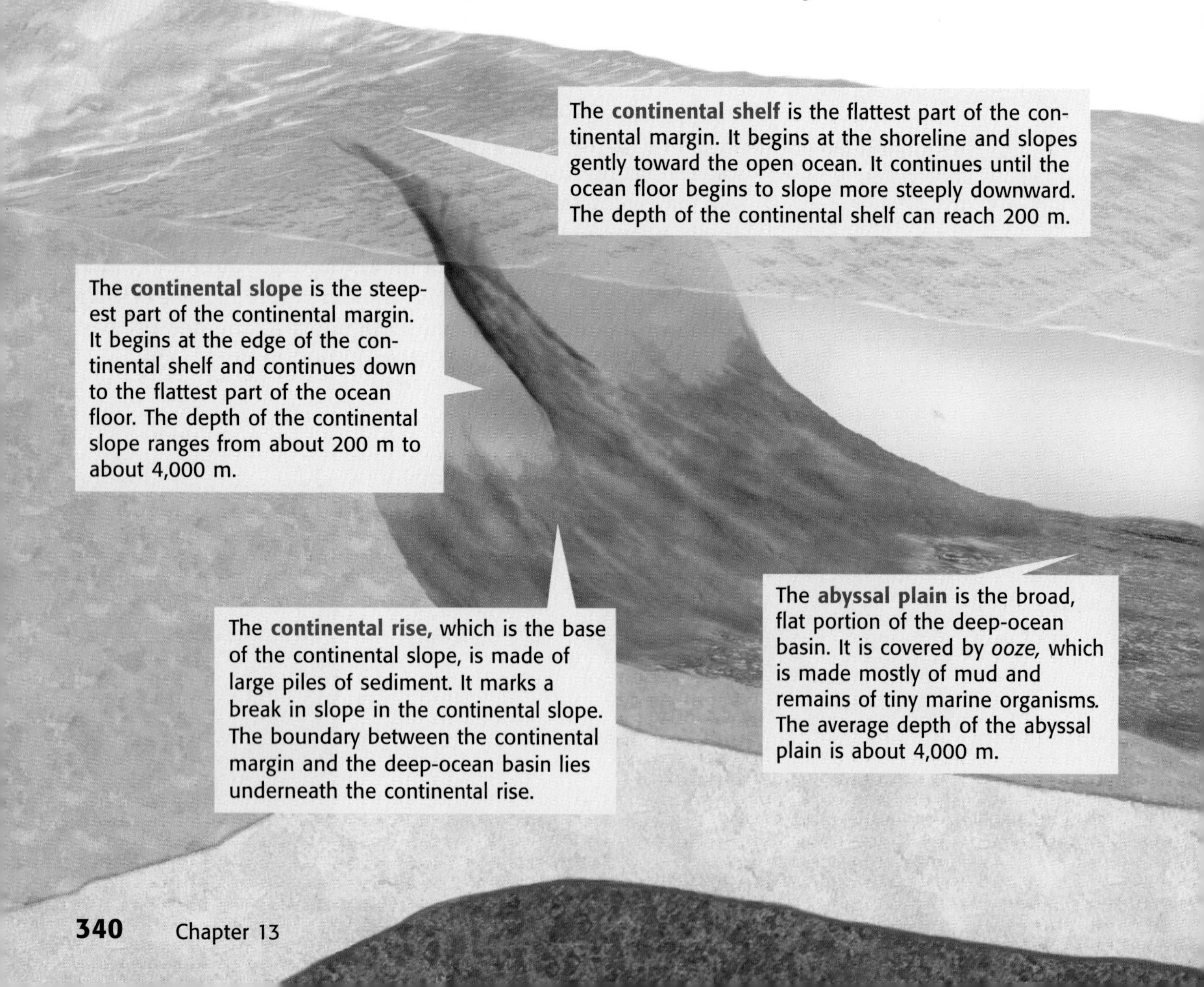

Figure 7 *The continental margin is subdivided into three depth zones, and the deep-ocean basin consists of one depth zone with several features.*

The **continental shelf** is the flattest part of the continental margin. It begins at the shoreline and slopes gently toward the open ocean. It continues until the ocean floor begins to slope more steeply downward. The depth of the continental shelf can reach 200 m.

The **continental slope** is the steepest part of the continental margin. It begins at the edge of the continental shelf and continues down to the flattest part of the ocean floor. The depth of the continental slope ranges from about 200 m to about 4,000 m.

The **continental rise**, which is the base of the continental slope, is made of large piles of sediment. It marks a break in slope in the continental slope. The boundary between the continental margin and the deep-ocean basin lies underneath the continental rise.

The **abyssal plain** is the broad, flat portion of the deep-ocean basin. It is covered by *ooze*, which is made mostly of mud and remains of tiny marine organisms. The average depth of the abyssal plain is about 4,000 m.

Underwater Real Estate As you can see, the continental margin is subdivided into the continental shelf, the continental slope, and the continental rise based on depth and changes in slope. The deep-ocean basin consists of the abyssal plain, with features such as mid-ocean ridges, rift valleys, and ocean trenches that form near the boundaries of Earth's *tectonic plates*. On parts of the abyssal plain that are not near plate boundaries, thousands of seamounts are found on the ocean floor.

Explore

To get an idea of how deep parts of the ocean are, use an encyclopedia to find out how deep the Grand Canyon is. Compare this depth with that of the Mariana Trench, which is more than 11,000 m deep!

✔ Self-Check

How do the locations of rift valleys and ocean trenches differ? *(See page 564 to check your answer.)*

Mid-ocean ridges are mountain chains formed where *tectonic plates* pull apart. This pulling motion creates cracks in the ocean floor called *rift zones.* Directly below rift zones, molten rock called *magma* rises from below the crust and erupts through the cracks as *lava.* The lava then cools as it enters the water, becoming new oceanic crust. As plates on either side of rift zones continue to pull apart, more magma rises to fill in the spaces. Heat from the magma causes the crust on either side of the rifts to expand, forming the ridges.

Seamounts are individual mountains of volcanic material that are scattered across the abyssal plain. They form where magma pushes its way through or between tectonic plates. If a seamount builds up above sea level, it becomes a volcanic island. The Hawaiian Islands formed this way.

Ocean trenches are deep troughs in the deep-ocean basin. These narrow features sometimes reach thousands of kilometers in length and are the deepest places on Earth. Ocean trenches form where one oceanic plate is forced underneath a continental plate or another oceanic plate.

As mountains build up, a **rift valley** forms between them in the rift zone.

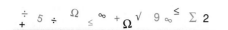

MATH BREAK

Depths of the Deep

The depths in a sea profile are calculated using the following simple formula:

$$D = \frac{1}{2}t \times v$$

D is the depth of the ocean floor, t is the time it takes for the sound to reach the bottom and return to the surface, and v equals the speed of sound in water (1,500 m/s). Calculate D for the following three parts of the ocean floor:

1. a mid-ocean ridge ($t = 2$ s)
2. an ocean trench ($t = 14$ s)
3. an abyssal plain ($t = 5.3$ s)

Viewing the Ocean Floor from Above

In spite of the great success of underwater exploration, sending scientists into deep water is still risky. Fortunately, there are ways to survey the underwater realm from the surface and from high above in space. Read on to learn about two technologies—sonar and satellites—that enable scientists to study the ocean floor without going below the surface.

Seeing by Sonar *Sonar,* which stands for "sound navigation and ranging," is a technology based on the echo-ranging behavior of bats. Scientists use sonar to determine the ocean's depth by sending high-frequency sound pulses from a ship down into the ocean. The sound travels through the water, bounces off the ocean floor, and returns to the ship. The deeper the water is, the longer the round trip takes. Scientists then calculate the depth by multiplying half the travel time by the speed of sound in water (about 1,500 m/s). This process is shown in the illustration below.

1 To map a section of the ocean floor, scientists travel by ship across the ocean's surface, repeatedly sending sonar signals to the ocean floor.

2 The longer it takes for the sound to bounce off the ocean floor and return to the ship, the deeper the floor is in that spot.

3 Scientists make a bathymetric profile like this one by plotting the different depths that they discover using these sonar signals. A *bathymetric profile* is basically a map of the ocean floor showing its depth variations.

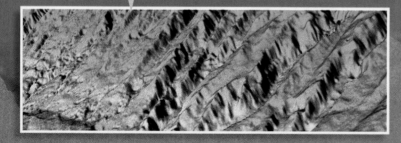

Oceanography via Satellite In the 1970s, scientists began studying Earth from satellites in orbit around the Earth. In 1972, *Landsat 1* orbited the Earth and sent back information about Earth's natural resources. In 1978, scientists launched the satellite *Seasat.* This satellite focused on the ocean, sending images back to Earth that allowed scientists to measure the direction and speed of ocean currents and detect changes in the polar icecaps.

Geosat, once a top-secret military satellite, has been used to measure slight changes in the height of the ocean's surface. Different underwater features, such as mountains and trenches, affect the height of the water above them. For example, the height of the ocean surface is higher over mountains than over the abyssal plains, thus reflecting the underwater topography of the ocean floor. Scientists measure the different heights of the ocean surface and use the measurements to make highly detailed maps of the ocean floor. As illustrated in **Figure 8,** oceanographers can make maps that cover a lot more territory by using satellites than by using ship-based sonar readings.

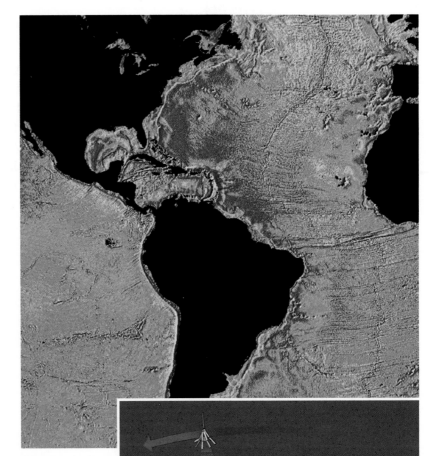

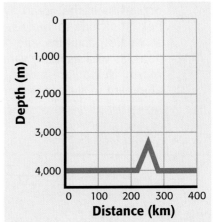

Figure 8 *The map above was generated by satellite measurements of different heights of the ocean surface.*

REVIEW

1. Name the two major regions of the ocean floor.

2. List the subdivisions of the continental margin.

3. List three technologies for studying the ocean floor, and explain how they are used.

4. **Interpreting Graphics** What part of the ocean floor would the bathymetric profile at right represent?

Bathymetric Profile

(Graph: Depth (m) on vertical axis from 0 to 4,000; Distance (km) on horizontal axis from 0 to 400. Profile shows a flat ocean floor at about 4,000 m with a narrow peak rising to about 3,500 m near 250 km.)

Life in the Ocean

The ocean contains a wide variety of life-forms, many of which we know little about. Trying to study them can be quite a challenge for scientists. To make things easier, scientists classify marine organisms into three main groups. Scientists also divide the ocean into two main environments based on the types of organisms that live in them. These two main environments are further subdivided into ecological zones based on locations of different organisms.

The Three Groups of Marine Life

The three main groups of marine life are plankton, nekton, and benthos. Marine organisms are placed into one of these three groups according to where they live and how they move. Carefully examine the figure below to understand the differences between these groups.

NEW TERMS

plankton   benthic environment
nekton   pelagic environment
benthos

OBJECTIVES

- Identify and describe the three groups of marine organisms.
- Identify and describe the benthic and pelagic environments.
- Classify the zones of the benthic and pelagic environments.

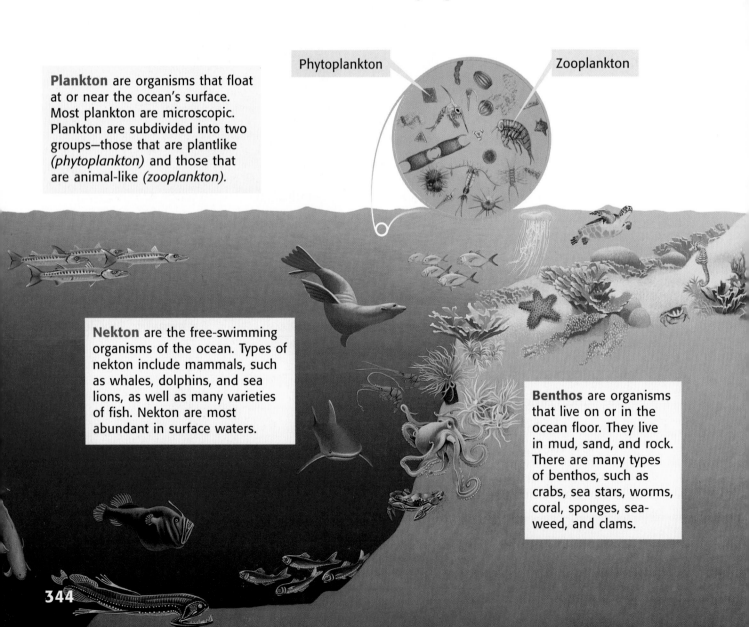

Phytoplankton   Zooplankton

Plankton are organisms that float at or near the ocean's surface. Most plankton are microscopic. Plankton are subdivided into two groups—those that are plantlike (*phytoplankton*) and those that are animal-like *(zooplankton).*

Nekton are the free-swimming organisms of the ocean. Types of nekton include mammals, such as whales, dolphins, and sea lions, as well as many varieties of fish. Nekton are most abundant in surface waters.

Benthos are organisms that live on or in the ocean floor. They live in mud, sand, and rock. There are many types of benthos, such as crabs, sea stars, worms, coral, sponges, seaweed, and clams.

The Benthic Environment

In addition to being divided into zones based on depth, the ocean floor is divided into ecological zones based on where different types of benthos live. These zones are grouped into one major marine environment—the benthic environment. The **benthic environment,** or bottom environment, is the ocean floor and all the organisms that live on or in it.

Intertidal Zone The shallowest benthic zone, the *intertidal zone,* is located between the low-tide and high-tide limits. Twice a day, the intertidal zone transforms. As the tide flows in, the zone is covered with ocean water, and as the tide retreats, the intertidal zone is exposed to the air and sun.

Intertidal organisms must be able to live both underwater and on exposed land. Some organisms attach themselves to rocks and reefs to avoid being washed out to sea during low tide, as shown in **Figure 9.** Clams, oysters, barnacles, and crabs have tough shells that give them protection against strong waves during high tide and against harsh sunlight during low tide. Some animals can burrow in sand or between rocks. Plants such as seaweed have strong *holdfasts* (rootlike structures) that allow them to grow in this zone.

Sublittoral Zone The *sublittoral zone* begins where the intertidal zones ends, at the low-tide limit, and extends to the edge of the continental shelf. This benthic zone is more stable than the intertidal zone; the temperature, water pressure, and amount of sunlight remain fairly constant. Consequently, sublittoral organisms, such as corals, shown in **Figure 10,** do not have to cope with as much change as intertidal organisms. Although the sublittoral zone extends down 200 m below sea level, plants and most animals stay in the upper 100 m, where sunlight reaches the ocean floor.

life science
CONNECTION

Coral reefs, found in shallow marine waters, have the largest concentration of life in the ocean. Layers of skeletons from animals called *corals* form the reefs, which are the largest animal structures on Earth. Many other organisms live on, around, and even in coral reefs.

Figure 9 *Organisms such as sea anemones and starfish attach themselves to rocks and reefs. These organisms must be able to survive wet and dry conditions.*

Figure 10 *Corals, like many other types of organisms, can live in both the sublittoral zone and the intertidal zone. However, they are more common in the sublittoral zone.*

Figure 11 *Octopuses are one of the animals common to the bathyal zone.*

Figure 12 *Tube worms can tolerate higher temperatures than most other organisms. These animals survive in water as hot as 81°C.*

Figure 13 *These clams are one of the few types of organisms known to live in the hadal zone.*

Bathyal Zone The *bathyal zone* extends from the edge of the continental shelf to the abyssal plain. The depth of this zone ranges from 200 m to 4,000 m below sea level. Because of the lack of sunlight at these depths, plant life is scarce in this part of the benthic environment. Animals in this zone include sponges, *brachiopods,* sea stars, *echinoids,* and octopuses, such as the one shown in **Figure 11.**

Abyssal Zone No plants and very few animals live in the *abyssal zone,* which is on the abyssal plain. Among the abyssal animal types are crabs, sponges, worms, and sea cucumbers. Many of these organisms, such as the tube worms shown in **Figure 12,** live around hot-water vents called *black smokers.* The abyssal zone can reach 6,000 m in depth. Scientists know very little about this benthic zone because it is so deep and dark.

Hadal Zone The deepest benthic zone is the *hadal zone.* This zone consists of the floor of the ocean trenches and any organisms found there. Scientists know even less about the hadal zone than they do about the abyssal zone. So far, scientists have discovered a type of sponge, a few species of worms, and a type of clam, which is shown in **Figure 13.**

The Pelagic Environment

The **pelagic environment,** or water environment, is the entire volume of water in the ocean and the marine organisms that live above the ocean floor. There are two major zones in the pelagic environment—the *neritic zone* and the *oceanic zone.*

Neritic Zone The neritic zone includes the volume of water that covers the continental shelf. This warm, shallow pelagic zone contains the largest concentration of marine life. This is due in part to an abundance of sunlight and in part to the many benthos below the neritic zone that serve as a food supply. Fish, plankton, and marine mammals, such as the one in **Figure 14,** are just a few of the animal groups found here. Most seafood is harvested from the neritic zone.

Figure 14 *Many marine mammals, such as this dolphin, live in the neritic zone.*

Oceanic Zone The oceanic zone includes the volume of water that covers the entire sea floor except for the continental shelf. In the deeper parts of the oceanic zone, the water temperature is colder and the pressure is much greater than in the neritic zone. Also, organisms are more spread out in the oceanic zone than in the neritic zone. While many of the same organisms that live in the neritic zone are found throughout the upper regions, some strange animals lurk in the darker depths. For example, the anglerfish, shown in **Figure 15,** is a tricky predator that uses a natural lure attached to its head to attract prey. And the *Gigantura,* a fish with long, tubular eyes and flexible skin, can expand its body to swallow animals larger than itself! Other animals in the deeper parts of this zone include giant squids and some whale species.

Figure 15 *The anglerfish lives deep in the oceanic zone.*

REVIEW

1. List and briefly describe the three main groups of marine organisms.

2. Name the two ocean environments. List the zones of each environment.

3. **Making Predictions** How would the ocean's ecological zones change if sea level dropped 300 m?

Resources from the Ocean

NEW TERMS
desalination

OBJECTIVES

- List two methods of harvesting the ocean's living resources.
- List nonliving resources in the ocean.
- Describe the ocean's energy resources.

The ocean offers a seemingly endless supply of resources. Food, raw materials, energy, and drinkable water all are harvested from the ocean. And there are probably undiscovered resources in unexplored regions of the ocean. As human populations have grown, however, the demand for these resources has increased while the availability has decreased.

Living Resources

People have been harvesting marine plants and animals for food for thousands of years. Many civilizations formed in coastal regions that were rich enough in marine life to support growing human populations. Read on to learn how humans harvest marine life today.

Fishing the Ocean Harvesting food from the ocean is a multi-billion-dollar industry. Of all the seafood taken from the ocean, fish are the most abundant. Almost 75 million tons of fish is harvested each year. With improved technology, such as sonar and drift nets, fishermen have become better at locating and taking fish from the ocean. **Figure 16** illustrates how drift nets are used. In recent years, many people have become concerned that we are overfishing the ocean—taking more fish than can be naturally replaced. Also, a few years ago, the public became aware that animals other than fish, especially dolphins and turtles, were accidentally being caught in drift nets. Today the fishing industry is making efforts to prevent overfishing and damage to other wildlife from drift nets.

Figure 16 *Drift nets are fishing nets that cover kilometers of ocean. Fishermen can harvest entire schools of fish in one drift net.*

Farming the Ocean As overfishing reduces fish populations and laws regulating fishing become stricter, it is becoming more difficult to supply our demand for fish. To compensate for this, many ocean fish, such as salmon and turbot, are being captively bred in fish farms. Fish farming requires several holding ponds, each containing fish at a certain level of development. **Figure 17** shows a holding pond in a fish farm. When the fish are old enough, they are harvested and packaged for shipping.

Figure 17 *Consuming fish raised in a fish farm helps reduce the number of fish harvested from the ocean.*

Fish are not the only seafood harvested in a farmlike setting. Shrimp, oysters, crabs, and mussels are raised in enclosed areas near the shore. Mussels and oysters are grown attached to ropes, as shown in **Figure 18.** Huge nets line the nursery area, preventing the animals from being eaten by their natural predators.

Many species of algae, commonly known as seaweed, are also harvested from the ocean. For example, kelp, a seaweed that grows as much as 33 cm a day, is harvested and used as a thickener in jellies, ice cream, and similar products that have a smooth, gel-like composition. The next time you enjoy your favorite chocolate-ripple ice cream, remember that without seaweed, it would be a runny mess! Seaweed is rich in protein, and several species of seaweed are staples of the Japanese diet. For example, the rolled varieties of sushi, a Japanese dish, are wrapped in seaweed.

Figure 18 *In addition to fish, there are many other types of seafood, such as these mussels, that are raised in farms.*

Nonliving Resources

Humans harvest many types of nonliving resources from the ocean. These resources provide raw materials, drinkable water, and energy for our expanding population. Some resources are easily obtained, while others are rare or difficult to harvest.

Oil and Natural Gas Modern civilization continues to be very dependent on oil and natural gas as major sources of energy. Oil and natural gas are *nonrenewable resources,* which means that they are used up faster than they can be replenished naturally. However, drilling for oil and gas on the ocean floor as well as on land is still profitable. Much of Earth's oil and gas began to form beneath the sea millions of years ago when dead organisms on the ocean floor were covered by sediment. This organic matter was crushed and buried deep beneath the surface by the overlying sediment. Heat was generated during this process, and the animal and plant matter eventually turned into oil or natural gas. These two resources are trapped under layers of impermeable rock. Petroleum engineers must drill through this rock in order to reach the resources.

But how do petroleum engineers know where to drill? Ships with seismic equipment are used for this purpose. Special devices send powerful pulses of sound to the ocean floor. The pulses travel through the water and penetrate the rocks below. The pulses are then reflected back toward the ship, where they are recorded by electronic equipment and analyzed by a computer. The computer readings indicate how rock layers are arranged below the ocean floor. Petroleum geologists look for readings that indicate arrangements that might trap oil and gas, such as the reading in **Figure 19.** They then recommend drilling in a spot that could contain a lot of oil or gas.

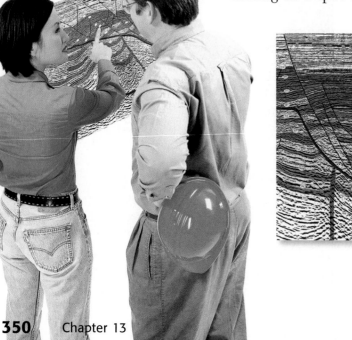

Figure 19 *Petroleum geologists look at seismic readings to decide where on the ocean floor to drill for oil and gas. This reading shows some promise!*

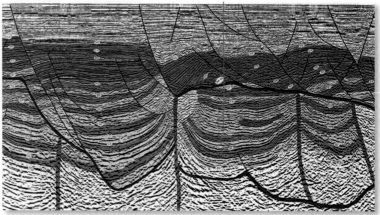

Fresh Water and Desalination In some areas of the world where fresh water is limited, people desalinate ocean water. **Desalination** is the process of evaporating sea water so that the water and the salt separate. As the water cools and condenses, it is collected and processed for human use. But desalination is not as simple as it sounds, and it is very costly. Countries with an adequate amount of annual rainfall rely on the fresh water provided by precipitation and therefore do not need costly desalination plants. But some countries located in arid regions of the world must build desalination plants to provide an adequate supply of fresh water. Saudi Arabia, located in the desert region of the Middle East, has one of the largest desalination plants in the world. Look at a world map, and try to identify other areas that might depend on desalination.

Sea-Floor Minerals Scientists are very interested in mineral nodules that are lying on the ocean floor. These nodules are made mostly of manganese, which can be used to make certain types of steel. They also contain iron, copper, nickel, and cobalt. Other nodules are made of phosphates, which are used in making fertilizer.

Nodules are formed from dissolved substances in sea water that stick to solid objects, such as pebbles. As more substances stick to the coated pebble, a nodule begins to grow. Manganese nodules range from the size of a marble to the size of a soccer ball. The nodules were discovered nearly 130 years ago when HMS *Challenger,* a British exploration ship, dredged them up while exploring the Pacific Ocean. The photograph in **Figure 20** shows a number of nodules scattered across the ocean floor. It is believed that 15 percent of the ocean floor is covered with these nodules. However, they are located in the deeper parts of the ocean, and mining them is costly and difficult.

Quick Lab

How Much Fresh Water Is There?

1. Fill a large **beaker** with 1,000 mL of **water.** This represents all the water on Earth.
2. Carefully pour 970 mL from the beaker into a **graduated cylinder.** This represents the amount of water in the ocean.
3. Pour another 20 mL from the beaker into a **second graduated cylinder.** This represents the amount of water frozen in icecaps and glaciers.
4. Pour another 5 mL into a **third graduated cylinder.** This represents nonconsumable water on land.
5. Take a look at the leftover water. This represents Earth's supply of fresh water.

Put freshwater problems on ice! Turn to page 363 to find out how.

Figure 20 *These manganese nodules could make you wealthy if you knew an affordable way to mine them.*

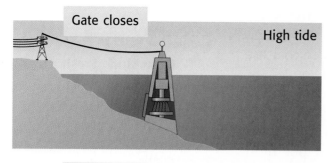

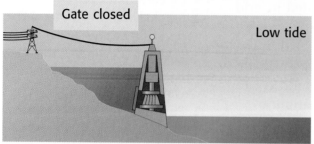

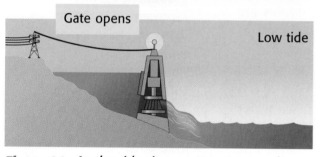

Figure 21 *As the tide rises, water enters a bay behind a dam. The gates then close at high tide. The gates remain closed as the tide lowers. At low tide, the gates open, and the water rushes through the dam, moving the turbines, which in turn create electricity.*

BRAIN FOOD

The difference between high and low tide in the Bay of Fundy, in New Brunswick, Canada, can be greater than 15 m! This tidal range is the world's largest.

Tidal Energy The ocean creates several types of energy resources simply because of its constant movement. The gravitational pull of the sun and moon causes the ocean to rise and fall as tides. *Tidal energy,* energy generated from the movement of tides, is an excellent alternative source of energy. If the water during high tide can be rushed through a narrow coastal passageway, the water's force can be powerful enough to generate electricity. **Figure 21** shows how this works. Tidal energy is a clean, inexpensive, and renewable resource once the dam is built. A *renewable resource* can be replenished, in time, after being used. Unfortunately, tidal energy is practical only in a few areas of the world, where the coastline has shallow, narrow channels. For example, the coastline at Cook Inlet, in Alaska, is perfect for generating tidal power.

Wave Energy Have you ever stood on the beach and watched as waves crashed onto the shore? This constant motion, which has been occurring since the oceans formed billions of years ago, is an energy resource. Wave energy, like tidal energy, is a clean, renewable resource.

Recently, computer programs have been developed to analyze the energy of waves. Researchers have located certain areas of the world where wave energy can generate enough electricity to make it worthwhile to build power plants. Wave energy in the North Sea is strong enough to produce power for parts of Scotland and England.

REVIEW

1. List two methods of harvesting the ocean's living resources.

2. Name four nonliving resources in the ocean.

3. **Interpreting Graphics** Take another look at Figure 21. As the tide is rising, will the gate be open or closed? How might this affect the turbines?

Ocean Pollution

Humans have used the ocean for waste disposal for hundreds, if not thousands, of years. This has harmed the organisms that live in the oceans as well as animals that depend on marine organisms. People are also affected by polluted oceans. Fortunately, we are becoming more aware of ocean pollution, and we are learning from our mistakes.

Sources of Ocean Pollution

There are many sources of ocean pollution. Some of these sources are easily identified, but others are more difficult to pinpoint. Read on to find out where different types of ocean pollution come from and how they affect the ocean.

Trash Dumping People dump trash in many places, including the ocean. In the 1980s, scientists became alarmed by the kind of trash that was washing up on beaches. Bandages, vials of blood, and syringes (needles) were found among the waste. Some of the blood in the vials even contained the AIDS virus. The Environmental Protection Agency (EPA) began an investigation and discovered that hospitals in the United States produce an average of 3 million tons of medical waste each year. And where does some of this trash end up? You guessed it—in the ocean. Because of stricter laws, much of this medical waste is now buried in sanitary landfills. However, dumping trash in the deeper part of the ocean is still a common practice in many countries.

Figure 22 *This barge is headed out to the open ocean, where it will dump the trash it carries.*

In Austin, Texas, sludge is used to make a compost called *Dillo Dirt*. (*Dillo* refers to *armadillo*, a small aardvark-like mammal common in Texas.) Instead of polluting the Gulf of Mexico, Austinites are using sludge to grow beautiful and beneficial gardens.

Sludge Dumping By 1990, the United States alone had discharged 38 trillion liters of treated sludge into the waters along its coasts. What is sludge, and why is it so bad? To answer this question, we need to define *raw sewage*.

Raw sewage refers to all the liquid and solid wastes that are flushed down toilets and poured down drains. After collecting in sewer drains, raw sewage is sent through a treatment plant, where it undergoes a cleaning process that removes the solid waste. Once the liquid is sufficiently treated, it is released into nearby waterways. The remaining solid waste, which is called *sludge,* still contains toxins and bacteria that can cause diseases. In many areas, people dump sludge into the ocean several kilometers offshore, intending for it to settle to and stay on the ocean floor. Unfortunately, this sludge does not always stay on the ocean floor. Sometimes currents stir the sludge up and move it closer to shore. This can pollute beaches and kill marine life. Many countries have banned sludge dumping, but it continues to occur in many areas of the world.

Nonpoint-Source Pollution Did you know that every time you wash a car or fertilize your lawn you contribute to ocean pollution? Unfortunately, it's true. We usually think of water pollution as coming from large factories, but you may be surprised to know that most of the pollution comes from everyday citizens doing everyday things. This type of pollution, which is shown in **Figure 23,** is called **nonpoint-source pollution** because you cannot pinpoint its exact source. But if the source of pollution is everyday activities at people's homes, how does the pollution get into the ocean? All waste water and runoff eventually enter a body of water, usually a stream. Every stream leads to a river, and every river leads to the ocean.

Figure 23 Nonpoint-source pollution contributes significantly to ocean pollution. What can you do to cut down on nonpoint-source pollution?

Oil Spills Because oil is in such high demand across the world, large tankers must transport billions of barrels of it across the oceans. If not handled properly, these transports can quickly turn disastrous. In 1989, the United States experienced a large oil spill in Prince William Sound, a waterway on the Alaskan coast. The *Exxon Valdez,* a supertanker, struck a reef and spilled more than 260,000 barrels of crude oil. The effect of this accident on wildlife was catastrophic. Many animals were covered in oil and started dying immediately. Animals that fed on these oil-contaminated animals also died. Many Alaskans who made their living from fishing lost their businesses and, in some cases, their traditional way of life. Although many animals were saved, as shown in **Figure 24,** and the Exxon Oil Company spent $2.5 billion to try to clean up the mess, Alaska's wildlife and economy will continue to suffer for decades.

Figure 24 *Many oil-covered animals were rescued and cleaned after the* Exxon Valdez *spill.*

Today many oil companies are using new technology to safeguard against oil spills. Tankers are now being built with two hulls instead of one. This prevents oil from spilling into the ocean if the outside hull of the ship is damaged. **Figure 25** illustrates the design of a double-hulled tanker.

Figure 25 *If the outside hull of a double-hulled tanker is punctured, the oil will still be contained within the inside hull.*

Saving Our Ocean Resources

Although humans have done much to harm the ocean's resources, we have also begun to do more to save them. From international treaties to volunteer cleanups, efforts to conserve the ocean's resources are making an impact around the world.

Nations Take Notice When ocean pollution reached an all-time high, many countries recognized the need to work together to solve the problem. In 1989, 64 countries ratified a treaty that prohibits the dumping of mercury, cadmium compounds, certain plastics, oil, and high-level radioactive wastes into the ocean. Many other international agreements restricting ocean pollution have been made, but enforcing them is often difficult.

In spite of efforts to protect the ocean, waste dumping and oil spills still occur, and contaminated organisms continue to wash ashore. Why are the laws not working as well as they should? Enforcing these laws takes money and human resources, and many agencies are lacking in both.

Action in the United States The United States, like many other countries, has taken additional measures to control local pollution. In 1972, Congress passed the Clean Water Act, which put the EPA in charge of issuing permits for any dumping of trash into the ocean. Later that year, a stricter law was passed. The U.S. Marine Protection, Research, and Sanctuaries Act prohibits the dumping of any material that would affect human health or welfare, the marine environment or ecosystems, or businesses that depend on the ocean.

Why worry about a few drops of oil? You might be surprised that a little goes a long way. Turn to page 540 in the LabBook to learn more.

Get together with your classmates and divide yourselves into three groups: Nation A, Nation B, and Nation C. All three nations are located near the ocean, and all three nations share borders. Nation A has a very rich supply of oil, which it transports around the world. Nation B currently depends on nuclear energy and has many nuclear power plants near its shores. Nation B has no place on land to store radioactive waste from its nuclear power plants. Nation C sells nuclear technology to Nation B, buys oil from Nation A, and has the world's most diverse coastal ecosystem. The three nations must form a treaty to safeguard against ocean pollution without seriously harming any of their economies. Can you do it?

Figure 26 *The Adopt-a-Beach program in Texas has been a huge success.*

Citizens Take Charge Citizens of many countries have demanded that their governments do more to solve the growing problem of ocean pollution. Because of public outcry, the United States now spends more than $130 million each year monitoring the oceans. United States citizens have also begun to take the matter into their own hands. In the early 1980s, citizens began organizing beach cleanups. One of the largest cleanups is the semiannual Adopt-a-Beach program, shown in **Figure 26,** that originated with the Texas Coastal Cleanup campaign. Millions of tons of trash have been gathered from the beaches, and people are being educated about the hazards of ocean dumping.

Though governments pass laws against ocean dumping, keeping the oceans clean is everyone's responsibility. The next time you and your family visit the beach, make sure the only items you leave behind on the sand are hermit crabs, shells, and maybe a few sand dollars.

REVIEW

1. List three types of ocean pollution. How can each of these types be prevented or minimized?

2. Which type of ocean pollution is most common?

3. **Summarizing Data** List and describe three measures that governments have taken to control ocean pollution.

Chapter Highlights

Vocabulary

salinity *(p. 334)*

thermocline *(p. 335)*

water cycle *(p. 337)*

Section Notes

- The four oceans as we know them today formed within the last 300 million years.

- Salts have been added to the ocean for billions of years.

- The three temperature zones of ocean water are the surface zone, thermocline, and deep zone.

- The ocean plays the largest role in the water cycle.

- The ocean stabilizes Earth's conditions by absorbing and retaining heat.

Vocabulary

continental shelf *(p. 340)*

continental slope *(p. 340)*

continental rise *(p. 340)*

abyssal plain *(p. 340)*

mid-ocean ridge *(p. 341)*

rift valley *(p. 341)*

seamount *(p. 341)*

ocean trench *(p. 341)*

Section Notes

- The ocean floor is divided into zones based on depth and slope.

- The continental margin consists of the continental shelf, the continental slope, and the continental rise.

- The deep-ocean basin consists of the abyssal plain, with features such as mid-ocean ridges, rift valleys, seamounts, and ocean trenches.

- In addition to directly studying the ocean floor, scientists indirectly study the ocean floor using sonar and satellites.

Labs

Probing the Depths *(p. 538)*

☑ Skills Check

Math Concepts

PERCENTAGES Percentages are a way of describing the parts within a whole. Percentages are expressed in hundredths. Take another look at Figure 1 on page 334. The pie chart shows the percentages of dissolved solids in ocean water. The amount of chlorine (Cl) dissolved in the ocean is 55 percent. This means that 55 of every 100 parts of dissolved solids in the ocean are chlorine.

Visual Understanding

RETAINING HEAT The ocean retains heat better than air or dry land. Look at Figure 4 on page 338. Notice how the line representing sea temperatures varies little from day to day. On the other hand, the lines representing air and soil temperatures vary significantly from day to day.

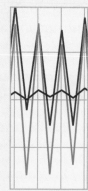

SECTION 3

Vocabulary

plankton *(p. 344)*

nekton *(p. 344)*

benthos *(p. 344)*

benthic environment *(p. 345)*

pelagic environment *(p. 347)*

Section Notes

- There are three main groups of marine life—plankton, nekton, and benthos.

- The two main ocean environments—the benthic and pelagic environments—are divided into ecological zones based on the locations of organisms that live in the environments.

SECTION 4

Vocabulary

desalination *(p. 351)*

Section Notes

- Humans depend on the ocean for living and non-living resources.

- Ocean farms raise fish and other marine life to help feed growing human populations.

- Nonliving ocean resources include oil and natural gas, fresh water, minerals, and tidal and wave energy.

SECTION 5

Vocabulary

nonpoint-source pollution *(p. 354)*

Section Notes

- Types of ocean pollution include trash dumping, sludge dumping, nonpoint-source pollution, and oil spills.

- Nonpoint-source pollution cannot be traced to specific points of origin.

- Efforts to save ocean resources include international treaties and volunteer cleanups.

Labs

Investigating an Oil Spill *(p. 540)*

---

internet**connect**

 GO TO: go.hrw.com

Visit the **HRW** Web site for a variety of learning tools related to this chapter. Just type in the keyword:

KEYWORD: HSTOCE

 GO TO: www.scilinks.org

Visit the **National Science Teachers Association** on-line Web site for Internet resources related to this chapter. Just type in the *sci*LINKS number for more information about the topic:

TOPIC: Exploring Earth's Oceans	*sci*LINKS NUMBER: HSTE305
TOPIC: The Ocean Floor	*sci*LINKS NUMBER: HSTE310
TOPIC: Life in the Oceans	*sci*LINKS NUMBER: HSTE315
TOPIC: Ocean Resources	*sci*LINKS NUMBER: HSTE320
TOPIC: Jacques Cousteau: Ocean Explorer	*sci*LINKS NUMBER: HSTE325

Chapter Review

To complete the following sentences, choose the correct term from each pair of terms listed below:

1. The region of the ocean floor that is closest to the shoreline is the __?__. *(continental shelf* or *continental slope)*

2. Below the surface layer of the ocean is a layer of water that gets colder with depth and extends to a depth of 700 m. This layer is called the __?__. *(thermocline* or *benthic environment)*

3. __?__ typically float at or near the ocean's surface. *(Plankton* or *Nekton)*

Correct the wrong terminology in each of the following sentences. A word bank is provided.

4. The water cycle is the process of evaporating sea water so that the water and salt separate.

5. Types of nekton include sea stars and clams.

Word bank: non-point-source pollution, plankton, desalination, benthos

Explain the difference between the words in each of the following pairs:

6. ocean trench/rift valley

7. salinity/desalination

8. nekton/benthos

9. pelagic environment/benthic environment

Multiple Choice

10. The largest ocean is the
    a. Indian Ocean.   c. Atlantic Ocean.
    b. Pacific Ocean.   d. Arctic Ocean.

11. The average salinity of ocean water is
    a. 45‰.   c. 35‰.
    b. 24‰.   d. None of the above

12. Which of the following affects the ocean's salinity?
    a. fresh water added by rivers
    b. currents
    c. evaporation
    d. All of the above

13. Most precipitation falls
    a. on land.
    b. into lakes and rivers.
    c. into the ocean.
    d. in rain forests.

14. Which benthic zone has a depth range between 200 m and 4,000 m?
    a. bathyal zone   c. hadal zone
    b. abyssal zone   d. sublittoral zone

Short Answer

15. Why does coastal water in areas with hotter, drier climates typically have a higher salinity than coastal water in cooler, more humid areas?

16. What is the difference between the abyssal plain and the abyssal zone?

17. How do the continental shelf, the continental slope, the continental rise, and the continental margin relate to each other?

Concept Mapping

18. Use the following terms to create a concept map: marine life, plankton, nekton, benthos, benthic environment, pelagic environment.

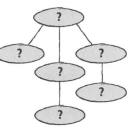

CRITICAL THINKING AND PROBLEM SOLVING

Write one or two sentences to answer the following questions:

19. Other than obtaining fresh water, what benefit comes from desalination?

20. Explain the difference between a bathymetric profile and a seismic reading.

MATH IN SCIENCE

21. Imagine that you are in the kelp-farming business and that your kelp grows 33 cm per day. You begin harvesting when your plants are 50 cm tall. During the first seven days of harvest, you cut 10 cm off the top of your kelp plants each day. How tall would your kelp plants be after the seventh day of harvesting?

INTERPRETING GRAPHICS

Examine the image below, and answer the questions that follow:

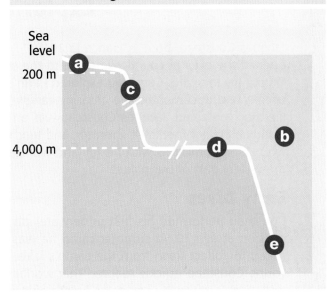

Ecological Zones of the Ocean

22. At which point (*a, b, c, d, or e*) would you most likely find an anglerfish?

23. At which point would you most likely find tube worms?

24. Which ecological zone is at point *c*? Which depth zone is at point *c*?

25. Name a type of organism you might find at point *e*.

NOW What Do You Think?

Take a minute to review your answers to the ScienceLog questions on page 331. Have your answers changed? If necessary, revise your answers based on what you have learned since you began this chapter.

Exploring Ocean Life

Jacques Cousteau, born in France in 1910, opened the eyes of countless people to the sea. During his long life, Cousteau explored Earth's oceans and documented the amazing variety of life they contained. Jacques Cousteau was an explorer, environmentalist, inventor, and teacher who inspired millions with his joy and wonder at the watery part of our planet.

Early Dives

Cousteau performed his first underwater diving mission at age 10. At summer camp he was asked to collect trash from the camp's lake. The young Cousteau quickly realized that working underwater without goggles or breathing equipment was a tremendous challenge.

Cousteau had another early underwater experience when he visited Southeast Asia. He saw people diving into the water to catch fish with their bare hands. This fascinated Cousteau. Even at a young age, he was thinking about how to make equipment that would let a person breathe underwater.

▲ *Cousteau in front of the* Calypso II

Underwater Flight

As a young man, Cousteau and some friends developed the aqualung, a self-contained breathing system for underwater exploration. As someone who had often dreamed of flying, Cousteau was thrilled with his invention. After one of his first dives, Cousteau explained, "I experimented with all possible maneuvers— loops, somersaults, and barrel rolls. . . . Delivered from gravity and buoyancy, I flew around in space."

Using the aqualung and other underwater equipment he developed, Cousteau began making underwater films. In 1950, he bought a boat named *Calypso,* which became his home and floating laboratory. For the next 40 years, through his films and television series, Cousteau brought what he called "the silent world" of the oceans and seas to living rooms everywhere.

A Protector of Life

Cousteau was long an outspoken defender of the environment. "When I saw all this beauty under the sea, I fell in love with it. And finally, when I realized to what extent the oceans were threatened, I decided to campaign as vigorously as I could against everything that threatened what I loved."

Jacques Cousteau died in 1997 at age 87. Before his death, he dedicated the *Calypso II,* a new research vessel, to the children of the world.

Write About It

▶ Ocean pollution and overfishing are subjects of intense debate. Think about these issues, and discuss them with your classmates. Then write an essay in which you try to convince readers of your point of view.

EYE ON THE ENVIRONMENT

Putting Freshwater Problems on Ice

Imagine how different your life would be if you couldn't get fresh water. What would you drink? How would you clean things? The Earth has enough fresh water to supply 100 billion liters to each person, yet water shortages affect millions of people every day. So what's the problem?

The Ice-Water Planet

Three-quarters of Earth's fresh water is frozen in polar icecaps. Plenty of fresh water is there, but people can't use water that is frozen and thousands of kilometers away.

The ice sheet that covers Antarctica is thousands of meters thick and is almost twice the size of the United States. Hundreds of huge chunks break off its edges every year. These icebergs, which are made up entirely of frozen fresh water, float away into the sea and eventually melt. Water from 1 year's worth of these icebergs would be enough to supply all of southern California for more than a century. So why not use it?

Obvious but Not Easy

Transporting icebergs to areas that need fresh water is harder than it sounds. For one thing, many of the icebergs are huge. The largest ever recorded was about the size of Connecticut. Even small icebergs may be 2 km long and 1 km wide.

Researchers have considered many methods of transporting icebergs. Most of the ideas involve pushing or towing icebergs through the water. A few ideas involve attaching engines and propellers directly to the icebergs.

However, because icebergs are so large, it takes a long time to move them. And when an iceberg finally does get somewhere, a considerable amount of it has melted. To prevent melting, insulating materials could be wrapped around an iceberg.

▲ *Icebergs such as this one might provide water in the future.*

A Worthy Investment

Lakes and groundwater still provide the cheapest fresh water in most areas. However, if there is no lake, river, or well water available, icebergs may then be a reasonable option to consider. Even though transporting icebergs is difficult, it may still be worthwhile to try. Irrigating 100 km^2 of desert with water from icebergs might cost as much as $1 million, but purifying enough sea water to irrigate that amount of desert could cost over $1 billion.

People in arid regions have spent considerable time on iceberg research. So far, no one has set up a program for harvesting icebergs. But someday water from icebergs may flow from our household faucets.

An Icy Investigation

▶ Float an ice cube in a bowl of cold water, and record the time it takes the cube to melt. Then try to insulate other ice cubes with different materials, such as cloth, plastic wrap, and aluminum foil. Which material works best? How could this material be used on real icebergs?

14 The Movement of Ocean Water

This Really Happened!

On February 3, 1963, the ocean tanker SS *Marine Sulphur Queen* sailed eastward around the Florida Keys bound for Virginia. Soon after the ship entered the Atlantic, all radio contact with it was lost. Coast Guard rescuers who tried to locate the ship found only life jackets, oil cans, and debris in the area of the tanker's last known position. No survivors were ever found. Several explanations for the *Queen*'s disappearance were offered, but very little evidence supported any of them. The only certainty was that the

ship entered the Bermuda Triangle, never to be heard from again.

The Bermuda Triangle is a part of the Atlantic Ocean extending from the Florida coast to Bermuda and Puerto Rico. Many ships have sailed into this area only to vanish. Is there an explanation for this?

In the western part of the triangle, a wide ocean current called the Gulf Stream is squeezed into the narrow area between Florida and the Great Bahama Banks as it flows northward. Winds blowing southward across the ocean surface in this area sometimes create large, dangerous waves when they meet the Gulf Stream. The Bermuda Triangle also has a reputation for unpredictable weather. Many sailors have been stranded there without wind for their sails. Strong thunderstorms and *waterspouts*, which are like tornadoes on the surface of the ocean, occur with little warning. To make matters worse, the ocean floor beneath the triangle is a maze of deep trenches that can hide a shipwreck.

The Bermuda Triangle

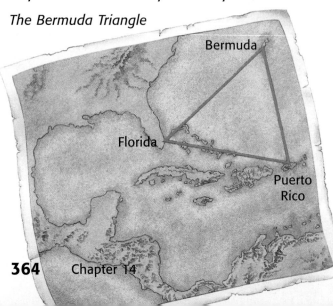

While many people link the Bermuda Triangle to the supernatural, the disappearance of ships there is probably best explained by scientific facts—dangerous waves and weather are capable of sinking ships. In this chapter you will learn about waves and other movements of ocean water.

What Do You Think?

In your ScienceLog, try to answer the following questions based on what you already know:

1. What factors control ocean currents?

2. What causes the ocean tides?

When Two *Whirls* Collide

Ocean currents in the Northern Hemisphere flow in a clockwise direction, while ocean currents in the Southern Hemisphere flow in a counterclockwise direction. In certain parts of the ocean, however, southern currents flow across the equator into the Northern Hemisphere and begin flowing clockwise. In this activity you and your lab partner will demonstrate how two currents flowing in opposite directions affect one another.

Procedure

1. Fill a large **tub** 5 cm full with **water.**

2. Add 10 drops of **red food coloring** to the water on one end of the tub.

3. Add 10 drops of **blue food coloring** to the water at the other end of the tub.

4. Using a **pencil,** quickly stir the water at the end of the tub with the red food coloring in a clockwise direction while your partner stirs the water at the other end in a counterclockwise direction. Stir both ends steadily for about 5 seconds.

5. In your ScienceLog, draw what you see happening in the tub immediately after you stop stirring. (Both ends should still be swirling.)

Analysis

6. How did the blue water and the red water interact?

7. How does this relate to the ocean currents in the Northern and Southern Hemispheres?

Currents

NEW TERMS

surface current   upwelling
Coriolis effect   El Niño
deep current

OBJECTIVES

- Describe surface currents, and list the three factors that control them.
- Describe deep currents.
- Illustrate the factors involved in deep-current movement.
- Explain how currents affect climate.

Imagine that you are stranded on a desert island. You stuff a distress message into a bottle and throw it into the ocean, hoping it will find its way to someone who will send help. What are the forces that would send your bottle across the ocean, bobbing up and down as it traveled? Is there any way to predict where your bottle may land?

Earlier this century, a Norwegian explorer named Thor Heyerdahl tried to answer similar questions that involved human migration across the ocean. Heyerdahl theorized that the inhabitants of Polynesia originally sailed from Peru on rafts powered only by the wind and ocean currents. Unable to convince scientists of his theory, he decided to prove it. In 1947, Heyerdahl and a crew of five people set sail from Peru on a handcrafted raft. The raft, shown in **Figure 1,** was named the *Kon-Tiki,* after the Peruvian sun god.

Figure 1 *The handcrafted* Kon-Tiki *was made mainly from materials that would have been available to ancient Peruvians.*

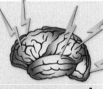

On the 97th day of their expedition, Heyerdahl and his crew landed on an island in Polynesia. The Humboldt and South Equatorial Currents had carried the raft westward more than 6,000 km across the South Pacific. This supported Heyerdahl's theory that ocean-surface currents carried the ancient Peruvians across the Pacific to Polynesia. But how did Heyerdahl know the direction of the currents? What forces created these currents? To answer these questions about ocean currents, and others you may have, let's examine what causes ocean currents, the different types of ocean currents, and how ocean currents affect climate.

Surface Currents

Surface currents are streamlike movements of water that occur at or near the surface of the ocean. Some surface currents are several thousand kilometers in length, traveling across entire oceans. The Gulf Stream, one of the longest surface currents, transports 25 times more water than all the rivers in the world. Surface currents are controlled by three factors: global winds, the Coriolis effect, and continental deflections. These three factors keep surface currents flowing continuously in distinct patterns around the Earth.

Global Winds Have you ever blown gently on a cup of hot chocolate? You may have noticed ripples moving across the surface. These ripples are caused by a tiny surface current created by your breath. In much the same way, winds blowing across the Earth's surface create surface currents in the ocean. Surface currents can reach depths of several hundred meters and lengths of several thousand kilometers. That's quite a bit larger than the current in your cup of hot chocolate!

Wind has the power to move large quantities of water. Different winds cause currents to flow in different directions. Near the equator, the winds blow ocean water east to west, but closer to the poles, ocean water is blown west to east, as shown in **Figure 2.** Merchant ships often use these currents to travel more quickly back and forth across the oceans.

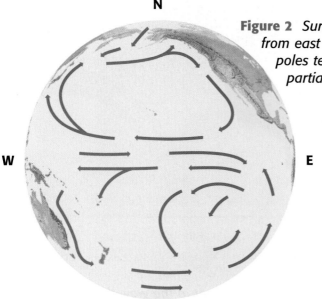

Figure 2 *Surface currents near the equator generally flow from east to west, but surface currents closer to the poles tend to flow from west to east. This pattern is partially a result of global wind patterns.*

Self-Check

Take another look at Figure 2. As Heyerdahl made his journey in 1947, from what direction would he have noticed the wind blowing? (See page 564 to check your answer.)

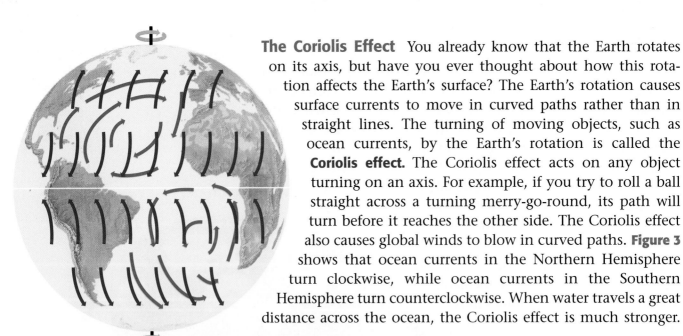

Figure 3 *The rotation of the Earth causes ocean currents (red arrows) and global winds (purple arrows) to move in opposite directions on either side of the equator.*

The Coriolis Effect

You already know that the Earth rotates on its axis, but have you ever thought about how this rotation affects the Earth's surface? The Earth's rotation causes surface currents to move in curved paths rather than in straight lines. The turning of moving objects, such as ocean currents, by the Earth's rotation is called the **Coriolis effect.** The Coriolis effect acts on any object turning on an axis. For example, if you try to roll a ball straight across a turning merry-go-round, its path will turn before it reaches the other side. The Coriolis effect also causes global winds to blow in curved paths. **Figure 3** shows that ocean currents in the Northern Hemisphere turn clockwise, while ocean currents in the Southern Hemisphere turn counterclockwise. When water travels a great distance across the ocean, the Coriolis effect is much stronger.

Continental Deflections

If the Earth's surface were covered only with water, surface currents would travel freely across the globe in a very uniform pattern. However, we know that this is not the case—continents rise above sea level over roughly one-third of the Earth's surface. When surface currents meet continents, they *deflect,* or change direction. Notice in **Figure 4** how the Brazil Current deflects southward as it meets the east coast of South America.

Explore

Some people think the Coriolis effect can be seen in sinks; that is, water draining from sinks turns clockwise in the Northern Hemisphere and counterclockwise in the Southern Hemisphere. Is this true? Research this question at the library, on the Internet, and in your sinks and tubs at home.

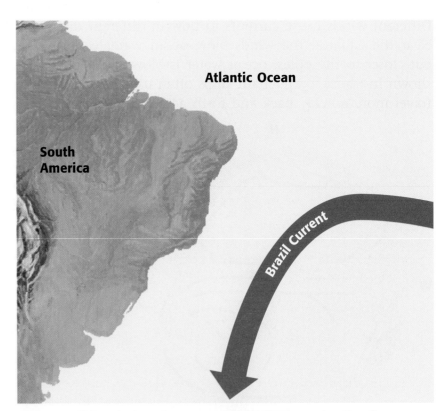

Figure 4 *If South America were not in the way, the Brazil Current would probably flow farther west.*

Taking Temperatures All three factors—global winds, the Coriolis effect, and continental deflections—work together to form a pattern of surface currents on Earth. But currents are also affected by the temperature of the water in which they arise. Warm-water currents begin near the equator and carry warm water to other parts of the ocean. Cold-water currents begin closer to the poles and carry cool water to other parts of the ocean. As you can see on the map in **Figure 5,** all the oceans are connected, and both warm-water and cold-water currents travel from one ocean to another.

physical science
CONNECTION

While winds are responsible for ocean currents, the sun is the initial energy source of the currents. Because the sun heats the Earth more in some places than in others, convection currents are formed, which cause winds to blow.

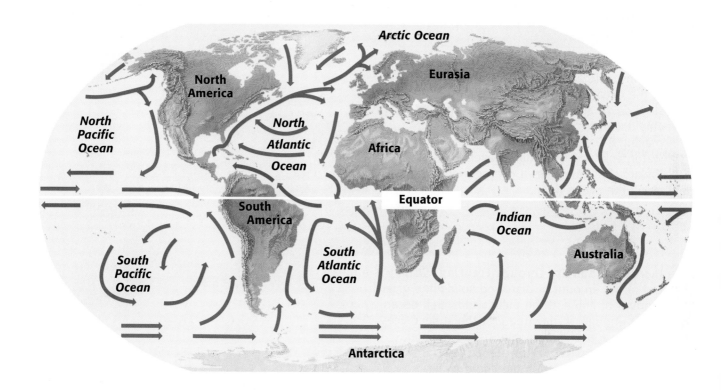

Figure 5 *This map shows Earth's surface currents. Warm-water currents are shown as red arrows, and cold-water currents are shown as blue arrows.*

REVIEW

1. List the three factors that control surface currents.

2. Explain how the Earth's rotation affects the patterns of surface currents.

3. **Inferring Conclusions** If there were no land on Earth's surface, what would the pattern of surface currents look like? Explain.

Turn to page 542 in the LabBook to demonstrate how temperature and salinity affect ocean water.

Deep Currents

Deep currents are streamlike movements of ocean water far below the surface. Unlike surface currents, deep currents are not directly controlled by wind or the Coriolis effect. Instead, they form in parts of the ocean where water density increases. *Density* is the ratio of the mass of a substance to its volume. Two main factors—temperature and salinity—combine to affect the density of ocean water, as shown below. As you can see, both decreasing the temperature of ocean water and increasing the water's salinity increase the water's density.

How Deep Currents Form

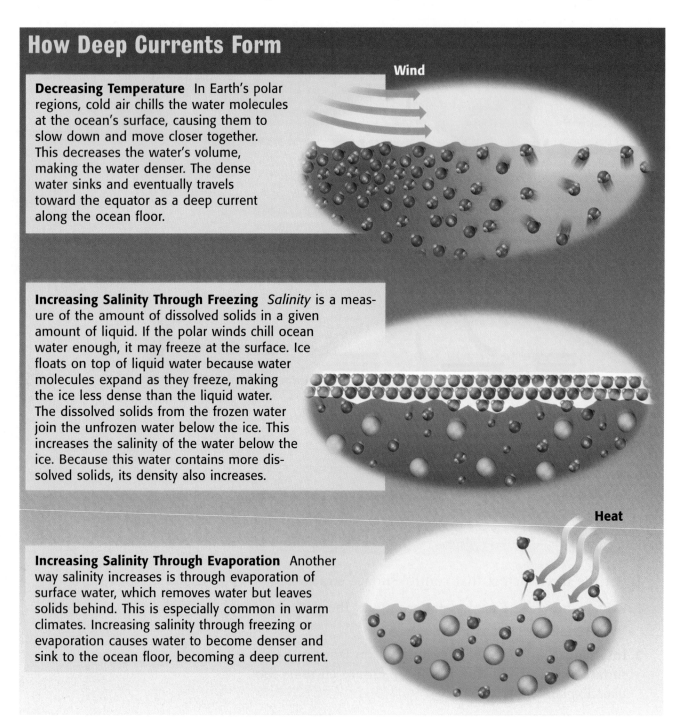

Decreasing Temperature In Earth's polar regions, cold air chills the water molecules at the ocean's surface, causing them to slow down and move closer together. This decreases the water's volume, making the water denser. The dense water sinks and eventually travels toward the equator as a deep current along the ocean floor.

Wind

Increasing Salinity Through Freezing *Salinity* is a measure of the amount of dissolved solids in a given amount of liquid. If the polar winds chill ocean water enough, it may freeze at the surface. Ice floats on top of liquid water because water molecules expand as they freeze, making the ice less dense than the liquid water. The dissolved solids from the frozen water join the unfrozen water below the ice. This increases the salinity of the water below the ice. Because this water contains more dissolved solids, its density also increases.

Heat

Increasing Salinity Through Evaporation Another way salinity increases is through evaporation of surface water, which removes water but leaves solids behind. This is especially common in warm climates. Increasing salinity through freezing or evaporation causes water to become denser and sink to the ocean floor, becoming a deep current.

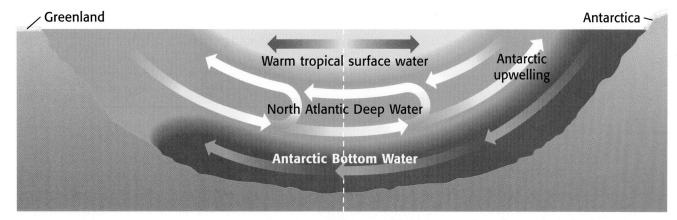

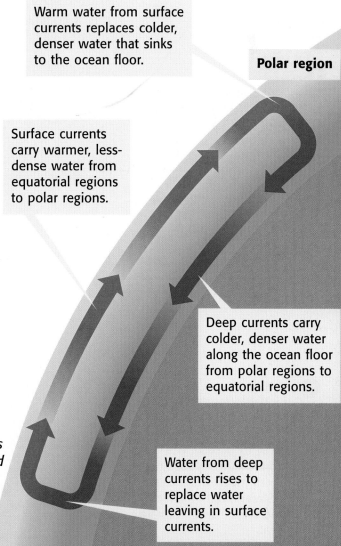

Greenland

Antarctica

Warm tropical surface water

Antarctic upwelling

North Atlantic Deep Water

Antarctic Bottom Water

Figure 6 *This cross section shows that the less-dense North Atlantic Deep Water, which forms in the Arctic Ocean near Greenland, flows on top of the denser Antarctic Bottom Water when the two currents meet.*

Movement of Deep Currents The movement of deep currents as they travel along the ocean floor is very complex. Differences in temperature and salinity, and therefore in density, cause variations in deep currents. For example, the deepest current, the Antarctic Bottom Water, is denser than the North Atlantic Deep Water. Both currents spread out across the ocean floor as they flow toward the same equatorial region. But when the currents meet, the North Atlantic Deep Water actually flows on top of the denser Antarctic Bottom Water, as shown in **Figure 6.** The main thermocline is a barrier that keeps warm surface waters from mixing efficiently with cold deep currents. It takes about 1,000 years for water from cold regions to cycle through warm regions.

Currents Trading Places Now that you understand how deep currents form and how they move along the ocean floor, you can learn how they trade places with surface currents. To see how this works, study **Figure 7.**

Figure 7 *This cross section shows the movement of warm water and cold water between polar and equatorial regions.*

Warm water from surface currents replaces colder, denser water that sinks to the ocean floor.

Polar region

Surface currents carry warmer, less-dense water from equatorial regions to polar regions.

Deep currents carry colder, denser water along the ocean floor from polar regions to equatorial regions.

Water from deep currents rises to replace water leaving in surface currents.

Equatorial region

Surface Currents and Climate

Surface currents greatly affect the climate in many parts of the world. Some surface currents warm or cool coastal areas year-round. Other surface currents sometimes change their circulation pattern. This causes changes in the atmosphere that disrupt the climate in many parts of the world.

Currents That Stabilize Climate Although surface currents are generally much warmer than deep currents, their temperatures do vary. Surface currents are classified as warm-water currents or cold-water currents. Look back at Figure 5 to see where each type is located. Because they are warm or cold, surface currents affect the climate of the land near the area where they flow. For example, warm-water currents create warmer climates in coastal areas that would otherwise be much cooler. Likewise, cold-water currents create cooler climates in coastal areas that would otherwise be much warmer. **Figure 8** shows how a warm-water current and a cold-water current affect coastal climates.

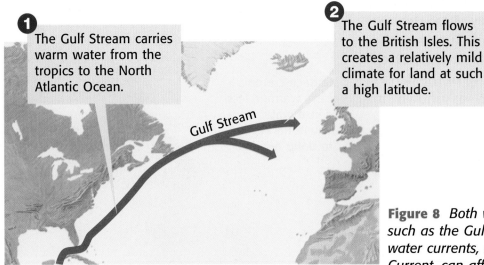

1 The Gulf Stream carries warm water from the tropics to the North Atlantic Ocean.

2 The Gulf Stream flows to the British Isles. This creates a relatively mild climate for land at such a high latitude.

Figure 8 *Both warm-water currents, such as the Gulf Stream, and cold-water currents, such as the California Current, can affect the climate of coastal regions.*

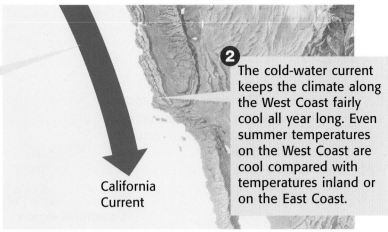

1 Cold water from the north is carried southward by the California Current, all the way to Mexico. The California Current does not move as much water as the Gulf Stream, but its effect on the West Coast's climate is great.

2 The cold-water current keeps the climate along the West Coast fairly cool all year long. Even summer temperatures on the West Coast are cool compared with temperatures inland or on the East Coast.

California Current

Current Variations—El Niño The surface currents in the tropical region of the Pacific Ocean usually travel with the trade winds from east to west. This builds up warm water in the western Pacific and causes upwelling in the eastern Pacific. **Upwelling** is a near-shore process in which cold, nutrient-rich water from the deep ocean rises to the surface to replace warm surface water that is blown farther out to sea by prevailing winds. But every 2 to 12 years, the South Pacific trade winds relax and move less surface water to the western Pacific. This reduces upwelling along the coast of South America, causing surface water temperatures there to rise. Gradually, this warming spreads westward. This periodic change in the location of warm and cool surface waters in the Pacific Ocean is called **El Niño.** El Niño not only affects surface waters but also alters the interaction between the ocean and the atmosphere, causing changes in the atmosphere's circulation. Global weather patterns change as a result of El Niño conditions.

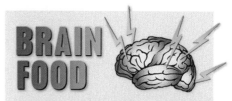

BRAIN FOOD

El Niño means "The Child" in Spanish. The term originally referred to a warm current that arrived each year during the Christmas season off the coast of Ecuador and Peru.

Effects of El Niño Scientists are concerned about the global climatic changes caused by El Niño because the changes alter weather patterns. These changing weather patterns cause disasters, such as flash floods and mudslides in areas of the world that normally receive little rain. **Figure 9** shows homes destroyed by a mudslide in Southern California, an area that usually receives little rainfall. While some regions flood, regions that usually receive a lot of rain may experience droughts, which can lead to crop failures. For example, the country of Indonesia (located in the Pacific Ocean along the equator) depends on annual monsoon rains for growing crops. During an El Niño season, these rains are blown over the middle of the Pacific Ocean, missing Southeast Asia altogether.

Figure 9 *In 1997, an El Niño caused excessive rain in Southern California. These homes were destroyed by rain-generated mudslides.*

REVIEW

1. How do temperature and salinity relate to deep-current movement?

2. Why is the climate in Scotland relatively mild even though the country is located at a high latitude?

3. **Applying Concepts** Many marine organisms depend on upwelling to bring nutrients to the surface. How might an El Niño affect Peruvians' way of life?

The Movement of Ocean Water **373**

Waves

NEW TERMS

crest   surf
trough   whitecap
wavelength   swells
wave height   tsunami
wave period   storm surge
breaker zone

OBJECTIVES

- Identify wave components, and explain how they relate to wave movement.
- Describe how ocean waves form and how they move.
- Classify types of waves.
- Analyze types of dangerous waves.

We all know what ocean waves look like. Even if you've never been to the seashore, you've most likely seen waves on television. But what are ocean waves? How do they form and move? Are all waves the same? And what do they do besides drop shells and sand dollars on the beach? Let us examine ocean waves so that we can answer these questions.

Anatomy of a Wave

Waves are made up of two main components—crests and troughs. A **crest** is the highest point of a wave, and a **trough** is the lowest point. Imagine a thrilling roller coaster designed with many rises and dips. The top of a rise on a roller-coaster track is similar to

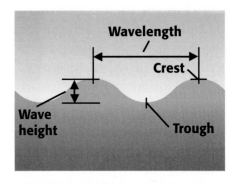

the crest of a wave, and the bottom of a dip in the track resembles the trough of a wave. The distance between two adjacent wave crests or wave troughs is a **wavelength.** The vertical distance between a wave's crest and its trough is a **wave height.**

Wave Formation and Movement

If you have watched ocean waves before, you may have noticed that water appears to move across the ocean's surface. However, this movement is only an illusion. Most waves form as wind blows across the water's surface, transferring energy to the water. As the energy moves through the water, so do the waves. But the water itself stays behind, rising and falling in circular movements. Notice in **Figure 10** that the floating bottle remains in the same spot as the waves travel from left to right. The circle of moving water that the bottle moves with has a diameter that is equal to the height of the waves that created it. Underneath this circle are smaller circles of moving water. The diameters of these circles get smaller with depth because wave energy decreases with depth. Wave energy only reaches to a certain depth. Below that depth, the water is not affected by wave energy.

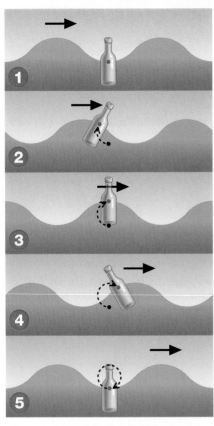

Figure 10 *Like the bottle in this figure, water remains in the same place as waves travel through it.*

Specifics of Wave Movement

Waves not only come in different sizes but also travel at different speeds. To calculate wave speed, scientists must know the wavelength and the wave period. **Wave period** is the time between the passage of two wave crests (or troughs) at a fixed point, as shown in **Figure 11.** Dividing wavelength by wave period gives you wave speed, as shown below.

$$\frac{\text{wavelength (m)}}{\text{wave period (s)}} = \text{wave speed (m/s)}$$

For any given wavelength, an increase in wave period will decrease the wave speed, and a decrease in wave period will increase the wave speed.

MATH BREAK

Wave Speed

Imagine you are in a rowboat on the open ocean. You count 2 waves traveling right under your boat in 10 seconds. You estimate the wavelength to be 3 m. What is the wave speed?

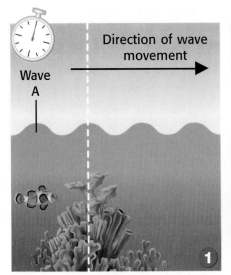
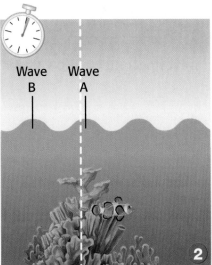

Figure 11 *Notice in frame 1 that the waves are moving from left to right. In frame 2, the clock begins running as Wave A passes the reef's peak. The clock stops in frame 3 as Wave B passes the reef's peak. The time shown on the clock (5 seconds) represents the wave period.*

Ocean waves travel in the direction the wind blows. If the wind is constantly blowing, wavelength, wave height, and the energy of the waves increase. Wave height depends on the *fetch,* the distance the wind is able to blow and waves are able to travel without interruption. The greater the fetch is, the higher the waves are.

Types of Waves

As you learned earlier in this section, wind forms most ocean waves. However, waves can form by other mechanisms. Underwater earthquakes and landslides as well as impacts by cosmic bodies can form different types of waves. The sizes of the different types of waves can vary, but most move the same way. Depending on their size and the angle at which they hit the shore, waves can generate a variety of near-shore events, some of which can be dangerous to humans.

Deep-Water Waves and Shallow-Water Waves Have you ever wondered why waves increase in height as they approach the shore? The answer has to do with the depth of the water. *Deep-water waves* are waves that move in water that is deeper than one-half of their wavelength. But as the waves move closer to shore, the water becomes shallower. When the waves reach water that is shallower than one-half of their wavelength, they begin to interact with the ocean floor. These waves are called *shallow-water waves.*

As deep-water waves become shallow-water waves, the water particles slow down and build up, forcing more water between wave crests and increasing wave height. Gravity eventually pulls the high wave crests down, causing them to crash into the ocean floor as *breakers.* The near-shore area where waves first begin to tumble downward, or break, is called the **breaker zone.** Waves continue to break as they move from the breaker zone to the shore. The area between the breaker zone and the shore is called the **surf. Figure 12** illustrates how deep-water waves become shallow-water waves that eventually break.

Figure 12 *Deep-water waves become shallow-water waves when they reach depths of less than half of their wavelength. Heightened shallow-water waves begin to tumble in the breaker zone. In the surf, water moves toward the shore.*

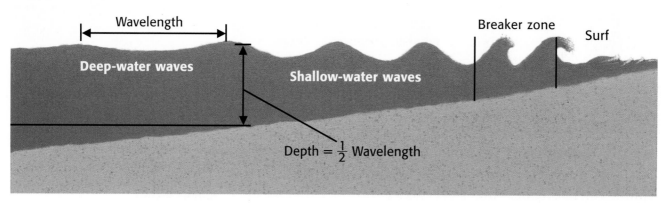

Wavelength

Deep-water waves

Shallow-water waves

Breaker zone

Surf

Depth $= \frac{1}{2}$ Wavelength

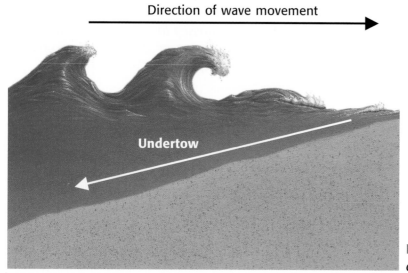

Direction of wave movement

Undertow

When waves crash on the beach head-on, the water they moved through flows back to the ocean underneath new incoming waves. This receding movement of water, which carries sand, rock particles, and plankton away from the shore, is called an *undertow.* **Figure 13** illustrates the back-and-forth movement of water at the shore.

Figure 13 *Head-on waves create an undertow.*

When waves hit the shore at an angle, they cause water to move along the shore in a current called a *longshore current*. This process is shown in **Figure 14.** Longshore currents are responsible for most sediment transport in beach environments. This movement of sand and other sediment both tears down and builds up the coastline. Unfortunately, longshore currents also carry trash and other types of ocean pollution, spreading it along the shore.

Figure 14 *Longshore currents form where waves approach beaches at an angle.*

Open-Ocean Waves Sometimes waves called whitecaps form in the open ocean. **Whitecaps** are white, foaming waves with very steep crests that break in the open ocean before the waves get close to the shore. These waves usually form during stormy weather, and they are usually short-lived. Calmer winds form waves called swells. **Swells** are rolling waves that move in a steady procession across the ocean. Swells have longer wavelengths than whitecaps and can travel for thousands of kilometers. **Figure 15** shows how whitecaps and swells differ.

environmental science
CONNECTION

Not far offshore from Galveston Island, Texas, engineers use huge suction machines called dredges to collect sand from the ocean floor. This sand is then pumped onto the shoreline, rebuilding the beaches that have been eroded by longshore currents.

Figure 15 *Whitecaps, shown in the photo above, break in the open ocean, while swells, shown in the photo at right, roll gently in the open ocean.*

Turn to page 388 to learn about a scientist who studies earthquakes that cause tsunamis.

Figure 16 *An upward shift in the ocean floor creates an earthquake. The energy released by the earthquake pushes a large volume of water upward, creating a series of tsunamis.*

Tsunamis Professional surfers often travel to Hawaii to catch some of the highest waves in the world. But even the best surfers would not be able to handle a giant tsunami. **Tsunamis** are waves that form when a large volume of ocean water is suddenly moved up or down. This movement can be caused by underwater earthquakes, volcanic eruptions, landslides, underwater explosions, or the impact of a cosmic body, such as a meteorite or comet. The majority of tsunamis occur in the Pacific Ocean because of the greater number of earthquakes in that region. **Figure 16** shows how an earthquake can generate a tsunami.

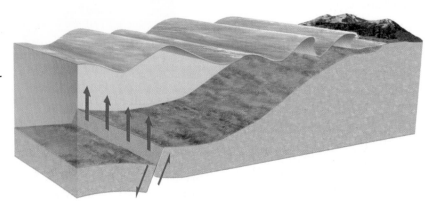

Although tsunami wavelengths can be more than 150 km, tsunamis behave much like wind-generated waves. When tsunamis near continents, they slow down and their wavelengths shorten as they interact with the ocean floor. As tsunamis get closer together, the water is compressed into a smaller space, increasing their wave height. Tsunamis can reach more than 30 m in height as they slam into the coast, destroying just about everything in their path. The powerful undertow created by a tsunami can be as destructive as the tsunami itself. **Figure 17** shows a coastal community devastated by a tsunami.

Figure 17 *Imagine the strength of the tsunami that carried this boat so far inland!*

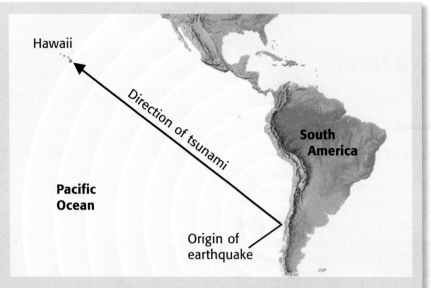

On May 22, 1960, an earthquake off the coast of South America generated a tsunami that completely crossed the Pacific Ocean. Ten thousand kilometers away from the origin of the earthquake, the tsunami hit the city of Hilo on the coast of Hawaii, causing extensive damage. If the tsunami traveled at a speed of 188 m/s, how long after the earthquake occurred did the tsunami reach Hilo? If the residents of Hilo heard about the earthquake as soon as it happened, do you think they had enough warning time? What might be done to ensure that this amount of time would be sufficient warning for a tsunami?

Storm Surges

A **storm surge** is a local rise in sea level near the shore that is caused by strong winds from a storm, such as a hurricane. Winds form a storm surge by blowing water into a big pile under the storm. As the storm moves onto shore, so does the giant mass of water beneath it. Storm surges often disappear as quickly as they form, making them difficult to study. Storm surges contain a lot of energy and can reach about 8 m in height. This often makes them the most destructive part of hurricanes.

REVIEW

1. Explain how water moves as waves travel through it.

2. Where do deep-water waves become shallow-water waves?

3. Name five events that can cause a tsunami.

4. **Doing Calculations** Look again at Figure 11. If the wave speed is 0.8 m/s, what is the wavelength?

Quick Lab

Do the Wave

1. Tie one end of a thin piece of **rope** to a doorknob.

2. Tie a **ribbon** around the rope halfway between the doorknob and the other end of the rope.

3. Holding the rope at the untied end, quickly move the rope up and down, and observe the ribbon.

4. How does the movement of the rope and ribbon relate to the movement of water and deep-water waves?

5. Repeat step 3, but move the rope higher and lower this time.

6. How does this affect the waves in the rope?

Tides

You haved learned how winds and earthquakes can move ocean water. But there are less-obvious forces that continually move ocean water in regular patterns called tides. **Tides** are daily movements of ocean water that change the level of the ocean's surface. Tides are influenced by the sun and the moon, and they occur in a variety of cycles.

NEW TERMS

tides   neap tides
tidal range   tidal bore
spring tides

OBJECTIVES

- Explain tides and their relationship with the Earth, the sun, and the moon.
- Classify different types of tides.
- Analyze the relationship between tides and coastal land.

Gravitational forces from both the sun and the moon continuously pull on the Earth. Although the moon is much smaller than the sun, the moon's gravity is the dominant force behind Earth's tides.

The Lure of the Moon

The phases of the moon and their relationship to the tides were first discovered more than 2,000 years ago by a Greek explorer named Pytheas. But Pytheas and other early investigators could not explain the relationship. A scientific explanation was not given until 1687, when Sir Isaac Newton's theories on the principle of gravitational pull were published. The gravity of the moon pulls on every particle of the Earth, but the pull is much more noticeable in liquids than in solids. This is because liquids move more easily. Even the liquid in an open soft drink is slightly pulled by the moon's gravity.

High Tide and Low Tide How high tides get and how often they occur depend on the position of the moon as it revolves around the Earth. The moon's pull is strongest on the part of the Earth directly facing the moon. When that part happens to be a portion of the ocean, the water there bulges toward the moon. At the same time, water on the opposite side of the Earth bulges due to the motion of the Earth and the moon around each other. These bulges are called *high tides*. Notice in **Figure 18** how the position of the moon causes the water to bulge. Also notice that when high tides occur, water is drawn away from the area between the high tides, causing *low tides* to form.

Puzzled about why high tide also occurs on the side of the Earth opposite the moon? Turn to page 544 to see how you can find out for yourself.

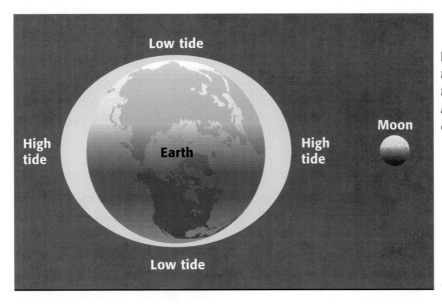

Figure 18 *High tide occurs on the part of Earth that is closest to the moon. At the same time, high tide also occurs on the opposite side of Earth.*

The rotation of the Earth and the revolving of the moon around the Earth determine when tides occur. If the Earth rotated at the same speed that the moon revolves around the Earth, tides would continuously occur at the same spots on Earth. But the moon revolves around the Earth much more slowly than the Earth rotates. **Figure 19** shows that it takes 24 hours and 50 minutes for a spot on Earth that is facing the moon to rotate so that it is facing the moon again.

BRAIN FOOD

Even dry land has tides. For example, the land in Oklahoma moves up and down several centimeters throughout the day, corresponding with the tides. Tides on the solid part of Earth's surface are usually about one-third the size of ocean tides.

Tuesday, 11:00 A.M.

Wednesday, 11:50 A.M.

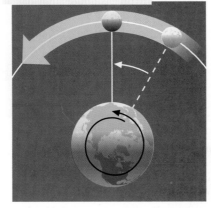

Figure 19 *The tide at any point on the Earth will occur about 1 hour later each day because as the Earth rotates under the moon, the moon revolves farther around the Earth.*

The Movement of Ocean Water **381**

Tidal Variations

The sun also affects tides. The sun is much larger than the moon, but it is also much farther away. As a result, the sun's influence on tides is less powerful than the moon's influence. The combined forces of the sun and the moon on the Earth result in tidal ranges that vary based on the positions of all three bodies. A **tidal range** is the difference between levels of ocean water at high tide and low tide.

Figure 20 *During spring tides, the gravitational forces of the sun and moon pull on the Earth either from the same direction (left) or from opposite directions (right).*

Spring Tides When the sun, Earth, and moon are in alignment with one another, spring tides occur. **Spring tides** are tides with maximum daily tidal range that occur during the new and full moons. Spring tides occur every 14 days. The first time spring tides occur is when the moon is between the sun and Earth. The second time spring tides occur is when the moon and the sun are on opposite sides of the Earth. **Figure 20** shows the positions of the sun and moon during spring tides.

Figure 21 *During neap tides, the sun and moon are at right angles with respect to the Earth. This arrangement minimizes their gravitational effect on the Earth.*

Neap Tides When the sun, Earth, and moon form a 90° angle, as shown in **Figure 21,** neap tides occur. **Neap tides** are tides with minimum daily tidal range that occur during the first and third quarters of the moon. Neap tides occur halfway between the occurrence of spring tides. When neap tides occur, the gravitational forces on the Earth by the sun and the moon work against each other—they do not pull along the same line as they do during spring tides.

Tides and Topography

Tides can be accurately predicted once the tidal range has been measured at a certain point over a period of time. This information can be useful for people who live near or visit the coast, as illustrated in **Figure 22.**

Figure 22 *It's a good thing the people on the beach (left) knew when high tide occurred (right). These photos show the Bay of Fundy, in New Brunswick, Canada. The Bay of Fundy has the greatest tidal range on Earth.*

In some coastal areas with shallow bays that are just the right length, movements of water called tidal bores occur. A **tidal bore** is a body of water that rushes up through a narrow bay, estuary, or river channel during the rise of high tide, causing a very sudden tidal rise. Sometimes tidal bores form waves that rush up the inlets, as shown in **Figure 23.** Tidal bores occur in coastal areas of China, the British Isles, France, and Canada.

Figure 23 *Surf's up! These people are riding a wave created by a tidal bore.*

REVIEW

1. Why are spring tides so much larger than neap tides?

2. What causes tidal bores?

3. **Applying Concepts** How many days pass between minimum and maximum tidal range in any given area? Explain.

Chapter Highlights

SECTION 1

Vocabulary

surface current *(p. 367)*

Coriolis effect *(p. 368)*

deep current *(p. 370)*

upwelling *(p. 373)*

El Niño *(p. 373)*

Section Notes

- Currents are classified as surface currents and deep currents.

- Surface currents are controlled by three factors: global winds, the Coriolis effect, and continental deflections.

- Surface currents, such as the Gulf Stream, can be several thousand kilometers in length.

- Deep currents form where the density of ocean water increases. Water density depends on temperature and salinity.

- Surface currents affect the climate of the land near which they flow.

Labs

Up from the Depths *(p. 542)*

SECTION 2

Vocabulary

crest *(p. 374)*

trough *(p. 374)*

wavelength *(p. 374)*

wave height *(p. 374)*

wave period *(p. 375)*

breaker zone *(p. 376)*

surf *(p. 376)*

whitecap *(p. 377)*

swells *(p. 377)*

tsunami *(p. 378)*

storm surge *(p. 379)*

Section Notes

- Waves are made up of two main components—crests and troughs.

- Waves are usually created by the transfer of the wind's energy across the surface of the ocean.

☑ Skills Check

Math Concepts

TWO OUT OF THREE The wave equation on page 375 has three variables. If you know two of these variables, you can figure out the third. Take a look at the examples below.

1. wave speed = 0.6 m/s, wave period = 10 s
   wavelength = wave speed × wave period
   = 6 m

2. wave speed = 0.6 m/s, wavelength = 6 m
   wave period = $\dfrac{\text{wavelength}}{}$ = 10 s

Visual Understanding

BREAKING WAVES Before shallow-water waves break, their wave height increases and their wavelength decreases. Look at Figure 12 on page 376 again. Notice that the waves are taller and that their crests are closer together near the breaker zone.

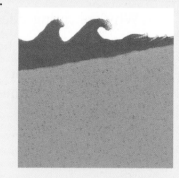

- Waves travel through water near the water's surface, while the water itself rises and falls in circular movements.

- Waves travel in the direction the wind blows. If the wind blows over a long distance, the wavelength becomes very large and the waves travel quickly.

- Wind-generated waves are classified as deep-water and shallow-water waves.

- Tsunamis are dangerous waves that can be very destructive to coastal communities.

Vocabulary

tides (p. 380)

tidal range (p. 382)

spring tides (p. 382)

neap tides (p. 382)

tidal bore (p. 383)

Section Notes

- Tides are caused by the gravitational forces of the moon and sun tugging on the Earth.

- The moon's gravity is the main force behind tides.

- The relative positions of the sun and moon with respect to Earth cause different tidal ranges.

- Maximum tidal range occurs during spring tides.

- Minimum tidal range occurs during neap tides.

- Tidal bores occur as high tide rises in narrow coastal inlets.

Labs

Turning the Tides (p. 544)

 internet **connect**

go.hrw.com

GO TO: go.hrw.com

Visit the **HRW** Web site for a variety of learning tools related to this chapter. Just type in the keyword:

KEYWORD: HSTH2O

SCI LINKS

NSTA

GO TO: www.scilinks.org

Visit the **National Science Teachers Association** on-line Web site for Internet resources related to this chapter. Just type in the *sci*LINKS number for more information about the topic:

TOPIC: Ocean Currents	*sci*LINKS NUMBER: HSTE330
TOPIC: El Niño	*sci*LINKS NUMBER: HSTE335
TOPIC: Ocean Waves	*sci*LINKS NUMBER: HSTE340
TOPIC: Tsunamis	*sci*LINKS NUMBER: HSTE345
TOPIC: The Tides	*sci*LINKS NUMBER: HSTE350

Chapter Review

USING VOCABULARY

For each pair of terms, explain the difference in their meaning.

1. wavelength/wave height

2. whitecap/swell

3. tsunami/storm surge

4. spring tide/neap tide

Replace the incorrect term in each of the following sentences with the correct term provided in the word bank below:

5. Deep currents are directly controlled by wind.

6. The Coriolis effect reduces upwelling along the coast of South America.

7. Neap tides occur when the moon is between the Earth and the sun.

8. A tidal bore is the difference between levels of ocean water at high tide and low tide.

Word bank: breaker zone, spring tides, tsunamis, surface currents, tidal range, El Niño.

UNDERSTANDING CONCEPTS

Multiple Choice

9. Surface currents are formed by
   a. the moon's gravity.
   b. the sun's gravity.
   c. wind.
   d. increased water density.

10. Deep currents form when
    a. cold air decreases water density.
    b. warm air increases water density.
    c. the ocean surface freezes and solids from the water underneath are removed.
    d. salinity increases.

11. When waves come near the shore,
    a. they speed up.
    b. they maintain their speed.
    c. their wavelength increases.
    d. their wave height increases.

12. Longshore currents transport sediment
    a. out to the open ocean.
    b. along the shore.
    c. during low tide only.
    d. during high tide only.

13. Whitecaps break
    a. in the surf.
    b. in the breaker zone.
    c. in the open ocean.
    d. as their wavelength increases.

14. Tidal range is greatest during
    a. spring tide.
    b. neap tide.
    c. a tidal bore.
    d. the day only.

Short Answer

15. Explain the relationship between upwelling and El Niño.

16. Explain what happens when the North Atlantic Deep Water meets the Antarctic Bottom Water.

17. Describe the relative positions of the Earth, the moon, and the sun during neap tide. Where do high tide and low tide occur during this time?

18. Explain the difference between the breaker zone and the surf.

Concept Mapping

19. Use the following terms to create a concept map: wind, deep currents, sun's gravity, types of ocean-water movement, surface currents, tides, increasing water density, waves, moon's gravity.

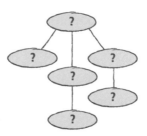

CRITICAL THINKING AND PROBLEM SOLVING

Write one or two sentences to answer the following questions:

20. What would happen to surface currents if the Earth reversed its rotation? Be specific.

21. How would you explain a bottle moving across the water in the same direction the waves are traveling?

22. You and a friend are planning a fishing trip to the ocean. Your friend tells you that the fish bite more in his secret fishing spot during low tide. If low tide occurred at the spot at 7 A.M. today and you are going to fish there in one week, at what time will low tide occur in that spot?

MATH IN SCIENCE

23. If a barrier island that is 1 km wide and 10 km long loses 1.5 m of its width per year to erosion by longshore current, how long will it take for the island to lose one-fourth of its width?

INTERPRETING GRAPHICS

Study the diagram below, and answer the questions that follow.

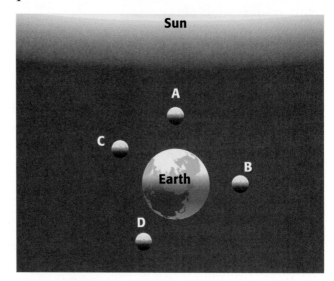

24. At which position (A, B, C, or D) would the moon be during a neap tide?

25. At which position (A, B, C, or D) would the moon be during a spring tide?

26. Would tidal range be greater with the moon at position C or position D? Why?

NOW What Do You Think?

Take a minute to review your answers to the ScienceLog questions on page 365. Have your answers changed? If necessary, revise your answers based on what you have learned since you began this chapter.

CAREERS

SEISMOLOGIST

As a seismologist, **Hiroo Kanamori** studies how earthquakes occur and tries to reduce their impact on our society. He also analyzes the effects of earthquakes on oceans and how earthquakes cause tsunamis (tsoo NAH mes). He has discovered that even weak earthquakes can create tsunamis.

Since most tsunamis are caused by underwater earthquakes, scientists can monitor earthquakes to predict when and where a tsunami will hit land. But the predictions are not always accurate. Very weak earthquakes should not create powerful tsunamis, yet they do. Kanamori calls these special events *tsunami earthquakes,* and he has learned how to predict the size of the resulting tsunamis.

A tsunami can be more dangerous than an earthquake. When people feel the tremors created when the plates slide, they don't always realize that a large tsunami may be on the way. Because of this, people don't expect a tsunami and don't leave the area.

Measuring Tsunami Earthquakes

As tectonic plates grind against each other, they send out seismic waves. These waves travel through the earth's crust and can be recorded by a sensitive machine. But when the plates grind very slowly, only long period seismic waves are recorded. When Kanamori sees a long period wave, he knows that a tsunami will form.

"The speed of the average tsunami is about 800 kilometers per hour, which is much slower than the speed of the long period waves at 15,000 kilometers per hour. So these special seismic waves arrive at distant recording stations much earlier than a tsunami," explains Kanamori. This important fact lets scientists like Kanamori warn people in the tsunami's path so they can leave the area.

An Interesting Career

Kanamori finds his work very rewarding. "It is always good to see how what we learned in the classroom can solve our real-life problems," he explains. "We can see how physics and mathematics work to explain seemingly complex natural events, such as earthquakes, volcanoes, and tsunamis."

A Challenge

▶ The depth of an ocean influences how fast a tsunami travels. To investigate, fill a 0.5 m long tub with 5 cm of water. Tap the tub. How long does it take for the wave to go back and forth? Add more water, and tap it again. Did the wave move faster or slower?

▶ *Monster waves are well-known in many communities along the Pacific coast.*

Health

Red Tides

Imagine going to the beach only to find that the ocean water has turned red and fish are floating belly up all over the place. This is not an imaginary scene. It really happens. What could cause such widespread damage to the ocean? Single-cell algae, that's what!

Blooming Algae

When certain algae grow rapidly, they clump together on the ocean's surface in an algal bloom that changes the color of the water. People called these algal blooms red tides because the blooms often turned the water red or reddish-brown. They also believed that tidal conditions caused the blooms. Scientists now call these algae explosions harmful algal blooms (HABs) because HABs are not always red, and they are not directly related to tides. The blooms are harmful because certain species of algae produce toxins that can poison fish, shellfish, and people.

Scientists also have learned that the ocean's natural currents may carry HABs hundreds of miles along a coastline. For example, in 1987, the Gulf Stream off the Atlantic coast of Florida carried a toxic bloom up the coast to North Carolina.

Troublesome Toxins

Some people who ate tainted shellfish from the North Carolina coast in 1987 suffered from muscular aches, anxiety, sweating, dizziness, diarrhea, vomiting, and abdominal pain. Some algae toxins can even kill people who eat the tainted seafood. Another HAB occurred in 1987 in Nova Scotia, Canada. Four people died from

▲ *Harmful algal blooms are caused by algae like the one shown above right.*

eating contaminated shellfish, and another 150 people suffered from symptoms such as dizziness, headaches, seizures, short-term memory loss, and comas.

In the 1990s, Texas, Maryland, Alaska, and many other coastal states experienced HABs. However, the problem is not confined to North America. Throughout the 1990s, HABs caused health problems in South Africa, Argentina, India, New Zealand, and France.

No Signs to Read

Fish and shellfish are major sources of protein for people all over the world. Unfortunately, there are no outward signs when seafood is contaminated. The toxins don't change the flavor, and cooking the seafood doesn't eliminate the toxins. Sometimes a HAB rides into an area on an ocean current, causing fish to die and people to become ill before authorities are aware of the problem.

Fortunately, scientists all over the world are working on ways to monitor and even predict HABs. As a result, people eventually may be able to eat fish and shellfish without worrying about toxic algae.

Find Out More

▶ Some people think that human activities are causing more HABs than occurred in the past. Other people disagree. Find out more about this issue, and have a class debate about the role humans play in creating HABs.

UNIT 6

Weather and Climate

In this unit, you will learn more about the ocean of air in which we live. You will learn about the atmosphere and how it affects conditions on the Earth's surface. The constantly changing weather is always a good topic for conversation. It is also the subject of the science of meteorology. Forecasting the weather is not an easy task. Climate, on the other hand, is much more predictable. This timeline shows some of the events that have occurred as scientists have tried to better understand weather and climate.

1656

Saturn's rings are recognized as such. Galileo had seen them in 1612, but his telescope was not strong enough to make them out as rings.

1281

A sudden typhoon destroys a fleet of Mongolian ships about to reach Japan. This "divine wind," or *kamikaze* in Japanese, saves the country from invasion and conquest.

1945

First atmospheric test of an atomic bomb takes place near Alamogordo, New Mexico.

1974

Chlorofluorocarbons (CFCs) are recognized as harmful to the ozone layer.

1982

Weather information becomes available 24 hours a day, 7 days a week on commercial television.

1714
Gabriel Fahrenheit builds the first mercury thermometer.

1749
Benjamin Franklin explains how updrafts of air are caused by the sun's heating of the local atmosphere.

1778
Karl Sheele and Antoine Lavoisier separately conclude that air is mostly made of nitrogen and oxygen.

1938
The cause of ice ages as a periodic result of the Earth's motion through space is determined by Yugoslav scientist Milutin Milankovitch.

1838
John James Audubon publishes *The Birds of America.*

1999
The first nonstop balloon trip around the world is successfully completed when Brian Jones and Bertrand Piccard land in Egypt.

1985
Scientists discover an ozone hole over Antarctica.

1986
The world's worst nuclear accident takes place at Chernobyl, Ukraine, spreading radiation through the atmosphere as far as the western United States.

15 The Atmosphere

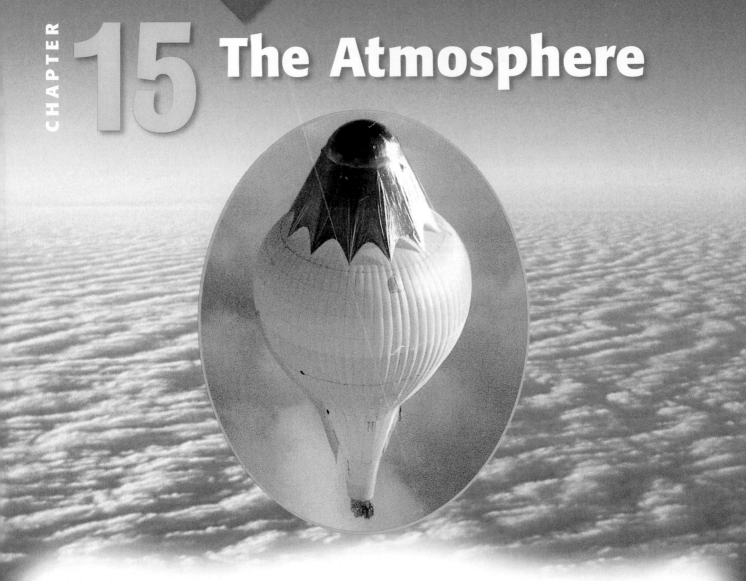

This Really Happened!

On August 17, 1998, Steve Fossett was well on his way to making the first around-the-world balloon flight. It was his fourth attempt, and after 10 days and 22,910 km he had already traveled two-thirds of the way. At the time, this was farther than any other balloonist had traveled in history. But something happened in the dark morning hours that ended Fossett's flight and nearly cost him his life.

While floating over the Pacific Ocean at 8,839 m above sea level, Fossett noticed a row of thunderstorms below. Suddenly his balloon, the *Solo Spirit,* hit an unexpected air disturbance and was sucked downward at a rate of more than 420 km/h. Knowing he was in danger, Fossett climbed out of his bubble hatch and cut loose the heavy tanks of fuel and oxygen to slow the balloon's fall. He then prepared himself for the crash.

When Fossett regained consciousness, his capsule was upside down, half-full of water, and on fire. With a satellite radio beacon to give his location and a small life boat, Fossett scrambled out of the capsule to await his rescue.

Fossett experienced firsthand how unpredictable our atmosphere can be. He was fortunate to have survived. The atmosphere can be unpredictable and dangerous, but it also provides us with gases needed for our survival on Earth. In this chapter you will learn how the Earth's atmosphere affects you and how you affect it.

What Do You Think?

In your ScienceLog, try to answer the following questions based on what you already know:

1. What is air made of?

2. How is the atmosphere organized?

3. What is wind and how does it move?

Better Part of Air

You might wonder how Steve Fossett got his hot air balloon to rise. When you heat a balloon, the air inside the balloon becomes less dense, causing the balloon to rise. When you want to land, you just cool the air to make it more dense, causing the balloon to sink. But with a given mass at the same pressure, what takes up more volume, warm air or cool air? You can find out by doing this simple experiment.

Procedure

1. Using **adhesive putty,** place a **candle** in the center of an **aluminum pie plate.**

2. Fill the pie plate almost one-quarter full with **water.**

3. Light the candle, and place the open end of a **beaker** over it. Notice the level of the water inside the beaker.

4. After the candle goes out, record your observations in your ScienceLog.

Analysis

5. What is happening to the air temperature when the candle goes out?

6. Why does the water rise in the beaker?

7. What takes up more volume, warm air or cool air? Explain.

8. How does the change in air temperature affect a hot air balloon compared with a glass beaker?

Characteristics of the Atmosphere

NEW TERMS

atmosphere   stratosphere
air pressure   ozone
altitude   mesosphere
troposphere   thermosphere

OBJECTIVES

- Discuss the composition of the Earth's atmosphere.
- Explain why pressure changes with altitude.
- Explain how temperature changes with altitude.
- Describe the layers of the atmosphere.

If you were lost in the desert, you could survive for a few days without food and water. But you wouldn't last more than 5 minutes without the *atmosphere*. The **atmosphere** is a mixture of gases that surrounds the Earth. In addition to containing the oxygen we need to breathe, it protects us from the sun's harmful rays. But the atmosphere is always changing. Every breath we take, every tree we plant, and every motor vehicle we ride in affects the composition of our atmosphere. Later you will find out how the atmosphere is changing. But first you need to learn about the atmosphere's composition and structure.

Composition of the Atmosphere

Figure 1 shows the relative amounts of the gases that make up the atmosphere. Besides gases, the atmosphere also contains small amounts of solids and liquids. Tiny solid particles, such as dust, volcanic ash, sea salt, dirt, and smoke, are carried in the air. Next time you turn off the lights at night, shine a flashlight and you will see some of these tiny particles floating in the air.

Figure 1 *Two gases—nitrogen and oxygen—make up 99 percent of the air we breathe.*

Oxygen, the second most common gas in the atmosphere, is produced mainly by plants.

Nitrogen is the most abundant gas in the atmosphere. It is released into the atmosphere by volcanic eruptions and when dead plants and dead animals decay.

The **remaining 1 percent** of the atmosphere is made up of argon, carbon dioxide, water vapor, and other gases.

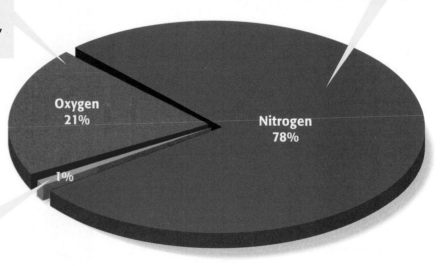

Oxygen 21%

1%

Nitrogen 78%

The most common liquid in the atmosphere is water. Liquid water is found as water droplets in clouds. When the water droplets become too big and heavy for the clouds to hold, they fall as rain. Remember that liquid water is different from water vapor. Water vapor, which is also found in the atmosphere, is a gas and is not visible.

Atmospheric Pressure and Temperature

Have you ever been in an elevator in a tall building? If you have, you probably remember the "popping" in your ears as you went up or down. As you move up or down in an elevator, the air pressure outside your ears changes, while the air pressure inside your ears stays the same. **Air pressure** is the measure of the force with which the air molecules push on a surface. Your ears pop when the pressure inside and outside of your ears suddenly becomes equal. Air pressure changes throughout the atmosphere. Temperature and the kinds of gases present also change. Why do these changes occur? Read on to find out.

Pressure Think of air pressure as a human pyramid, as shown in **Figure 2**. The people at the bottom of the pyramid can feel all the weight and pressure of the people on top. The person on top doesn't feel any weight because there isn't anyone above. The atmosphere works in a similar way.

The Earth's atmosphere is held around the planet by gravity. Gravity pulls the gas molecules in the atmosphere toward the Earth's surface, giving them weight. This weight causes the air to push against the Earth's surface. As you move farther away from the Earth's surface, air pressure decreases because fewer gas molecules are pushing on you. **Altitude** is the height of an object above the Earth's surface. As altitude increases, air pressure decreases.

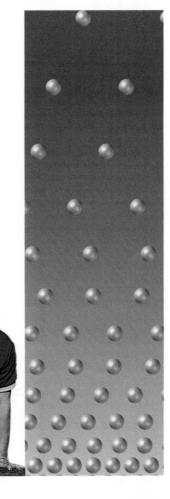

Figure 2 *Like the bottom row of the human pyramid, the lower atmosphere has more molecules pushing on it and therefore experiences greater pressure than the upper atmosphere.*

Self-Check

Does air become more or less dense as you climb a mountain? Why? (See page 564 to check your answer.)

Air Temperature Air temperature also changes as you increase altitude. As you pass through the atmosphere, air temperature changes between warmer and colder conditions. The temperature differences result mainly from the way solar energy is absorbed as it moves downward through the atmosphere. Some parts of the atmosphere are warmer because they contain gases that absorb solar energy. Other parts do not contain these gases and are therefore cooler.

Layers of the Atmosphere

Based on temperature changes, the Earth's atmosphere is divided into four layers—the troposphere, stratosphere, mesosphere, and thermosphere. **Figure 3** illustrates the four atmospheric layers, showing their altitude and temperature. As you can see, each layer has unique characteristics.

Figure 3 Profile of the Earth's Atmosphere

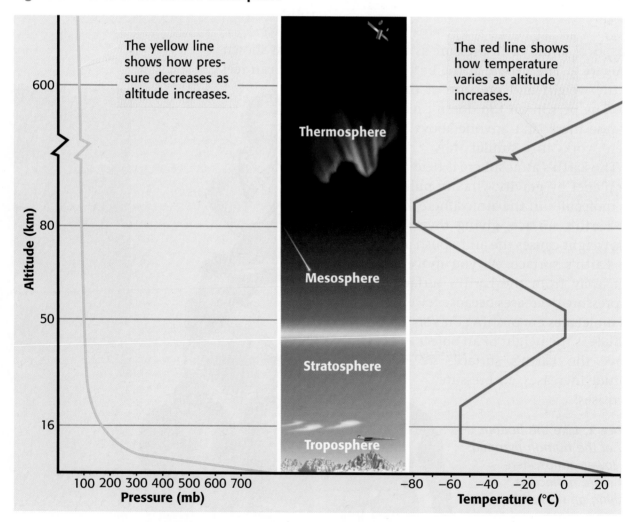

The yellow line shows how pressure decreases as altitude increases.

Thermosphere

Mesosphere

Stratosphere

Troposphere

The red line shows how temperature varies as altitude increases.

Pressure (mb)

Temperature (°C)

Altitude (km)

Troposphere The **troposphere,** which lies next to the Earth's surface, is the lowest layer of the atmosphere. The troposphere is also the densest atmospheric layer, containing almost 90 percent of the atmosphere's total mass. Almost all of Earth's carbon dioxide, water vapor, clouds, air pollution, weather, and life-forms are found in the troposphere. In fact, the troposphere is the layer in which you live. **Figure 4** shows the effects of altitude on temperature in the troposphere.

Stratosphere The atmospheric layer above the troposphere is called the **stratosphere.** In the stratosphere, the air is very thin and contains little moisture. The lower stratosphere is extremely cold, measuring about −60°C. In the stratosphere, the temperature rises with increasing altitude. This occurs because of ozone. **Ozone** is a molecule that is made up of three oxygen atoms, as shown in **Figure 5.** Almost all of the ozone in the atmosphere is contained in the *ozone layer* of the stratosphere. Ozone absorbs solar energy in the form of ultraviolet radiation, warming the air. By absorbing the ultraviolet radiation, the ozone layer also protects life at the Earth's surface.

Figure 4 *Snow and ice can remain year-round on a high mountain while forests grow on its lower slopes and base. That is because as altitude increases, the atmosphere thins, losing its ability to absorb and transfer heat.*

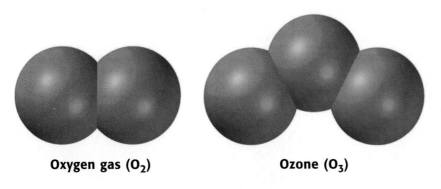

Oxygen gas (O₂)   **Ozone (O₃)**

Figure 5 *While ozone is made up of three oxygen atoms, the oxygen in the air you breathe is made up of two oxygen atoms.*

People protect themselves from the sun's damaging rays by applying sunblock. Exposure of unprotected skin to the sun's ultraviolet rays over a long period of time can cause skin cancer. The breakdown of the Earth's ozone layer is thinning the layer, which allows some harmful ultraviolet radiation to reach the Earth's surface. Sunblocks contain different ratings of SPFs, or skin protection factors. What do the SPF ratings mean?

Mesosphere Above the stratosphere is the mesosphere. The **mesosphere** is the coldest layer of the atmosphere. As in the troposphere, the temperature drops with increasing altitude. Temperatures can be as low as –93°C at the top of the mesosphere. Scientists have recently discovered large wind storms in the mesosphere with winds reaching speeds of more than 320 km/h.

Thermosphere The uppermost atmospheric layer is the **thermosphere.** Here temperature again increases with altitude because many of the gases are absorbing solar radiation. Temperatures in this layer can reach 1,700°C. When you think of an area with high temperatures, you probably think of a place that is very hot. While the thermosphere has very high temperatures, it would not feel hot. Temperature and heat are not the same thing. Temperature is a measure of the average energy of particles in motion. A high temperature means that the particles are moving very fast. Heat, on the other hand, involves the transfer of energy between objects at different temperatures. But in order to transfer energy, particles must touch one another. The air in the thermosphere is very thin, meaning particles are far apart. So even though the particles are moving very fast, they rarely transfer energy because the particles rarely collide. **Figure 6** illustrates how the density of particles affects the heating of the atmosphere.

Figure 6 *Temperatures in the thermosphere are higher than those in the troposphere, but the air particles are too far apart for heat to be transferred.*

The **thermosphere** contains relatively few particles, all of which are moving fast. The temperature of this layer is high due to the speed of its particles. But because the particles aren't close enough together to touch one another, the thermosphere does not give off much heat.

The **troposphere** contains more particles, all of which travel at a slower speed. The temperature of this layer is lower than that of the thermosphere. But because the particles are bumping into one another, the troposphere transfers much more heat.

In the upper mesosphere and the lower thermosphere, nitrogen and oxygen atoms absorb harmful solar energy. This absorption not only contributes to the thermosphere's high temperatures but also causes the gas particles to become electrically charged. Electrically charged particles are called ions; therefore, this part of the thermosphere is referred to as the *ionosphere*. Sometimes these ions radiate energy as light of different colors, as shown in **Figure 7.**

Figure 7 *Aurora borealis (northern lights) and aurora australis (southern lights) occur in the ionosphere. The auroras generally occur near the poles between 65° and 90° north and south latitude.*

The ionosphere also reflects certain radio waves, such as AM radio waves. If you have ever listened to an AM radio station, you can be sure that the ionosphere had something to do with how clear it sounded. When conditions are right, an AM radio wave can travel around the world after being reflected off the ionosphere. These radio signals bounce off the ionosphere and are sent back to Earth.

There is no definite boundary between the atmosphere and space. In the upper thermosphere, the air becomes thinner and thinner, eventually blending into space.

REVIEW

1. Explain why pressure decreases but temperature varies as altitude increases.

2. What causes air pressure?

3. How can the thermosphere have high temperatures but not feel hot?

4. **Analyzing Relationships** Identify one characteristic of each layer of the atmosphere, and explain how that characteristic affects life on Earth.

Section 2

Heating of the Atmosphere

NEW TERMS

radiation
conduction
convection
greenhouse effect
global warming

OBJECTIVES

- Describe what happens to radiation that reaches the Earth.
- Summarize the processes of radiation, conduction, and convection.
- Explain how the greenhouse effect could contribute to global warming.

Have you ever walked barefoot across a sidewalk on a sunny day? If so, your foot felt the warmth of the hot pavement. How did the sidewalk become so warm? Solar energy was changed into heat. The Earth's atmosphere is also heated in several ways by the transfer of energy from the sun. In this section you will find out what happens to the solar energy as it enters the Earth's atmosphere, how the energy is transferred through the atmosphere, and why it seems to be getting hotter every year.

Energy in the Atmosphere

The Earth receives energy from the sun in the form of radiation. **Radiation** is energy that is transferred as electromagnetic waves. The primary types of radiation reaching the Earth's surface from the sun are known as visible light. Although the sun releases a huge amount of radiation, the Earth receives only about two-billionths of this energy. Yet even this small amount of radiation contains a very large amount of energy. **Figure 8** shows what happens to all this radiation once it enters the atmosphere.

When radiation is absorbed, its energy is changed into heat. For example, when you stand in the sun on a cool day, you can feel the sun's rays warming your body. Your skin

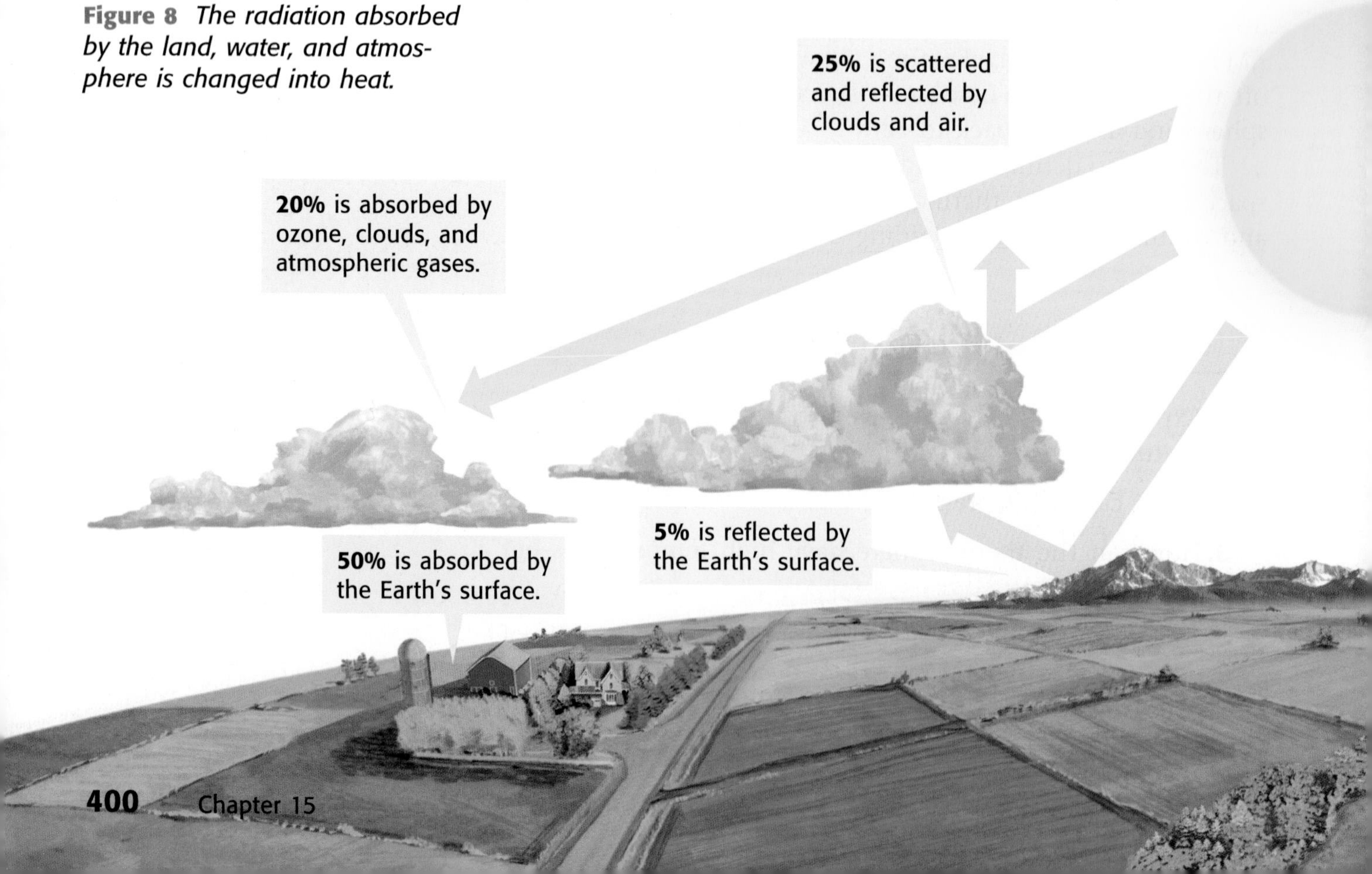

25% is scattered and reflected by clouds and air.
20% is absorbed by ozone, clouds, and atmospheric gases.
5% is reflected by the Earth's surface.
50% is absorbed by the Earth's surface.

Figure 8 *The radiation absorbed by the land, water, and atmosphere is changed into heat.*

absorbs the radiation, causing your skin's molecules to move faster. You feel this as an increase in temperature. The same thing happens when radiation is absorbed by the Earth's surface. The Earth's surface is heated as it absorbs energy from the sun. The Earth transfers energy to the lower atmosphere, heating it, and causing convection.

Moving the Energy Around Most heat in the atmosphere moves by *convection.* **Convection** is the transfer of heat by the circulation or movement of a liquid or a gas. For instance, as air is heated, it becomes less dense and rises. Cool air is more dense and sinks. As the cool air sinks, it pushes the warm air up. The cool air is heated by the Earth and begins to rise. This continual process of warm air rising and cool air sinking causes air to move in a circular pattern called a *convection current.*

As shown in **Figure 9,** convection is only one of several processes responsible for redistributing energy on the Earth. Once incoming solar radiation passes through the atmosphere and is absorbed by the Earth's surface, the energy is transferred to the atmosphere by several methods. These methods include evaporation of surface water and its condensation in the atmosphere; emission of infrared waves, which are then absorbed by atmospheric gases; and conduction as cool air comes in contact with warm surfaces. **Conduction** is the transfer of thermal energy from one substance to another through direct contact. When cool air comes in contact with warm land and ocean surfaces, energy is transferred from the land or ocean to the atmosphere.

Figure 9 *There are several important processes involved in heating the Earth and its atmosphere.*

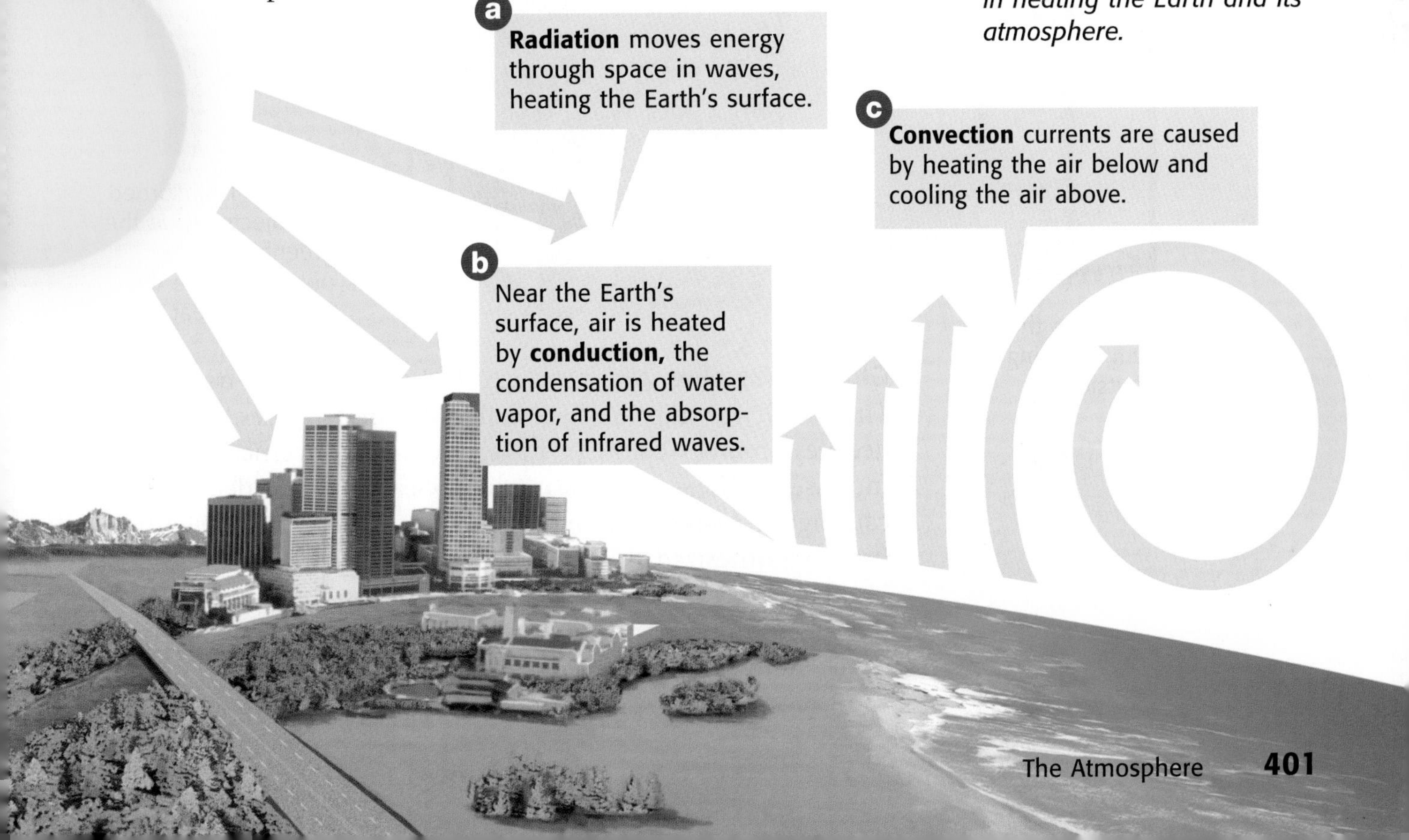

a **Radiation** moves energy through space in waves, heating the Earth's surface.

c **Convection** currents are caused by heating the air below and cooling the air above.

b Near the Earth's surface, air is heated by **conduction,** the condensation of water vapor, and the absorption of infrared waves.

The Greenhouse Effect

As you saw in Figure 8, about 70 percent of the solar energy reaching the Earth is absorbed by the land, oceans, and atmosphere. At the same time, the Earth emits an equal amount of energy back to space as infrared waves. If this did not happen, the planet would continue to get warmer. Atmospheric gases, such as carbon dioxide and water vapor, stop the escape of some of this energy by absorbing it and radiating it back to the Earth. As a result, the Earth is warmer than it would be if there were no atmosphere. It is similar to how a blanket keeps you warm at night. This process, in which the gases in the atmosphere trap thermal energy, is known as the **greenhouse effect.** This term is used because the atmosphere works much like a greenhouse, as shown in **Figure 10.**

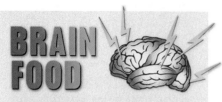
Figure 10 *The gases in the atmosphere act like a layer of glass. Both glass and the gases in the atmosphere allow solar energy to pass through. But glass and some of the gases in the atmosphere absorb heat and stop it from escaping to space.*

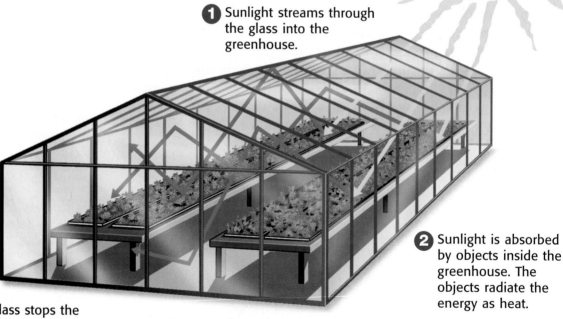

1 Sunlight streams through the glass into the greenhouse.

2 Sunlight is absorbed by objects inside the greenhouse. The objects radiate the energy as heat.

3 The glass stops the heat from escaping to the outside.

Global Warming Not every gas in the atmosphere traps heat. Those that do trap heat are called *greenhouse gases*. In recent decades, many scientists have become concerned that an increase of these gases, particularly carbon dioxide, may be causing an increase in the greenhouse effect. These scientists have hypothesized that a rise in carbon dioxide as a result of human activity has led to increased global temperatures. A rise in average global temperatures is called **global warming.** If there were an increase in the greenhouse effect, global warming would result.

If the average global temperatures continue to rise, the ice-caps could melt, causing a rise in sea level that could flood coastal areas. A rise in global temperatures could also cause climate and weather changes. Later in this chapter you will learn about the human activities that are contributing to an increase in greenhouse gases.

Keeping the Earth Livable For the Earth to remain livable, the amount of solar energy received and the amount of thermal radiation returned to space must be equal. As you saw in Figure 8, about 30 percent of the incoming radiation is reflected back into space. Most of the 70 percent that is absorbed by the Earth and its atmosphere is sent back into space in the form of heat. The balance between incoming radiation and outgoing heat is known as the *radiation balance.* If greenhouse gases, such as carbon dioxide, continue to increase in the atmosphere, the radiation balance may be affected. Some of the energy that once escaped into space could be trapped. The Earth's temperatures would continue to rise, causing major changes in plant and animal communities.

Some scientists argue that the Earth had warmer periods before humans ever walked the planet, so global warming may be a natural process. Nevertheless, many of the world's nations have signed a treaty to reduce activities that increase greenhouse gases in the atmosphere. Another step that is being taken to reduce high carbon dioxide levels in the atmosphere is the planting of millions of trees by volunteers, as shown in **Figure 11.**

Figure 11 *Plants take in harmful carbon dioxide and give off oxygen, which we need to breathe.*

REVIEW

1. Describe three things that can happen to radiation when it reaches the Earth's atmosphere.

2. How is energy transferred through the atmosphere?

3. What is the greenhouse effect?

4. **Inferring Relationships** How does the process of convection rely on conduction?

Atmospheric Pressure and Winds

Sometimes it cools you. Other times it scatters tidy piles of newly swept trash. Still other times it uproots trees and flattens buildings, as shown in **Figure 12**. **Wind** is moving air. In this section you will learn about air movement and about the similarities and differences between different kinds of winds.

Figure 12 *In 1998, the winds from Hurricane Mitch reached speeds of 288 km/h, destroying entire towns in Honduras.*

Why Air Moves

Wind is created by differences in air pressure. These differences in air pressure are generally caused by the unequal heating of the Earth. For example, because the Earth receives more direct solar energy at the equator than at the poles, the air at the equator is warmer and less dense. This warm, less-dense air rises. As it rises it creates an area of low pressure. At the poles, however, the same amount of solar energy that the equator receives is spread over a larger area. Thus, the air is colder and more dense. Colder, more-dense air is heavier and sinks. This cold, sinking air creates areas of high pressure. Pressure differences in the atmosphere at the equator and at the poles cause air to move. Because air moves from areas of high pressure to areas of low pressure, winds generally move from the poles to the equator, as shown in **Figure 13**.

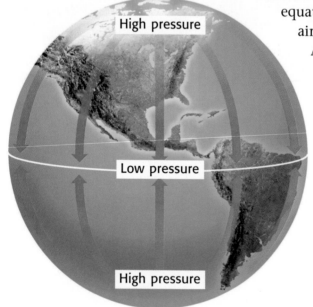

High pressure

Low pressure

High pressure

Figure 13 *Surface winds blow from polar high-pressure areas to equatorial low-pressure areas.*

The speed of the wind is determined by the pressure difference between the area of high pressure and the area of low pressure. The greater the pressure difference is, the faster the wind moves.

Pressure Belts You may be imagining wind moving in one huge, circular pattern, from the poles to the equator. In fact, the pattern is much more complex. As warm air rises over the equator, it begins to cool. Eventually, it stops rising and moves toward the poles. At about 30° north and 30° south latitude, some of the cool air begins to sink. This cool, sinking air causes a high pressure belt near 30° north and 30° south latitude.

At the poles, cold air sinks. As this air moves away from the poles and along the Earth's surface, it begins to warm. As the air warms, the pressure drops, creating a low-pressure belt around 60° north and 60° south latitude. The circular patterns caused by the rising and sinking of air are called *convection cells,* as shown in **Figure 14.**

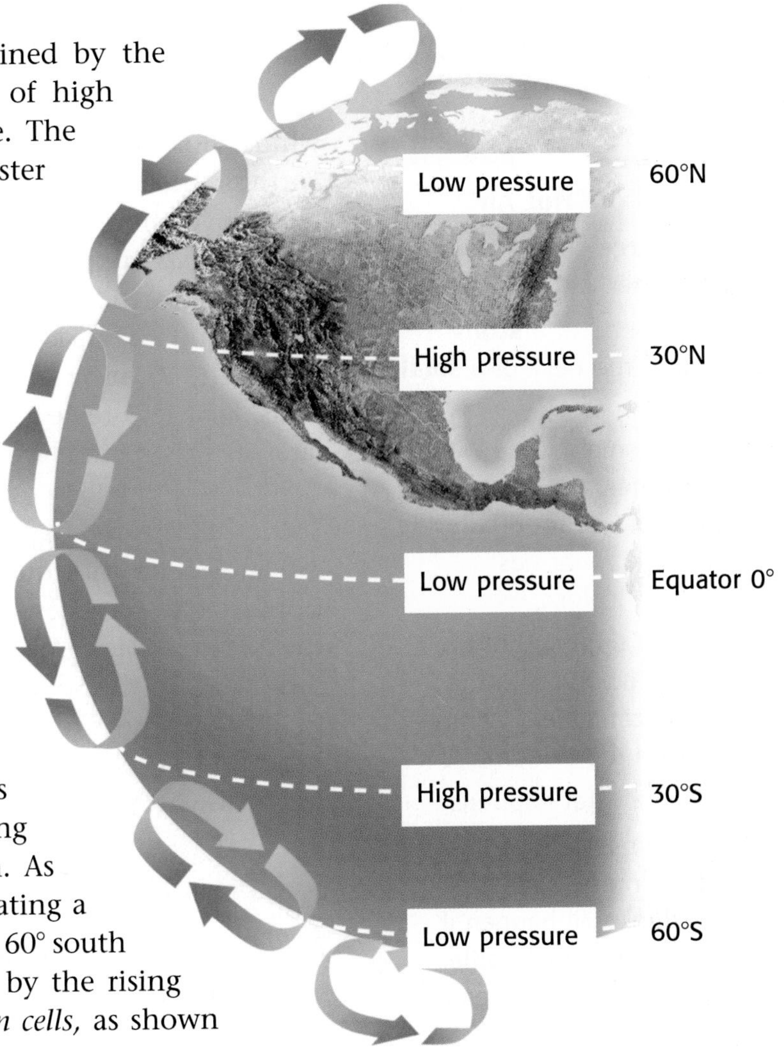

Low pressure — 60°N

High pressure — 30°N

Low pressure — Equator 0°

High pressure — 30°S

Low pressure — 60°S

Figure 14 *The uneven heating of the Earth produces pressure belts. These belts occur at about every 30° of latitude.*

Coriolis Effect Winds don't blow directly north or south. The movement of wind is affected by the rotation of the Earth. The Earth's rotation causes wind to travel in a curved path rather than in a straight line. The curving of moving objects, such as wind, by the Earth's rotation is called the **Coriolis effect.** Because of the Coriolis effect, the winds in the Northern Hemisphere curve to the right, and those in the Southern Hemisphere curve to the left.

To better understand how the Coriolis effect works, imagine rolling a marble across a Lazy Susan while it is spinning. What you might observe is shown in **Figure 15.**

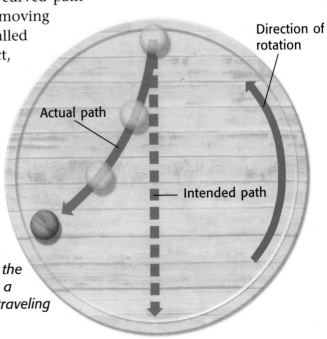

Direction of rotation

Actual path

Intended path

Figure 15 *Because of the Lazy Susan's rotation, the path of the marble curves instead of traveling in a straight line. The Earth's rotation affects objects traveling on or near its surface in much the same way.*

The Atmosphere   **405**

Types of Winds

There are two main types of winds: local winds and global winds. Both types are caused by the uneven heating of the Earth's surface and by pressure differences. *Local winds* generally move short distances and can blow from any direction. *Global winds* are part of a pattern of air circulation that moves across the Earth. These winds travel longer distances than local winds, and they each travel in a specific direction. **Figure 16** shows the location and movement of major global wind systems. First let's review the different types of global winds, and later in this section we will discuss local winds.

Trade Winds In both hemispheres, the winds that blow from 30° latitude to the equator are called **trade winds.** Because the Coriolis effect makes the trade winds curve to the right in the Northern Hemisphere, they move from the northeast to the southwest. In the Southern Hemisphere, the trade winds curve to the left and move from the southeast to the northwest. Early traders used the trade winds to sail from Europe to the Americas, hence the name.

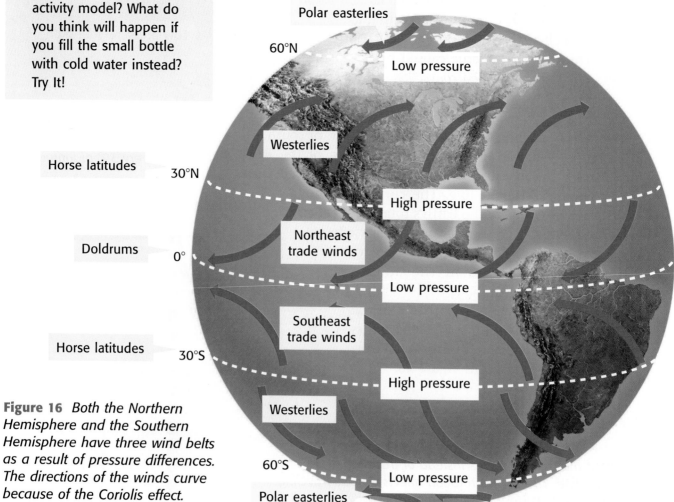

Figure 16 *Both the Northern Hemisphere and the Southern Hemisphere have three wind belts as a result of pressure differences. The directions of the winds curve because of the Coriolis effect.*

The trade winds of the Northern and Southern Hemispheres meet in an area of low pressure around the equator called the *doldrums*. In the doldrums there is very little wind because of the warm rising air. *Doldrums* comes from an Old English word meaning "foolish." Sailors were considered foolish if they got their ship stuck in these areas of little wind.

At about 30° north and 30° south latitude, sinking air creates an area of high pressure. This area is called the *horse latitudes*. Here the winds are weak. Legend has it that the name horse latitudes was given to these areas when sailing ships carried horses from Europe to the Americas. When the ships were stuck in this area due to lack of wind, horses were sometimes thrown overboard to save drinking water for the sailors.

Westerlies The **westerlies** are wind belts found in both the Northern and Southern Hemispheres between 30° and 60° latitude. The westerlies flow toward the poles in the opposite direction of the trade winds. In the Northern Hemisphere, the westerlies blow from the southwest to the northeast. In the Southern Hemisphere, they blow from the northwest to the southeast. The westerlies helped early traders return to Europe. Sailing ships, like the one in **Figure 17,** were designed to best use the wind to move the ship forward.

Figure 17 *This ship is a replica of Columbus's* Santa Maria, *which used the trade winds to sail to the New World.*

Polar Easterlies The **polar easterlies** are wind belts that extend from the poles to 60° latitude in both hemispheres. The polar easterlies are formed from cold, sinking air moving from the poles toward 60° north and 60° south latitude. The polar easterlies blow from the northeast to the southwest in the Northern Hemisphere. In the Southern Hemisphere, these winds blow from the southeast to the northwest.

To find out how to build a device that measures wind speed, turn to page 548 of the LabBook.

Jet Streams The **jet streams** are narrow belts of high-speed winds that blow in the upper troposphere and lower stratosphere over both the Northern Hemisphere and the Southern Hemisphere, as shown in **Figure 18**. These winds often change speed and can reach maximum speeds of 500 km/h. Unlike other global winds, the jet streams do not follow regular paths around the Earth, but change both their latitude and altitude.

Knowing the position of the jet stream is important to both meteorologists and airline pilots. Because the jet stream controls the movement of storms, meteorologists can track a storm if they know the location of the jet stream. By flying in the direction of the jet stream, pilots can save time and fuel. On the other hand, pilots flying against the jet stream will use more fuel and take longer to reach their destination.

Local Winds Local winds are influenced by the geography of an area. An area's geography, such as a shoreline or a mountain, sometimes produces temperature differences that cause local winds like land and sea breezes, as shown in **Figure 19**. During the day, land heats up faster than water. The land heats the air above it. At night, land cools faster than water, cooling the air above the land.

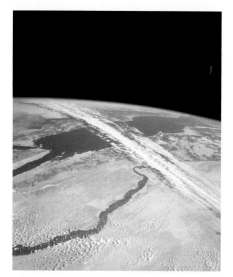

Figure 18 *The large pressure differences between cold air from the poles and warm air from the middle latitudes produce fast-moving jet streams.*

Figure 19 Sea and Land Breezes

Warm air

The cool air moves toward the land, producing a *sea breeze.*

Cool air

As warm air rises, it creates an area of low pressure over the land.

Air over the water is cooler and creates an area of high pressure.

Cool air

The cool air moves toward the water, producing a *land breeze.*

Warm air

Air over land is cooler and creates an area of high pressure.

Air over the water is warmer and creates an area of low pressure.

Mountain and valley breezes are another example of local winds caused by an area's geography. Campers in mountain areas may feel a warm afternoon change into a cold night soon after the sun sets. The illustrations in **Figure 20** show you why.

MATH **BREAK**

Calculating Groundspeed
An airplane has an airspeed of 500 km/h and is moving into a 150 km/h head wind due to the jet stream. What is the actual groundspeed of the plane? Over a 3-hour flight, how far would the plane actually travel? (Hint: To calculate actual ground-speed, subtract head-wind speed from airspeed.)

Warm air

During the day, the sun heats the valley floor and warms the air above it.

Warm air from the valley moves upslope, creating a *valley breeze.*

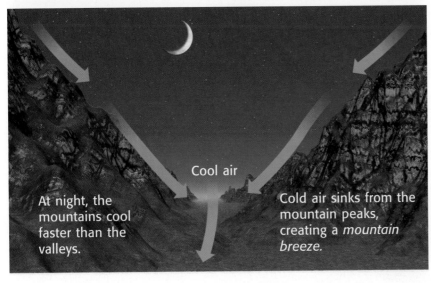

Cool air

At night, the mountains cool faster than the valleys.

Cold air sinks from the mountain peaks, creating a *mountain breeze.*

Figure 20 *During the day, a gentle breeze blows up the slopes. At night, cold air flows downslope and settles in the valley.*

REVIEW

1. How does the Coriolis effect affect wind movement?

2. What causes winds?

3. Compare and contrast global winds and local winds.

4. **Applying Concepts** Suppose you are vacationing at the beach. It is daytime and you want to go swimming in the ocean. You know the beach is near your hotel, but you don't know what direction it is in. How might the local wind help you find the ocean?

The Air We Breathe

NEW TERMS
primary pollutants
secondary pollutants
acid precipitation
scrubber

OBJECTIVES
- Describe the major types of air pollution.
- Name the major causes of air pollution.
- Explain how air pollution can affect human health.
- Explain how air pollution can be reduced.

Air pollution, as shown in **Figure 21,** is not a new problem. By the middle of the 1700s, many of the world's large cities suffered from poor air quality. Most of the pollutants were released from factories and homes that burned coal for heat. Even 2,000 years ago, the Romans were complaining about the bad air in their cities. At that time the air was thick with the smoke from fires and the smell of open sewers. So you see, cities have always been troubled with air pollution. In this section you will learn about the different types of air pollution, their sources, and what the world is doing to reduce them.

Figure 21 *The air pollution in Mexico City is sometimes so dangerous that some people wear surgical masks when they go outside.*

Air Quality

Even "clean" air is not perfectly clean. It contains many pollutants from natural sources. These pollutants include dust, sea salt, volcanic gases and ash, smoke from forest fires, pollen, swamp gas, and many other materials. In fact, natural sources produce a greater amount of pollutants than humans do. But we have adapted to many of these natural pollutants.

Most of the air pollution mentioned in the news is a result of human activities. Pollutants caused by human activities can be solids, liquids, or gases. Human-caused air pollution, such as that shown in Figure 21, is most common in cities. As more people move to cities, urban air pollution increases.

Types of Air Pollution

Air pollutants are generally described as either *primary pollutants* or *secondary pollutants*. **Primary pollutants** are pollutants that are put directly into the air by human or natural activity. **Figure 22** shows some examples of primary air pollutants.

Figure 22 *Exhaust from vehicles, ash from volcanic eruptions, and soot from smoke are all examples of primary pollutants.*

Secondary pollutants are pollutants that form from chemical reactions that occur when primary pollutants come in contact with other primary pollutants or with naturally occurring substances, such as water vapor. Many secondary pollutants are formed when a primary pollutant reacts with sunlight. Ozone and smog are examples of secondary pollutants. As you read at the beginning of this chapter, ozone is a gas in the stratosphere that is helpful and absorbs harmful rays from the sun. Near the ground, however, ozone is a dangerous pollutant that affects the health of all organisms. Ozone and smog are produced when sunlight reacts with automobile exhaust, as illustrated in **Figure 23.**

Figure 23 *Many large cities suffer from smog, especially those with a sunny climate and millions of automobiles, such as Los Angeles and Rome.*

2 Ozone reacts with automobile exhaust to form smog.

Smog

1 Automobile exhaust reacts with air and sunlight to form ozone.

Automobile exhaust

Ozone

Sources of Human-Caused Air Pollution

Human-caused air pollution comes from a variety of sources. The major source of air pollution today is transportation, as shown in **Figure 24.** Cars contribute about 60 percent of the human-caused air pollution in the United States. The oxides that come from car exhaust, such as nitrogen oxide, contribute to smog and acid rain. *Oxides* are chemical compounds that contain oxygen and other elements.

Industrial Air Pollution Many industrial plants and electric power plants burn fossil fuels to get their energy. But burning fossil fuels causes large amounts of oxides to be released into the air, as shown in **Figure 25.** In fact, the burning of fossil fuels in industrial and electric power plants is responsible for 96 percent of the sulfur oxides released into the atmosphere.

Some industries also produce chemicals that form poisonous fumes. The chemicals used by oil refineries, chemical manufacturing plants, dry-cleaning businesses, furniture refinishers, and auto-body shops can add poisonous fumes to the air.

Figure 24 *Seventy percent of the carbon monoxide in the United States is produced by transportation.*

Figure 25 *This power plant burns coal to get its energy and releases sulfur oxides and particulates into the atmosphere.*

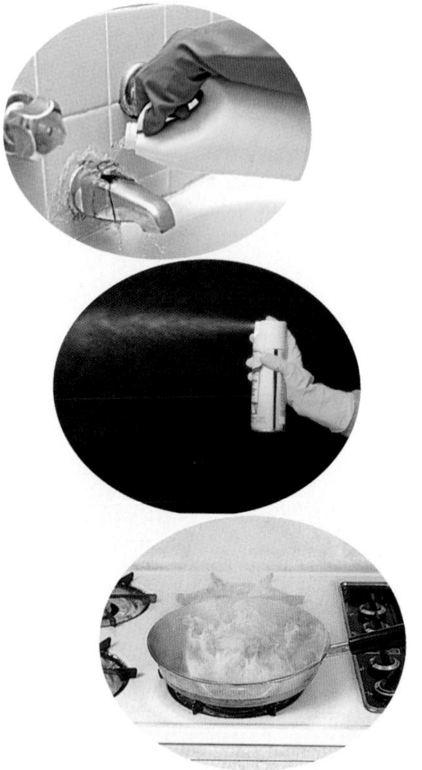

Figure 26 *Household cleaners, air fresheners, and smoke from cooking all contribute to indoor air pollution.*

Indoor Air Pollution Air pollution is not limited to the outdoors. Our homes, schools, and buildings have air pollution too. Sometimes the air inside a building is even worse than the air outside. As shown in **Figure 26,** many of the products that you use every day contribute to air pollution. Industrial compounds found in carpets, paints, building materials, and furniture also pollute the air, especially when they are new.

In buildings where the windows are tightly sealed to reduce air leaks and keep electric bills low, pollutants can sometimes reach higher levels inside than outside.

The Air Pollution Problem

Air pollution is both a local and global concern. As you have already learned, local air pollution, such as smog, generally affects large cities. Air pollution becomes a global concern when local pollution moves away from its source. How does this happen? What effect does it have? You will soon find out.

Winds can move pollutants from one place to another, sometimes reducing the amount of pollution in the source area but increasing it in another place. For example, the prevailing winds carry air pollution created in the midwestern United States hundreds of miles to Canada. One such form of this pollution is acid precipitation.

Acid precipitation is precipitation, such as rain, sleet, or snow, that contains acids from air pollution. When fossil fuels are burned, they release oxides of sulfur and nitrogen into the atmosphere. When these oxides combine with water droplets in the atmosphere, they form sulfuric acid and nitric acid, which fall as precipitation. Acid precipitation has many negative effects on the environment, as shown in **Figure 27.**

Figure 27 *Acid precipitation can kill living things, such as fish and trees, by making their environment too acidic to live in. Acid rain can also damage buildings by chemically weathering the concrete and limestone.*

The Ozone Hole Other global concerns brought about by air pollution include the warming of our planet, mentioned earlier in this chapter, and the ozone hole in the stratosphere. Remember, the ozone layer in the stratosphere protects you from the sun's harmful ultraviolet rays. In the 1970s, scientists determined that some chemicals released into the atmosphere react with ozone in the ozone layer. The reaction results in a breakdown of ozone into oxygen, which does not block ultraviolet rays. The loss of ozone creates an ozone hole, which allows more ultraviolet rays to reach the Earth's surface. During the 1980s, scientists found that the ozone layer above the South Pole had thinned by 50 to 98 percent. **Figure 28** shows a satellite image of the ozone hole.

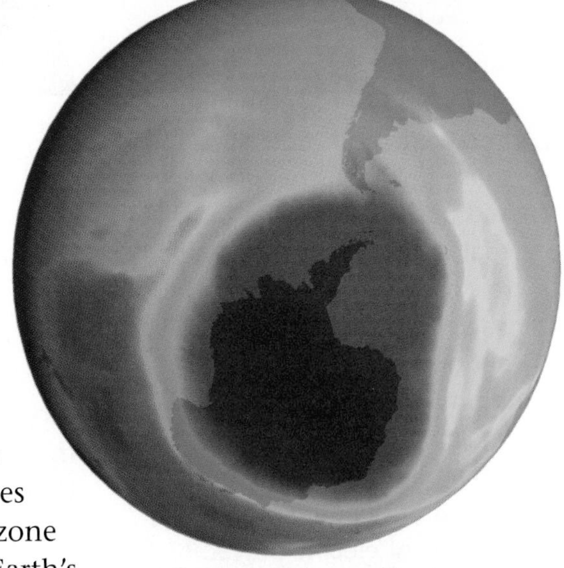

Figure 28 *This satellite image, taken in 1998, shows that the ozone hole, the dark blue area, is still growing.*

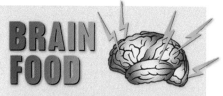
Effects on Human Health You step outside and notice a smoky haze. When you take a deep breath, your throat tingles and you begin to cough. Air pollution like this affects many cities around the world. For example, on March 17, 1992, in Mexico City, all children under the age of 14 were prohibited from going to school because of extremely high levels of air pollution. This is an extreme case, but daily exposure to small amounts of air pollution can cause serious health problems. Children, elderly people, and people with allergies, lung problems, and heart problems are especially vulnerable to the effects of air pollution. **Figure 29** illustrates some of the effects that air pollution has on the human body.

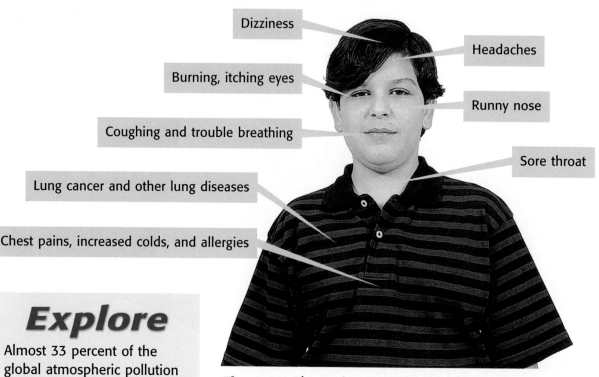

Dizziness

Headaches

Burning, itching eyes

Runny nose

Coughing and trouble breathing

Sore throat

Lung cancer and other lung diseases

Chest pains, increased colds, and allergies

Figure 29 *The Environmental Protection Agency blames air pollution for at least 2,000 new cases of cancer each year.*

Explore

Almost 33 percent of the global atmospheric pollution from carbon dioxide is caused by industrial plants and power plants that burn coal or other fossil fuels. We rely on these sources of power for a better way of life, but our use of them is polluting our air and worsening our quality of life. Use your school library or the Internet to find out about some other sources of electric power. What special problems does each source of energy bring with it?

Cleaning Up Our Act

Is all this talk about bad air making you a little choked up? Don't worry, help is on the way! In the United States, progress has been made in cleaning up the air. One reason for this progress is the Clean Air Act, which was passed by Congress in 1970. The Clean Air Act is a law that gives the Environmental Protection Agency (EPA) the authority to control the amount of air pollutants that can be released from any source, such as cars and factories. The EPA also checks air quality. If air quality worsens, the EPA can set stricter standards. What are car manufacturers and factories doing to improve air quality? Read on to find out.

Controlling Air Pollution from Vehicles The EPA has required car manufacturers to meet a certain standard for the exhaust that comes out of the tailpipe on cars. New cars now have devices that remove most of the pollutants from the car's exhaust as it exits the tailpipe. Car manufacturers are also making cars that run on fuels other than gasoline. Some of these cars run on hydrogen and natural gas, while others run on batteries powered by solar energy. The car shown in **Figure 30** is electric.

Are electric cars the cure for air pollution? Turn to page 421 and decide for yourself.

Figure 30 *Instead of having to refuel at a gas station, an electric car is plugged in to a recharging outlet.*

Controlling Air Pollution from Industry The Clean Air Act requires many industries to use *scrubbers*. A **scrubber,** shown in **Figure 31,** is a device that attaches to smokestacks to remove some of the more harmful pollutants before they are released into the air. One such scrubber is used in coal-burning power plants in the United States to remove ash and other particles from the smokestacks. Scrubbers prevent 22 million metric tons of ash from being released into the air each year.

Although we have a long way to go, we're taking steps in the right direction to keep the air clean for future generations.

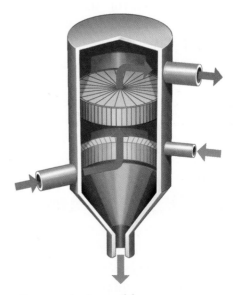

Figure 31 *A scrubber moves gases through a spray of water that dissolves many of the pollutants the gases contain.*

REVIEW

1. How can the air inside a building be more polluted than the air outside?

2. Why might it be difficult to establish a direct link between air pollution and health problems?

3. How has the Clean Air Act helped to reduce air pollution?

4. **Applying Concepts** How is the water cycle affected by air pollution?

Chapter Highlights

SECTION 1

Vocabulary

atmosphere (p. 394)

air pressure (p. 395)

altitude (p. 395)

troposphere (p. 397)

stratosphere (p. 397)

ozone (p. 397)

mesosphere (p. 398)

thermosphere (p. 398)

Section Notes

- The atmosphere is a mixture of gases.

- Nitrogen and oxygen are the two most abundant atmospheric gases.

- Throughout the atmosphere, there are changes in air pressure, temperature, and gases.

- Air pressure decreases as altitude increases.

- Temperature differences in the atmosphere are a result of the way solar energy is absorbed as it moves downward through the atmosphere.

- The troposphere is the lowest and densest layer of the atmosphere. All weather occurs in the troposphere.

- The stratosphere contains the ozone layer, which protects us from harmful radiation.

- The mesosphere is the coldest layer of the atmosphere.

- The uppermost atmospheric layer is the thermosphere.

Labs

Under Pressure! (p. 550)

SECTION 2

Vocabulary

radiation (p. 400)

conduction (p. 401)

convection (p. 401)

greenhouse effect (p. 402)

global warming (p. 402)

Section Notes

- The Earth receives energy from the sun in the form of radiation.

- Radiation that reaches the Earth's surface is absorbed or reflected.

- Heat is transferred through the atmosphere by conduction and convection.

- The greenhouse effect is caused by gases in the atmosphere that trap heat that is reflected off and radiated from the Earth's surface.

Labs

Boiling Over! (p. 546)

☑ Skills Check

Math Concepts

FLYING AGAINST THE JET STREAM The groundspeed of an airplane can be affected by the jet stream. The jet stream can push an airplane toward its final destination or slow it down. To find the groundspeed of an airplane, you either add or subtract the wind speed, depending on whether the airplane is moving with or against the jet stream. For example, if an airplane is traveling at an airspeed of 400 km/h and is moving with a 100 km/h jet stream, you would add the jet stream speed to the airspeed of the airplane to calculate the groundspeed.

$$400 \text{ km/h} + 100 \text{ km/h} = 500 \text{ km/h}$$

To calculate the groundspeed of an airplane traveling at 400 km/h that is moving into a 100 km/h jet stream, you would subtract the jet-stream speed from the airspeed of the airplane.

$$400 \text{ km/h} - 100 \text{ km/h} = 300 \text{ km/h}$$

Visual Understanding

GLOBAL WINDS Study Figure 16 on page 406 to review the global wind belts that result from air pressure differences.

SECTION 3

Vocabulary

wind (*p. 404*)

Coriolis effect (*p. 405*)

trade winds (*p. 406*)

westerlies (*p. 407*)

polar easterlies (*p. 407*)

jet streams (*p. 408*)

Section Notes

- At the Earth's surface, winds blow from areas of high pressure to areas of low pressure.

- Pressure belts exist approximately every 30° of latitude.

- The Coriolis effect makes wind curve as it moves across the Earth's surface.

- Global winds are part of a pattern of air circulation across the Earth and include the trade winds, the westerlies, and the polar easterlies.

- Local winds move short distances, can blow in any direction, and are influenced by geography.

Labs

Go Fly a Bike! (*p. 548*)

SECTION 4

Vocabulary

primary pollutants (*p. 411*)

secondary pollutants (*p. 411*)

acid precipitation (*p. 413*)

scrubber (*p. 415*)

Section Notes

- Air pollutants are generally classified as primary or secondary pollutants.

- Human-caused pollution comes from a variety of sources, including factories, cars, and homes.

- Air pollution can heighten problems associated with allergies, lung problems, and heart problems.

- The Clean Air Act has reduced air pollution by controlling the amount of pollutants that can be released from cars and factories.

---

 internetconnect

go.hrw.com **GO TO:** go.hrw.com

 SCiLINKS **NSTA** **GO TO:** www.scilinks.org

Visit the **HRW** Web site for a variety of learning tools related to this chapter. Just type in the keyword:

KEYWORD: HSTATM

Visit the **National Science Teachers Association** on-line Web site for Internet resources related to this chapter. Just type in the *sci*LINKS number for more information about the topic:

TOPIC:	**sciLINKS NUMBER:**
TOPIC: Composition of the Atmosphere	*sci*LINKS NUMBER: HSTE355
TOPIC: Energy in the Atmosphere	*sci*LINKS NUMBER: HSTE360
TOPIC: The Greenhouse Effect	*sci*LINKS NUMBER: HSTE365
TOPIC: Atmospheric Pressure and Winds	*sci*LINKS NUMBER: HSTE370
TOPIC: Air Pollution	*sci*LINKS NUMBER: HSTE375

Chapter Review

USING VOCABULARY

Explain the difference between the following sets of words:

1. air pressure/altitude

2. troposphere/thermosphere

3. greenhouse effect/global warming

4. convection/conduction

5. global wind/local wind

6. primary pollutant/secondary pollutant

UNDERSTANDING CONCEPTS

Multiple Choice

7. What is the most abundant gas in the air that we breathe?
   a. oxygen
   c. hydrogen
   b. nitrogen
   d. carbon dioxide

8. The major source of oxygen for the Earth's atmosphere is
   a. sea water.
   c. plants.
   b. the sun.
   d. animals.

9. The bottom layer of the atmosphere, where almost all weather occurs, is the
   a. stratosphere.
   b. troposphere.
   c. thermosphere.
   d. mesosphere.

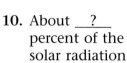

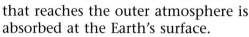

10. About __?__ percent of the solar radiation that reaches the outer atmosphere is absorbed at the Earth's surface.
    a. 20
    b. 30
    c. 50
    d. 70

11. The ozone layer is located in the
    a. stratosphere.
    b. troposphere.
    c. thermosphere.
    d. mesosphere.

12. How does most heat energy in the atmosphere move?
    a. conduction
    b. convection
    c. advection
    d. radiation

13. The balance between incoming radiation and outgoing heat energy is called __?__.
    a. convection
    b. conduction
    c. greenhouse effect
    d. radiation balance

14. Most of the United States is located in which prevailing wind belt?
    a. westerlies
    b. northeast trade winds
    c. southeast trade winds
    d. doldrums

15. Which of the following is not a primary pollutant?
    a. car exhaust
    b. acid precipitation
    c. smoke from a factory
    d. fumes from burning plastic

16. The Clean Air Act
    a. controls the amount of air pollutants that can be released from most sources.
    b. requires cars to run on fuels other than gasoline.
    c. requires many industries to use scrubbers.
    d. (a) and (c) only

Short Answer

17. Why does the atmosphere become less dense as altitude increases?

18. Explain why air rises when it is heated.

19. What causes temperature changes in the atmosphere?

20. What are secondary pollutants, and how are they formed? Give an example.

Concept Mapping

21. Use the following terms to create a concept map: altitude, air pressure, temperature, atmosphere.

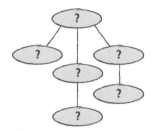

CRITICAL THINKING AND PROBLEM SOLVING

Write one or two sentences to answer the following questions:

22. What is the relationship between the greenhouse effect and global warming?

23. How do you think the Coriolis effect would change if the Earth were to rotate twice as fast? Explain.

24. Without the atmosphere, the Earth's surface would be very different. What are several ways that the atmosphere affects the Earth?

MATH IN SCIENCE

25. Wind speed is measured in miles per hour and in knots. One mile (statute mile or land mile) is 5,280 ft. One nautical mile (or sea mile) is 6,076 ft. Speed in nautical miles is measured in knots. Calculate the wind speed in knots if the wind is blowing at 25 mi/h.

INTERPRETING GRAPHICS

Use the wind-chill chart to answer the questions below.

Wind-Chill Chart

Wind Speed		Actual thermometer reading (°F)				
		40	30	20	10	0
Knots	mph	Equivalent temperature (°F)				
Calm		40	30	20	10	0
4	5	37	27	16	6	−5
9	10	28	16	4	−9	−21
13	15	22	9	−5	−18	−36
17	20	18	4	−10	−25	−39
22	25	16	0	−15	−29	−44
26	30	13	−2	−18	−33	−48
30	35	11	−4	−20	−35	−49

26. If the wind speed is 20 mi/h and the temperature is 40°F, how cold will the air seem?

27. If the wind speed is 30 mi/h and the temperature is 20°F, how cold will the air seem?

NOW What Do You Think?

Take a minute to review your answers to the ScienceLog questions on page 393. Have your answers changed? If necessary, revise your answers based on what you have learned since you began this chapter.

Particles in the Air

Take a deep breath. You have probably just inhaled thousands of tiny specks of dust, pollen, and other particles. These particles, called particulates, are harmless under normal conditions. But if concentrations of particulates get too high or if they consist of harmful materials, they are considered to be a type of air pollution.

Because many particulates are very small, our bodies' natural filters, such as nasal hairs and mucous membranes, cannot filter all of them out. When inhaled, particulates can cause irritation in the lungs. Over time, this irritation can lead to diseases such as bronchitis, asthma, and emphysema. The danger increases as the level of particulates in the air increases.

Where There's Smoke…

Unfortunately, dust and pollen are not the only forms of particulates. Many of the particulates in the air come from the burning of various materials. For example, when wood is burned, it releases particles of smoke, soot, and ash into the air. Some of these are so small that they can float in the air for days. The burning of fuels such as coal, oil, and gasoline also creates particulates. The particulates from these sources can be very dangerous in high concentrations. That's why particulate concentrations are one measure of air quality. Large concentrations of particulates are visible in the air. Along with other pollutants, particulates are

▲ *When the ash from Mount St. Helens settled from the air, it created scenes like this one.*

what make polluted air look brown or yellowish brown. But don't be fooled—even air that appears clean can be polluted.

Eruptions of Particulates

Volcanoes can be the source of incredible amounts of particulates. For example, when Mount St. Helens erupted in 1980, it launched thousands of tons of ash into the surrounding air. The air was so thick with ash that the area became as dark as night. For several hours, the ash completely blocked the light from the sun. When the ash finally settled from the air, it covered the surrounding landscape like a thick blanket of snow. This layer of ash killed plants and livestock for several kilometers around the volcano.

One theory to explain the extinction of dinosaurs is that a gargantuan meteorite hit the Earth with such velocity that the resulting impact created enough dust to block out the sun for years. During this dark period, plants were unable to grow and therefore could not support the normal food chains. Consequently, the dinosaurs died out.

Do Filters Really Filter?

▶ Since the burning of most substances creates particulates, there must be particulates in cigarette smoke. Do some research to find out if the filters on cigarettes are effective at preventing particulates from entering the smoker's body. Your findings may surprise you!

A Cure for Air Pollution?

Automobile emissions are responsible for at least half of all urban air pollution and a quarter of all carbon dioxide released into the atmosphere. Therefore, the production of a car that emits no polluting gases in its exhaust is a significant accomplishment. The only such vehicle currently available is the electric car. Electric cars are powered by batteries, so they do not produce exhaust gases. Supporters believe that switching to electric cars will reduce air pollution in this country. But critics believe that taxpayers will pay an unfair share for this switch and that the reduction in pollution won't be as great as promised.

▲ *Will a switch to electric cars such as this one reduce air pollution?*

Electric Cars Will Reduce Air Pollution

Even the cleanest and most modern cars emit pollutants into the air. Supporters of a switch to electric cars believe the switch will reduce pollution in congested cities. But some critics suggest that a switch to electric cars will simply move the source of pollution from a car's tailpipe to the power plant's smokestack. This is because most electricity is generated by burning coal.

In California, electric cars would have the greatest impact. Here most electricity is produced by burning natural gas, which releases less air pollution than burning coal.

Nuclear plants and dams release no pollutants in the air when they generate electricity. Solar power and wind power are also emission-free ways to generate electricity. Supporters argue that a switch to electric cars will reduce air pollution immediately and that a further reduction will occur when power plants convert to these cleaner sources of energy.

Electric Cars Won't Solve the Problem

Electric cars are inconvenient because the batteries have to be recharged so often. The batteries also have to be replaced every 2 to 3 years. The nation's landfills are already crowded with conventional car batteries, which contain acid and metals that may pollute ground water. A switch to electric cars would aggravate this pollution problem because the batteries have to be replaced so often.

Also, electric cars will likely replace the cleanest cars on the road, not the dirtiest. A new car may emit only one-tenth of the pollution emitted by an older model. If an older car's pollution-control equipment does not work properly, it may emit 100 times more pollution than a new car. But people who drive older, poorly maintained cars probably won't be able to afford expensive electric cars. Therefore, the worst offenders will stay on the road, continuing to pollute the air.

Analyze the Issue

▶ Do you think electric cars are the best solution to the air pollution problem? Why or why not? What are some alternative solutions for reducing air pollution?

16 Understanding Weather

Would You Believe . . .

In May of 1997, a springtime tornado wreaked havoc on Jarrell, Texas. The Jarrell tornado was one of the rarest and most powerful tornadoes, with winds estimated at more than 410 km/h. The twister peeled the asphalt from paved roads, stripped fields of corn bare, and destroyed an entire neighborhood.

North America experiences more tornadoes than any other continent—averaging about 700 per year. Most of these tornadoes hit an area in the central United States called Tornado Alley. Tornado Alley covers most of the Great Plains, extending from Texas across Oklahoma, Kansas, southern Nebraska, Iowa, and South Dakota. But what causes these tornadoes, and why is the Great Plains area so vulnerable?

In the spring and early summer, cold, dry air from the North Pole clashes with warm, moist air from the Tropics. This clash forces the warm air to rise and become unstable. When there is a large contrast between the two clashing air masses, the chances that a tornado will form are increased.

Tornado Alley experiences more tornadoes than any other area because its flatness and location on the Earth's surface make it possible for warm and cold air masses to collide with one another.

In this chapter you will learn about what causes weather, the different types of air masses, and how weather can suddenly turn violent.

What Do You Think?

In your ScienceLog, try to answer the following questions based on what you already know:

1. Name some different types of clouds. How are they different?

2. What causes weather?

2. Light a long **match** at the mouth of the bottle. Blow it out and then insert it inside the bottle, holding it there for several seconds.

3. After removing the match, put your mouth over the opening and blow into the bottle several times. Have your partner observe and record what happens as you blow into the bottle. Record what happens in your ScienceLog.

Analysis

4. Describe what happened after you blew into the bottle.

5. What role did water play in this lab?

6. What role did smoke play in this lab?

7. Write your explanation for the formation of the cloud in the bottle. See if your explanation matches the explanation found in this chapter.

Investigate!

Cloud in a Bottle

Some tornadoes, like the one that struck the town of Jarrell, Texas, are classified as violent tornadoes. Only 2 percent of the tornadoes that occur in the United States fall into the violent category. You have already learned that tornadoes can occur when two different air masses collide, but how do tornadoes form? Tornadoes form from clouds. And how do clouds form? Try this simple experiment to find out.

Procedure

1. Pour some **water** into a **large clear-plastic bottle.** Rinse the water around, and then pour it out.

Water in the Air

There might not be a pot of gold at the end of a rainbow, but rainbows hold another secret that you might not be aware of. Rainbows are evidence that the air contains water. Water droplets break up sunlight into the different colors that you can see in a rainbow. Water can exist in the air as a solid, liquid, or gas. Ice, a solid, is found in clouds as snowflakes. Liquid water exists in clouds as water droplets. And water in gaseous form exists in the air as water vapor. Water in the air affects the weather. **Weather** is the condition of the atmosphere at a particular time and place. In this section you will learn how water affects the weather.

The Water Cycle

Water in liquid, solid, and gaseous states is constantly being recycled through the water cycle. The **water cycle** is the continuous movement of water from water sources, such as lakes and oceans, into the air, onto and over land, into the ground, and back to the water sources. Look at **Figure 1** below to see how water moves through the water cycle.

Figure 1 *In the water cycle, water is returned to the Earth's surface through precipitation.*

Condensation occurs when water vapor cools and changes back into liquid droplets. This is how clouds form.

Evaporation occurs when liquid water changes into water vapor, which is a gas.

Transpiration is the process by which plants release water vapor into the air through their leaves.

Precipitation occurs when rain, snow, sleet, or hail falls from the clouds onto the Earth's surface.

Runoff is water, usually from precipitation, that flows across land and collects in rivers, streams, and eventually the ocean.

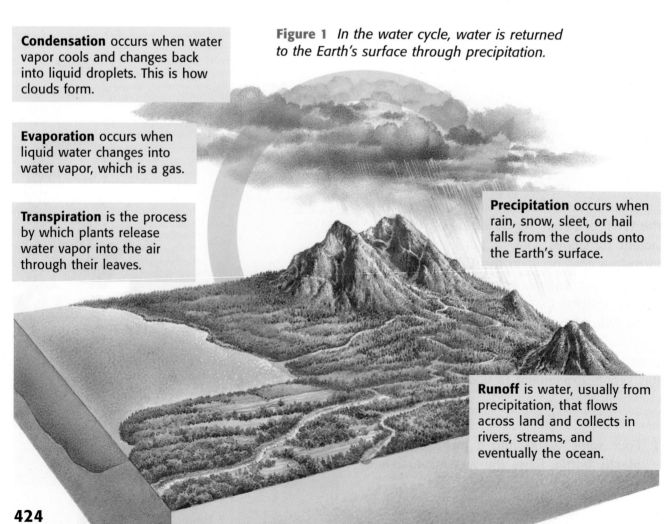

Humidity

Have you ever spent a long time styling your hair before school and had a bad hair day anyway? You walked outside and—wham—your straight hair became limp, or your curly hair became frizzy. Most bad hair days can be blamed on humidity. **Humidity** is the amount of water vapor or moisture in the air. And it is the moisture in the air that makes your hair go crazy, as shown in **Figure 2.**

As water evaporates, the humidity of the air increases. But air's ability to hold water vapor depends on air temperature. As temperature increases, the air's ability to hold water also increases. **Figure 3** shows the relationship between air temperature and air's ability to hold water.

Figure 2 *When there is more water in the air, your hair absorbs moisture and becomes longer.*

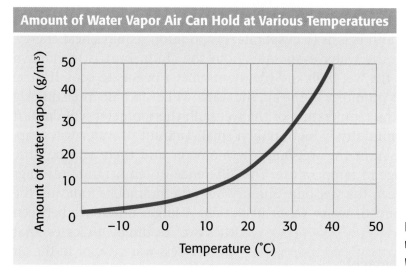

Amount of Water Vapor Air Can Hold at Various Temperatures

Amount of water vapor (g/m³) vs. Temperature (°C)

Self-Check

How does humidity relate to the water cycle? *(Turn to page 564 to check your answer.)*

Figure 3 *This graph shows that warmer air can hold more water vapor than cooler air.*

Relative Humidity   **Relative humidity** is the amount of moisture the air contains compared with the maximum amount it can hold at a particular temperature. Relative humidity is given as a percentage. When air holds all the water it can at a given temperature, the air is said to be *saturated.* Saturated air has a relative humidity of 100 percent. But how do you find the relative humidity of air that is not saturated? If you know the maximum amount of water vapor air can hold at a particular temperature and you know how much water vapor the air is actually holding, you can calculate the relative humidity.

Suppose that 1 m³ of air at a certain temperature can hold 24 g of water vapor. However, you know that the air actually contains 18 g of water vapor. You can calculate the relative humidity using the following formula:

$$\frac{\text{(present) } 18 \text{ g/m}^3}{\text{(saturated) } 24 \text{ g/m}^3} \times 100 = \text{(relative humidity) } 75\%$$

$\div\ 5\ \div\quad \Omega\quad \leq\quad \infty\quad +_\Omega\quad ^{\sqrt{}}\ 9\ _\infty\ ^{\leq}\ \Sigma\ 2$

MATH BREAK

Relating Relative Humidity
Assume that a sample of air 1 m³ at 25°C, contains 11 g of water vapor. Calculate the relative humidity of the air using the value for saturated air shown in Figure 3.

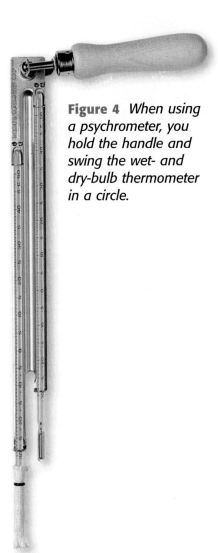

Figure 4 *When using a psychrometer, you hold the handle and swing the wet- and dry-bulb thermometer in a circle.*

If the temperature stays the same, relative humidity changes as water vapor enters or leaves the air. The more water vapor that is in the air at a particular temperature, the higher the relative humidity is. Relative humidity is also affected by changes in temperature. If the amount of water vapor in the air stays the same, the relative humidity decreases as the temperature rises and increases as the temperature drops.

Measuring Relative Humidity A **psychrometer** is an instrument used to measure relative humidity. As you can see in **Figure 4,** a psychrometer consists of two thermometers. The bulb of one thermometer is covered with a damp cloth. This thermometer is called a wet-bulb thermometer. The other thermometer is a dry-bulb thermometer. The dry-bulb thermometer measures air temperature.

As air passes over the wet-bulb thermometer, the water in the cloth begins to evaporate. Evaporation requires heat energy. So as the water evaporates from the cloth, heat is withdrawn from the wet-bulb and the thermometer begins to cool. If there is less humidity in the air, the water will evaporate more quickly and the temperature of the wet-bulb thermometer will drop. If the humidity is high, only a small amount of water will evaporate from the wet-bulb thermometer and there will be little change in temperature. The difference in temperature readings between the wet-bulb and dry-bulb thermometers indicates the amount of water vapor in the air. A larger difference between the two readings indicates that there is less water vapor in the air and thus lower humidity.

Relative humidity can be determined using a table such as the one in **Figure 5.** The numbers across the top of the table represent the differences between the wet-bulb and dry-bulb temperatures in degrees Celsius. The numbers along the left side of the table indicate the dry-bulb temperature readings in degrees Celsius.

Relative Humidity (in percentage)										
Dry-bulb reading (°C)	Difference between wet-bulb reading and dry-bulb reading (°C)									
	1	2	3	4	5	6	7	8	9	10
0	81	64	46	29	13					
2	84	68	52	37	22	7				
4	85	71	57	43	29	16				
6	86	73	60	48	35	24	11			
8	87	75	63	51	40	29	19	8		
10	88	77	66	55	44	34	24	15	6	
12	89	78	68	58	48	39	29	21	12	
14	90	79	70	60	51	42	34	26	18	10
16	90	81	71	63	54	46	38	30	23	15
18	91	82	73	65	57	49	41	34	27	20
20	91	83	74	66	59	51	44	37	31	24
22	92	83	76	68	61	54	47	40	34	28
24	92	84	77	69	62	56	49	43	37	31
26	92	85	78	71	64	58	51	46	40	34
28	93	85	78	72	65	59	53	48	42	37
30	93	86	79	73	67	61	55	50	44	39

Figure 5 *Locate the column that shows the difference between the wet-bulb and dry-bulb readings. Then locate the row that lists the temperature reading on the dry-bulb thermometer. The value where the column and row intersect is the relative humidity.*

The Process of Condensation

You have probably seen water droplets form on the outside of a glass of ice water, as shown in **Figure 6.** Did you ever wonder where those water droplets came from? The water came from the surrounding air, and droplets formed because of condensation. **Condensation** is the process by which a gas, such as water vapor, becomes a liquid. Before condensation can occur, the air must be saturated; it must have a relative humidity of 100 percent. Condensation occurs when saturated air cools further.

Air can become saturated when water vapor is added to the air through evaporation or transpiration. Air can also become saturated, as in the case of the glass of ice water, when it cools to its dew point. The **dew point** is the temperature to which air must cool to be completely saturated. The ice in the glass of water causes the air surrounding the glass to cool to its dew point.

Before it can condense, water vapor must also have a surface to condense on. On the glass of ice water, water vapor condenses on the sides of the glass. Another example you may already be familiar with is water vapor condensing on grass, forming small water droplets called *dew,* as shown in **Figure 7.**

Figure 6 *Condensation occurred when the air next to the glass cooled to below its dew point.*

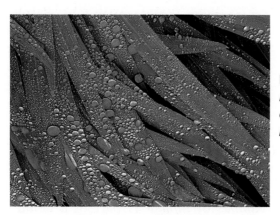

Figure 7 *Dew is most likely to form on cool, clear nights when there is little wind.*

REVIEW

1. What is the difference between humidity and relative humidity?

2. What are two ways that air can become saturated with water vapor?

3. What does a relative humidity of 75 percent mean?

4. How does the water cycle contribute to condensation?

5. **Analyzing Relationships** What happens to relative humidity as the air temperature drops below the dew point?

Quick **Lab**

Out of Thin Air

1. Take a **plastic container,** such as a jar or drinking glass, and fill it almost to the top with room-temperature **water.**

2. Observe the outside of the can or container. Record your observations.

3. Add one or two **ice cubes,** and watch the outside of the container for any changes.

4. What happened to the outside of the container?

5. What is the liquid?

6. Where did the liquid come from? Why?

Clouds

Some look like cotton balls, some look like locks of hair, and others look like blankets of gray blocking out the sun. But what *are* clouds and how do they form? And why are there so many different-looking clouds? A **cloud** is a collection of millions of tiny water droplets or ice crystals. Clouds form as warm air rises and cools. As the rising air cools, it becomes saturated. This is because cooler air cannot hold as much water vapor as warm air. At saturation—that is, 100 percent relative humidity—the water vapor changes to a liquid or a solid depending on the air temperature. In order for water vapor to change physical states, it needs a surface on which to change. These surfaces, called *condensation nuclei,* are small particles, such as dust, smoke, and salt, suspended in the air. At higher temperatures, water vapor condenses on small particles as tiny water droplets. At temperatures below freezing, water vapor changes directly to a solid, forming ice crystals.

Cumulus

Figure 8 *Cumulus clouds look like piles of cotton balls.*

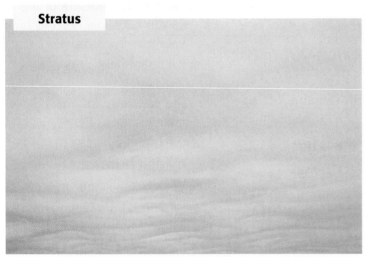

Stratus

Figure 9 *Although stratus clouds are not as tall as cumulus clouds, they cover more area.*

Kinds of Clouds Although there are many different-looking clouds, all clouds are classified according to three basic types—cumulus, stratus, and cirrus. **Cumulus** (KYOO myoo luhs) **clouds,** as shown in **Figure 8,** are puffy, white clouds that tend to have flat bottoms. Cumulus clouds form when warm air rises. These clouds generally indicate fair weather. However, when these clouds get larger they produce thunderstorms. A cumulus cloud that produces thunderstorms is called a *cumulonimbus cloud.* As a rule, when *-nimbus* or *nimbo-* is part of a cloud's name, it means that precipitation might fall from the cloud.

Stratus (STRAT uhs) **clouds,** as shown in **Figure 9,** are clouds that form in layers. Stratus clouds cover large areas of the sky, often blocking out the sun. These clouds are caused by a gentle lifting of a large body of air into the atmosphere. *Nimbostratus clouds* are dark stratus clouds that usually produce light to heavy, continuous rain. When water vapor condenses near the ground, it forms a stratus cloud called *fog.*

As you can see in **Figure 10, cirrus** (SIR uhs) **clouds** are thin, feathery, white clouds found at high altitudes. Cirrus clouds form when the wind is strong. Cirrus clouds may indicate approaching bad weather if they thicken and lower in altitude.

Clouds are also classified by the altitude at which they form. The illustration in **Figure 11** shows the three altitude groups used to categorize clouds.

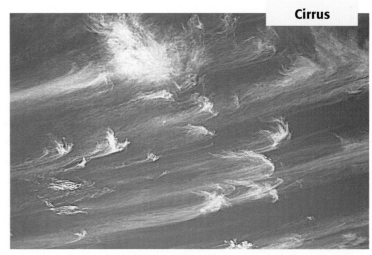

Cirrus

Figure 10 *Cirrus clouds are made of ice crystals because they form at high altitudes where the temperature is below freezing.*

Figure 11 Cloud Types Based on Form and Altitude

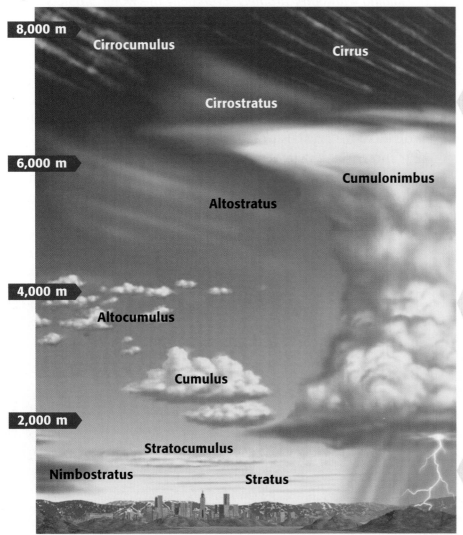

8,000 m

Cirrocumulus

Cirrus

Cirrostratus

6,000 m

Cumulonimbus

Altostratus

4,000 m

Altocumulus

Cumulus

2,000 m

Stratocumulus

Nimbostratus

Stratus

The prefix *cirro-* is used to describe high clouds that form above 6,000 m. Because of the cold temperatures at high altitude, high clouds are made up of ice crystals.

Middle clouds form between 2,000 m and 6,000 m. Middle clouds can be made up of both water droplets and ice crystals. The prefix *alto-* is used to describe clouds within this altitude range.

Low clouds form below 2,000 m. These clouds are made up of water droplets. The prefix *strato-* is commonly used to describe these types of clouds.

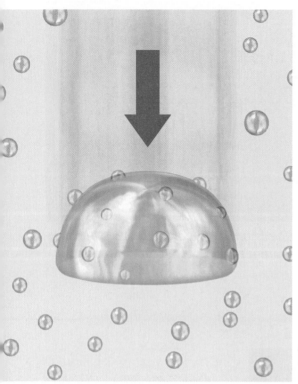

Precipitation

Water vapor that condenses to form clouds can eventually fall to the ground as precipitation. **Precipitation** is water, in solid or liquid form, that falls from the air to the Earth. There are four major forms of precipitation—rain, snow, sleet, and hail.

Rain, the most common form of precipitation, is liquid water that falls from the clouds to Earth. A cloud produces rain when its water droplets become large enough to fall. A cloud droplet begins as a water droplet smaller than the period at the end of this sentence. Before a cloud droplet falls as precipitation, it must increase in size to about 100 times its normal diameter. **Figure 12** illustrates how a water droplet increases in size until it is finally large enough to fall as precipitation.

Figure 12 *Cloud droplets get larger by colliding and joining with other droplets. Eventually the water droplets become too heavy to remain suspended in the cloud and fall as precipitation.*

Snow, Sleet, and Hail The most common form of solid precipitation is *snow.* Snow forms when temperatures are so cold that water vapor changes directly to a solid. Snow can fall as individual ice crystals or combine to form snowflakes, like the one shown in **Figure 13.**

Sleet, also called freezing rain, forms when rain falls through a layer of freezing air. The rain freezes, producing falling ice. Sometimes rain does not freeze until it hits a surface near the ground. When this happens, the rain changes into a layer of ice called *glaze,* as shown in **Figure 14.**

Figure 13 *Snowflakes are six-sided ice crystals that range in size from several millimeters to several centimeters.*

Figure 14 *Glaze ice forms as rain freezes on surfaces near the ground.*

Hail, as shown in **Figure 15,** is solid precipitation that falls as balls or lumps of ice. Hail usually forms in cumulonimbus clouds. Updrafts of air in the clouds carry raindrops to high altitudes in the cloud, where they freeze. As the frozen raindrops fall, they collide and combine with water droplets. Another updraft of air can send the hail up again high into the cloud. Here the water drops collected by the hail freeze, forming another layer of frozen ice. If the upward movement of air is strong enough, the hail can accumulate many layers of ice. Eventually, the hail becomes too heavy and falls to the Earth's surface. Hail is usually associated with warm weather and most often occurs during the spring and summer months.

Figure 15 *Hail is one of the most destructive forms of precipitation. The impact of large hailstones can damage property and crops.*

Measuring Precipitation A *rain gauge* is an instrument for measuring the amount of rainfall. Although there are many types of rain gauges, a rain gauge typically consists of a funnel and a cylinder, as shown in **Figure 16.** Rain falls into the funnel and collects in the cylinder. Markings on the cylinder indicate how much rain has fallen.

Snow is measured by both depth and water content. The depth of snow is measured using a measuring stick. The snow's water content is determined by melting the snow and measuring the amount of water. The amount of liquid water resulting from a snowmelt depends on the type of snow. Dry snow produces much less water than wet snow. For example, as much as 20 cm of dry snow is needed to produce 1 cm of liquid water. But only 6 cm of wet snow is needed to produce the same amount of water.

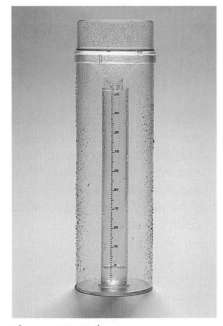

Figure 16 *Rain gauges measure only the precipitation that falls in a particular place.*

> ### REVIEW
>
> 1. How do clouds form?
>
> 2. Why are some clouds formed from water droplets, while others are made up of ice crystals?
>
> 3. Describe how rain forms.
>
> 4. **Applying Concepts** How can rain and hail fall from the same cumulonimbus cloud?

Air Masses and Fronts

Have you ever wondered how the weather can change so fast? One day the sun is shining and you are wearing shorts, and the next day it is so cold you need a coat. Changes in weather are caused by the movement and interaction of air masses. An **air mass** is a large body of air that has similar temperature and moisture throughout. In this section you will learn about air masses and how their interaction influences the weather.

Air Masses

An air mass gets its moisture and temperature characteristics from the area over which it forms. These areas are called *source regions*. For example, an air mass that develops over the Gulf of Mexico is warm and wet because this area is warm and has a lot of water that evaporates into the air. There are many types of air masses, each associated with a particular source region. And each of these masses can be identified by its moisture and temperature characteristics. The characteristics of these air masses are represented on maps with a two-letter symbol, as shown in **Figure 17.** The first letter indicates the moisture characteristics of the air mass, and the second symbol represents the temperature characteristics of the air mass.

NEW TERMS

air mass
front

OBJECTIVES

- Explain how air masses are characterized.
- Describe the four major types of air masses that influence weather in the United States.
- Describe the four major types of fronts.
- Relate fronts to weather changes.

Figure 17 *This map shows the source regions for air masses that influence weather in North America. Air masses keep their moisture and temperature characteristics as they move over the Earth's surface.*

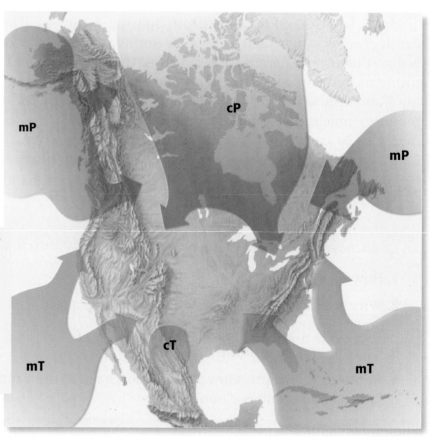

maritime (m)–forms over water; wet

continental (c)–forms over land; dry

polar (P)–forms over the polar regions; cold

tropical (T)–develops over the Tropics; warm

Cold Air Masses Most of the cold winter weather in the United States is influenced by three polar air masses. One of these air masses develops over land, while the other two form over oceans. The source regions for these air masses are Canada, the North Pacific Ocean, and the North Atlantic Ocean.

A continental polar air mass develops over land in northern Canada. In the winter, this air brings extremely cold weather to the United States, as shown in **Figure 18.** In the summer, it generally brings cool, dry weather.

A maritime polar air mass that forms over the North Pacific Ocean mostly affects the Pacific Coast. This air mass is very wet, but not as cold as the air mass that develops over Canada. In the winter, this air mass brings rain and snow to the Pacific Coast. In the summer, it brings cool, foggy weather.

A maritime polar air mass that forms over the North Atlantic Ocean usually affects New England and eastern Canada. In the winter, it produces cold, cloudy weather with precipitation. In the summer, the air mass brings cool weather with fog.

Figure 18 *A cP air mass generally moves southeastward across Canada and into the northern United States.*

Warm Air Masses Four warm air masses influence the weather in the United States. Three of these air masses develop over water, while only one forms over land. The source regions for these air masses are the Atlantic Ocean, the Pacific Ocean, the Gulf of Mexico, and the desert region of Mexico and the southwestern United States.

A maritime tropical air mass that develops over warm areas in the North Pacific Ocean is lower in moisture content and weaker than the maritime polar air mass. As a result, southern California receives less precipitation than the rest of California.

Other maritime tropical air masses develop over the warm waters of the Gulf of Mexico and the North Atlantic Ocean. These air masses move north across the East Coast and into the Midwest. In the summer, they bring hot and humid weather, thunderstorms, and hurricanes, as shown in **Figure 19.** In the winter, they bring mild, often cloudy weather.

Figure 19 *People in Houston, Texas, experience the many thunderstorms brought by mT air masses from the Gulf of Mexico.*

A continental tropical air mass forms over the deserts of northern Mexico and the southwestern United States. This air mass influences weather in the United States only during the summer. It generally moves northeastward, bringing clear, dry, and very hot weather.

Fronts

Air masses with different characteristics, such as temperature and humidity, do not usually mix. So when two different air masses meet, a boundary forms between them. This boundary is called a **front.** Weather at a front is usually cloudy and stormy. **Figure 20** illustrates the four different types of fronts—cold fronts, warm fronts, occluded fronts, and stationary fronts. Fronts are usually associated with weather in the middle latitudes, where there are both cold and warm air masses. Fronts do not occur in the Tropics because only warm air masses exist there.

A **cold front** forms when a cold air mass meets and displaces a warm air mass. Because the moving cold air is more dense, it moves under the less-dense warm air, pushing it up. Cold fronts can move fast, producing large cumulonimbus clouds with thunderstorms, heavy rain, or snow. Cooler weather usually follows a cold front because the warm air is pushed away from the Earth's surface.

A **warm front** forms when a warm air mass meets and overrides a cold air mass. The warm, less-dense air moves over the cold, denser air. The warm air gradually replaces the cold air. Warm fronts generally bring nimbostratus clouds and drizzly precipitation. After the front passes, weather conditions are clear and warm.

Figure 20   Different Types of Fronts

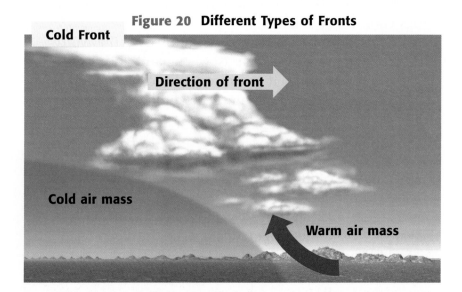

Cold Front
Direction of front
Cold air mass
Warm air mass

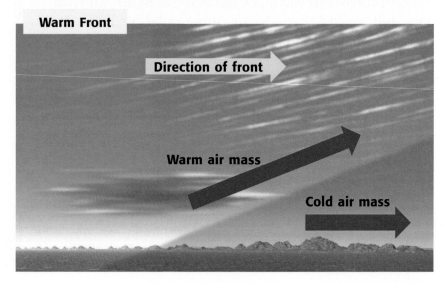

Warm Front
Direction of front
Warm air mass
Cold air mass

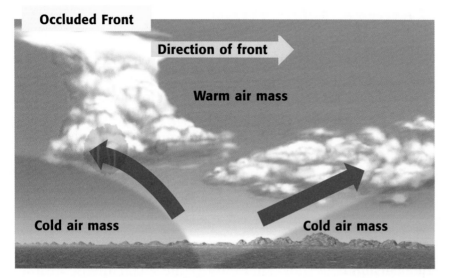

Occluded Front

Direction of front

Warm air mass

Cold air mass   **Cold air mass**

An **occluded front** forms when a faster-moving cold front overtakes a slower-moving warm front and forces the warm air up. The cold front then continues advancing until it meets a cold air mass that is warmer. The cold front then forces this air mass to rise. An occluded front has cool temperatures and large amounts of precipitation.

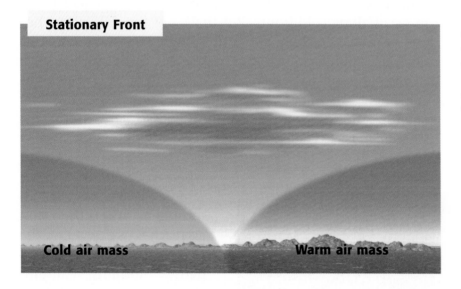

Stationary Front

Cold air mass   **Warm air mass**

A **stationary front** forms when a cold air mass meets a warm air mass and little horizontal movement occurs. The weather associated with a stationary front is similar to that produced by a warm front.

REVIEW

1. What are the characteristics that define air masses?

2. What are the major air masses that influence the weather in the United States?

3. What are fronts, and what causes them?

4. What kind of front forms when a cold air mass displaces a warm air mass?

5. **Analyzing Relationships** Explain why the Pacific Coast has cool, wet winters and warm, dry summers.

Severe Weather

Weather in the mid-latitudes can change from day to day. These changes result from the continual shifting of air masses. Sometimes a series of storms will develop along a front and bring severe weather. **Severe weather** is weather that can cause property damage and even death. Examples of severe weather include thunderstorms, tornadoes, and hurricanes. In this section you will learn about the different types of severe weather and how each type forms.

Thunderstorms

Thunderstorms, as shown in **Figure 21,** are small, intense weather systems that produce strong winds, heavy rain, lightning, and thunder. As you learned in the previous section, thunderstorms can occur along cold fronts. But that's not the only place they develop. There are only two atmospheric conditions required to produce thunderstorms: the air near the Earth's surface must be warm and moist, and the atmosphere must be unstable. The atmosphere is unstable when the surrounding air is colder than the rising air mass. As long as the air surrounding the rising air mass is colder, the air mass will continue to rise.

Thunderstorms occur when warm, moist air rises rapidly in an unstable atmosphere. When the warm air reaches its dew point, the water vapor in the air condenses, forming cumulus clouds. If the atmosphere is extremely unstable, the warm air will continue to rise, causing the cloud to grow into a dark, cumulonimbus cloud. These clouds can reach heights of more than 15 km.

NEW TERMS

severe weather
thunderstorms
lightning

thunder
tornado
hurricane

OBJECTIVES

- Explain what lightning is.
- Describe the formation of thunderstorms, tornadoes, and hurricanes.
- Describe the characteristics of thunderstorms, tornadoes, and hurricanes.

Figure 21 *A typical thunderstorm produces approximately 470 million liters of water and enough electricity to provide power to the entire United States for 20 minutes.*

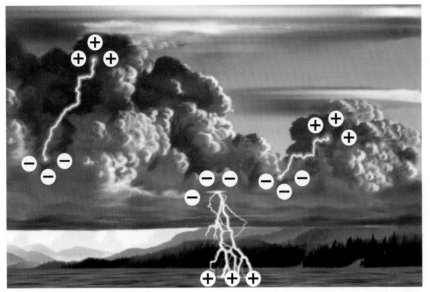

Figure 22 *The upper part of a cloud usually carries a positive electrical charge, while the lower part of the cloud carries mainly negative charges.*

How would you feel if your entire summer was crammed into 1 day every few years? Turn to page 451 to find out how one person felt.

Lightning Thunderstorms are very active electrically. **Lightning** is a large electrical discharge that occurs between two oppositely charged surfaces, as shown in **Figure 22.** Have you ever touched someone after scuffing your feet on the carpet and received a mild shock? If so, you have experienced how lightning forms. While walking around, friction between the floor and your shoes builds up an electrical charge in your body. When you touch someone else, the charge is released.

When lightning strikes, energy is released. This energy is transferred to the air and causes the air to expand rapidly and send out sound waves. **Thunder** is the sound that results from the rapid expansion of air along the lightning strike.

physical science
CONNECTION

Have you ever wondered why you don't see lightning and hear thunder at the same time? Well, there's an easy explanation. Light travels faster than sound. The light reaches you almost instantly, but the sound travels only 1 km every 3 seconds. The closer the lightning is to where you are, the sooner you will hear the thunder.

Severe Thunderstorms Only about 10 percent of thunderstorms are considered severe. Severe thunderstorms produce one or more of the following conditions—high winds, hail, flash floods, and tornadoes. Hailstorms damage crops, dent the metal on cars, and break windows. Sudden flash flooding due to heavy rains causes millions of dollars in property damage annually and is the biggest cause of weather-related deaths.

Lightning, which occurs with all thunderstorms, is responsible for thousands of forest fires each year in the United States. Lightning also kills or injures hundreds of people a year in the United States. **Figure 23** shows how easily lightning can strike an object at the Earth's surface.

Figure 23 *Lightning often strikes the highest object in an area.*

Tornadoes

Tornadoes are produced in only 1 percent of all thunderstorms. A **tornado** is a small, rotating column of air that has high wind speeds and low central pressure and that touches the ground. A tornado starts out as a funnel cloud that pokes through the bottom of a cumulonimbus cloud and hangs in the air. It is called a tornado when it makes contact with the Earth's surface. **Figure 24** shows the development of a tornado.

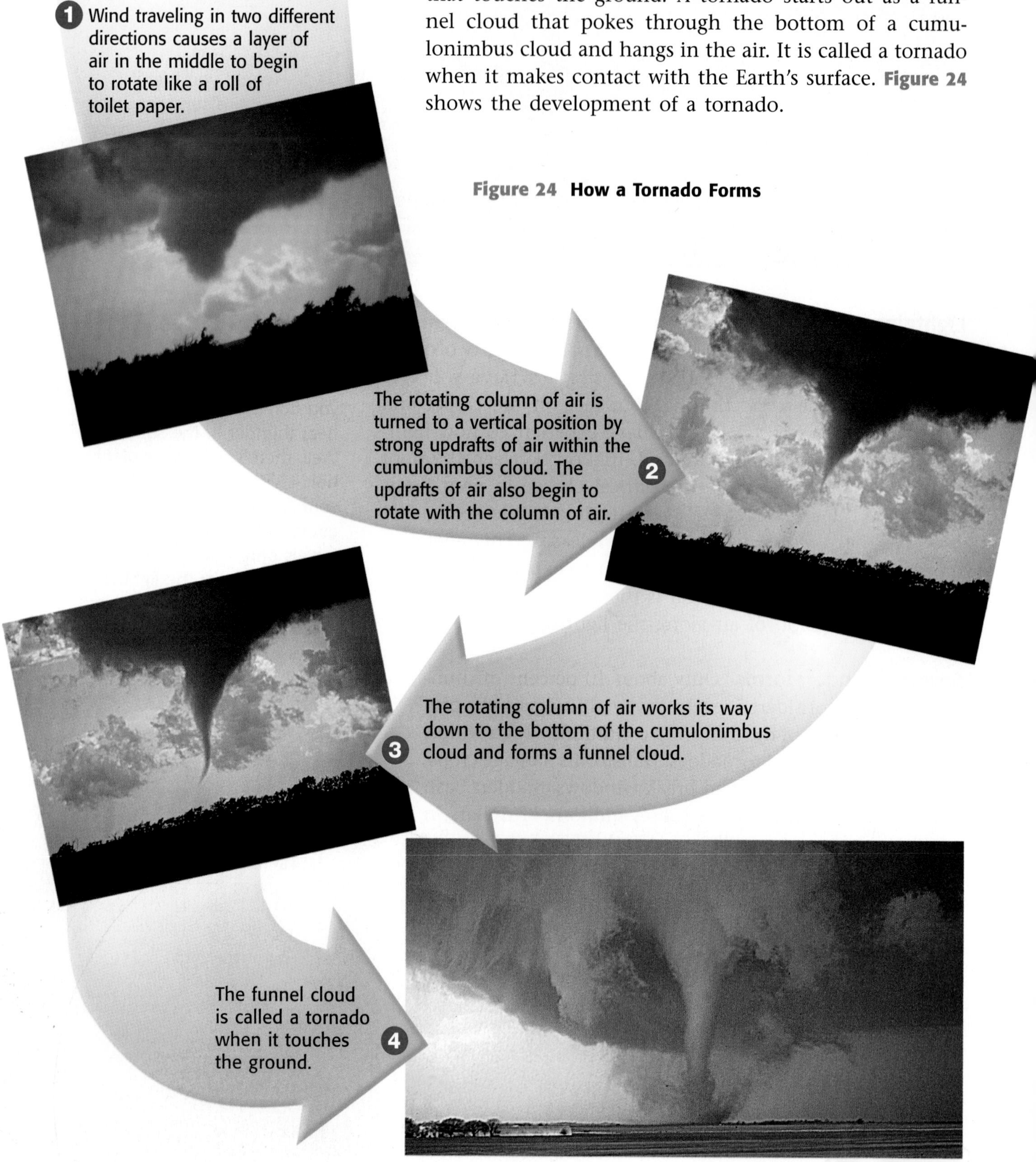

Figure 24 How a Tornado Forms

1. Wind traveling in two different directions causes a layer of air in the middle to begin to rotate like a roll of toilet paper.

2. The rotating column of air is turned to a vertical position by strong updrafts of air within the cumulonimbus cloud. The updrafts of air also begin to rotate with the column of air.

3. The rotating column of air works its way down to the bottom of the cumulonimbus cloud and forms a funnel cloud.

4. The funnel cloud is called a tornado when it touches the ground.

About 75 percent of the world's tornadoes occur in the United States. The majority of these tornadoes happen in the spring and early summer when cold, dry air from Canada collides with warm, moist air from the Tropics. The length of a tornado's path of destruction can vary, but it is usually about 8 km long and 10–60 m wide. Although most tornadoes last only a few minutes, they can cause a lot of damage. This is due to their strong spinning winds. The average tornado has wind speeds of between 120 and 180 km/h, but rarer, more violent tornadoes can have spinning winds of up to 500 km/h. The winds of tornadoes have been known to uproot trees and destroy buildings, as shown in **Figure 25.** Tornadoes are capable of picking up heavy objects, such as houses, cars, and store signs, and hurling them through the air.

Hurricanes

A **hurricane,** as shown in **Figure 26,** is a large, rotating tropical weather system with wind speeds of at least 119 km/h. Hurricanes are the most powerful storms on Earth. Hurricanes have different names in other parts of the world. In the western Pacific Ocean, they are called *typhoons.* Hurricanes that form over the Indian Ocean are called *cyclones.*

Hurricanes generally form in the area between 5° and 20° north and south latitude over warm, tropical oceans. At higher latitudes, the water is too cold for hurricanes to form. Hurricanes vary in size from 160 km to 1,500 km in diameter, and they can travel for thousands of miles.

Figure 25 *The tornado that hit Kissimmee, Florida, in 1998 had wind speeds of up to 416 km/h.*

Did you know that fish have been known to fall from the sky? Some scientists think the phenomenon of raining fish is caused by waterspouts. A waterspout is a tornado that occurs over water. When the funnel comes into contact with the surface of the water, it causes the water to spray several meters upward.

Figure 26 Hurricane Fran Photographed from Space

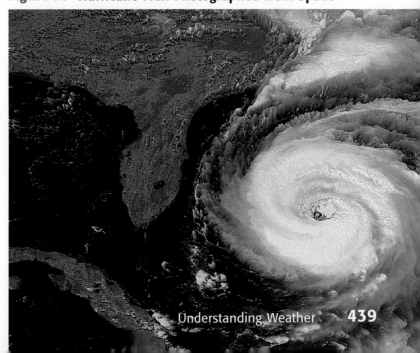

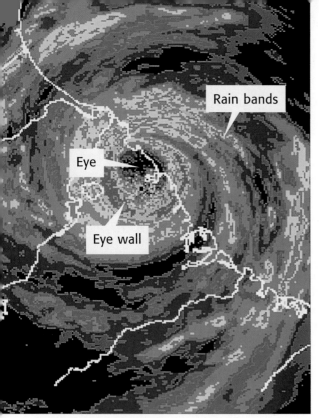

Rain bands

Eye

Eye wall

Figure 27 *The photo above gives you a bird's-eye view of a hurricane.*

Formation of a Hurricane A hurricane begins as a group of thunderstorms moving over tropical ocean waters. Winds traveling in two different directions collide, causing the storm to rotate over an area of low pressure. Because of the Coriolis effect, the storm turns counterclockwise in the Northern Hemisphere and clockwise in the Southern Hemisphere.

Hurricanes get their energy from the condensation of water vapor. Once formed, the hurricane is fueled through contact with the warm ocean water. Moisture is added to the warm air by evaporation from the ocean. As the warm, moist air rises, the water vapor condenses, releasing large amounts of heat energy. The hurricane continues to grow as long as it is over its source of warm, moist air. When the hurricane moves into colder waters or over land, it begins to die because it has lost its source of energy. **Figure 27** and **Figure 28** show two views of a hurricane.

Figure 28 *The view below shows how a hurricane would look if you cut it in half and looked at it from the side. The arrows indicate the flow of air.*

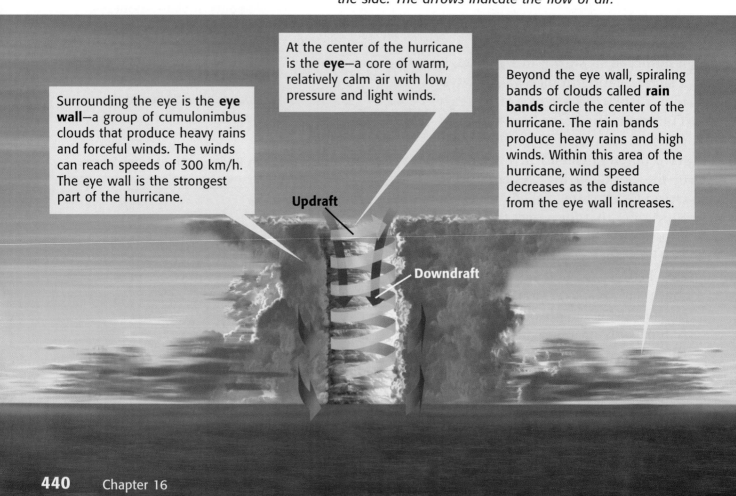

At the center of the hurricane is the **eye**—a core of warm, relatively calm air with low pressure and light winds.

Beyond the eye wall, spiraling bands of clouds called **rain bands** circle the center of the hurricane. The rain bands produce heavy rains and high winds. Within this area of the hurricane, wind speed decreases as the distance from the eye wall increases.

Surrounding the eye is the **eye wall**—a group of cumulonimbus clouds that produce heavy rains and forceful winds. The winds can reach speeds of 300 km/h. The eye wall is the strongest part of the hurricane.

Updraft

Downdraft

Damage Caused by Hurricanes Hurricanes can cause a lot of damage when they move near or onto land. The speed of the steady winds of most hurricanes ranges from 120 km/h to 150 km/h, and they can reach speeds as high as 300 km/h. Hurricane winds can knock down trees and telephone poles and can damage and destroy buildings and homes.

While high winds cause a great deal of damage, most hurricane damage is caused by flooding associated with heavy rains and storm surges. A *storm surge* is a wall of water that builds up over the ocean due to the heavy winds and low atmospheric pressure. The wall of water gets bigger and bigger as it nears the shore, reaching its greatest height when it crashes onto the shore. Depending on the strength of the hurricane, a storm surge can be 1 m to 8 m high. A storm surge can affect a 65 km–160 km stretch of coastline. Flooding causes tremendous damage to property and lives when a storm surge moves onto shore. Flooding can be increased by the heavy rains that usually accompany hurricanes, as shown in **Figure 29.**

astronomy CONNECTION

The weather on Jupiter is more exciting than that on Earth. Wind speeds reach up to 540 km/h. Storms last for decades, and one—the Great Red Spot of Jupiter—has been swirling around since it was first discovered, in 1664. The Great Red Spot has a diameter of more than one and a half times that of the Earth. It is like a hurricane that has lasted more than 300 years.

Figure 29 *In 1998, the flooding associated with Hurricane Mitch devastated Central America. Whole villages were swept away by the flood waters and mudslides. Total rainfall for the storm was reported to be as high as 190 cm in some areas. Thousands of people were killed, and damages were estimated to be more than $5 billion.*

REVIEW

1. What is lightning?

2. Describe how tornadoes develop. What is the difference between a funnel cloud and a tornado?

3. Why do hurricanes form only over certain areas?

4. **Inferring Relationships** What happens to a hurricane as it moves over land? Why?

Forecasting the Weather

Have you ever left your house in the morning wearing a short-sleeved shirt, only to need a sweater in the afternoon? At some time in your life, you have been caught off guard by the weather. Weather affects how you dress and your daily plans, so it is important that you get accurate weather forecasts. A **weather forecast** is a prediction of weather conditions over the next 3 to 5 days. Meteorologists observe and collect data on current weather conditions in order to provide reliable predictions. In this section you will learn about some of the methods used to collect weather data and how those data are displayed.

Weather Forecasting Technology

In order for meteorologists to accurately forecast the weather, they need to measure various atmospheric conditions, such as air pressure, humidity, precipitation, temperature, wind speed, and wind direction. Meteorologists use special instruments to collect data on weather conditions both near and far above the Earth's surface. You have already learned about two tools that meteorologists use near the Earth's surface—psychrometers, which are used to measure relative humidity, and rain gauges, which are used to measure precipitation. Read on to learn about other methods meteorologists use to collect data.

Measuring Air Temperature A **thermometer** is a tool used to measure air temperature. A common type of thermometer uses a liquid sealed in a narrow glass tube, as shown in **Figure 30.** When air temperature increases, the liquid expands and moves up the glass tube. As air temperature decreases, the liquid shrinks and moves down the tube.

Air temperature is measured in both degrees Celsius and degrees Fahrenheit. In the United States, television weather forecasters generally report air temperature in degrees Fahrenheit.

NEW TERMS

weather forecast   wind vane
thermometer   anemometer
barometer   station model
windsock   isobars

OBJECTIVES

- Describe the different types of instruments used to take weather measurements.
- Explain how to interpret a weather map.
- Explain why weather maps are useful.

Figure 30 *A liquid thermometer is usually filled with alcohol that is colored red, or mercury, which is silver.*

Measuring Air Pressure A **barometer** is an instrument used to measure air pressure. The mercurial barometer, as shown in **Figure 31,** provides the most accurate method of measuring air pressure. A mercurial barometer consists of a glass tube sealed at one end that is placed in a container full of mercury. The air pressure pushes on the mercury inside the container, causing the mercury to move up the glass tube. The greater the air pressure is, the higher the mercury will rise.

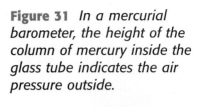

Figure 31 *In a mercurial barometer, the height of the column of mercury inside the glass tube indicates the air pressure outside.*

Measuring Wind Direction and Wind Speed Wind direction can be measured using a **windsock** or a **wind vane.** A windsock, as shown in **Figure 32,** is a cone-shaped cloth bag open at both ends. The wind enters through the wide end and leaves through the narrow end. Therefore, the wide end points into the wind.

A wind vane is shaped like an arrow with a large tail and is attached to a pole. The wind pushes the tail of the wind vane, spinning it on the pole until the arrow points into the wind.

Figure 32 *You can make a windsock by stretching a piece of weatherproof material over a series of increasingly large rings to form a cone shape.*

Wind speed is measured by a device called an **anemometer.** An anemometer, as shown in **Figure 33,** consists of three or four cups connected by spokes to a pole. The wind pushes on the hollow sides of the cups, causing them to rotate on the pole. The motion sends a weak electrical current that is measured and displayed on a dial.

Measuring Weather in the Upper Atmosphere You have learned how weather conditions are recorded near the Earth's surface. But in order for meteorologists to better understand weather patterns, they must collect data from higher altitudes. Studying weather at higher altitudes requires the use of more-sophisticated equipment.

Figure 33 *The faster the wind speed is, the faster the cups of the anemometer spin.*

Figure 34 *Radiosondes have radio transmitters that send measurements to stations on the ground.*

Weather balloons carry electronic equipment called *radiosondes* to measure weather conditions as high as 30 km above the Earth's surface. Radiosondes, as shown in **Figure 34,** measure temperature, air pressure, and relative humidity.

Radar is used to find the location, movement, and intensity of precipitation. Radar can also detect what form of precipitation a weather system is carrying. Radar is often used for monitoring severe weather systems, such as hurricanes. You might be familiar with a type of radar called Doppler radar. Many television weather reports use Doppler radar to show the direction, velocity, and intensity of precipitation, as shown in **Figure 35.**

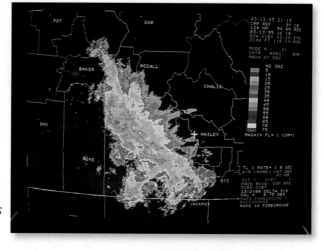

Figure 35 *Doppler radar is used to detect funnel clouds and tornadoes. Using Doppler radar, meteorologists can predict a tornado up to 20 minutes before it touches the ground.*

Weather satellites orbiting the Earth provide weather information that cannot be obtained from the ground. These satellites take images of the swirling clouds you see on television weather reports. Satellites can not only measure wind speeds and humidity but also determine temperatures at various altitudes, from the tops of clouds down to ground level and ocean surfaces.

Weather Maps

As you have learned, meteorologists base their forecasts on information gathered from many sources. In the United States, the National Weather Service (NWS) and the National Oceanic and Atmospheric Administration (NOAA) collect and analyze weather data. The NWS produces weather maps based on information gathered from about 1,000 weather stations across the United States. On these maps, each station is represented by a station model. A **station model,** as shown in **Figure 36,** is a small circle, which shows the location of the weather station, with a set of symbols and numbers surrounding it, which represent the weather data.

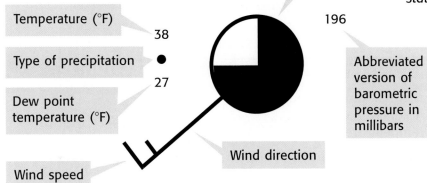

Amount of cloud cover

Temperature (°F) 38

Type of precipitation ●

Dew point temperature (°F) 27

Wind speed

Wind direction

196

Abbreviated version of barometric pressure in millibars

Figure 36 *Weather conditions at a station are represented by symbols.*

Weather maps also include lines called isobars. Isobars are similar to contour lines on a topographical map, except **isobars** are lines that connect points of equal air pressure rather than equal elevation. Isobar lines that form closed circles represent areas of high or low pressure. These areas are usually marked on a map with a capital *H* or *L*. Fronts are also labeled on weather maps. Weather maps, like the one shown in **Figure 37,** provide useful information for making accurate weather forecasts.

Figure 37 *Can you identify the different fronts on the weather map?*

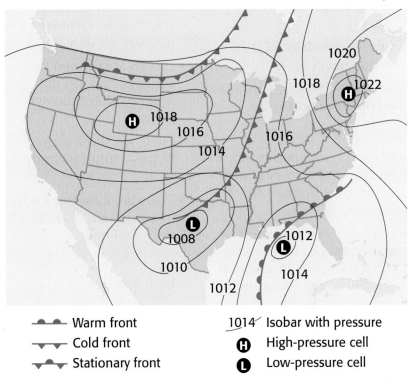

🔺🔺 Warm front
🔻 Cold front
🔻🔺 Stationary front

1014 Isobar with pressure
Ⓗ High-pressure cell
Ⓛ Low-pressure cell

REVIEW

1. What are three methods meteorologists use to collect weather data?

2. What are weather maps based on?

3. What does a station model represent?

4. **Inferring Conclusions** Why would a meteorologist compare a new weather map with one 24 hours old?

To learn more about station models and their symbols, turn to page 552 in the LabBook.

Chapter Highlights

SECTION 1

Vocabulary

weather *(p. 424)*

water cycle *(p. 424)*

humidity *(p. 425)*

relative humidity *(p. 425)*

psychrometer *(p. 426)*

condensation *(p. 427)*

dew point *(p. 427)*

cloud *(p. 428)*

cumulus clouds *(p. 428)*

stratus clouds *(p. 428)*

cirrus clouds *(p. 429)*

precipitation *(p. 430)*

Section Notes

- Water is continuously moving and changing state as it moves through the water cycle.

- Humidity is the amount of water vapor or moisture in the air. Relative humidity is the amount of moisture the air contains compared with the maximum amount it can hold at a particular temperature.

- Water droplets form because of condensation.

- Dew point is the temperature at which air is saturated.

- Condensation occurs when the air next to a surface cools to below its dew point.

- Clouds are formed from condensation on dust and other particles above the ground.

- There are three major cloud forms—cumulus, stratus, and cirrus.

- There are four major forms of precipitation—rain, snow, sleet, and hail.

Labs

Let It Snow! *(p. 555)*

SECTION 2

Vocabulary

air mass *(p. 432)*

front *(p. 434)*

Section Notes

- Air masses form over source regions. An air mass has similar temperature and moisture content throughout.

- Four major types of air masses influence weather in the United States—maritime polar, maritime tropical, continental polar, continental tropical.

- A front is a boundary between contrasting air masses.

- There are four types of fronts—cold fronts, warm fronts, occluded fronts, and stationary fronts.

- Specific types of weather are associated with each front.

☑ Skills Check

Math Concepts

RELATIVE HUMIDITY Relative humidity is the amount of moisture the air is holding compared with the amount it can hold at a particular temperature. The relative humidity of air that is holding all the water it can at a given temperature is 100 percent, meaning it is saturated. You can calculate relative humidity with the following equation:

$$\frac{\text{(present) g/m}^3}{\text{(saturated) g/m}^3} \times 100 = \text{relative humidity}$$

Visual Understanding

HURRICANE HORSE-POWER Hurricanes are the most powerful storms on Earth. A cross-sectional view helps you identify the different parts of a hurricane. The diagram on page 440 shows a side view of a hurricane.

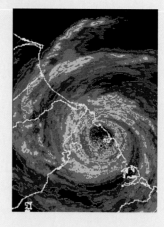

Vocabulary

severe weather *(p. 436)*

thunderstorms *(p. 436)*

lightning *(p. 437)*

thunder *(p. 437)*

tornado *(p. 438)*

hurricane *(p. 439)*

Section Notes

- Severe weather is weather that can cause property damage and even death.

- Thunderstorms are small, intense storm systems that produce lightning, thunder, strong winds, and heavy rain.

- Lightning is a large electrical discharge that occurs between two oppositely charged surfaces.

- Thunder is the sound that results from the expansion of air along a lightning strike.

- A tornado is a rotating funnel cloud that touches the ground.

- Hurricanes are large, rotating, tropical weather systems that form over the tropical oceans.

Vocabulary

weather forecast *(p. 442)*

thermometer *(p. 442)*

barometer *(p. 443)*

windsock *(p. 443)*

wind vane *(p. 443)*

anemometer *(p. 443)*

station model *(p. 444)*

isobars *(p. 445)*

Section Notes

- Radiosondes, radar, and weather satellites take weather measurements at high altitudes.

- Meteorologists present weather data gathered from stations as station models on weather maps.

Labs

Watching the Weather *(p. 552)*

Gone with the Wind *(p. 556)*

---

 internet connect

 GO TO: go.hrw.com

GO TO: www.scilinks.org

Visit the **HRW** Web site for a variety of learning tools related to this chapter. Just type in the keyword:

KEYWORD: HSTWEA

Visit the **National Science Teachers Association** on-line Web site for Internet resources related to this chapter. Just type in the *sci*LINKS number for more information about the topic:

TOPIC: Collecting Weather Data	*sci*LINKS NUMBER: HSTE380
TOPIC: Air Masses and Fronts	*sci*LINKS NUMBER: HSTE385
TOPIC: Severe Weather	*sci*LINKS NUMBER: HSTE390
TOPIC: Forecasting the Weather	*sci*LINKS NUMBER: HSTE395

Chapter Review

USING VOCABULARY

Explain the difference between the following sets of words:

1. relative humidity/dew point

2. cumulus clouds/stratus clouds

3. air mass/front

4. lightning/thunder

5. tornado/hurricane

6. barometer/anemometer

UNDERSTANDING CONCEPTS

Multiple Choice

7. The process of liquid water changing to gas is called
   a. precipitation.
   b. condensation.
   c. evaporation.
   d. water vapor.

8. What is the relative humidity of air at its dew-point temperature?
   a. 0%
   b. 50%
   c. 75%
   d. 100%

9. Which of the following is not a type of condensation?
   a. fog
   b. cloud
   c. snow
   d. dew

10. High clouds made of ice crystals are called __?__ clouds.
    a. stratus
    b. cumulus
    c. nimbostratus
    d. cirrus

11. Large thunderhead clouds that produce precipitation are called __?__ clouds.
    a. nimbostratus
    b. cumulonimbus
    c. cumulus
    d. stratus

12. Strong updrafts within a thunderhead can produce
    a. snow.
    b. rain.
    c. sleet.
    d. hail.

13. A maritime tropical air mass contains
    a. warm, wet air.
    b. cold, moist air.
    c. warm, dry air.
    d. cold, dry air.

14. A front that forms when a warm air mass is trapped between cold air masses and forced high up into the atmosphere is called a(n)
    a. stationary front.
    b. warm front.
    c. occluded front.
    d. cold front.

15. A severe storm that forms as a rapidly rotating funnel cloud is called a
    a. hurricane.
    b. tornado.
    c. typhoon.
    d. thunderstorm.

16. The lines on a weather map connecting points of equal atmospheric pressure are called
    a. contour lines.
    b. highs.
    c. isobars.
    d. lows.

Short Answer

17. Explain the relationship between condensation and the dew point.

18. Describe the conditions along a stationary front.

19. What are the characteristics of an air mass that forms over the Gulf of Mexico?

20. Explain how a hurricane develops.

Concept Mapping

21. Use the following terms to create a concept map: evaporation, relative humidity, water vapor, dew, psychrometer, clouds, fog.

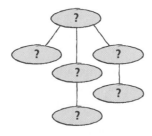

Write one or two sentences to answer the following questions:

22. If both the air temperature and the amount of water vapor in the air change, is it possible for the relative humidity to stay the same? Explain.

23. What can you assume about the amount of water vapor in the air if there is no difference between the wet- and dry-bulb readings of a psychrometer?

24. List the major similarities and differences between hurricanes and tornadoes.

MATH IN SCIENCE

You always see lightning before you hear thunder. That's because light travels at about 300,000,000 m/s, while sound travels only 330 m/s. One way you can determine how close you are to the thunderstorm is by counting how many seconds there are between the lightning and thunder. Usually, it takes thunder about 3 seconds to cover 1 km. Answer the following questions based on this estimate.

25. If you hear thunder 12 seconds after you see the flash of lightning, how far away is the thunderstorm?

26. If you hear thunder 36 seconds after you see the flash of lightning, how far away is the thunderstorm?

INTERPRETING GRAPHICS

Use the weather map below to answer the questions that follow.

⚬⚬⚬ Warm front

▽▽▽ Cold front

▽⚬▽ Stationary front

27. Where are thunderstorms most likely to occur? Explain your answer.

28. What are the weather conditions like in Tulsa, Oklahoma? Explain your answer.

NOW What Do You Think?

Take a minute to review your answers to the ScienceLog questions on page 423. Have your answers changed? If necessary, revise your answers based on what you have learned since you began this chapter.

CAREERS

METEOROLOGIST

Predicting floods, observing a tornado develop inside a storm, watching the growth of a hurricane, and issuing flood warnings are all in a day's work for **Cristy Mitchell.** As a meteorologist for the National Weather Service, Mitchell spends each working day observing the powerful forces of nature.

In addition to using computers, Mitchell also uses radar and satellite imagery to show regional and national weather. Meteorologists also use computerized models of the world's atmosphere to help forecast the weather.

Find Out for Yourself

▶ Use the library or the Internet to find information about hurricanes, tornadoes, or thunderstorms. How do meteorologists define these storms? What trends in air pressure, temperature, and humidity do meteorologists use to forecast storms?

When asked what made her job interesting, Mitchell replied, "There's nothing like the adrenaline rush you get when you see a tornado coming! I would say that witnessing the powerful forces of nature is what really makes my job interesting."

Meteorology is the study of natural forces in Earth's atmosphere. Perhaps the most familiar field of meteorology is weather forecasting. However, meteorology is also used in air-pollution control, agricultural planning, and air and sea transportation, and criminal and civil investigations. Meteorologists also study trends in Earth's climate, such as global warming and ozone depletion.

Collecting the Data

Meteorologists collect data on air pressure, temperature, humidity, and wind velocity. By applying what they know about the physical properties of the atmosphere and analyzing the mathematical relationships in the data, they are able to forecast the weather.

Meteorologists use a variety of tools, such as computers and satellites, to collect the data they need to make accurate weather forecasts. Mitchell explained, "The computer is an invaluable tool for me. Through it, I receive maps and detailed information, including temperature, wind speed, air pressure, lightning activity, and general sky conditions for a specific region."

▲ *This photograph of Hurricane Elena was taken from the space shuttle* Discovery *in September 1985.*

Science Fiction

"All Summer in a Day"

by Ray Bradbury

It is raining, just like it has been for 7 long years. That is 2,555 days of nonstop rain. For the men, women, and children who came to build a civilization on Venus, constant rain is a fact of life. But there is one special day—a day when it stops raining and the sun shines gloriously. This day comes about only once every 7 years. And today is that day!

At school the students have been looking forward to this day for weeks. In one class they've read about how the sun is like a lemon, and how hot it is. They've written stories and poems about what it might be like to see the sun.

And now that the day has finally arrived, all of the children in that class are peering through the window, searching for the sun. The children are 9 years old, and all of them but Margot have lived on Venus all their lives. None of them remember the day 7 years ago when the rain stopped. They only recall stories about the sunshine, and now they just can't wait to see it for themselves!

But Margot is different. She longs to see the sun even more than the others. The reason makes the other kids jealous. And jealous kids can be cruel. . . .

What happens to Margot? Find out for yourself by reading Ray Bradbury's "All Summer in a Day" in the *Holt Anthology of Science Fiction.*

17 Climate

What If . . . ?

The brochure boasts of the most adventurous summer camp in the world. You can't wait to lace up your hiking boots and head for the outdoors. But before you fly halfway around the world, you check the recommended supply list: light summer clothes, sunscreen, rain gear, heavy down-filled jacket, ski mask, and thick gloves. Wait a minute! You are traveling to only one destination, so why are you required to bring such a wide variety of clothes? On further investigation, you learn that your outdoor adventure advertises the opportunity to "climb the climates of the world in just three days."

Your destination is Africa's tallest mountain, Kilimanjaro, which is 5,895 m above sea level. But you can leave your heavy climbing gear at home because the summit is a slightly inclined slope that can be reached without the aid of special equipment.

The trek starts at 2,700 m above sea level, where you spend the first day hiking through a hot, sweltering rain forest. Day two finds you treading through a grassy meadow that slopes up the side of the first peak, called Mawensii. On the third day, you start to get cold. The frozen ground crunches under your feet. Within 2 hours your feet feel like blocks of ice, and breathing is difficult. You finally reach the summit just as the clouds part, revealing steam rising off the rain forest 3,000 m below. Maybe the trip was worth the effort after all!

Climate changes as elevation increases, just as it changes from the equator to the poles. In this chapter you will learn what factors affect climate, how climate is influenced by human and natural activity, and what type of environment is found in which climate.

Investigate!

What's Your Angle?

Because the Earth is round, the sun's solar rays strike the Earth's surface at different angles. Therefore, different amounts of solar energy reach the Earth's surface at different places. The area around the equator receives the direct rays of the sun. The energy is more concentrated because it is spread over a smaller area. This results in high temperatures. At the poles, the sun's rays strike the surface at a lower angle. The energy is therefore less concentrated, resulting in low temperatures. Try this simple experiment to find out how the amount of solar energy received at the equator differs from the amount received at the poles.

Procedure

1. Plug in a **lamp**, and position it 30 cm from a **globe**.

2. Point the lamp so that the light shines directly on the globe's equator, as shown in the diagram.

3. Using **adhesive putty**, attach one **thermometer** to the globe's equator and another **thermometer** to the globe's north pole.

4. Record the temperature reading of each thermometer in your ScienceLog.

5. Turn on the lamp, and let the light shine on the globe for 3 minutes.

6. When the time is up, turn off the lamp, and record the temperature reading of each thermometer again in your ScienceLog.

Analysis

7. Was there a difference between the starting temperatures and the final temperatures? Explain your results.

8. Was there a difference between the final temperature at the globe's north pole and that at the globe's equator? If so, what was it?

9. How does this experiment relate to solar radiation striking the Earth?

10. Based on the experiment, what temperature changes would you expect if you traveled from the equator to the polar regions?

What Is Climate?

NEW TERMS

weather   prevailing winds
climate   elevation
latitude   surface currents

OBJECTIVES

- Explain the difference between weather and climate.
- Identify the factors that determine climates.

You have just received a call from a friend who is coming to visit you tomorrow. He is wondering what clothing to bring and wants to know about the current weather in your area. You step outside, check to see if there are rain clouds in the sky, and note the temperature. But what if your friend asked you about the climate in your area? What is the difference between weather and climate?

The best way to distinguish between weather and climate is to think in terms of time. **Weather** is the condition of the atmosphere at a particular time and place. A typical weather report might read, "Today will be hot and humid, with a 20 percent chance of rain." Weather conditions vary from day to day. **Climate,** on the other hand, is the average weather conditions in a certain area over a long period of time. Climate is determined by two main factors, temperature and precipitation. Study the map in **Figure 1,** and see if you can describe the climate in northern Africa.

Figure 1 *How does the climate in northern Africa differ from the climate where you live?*

As you can see in **Figure 2,** if you were to take a trip around the world, or even across the United States, you would experience different climates. For example, if you visited the Texas coast in the summer, you would find it hot and humid. But if you visited interior Alaska during the summer, it would probably be much cooler and less humid. Why are the climates so different? The answer is complicated. It includes factors such as latitude, wind patterns, geography, and ocean currents.

Figure 2 *Summer in Texas is very different from summer in Alaska.*

Latitude

Think of the last time you looked at a globe. Do you recall the thin horizontal lines that circle the globe? These horizontal lines are called lines of latitude. **Latitude** is the distance north or south, measured in degrees, from the equator. In general, the temperature of an area depends on its latitude. The higher the latitude is, the colder the climate is. For example, the two coldest places on Earth, the North Pole and the South Pole, are at 90° north and south of the equator, respectively. On the other hand, the equator, which has a latitude of 0°, is hot.

Why are there such temperature differences at different latitudes? The answer has to do with solar energy. Solar energy heats the Earth. Latitude determines the amount of solar energy a particular area receives. You can see how this works in **Figure 3.** Notice that the sun's rays hit the area around the equator directly, at nearly a 90° angle. At this angle, a small area of the Earth's surface receives more direct solar energy, resulting in high temperatures. Near the poles, however, the sun's rays strike the surface at a lesser angle than at the equator. This lesser angle spreads the same amount of solar energy over a larger area, resulting in lower temperatures.

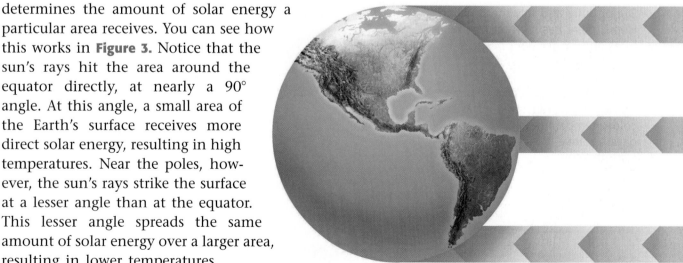

Figure 3 *The sun's rays strike the Earth's surface at different angles because the surface is curved.*

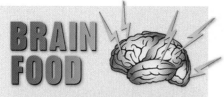
Seasons and Latitude In most places in the United States, the year consists of four seasons. Winter is probably cooler than summer where you live. But there are places in the world that do not have such seasonal changes. For example, areas near the equator have approximately the same temperatures and same amount of daylight year-round. **Figure 4** shows how latitude determines the seasons.

Figure 4 *The Earth is tilted on its axis at a 23.5° angle. This tilt affects how much solar energy an area receives as the Earth moves around the sun.*

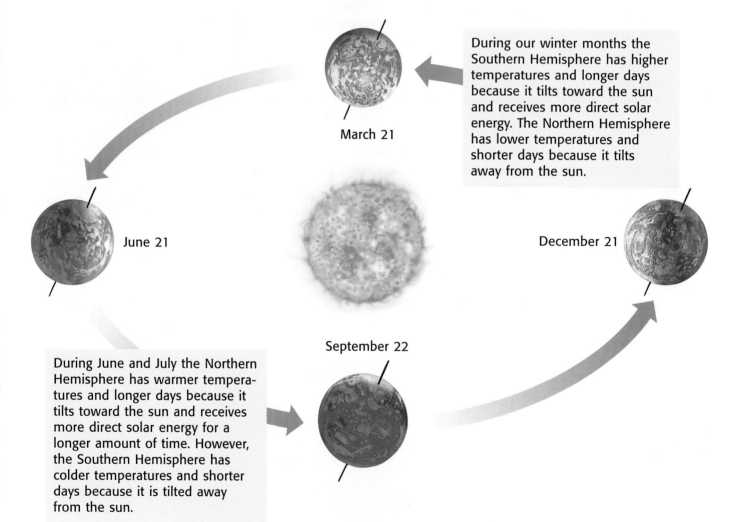

March 21

During our winter months the Southern Hemisphere has higher temperatures and longer days because it tilts toward the sun and receives more direct solar energy. The Northern Hemisphere has lower temperatures and shorter days because it tilts away from the sun.

June 21

December 21

September 22

During June and July the Northern Hemisphere has warmer temperatures and longer days because it tilts toward the sun and receives more direct solar energy for a longer amount of time. However, the Southern Hemisphere has colder temperatures and shorter days because it is tilted away from the sun.

Self-Check

During what months does Australia have summer? *(See page 564 to check your answer.)*

Prevailing Winds

Prevailing winds are winds that blow mainly from one direction. These winds influence an area's moisture and temperature. Before you learn how the prevailing winds affect climate, take a look at **Figure 5** to learn about some of the basic properties of air.

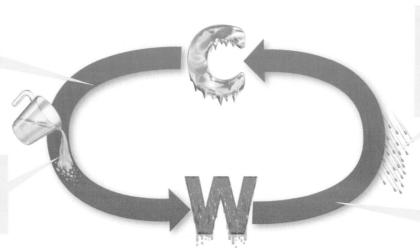

Figure 5 *Because warm air is less dense, it tends to rise. Cooler, denser air tends to sink.*

Cold air sinks, and as it sinks it warms.

When cold air is heated, it gains the ability to hold water vapor.

When warm air cools, it loses the ability to hold water vapor. This results in *precipitation*.

Warm air rises, and as it rises it cools.

Prevailing winds affect the amount of precipitation that a region receives. If the prevailing winds form from warm air, they will carry moisture. If the prevailing winds form from cold air, they will probably be dry. Precipitation is more likely to occur when the prevailing winds are warm and moist.

The amount of moisture in prevailing winds is also affected by whether the winds blow across land or across a large body of water. Winds that travel across large bodies of water, such as the ocean, absorb moisture. Winds that travel across land tend to be dry. Even if a region borders the ocean, the area might be dry if the prevailing winds blow across the land, as shown in **Figure 6**.

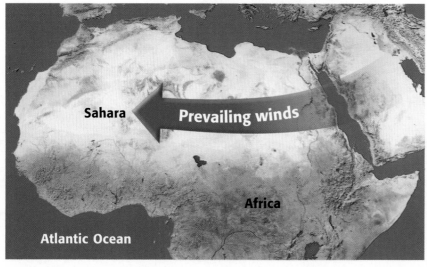

Sahara — Prevailing winds

Africa

Atlantic Ocean

Figure 6 *The Sahara Desert, in northern Africa, is extremely dry because the prevailing winds blow across the continent from east to west and is formed from cold, sinking air.*

Quick Lab

A Cool Breeze

1. Hold a **thermometer** next to the top edge of a **cup of water** containing **two ice cubes.** Read the temperature next to the cup.

2. Have your lab partner fan the surface of the cup with a **paper fan.** Read the temperature again. Has the temperature changed? Why? Record your answer in your ScienceLog.

Mountains can influence an area's climate by affecting both temperature and precipitation. For example, Kilimanjaro, the tallest mountain in Africa, has snow-covered peaks year-round, even though it is only about 3° (320 km) south of the equator. Temperatures on Kilimanjaro and in other mountainous areas are affected by elevation. **Elevation** is the height of surface landforms above sea level. At higher elevations, atmospheric pressure decreases, allowing air to expand. This results in the atmosphere being less dense. When the atmosphere is less dense, its ability to hold heat is reduced and temperatures are therefore lower than they would be at lower elevations.

Mountains also affect the climate of nearby areas by influencing the distribution of precipitation. As air rises, it expands and cools, decreasing its ability to carry water vapor. **Figure 7** shows how the climates on two sides of a mountain can be very different.

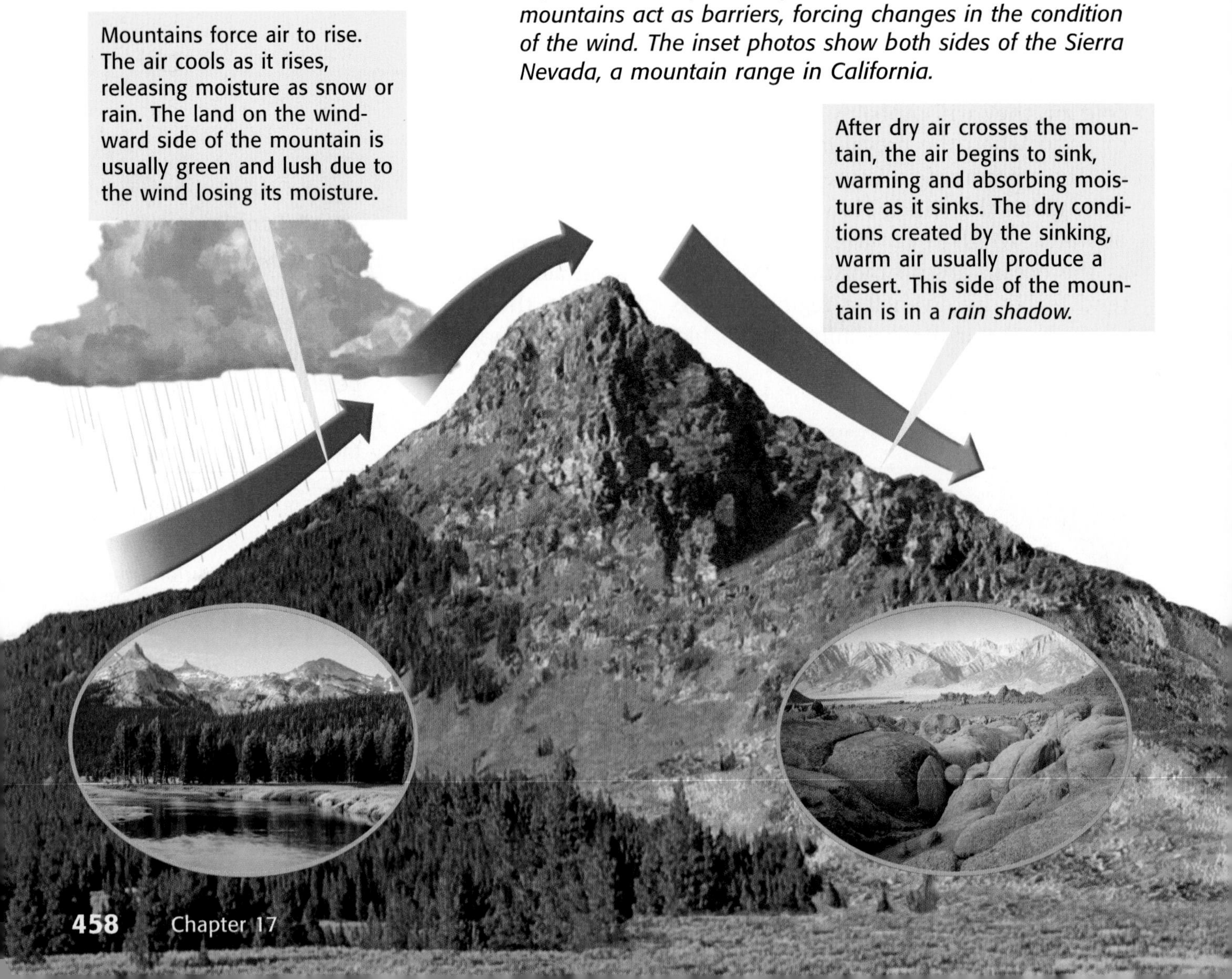

Explore

Using a physical map, locate the mountain ranges in the United States. Does climate vary from one side of a mountain range to the other? If so, what does this tell you about the climatic conditions on either side of the mountain? From what direction are the prevailing winds blowing?

Figure 7 *As the prevailing winds blow across a continent, mountains act as barriers, forcing changes in the condition of the wind. The inset photos show both sides of the Sierra Nevada, a mountain range in California.*

Mountains force air to rise. The air cools as it rises, releasing moisture as snow or rain. The land on the windward side of the mountain is usually green and lush due to the wind losing its moisture.

After dry air crosses the mountain, the air begins to sink, warming and absorbing moisture as it sinks. The dry conditions created by the sinking, warm air usually produce a desert. This side of the mountain is in a *rain shadow*.

Ocean Currents

Because of water's ability to absorb and release heat, the circulation of ocean surface currents has an enormous effect on an area's climate. **Surface currents,** which can be either warm or cold, are streamlike movements of water that occur at or near the surface of the ocean. **Figure 8** shows the pattern of the major warm and cold ocean currents.

The movement of surface currents is affected by three factors—wind, the Earth's rotation, and the location of continents. As surface currents move, they carry warm or cool water to different locations. The surface temperature of the water affects the temperature of the air above it. Warm currents heat the surrounding air and cause warmer temperatures, while cool currents cool the surrounding air and cause cooler temperatures. For example, the Gulf Stream current carries warm water northward off the east coast of North America past Iceland, an island country located just below the Arctic Circle. The warm water from the Gulf Stream heats the surrounding air, creating warmer temperatures in southern Iceland. Temperatures in Iceland are milder than in its neighboring country, Greenland, where the climate is not influenced by the Gulf Stream.

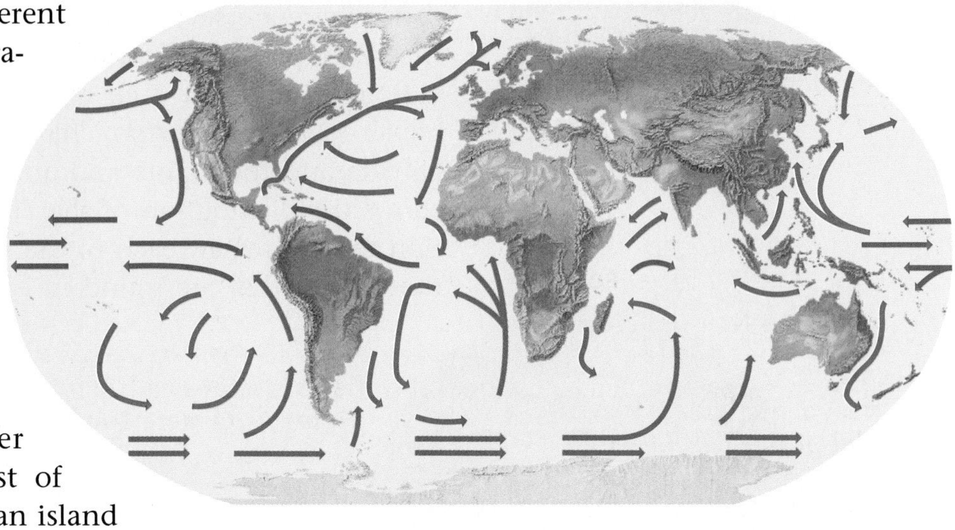

Figure 8 *The red arrows represent the movement of warm ocean currents. The blue arrows represent the movement of cold ocean currents.*

REVIEW

1. What is the difference between weather and climate?

2. How do mountains affect climate?

3. Describe how air temperature is affected by ocean currents.

4. **Analyzing Relationships** How would seasons be different if the Earth did not tilt on its axis?

across the sciences
C O N N E C T I O N

What is El Niño? Can it affect our health? Turn to page 478 to find out.

Climates of the World

Have you ever wondered why the types of plants and animals in one part of the world are different from those found in another part? One reason involves climate. Plants and animals that have adapted to one climate may not be able to live in another climate. For instance, frogs do not live in Antarctica. **Figure 9** illustrates the three major climate zones of Earth—tropical, temperate, and polar. Each zone has a temperature range that relates to its latitude. However, in each of these zones there are several types of climates due to differences in the geography and the amount of precipitation. Because of the various climates in each zone, there are different biomes. A **biome** is a large region characterized by a specific type of climate and the plants and animals that live there. **Figure 10** shows the distribution of the Earth's land biomes. In this section we will review each of the three major climate zones and the biomes that are found in each zone.

NEW TERMS

biome
tropical zone
temperate zone
deciduous
evergreens
polar zone
microclimates

OBJECTIVES

- Locate and describe the three major climate zones.
- Describe the different biomes found in each climate zone.

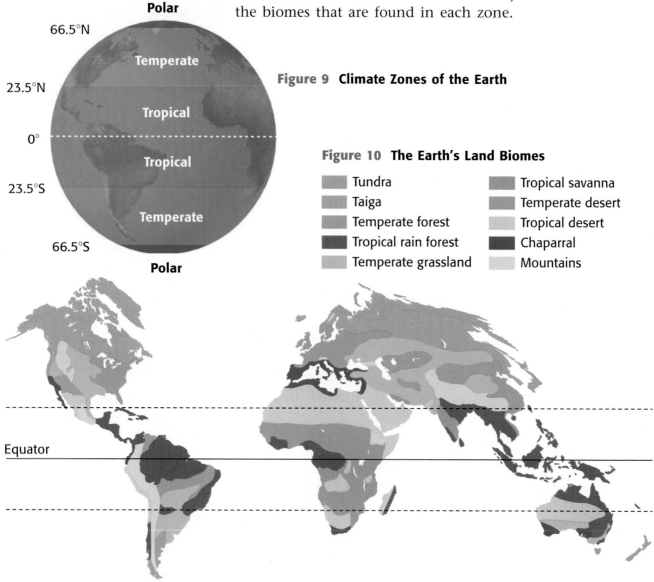

Polar

66.5°N

Temperate

23.5°N

Tropical

0°

Tropical

23.5°S

Temperate

66.5°S

Polar

Figure 9 Climate Zones of the Earth

Figure 10 The Earth's Land Biomes

- Tundra
- Taiga
- Temperate forest
- Tropical rain forest
- Temperate grassland
- Tropical savanna
- Temperate desert
- Tropical desert
- Chaparral
- Mountains

Equator

The Tropical Zone

The **tropical zone,** or the *Tropics,* is the warm zone located around the equator, as shown in **Figure 11.** This zone extends from the tropic of Cancer to the tropic of Capricorn. As you have learned, latitudes in this zone receive the most solar radiation. Temperatures are therefore usually hot, except at high elevations. Within the tropical zone there are three types of biomes—tropical rain forest, tropical desert, and tropical savanna. **Figure 12** shows the distribution of these biomes.

Figure 11 The Earth's Tropical Zone

23.5°N

Tropical

0°

Tropical

23.5°S

Figure 12 Biomes of the Tropical Zone

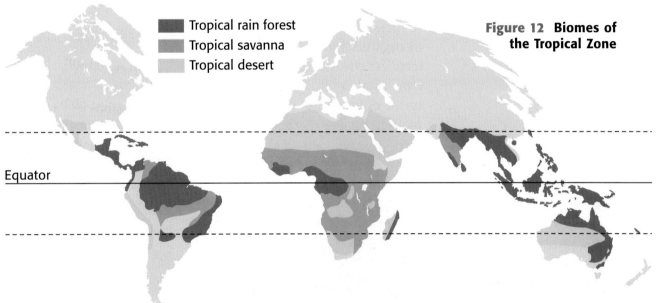

Tropical rain forest

Tropical savanna

Tropical desert

Equator

Tropical Rain Forest Tropical rain forests are always warm and wet. Because they are located near the equator, they receive strong sunlight year-round, causing little difference between seasons. Tropical rain forests contain the greatest number of plant and animal species of any biome. But in spite of the lush vegetation, shown in **Figure 13,** the soil in rain forests is poor. The rapid decay of plants and animals returns nutrients to the soil, but these nutrients are quickly absorbed and used by the plants. The nutrients that are not immediately used by the plants are washed away by the heavy rains, leaving soil that is thin and nutrient poor.

Figure 13 *In tropical rain forests, many of the trees form aboveground roots that grow horizontally from the trees to provide extra support for the trees in the thin soil.*

Avg. Temperature Range: 25°C–28°C (77°F–82°F)

Avg. Yearly Precipitation: 200 cm or more

Soil Characteristics: thin and nutrient poor

Vegetation: mahogany, ebony, rosewood, and balsa trees; vines, ferns, and bamboo

Animals: monkeys, lemurs, parrots, snakes, tree frogs, bats, pigs, small antelopes, tigers, jaguars, and leopards

Tropical Deserts A desert is an area that receives less than 25 cm of rainfall per year. Because of this low yearly rainfall, deserts are the driest places on Earth. Desert plants, shown in **Figure 14,** are adapted to survive in a place with little water. Deserts can be divided into hot deserts and cold deserts. The majority of hot deserts, such as the Sahara, in Africa, are tropical deserts. Hot deserts are caused by cool sinking air masses. Daily temperatures in tropical deserts vary from very hot daytime temperatures (50°C) to cool nighttime temperatures (20°C). Winters in hot deserts are usually mild. Because of the dryness, the soil is poor in organic matter, which fertilizes the soil. The dryness makes it hard to break down dead organic matter.

Avg. Temperature Range:
16°C–50°C (61°F–120°F)

Avg. Yearly Precipitation:
0–25 cm

Soil Characteristics: poor in organic matter

Vegetation: succulents (cactus and euphorbia), shrubs, thorny trees

Animals: kangaroo rats, lizards, scorpions, snakes, birds, bats, toads

life science CONNECTION

Some desert animals, such as the spadefoot toad, survive the scorching summer heat by burying themselves in the ground and sleeping through the dry season.

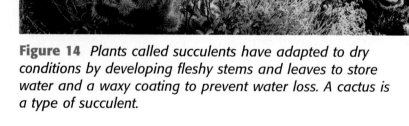

Figure 14 *Plants called succulents have adapted to dry conditions by developing fleshy stems and leaves to store water and a waxy coating to prevent water loss. A cactus is a type of succulent.*

✔**Self-Check**

If desert soil is so nutrient rich, why are deserts not suitable for agriculture? *(See page 564 to check your answer.)*

Tropical Savannas Tropical savannas, sometimes referred to as grasslands, are dominated by tall grasses, with trees scattered here and there. **Figure 15** is a photo of an African savanna. The climate is usually very warm, with a dry season that lasts four to eight months followed by short periods of rain. Savanna soils are generally nutrient poor, but grass fires, which are common during the dry season, leave the soils nutrient enriched. Many plants have adapted to fire and use it to reproduce. Grasses sprout from their roots after the upper part of the plant is burned. The seeds of some plant species require fire in order to grow. For example, some species need fire to break open the seed's outer skin. Only after this skin is broken can the seed grow. Other species drop their seeds at the end of fire season. The heat from the fire triggers the plants to drop their seeds into the newly enriched soil.

Avg. Temperature Range: 27°C–32°C (80°F–90°F)

Avg. Yearly Precipitation: 100 cm

Soil Characteristics: generally nutrient poor

Vegetation: tall grasses (3–5 m), trees, thorny shrubs

Animals: gazelles, rhinoceroses, giraffes, lions, hyenas, ostriches, crocodiles, elephants

Figure 15 *The grass of a tropical savanna is 3–5 m tall, much taller than that of a temperate grassland.*

REVIEW

1. What are the soil characteristics of a tropical rain forest?

2. In what way has savanna vegetation adapted to fire?

3. **Summarizing Data** How do each of the tropical biomes differ?

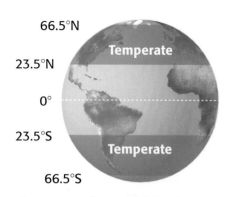

The Temperate Zone

The **temperate zone,** as shown in **Figure 16,** is the climate zone between the Tropics and the polar zone. Temperatures in the temperate zone tend to be moderate. The continental United States is in the temperate zone, which includes the following four biomes: temperate forest, temperate grassland, chaparral, and temperate desert. **Figure 17** shows the distribution of the biomes found in the temperate zone.

Figure 16 The Earth's Temperate Zones

Figure 17 Biomes of the Temperate Zone

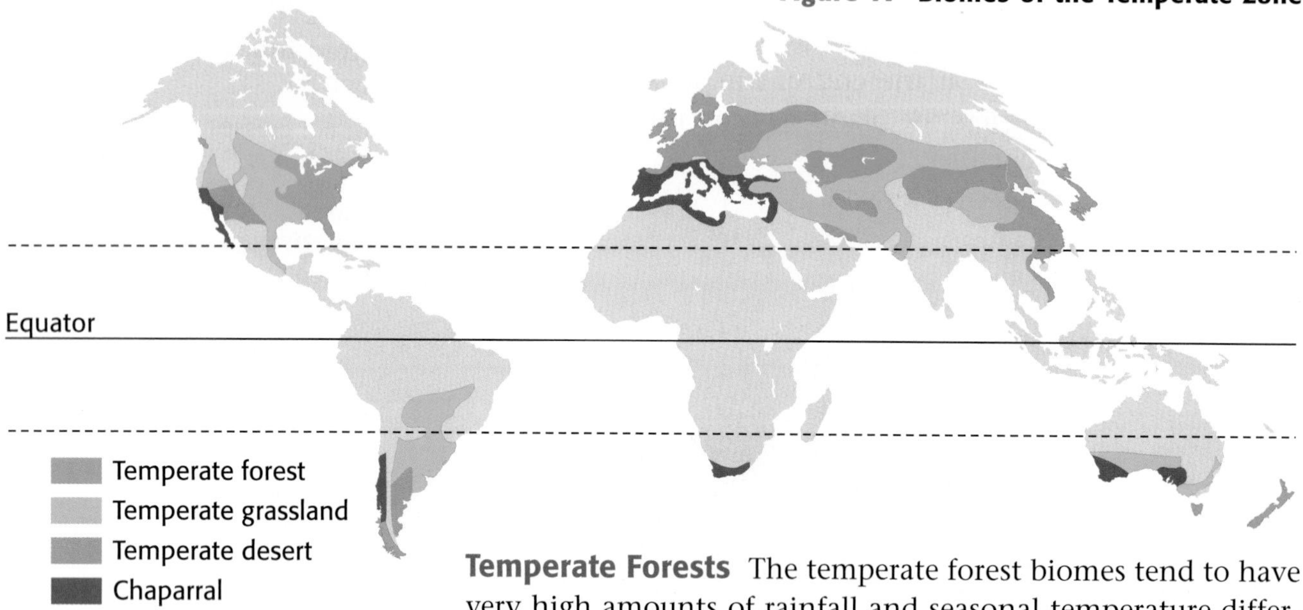

Equator

- Temperate forest
- Temperate grassland
- Temperate desert
- Chaparral

Temperate Forests The temperate forest biomes tend to have very high amounts of rainfall and seasonal temperature differences. Because of these distinct seasonal changes, summers are usually warm and winters are usually cold. The largest temperate forests are deciduous, such as the one shown in **Figure 18.** **Deciduous** trees are trees that lose their leaves when the weather becomes cold. These trees tend to be broad-leaved. The soils in deciduous forests are usually quite fertile because of the high organic content contributed by decaying leaves that drop every winter.

Another type of temperate forest is the evergreen forest. **Evergreens** are trees that keep their leaves year-round. Evergreens can be either broad-leaved trees or needle-leaved trees, such as pine trees. Mixed forests of broad-leaved and needle-leaved trees can be found in humid climates, such as Florida, where winter temperatures rarely fall below freezing.

Figure 18 *Deciduous trees have leaves that change color and drop when temperatures become cold.*

Avg. Temperature Range: 0°C–28°C (32°F–82°F)

Avg. Yearly Precipitation: 76–250 cm

Soil Characteristics: very fertile, organically rich

Vegetation: deciduous and evergreen trees, shrubs, herbs

Animals: deer, bears, boars, badgers, squirrels, wolves, wild cats, red foxes, owls, and many other birds

Temperate Grasslands Temperate grasslands, such as those shown in **Figure 19,** occur in regions that receive too little rainfall for trees to grow. This biome has warm summers and cold winters. The temperate grasslands are known by many local names—the *prairies* of North America, the *steppes* of Eurasia, the *veldt* of Africa, and the *pampas* of South America. Grasses are the most common type of vegetation found in this biome. Because grasslands have the most fertile soils of all biomes, much of the temperate grassland has been plowed to make room for croplands.

Avg. Temperature Range: −6°C–26°C (21°F–78°F)

Avg. Yearly Precipitation: 38–76 cm

Soil Characteristics: most fertile soils of all biomes

Vegetation: grasses

Animals: large grazing animals, including the bison of North America, the kangaroo of Australia, and the antelope of Africa

Figure 19 *The world's grasslands once covered about 42 percent of Earth's total land surface. Today they occupy only about 12 percent of the Earth's surface.*

Chaparrals Chaparral regions, as shown in **Figure 20,** have cool, wet winters and hot, dry summers. The vegetation is mainly evergreen shrubs, which are short, woody plants with thick, waxy leaves. The waxy leaves are adaptations that help prevent water loss in dry conditions. These shrubs grow in rocky, nutrient-poor soil. Like tropical-savanna vegetation, chaparral vegetation has adapted to fire. In fact, some plants, such as chamise, can grow back from their roots after a fire.

Avg. Temperature Range: 11°C–26°C (51°F–78°F)

Avg. Yearly Precipitation: 48–56 cm

Soil Characteristics: rocky, nutrient-poor soils

Vegetation: evergreen shrubs, scrubby trees, herbs

Animals: ground squirrels, deer, elk, mountain lions, coyotes, wolves

Figure 20 *Some plant species found in chaparral produce substances that help them catch on fire. These species require fire to reproduce.*

Temperate Deserts The temperate desert biomes, like the one shown in **Figure 21,** tend to be cold deserts. Like all deserts, cold deserts receive less than 25 cm of rainfall annually. Temperate deserts can be very hot in the daytime, but—unlike hot deserts—they tend to be very cold at night.

Avg. Temperature Range:
1°C–50°C (34°F–120°F)

Avg. Yearly Precipitation:
0–25 cm

Soil Characteristics: poor in organic matter

Vegetation: succulents (cactus), shrubs, thorny trees

Animals: kangaroo rats, lizards, scorpions, snakes, birds, bats, toads

Figure 21 *The Great Basin Desert is in the rain shadow of the Sierra Nevada.*

The temperatures sometimes drop below freezing. This large change in temperature between day and night is caused by low humidity and cloudless skies. These conditions allow for a large amount of energy to reach, and thus heat, the Earth's surface during the day. However, these same characteristics allow the heat to escape at night, causing temperatures to drop. You probably rarely think of snow and deserts together, but temperate deserts often receive light snow during the winter.

Temperate deserts are dry because they are generally located inland, far away from a moisture source, or are located on the rain-shadow side of a mountain range.

The Polar Zone

The **polar zone** includes the northernmost and southernmost climate zones, as shown in **Figure 22.** Polar climates have the coldest average temperatures. The temperatures in the winter stay below freezing, and the temperatures during the summer months remain chilly. **Figure 23,** on the next page, shows the distribution of the biomes found in the polar zone.

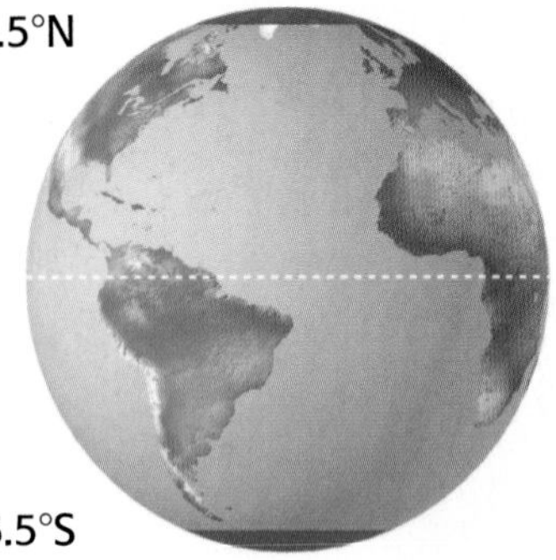

Polar

66.5°N

0°

66.5°S

Polar

Figure 22 The Earth's Polar Zones

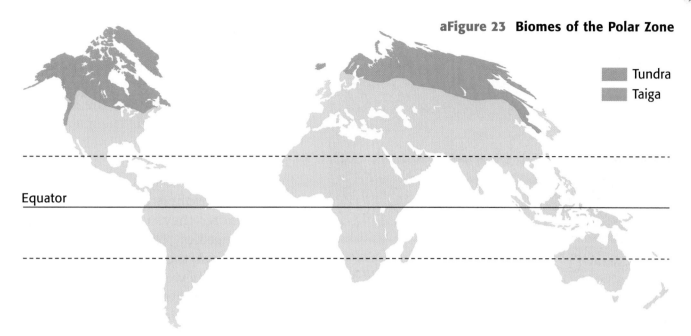

Tundra
Taiga

Equator

Tundra Next to deserts, the tundra, as shown in **Figure 24,** is the driest place on Earth. This biome has long, cold winters with almost 24 hours of night and short, cool summers with almost 24 hours of daylight. In the summer, only the top meter of soil thaws. Underneath the thawed soil lies a permanently frozen layer of soil, called *permafrost*. This frozen layer prevents the water in the thawed soil from draining. Because of the poor drainage, the upper soil layer is muddy and is therefore an excellent breeding ground for insects, such as mosquitoes. Many birds migrate to the tundra during the summer to feed on the insects.

oceanography
CONNECTION

Subfreezing climates contain almost no decomposing bacteria. The well-preserved body of John Torrington, a member of an expedition that explored the Northwest Passage in Canada in the 1840s, was uncovered in 1984, appearing much as it did when he died, more than 140 years earlier.

Avg. Temperature Range: −27°C–5°C (−17°F–41°F)

Avg. Yearly Precipitation: 0–25 cm

Soil Characteristics: frozen

Vegetation: mosses, lichens, sedges, and dwarf trees

Animals: rabbits, lemmings, reindeer, caribou, musk oxen, wolves, foxes, birds, and polar bears

Figure 24 *In the tundra, mosses and lichens cover rocks. Dwarf trees grow close to the ground to protect themselves from strong winds and to absorb heat from the Earth's sunlit surface.*

Figure 25 *The taiga is the major source of wood for paper.*

Avg. Temperature Range:
−10°C–15°C (14°F–59°F)

Avg. Yearly Precipitation:
40–61 cm

Soil Characteristics: acidic soil

Vegetation: mosses, lichens, conifers

Animals: birds, rabbits, moose, elk, wolves, lynxes, and bears

Taiga (Northern Coniferous Forest)

Just south of the tundra lies the taiga biome. The taiga, as shown in **Figure 25,** has long, cold winters and short, warm summers. Like the tundra, the soil during the winter is frozen. The majority of the trees are evergreen needle-leaved trees called *conifers,* such as pine, spruce, and fir trees. The needles and bendable branches allow these trees to shed heavy snow before they can be damaged. Conifer needles contain acidic substances. When the needles die and fall to the soil, they make the soil acidic. Most plants cannot grow in acidic soil, and therefore the forest floor is bare except for some mosses and lichens.

Microclimates

You have learned the types of biomes that are found in each climate zone. But the climate and the biome of a particular place can also be influenced by local conditions. **Microclimates** are small regions with unique climatic characteristics. For example, elevation can affect an area's climate and therefore its biome. Tundra and taiga biomes exist in the Tropics on high mountains. How is this possible? Remember that as the elevation increases, the atmosphere loses its ability to absorb and hold heat. This results in lower temperatures.

Cities are also microclimates. In a city, temperatures can be 1°C to 2°C warmer than the surrounding rural areas. This is because buildings and pavement made of dark materials absorb solar radiation instead of reflecting it. There is also less vegetation to take in the sun's rays. This absorption of the sun's rays by buildings and pavement heats the surrounding air and causes temperatures to rise.

physical science
CONNECTION

Roof temperatures can get so hot that you can fry an egg on them! In a study of roofs on a sunny day when the air temperature was 13°C, scientists recorded roof temperatures ranging from 18°C to 61°C depending on color and material of the roof.

To find out more about microclimates, turn to page 559 of the LabBook.

REVIEW

1. Describe how tropical deserts and temperate deserts differ.

2. List and describe the three major climate zones.

3. **Inferring Conclusions** Rank each biome according to how suitable it would be for growing crops. Explain your reasoning.

Changes in Climate

NEW TERMS

ice age
global warming
greenhouse effect

OBJECTIVES

- Describe how the Earth's climate has changed over time.
- Summarize the different theories that attempt to explain why the Earth's climate has changed.
- Explain the greenhouse effect and its role in global warming.

As you know, the weather constantly changes—sometimes several times in one day. Saturday, your morning baseball game was canceled because of rain, but by that afternoon the sun was shining. Now think about the climate where you live. You probably haven't noticed a change in climate, because climates change slowly. What causes climates to change? Until recently, climatic changes were connected only to natural causes. However, studies indicate that human activities, such as the burning of fossil fuels, may have an influence on climatic change. In this section, you will learn how natural and human factors may influence climatic change.

Ice Ages

The geologic record indicates that the Earth's climate has been much colder than it is today. In fact, much of the Earth was covered by sheets of ice during certain periods. An **ice age** is a period during which ice collects in high latitudes and moves toward lower latitudes. This movement is characterized by episodes of advance and retreat. Scientists have found evidence of many major ice ages throughout the Earth's geologic history. The most recent ice age began about 2 million years ago. During an ice age, there are periods of cold, when much of the Earth's surface is covered by ice, and periods of warmth, when the ice melts. These periods are called glacial and interglacial periods. During *glacial periods,* the enormous sheets of ice advance, covering a larger area. Ice sheets gain their water from the ocean, so sea level may drop by more than 100 m during glacial periods. **Figure 26** shows that during the last glacial period, which began about 115,000 years ago and ended about 10,000 years ago, huge sheets of ice covered much of the northern United States.

Figure 26 *During the last glacial period, the Great Lakes were covered by an enormous block of ice that was 1.5 km high.*

Interglacial periods are warmer times that occur between glacial periods. During an interglacial period, the ice begins to melt back, or retreat. As the ice melts, the sea level rises again. The last interglacial period began 10,000 years ago and is still occurring. Why does this periodic change in temperature occur? Will the Earth experience another glacial period in the future? To answer these questions, let's examine the theories that scientists have been debating for the past 200 years.

Causes of Ice Ages There are many theories about the causes of ice ages. Each theory attempts to explain the gradual cooling that leads to the development of enormous ice sheets that periodically cover large areas of the Earth's surface. The *Milankovitch theory* explains why an ice age isn't just one long cold spell but instead alternates between cold and warm periods. Milutin Milankovitch, a Yugoslavian scientist, proposed that changes in the Earth's orbit and in the tilt of the Earth's axis cause ice ages, as illustrated in **Figure 27.**

Figure 27 *According to the Milankovitch theory, the amount of solar radiation the Earth receives varies due to three kinds of changes in the Earth's orbit.*

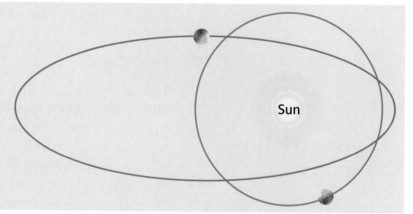

1 Over a period of 100,000 years, the Earth's orbit slowly changes from a more circular shape to a more elliptical shape. When the orbit is more elliptical, summers are hotter and winters are cooler. When the orbit is more circular, there is not as much seasonal change.

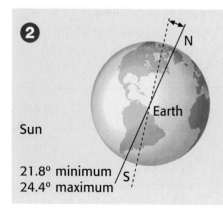

2 Over a period of 41,000 years, the tilt of the Earth's axis varies between 21.8° and 24.4°. When the tilt is at 24.4°, the poles receive more solar energy.

21.8° minimum
24.4° maximum

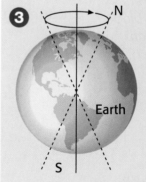

3 The circular motion of the Earth's axis causes the Earth to change position. The Earth's axis traces a complete circle every 26,000 years. The circular motion of the Earth's axis determines the time of year that the Earth is closest to the sun.

✓ Self-Check

How do you think the Earth's elliptical orbit affects the amount of solar radiation that reaches the surface?
(See page 564 to check your answer.)

There are many natural factors that can affect global climate. Some of these factors are thought to have contributed to the Earth's cooling that led to the ice ages. Catastrophic events, such as volcanic eruptions, can influence climate. Volcanic eruptions send large amounts of dust, ash, and smoke into the atmosphere. Once in the atmosphere, the dust, smoke, and ash particles act as a shield, blocking out so much of the sun's rays that the Earth cools. **Figure 28** shows how dust particles from a volcanic eruption block the sun.

Figure 28 *Volcanic eruptions, such as the one that occurred at Mount St. Helens, shown above, produce dust that reflects sunlight, as shown at left.*

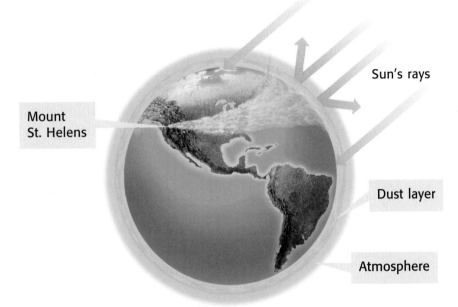

Sun's rays

Mount St. Helens

Dust layer

Atmosphere

Changes in the sun's energy output also affect global climate. When the sun is radiating a lot of energy, temperatures increase. But when the sun's energy output decreases, temperatures drop.

The Earth's climate is further influenced by plate tectonics and continental drift. One theory proposes that ice ages occur when the continents are positioned closer to the polar regions. For example, approximately 250 million years ago, all the continents were connected near the South Pole in one giant landmass called Pangaea, as shown in **Figure 29**. During this time, ice covered a large area of the Earth's surface. As Pangaea broke apart, the continents moved toward the equator, and the ice age ended. During the last ice age, many large landmasses were positioned in the polar zones. Antarctica, northern North America, Europe, and Asia all were covered with large sheets of ice.

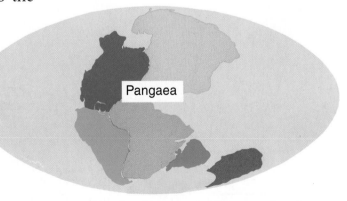

Pangaea

Figure 29 *Much of Pangaea—the part that is now Africa, South America, India, Antarctica, Australia, and Saudi Arabia—was covered by continental ice sheets.*

MATH BREAK

The Ride to School

Find out how much carbon dioxide is released into the atmosphere each month from the car or bus that transports you to school.

1. Figure out the distance from your home to school.
2. From this figure, calculate how many kilometers you travel to and from school, in a car or bus, per month.
3. Divide this number by 20. This represents approximately how many gallons of gas are used during your trips to school.
4. If burning 1 gal of gasoline produces 9 kg of carbon dioxide, how much carbon dioxide is released?

Global Warming

Is the Earth really experiencing global warming? **Global warming** is a rise in average global temperatures that can result from an increase in the greenhouse effect. To understand how global warming works, you must first learn about the greenhouse effect.

Greenhouse Effect   The **greenhouse effect** is the Earth's natural heating process, in which gases in the atmosphere trap heat. Think about the case illustrated in **Figure 30**. It's a hot summer day, and you are about to go for a ride in the car with your brother. As you crawl into the back seat, you notice that it feels hotter inside the car than outside. Then you sit down and—ouch!—burn yourself on the seat. If you have experienced this, then you already know something about the greenhouse effect. The Earth's atmosphere performs the same function as the glass windows in a car.

Figure 30 *Sunlight streams into the car through the clear glass windows. The seats absorb the radiant energy and change it into heat energy. The heat is then trapped in the car.*

Greenhouse gases allow sunlight to pass through the atmosphere. It is absorbed by the Earth's surface and reradiated as heat energy. Greenhouse gases absorb the heat as it moves out of the atmosphere. An increase in the greenhouse effect occurs when there is an increase in greenhouse gases in the atmosphere. Many scientists hypothesize that the rise in global temperatures is due to an increase of carbon dioxide, a greenhouse gas, as a result of human activity. Most evidence indicates that the increase in carbon dioxide is caused by the burning of fossil fuels, such as coal, oil, and natural gas, which releases carbon dioxide into the atmosphere. But the burning of fossil fuels is not the only reason for the increase in carbon dioxide.

LabBook

Are global temperatures really on the rise? Turn to page 558 of the LabBook to find out.

A city just received a warning from the Environmental Protection Agency for exceeding the automobile fuel emissions standards. If you were the city manager, what suggestions would you make to reduce the amount of automobile emissions?

Another contributing factor might be deforestation. *Deforestation* is the process of clearing forests, as shown in **Figure 31.** In many countries around the world, forests are being burned to clear land for agriculture. All types of burning release carbon dioxide into the atmosphere, thereby increasing the greenhouse effect. Plants use carbon dioxide to make food. As plants are removed from the Earth, the carbon dioxide that would have been used by the plants builds up in the atmosphere.

Consequences of Global Warming If the average global temperature continues to rise, some regions of the world might experience flooding. Warmer temperatures could cause the icecaps to melt, raising the sea level and flooding low-lying areas, such as the coasts.

Figure 31 *Clearing land by burning leads to increased levels of carbon dioxide in the atmosphere.*

Areas that receive little rainfall, such as deserts, might receive even less due to increased evaporation. Scientists predict that the Midwest, an agricultural area, could experience warmer, drier conditions. A change in climate such as this could harm crops. But farther north, such as in Canada, weather conditions for farming would improve.

REVIEW

1. How has the Earth's climate changed over time? What might have caused these changes?

2. Explain how the greenhouse effect warms the Earth.

3. What are two ways that humans contribute to the increase in carbon dioxide levels in the atmosphere?

4. **Analyzing Relationships** How will the warming of the Earth affect agriculture in different parts of the world?

Chapter Highlights

Vocabulary

weather *(p. 454)*

climate *(p. 454)*

latitude *(p. 455)*

prevailing winds *(p. 457)*

elevation *(p. 458)*

surface currents *(p. 459)*

Section Notes

• Weather is the condition of the atmosphere at a particular time and place. Climate is the average weather conditions in a certain area over a long period of time.

• Climate is determined by temperature and precipitation.

• Climate is controlled by factors such as latitude, elevation, wind patterns, local geography, and ocean currents.

• The amount of solar energy an area receives is determined by the area's latitude.

• The seasons are a result of the tilt of the Earth's axis and its path around the sun.

• The amount of moisture carried by prevailing winds affects the amount of precipitation that falls.

• As elevation increases, temperature decreases.

• Mountains affect the distribution of precipitation. The dry side of the mountain is called the rain shadow.

• As ocean currents move across the Earth, they redistribute warm and cool water. The temperature of the surface water affects the air temperature.

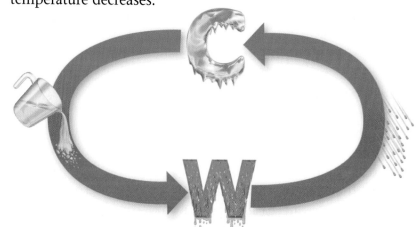

☑ Skills Check

Visual Understanding

THE SEASONS Seasons are determined by latitude. The diagram on page 456 shows how the tilt of the Earth affects how much solar energy an area receives as the Earth moves around the sun.

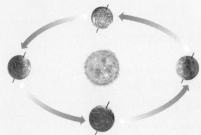

THE RAIN SHADOW The illustration on page 458 shows how the climates on two sides of a mountain can be very different. A mountain can affect the climate of areas nearby by influencing the amount of precipitation these areas receive.

LAND BIOMES OF THE EARTH Look back at Figure 10 on page 460 to review the distribution of the Earth's Land Biomes.

SECTION 2

Vocabulary

biome *(p. 460)*

tropical zone *(p. 461)*

temperate zone *(p. 464)*

deciduous *(p. 464)*

evergreens *(p. 464)*

polar zone *(p. 466)*

microclimates *(p. 468)*

Section Notes

- The Earth is divided into three climate zones according to latitude—the tropical zone, the temperate zone, and the polar zone.

- The tropical zone is the zone around the equator. The tropical rain forest, tropical desert, and tropical savanna are in this zone.

- The temperate zone is the zone between the tropical zone and the polar zone. The temperate forest, temperate grassland, chaparral, and temperate desert are in this zone.

- The polar zones are the northernmost and southernmost zones. The taiga and tundra are in this zone.

Labs

For the Birds *(p. 559)*

Biome Business *(p. 562)*

SECTION 3

Vocabulary

ice age *(p. 469)*

global warming *(p. 472)*

greenhouse effect *(p. 472)*

Section Notes

- Explanations for the occurrence of ice ages include changes in the Earth's orbit, volcanic eruptions, changes in the sun's energy output, and plate tectonics and continental drift.

- Some scientists believe that global warming is occurring as a result of an increase in carbon dioxide from human activity.

- If global warming continues, it could drastically change climates, causing either floods or drought.

Labs

Global Impact *(p. 558)*

---

 internet connect

go. hrw .com **GO TO:** go.hrw.com

Visit the **HRW** Web site for a variety of learning tools related to this chapter. Just type in the keyword:

KEYWORD: HSTCLM

SCI LINKS **NSTA** **GO TO:** www.scilinks.org

Visit the **National Science Teachers Association** on-line Web site for Internet resources related to this chapter. Just type in the *sci*LINKS number for more information about the topic:

TOPIC: What Is Climate?	*sci*LINKS NUMBER: HSTE405
TOPIC: Climates of the World	*sci*LINKS NUMBER: HSTE410
TOPIC: Changes in Climate	*sci*LINKS NUMBER: HSTE415
TOPIC: Modeling Earth's Climate	*sci*LINKS NUMBER: HSTE420

Chapter Review

USING VOCABULARY

To complete the following sentences, choose the correct term from each pair of terms listed below:

1. __?__ is the condition of the atmosphere in a certain area over a long period of time. (*Weather* or *Climate*)

2. __?__ is the distance north and south from the equator measured in degrees. (*Longitude* or *Latitude*)

3. Savannas are grasslands located in the __?__ zone between 23.5° north latitude and 23.5° south latitude. (*temperate* or *tropical*)

4. Trees that lose their leaves are found in a(n)__?__ forest. (*deciduous* or *evergreen*)

5. Frozen land in the polar zone is most often found in a __?__. (*taiga* or *tundra*)

6. A rise in global temperatures due to an increase in carbon dioxide is called __?__. (*global warming* or *the greenhouse effect*)

UNDERSTANDING CONCEPTS

Multiple Choice

7. The tilt of Earth as it orbits the sun causes
   a. global warming.
   b. different seasons.
   c. a rain shadow.
   d. the greenhouse effect.

8. What factor affects the prevailing winds as they blow across a continent, producing different climates?
   a. latitude
   b. mountains
   c. forests
   d. glaciers

9. What factor determines the amount of solar energy an area receives?
   a. latitude
   b. wind patterns
   c. mountains
   d. ocean currents

10. What climate zone has the coldest average temperature?
    a. tropical
    b. polar
    c. temperate
    d. tundra

11. What biome is not located in the tropical zone?
    a. rain forest
    b. savanna
    c. chaparral
    d. desert

12. What biome contains the greatest number of plant and animal species?
    a. rain forest
    b. temperate forest
    c. grassland
    d. tundra

13. Which of the following is not a theory for the cause of ice ages?
    a. the Milankovitch theory
    b. volcanic eruptions
    c. plate tectonics
    d. the greenhouse effect

14. Which of the following is thought to contribute to global warming?
    a. wind patterns
    b. deforestation
    c. ocean surface currents
    d. microclimates

Short Answer

15. Why do higher latitudes receive less solar radiation than lower latitudes?

16. How does wind influence precipitation patterns?

17. Why do tropical rain forests contain the greatest number of plant and animal species on the planet?

18. How have desert plants and animals adapted to this biome?

19. How are tundra and deserts similar?

Concept Mapping

20. Use the following terms to create a concept map: climate, global warming, deforestation, greenhouse effect, flooding.

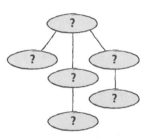

CRITICAL THINKING AND PROBLEM SOLVING

Write one or two sentences to answer the following questions:

21. Explain how ocean surface currents are responsible for milder climates.

22. In your own words, explain how a change in the Earth's orbit can affect the Earth's climates as proposed by Milutin Milankovitch.

23. Explain why the climate differs drastically on each side of the Rocky Mountains.

24. What are some steps you and your family can take to reduce the amount of carbon dioxide that is released into the atmosphere?

MATH IN SCIENCE

25. If the air temperature near the shore of a lake measures 24°C, and if the temperature increases by 0.05°C every 10 m traveled away from the lake, what would the air temperature be 1 km from the lake?

INTERPRETING GRAPHICS

The following illustration shows the Earth's orbit around the sun.

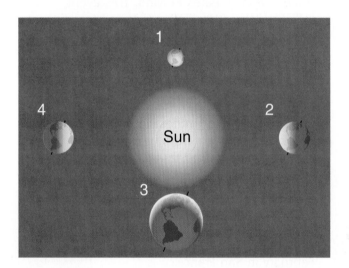

26. At what position, **1**, **2**, **3**, or **4**, is it spring in the Southern Hemisphere?

27. At what position does the South Pole receive almost 24 hours of daylight?

28. Explain what is happening in each climate zone in both the Northern Hemisphere and Southern Hemisphere at position **4**.

NOW What Do You Think?

Take a minute to review your answers to the ScienceLog questions on page 453. Have your answers changed? If necessary, revise your answers based on what you have learned since you began this chapter.

Blame "The Child"

El Niño, which is Spanish for "the child," is the name of a weather event that occurs in the Pacific Ocean. Every 2 to 12 years, the interaction between the ocean surface and atmospheric winds creates El Niño. This event influences weather patterns in many regions of the world.

Difficult Breathing

For Indonesia and Malaysia, El Niño meant droughts and forest fires in 1998. Thousands of people in these countries suffered from respiratory ailments from breathing the smoke caused by these fires. Heavy rains in San Francisco created extremely high mold-spore counts. These spores cause problems for people with allergies. The spore count in February in San Francisco is usually between 0 and 100. In 1998, the count was often higher than 8,000!

Rodent Invasion

In areas where El Niño creates heavy rains, the result is lush vegetation. This lush vegetation provides even more food and shelter for rodents. As the rodent population increases, so does the threat of the diseases they spread. In states like Arizona, Colorado, and New Mexico, this means there is a greater chance among humans of contracting hantaviral pulmonary syndrome (HPS).

HPS is carried by deer mice and remains in their urine and feces. People are infected when they inhale dust contaminated with mouse feces or urine. Once infected, a person experiences flulike symptoms that can sometimes lead to fatal kidney or lung disease.

More Rodents and Insects

Heavy rains near Los Angeles might encourage a rodent-population explosion in the mountains east of the city. If so, there could be an increase in the number of rodents infected with bubonic plague. More infected rodents means more infected fleas, which carry bubonic plague to humans.

Ticks and mosquitoes could also increase in number. These insects can spread disease too. For example, ticks can carry Lyme disease, ehrlichiosis, babesiosis, and Rocky Mountain spotted fever. Mosquitoes can spread malaria, dengue fever, encephalitis, and Rift Valley fever.

◀ *If this flea carries bubonic plague bacteria, just one bite can infect a person.*

What About Camping?

Because all of these diseases can be fatal to humans, people must take precautions. Camping in the great outdoors increases the risk of infection. Campers should steer clear of rodents and their burrows. Don't forget to dust family pets with flea powder, and don't let them roam free. Try to remember that an ounce of prevention is worth a pound of cure.

Find Out More

▶ How do you think El Niño affects the fish and mammals that live in the ocean? Write your answer in your ScienceLog, and then do some research to see if you are correct.

Science, Technology, and Society

Some Say Fire, Some Say Ice . . .

The Earth's climate has undergone many drastic changes. For example, 6,000 years ago in the part of North Africa that is now a desert, hippos, crocodiles, and early Stone Age people shared shallow lakes that covered the area. Grasslands stretched as far as the eye could see.

Scientists have known for many years that Earth's climate has changed. What they didn't know was why. Using supercomputers and complex computer programs, scientists may now be able to explain why North Africa's lakes and grasslands became a desert. And that information may be useful for predicting future heat waves and ice ages.

Climate Models

Scientists who study Earth's atmosphere have developed climate models to try to imitate Earth's climate. A climate model is like a very complicated recipe with thousands of ingredients. These models do not make exact predictions about future climates, but they do estimate what might happen.

What ingredients are included in a climate model? One important ingredient is the level of greenhouse gases (especially carbon dioxide) in the atmosphere. Land and ocean water temperatures from around the globe are other ingredients. So is information about clouds, cloud cover, snow, and ice cover. And in more recent models, scientists have included information about ocean currents.

A Challenge to Scientists

Earth's atmosphere-ocean climate system is extremely complex. One challenge for scientists is to understand all the system's parts. Another is to understand how those parts work together. But understanding Earth's climate system is critical. An accurate climate model should help scientists predict heat waves, floods, and droughts.

Even the best available climate models must be improved. The more information scientists can include in a climate model, the more accurate the results. Today data are available from more locations, and scientists need more-powerful computers to process all the data.

As more-powerful computers are developed to handle all the data in a climate model, scientists' understanding of Earth's climate changes will improve. This knowledge should help scientists better predict the impact human activities have on global climate. And these models could help scientists prevent some of the worst effects of climate change, such as global warming or another ice age.

▲ *This meteorologist is using a high-powered supercomputer to do climate modeling.*

A Challenge for You

▶ Earth's oceans are a major part of the climate model. Find out some of the ways oceans affect climate. Do you think human activities are changing the oceans?

LabBook

Contents

Exploring, inventing, and investigating are essential to the study of science. However, these activities can also be dangerous. To make sure that your experiments and explorations are safe, you must be aware of a variety of safety guidelines.

You have probably heard of the saying, "It is better to be safe than sorry." This is particularly true in a science classroom where experiments and explorations are being performed. Being uninformed and careless can result in serious injuries. Don't take chances with your own safety or with anyone else's.

Following are important guidelines for staying safe in the science classroom. Your teacher may also have safety guidelines and tips that are specific to your classroom and laboratory. Take the time to be safe.

Safety Rules!

Start Out Right

Always get your teacher's permission before attempting any laboratory exploration. Read the procedures carefully, and pay particular attention to safety information and caution statements. If you are unsure about what a safety symbol means, look it up or ask your teacher. You cannot be too careful when it comes to safety. If an accident does occur, inform your teacher immediately, regardless of how minor you think the accident is.

Safety Symbols

All of the experiments and investigations in this book and their related worksheets include important safety symbols to alert you to particular safety concerns. Become familiar with these symbols so that when you see them, you will know what they mean and what to do. It is important that you read this entire safety section to learn about specific dangers in the laboratory.

If you are instructed to note the odor of a substance, wave the fumes toward your nose with your hand. Never put your nose close to the source.

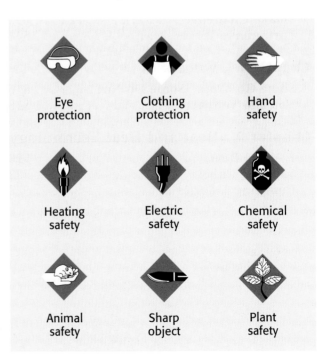

Eye protection	Clothing protection	Hand safety
Heating safety	Electric safety	Chemical safety
Animal safety	Sharp object	Plant safety

Eye Safety

Wear safety goggles when working around chemicals, acids, bases, or any type of flame or heating device. Wear safety goggles any time there is even the slightest chance that harm could come to your eyes. If any substance gets into your eyes, notify your teacher immediately, and flush your eyes with running water for at least 15 minutes. Treat any unknown chemical as if it were a dangerous chemical. Never look directly into the sun. Doing so could cause permanent blindness.

Avoid wearing contact lenses in a laboratory situation. Even if you are wearing safety goggles, chemicals can get between the contact lenses and your eyes. If your doctor requires that you wear contact lenses instead of glasses, wear eye-cup safety goggles in the lab.

Safety Equipment

Know the locations of the nearest fire alarms and any other safety equipment, such as fire blankets and eyewash fountains, as identified by your teacher, and know the procedures for using them.

Be extra careful when using any glassware. When adding a heavy object to a graduated cylinder, tilt the cylinder so the object slides slowly to the bottom.

Neatness

Keep your work area free of all unnecessary books and papers. Tie back long hair, and secure loose sleeves or other loose articles of clothing, such as ties and bows. Remove dangling jewelry. Don't wear open-toed shoes or sandals in the laboratory. Never eat, drink, or apply cosmetics in a laboratory setting. Food, drink, and cosmetics can easily become contaminated with dangerous materials.

Certain hair products (such as aerosol hair spray) are flammable and should not be worn while working near an open flame. Avoid wearing hair spray or hair gel on lab days.

Sharp/Pointed Objects

Use knives and other sharp instruments with extreme care. Never cut objects while holding them in your hands. Place objects on a suitable work surface for cutting.

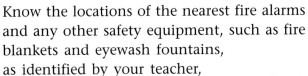

Heat

Wear safety goggles when using a heating device or a flame. Whenever possible, use an electric hot plate as a heat source instead of an open flame. When heating materials in a test tube, always angle the test tube away from yourself and others. In order to avoid burns, wear heat-resistant gloves whenever instructed to do so.

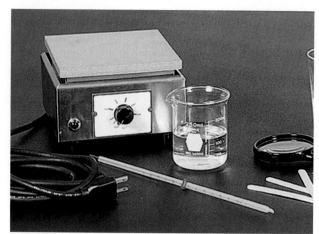

Electricity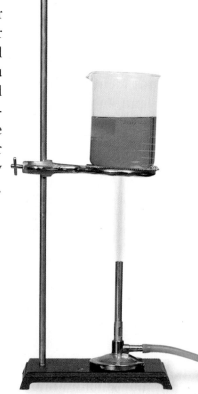

Be careful with electrical cords. When using a microscope with a lamp, do not place the cord where it could trip someone. Do not let cords hang over a table edge in a way that could cause equipment to fall if the cord is accidentally pulled. Do not use equipment with damaged cords. Be sure your hands are dry and that the electrical equipment is in the "off" position before plugging it in. Turn off and unplug electrical equipment when you are finished.

Chemicals

Wear safety goggles when handling any potentially dangerous chemicals, acids, or bases. If a chemical is unknown, handle it as you would a dangerous chemical. Wear an apron and safety gloves when working with acids or bases or whenever you are told to do so. If a spill gets on your skin or clothing, rinse it off immediately with water for at least 5 minutes while calling to your teacher.

Never mix chemicals unless your teacher tells you to do so. Never taste, touch, or smell chemicals unless you are specifically directed to do so. Before working with a flammable liquid or gas, check for the presence of any source of flame, spark, or heat.

Animal Safety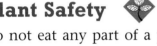

Always obtain your teacher's permission before bringing any animal into the school building. Handle animals only as your teacher directs. Always treat animals carefully and with respect. Wash your hands thoroughly after handling any animal.

Plant Safety

Do not eat any part of a plant or plant seed used in the laboratory. Wash hands thoroughly after handling any part of a plant. When in nature, do not pick any wild plants unless your teacher instructs you to do so.

Glassware

Examine all glassware before use. Be sure that glassware is clean and free of chips and cracks. Report damaged glassware to your teacher. Glass containers used for heating should be made of heat-resistant glass.

Using the Scientific Method

Geologists often use a technique called *core sampling* to learn what underground rock layers look like. This technique involves drilling several holes in the ground in different places and taking samples of the underground rock or soil. Geologists then compare the samples from each hole to construct a diagram that shows the bigger picture.

In this activity, you will model the process geologists use to diagram underground rock layers. You will first use modeling clay to form a rock-layer model. You will then exchange models with a classmate, take core samples, and draw a diagram of your classmate's layers.

Materials

- 3 colored pencils or markers
- nontransparent pan or box
- modeling clay in three colors
- 1/2 in. PVC pipe
- plastic knife

SCIENTIFIC METHOD

Ask a Question

1. Can unseen features be revealed by sampling parts of the whole?

Form a Hypothesis

2. Form a hypotheses on whether taking core samples from several locations will give a good indication of the entire hidden feature.

Test the Hypothesis

3. To test your hypothesis, you will take core samples from a model of underground rock layers, draw a diagram of the entire rock-layer sequence, and then compare your drawing with the actual model.

Build a Model

The model rock layers should be formed out of view of the classmates who will be taking the core samples.

4. Form a plan for your rock layers, and sketch the layers in your ScienceLog. Your sketch should include the three colors in several layers of varying thicknesses.

5. In the pan or box, mold the clay into the shape of the lowest layer in your sketch.

6. Repeat step 5 for each additional layer of clay. You now have a rock-layer model. Exchange models with a classmate.

Collect Data

7. Choose three places on the surface of the clay to drill holes. The holes should be far apart and in a straight line. (You do not need to remove the clay from the pan or box.)

8. Use the PVC pipe to "drill" a vertical hole in the clay at one of the chosen locations by slowly pushing the pipe through all the layers of clay. Slowly remove the pipe.

9. Remove the core sample from the pipe by gently pushing the clay out of the pipe with an unsharpened pencil.

10. Draw the core sample in your ScienceLog, and record your observations. Be sure to use a different color of pencil or marker for each layer.

11. Repeat steps 8–10 for the next two core samples. Make sure your drawings are side by side in your ScienceLog in the same order as the samples in the model.

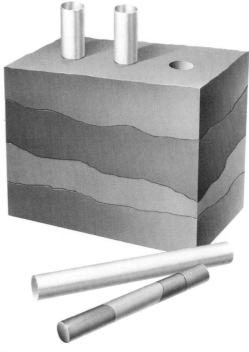

Analyze the Results

12. Look at the pattern of rock layers in each of your core samples. Think about how the rock layers between the core samples might look. Then construct a diagram of the rock layers.

13. Complete your diagram by coloring the rest of the rock layers.

Draw Conclusions

14. Use the plastic knife to cut the clay model along a line connecting the three holes and remove one side of the model. The rock layers should now be visible.

15. How well does your rock-layer diagram match the model? Explain.

16. Is it necessary to revise your diagram from step 13? If so, how?

17. Do your conclusions support your hypothesis? Why or why not?

Going Further
What are two ways that the core-sampling method could be improved?

Round or Flat?

Eratosthenes thought he could measure the circumference of the Earth. He came up with the idea while reading that a deep vertical well in southern Egypt was entirely lit up by the sun at noon once each year. He realized that for this to happen, the sun must be directly over the well at that moment! But at the same moment, in a city just north of this well, a tall monument cast a shadow. Eratosthenes reasoned that the sun could not be directly over both the monument and the well at noon on the same day. In this experiment, you will test his idea and see for yourself how his experiment works.

Materials

- basketball
- 2 books or notebooks
- modeling clay
- 2 unsharpened pencils
- metric ruler
- meterstick
- masking tape
- flashlight or small lamp
- string, 10 cm long
- protractor
- tape measure
- calculator (optional)

SCIENTIFIC METHOD

Ask a Question

1. How could I use Eratosthenes' experiment to measure the size of the Earth?

Conduct an Experiment

2. Set the basketball on a table, and place a book or notebook on either side to hold the ball in place. The ball represents the Earth.

3. Use modeling clay to attach a pencil to the "equator" of the ball so that it sticks directly outward.

4. Attach the second pencil to the ball 5 cm above the first pencil. This second pencil should also stick directly outward, as shown on the next page.

5. Use a meterstick to measure 1 m away from the ball. Mark this position with masking tape, and label it "sun." Place the flashlight here.

6. When your teacher turns out the lights, turn on your flashlight, and point it so that the pencil on the equator does not cast a shadow. Ask a partner to hold the flashlight in this position. The second pencil should cast a shadow on the ball.

7. Tape one end of the string to the top of the second pencil. Hold the other end of the string against the ball at the far edge of the shadow. Make sure that the string is taut, but be careful not to pull the pencil over.

8. Use a protractor to measure the angle between the string and the pencil. Record this angle in your ScienceLog.

9. Use the following formula to calculate the *experimental circumference* of the ball:

$$\text{Circumference} = \frac{360° \times 5 \text{ cm}}{\text{angle between pencil and string}}$$

Record this circumference in your ScienceLog.

10. Wrap the tape measure around the ball's "equator" to measure the *actual circumference* of the ball. Record this circumference in your ScienceLog.

Analyze the Results

11. In your ScienceLog, compare the experimental circumference with the actual circumference.

12. What could have caused your experimental circumference to be different from the actual value?

13. What are some of the advantages and disadvantages of taking measurements this way?

Draw Conclusions

14. Was this an effective method for Eratosthenes to measure the Earth's circumference? Explain your answer.

Going Further

You can calculate the circumference of Earth by doing Eratosthenes' experiment with other schools around the world during the fall and spring equinoxes. To find out more, search for "Eratosthenes' experiment" on the Internet. The experiment is conducted each year.

Orient Yourself!

You have been invited to attend an orienteering event with your neighbors. In orienteering events, participants use maps and compasses to find their way along a course. There are several control points that each participant must reach. The object is to reach each control point and then the finish line. Orienteering events are often timed competitions. In order to find the fastest route through the course, the participants must read the map and use their compass correctly. Being the fastest runner does not necessarily guarantee finishing first. You also must choose the most direct route to follow.

Your neighbors participate in several orienteering events each year. They always come home raving about how much fun they had. You would like to join them, but you will need to learn how to use your compass first.

Materials

- magnetic compass
- course map
- ruler
- 2 colored pencils or markers

Procedure

1. Together as a class, go outside to the orienteering course your teacher has made.

2. Hold your compass flat in your hand. Turn the compass until the N is pointing straight in front of you. (The needle in your compass will always point north.) Turn your body until the needle lines up with the N on your compass. You are now facing north.

3. Regardless of which direction you want to face, you should always align the end of the needle with the N on your compass. If you are facing south, the needle will be pointing directly toward your body. When the N is aligned with the needle, the S will be directly in front of you, and you will be facing south.

4. Use your compass to face east. Align the needle with the N. Where is the E? Turn to face that direction. When the needle and the N are aligned and the E is directly in front of you, you are facing east.

5. In an orienteering competition, you will need to know how to determine which direction you are traveling. Now, face any direction you choose.

6. Do not move, but rotate the compass to align the needle on your compass with the N. What direction are you facing? You are probably not facing directly north, south, east, or west. If you are facing between north and west, you are facing northwest. If you are facing between north and east, you are facing northeast.

7. Find a partner or partners to follow the course your teacher has made. Get a copy of the course map from your teacher. It will show several control points. You must stop at each one. You will need to follow this map to find your way through the course. Find and stand at the starting point.

8. Face the next control point on your map. Rotate your compass to align the needle on your compass with the N. What direction are you facing?

9. Use the ruler to draw a line on your map between the two control points. Write the direction between the starting point and the next control point on your map.

10. Walk toward the control point. Keep your eyes on the horizon, not on your compass. You might need to go around obstacles such as a fence or building. Use the map to find the easiest way around.

11. Record the color or code word you find at the control point next to the control point symbol on your map.

12. Repeat steps 8–11 for each control point. Follow the points in order as they are labeled. For example, determine the direction from control point 1 to control point 2. Be sure to include the direction between the final control point and the starting point.

Analysis

13. The object of an orienteering competition is to arrive at the finish line first. The maps provided at these events do not instruct the participants to follow a specific path. In one form of orienteering, called "score orienteering," competitors may find the control points in any order. Look at your map. If this course were used for a score-orienteering competition, would you change your route? Explain.

14. If there is time, follow the map again. This time, use your own path to find the control points. Draw this path and the directions on your map in a different color. Do you believe this route was faster? Why?

Going Further

Do some research to find out about orienteering events in your area. The Internet and local newspapers may be good sources for the information. Are there any events that you would like to attend?

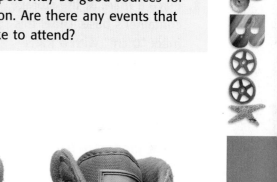

Topographic Tuber

Imagine that you live on top of a tall mountain and often look down on the lake below. Every summer, an island appears. You call it Sometimes Island because it goes away again during heavy fall rains. This summer you begin to wonder if you could make a topographic map of Sometimes Island. You don't have fancy equipment to make the map, but you have an idea. What if you place a meterstick with the 0 m mark at the water level in the summer? Then as the expected fall rains come, you could draw the island from above as the water rises. Would this idea really work?

Materials

- clear plastic storage container with transparent lid
- transparency marker
- metric ruler
- potato, cut in half
- water
- tracing paper

SCIENTIFIC METHOD

Ask a Question

1. How do I make a topographic map?

Conduct an Experiment

2. Place a mark at the storage container's base. Label this mark "0 cm" with a transparency marker.

3. Measure and mark 1 cm increments up the side of the container until you reach the top of the container. Label these marks "1 cm," "2 cm," "3 cm," and so on.

4. Place the potato flat side down in the center of the container.

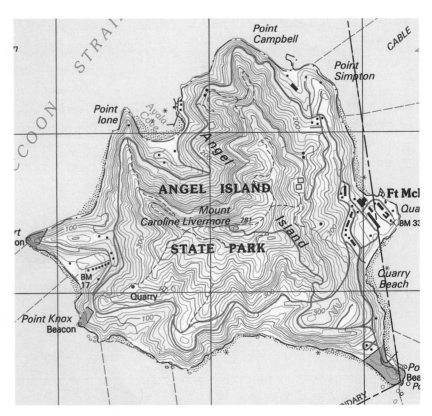

5. Pour water into the container until it reaches the line labeled "1 cm."

6. Place the lid on the container, and seal it. Part of the potato will be sticking out above the water. Viewing the potato from above, use the transparency marker to trace the part of the potato that touches the top of the water.

7. The scale for your map will be 1 cm = 10 m. Draw a 2 cm line in the bottom right-hand corner of the lid. Place hash marks at 0 cm, 1 cm, and 2 cm. Label these marks "0 m," "10 m," and "20 m."

8. Label the elevation of the contour line you drew in step 6. According to the scale, the elevation is 10 m.

9. Remove the lid. Carefully pour water into the container until it reaches the line labeled "2 cm."

10. Place the lid on the container, and seal it. Viewing the potato from above, trace the part of the potato that touches the top of the water at this level.

11. Use the scale to calculate the elevation of this line. Label the elevation on your drawing.

12. Repeat steps 9–11, adding 1 cm to the depth of the water each time. Stop when the potato is completely covered.

13. Remove the lid, and set it on a tabletop. Place tracing paper on top of the lid. Trace the contours from the lid onto the paper. Label the elevation of each contour line. Congratulations! You have just made a topographic map!

Analyze the Results

14. What is the contour interval of this topographic map?

15. By looking at the contour lines, how can you tell which parts of the potato are steeper?

Draw Conclusions

16. Do all topographic maps have a 0 m elevation contour line as a starting point? How would this affect a topographic map of Sometimes Island? Explain your answer.

17. Would this be an effective way to make a topographic map of Sometimes Island? Why or why not?

18. What is the elevation of the highest point on your map?

Going Further
Place all of the potatoes on a table or desk at the front of the room. Your teacher will mix up the potatoes as you trade topographic maps with another group. By reading the topographic map you just received, can you pick out the matching potato?

Mysterious Minerals

Imagine sitting on a rocky hilltop, gazing at the ground below you. You can see dozens of different types of rocks. How can scientists possibly identify the countless variations? It's a mystery!

In this activity you'll use your powers of observation and a few simple tests to determine the identities of rocks and minerals. Take a look at the Mineral Identification Key on the next page. That key will help you use clues to discover the identity of several minerals.

Materials

- several sample minerals
- glass microscope slides
- streak plate
- safety gloves
- iron filings

Procedure

1. In your ScienceLog, create a data chart like the one below.

2. Choose one mineral sample, and locate its column in your data chart.

3. Follow the Mineral Identification Key to find the identity of your sample. When you are finished, record the mineral's name and primary characteristics in the appropriate column in your data chart. **Caution:** Put on your gloves when scratching the glass slide.

4. Select another mineral sample, and repeat steps 3 and 4 until your data table is complete.

Analysis

5. Were some minerals easier to identify than others? Explain.

6. A streak test is a better indicator of a mineral's true color than visual observation. Why isn't a streak test used to help identify every mineral?

7. In your ScienceLog, summarize what you learned about the various characteristics of each mineral sample you identified.

Mineral Summary Chart						
Characteristics	1	2	3	4	5	6
Mineral name						
Luster						
Color						
Streak						
Hardness						
Cleavage						
Special properties						

DO NOT WRITE IN BOOK

Mineral Identification Key

1. **a.** If your mineral has a metallic luster, **GO TO STEP 2.**
    b. If your mineral has a nonmetallic luster, **GO TO STEP 3.**

2. **a.** If your mineral is black, **GO TO STEP 4.**
    b. If your mineral is yellow, it is **PYRITE.**
    c. If your mineral is silver, it is **GALENA.**

3. **a.** If your mineral is light in color, **GO TO STEP 5.**
    b. If your mineral is dark in color, **GO TO STEP 6.**

4. **a.** If your mineral leaves a red-brown line on the streak plate, it is **HEMATITE.**
    b. If your mineral leaves a black line on the streak plate, it is **MAGNETITE.** Test your sample for its magnetic properties by holding it near some iron filings.

5. **a.** If your mineral scratches the glass microscope slide, **GO TO STEP 7.**
    b. If your mineral does not scratch the glass microscope slide, **GO TO STEP 8.**

6. **a.** If your mineral scratches the glass slide, **GO TO STEP 9.**
    b. If your mineral does not scratch the glass slide, **GO TO STEP 10.**

7. **a.** If your mineral shows signs of cleavage, it is **ORTHOCLASE FELDSPAR.**
    b. If your mineral does not show signs of cleavage, it is **QUARTZ.**

8. **a.** If your mineral shows signs of cleavage, it is **MUSCOVITE.** Examine this sample for twin sheets.
    b. If your mineral does not show signs of cleavage, it is **GYPSUM.**

9. **a.** If your mineral shows signs of cleavage, it is **HORNBLENDE.**
    b. If your mineral does not show signs of cleavage, it is **GARNET.**

10. **a.** If your mineral shows signs of cleavage, it is **BIOTITE.** Examine your sample for twin sheets.
    b. If your mineral does not show signs of cleavage, it is **GRAPHITE.**

Going Further

Using your textbook and other reference books, research other methods of identifying different types of minerals. Based on your findings, create a new identification key. Give it to a friend along with a few sample minerals, and see if your friend can unravel the mystery!

Is It Fool's Gold?—A Dense Situation

Have you heard of fool's gold? Maybe you've seen a piece of it. This notorious mineral was often passed off as real gold. There are, however, simple tests you can do to keep from being tricked. Minerals can be identified by their properties. Some properties, such as color, vary between different samples of the same mineral. Other properties, such as density and specific gravity, remain consistent from one sample to another. In this activity, you will try to verify the identity of some mineral samples.

Ask a Question

1. How can I determine if an unknown mineral is not gold or silver?

Make Observations

2. Copy the data table below into your ScienceLog. Use it to record your observations.

Observation Chart		
Measurement	**Galena**	**Pyrite**
Mass in air (g)		
Weight in air (N)		
Beginning volume of water (mL)		
Final volume of water (mL)		
Volume of mineral (mL)		
Weight in water (N)		

DO NOT WRITE IN BOOK

3. Find the mass of each sample by laying the mineral on the balance. Record the mass of each in your data table.

4. Attach the spring scale to the ring stand.

5. Tie a string around the sample of galena, leaving a loop at the loose end. Suspend the galena from the spring scale, and find its weight in air. Do not remove the sample from the spring scale yet. Enter these data in your data table.

Materials

- spring scale
- ring stand
- pyrite sample
- galena sample
- balance
- string
- 400 mL beaker
- 400 mL of water

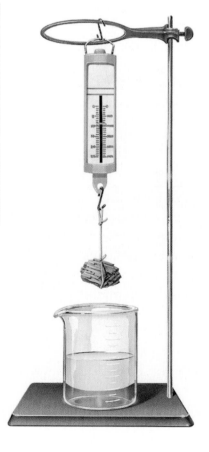

6. Fill a beaker halfway with water. Record the beginning volume of water in your data table.

7. Carefully lift the beaker around the galena until the mineral is completely submerged. Be careful not to splash any water out of the beaker! Be sure the mineral does not touch the beaker.

8. Record the new volume and weight in your data table.

9. Subtract the original volume of water from the new volume to find the amount of water displaced by the mineral. This is the volume of the mineral sample itself. Record this value in your data table.

10. Repeat steps 5–9 for the sample of pyrite.

Analyze the Results

11. Copy the data table below into your ScienceLog.
    Note: 1 mL = 1 cm^3

12. Use the following equations to calculate the density and specific gravity of each mineral, and record your answers in your data table.

$$\text{Density} = \frac{\text{mass in air}}{\text{volume}}$$

$$\text{Specific gravity} = \frac{\text{weight in air}}{\text{weight in air} - \text{weight in water}}$$

Mineral	Density (g/cm^3)	Specific gravity
Silver	10.5	10.5
Galena		
Pyrite		
Gold	19.3	19.3

DO NOT WRITE IN BOOK

Draw Conclusions

13. The density of pure gold is 19.3 g/cm^3. How can you use this information to prove that your sample of pyrite is not gold?

14. The density of pure silver is 10.5 g/cm^3. How can you use this information to prove that your sample of galena is not silver?

15. If you found a gold-colored nugget, how could you find out if the nugget was real gold or fool's gold?

Going Further

Sugar cubes dissolve in water. Explain how you would find the density of a sugar cube.

Crystal Growth

Magma forms deep below the Earth's surface at depths of 25 to 160 km and at extremely high temperatures. Some magma reaches the surface and cools quickly. Other magma gets trapped in cracks or magma chambers beneath the surface and cools very slowly. In both cases, the magma forms crystals as it cools and solidifies. The size of the crystals found in igneous rocks gives geologists clues about where and how the crystals formed.

When magma cools slowly, large, well-developed crystals form. On the other hand, when magma erupts onto the surface, heat is lost rapidly to the air or water. There is not enough time for large crystals to grow.

In this experiment, you will demonstrate how the rate of cooling affects the size of crystals in igneous rocks by cooling crystals of magnesium sulfate at two different rates.

Make a Prediction

1. Suppose you have two solutions that are identical in every way except for temperature. How will the temperature of a solution affect the size of the crystals and the rate at which they form?

Make Observations

2. Put on your gloves, apron, and goggles.

3. Fill the beaker halfway with tap water. Place the beaker on the hot plate, and let it begin to warm. The temperature of the water should be between 40°C and 50°C. **Caution:** Make sure the hot plate is away from the edge of the lab table.

4. Examine two or three crystals of the magnesium sulfate with your hand lens. In your ScienceLog, describe the color, shape, luster, and other interesting features of the crystals.

5. Draw a sketch of the magnesium sulfate crystals in your ScienceLog.

Conduct an Experiment

6. Use the pointed laboratory scoop to fill the test tube about halfway with the magnesium sulfate. Add an equal amount of distilled water.

Materials

- heat-resistant gloves
- 400 mL beaker
- 200 mL of tap water
- hot plate
- Celsius thermometer
- magnesium sulfate (MgSO$_4$) (Epsom salts)
- hand lens
- pointed laboratory scoop
- medium test tube
- distilled water
- watch or clock
- aluminum foil
- test-tube tongs
- dark marker
- masking tape
- basalt
- pumice
- granite

7. Hold the test tube in one hand, and use one finger from your other hand to tap the test tube gently. Observe the solution mixing as you continue to tap the test tube.

8. Place the test tube in the beaker of hot water, and heat it for approximately 3 minutes. **Caution:** Be sure to direct the opening of the test tube away from you and other students.

9. While the test tube is heating, shape your aluminum foil into two small boatlike containers by doubling the foil and turning up each edge.

10. If all the magnesium sulfate is not dissolved after 3 minutes, tap the test tube again, and heat it for 3 more minutes. **Caution:** Use the test-tube tongs to handle the hot test tube.

11. With a marker and a piece of masking tape, label one of your aluminum boats "Sample 1", and place it on the hot plate. Turn the hot plate off.

12. Label the other aluminum boat "Sample 2," and place it on the lab table.

13. Using the test-tube tongs, remove the test tube from the beaker of water, and evenly distribute the contents to each of your foil boats. Carefully pour the hot water in the beaker down the drain. Do not move or disturb either of your foil boats.

14. Copy the table below into your ScienceLog. Using the hand lens, carefully observe the foil boats. Record the time it takes for the first crystals to appear.

15. If crystals have not formed in the boats before class is over, carefully place the boats in a safe place. You may then record the time in days instead of in minutes.

16. When crystals have formed in both boats, use your hand lens to examine the crystals carefully.

Crystal-Formation Table			
Crystal formation	**Time**	**Size and appearance of crystals**	**Sketch of crystals**
Sample 1			
Sample 2			

DO NOT WRITE IN BOOK

Analyze the Results

17. Was your prediction correct? Explain.

18. Compare the size and shape of the crystals in Samples 1 and 2 with the size and shape of the crystals you examined in step 4. How long do you think the formation of the original crystals must have taken?

Draw Conclusions

19. Granite, basalt, and pumice are all igneous rocks. The most distinctive feature of each is the size of their crystals. Different igneous rocks form when magma cools at different rates. Examine a sample of each with your hand lens.

20. Copy the table below into your ScienceLog, and sketch each rock sample.

21. Use what you have learned in this activity to explain how each rock sample formed and how long it took for the crystals to form. Record your answers in your table.

Igneous Rock Observations			
	Granite	**Basalt**	**Pumice**
Sketch			
How did the rock sample form?			
Rate of cooling			

Going Further

Describe the size and shape of the crystals you would expect to find when a volcano erupts and sends material into the air and when magma oozes down the volcano's slope.

Let's Get Sedimental

Superposition makes a lot of sense. Consider the following statement: "In an undisturbed column of sedimentary rock, the oldest rock has to be on the bottom." You cannot drop sediment on top of something that isn't there any more than you can sit on a chair that isn't there. But notice the word *undisturbed.* That means the layers of sediment today look exactly like they did when they first settled—there has been no folding and no flipping over. But how do we determine if sedimentary rocks are undisturbed? The best way is to be sure that the top of the layer still points up. This experiment will show you how to read rock features that say, in effect, "This side up." Then you can look for the signs at a real outcrop.

Materials

- sand
- gravel
- soil (clay-rich, if available)
- 3 L mixing bowl
- plastic pickle jar or 3 L plastic soda bottle with a cap
- water
- scissors
- dropper pipet
- magnifying lens

Procedure

1. Thoroughly mix the sand, gravel, and soil together, and fill the plastic container about one-third full of the mixture.

2. Add water until the container is two-thirds full. Twist the cap back onto the container, and shake the container vigorously until all of the sediment is mixed in the rapidly moving water.

3. Place the container on a tabletop. Using the scissors, carefully cut the top off the container a few centimeters above the water, as shown at right. This will promote evaporation.

4. Do not disturb the container. Allow the water to evaporate. (You may accelerate the process by carefully using the dropper pipet to siphon off some of the clear water after allowing the container to sit for at least 24 hours.)

5. Immediately after you set the bottle on the desk, describe what you see from above and through the sides of the bottle. Do this at least once each day. Record your observations in your ScienceLog.

6. After the sediment has dried and hardened, describe its surface in your ScienceLog.

7. Carefully lay the container on its side, and cut a strip of plastic out of the side to expose the sediments in the bottle. You may find it easier if you place pieces of clay on either side of the bottle to stabilize it.

8. Brush away the loose material from the sediment, and gently blow on the surface until it is clean. Examine the surface, and record your observations in your ScienceLog.

Analysis

9. Do you see anything through the side of the bottle that could help you determine if a sedimentary rock is undisturbed? Explain.

10. What structures do you see on the surface of the sediment that you would not expect to find at the bottom?

11. Explain how these features might be used to identify the top of the sedimentary bed in a real outcrop and to decide if the bed has been disturbed.

12. Did you see any structures on the side of the container that might indicate which direction is up?

13. After removing the side of the bottle, use the magnifying glass to examine the boundaries between the gravel, sand, and silt. What do you see? Do the size and type of sediment change quickly or gradually?

Going Further

Explain why the following statement is true: "If the top of a layer can't be found, finding the bottom of it works just as well." Imagine that a layer was deposited directly above the layers in your container. Describe the bottom of this layer.

Metamorphic Mash

Metamorphism is a complex process that takes place deep within the Earth, where the temperature and pressure would turn a human into a crispy pancake. The effects of this extreme temperature and pressure are obvious in some metamorphic rocks. One of these effects is the reorganization of mineral grains within the rock fabric. In this activity, you will investigate the process of metamorphism without being charred, flattened, or buried.

Materials

- modeling clay
- sequins or other small flat objects
- plastic knife
- small pieces of very stiff cardboard or plywood

Procedure

1. Flatten the clay into a layer about 1 cm thick. Sprinkle the surface with sequins.

2. Roll the corners of the clay toward the middle to form a neat ball.

3. Carefully use the plastic knife to cut the ball in half. In your ScienceLog, describe the position and location of the sequins inside the ball.

4. Put the ball back together, and use the sheets of cardboard or plywood to flatten the ball until it is about 2 cm thick.

5. Using the plastic knife, slice open the slab of clay in several places. In your ScienceLog, describe the position and location of the sequins in the slab.

Analysis

6. What physical process does flattening the ball represent?

7. Describe any changes in the position and location of the sequins that occurred as the clay ball was flattened into a slab.

8. How are the sequins oriented in relation to the force you put on the ball to flatten it?

9. Do you think the orientation of the mineral grains in a foliated metamorphic rock tells you anything about the rock? Defend your answer.

Going Further

Suppose you find a foliated metamorphic rock that has grains running in two distinct directions. Use what you have learned in this activity to offer a possible explanation for this observation.

Make a Water Wheel

Lift Enterprises is planning to build a water wheel that will lift objects like a crane does. City planners feel that this would make very good use of the energy supplied by the river that flows through town. Development of the water wheel is in the early stages. The president of the company has asked you to modify the basic water-wheel design so that the final product will lift objects more quickly.

Ask a Question

1. What factors influence the rate at which a water wheel lifts a weight?

Form a Hypothesis

2. In your ScienceLog, change the question above into a statement giving your "best guess" as to what factors will have the greatest effect on your water wheel.

Build a Model

3. Measure and mark a 5 × 5 cm square on an index card. Cut the square out of the card.

4. Fold the square in half to form a triangle.

5. Measure and mark a line 8 cm from the bottom of the plastic jug. Use scissors to cut along this line. (Your teacher may need to use a safety razor to start this cut for you.) Keep both sections of the jug.

6. Use the permanent marker to trace four triangles onto the flat parts of the top section of the plastic jug. Use the paper triangle you made in step 4 as a template. Cut the triangles out of the plastic to form four fins.

7. Use a thumbtack to attach one corner of each plastic fin to the round edge of the cork, as shown at right. Make sure the fins are equally spaced around the cork.

8. Press a thumbtack into one of the flat sides of the cork. Jiggle the thumbtack to widen the hole in the cork, and then remove the thumbtack.

9. Repeat step 8 on the other side of the cork.

Materials

- index card
- metric ruler
- scissors
- safety razor (for teacher)
- large plastic milk jug
- permanent marker
- 5 thumbtacks
- cork
- glue
- 2 wooden skewers
- hole punch
- modeling clay
- transparent tape
- 20 cm of thread
- coin
- 2 L bottle filled with water
- watch or clock that indicates seconds

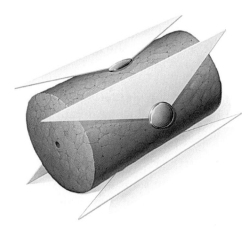

10. Place a drop of glue on the end of a skewer, and insert the skewer into one of the holes in the end of the cork. Insert the second skewer into the hole in the other end.

11. Use a hole punch to carefully punch two holes in the bottom section of the plastic jug. Punch each hole 1 cm from the top edge of the jug, directly across from one another.

12. Carefully push the skewers through the holes, and suspend the cork in the center of the jug.

13. Attach a small ball of clay to the end of each skewer. The clay balls should be the same size.

14. Tape one end of the thread to one skewer on the outside of the jug next to the clay ball. Wrap the thread around the clay ball three times. (As the water wheel turns, the thread should continue to wrap around the clay. The other ball of clay balances the weight and helps to keep the water wheel turning smoothly.)

15. Tape the free end of the thread to a coin. Wrap the thread around the coin once, and tape it again. You are now ready to test your hypothesis.

Test the Hypothesis

16. Slowly and carefully pour water from the 2 L bottle onto the fins so that the water wheel spins. What happens to the coin? Record your observations in your ScienceLog.

17. Lower the coin back to the starting position. Add more clay to the skewer to increase the diameter of the wheel. Repeat step 16. Did the coin rise faster or slower this time?

18. Lower the coin back to the starting position. Modify the shape of the clay, and repeat step 16. Does the shape of the clay affect how quickly the coin rises? Explain your answer.

19. What happens if you remove two of the fins from opposite sides? What happens if you add more fins? Modify your water wheel to find out.

20. Experiment with another fin shape. How does a different fin shape affect how quickly the coin rises?

Analyze the Results

21. What factors influence how quickly you can lift the coin?

Draw Conclusions

22. What recommendations would you make to Lift Enterprises to improve its water wheel?

Going Further
Design and build your own water wheel using the materials from this activity. Decide how many fins to use and what shape the fins should be. As a class, hold a competition to see which wheel can lift the most weight.

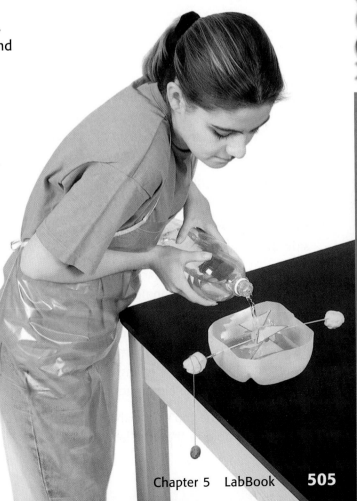

Power of the Sun

The sun radiates energy in every direction. Like the sun, the energy radiated by a light bulb spreads out in all directions. But how much energy an object receives depends on how close that object is to the source. As you move farther from the source, the amount of energy you receive decreases. For example, if you measure the amount of energy that reaches you from a light and then move three times farther away, you will discover that nine times less energy will reach you at your second position. Energy from the sun travels as light energy. When light energy is absorbed by an object it is converted into heat energy. *Power* is the rate at which one form of energy is converted to another, and it is measured in *watts*. Because power is related to distance, nearby objects can be used to measure the power of far-away objects. In this lab you will calculate the power of the sun using an ordinary 100-watt light bulb.

Materials

- protective gloves
- aluminum strip, 2 × 8 cm
- pencil
- black permanent marker
- Celsius thermometer
- mason jar, cap, and lid with hole in center
- modeling clay
- desk lamp with a 100 W bulb and removable shade
- metric ruler
- watch or clock that indicates seconds
- scientific calculator

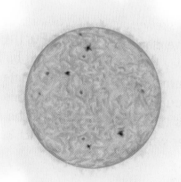

Procedure

1. Gently shape the piece of aluminum around a pencil so that it holds on in the middle and has two wings, one on either side of the pencil.

2. Bend the wings outward so that they can catch as much sunlight as possible.

3. Use the marker to color both wings on one side of the aluminum strip black.

4. Remove the pencil and place the aluminum snugly around the thermometer near the bulb.
   Caution: Do not press too hard—you do not want to break the thermometer! Wear protective gloves when working with the thermometer and the aluminum.

5. Carefully slide the top of the thermometer through the hole in the lid. Place the lid on the jar so that the thermometer bulb is inside the jar, and screw down the cap.

6. Secure the thermometer to the jar lid by molding clay around the thermometer on the outside of the lid. The aluminum wings should be in the center of the jar.

7. Read the temperature on the thermometer. Record this as room temperature.

8. Place the jar on a windowsill in the sunlight. Turn the jar so that the black wings are angled toward the sun.

9. Watch the thermometer until the temperature reading stops rising. Record the temperature in your ScienceLog.

10. Remove the jar from direct sunlight, and allow it to return to room temperature.

11. Remove any shade or reflector from the lamp. Place the lamp at one end of a table.

12. Place the jar about 30 cm from the lamp. Turn the jar so that the wings are angled toward the lamp.

13. Turn on the lamp, and wait about 1 minute.

14. Move the jar a few centimeters toward the lamp until the temperature reading starts to rise. When the temperature stops rising, compare it with the reading you took in step 9.

15. Repeat step 14 until the temperature matches the temperature you recorded in step 9.

16. If the temperature reading rises too high, move the jar away from the lamp and allow it to cool. Once the reading has dropped to at least 5°C below the temperature you recorded in step 9, you may begin again at step 12.

17. When the temperature in the jar matches the temperature you recorded in step 9, record the distance between the center of the light bulb and the thermometer bulb in your ScienceLog.

Analysis

18. The thermometer measured the same amount of energy absorbed by the jar at the distance you measured to the lamp. In other words, your jar absorbed as much energy from the sun at a distance of 150 million kilometers as it did from the 100 W light bulb at the distance you recorded in step 17.

19. Use the following formula to calculate the power of the sun (be sure to show your work):

$$\frac{\text{power of the sun}}{(\text{distance to the sun})^2} = \frac{\text{power of the lamp}}{(\text{distance to the lamp})^2}$$

Hint: (distance)^2 means that you multiply the distance by itself. If you found that the lamp was 5 cm away from the jar, for example, the (distance)^2 would be 25.

Hint: Convert 150,000,000 km to 15,000,000,000,000 cm.

20. Review the discussion of scientific notation in the Math Refresher found in the Appendix at the back of this book. You will need to understand this technique for writing large numbers in order to compare your calculation with the actual figure. For practice, convert the distance to the sun given in step 19 to scientific notation.

15,000,000,000,000 cm = $1.5 \times 10^{\underline{?}}$ cm

21. The sun emits 3.7×10^{26} W of power. Compare your answer in step 19 with this value. Was this a good way to calculate the power of the sun? Explain.

Convection Connection

Some scientists think convection currents within the Earth's mantle are responsible for the movement of tectonic plates. Because these convection currents cannot be observed, scientists use models to simulate the process. In this activity, you will make your own model to simulate tectonic-plate movement.

Materials

- heat-resistant gloves
- 2 small hot plates
- rectangular aluminum pan
- wooden blocks
- cold water
- 2 craft sticks
- pencil
- metric ruler
- food coloring
- 3 thermometers

Procedure

1. Place two hot plates side by side in the center of your lab table. Be sure they are safely away from the edge of the table.

2. Place the pan on top of the hot plates. Slide the wooden blocks under the pan to support the ends. Make sure the pan is level and secure.

3. Fill the pan with cold water. The water should be at least 4 cm deep. Turn on the hot plates, and put on your gloves.

4. After a minute or two, tiny bubbles will begin to rise in the water above the hot plates. Gently place two craft sticks on the water's surface.

5. Use the pencil to align the sticks parallel to the short ends of the pan. The sticks should be about 3 cm apart and near the center of the pan.

6. As soon as the sticks begin to move, place a drop of food coloring in the water at the center of the pan. Observe what happens to the food coloring.

7. With the help of a partner, hold one thermometer bulb just under the water at the center of the pan. Hold the other two thermometers just under the water near the ends of the pan. Record the temperatures.

8. When you are finished, turn off the hot plates. After the water has completely cooled, carefully empty the water into a sink.

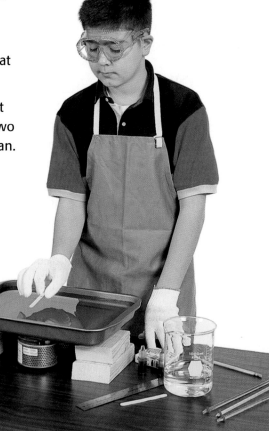

Analysis

9. Based on your observations of the motion of the food coloring, how does the temperature of the water affect the direction the water moves?

10. How does the motion of the craft sticks relate to the motion of the water?

11. How does this model relate to plate tectonics and the movement of the continents?

Oh, the Pressure!

When scientists want to understand natural processes, such as mountain formation, they often make models to help them. Models are useful in studying how rocks react to the forces of plate tectonics. In a short amount of time, a model can demonstrate geological processes that take millions of years. Do the following activity to find out how folding and faulting occur in the Earth's crust.

Materials

- modeling clay in 4 different colors
- 5 × 15 cm strip of poster board
- soup can or rolling pin
- newspaper
- colored pencils
- plastic knife
- 5 × 5 cm squares of poster board (2)

SCIENTIFIC METHOD

Ask a Question

1. How do synclines, anticlines, and faults form?

Conduct an Experiment

2. Use modeling clay of one color to form a long cylinder, and place the cylinder in the center of the glossy side of the poster-board strip.

3. Mold the clay to the strip. Try to make the clay layer the same thickness all along the strip; you can use the soup can or rolling pin to even it out. Pinch the sides of the clay so that it is the same width and length as the strip. Your strip should be at least 15 cm long and 5 cm wide.

4. Flip the strip over on the newspaper your teacher has placed across your desk. Carefully peel the strip from the modeling clay.

5. Repeat steps 2–4 with the other colors of modeling clay. Each member of your group should have a turn molding the clay. Each time you flip the strip over, stack the new clay layer on top of the previous one. When you are finished, you should have a block of clay made of four layers.

6. Lift the block of clay and hold it parallel to and just above the tabletop. Push gently on the block from opposite sides, as shown below.

7. Use the colored pencils to draw the results of step 6 in your ScienceLog. Use the terms *syncline* and *anticline* to label your diagram. Draw arrows to show the direction that each edge of the clay was pushed.

8. Repeat steps 2–5 to form a second block of clay.

9. Cut the second block of clay in two at a 45° angle as seen from the side of the block.

10. Press one poster-board square on the angled end of each of the block's two pieces. The poster board represents a fault. The two angled ends represent a hanging wall and a footwall. The model should resemble the one in the photograph on the next page.

11. Keeping the angled edges together, lift the blocks and hold them parallel to and just above the tabletop. Push gently on the two blocks until they move. Record your observations in your Sciencelog.

12. Now hold the two pieces of the clay block in their original position, and slowly pull them apart, allowing the hanging wall to move downward. Record your observations.

Analyze the Results

13. What happened to the first block of clay in step 6? What kind of force did you apply to it?

14. What happened to the pieces of the second block of clay in step 11? What kind of force did you apply to them?

15. What happened to the pieces of the second block of clay in step 12? Describe the forces that acted on the block and how the pieces of the block reacted.

Draw Conclusions

16. Summarize how the forces you applied to the blocks of clay relate to the way tectonic forces affect rock layers. Be sure to use the terms *fold, fault, anticline, syncline, hanging wall, footwall, tension,* and *compression* in your summary.

Quake Challenge

In many parts of the world, it is important that buildings be built with earthquakes in mind. Each building must be designed so that the structure is protected during an earthquake. Architects have improved the design of buildings a lot since 1906, when an earthquake destroyed much of San Francisco. In this activity you will use marshmallows and toothpicks to build a structure that can withstand a simulated earthquake. In the process, you will discover some of the ways a building can be built to withstand an earthquake.

Materials

- 10 marshmallows
- 10 toothpicks
- square of gelatin, approximately 8 × 8 cm
- paper plate

Ask a Question

1. What features help a building withstand an earthquake? How can I use this information to build my structure?

Form a Hypothesis

2. Brainstorm with a classmate to design a structure that will resist the simulated earthquake. Sketch your design in your ScienceLog. Write two or three sentences to describe your design.

Test the Hypothesis

3. Follow your design to build a structure using the toothpicks and marshmallows.

4. Set your structure on a square of gelatin.

5. Shake the square of gelatin to test whether your building will remain standing during a quake. Do not pick up the gelatin.

6. If your first design does not work well, change it until you find a design that does. Try to determine why your building is falling so that you can improve your design each time.

7. Sketch your final design in your ScienceLog.

8. After you have tested your final design, place your structure on the gelatin square on your teacher's desk.

9. When every group has added a structure to the teacher's gelatin, your teacher will simulate an earthquake by shaking the gelatin. Watch to see which buildings withstand the most severe quake.

Analyze the Results

10. Which buildings were still standing after the final earthquake? What features made them more stable?

11. How would you change your design to make your structure more stable?

Communicate Results

12. This was a simple model of a real-life problem for architects. Based on this activity, what advice would you give to those who design buildings in earthquake-prone areas?

Earthquake Waves

The energy from an earthquake travels as seismic waves in all directions through the Earth. Seismologists can use the properties of certain types of seismic waves to find the epicenter of an earthquake.

P waves travel more quickly than S waves and are always detected first. The average speed of P waves in the Earth's crust is 6.1 km/s. The average speed of S waves in the Earth's crust is 4.1 km/s. The difference in arrival time between P waves and S waves is called *lag time.*

In this activity you will use the S-P-time method to determine the location of an earthquake's epicenter.

Materials

- calculator (optional)
- compass
- metric ruler

Procedure

1. The illustration below shows seismographic records made in three cities following an earthquake. These traces begin at the left and show the arrival of P waves at time zero. The second set of waves on each record represents the arrival of S waves.

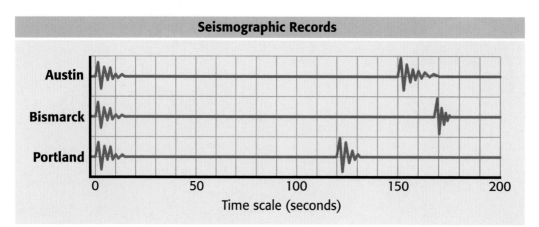

Seismographic Records

Austin

Bismarck

Portland

0   50   100   150   200

Time scale (seconds)

2. Copy the data table on the next page into your ScienceLog.

3. Use the time scale provided with the seismographic records to find the lag time between the P waves and the S waves for each city. Remember, the lag time is the time between the moment when the first P wave arrives and the moment when the first S wave arrives. Record this data in your table.

4. Use the following equation to calculate how long it takes each wave type to travel 100 km:

100 km ÷ average speed of the wave = time

5. To find lag time for earthquake waves at 100 km, subtract the time it takes P waves to travel 100 km from the time it takes S waves to travel 100 km. Record the lag time in your ScienceLog.

6. Use the following formula to find the distance from each city to the epicenter:

$$\text{distance} = \frac{\text{measured lag time (s)} \times 100 \text{ km}}{\text{lag time for 100 km (s)}}$$

In your Data Table, record the distance from each city to the epicenter.

7. Trace the map below into your ScienceLog.

8. Use the scale to adjust your compass so that the radius of a circle with Austin at the center is equal to the distance between Austin and the epicenter of the earthquake.

Epicenter Data Table		
City	Lag time (seconds)	Distance to the epicenter (km)
Austin, TX		
Bismarck, ND		
Portland, OR		

DO NOT WRITE IN BOOK

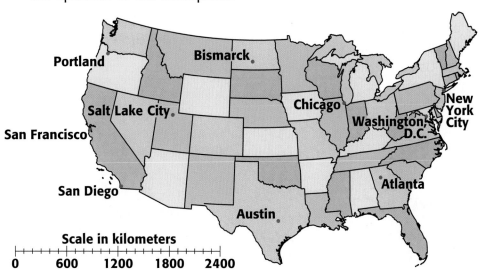

Scale in kilometers
0   600   1200   1800   2400

9. Put the point of your compass at Austin on your copy of the map, and draw a circle.

10. Repeat steps 8 and 9 for Bismarck and Portland. The epicenter of the earthquake is located near the point where the three circles meet.

Analysis

11. Which city is closest to the epicenter?

12. Why do seismologists need measurements from three different locations to find the epicenter of an earthquake?

Some Go "Pop," Some Do Not

DISCOVERY LAB

Volcanic eruptions range from mild to violent. When volcanoes erupt, the materials left behind provide information to scientists studying the Earth's crust. Mild, or nonexplosive, eruptions produce thin, runny lava that is low in silica. During nonexplosive eruptions, lava simply flows down the side of the volcano. Explosive eruptions, on the other hand, do not produce much lava. Instead, the explosions hurl ash and debris into the air. The materials left behind are light in color and high in silica. These materials help geologists determine the composition of the crust underneath the volcanoes.

Materials

- graph paper
- metric ruler
- red, yellow, and orange colored pencils or markers

Procedure

1. Copy the map below onto graph paper. Take care to line the grid up properly.

2. Locate each volcano from the list on the next page by drawing a circle with a diameter of about 1 cm in the proper location on your copy of the map. Use the latitude and longitude grids to help you.

3. Review all the eruptions for each volcano. For each explosive eruption, color the circle red. For each quiet volcano, color the circle yellow. For volcanoes that have erupted in both ways, color the circle orange.

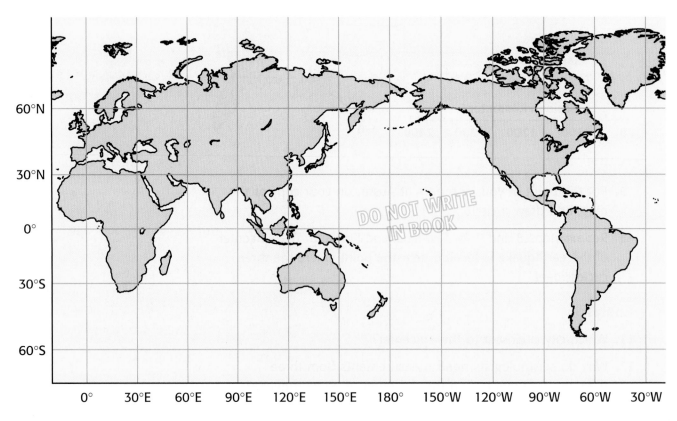

60°N   30°N   0°   30°S   60°S

0°   30°E   60°E   90°E   120°E   150°E   180°   150°W   120°W   90°W   60°W   30°W

Volcanic Activity Chart

Volcano name	Location	Description
Mount St. Helens	46°N 122°W	An explosive eruption blew the top off the mountain. Light-colored ash covered thousands of square kilometers. Another eruption sent a lava flow down the southeast side of the mountain.
Kilauea	19°N 155°W	One small eruption sent a lava flow along 12 km of highway.
Rabaul caldera	4°S 152°E	Explosive eruptions have caused tsunamis and have left 1–2 m of ash on nearby buildings.
Popocatépetl	19°N 98°W	During one explosion, Mexico City closed the airport for 14 hours because huge columns of ash made it too difficult for pilots to see. Eruptions from this volcano have also caused damaging avalanches.
Soufriere Hills	16°N 62°W	Small eruptions have sent lava flows down the hills. Other explosive eruptions have sent large columns of ash into the air.
Long Valley caldera	37°N 119°W	Explosive eruptions have sent ash into the air.
Okmok	53°N 168°W	Recently, there have been slow lava flows from this volcano. Twenty-five hundred years ago, ash and debris exploded from the top of this volcano.
Pavlof	55°N 161°W	Eruption clouds have been sent 200 m above the summit. Eruptions have sent ash columns 10 km into the air. Occasionally, small eruptions have caused lava flows.
Fernandina	42°N 12°E	Eruptions have ejected large blocks of rock from this volcano.
Mount Pinatubo	15°N 120°E	Ash and debris from an explosive eruption destroyed homes, crops, and roads within 52,000 km^2 around the volcano.

Analysis

4. According to your map, where are volcanoes that always have nonexplosive eruptions located?

5. Where are volcanoes that always erupt explosively located?

6. Where are volcanoes that erupt in both ways located?

7. If volcanoes get their magma from the crust below them, what can you say about the silica content of Earth's crust under the oceans?

8. What is the composition of the crust under the continents? How do we know?

9. What is the source of materials for volcanoes that erupt in both ways? How do you know?

10. Do the locations of volcanoes that erupt in both ways make sense based on your answers to questions 7 and 8? Explain.

Going Further

Volcanoes are present on other planets. If a planet had only nonexplosive volcanoes on its surface, what would we be able to infer about the planet? If a planet had volcanoes that ranged from nonexplosive to explosive, what might that tell us about the planet?

Volcano Verdict

You will need to pair up with a partner for this exploration. You and your partner will act as geologists who work in a city located near a volcano. City officials are counting on you to predict when the volcano will erupt next. You and your partner have decided to use limewater as a gas-emissions tester. You will use this tester to measure the levels of carbon dioxide emitted from a simulated volcano. The more active the volcano is, the more carbon dioxide it releases.

Materials

- 1 L of limewater
- 9 oz clear plastic cup
- graduated cylinder
- 100 mL of water
- 140 mL of white vinegar
- 16 oz drink bottle
- modeling clay
- flexible drinking straw
- 15 mL of baking soda
- 2 sheets of bathroom tissue
- coin
- box or stand for plastic cup

Procedure

1. Put on your safety goggles, and carefully pour limewater into the plastic cup until the cup is three-fourths full. This is your gas-emissions tester.

2. Now build a model volcano. Begin by pouring 50 mL of water and 70 mL of vinegar into the drink bottle.

3. Form a plug of clay around the short end of the straw, as shown below. The clay plug must be large enough to cover the opening of the bottle. Be careful not to get the clay wet.

4. Sprinkle 5 mL of baking soda along the center of a single section of bathroom tissue. Then roll the tissue and twist the ends so that the baking soda can't fall out.

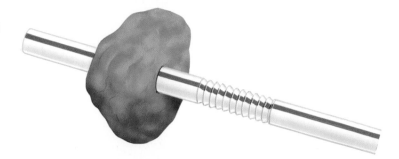

5. Drop the tissue into the drink bottle, and immediately put the short end of the straw inside the bottle, making a seal with the clay.

6. Put the other end of the straw into the limewater, as shown at right.

7. You have just taken your first measurement of gas levels from the volcano. Record your observations in your ScienceLog.

8. Imagine that it is several days later and you need to test the volcano again to collect more data. Before you continue, toss a coin. If it lands heads up, go to step 9a. If it lands tails up, go to step 9b. Write the step you take in your ScienceLog.

9a. Repeat steps 1–7. This time add 2 mL of baking soda to the vinegar and water. **Note:** You must use fresh water, vinegar, and limewater. Describe your observations in your ScienceLog. Go to step 10.

9b. Repeat steps 1–7. This time add 8 mL of baking soda to the vinegar and water. **Note:** You must use fresh water, vinegar, and limewater. Describe your observations in your ScienceLog. Go to step 10.

Analysis

10. How do you explain the difference in the appearance of the limewater from one trial to the next?

11. What do your measurements indicate about the activity in the volcano?

12. Based on your results, do you think it would be necessary to evacuate the city?

13. How would a geologist use a gas-emissions tester to forecast volcanic eruptions?

Feel the Heat

Energy is transferred between objects at different temperatures. Energy moves from objects at higher temperatures to objects at lower temperatures. If two objects are left in contact for a while, the warmer object will cool down, and the cooler object will warm up until they eventually reach the same temperature. In this activity, you will combine equal masses of water and iron nails at different temperatures to determine which has a greater effect on the final temperature.

Make a Prediction

1. When you combine substances at two different temperatures, will the final temperature be closer to the initial temperature of the warmer substance, the colder substance, or halfway in between? Write your prediction in your ScienceLog.

Conduct an Experiment/Collect Data

2. Copy the table below into your ScienceLog.

Materials

- rubber band
- 10–12 nails
- metric balance
- 30 cm of string
- 9 oz plastic-foam cups (2)
- hot water
- 100 mL graduated cylinder
- cold water
- thermometer
- paper towels

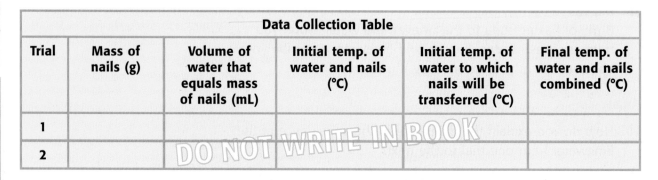

		Data Collection Table			
Trial	Mass of nails (g)	Volume of water that equals mass of nails (mL)	Initial temp. of water and nails (°C)	Initial temp. of water to which nails will be transferred (°C)	Final temp. of water and nails combined (°C)
1					
2					

3. Use the rubber band to bundle the nails together. Find and record the mass of the bundle. Tie a length of string around the bundle, leaving one end 15 cm long.

4. Put the bundle of nails into one of the cups, letting the string dangle outside the cup. Fill the cup with enough hot water to cover the nails, and set it aside for at least 5 minutes.

5. Use the graduated cylinder to measure enough cold water to exactly equal the mass of the nails (1 mL of water = 1 g). Record this volume in the table.

6. Measure and record the temperature of the hot water with the nails and the temperature of the cold water.

7. Use the string to transfer the bundle of nails to the cup of cold water. Use the thermometer to monitor the temperature of the water-nail mixture. When the temperature stops changing, record this as the final temperature in the table.

8. Empty the cups, and dry the nails.

9. For Trial 2, repeat steps 3 through 8, but this time switch the hot and cold water. Record all your measurements.

Analyze the Results

10. In Trial 1, you used equal masses of cold water and nails. Did the final temperature support your initial prediction? Explain.

11. In Trial 2 you used equal masses of hot water and nails. Did the final temperature support your initial prediction? Explain.

12. In Trial 1, which material—the water or the nails—changed temperature the most after you transferred the nails? What about in Trial 2? Explain your answers.

Draw Conclusions

13. The cold water in Trial 1 gained energy. Where did the energy come from?

14. How does the energy gained by the nails in Trial 2 compare with the energy lost by the hot water in Trial 2? Explain.

15. Which material seems to be able to hold energy better? Explain your answer.

16. Specific heat capacity is a property of matter that tells how much energy is required to change the temperature of 1 kg of a material by 1°C. Which material in this activity has a higher specific heat capacity (changes temperature less for the same amount of energy)?

17. Would it be better to have pots and pans made from a material with a high specific heat capacity or a low specific heat capacity? Explain your answer. (Hint: Do you want the pan or the food in the pan to absorb all the energy from the stove?)

Communicate Results

18. Share your results with your classmates. Discuss how you would change your prediction to include your knowledge of specific heat capacity.

Save the Cube!

The biggest enemy of an ice cube is the transfer of thermal energy—heat. Energy can be transferred to an ice cube in three ways: conduction (the transfer of energy through direct contact), convection (the transfer of energy by the movement of a liquid or gas), and radiation (the transfer of energy through space). Your challenge in this activity is to design a way to protect an ice cube as much as possible from all three types of energy transfer.

Materials

- small plastic bag
- ice cube
- assorted materials provided by your teacher
- empty half-pint milk carton
- metric balance
- small plastic or paper cup

Procedure

1. The guidelines for your design are as follows: You must use a plastic bag to hold the ice cube and any water from its melting. You may use any of the available materials to protect the ice cube. The ice cube, bag, and protection must be small enough to all fit inside the milk carton.

2. Write a description of your proposed design in your ScienceLog. Be sure to describe how your design protects against each type of energy transfer.

3. Find the mass of the empty cup, and record it in your ScienceLog. Then find and record the mass of an empty plastic bag.

4. Place an ice cube in the bag. Quickly find and record their mass together.

5. Quickly wrap the bag (and the ice cube inside) with the protection. Remember that the package must fit in the milk carton.

6. Place your protected ice cube in the "thermal zone" set up by your teacher. After 10 minutes, carefully remove the protected cube from the thermal zone, and remove the protection from the plastic bag and ice cube.

7. Open the bag. Pour any water into the cup. Find and record the mass of the cup and water together.

8. Find and record the mass of the water by subtracting the mass of the empty cup from the mass of the cup and water.

9. Find and record the mass of the ice cube by subtracting the mass of the empty bag from the mass of the bag and ice cube.

10. Find the percentage of the ice cube that melted using the following equation:

$$\% \text{ melted} = \frac{\text{mass of water}}{\text{mass of ice cube}} \times 100$$

11. Record your percentage in your ScienceLog and on the board.

Analysis

12. Describe how well your design protected against each type of energy transfer compared with other designs in your class. How could you improve your design?

13. Why is a white plastic-foam cooler so useful for keeping ice frozen?

Counting Calories

Energy transferred by heat is often expressed in units called calories. In this lab, you will build a model of a device called a calorimeter. Scientists often use calorimeters to measure the amount of energy that can be transferred by a substance. In this experiment, you will construct your own calorimeter and test it by measuring the energy released by a hot penny.

Materials

- small plastic-foam cup with lid
- thermometer
- large plastic-foam cup
- water
- 100 mL graduated cylinder
- tongs
- heat source
- penny
- stopwatch

Procedure

1. Copy the table below into your ScienceLog.

Data Collection Table

Seconds	0	15	30	45	60	75	90	105	120
Water temp. (°C)									

DO NOT WRITE IN BOOK

2. Place the lid on the small plastic-foam cup, and insert a thermometer through the hole in the top of the lid. (The thermometer should not touch the bottom of the cup.) Place the small cup inside the large cup to complete the calorimeter.

3. Remove the lid from the small cup, and add 50 mL of room-temperature water to the cup. Measure the water's temperature, and record the value in the 0 seconds column of the table.

4. Using tongs, heat the penny carefully. Add the penny to the water in the small cup, and replace the lid. Start your stopwatch.

5. Every 15 seconds, measure and record the temperature. Gently swirl the large cup to stir the water, and continue recording temperatures for 2 minutes (120 seconds).

Analysis

6. What was the total temperature change of the water after 2 minutes?

7. The number of calories absorbed by water is the mass of the water (in grams) multiplied by the temperature change (in °C) of the water. How many calories were absorbed by the water? (Hint: 1 mL of water = 1 g of water.)

8. In terms of heat, explain where the calories to change the water temperature came from.

Water Cycle—
What Goes Up . . .

Why does a bathroom mirror "fog up"? What happens when water "dries up"? Where does rain come from, and why doesn't it just "run out"? These questions relate to the major parts of the water cycle—condensation, evaporation, and precipitation. In this activity, you will make a model of the water cycle and watch water as it moves through the model.

Materials

- graduated cylinder
- 50 mL of tap water
- heat-resistant gloves
- beaker
- hot plate
- glass plate or watch glass
- tongs or forceps

Procedure

1. Use the graduated cylinder to pour 50 mL of water into the beaker. Note the water level in the beaker.

2. Put on your gloves, and place the beaker securely on the hot plate. Turn on the heat to medium, and bring the water to a boil.

3. While waiting for the water to boil, practice picking up and handling the glass plate or watch glass with the tongs. Hold the glass plate a few centimeters above the beaker, and tilt it so that the lowest edge of the glass is still above the beaker.

4. Observe the glass plate as the water in the beaker heats. In your ScienceLog, write down the changes you see in the beaker, in the air above the beaker, and on the glass plate held over the beaker. Write down any changes you see in the water.

5. Continue until you have observed steam rising off the water, the glass plate above the beaker becoming foggy, and water dripping from the glass plate.

6. Carefully set the glass plate on a counter or other safe surface as directed by your teacher.

7. Turn off the hot plate, and allow the beaker to cool. Move the hot beaker with gloves or tongs if directed to do so by your teacher.

8. Copy the illustration shown on the next page into your ScienceLog. On your sketch, draw and label the water cycle as it occurred in your model. Include arrows and labels for condensation, evaporation, and precipitation.

Analysis

9. Compare the water level in the beaker now with the water level at the beginning of the experiment. Was there a change? Explain why or why not.

10. If you had used a scale or balance to measure the mass of the water in the beaker before and after this activity, would the mass have changed? Why or why not?

11. How is your model similar to the Earth's water cycle? On your sketch of the illustration above, label where the processes shown in the model mimic the Earth's water cycle.

12. When you finished this experiment, the water in the beaker was still hot. What stores much of the heat in the Earth's water cycle?

Going Further

As rainwater runs over the land, the rainwater picks up minerals and salts. Do these minerals and salts evaporate, condense, and precipitate as part of the water cycle? Where do they go?

If the average global temperature on Earth gets warmer, how would you expect sea levels to change, and why? What if the average global temperature cools?

Clean Up Your Act

When you wash dishes, the family car, the bathroom sink, or your clothes, you wash them with water. But have you ever wondered how water gets clean? Two major methods of purifying water are filtration and evaporation. In this activity you will use both of these methods to test how well they remove pollutants from water. You will test detritus (decaying plant matter), soil, vinegar, and detergent. Your teacher may also ask you to test other pollutants.

SCIENTIFIC METHOD

Form a Hypothesis

1. Form a hypothesis about whether filtration and evaporation will clean each of the four pollutants from the water and how well they might do it. Then use the procedures below to test your hypothesis.

Method 1: Filtration

Filtration is a common method of removing various pollutants from water. It requires very little energy—gravity pulls water down through the layers of filter material. See how well this energy-efficient method works to clean your sample of polluted water.

Conduct an Experiment

2. Put on your gloves and goggles. Use scissors to cut the bottom out of the empty soda bottle carefully.

3. Carefully punch four or five small holes through the plastic cap of the bottle using a small nail and hammer. Screw the plastic cap onto the bottle.

4. Turn the bottle upside down, and set its neck in a ring on a ring stand, as shown on the next page. Put a handful of gravel into the inverted bottle. Add a layer of activated charcoal, followed by thick layers of sand and gravel. Place a 400 mL beaker under the neck of the bottle.

5. Fill each of the large beakers with 1,000 mL of clean water. Set one beaker aside to serve as the control. Add three or four spoonfuls of each of the following pollutants to the other beaker: detritus, soil, household vinegar, and dishwashing detergent.

Materials

- scissors
- plastic 2 L soda bottle with cap
- small nail
- hammer
- ring stand with ring
- gravel
- activated charcoal
- sand
- 400 mL beakers (2)
- 2,000 mL of water
- 1,000 mL beakers (2)
- detritus (grass and leaf clippings)
- soil
- household vinegar
- dishwashing detergent
- hand lens
- 2 plastic spoons
- pH test strips
- Erlenmeyer flask
- one-hole rubber stopper with a glass tube
- 1.5 m of plastic tubing
- heat-resistant gloves
- hot plate
- sealable plastic sandwich bag
- ice

Collect Data

6. Copy the table below into your ScienceLog, and record your observations for each beaker in the columns labeled "Before cleaning."

7. Observe the color of the water in each beaker.

8. Use a hand lens to examine the water for visible particles.

9. Smell the water, and note any unusual odors.

10. Stir the water in each beaker rapidly with a plastic spoon, and check for suds. Use a different spoon for each sample.

11. Use a pH test strip to find the pH of the water.

12. Gently stir the clean water, and then pour half of it through the filtration device.

13. Observe the water in the collection beaker for color, particles, odors, suds, and pH. Be patient. It may take several minutes for the water to travel through the filtration device.

14. Record your observations in the appropriate "After filtration" column in your table.

15. Repeat steps 12–14 using the polluted water.

Results Table						
	Before cleaning (clean water)	**Before cleaning (polluted water)**	**After filtration (clean water)**	**After filtration (polluted water)**	**After evaporation (clean water)**	**After evaporation (polluted water)**
Color						
Particles						
Odor						
Suds						
pH						

DO NOT WRITE IN BOOK

Analyze the Results

16. How did the color of the polluted water change after the filtration? Did the color of the clean water change?

17. Did the filtration method remove all of the particles from the polluted water? Explain.

18. How much did the pH of the polluted water change? Did the pH of the clean water change? Was the final pH of the polluted water the same as the pH of the clean water before cleaning? Explain.

Method 2: Evaporation

Cleaning water by evaporation is more expensive than cleaning water by filtration. Evaporation requires more energy, which can come from a variety of sources. In this activity, you will use an electric hot plate as the energy source. See how well this method works to clean your sample of polluted water.

Conduct an Experiment

19. Fill an Erlenmeyer flask with about 250 mL of the clean water, and insert the rubber stopper and glass tube into the flask.

20. Wearing goggles and gloves, connect about 1.5 m of plastic tubing to the glass tube.

21. Set the flask on the hot plate, and run the plastic tubing up and around the ring and down into a clean, empty 400 mL collection beaker.

22. Fill the sandwich bag with ice, seal the bag, and place the bag on the ring stand. Be sure the plastic bag and the tubing touch, as shown below.

23. Bring the water in the flask to a slow boil. As the water vapor passes by the bag of ice, the vapor will condense and drip into the collection beaker.

Collect Data

24. Observe the water in the collection beaker for color, particles, odor, suds, and pH. Record your observations in the appropriate "After evaporation" column in your data table.

25. Repeat steps 23–24 using the polluted water.

Analyze the Results

26. How did the color of the polluted water change after evaporation? Did the color of the clean water change after evaporation?

27. Did the evaporation method remove all of the particles from the polluted water? Explain.

28. How much did the pH of the polluted water change? Did the pH of the final clean water change? Was the final pH of the polluted water the same as the pH of the clean water before it was cleaned? Explain.

Draw Conclusions

29. Which method—filtration or evaporation—removed the most pollutants from the water? Explain your reasoning.

30. Describe any changes that occurred in the clean water during this experiment.

31. What do you think are the advantages and disadvantages of each method?

32. Explain how you think each material (sand, gravel, and charcoal) used in the filtration system helped clean the water.

33. List areas of the country where you think each method of purification would be the most and the least beneficial. Explain your reasoning.

Going Further

Do you think either purification method would remove oil from water? If time permits, repeat your experiment using several spoonfuls of cooking oil as the pollutant.

Filtration is only one step in the purification of water at water-treatment plants. Research other methods used to purify public water supplies.

Dune Movement

Have you ever heard news reporters talk about a hurricane or a thunderstorm that eroded a beach? Wind is always moving the sand along a beach. However, big storms produce strong winds that erode a beach and sand dunes more quickly than usual. Wind moves the sand by a process called *saltation.* The sand skips and bounces along the ground in the direction the wind is blowing. As the sand is blown across the beach, the dunes change. In this activity, you will investigate the effect wind has on a model sand dune.

Materials

- marker
- metric ruler
- shallow cardboard box
- fine sand
- paper bag, large enough to hold half the box
- filter mask
- hair dryer
- watch or clock that indicates seconds

Procedure

1. Use the marker to draw and label vertical lines 5 cm apart along one side of the box.

2. Fill the box about halfway with sand. Brush the sand into a dune shape about 10 cm from the end of the box.

3. Use the lines you drew along the edge of the box to measure the location of the dune's peak to the nearest centimeter.

4. Slide the box into the paper bag until only about half the box is exposed, as shown below.

5. Put on your safety goggles and filter mask. Hold the hair dryer so that it is level with the peak of the dune and about 10–20 cm from the open end of the box.

6. Turn on the hair dryer at the lowest speed, and direct the air toward the model sand dune for 1 minute.

7. Record the new location of the model dune in your ScienceLog.

8. Repeat steps 5 and 6 three times. After each trial, measure and record the location of the dune's peak.

Analysis

9. How far did the dune move during each trial?

10. How far did the dune move overall?

11. How might the dune's movement be affected if you were to turn the hair dryer to the highest speed?

Going Further

Flatten the sand. Place a barrier, such as a rock, in the sand. Position the hair dryer level with the top of the sand's surface. How does the rock affect the dune's movement?

Gliding Glaciers

A glacier is large moving mass of ice. Glaciers are responsible for shaping many of the Earth's natural features. Glaciers are set in motion by the pull of gravity. As a glacier moves it changes the landscape, eroding the surface over which it passes.

Materials

- 3 empty margarine containers
- sand
- gravel
- metric ruler
- water
- freezer
- rolling pin
- modeling clay
- small towel
- 3 bricks
- 3 pans
- 50 mL graduated cylinder
- timer

Slip-Sliding Away

The material that is carried by a glacier erodes the Earth's surface, gouging out grooves called *striations.* Different materials have varying effects on the landscape. By creating a model glacier, you will demonstrate the effects of glacial erosion by various materials.

Procedure

1. Fill one margarine container with sand to a depth of 1 cm. Fill another margarine container with gravel to a depth of 1 cm. Leave the third container empty. Fill the containers with water.

2. Put the three containers in a freezer, and leave them overnight.

3. Retrieve the containers from the freezer, and remove the three ice blocks from the containers.

4. Use a rolling pin to flatten the modeling clay.

5. Hold the plain ice block firmly with a towel, and press as you move it along the length of the clay. Do this three times. In your ScienceLog, sketch the pattern the ice block makes in the clay.

6. Repeat steps 4 and 5 with the ice block that contains sand. Sketch the pattern this ice block makes in the clay.

7. Repeat steps 4 and 5 with the ice block that contains gravel. Sketch the pattern this ice block makes in the clay.

Analysis

8. Did any material from the clay become mixed with the material in the ice blocks? Explain.

9. Was any material deposited on the clay surface? Explain.

10. What glacial features are represented in your clay model?

11. Compare the patterns formed by the three model glaciers. Do the patterns look like features carved by alpine glaciers or by continental glaciers? Explain.

Going Further

Replace the clay with different materials, such as soft wood or sand. How does each ice block affect the different surface materials? What types of surfaces do the different materials represent?

Slippery When Wet

As the layers of ice build up and the glacier gets larger, the glacier will eventually begin to melt. The water from the melted ice allows the glacier to move forward. In this activity, you'll learn about the effect of pressure on the melting rate of a glacier.

Procedure

12. Place one ice block upside down in each pan.

13. Place one brick on top of one of the ice blocks. Place two bricks on top of another ice block. Leave the third ice block alone.

14. After 15 minutes, remove the bricks from the ice blocks.

15. Measure the amount of water that has melted from each ice block using the graduated cylinder.

16. Record your findings in your ScienceLog.

Analysis

17. Which ice block produced the most water?

18. What did the bricks represent?

19. What part of the ice block melted first? Explain.

20. How could you relate this investigation to the melting rate of glaciers? Explain.

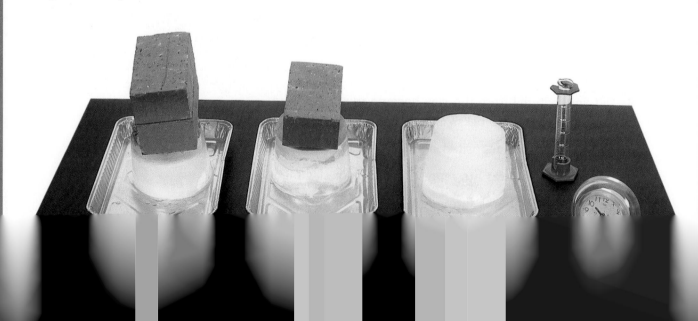

Creating a Kettle

As glaciers recede, they leave huge amounts of rock material behind. Sometimes receding glaciers form moraines by depositing some of the rock material in ridges. At other times, glaciers leave chunks of ice that form depressions called *kettles*. These depressions may form ponds or lakes. In this activity, you will create your own kettle and discover how they are formed by glaciers.

Materials

- small tub
- sand
- 4–5 ice cubes of various sizes
- metric ruler

Ask a Question

1. How are kettles formed?

Conduct an Experiment

2. Fill the tub three-quarters full with sand.

3. In your ScienceLog, describe the size and shape of the ice cubes.

4. Push the ice cubes to various depths in the sand.

5. Put the tub where it won't be disturbed overnight.

Make Observations

6. Look for the ice cubes the next day. Closely observe the sand around the area where you left each ice cube.

7. What happened to the ice cubes?

8. Use a metric ruler to measure the depth and diameter of the indentation left by the ice cubes.

Analyze the Results

9. How does this model relate to the size and shape of a natural kettle?

10. In what ways are your model kettles similar to real ones? How are they different?

Draw Conclusions

11. Based on your model, what can you conclude about the formation of kettles by receding glaciers?

Capturing the Wild Bean

When wildlife biologists study a group of organisms in an area, one of the things they need to know is how many organisms there are in the area. Occasionally, biologists worry that a certain organism is outgrowing the environment's carrying capacity. Other times, scientists need to know if an organism is becoming rare so steps can be taken to protect it. However, animals can be difficult to count because they can move around and hide. Because of this, biologists have developed methods to estimate the number of animals in a specific area. One of these counting methods is called the mark-recapture method.

In this activity, you will enter the territory of the wild pinto bean to get an estimation of the number of beans that live in their paper-bag habitat.

Materials

- small paper lunch bag
- pinto beans
- permanent marker
- pencil
- calculator

Procedure

1. Prepare a data table in your ScienceLog like the one below.

Mark-Recapture Data Table				
Number of animals in first capture	Total number of animals in recapture	Number of marked animals in recapture	Calculated estimate of population	Actual total population
	DO NOT WRITE IN BOOK			

2. Your teacher will provide you with a paper bag containing an unknown number of beans. Carefully reach into the bag and remove a handful of beans.

3. Count the number of beans you have "captured," and record this number in your data table under "Number of animals in first capture."

4. Use the permanent marker to carefully mark each bean that you have just counted. Allow the marks to dry completely. When you are certain that all the marks are dry, place the marked beans back into the bag.

5. Gently mix the beans in the bag so the marks won't rub off. Once again, reach into the bag, "capture," and remove a handful of beans.

6. Count the total number of beans in your "recapture." Record this number in your data table under "Total number of animals in recapture."

7. Count the number of beans in your recapture that have marks on them from the first capture. Record this number in your data table under "Number of marked animals in recapture."

8. Calculate your estimation of the total number of beans in the bag using the following equation:

$$\frac{\text{total number of beans in recapture} \times \text{total number of beans marked}}{\text{number of marked beans in recapture}} = \begin{array}{c}\text{calculated estimate of}\\\text{population}\end{array}$$

Enter this number in your data table under "Calculated estimate of population."

9. Replace all the beans in the bag. Then empty the bag on your work table. Be careful that no beans escape! Count each bean as you place them one at a time back into the bag. Record the number in your data table under "Actual total population."

Analysis

10. How close was your estimate to the actual number of beans?

11. If your estimate was not close to the actual number of beans, how might you change your mark-recapture procedure? If you did not recapture any marked beans, what might be the cause?

Going Further

How could you use the mark-recapture method to estimate the population of turtles in a small pond? Explain your procedure.

Adaptation: It's a Way of Life

MAKING MODELS

Since the beginning of life on Earth, species have had special characteristics called adaptations that have helped them survive changes in environmental conditions. Changes in a species' environment include climate changes, habitat destruction, or the extinction of prey. These things can cause a species to die out unless the species has a characteristic that helps it survive. For example, a species of bird may have an adaptation for eating sunflower seeds and ants. If the ant population dies out, the bird can still eat seeds and can therefore survive.

In this activity, you will explore several adaptations and design an organism with adaptations you choose. Then you will describe how these adaptations help the organism survive.

Materials

- poster board
- colored markers
- scissors
- magazines for cutouts
- other arts-and-crafts materials

Procedure

1. Study the chart below. Choose one adaptation from each column. For example, an organism might be a scavenger that burrows underground and has spikes on its tail!

Adaptations		
Diet	**Type of transportation**	**Special adaptation**
carnivore	flies	uses sensors to detect heat
herbivore	glides through the air	is active only at night and has excellent night vision
omnivore	burrows underground	changes colors to match its surroundings
scavenger	runs fast	has armor
decomposer	swims	has horns
	hops	can withstand extreme temperature changes
	walks	secretes a terrible and sickening scent
	climbs	has poison glands
	floats	has specialized front teeth
	slithers	has tail spikes
		stores oxygen in its cells so it does not have to breathe continuously
		one of your own invention

2. Design an organism that has the three adaptations you have chosen. Use poster board, colored markers, picture cutouts, or craft materials of your choosing to create your organism.

3. Write a caption on your poster describing your organism. Describe its appearance, its habitat, its niche, and how its adaptations help it survive. Give your animal a two-part "scientific" name based on its characteristics.

4. Display your creation in your classroom. Share with classmates how you chose the adaptations for your organism.

Analysis

5. What does your imaginary organism eat?

6. In what environment or habitat would your organism be most likely to survive—in the desert, tropical rain forest, plains, ice-caps, mountains, or ocean? Explain your answer.

7. Is your creature a mammal, a reptile, an amphibian, a bird, or a fish? What modern organism (on Earth today) or ancient organism (extinct) is your imaginary organism most like? Explain the similarities between the two organisms. Do some research outside of the lab, if necessary, to find out about a real organism that your imaginary organism may be similar to.

8. If a sudden climate change occurred, such as daily downpours of rain in a desert, would your imaginary organism survive? What adaptations for surviving such a change does it have?

Going Further

Call or write to an agency such as the U.S. Fish and Wildlife Service to get a list of endangered species in your area. Choose an organism on that list. Describe the organism's niche and any special adaptations it has that help it survive. Find out why it is endangered and what is being done to protect it.

Examine the illustration of the animal at right. Based on its physical characteristics, describe its habitat and niche. Is this a real animal?

Probing the Depths

In the 1870s, the crew of the ship the HMS *Challenger* used a wire and a weight to discover and map some of the deepest places in the world's oceans. Scientists tied a wire to a weight and dropped the weight overboard. When the weight reached the bottom of the ocean, they hauled the weight back up to the surface and measured the length of the wet wire. In this way, they were eventually able to map the ocean floor.

In this activity, you will model this traditional method of mapping by making a map of an ocean-floor model.

Materials

- modeling clay
- shoe box and lid
- scissors
- 8 unsharpened pencils
- metric ruler

Procedure

1. Use the clay to make a model ocean floor in the shoe box. Give the floor some mountains and valleys.

2. Cut eight holes in a line along the center of the lid. The holes should be just big enough to slide a pencil through. Close the box.

3. Exchange boxes with another student or group of students. Do not look into the box.

4. Copy the data table below into your ScienceLog. Also make a copy of the graph on the next page.

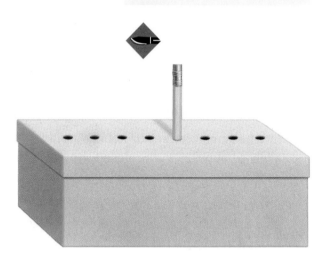

Ocean Depth Chart				
Hole position	Original length of probe	Amount of probe showing	Depth in centimeters	Depth in meters (cm × 200)
1				
2				
3				
4				
5				
6				
7				
8				

DO NOT WRITE IN BOOK

5. Measure the length of the probe (pencil) in centimeters. Record the length in your data table.

6. Gently insert the probe into the first hole position in the box until it touches the bottom. Do not force the probe down; this could affect your reading.

7. Making sure the probe is straight up and down, measure the length of probe showing above the lid. Record your data in the data table.

8. Use the following formula to calculate the depth in centimeters:

$$\text{original length of probe} - \text{amount of probe showing} = \text{depth in cm}$$

9. Use the scale 1 cm = 200 m to convert the depth in centimeters to meters to better represent real ocean depths. Add the data to your table.

10. Transfer the data to your graph for position 1.

11. Repeat steps 6–10 for the additional positions in the box.

12. After plotting all the points onto your graph, connect the points with a smooth curve.

13. Put a pencil in each of the holes in the shoe box. Compare the rise and fall of the set of pencils with your graph.

Analysis

14. What was the depth of your deepest point? your shallowest point?

15. Did your graph resemble the ocean-floor model, as shown by the pencils? If not, why not?

16. What difficulties might scientists have when measuring the real ocean floor? Do they ever get to "open the box"? Explain.

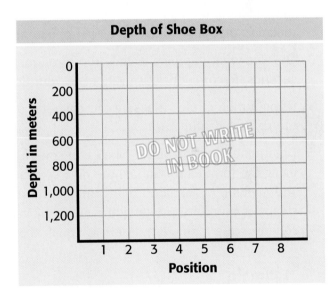

Depth of Shoe Box

DO NOT WRITE IN BOOK

Depth in meters: 0, 200, 400, 600, 800, 1,000, 1,200
Position: 1 2 3 4 5 6 7 8

Going Further

At the beginning of the twentieth century, scientists discovered that sound waves can be used to measure the depth of the ocean. By knowing the speed of sound and measuring the time it takes for the sound to travel to the bottom of the ocean and back, scientists can calculate the depth of the ocean. Do you think the speed of sound in water is constant (never changing)? If it does change, what might cause the change? How might the change affect the depth readings sonar provides?

Investigating an Oil Spill

Have you ever wondered why it is important to bring used motor oil to a recycling center rather than simply pouring it down the nearest drain or sewer? Or have you ever wondered why an oil spill of only a few thousand liters into an ocean containing many millions of liters of water can cause so much damage? The reason has to do with the fact that a little oil goes a long way.

Observing Oil and Water

You may have heard the expression "Oil and water don't mix." This is true—oil dropped on water will spread out thinly over the surface of the water. In this activity, you'll learn exactly how far oil can spread when it is in contact with water.

Procedure

1. Fill the pan two-thirds full with water. Be sure to wear your goggles and gloves.

2. Using the pipet, carefully add one drop of oil to the water in the middle of the pan. **Caution:** Machine oil is poisonous. Keep materials that have contacted oil out of your mouth and eyes.

3. Observe what happens to the drop of oil for the next few seconds. Record your observations in your ScienceLog.

4. Using a metric ruler, measure the diameter of the oil slick to the nearest centimeter.

5. Determine the area of the oil slick in square centimeters by using the formula for finding the area of a circle ($A = \pi r^2$). The radius (r) is equal to the diameter you measured in step 4 divided by 2. Multiply the radius by itself to get the square of the radius (r^2). Pi (π) is equal to 3.14.

> **Example**
> If your diameter is 10 cm,
> $r = 5$ cm, $r^2 = 25$ cm^2, $\pi = 3.14$
> $A = \pi r^2$
> $A = 3.14 \times 25$ cm^2
> $A = 78.5$ cm^2

6. Record your answers in your ScienceLog.

Materials

- safety gloves
- large pan (at least 22 cm in diameter)
- water
- pipet
- 15 mL light machine oil
- metric ruler
- graduated cylinder
- calculator (optional)

Analysis

7. What happened to the drop of oil when it came in contact with the water? Did this surprise you?

8. What total surface area was covered by the oil slick? (Be sure to show your calculations.)

9. What does this experiment tell you about the density of oil compared with the density of water? Explain.

Going Further

Can you devise a way to clean the oil from the water? Get permission from your teacher before testing your cleaning method.

Do you think oil behaves the same way in ocean water? Devise an experiment to test your hypothesis.

Finding the Number of Drops in a Liter

"It's only a few drops," you may think as you spill something toxic on the ground. But those drops eventually add up. Just how many drops does it take to make a difference? In this activity, you'll learn just what an impact a few drops can have.

Procedure

10. Using a clean pipet, count the number of water drops it takes to fill the graduated cylinder to 10 mL. Be sure to add the drops slowly so you get an accurate count.

11. Since there are 1,000 mL in a liter, multiply the number of drops in 10 mL by 100. This gives you the number of drops in a liter.

Analysis

12. How many drops of water from your pipet does it take to fill a 1 L container?

13. What would happen if someone spilled 4 L of oil into a lake?

Going Further

Find out how much oil supertankers contain. Can you imagine the size of an oil slick that would form if one of these tankers spilled its oil?

Up from the Depths

Every year, the water in certain parts of the ocean "turns over." This means that the water at the bottom rises to the top and the water at the top falls to the bottom. This yearly change brings fresh nutrients from the bottom of the ocean to the fish living near the surface. That makes it a great time for fishing! However, the water in some parts of the ocean never turns over. You will use this activity to find out why.

Some parts of the ocean are warmer at the bottom, and some are warmer at the top. Sometimes the saltiest water is at the bottom; sometimes it is not. You will investigate how these factors help determine whether the water will turn over.

Materials

- 400 mL beakers (5)
- tap water
- blue and red food coloring
- spoon
- bucket of ice
- watch or clock
- hot plate
- heat-resistant gloves
- 4 pieces of plastic wrap, approximately 30 × 20 cm
- salt

SCIENTIFIC METHOD

Ask a Question

1. Why do some parts of the ocean turn over, while others do not?

Conduct an Experiment

2. Label the beakers 1 through 5. Fill beakers 1 through 4 with tap water.

3. Add a drop of blue food coloring to the water in beakers 1 and 2. Stir.

4. Place beaker 1 in the bucket of ice for 10 minutes.

5. Add a drop of red food coloring to the water in beakers 3 and 4. Stir.

6. Set beaker 3 on a hot plate turned to a low setting for 10 minutes.

7. Add one spoonful of salt to the water in beaker 4, and stir.

8. While beaker 1 is cooling and beaker 3 is heating, copy the data table on the next page into your ScienceLog.

9. Pour half of the water in beaker 1 into beaker 5. Return beaker 1 to the bucket of ice.

10. Tuck a sheet of plastic wrap into beaker 5 so that the plastic rests on the surface of the water and lines the upper half of the beaker.

Observations Chart	
Mixture of water	**Observations**
Warm water placed above cold water	
Cold water placed above warm water	DO NOT WRITE IN BOOK
Salty water placed above fresh water	
Fresh water placed above salty water	

11. Put on your gloves. Slowly pour half of the water in beaker 3 into the plastic-lined upper half of beaker 5 to form two layers of water. Return beaker 3 to the hot plate, and remove your gloves.

12. Very carefully pull on one edge of the plastic wrap and remove it so that the warm, red water rests on the cold, blue water. **Caution:** The plastic wrap may be warm.

Make Observations

13. Wait about 5 minutes, and then observe the layers in beaker 5. Did one layer remain on top of the other? Was there any mixing or turning over? Record your observations in your data table.

14. Empty and rinse beaker 5 with clean tap water.

15. Repeat the procedure in steps 9–14, this time with warm, red water from beaker 3 on the bottom and cold, blue water from beaker 1 on top. (Use gloves when pouring warm water.)

16. Again repeat the procedure used in steps 9–14, this time with blue tap water from beaker 2 on the bottom and red, salty water from beaker 4 on top.

17. Repeat the procedure used in steps 9–14 a third time, this time with red, salty water from beaker 4 on the bottom and blue tap water from beaker 2 on top.

Analyze the Results

18. Compare the results of all four trials. Explain why the water turned over in some of the trials but not in all of them.

Draw Conclusions

19. What is the effect of temperature and salinity on the density of water?

20. What makes the temperature of ocean water decrease? What could make the salinity of ocean water increase?

21. What explanations can you give for the fact that some parts of the ocean turn over in the spring, while some do not?

Going Further

Suggest a method for setting up a model that tests the combined effects of temperature and salinity on the density of water. Consider using more than two water samples and dyes.

Turning the Tides

Daily tides are caused by two "bulges" on the ocean's surface—one on the side of the Earth facing the moon and the other on the opposite side. The bulge on the side facing the moon is caused by the moon's gravitational pull on the water. But the bulge on the opposite side is slightly more difficult to explain. Whereas the moon pulls the water on one side of the Earth, the combined rotation of the Earth and the moon "pushes" the water on the opposite side of the Earth. The sun also affects the tides, but because it is so far away from Earth, the sun's pull on the water is considerably weaker than the moon's. In this activity, you will model the motion of the Earth and the moon to investigate the tidal bulge on the side of Earth facing away from the moon.

Materials

- 2 disks of corrugated cardboard, one large and one small, with centers marked
- white glue
- piece of dowel, 1/4 in. in diameter and 36 cm long
- 5 cm length of string
- stapler with staples
- 1 × 1 cm piece of cardboard
- sharp pencil

Procedure

1. Draw a line from the center of each disk along the folds in the cardboard to the edge of the disk. This line is the radius.

2. Place a drop of white glue on one end of the dowel. Lay the larger disk flat, and align the dowel with the line for the radius you drew in step 1. Insert about 2.5 cm of the dowel into the edge of the disk.

3. Add a drop of glue to the other end of the dowel, and push that end into the smaller disk, again along its radius. The setup should look like a large two-headed lollipop, as shown below. This is a model of the Earth-moon system.

4. Staple the string to the edge of the large disk on the side opposite the dowel. Staple the cardboard square to the other end of the string. This smaller piece of cardboard represents the Earth's oceans that face away from the moon.

5. Place the tip of the pencil at the center of the large disk, as shown in the figure on the next page, and spin the model. **Caution:** Be sure you are at a safe distance from other people before spinning your model. You may poke a small hole in the bottom of the disk with your pencil, but DO NOT poke all the way through the cardboard. Record your observations in your ScienceLog.

6. Now find your model's *center of mass.* This is the point at which the model can be balanced on the end of the pencil. **Hint:** It might be easier to find the center of mass using the eraser end. Then use the sharpened end of the pencil to balance the model. This balance point should be just inside the edge of the larger disk.

7. Place the pencil at the center of mass, and spin the model around the pencil. Again, you may wish to poke a small hole in the disk. Record your observations in your ScienceLog.

Analysis

8. What happened when you tried to spin the model around the center of the large disk? This model, called the Earth-centered model, represents the incorrect view that the moon orbits the center of the Earth.

9. What happened when you tried to spin the model around its center of mass? This point, called the *barycenter,* is the point around which both the Earth and the moon rotate.

10. In each case, what happened to the string and cardboard square when the model was spun?

11. Which model—the Earth-centered model or the barycentric model—explains why the Earth has a tidal bulge on the side opposite the moon? Explain.

Moon

Earth

Tidal bulges

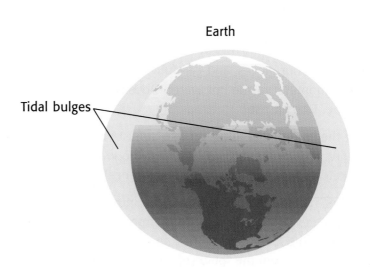

Boiling Over!

Safety Industries, Inc., would like to offer the public safer alternatives to the mercury thermometer. Many communities have complained that the glass thermometers are easy to break, and people are concerned about mercury poisoning. As a result, we would like your team of inventors to come up with a workable prototype that uses water instead of mercury. Safety Industries would like to offer a contract to the team that comes up with the best substitute for a mercury thermometer. In this activity, you will design and test your own water thermometer. Good luck!

Ask a Question

1. What conditions cause the liquid to rise in a thermometer? How can I use this information to build a thermometer?

Form a Hypothesis

2. Brainstorm with a classmate to design a thermometer that requires only water. Sketch your design in your ScienceLog. Write a one-sentence hypothesis that describes how your thermometer will work.

Test the Hypothesis

3. Follow your design to build a thermometer using only materials from the materials list. Like a mercury thermometer, your thermometer will need a bulb and a tube. However, the liquid in your thermometer will be water.

4. To test your design, place the aluminum pie pan on a hot plate. Carefully pour water into the pan until it is halfway full. Allow the water to heat.

5. Put on your gloves, and carefully place the "bulb" of your thermometer in the hot water. Observe the water level in the tube. Does it rise?

6. If the water level does not rise, adjust your design as necessary, and repeat steps 3–5. When the water level does rise, sketch your final design in your ScienceLog.

7. After you finalize your design, you must calibrate your thermometer with a laboratory thermometer by taping an index card to the thermometer tube so that the entire part of the tube protruding from the "bulb" of the thermometer touches the card.

Materials

- heat-resistant gloves
- aluminum pie pan
- hot plate
- water
- assorted containers, such as plastic bottles, soda cans, film canisters, medicine bottles, test tubes, balloons, and yogurt containers with lids
- assorted tubes, such as clear inflexible plastic straws or 5 mm diameter plastic tubing, 30 cm long
- modeling clay
- food coloring
- pitcher
- transparent tape
- index card
- Celsius thermometer
- a paper cone-shaped filter or funnel
- 2 large plastic-foam cups
- ice cubes
- metric ruler

8. Place the cone-shaped filter or funnel into the plastic-foam cup. Carefully pour hot water from the hot plate into the filter or funnel. Be sure that no water splashes or spills.

9. Place your own thermometer and a laboratory thermometer in the hot water. Mark the water level on the index card as it rises. Observe and record the temperature on the laboratory thermometer, and write this value on the card beside the mark.

10. Repeat steps 8–9 with warm water from the faucet.

11. Repeat steps 8–9 with ice water.

12. Divide the markings on the index card into equally sized increments, and write the corresponding temperatures on the index card.

Analyze the Results

13. How effective is your thermometer at measuring temperature?

14. Compare your thermometer design with other students' designs. How would you modify your design to make your thermometer measure temperature even better?

Draw Conclusions

15. Take a class vote to see which design should be chosen for a contract with Safety Industries. Why was this thermometer chosen? How did it differ from other designs in the class?

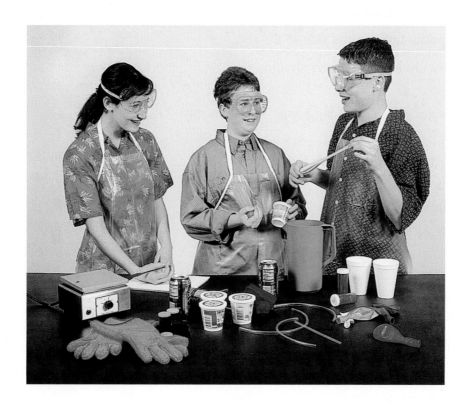

Go Fly a Bike!

Your friend Daniel just invented a bicycle that can fly! Trouble is, the bike can fly only when the wind speed is between 3 m/s and 10 m/s. If the wind is not blowing hard enough, the bike won't get enough lift to rise into the air, and if the wind is blowing too hard, the bike is difficult to control. Daniel needs to know if he can fly his bike today. Can you build a device that can estimate how fast the wind is blowing?

Materials

- scissors
- 5 small paper cups
- metric ruler
- hole punch
- 2 straight plastic straws
- colored marker
- small stapler
- thumbtack
- sharp pencil with an eraser
- modeling clay
- masking tape
- watch or clock that indicates seconds

SCIENTIFIC METHOD

Ask a Question

1. How can I construct a device to measure wind speed?

Construct an Anemometer

2. Cut off the rolled edges of all five paper cups. This will make them lighter, so that they can spin more easily.

3. Measure and place four equally spaced markings 1 cm below the rim of one of the paper cups.

4. Use the hole punch to punch a hole at each mark so that the cup has four equally spaced holes. Use the sharp pencil to carefully punch a hole in the center of the bottom of the cup.

5. Push a straw through two opposite holes in the side of the cup.

6. Repeat step 5 for the other two holes. The straws should form an X.

7. Measure 3 cm from the bottom of the remaining paper cups, and mark each spot with a dot.

8. At each dot, punch a hole in the paper cups with the hole punch.

9. Color the outside of one of the four cups.

10. Slide a cup on one of the straws by pushing the straw through the punched hole. Rotate the cup so that the bottom faces to the right.

11. Fold the end of the straw, and staple it to the inside of the cup directly across from the hole.

12. Repeat steps 10–11 for each of the remaining cups.

13. Push the tack through the intersection of the two straws.

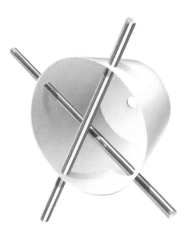

14. Push the eraser end of a pencil through the bottom hole in the center cup. Push the tack as far as it will go into the end of the eraser.

15. Push the sharpened end of the pencil into some modeling clay to form a base. This will allow the device to stand up without being knocked over, as shown at right.

16. Blow into the cups so that they spin. Adjust the tack so that the cups can freely spin without wobbling or falling apart. Congratulations! You have just constructed an anemometer.

Conduct an Experiment

17. Find a suitable area outside to place the anemometer vertically on a surface away from objects that would obstruct the wind, such as buildings and trees.

18. Mark the surface at the base of the anemometer with masking tape. Label the tape "starting point."

19. Hold the colored cup over the starting point while your partner holds the watch.

20. Release the colored cup. At the same time, your partner should look at the watch or clock. As the cups spin, count the number of times the colored cup crosses the starting point in 10 seconds.

Analyze the Results

21. How many times did the colored cup cross the starting point in 10 seconds?

22. Divide your answer in step 21 by 10 to get the number of revolutions in 1 second.

23. Measure the diameter of your anemometer (the distance between the outside edges of two opposite cups) in centimeters. Multiply this number by 3.14 to get the circumference of the circle made by the cups of your anemometer.

24. Multiply your answer from step 23 by the number of revolutions per second (step 22). Divide that answer by 100 to get wind speed in meters per second.

25. Compare your results with those of your classmates. Did you get the same result? What could account for any slight differences in your results?

Draw Conclusions

26. Could Daniel fly his bicycle today? Why or why not?

Under Pressure!

DISCOVERY LAB

You are planning a picnic with your friends, so you look in the newspaper for the weather forecast. The temperature this afternoon should be in the low 80s. This sounds quite comfortable! But you notice that the newspaper's forecast also includes the barometer reading. What does the reading tell you? In this activity, you will build your own barometer and discover what this instrument can tell you.

Materials

- balloon
- scissors
- large empty coffee can with 10 cm diameter
- masking tape or rubber band
- drinking straw
- transparent tape
- index card

SCIENTIFIC METHOD

Ask a Question

1. How can I construct a device that measures changes in atmospheric pressure?

Conduct an Experiment

2. Stretch and inflate the balloon. Let the air out. This will allow your barometer to be more sensitive to changes in atmospheric pressure.

3. Cut off the end of the balloon that you put in your mouth to inflate it. Stretch the balloon snugly over the mouth of the coffee can. Attach the balloon to the can with the tape or the rubber band.

4. Cut one end of the straw at an angle to form a pointer.

550 Chapter 15 LabBook

5. Place the straw with the pointer pointed away from the center of the stretched balloon so that 5 cm of the end of the straw hangs over the edge of the can, as shown at right. Tape the straw to the balloon.

6. Tape the index card to the can near the straw. Congratulations! You have just constructed a barometer!

7. Find a suitable area outside to place the barometer. Record the location of the straw for 3–4 days by marking it on the index card.

Analyze the Results

8. What factors affect how your barometer works? Explain your answer.

9. What does an upward movement of the straw indicate?

10. What does a downward movement of the straw indicate?

Draw Conclusions

11. Compare your results with the barometric pressures listed in your local newspaper. What kind of weather is associated with high pressure? What kind of weather is associated with low pressure?

Going Further

Now you can calibrate your barometer! Gather the weather section from your local newspaper for the same 3 or 4 days that you were testing your barometer. Find the barometer reading in the newspaper for each day, and record it beside that day's mark on your index card. Divide the markings on the index card into regular increments, and write the corresponding barometric pressures on the card.

Watching the Weather

Imagine that you own a private consulting firm that helps people plan for big occasions, such as weddings, parties, and celebrity events. One of your duties is making sure the weather doesn't put a damper on your clients' plans. In order to provide the best service possible, you have taken a crash course in reading weather maps. Will the celebrity golf match have to be delayed on account of rain? Will the wedding ceremony have to be moved inside so the blushing bride doesn't get soaked? It is your job to say "yea" or "nay."

Procedure

1. Study the station model and legend shown on the next page. You will use the legend to interpret the weather map on the final page of this activity.

2. Weather data is represented on a weather map by a station model. A station model is a small circle that shows the location of the weather station along with a set of symbols and numbers around the circle that represent the data collected at the weather station. Study the table below.

Weather-Map Symbols					
Weather conditions		**Cloud cover**		**Wind speed (mph)**	
••	Light rain	◯	No clouds	◎	Calm
∴	Moderate rain	◐	One-tenth or less		3–8
⁖	Heavy rain	◕	Two- to three-tenths		9–14
,	Drizzle	◒	Broken		15–20
✳ ✳	Light snow	◑	Nine-tenths		21–25
✳ ✳	Moderate snow	●	Overcast		32–37
⟁	Thunderstorm	⊗	Sky obscured		44–48
ᗬ	Freezing rain		**Special Symbols**		55–60
∞	Haze	▲▲▲▲	Cold front		66–71
≡	Fog	●●●●	Warm front		
		H	High pressure		
		L	Low pressure		
		ς	Hurricane		

Station Model

Wind speed is represented by whole and half tails.

A line indicates the direction the wind is coming from.

Air temperature

A symbol represents the current weather conditions. If there is no symbol, there is no precipitation.

Dew point temperature

Shading indicates the cloud coverage.

234

77

73

Atmospheric pressure in millibars (mbar). This number has been shortened on the station model. To read the number properly you must follow a few simple rules.

- If the first number is greater than 5, place a 9 in front of the number and a decimal point between the last two digits.
- If the first number is less than or equal to 5, place a 10 in front of the number and a decimal point between the last two digits.

Interpreting Station Models

The station model below is for Boston, Massachusetts. The current temperature in Boston is 42°F, and the dew point is 39°F. The barometric pressure is 1011.0 mbar. The sky is overcast, and there is a moderate rainfall. The wind is coming from the southwest at 15–20 mph.

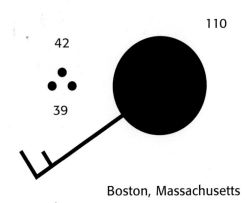

42

110

39

Boston, Massachusetts

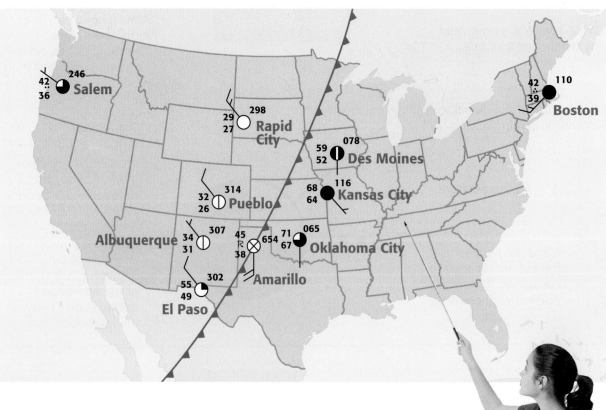

Analysis

3. Based on the weather for the entire United States, what time of year is it? Explain your answer.

4. Interpret the station model for Salem, Oregon. What is the temperature, dew point, cloud coverage, wind direction, wind speed, and atmospheric pressure? Is there any precipitation? If so, what kind?

5. What is happening to wind direction, temperature, and pressure as the cold front approaches? as it passes?

6. Interpret the station model for Amarillo, Texas.

Let It Snow!

While an inch of rain might be good for your garden, 7 or 8 cm could cause an unwelcome flood. But what about snow? How much snow is too much? A blizzard might drop 40 cm of snow overnight. Sure it's up to your knees, but how does this much snow compare with rain? This activity will help you find out.

Materials

- 150 mL of shaved ice
- 100 mL beaker
- metric ruler
- heat-resistant gloves
- hot plate
- graduated cylinder

Procedure

1. Pour 50 mL of shaved ice into your beaker. Do not pack the ice into the beaker. This ice will represent your snowfall.

2. Use the ruler to measure the height of the snow in the beaker.

3. Turn on the hot plate to a low setting.
   Caution: Wear heat-resistant gloves and goggles when working with the hot plate.

4. Place the beaker on the hot plate, and leave it there until all of the snow melts.

5. Pour the water into the graduated cylinder, and record the height and volume of the water in your ScienceLog.

6. Repeat steps 1–5 two more times.

Analysis

7. What was the difference in height before and after the snow melted in each of your three trials? What was the average difference?

8. Why did the volume change after the ice melted?

9. In this activity, what was the ratio of snow height to water height?

10. Use the ratio you found in step 9 to calculate how much water 50 cm of this snow would produce. Use the following equation to help.

$$\frac{\text{measured height of snow}}{\text{measured height of water}} = \frac{50 \text{ cm of snow}}{? \text{ cm of water}}$$

11. Why is it important to know the water content of a snowfall?

Going Further

Shaved ice isn't really snow. Research to find out how much water real snow would produce. Does every snowfall produce the same ratio of snow height to water depth?

Gone with the Wind

Pilots at the Fly Away Airport need your help—fast! Last night, lightning destroyed the orange windsock. This windsock helped pilots measure which direction the wind was blowing. But now the windsock is gone with the wind, and an incoming airplane needs to land. The pilot must know what direction the wind is blowing and is counting on you to make a device that can measure wind direction.

Materials

- paper plate
- drawing compass
- metric ruler
- protractor
- index card
- scissors
- stapler
- straight plastic straw
- sharpened pencil
- thumbtack or pushpin
- magnetic compass
- small rock

SCIENTIFIC METHOD

Ask a Question

1. How can I measure wind direction?

Conduct an Experiment

2. Find the center of the plate by tracing around its edge with a drawing compass. The pointed end of the compass should poke a small hole in the center of the plate.

3. Use a ruler to draw a line across the center of the plate.

4. Use a protractor to help you draw a second line through the center of the plate. This new line should be at a 90° angle to the line you drew in step 3.

5. Moving clockwise, label each line *N, E, S,* and *W.*

6. Use a protractor to help you draw two more lines through the center of the plate. These lines should be at a 45° angle to the lines you drew in steps 3 and 4.

7. Moving clockwise from *N,* label these new lines *NE, SE, SW,* and *NW.* The plate now resembles the face of a magnetic compass. This will be the base of your wind-direction indicator. It will help you read the direction of the wind at a glance.

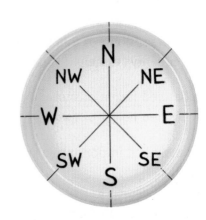

8. Measure and mark a 5 × 5 cm square on an index card. Cut the square out of the card. Fold the square in half to form a triangle.

9. Staple an open edge of the triangle to the straw so that one point of the triangle touches the end of the straw.

10. Hold the pencil at a 90° angle to the straw. The eraser should touch the balance point of the straw. Push a thumbtack or pushpin through the straw and into the eraser. The straw should spin without falling off.

11. Find a suitable area outside to measure the wind direction. The area should be clear of trees and buildings.

12. Press the sharpened end of the pencil through the center hole of the plate and into the ground. The labels on your paper plate should be facing the sky, as shown below.

13. Use a compass to find magnetic north. Rotate the plate so that the *N* on the plate points north. Place a small rock on top of the plate so that it does not turn.

14. Watch the straw as it rotates. The triangle will point in the direction the wind is blowing.

Analyze the Results

15. From what direction is the wind coming?

16. In what direction is the wind blowing?

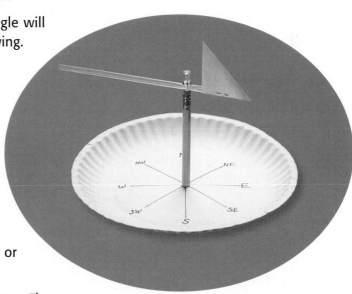

Draw Conclusions

17. Would this be an effective way for pilots to measure wind direction? Why or why not?

18. What improvements would you suggest to Fly Away Airport to measure wind direction more accurately?

Going Further

Use this tool to measure and record wind direction for several days. What changes in wind direction occur as a front approaches? as a front passes?

Review magnetic declination in the chapter titled "Maps as Models of the Earth." How might magnetic declination affect your design for a tool to measure wind direction?

Global Impact

For years scientists have debated the topic of global warming. Is the temperature of the Earth actually getting warmer? Sample sizes are a very important factor in any scientific study. In this activity, you will examine a chart to determine if the data indicate any trends. Be sure to notice how much the trends seem to change as you analyze different sets of data.

Materials

- 4 colored pencils
- metric ruler

Procedure

1. Look at the chart below. It shows average global temperatures recorded over the last 100 years.

2. Draw a graph in your ScienceLog. Label the horizontal axis "Time," and mark the grid in 5-year intervals. Label the vertical axis "Temperature (°C)," with values ranging from 13°C to 15°C.

3. Starting with 1900, use the numbers in red to plot the temperature in 20-year intervals. Connect the dots with straight lines.

4. Using a ruler, estimate the overall slope of temperatures, and draw a red line to represent the slope.

5. Using different colors, plot the temperatures at 10-year intervals and 5-year intervals on the same graph. Connect each set of dots, and draw the average slope for each set.

Analysis

6. Examine your completed graph, and explain any trends you see in the graphed data. Was there an increase or a decrease in average temperature over the last 100 years?

7. What differences did you see in each set of graphed data? what similarities?

8. What conclusions can you draw from the data you graphed in this activity?

9. What would happen if your graph were plotted in 1-year intervals? Try it!

Average Global Temperatures											
Year	**°C**	**Year**	**°C**	**Year**	**°C**	**Year**	**°C**	**Year**	**°C**	**Year**	**°C**
1900	14.0	1917	13.6	1934	14.0	1951	14.0	1968	13.9	1985	14.1
1901	13.9	1918	13.6	1935	13.9	1952	14.0	1969	14.0	1986	14.2
1902	13.8	1919	13.8	1936	14.0	1953	14.1	1970	14.0	1987	14.3
1903	13.6	1920	13.8	1937	14.1	1954	13.9	1971	13.9	1988	14.4
1904	13.5	1921	13.9	1938	14.1	1955	13.9	1972	13.9	1989	14.2
1905	13.7	1922	13.9	1939	14.0	1956	13.8	1973	14.2	1990	14.5
1906	13.8	1923	13.8	1940	14.1	1957	14.1	1974	13.9	1991	14.4
1907	13.6	1924	13.8	1941	14.1	1958	14.1	1975	14.0	1992	14.1
1908	13.7	1925	13.8	1942	14.1	1959	14.0	1976	13.8	1993	14.2
1909	13.7	1926	14.1	1943	14.0	1960	14.0	1977	14.2	1994	14.3
1910	13.7	1927	14.0	1944	14.1	1961	14.1	1978	14.1	1995	14.5
1911	13.7	1928	14.0	1945	14.0	1962	14.0	1979	14.1	1996	14.4
1912	13.7	1929	13.8	1946	14.0	1963	14.0	1980	14.3	1997	14.4
1913	13.8	1930	13.9	1947	14.1	1964	13.7	1981	14.4	1998	14.5
1914	14.0	1931	14.0	1948	14.0	1965	13.8	1982	14.1	1999	
1915	14.0	1932	14.0	1949	13.9	1966	13.9	1983	14.3	2000	
1916	13.8	1933	13.9	1950	13.8	1967	14.0	1984	14.1	2001	

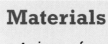

For the Birds

You and a partner have a new business building birdhouses. But your first clients have told you that birds do not want to live in the birdhouses you have made. The clients want their money back unless you can solve the problem. You need to come up with a solution right away!

You remember reading an article about microclimates in a science magazine. Cities often heat up because the pavement and buildings absorb so much solar radiation. Maybe the houses are too warm! How can the houses be kept cooler?

You decide to investigate the roofs; after all, changing the roofs would be a lot easier than building new houses. In order to help your clients and the birds, you decide to test different roof colors and materials to see how these variables affect a roof's ability to absorb the sun's rays.

One partner will test the color, and the other partner will test the materials. You will then share your results and make a recommendation together.

Part One: Color Test

Ask a Question

1. What color would be the best choice for the roof of a birdhouse?

Form a Hypothesis

2. In your ScienceLog, write down the color you think will keep a birdhouse coolest.

Test the Hypothesis

3. Paint one piece of cardboard black, another piece white, and a third light blue.

4. After the paint has dried, take the three pieces of cardboard outside, and place a thermometer on each piece.

5. In an area where there is no shade, place each piece at the same height so that all three receive the same amount of sunlight. Leave the pieces in the sunlight for 15 minutes.

6. Leave a fourth thermometer outside in the shade to measure the temperature of the air.

Materials

- 4 pieces of cardboard
- black, white, and light-blue tempera paint
- 4 Celsius thermometers
- watch or clock
- beige or tan wood
- beige or tan rubber

7. In your ScienceLog, record the reading of the thermometer on each piece of cardboard. Also record the outside temperature.

Analyze the Results

8. Did each of the three thermometers record the same temperature after 15 minutes? Explain.

9. Were the temperature readings on each of the three pieces of cardboard the same as the reading for the outside temperature? Explain.

Draw Conclusions

10. How do your observations compare with your hypothesis?

Part Two: Material Test

Ask a Question

11. Which material would be the best choice for the roof of a birdhouse?

Form a Hypothesis

12. In your ScienceLog, write down the material you think will keep a birdhouse coolest.

Test the Hypothesis

13. Take the rubber, wood, and the fourth piece of cardboard outside, and place a thermometer on each.

14. In an area where there is no shade, place each material at the same height so that they all receive the same amount of sunlight. Leave the materials in the sunlight for 15 minutes.

15. Leave a fourth thermometer outside in the shade to measure the temperature of the air.

16. In your ScienceLog, record the temperature of each material. Also record the outside temperature.

Analyze the Results

17. Did each of the thermometers on the three materials record the same temperature after 15 minutes? Explain.

18. Were the temperature readings on the rubber, wood, and cardboard the same as the reading for the outside temperature? Explain.

Draw Conclusions

19. How do your observations compare with your hypothesis?

Part Three: Sharing Information

Communicate Results

After you and your partner have finished your investigations, take a few minutes to share your results. Then work together to design a new roof.

20. Which material would you use to build the roofs for your birdhouses? Why?

21. Which color would you use to paint the new roofs? Why?

Going Further

Make three different-colored samples for each of the three materials. When you measure the temperatures for each sample, how do the colors compare for each material? Is the same color best for all three materials? How do your results compare with what you concluded in Part Three of this activity? What's more important, color or material?

Biome Business

You have just been hired as an assistant to a world-famous botanist. Your duties include collecting vegetation samples to study the effects of human activity on different plant species. Unfortunately, you were hired at the last minute, and no one has explained tomorrow's plan to you. You have been provided with climatographs for three biomes. A *climatograph* is a graph that shows the temperature and precipitation patterns for an area for a year. Each climatograph has two axes. The right axis indicates the temperature of the biome, while the left axis indicates the precipitation. You can use the information provided in the graphs to determine the type of climate in each biome. You also have a general map of the biomes, but nothing is labeled. Using this information, you must figure out what the environment will be like so that you can prepare yourself.

In this activity you will use climatographs and maps to determine where you will be traveling. You can find the exact locations by tracing the general maps and matching them to Figure 10 in the Climate chapter. Good luck!

Procedure

1. Look at each climatograph. The shaded areas show the average precipitation for the biome. The red line shows the average temperature.

2. Use the climatographs to determine the climate patterns for each biome. Compare the maps with the general map in Figure 10 to find the exact location of each region.

Analysis

3. Describe the precipitation patterns of each biome by answering the following questions:
   a. When does it rain the most in this biome?
   b. Do you think the biome is relatively dry, or do you think it rains a lot?

4. Describe the temperature patterns of each biome by answering the following questions:
   a. What are the warmest months of the year?
   b. Does the biome seem to have temperature cycles, like seasons, or is the temperature almost always the same?
   c. Do you think the biome is warm or cool? Explain.

5. Name each biome.

6. Where is each biome located?

Biome A

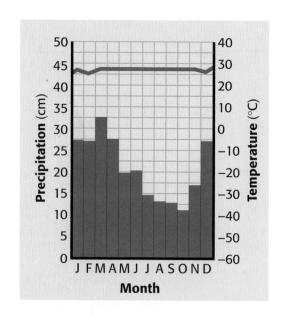

Biome B

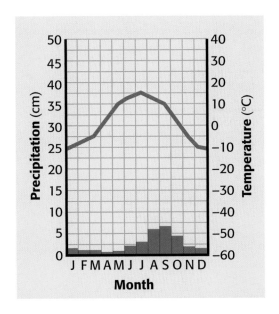

Biome C

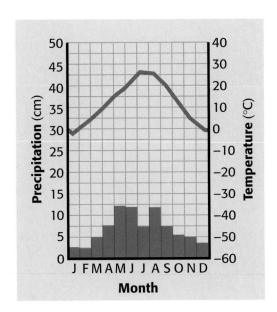

Going Further

In a cardboard box no bigger than a shoe box, build a model of one of the biomes that you investigated. Include things to represent the biome, such as the plants and animals that inhabit the area. Use magazines, photographs, colored pencils, plastic figurines, clay, or whatever you like. Be creative!

Self-Check Answers

Chapter 2—Maps as Models of the Earth

Page 36: The Earth rotates around the geographic poles.

Page 42: The measurements would be more accurate on a globe; there would be a certain amount of distortion on a world map.

Page 47: If the lines are close together, then the mapped area is steep. If the lines are far apart, the mapped area has a gradual slope or is flat.

Chapter 3—Minerals of the Earth's Crust

Page 69: These minerals form wherever salt water has evaporated.

Chapter 4—Rocks: Mineral Mixtures

Page 88: From fastest-cooled to slowest-cooled, the rocks in Figure 10 are: basalt, rhyolite, gabbro, and granite.

Page 96: A rock can come into contact with magma and also be subjected to pressure underground.

Chapter 5—Energy Resources

Page 123: Both devices harness energy from falling water.

Chapter 6—Plate Tectonics

Page 153: When folding occurs, sedimentary rock strata bend but do not break. When faulting occurs, sedimentary rock strata break along a fault, and the fault blocks on either side move relative to each other.

Chapter 7—Earthquakes

Page 169: Convergent motion creates reverse faults, while divergent motion creates normal faults. Convergent motion produces deep, strong earthquakes, while divergent motion produces shallow, weak earthquakes.

Page 176: 120

Chapter 8—Volcanoes

Page 201: 1. Solid rock may become magma when pressure is released, when the temperature rises above its melting point, or when its composition changes. 2. Magma forms in the lower crust and upper mantle, at depths between 25 and 160 km.

Chapter 9—Heat and Heat Technology

Page 227: Two substances can have the same temperature but different amounts of thermal energy. Unlike thermal energy, temperature does not depend on mass. A small amount of a substance at a particular temperature will have less thermal energy than a large amount of the substance at the same temperature.

Page 229: Steam can cause a more severe burn than boiling water because steam contains more energy per unit mass than does boiling water.

Chapter 10—The Flow of Fresh Water

Page 252: If a river slowed down, the suspended load would be deposited.

Page 256: A river might slow where there is a bend or where the river empties into a large body of water.

Page 260: The impermeable rock layer in the aquifer traps the water in the permeable layer below. This creates the pressure needed to form an artesian spring.

Chapter 11—Agents of Erosion and Deposition

Page 277: A large wave has more erosive energy than a small wave because a large wave releases more energy when it breaks.

Page 283: The roots of plants anchor sediment in place. Deflation hollows form in areas where there is little vegetation because there is nothing to anchor the sediment in place; the sediment blows away.

Page 289: When a moving glacier picks up speed or flows over a high point, a crevasse may form. This occurs because the ice cannot stretch quickly while it is moving and therefore cracks.

Chapter 12—Interactions of Living Things

Page 311: Humans are omnivores. An omnivore eats both plants and animals. Humans can eat meat and vegetables as well as animal products, such as milk and eggs, and plant products, such as grains and fruit.

Page 312: A food chain shows how energy moves in one direction from one organism to the next. A food web shows that there are many energy pathways between organisms.

Page 317: 1. If an area has only enough water to support 10 organisms, any additional organisms will cause some to go without water and move away or die. 2. Weather favorable for growing the food the deer eat will allow the forest to support more deer.

Chapter 13—Exploring the Oceans

Page 333: If North America and South America continue to drift westward and Asia continues to drift eastward, the continents will eventually collide on the other side of the Earth.

Page 341: Rift valleys form where tectonic plates pull apart, and ocean trenches form where one oceanic plate is forced underneath a continental plate or another oceanic plate.

Chapter 14—The Movement of Ocean Water

Page 367: Because he was traveling from Peru to a Polynesian island to the west, Heyerdahl would have noticed the wind blowing from the east.

Chapter 15—The Atmosphere

Page 396: As you climb a mountain, the air becomes less dense because there are fewer molecules to absorb heat. So even though cold air is generally more dense than warm air, it is less dense at higher elevations.

Chapter 16—Understanding Weather

Page 425: Evaporation occurs when liquid water changes into water vapor and returns to the air. Humidity is the amount of water vapor in the air.

Chapter 17—Climate

Page 456: Australia has summer during our winter months, December–February.

Page 462: Because of the dryness, desert soil is poor in organic matter, which fertilizes the soil. Without this natural fertilizer, crops would not be able to grow.

Page 470: The Earth's elliptical orbit causes increased seasonal differences. When the Earth's orbit is more elliptical, summers are hotter because the Earth is closer to the sun and receives more solar radiation. However, winters are cooler because the Earth is farther from the sun and receives less solar radiation.

CONTENTS

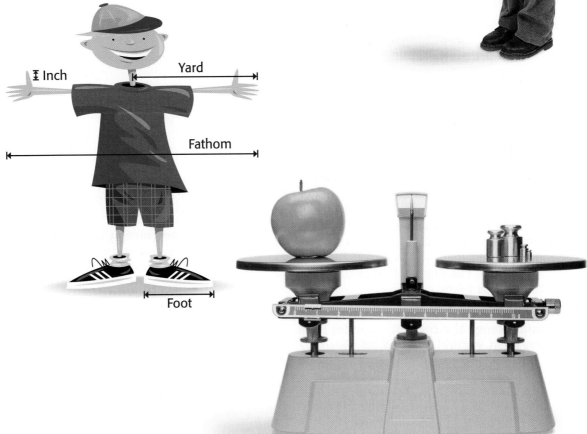

Concept Mapping: A Way to Bring Ideas Together

What Is a Concept Map?

Have you ever tried to tell someone about a book or a chapter you've just read and found that you can remember only a few isolated words and ideas? Or maybe you've memorized facts for a test, and then weeks later discover you're not even sure what topics those facts cover.

In both cases, you may have understood the ideas or concepts by themselves but not in relation to one another. If you could somehow link the ideas together, you would probably understand them better and remember them longer. This is something a concept map can help you do. A concept map is a way to see how ideas or concepts fit together. It can help you see the "big picture."

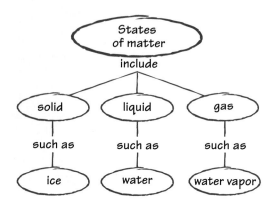

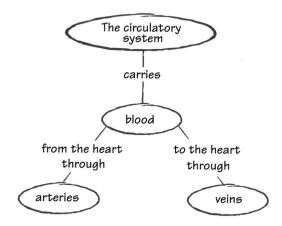

How to Make a Concept Map

❶ Make a list of the main ideas or concepts.

It might help to write each concept on its own slip of paper. This will make it easier to rearrange the concepts as many times as necessary to make sense of how the concepts are connected. After you've made a few concept maps this way, you can go directly from writing your list to actually making the map.

❷ Spread out the slips on a sheet of paper, and arrange the concepts in order from the most general to the most specific.

Put the most general concept at the top and circle it. Ask yourself, "How does this concept relate to the remaining concepts?" As you see the relationships, arrange the concepts in order from general to specific.

❸ Connect the related concepts with lines.

❹ On each line, write an action word or short phrase that shows how the concepts are related.

Look at the concept maps on this page, and then see if you can make one for the following terms:

plants, water, photosynthesis, carbon dioxide, sun's energy

One possible answer is provided at right, but don't look at it until you try the concept map yourself.

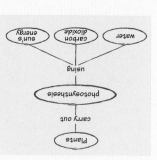

SI Measurement

The International System of Units, or SI, is the standard measuring system for many scientists. Using the same standards of measurement makes it easier for scientists to communicate with one another.

SI works by combining prefixes and base units. Each base unit can be used with different prefixes to define smaller and larger quantities. The table below lists common SI prefixes.

SI Prefixes			
Prefix	**Abbreviation**	**Factor**	**Example**
kilo-	k	1,000	kilogram, 1 kg = 1,000 g
hecto-	h	100	hectoliter, 1 hL = 100 L
deka-	da	10	dekameter, 1 dam = 10 m
		1	meter, liter
deci-	d	0.1	decigram, 1 dg = 0.1 g
centi-	c	0.01	centimeter, 1 cm = 0.01 m
milli-	m	0.001	milliliter, 1 mL = 0.001 L
micro-	µ	0.000001	micrometer, 1 µm = 0.000 001 m

SI Conversion Table		
SI units	**From SI to English**	**From English to SI**
Length		
kilometer (km) = 1,000 m	1 km = 0.621 mi	1 mi = 1.609 km
meter (m) = 100 cm	1 m = 3.281 ft	1 ft = 0.305 m
centimeter (cm) = 0.01 m	1 cm = 0.394 in.	1 in. = 2.540 cm
millimeter (mm) = 0.001 m	1 mm = 0.039 in.	
micrometer (µm) = 0.000 001 m		
nanometer (nm) = 0.000 000 001 m		
Area		
square kilometer (km^2) = 100 hectares	1 km^2 = 0.386 mi^2	1 mi^2 = 2.590 km^2
hectare (ha) = 10,000 m^2	1 ha = 2.471 acres	1 acre = 0.405 ha
square meter (m^2) = 10,000 cm^2	1 m^2 = 10.765 ft^2	1 ft^2 = 0.093 m^2
square centimeter (cm^2) = 100 mm^2	1 cm^2 = 0.155 in.^{2}	1 in.^{2} = 6.452 cm^2
Volume		
liter (L) = 1,000 mL = 1 dm^3	1 L = 1.057 fl qt	1 fl qt = 0.946 L
milliliter (mL) = 0.001 L = 1 cm^3	1 mL = 0.034 fl oz	1 fl oz = 29.575 mL
microliter (µL) = 0.000 001 L		
Mass		
kilogram (kg) = 1,000 g	1 kg = 2.205 lb	1 lb = 0.454 kg
gram (g) = 1,000 mg	1 g = 0.035 oz	1 oz = 28.349 g
milligram (mg) = 0.001 g		
microgram (µg) = 0.000 001 g		

Temperature Scales

Temperature can be expressed with three different scales: Fahrenheit, Celsius, and Kelvin. The SI unit for temperature is the kelvin (K).

Although 0 K is much colder than 0°C, a change of 1 K is equal to a change of 1°C.

Three Temperature Scales

	Fahrenheit	Celsius	Kelvin
Water boils	212°	100°	373
Body temperature	98.6°	37°	310
Room temperature	68°	20°	293
Water freezes	32°	0°	273

Temperature Conversions Table

To convert	Use this equation:	Example
Celsius to Fahrenheit °C ⟶ °F	$°F = \left(\dfrac{9}{5} \times °C\right) + 32$	Convert 45°C to °F. $°F = \left(\dfrac{9}{5} \times 45°C\right) + 32 = 113°F$
Fahrenheit to Celsius °F ⟶ °C	$°C = \dfrac{5}{9} \times (°F - 32)$	Convert 68°F to °C. $°C = \dfrac{5}{9} \times (68°F - 32) = 20°C$
Celsius to Kelvin °C ⟶ K	$K = °C + 273$	Convert 45°C to K. $K = 45°C + 273 = 318\ K$
Kelvin to Celsius K ⟶ °C	$°C = K - 273$	Convert 32 K to °C. $°C = 32\ K - 273 = -241°C$

Measuring Skills

Using a Graduated Cylinder

When using a graduated cylinder to measure volume, keep the following procedures in mind:

❶ Make sure the cylinder is on a flat, level surface.

❷ Move your head so that your eye is level with the surface of the liquid.

❸ Read the mark closest to the liquid level. On glass graduated clinders, read the mark closest to the center of the curve.

Using a Meterstick or Metric Ruler

When using a meterstick or metric ruler, keep the following procedures in mind:

❶ Place the ruler firmly against the object you are measuring.

❷ Align one edge of the object exactly with the zero end of the ruler.

❸ Look at the other edge of the object to see which of the marks on the ruler is closest to that edge. **Note:** Each small slash between the centimeters represents a millimeter, which is one-tenth of a centimeter.

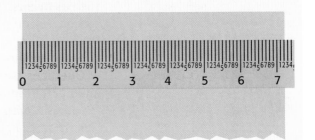

Using a Triple-Beam Balance

When using a triple-beam balance, keep the following procedures in mind:

❶ Make sure the balance is on a level surface.

❷ Place all of the countermasses at zero. Adjust the balancing knob until the pointer rests at zero.

❸ Place the object you wish to measure on the pan. **Caution:** Do not place hot objects or chemicals directly on the balance pan.

❹ Move the largest countermass along the beam to the right until it is at the last notch that does not tip the balance. Follow the same procedure with the next-largest countermass. Then move the smallest countermass until the pointer rests at zero.

❺ Add the readings from the three beams together to determine the mass of the object.

❻ When determining the mass of crystals or powders, use a piece of filter paper. First mass the paper. Then add the crystals or powder to the paper and remass. The actual mass of the crystals or powder is the total mass minus the mass of the paper. When finding the mass of liquids, first mass the empty container. Then mass the liquid and container together. The mass of the liquid is the total mass minus the mass of the container.

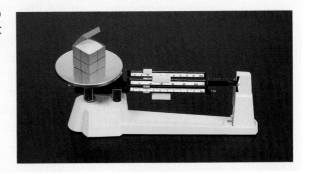

Scientific Method

The steps that scientists use to answer questions and solve problems is often called the **scientific method.** The scientific method is not a rigid procedure. Scientists may use all of the steps or just some of the steps of the scientific method. They may even repeat some of the steps. The goal of a scientific method is to come up with reliable answers and solutions.

Six Steps of a Scientific Method

1 **Ask a Question** Good questions come from careful **observations.** You make observations by using your senses to gather information. Sometimes you may use instruments, such as microscopes and telescopes, to extend the range of your senses. As you observe the natural world, you will discover that you have many more questions than answers. These questions drive the scientific method.

Questions beginning with *what, why, how,* and *when* are very important in focusing an investigation, and they often lead to a hypothesis. (You will learn what a hypothesis is in the next step.) Here is an example of a question that could lead to further investigation.

Question: How does acid rain affect plant growth?

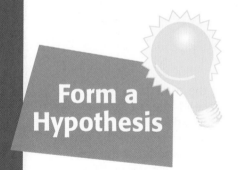

2 **Form a Hypothesis** After you come up with a question, you need to turn the question into a **hypothesis.** A hypothesis is a clear statement of what you expect the answer to your question to be. Your hypothesis will represent your best "educated guess" based on your observations and what you already know. A good hypothesis is one that is testable. If observations and information cannot be gathered or if an experiment cannot be designed to test your hypothesis, it is untestable, and the investigation can go no further.

Here is a hypothesis that could be formed from the question, "How does acid rain affect plant growth?"

Hypothesis: Acid rain causes plants to grow more slowly.

Notice that the hypothesis provides some specifics that lead to methods of testing. The hypothesis can also lead to predictions. A **prediction** is what you think will be the outcome of your experiment or data collection. Predictions are usually stated in an "if . . . then" format. For example, **if** meat is kept at room temperature, **then** it will spoil faster than meat kept in the refrigerator. More than one prediction can be made for a single hypothesis. Here is a sample prediction for the hypothesis that acid rain causes plants to grow more slowly.

Prediction: If a plant is watered with only acid rain (which has a pH of 4), then the plant will grow at half its normal rate.

3 **Test the Hypothesis** After you have formed a hypothesis and made a prediction, you should test your hypothesis. There are different ways to do this. Perhaps the most familiar way is to conduct a **controlled experiment.** A controlled experiment tests only one factor at a time. A controlled experiment has a **control group** and one or more **experimental groups.** All the factors for the control and experimental groups are the same except one factor, which is called the **variable.** By changing only one factor (the variable), you can see the results of just that one change.

Sometimes, the nature of an investigation makes a controlled experiment impossible. For example, dinosaurs have been extinct for millions of years, and the Earth's core is surrounded by thousands of meters of rock. It would be difficult if not impossible to conduct controlled experiments on such things. Under such circumstances, a hypothesis may be tested by making detailed observations. Taking measurements is one way of making observations.

Test Your Hypothesis

4 **Analyze the Results** After you have completed your experiments, made your observations, and collected your data, you must analyze all the information you have gathered. Tables and graphs are often used in this step to organize the data.

Analyze the Results

5 **Draw Conclusions** Based on the analysis of your data, you should conclude whether or not your results support your hypothesis. If your hypothesis is supported, you (or others) might want to repeat the observations or experiments to verify your results. If your hypothesis is not supported by the data, you may have to check your procedure for errors. You may even have to reject your hypothesis and make a new one. If you cannot draw a conclusion from your results, you may have to try the investigation again or carry out further observations or experiments.

Draw Conclusions

Do they support your hypothesis?

No

Yes

6 **Communicate Results** After any scientific investigation, you should report your results. By doing a written or oral report, you let others know what you have learned. They may want to repeat your investigation to see if they get the same results. Your report may even lead to another question, which in turn may lead to another investigation.

Communicate the Results

Scientific Method in Action

A scientific method is not a "straight line" of steps. It contains loops in which several steps may be repeated over and over again, while others may not be necessary. For example, sometimes scientists will find that testing one hypothesis raises new questions and new hypotheses to be tested. And sometimes, testing the hypothesis leads directly to a conclusion. Furthermore, the steps in a scientific method are not always used in the same order. Follow the steps in the diagram below, and see how many different directions a scientific method can take you.

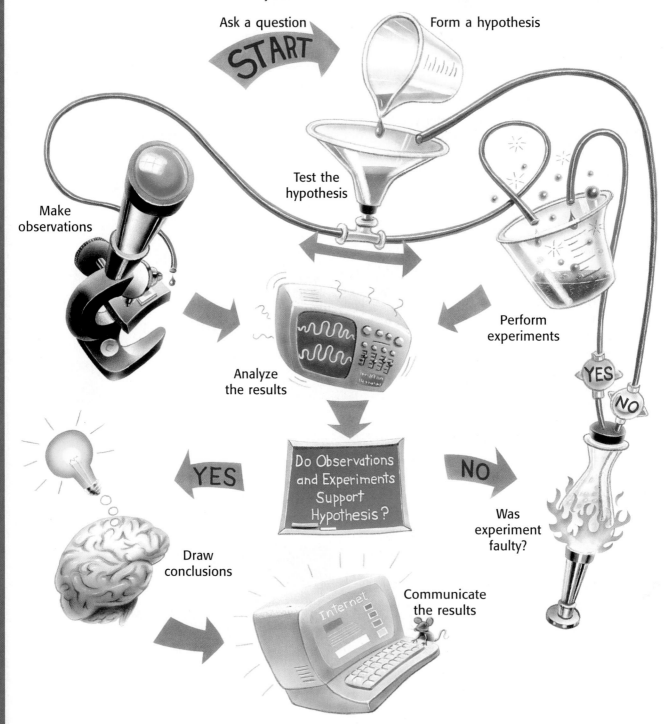

Ask a question

START

Form a hypothesis

Test the hypothesis

Make observations

Perform experiments

Analyze the results

YES   Do Observations and Experiments Support Hypothesis?   NO

Draw conclusions

Was experiment faulty?

Communicate the results

Making Charts and Graphs

Circle Graphs

A circle graph, or pie chart, shows how each group of data relates to all of the data. Each part of the circle represents a category of the data. The entire circle represents all of the data. For example, a biologist studying a hardwood forest in Wisconsin found that there were five different types of trees. The data table at right summarizes the biologist's findings.

Wisconsin Hardwood Trees	
Type of tree	**Number found**
Oak	600
Maple	750
Beech	300
Birch	1,200
Hickory	150
Total	3,000

How to Make a Circle Graph

1 In order to make a circle graph of this data, first find the percentage of each type of tree. To do this, divide the number of individual trees by the total number of trees and multiply by 100.

$$\frac{600 \text{ Oak}}{3,000 \text{ Trees}} \times 100 = 20\%$$

$$\frac{750 \text{ Maple}}{3,000 \text{ Trees}} \times 100 = 25\%$$

$$\frac{300 \text{ Beech}}{3,000 \text{ Trees}} \times 100 = 10\%$$

$$\frac{1,200 \text{ Birch}}{3,000 \text{ Trees}} \times 100 = 40\%$$

$$\frac{150 \text{ Hickory}}{3,000 \text{ Trees}} \times 100 = 5\%$$

2 Now determine the size of the pie shapes that make up the chart. Do this by multiplying each percentage by 360°. Remember that a circle contains 360°.

$20\% \times 360° = 72°$ $25\% \times 360° = 90°$
$10\% \times 360° = 36°$ $40\% \times 360° = 144°$
$5\% \times 360° = 18°$

3 Then check that the sum of the percentages is 100 and the sum of the degrees is 360.

$20\% + 25\% + 10\% + 40\% + 5\% = 100\%$
$72° + 90° + 36° + 144° + 18° = 360°$

4 Use a compass to draw a circle and mark its center.

5 Then use a protractor to draw angles of 72°, 90°, 36°, 144°, and 18° in the circle.

6 Finally, label each part of the graph and choose an appropriate title.

A Community of Wisconsin Hardwood Trees

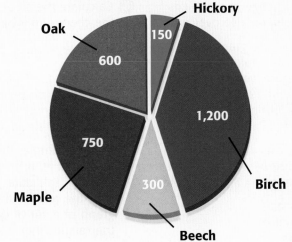

Line Graphs

Line graphs are most often used to demonstrate continuous change. For example, Mr. Smith's science class analyzed the population records for their hometown, Appleton, between 1900 and 2000. Examine the data at left.

Because the year and the population change, they are the *variables*. The population is determined by, or dependent on, the year. Therefore, the population is called the **dependent variable**, and the year is called the **independent variable**. Each set of data is called a **data pair**. To prepare a line graph, data pairs must first be organized in a table like the one at left.

Population of Appleton, 1900–2000	
Year	Population
1900	1,800
1920	2,500
1940	3,200
1960	3,900
1980	4,600
2000	5,300

How to Make a Line Graph

❶ Place the independent variable along the horizontal (x) axis. Place the dependent variable along the vertical (y) axis.

❷ Label the x-axis "Year" and the y-axis "Population." Look at your largest and smallest values for the population. Determine a scale for the y-axis that will provide enough space to show these values. You must use the same scale for the entire length of the axis. Find an appropriate scale for the x-axis too.

❸ Choose reasonable starting points for each axis.

❹ Plot the data pairs as accurately as possible.

❺ Choose a title that accurately represents the data.

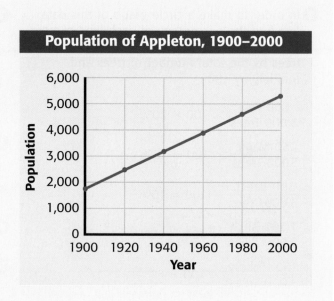

Population of Appleton, 1900–2000

How to Determine Slope

Slope is the ratio of the change in the y-axis to the change in the x-axis, or "rise over run."

❶ Choose two points on the line graph. For example, the population of Appleton in 2000 was 5,300 people. Therefore, you can define point *a* as (2000, 5,300). In 1900, the population was 1,800 people. Define point *b* as (1900, 1,800).

❷ Find the change in the y-axis.
(y at point *a*) − (y at point *b*)
5,300 people − 1,800 people = 3,500 people

❸ Find the change in the x-axis.
(x at point *a*) − (x at point *b*)
2000 − 1900 = 100 years

❹ Calculate the slope of the graph by dividing the change in y by the change in x.

$$slope = \frac{change\ in\ y}{change\ in\ x}$$

$$slope = \frac{3,500\ people}{100\ years}$$

$$slope = 35\ people\ per\ year$$

In this example, the population in Appleton increased by a fixed amount each year. The graph of this data is a straight line. Therefore, the relationship is **linear.** When the graph of a set of data is not a straight line, the relationship is **nonlinear.**

Using Algebra to Determine Slope

The equation in step 4 may also be arranged to be:

$$y = kx$$

where y represents the change in the y-axis, k represents the slope, and x represents the change in the x-axis.

$$\text{slope} = \frac{\text{change in } y}{\text{change in } x}$$

$$k = \frac{y}{x}$$

$$k \times x = \frac{y \times x}{x}$$

$$kx = y$$

Bar Graphs

Bar graphs are used to demonstrate change that is not continuous. These graphs can be used to indicate trends when the data are taken over a long period of time. A meteorologist gathered the precipitation records at right for Hartford, Connecticut, for April 1–15, 1996, and used a bar graph to represent the data.

Precipitation in Hartford, Connecticut April 1–15, 1996

Date	Precipitation (cm)	Date	Precipitation (cm)
April 1	0.5	April 9	0.25
April 2	1.25	April 10	0.0
April 3	0.0	April 11	1.0
April 4	0.0	April 12	0.0
April 5	0.0	April 13	0.25
April 6	0.0	April 14	0.0
April 7	0.0	April 15	6.50
April 8	1.75		

How to Make a Bar Graph

1 Use an appropriate scale and reasonable starting point for each axis.

2 Label the axes, and plot the data.

3 Choose a title that accurately represents the data.

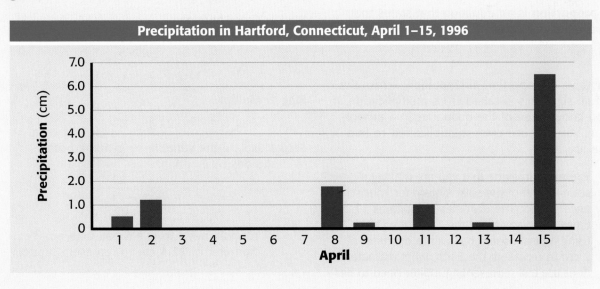

Precipitation in Hartford, Connecticut, April 1–15, 1996

Math Refresher

Science requires an understanding of many math concepts. The following pages will help you review some important math skills.

Averages

An **average,** or **mean,** simplifies a list of numbers into a single number that *approximates* their value.

> **Example:** Find the average of the following set of numbers: 5, 4, 7, 8.

Step 1: Find the sum.

$$5 + 4 + 7 + 8 = 24$$

Step 2: Divide the sum by the amount of numbers in your set. Because there are four numbers in this example, divide the sum by 4.

$$\frac{24}{4} = 6$$

The average, or mean, is **6.**

Ratios

A **ratio** is a comparison between numbers, and it is usually written as a fraction.

> **Example:** Find the ratio of thermometers to students if you have 36 thermometers and 48 students in your class.

Step 1: Make the ratio.

$$\frac{36 \text{ thermometers}}{48 \text{ students}}$$

Step 2: Reduce the fraction to its simplest form.

$$\frac{36}{48} = \frac{36 \div 12}{48 \div 12} = \frac{3}{4}$$

The ratio of thermometers to students is **3 to 4,** or $\frac{3}{4}$. The ratio may also be written in the form 3:4.

Proportions

A **proportion** is an equation that states that two ratios are equal.

$$\frac{3}{1} = \frac{12}{4}$$

To solve a proportion, first multiply across the equal sign. This is called cross-multiplication. If you know three of the quantities in a proportion, you can use cross-multiplication to find the fourth.

> **Example:** Imagine that you are making a scale model of the solar system for your science project. The diameter of Jupiter is 11.2 times the diameter of the Earth. If you are using a plastic-foam ball with a diameter of 2 cm to represent the Earth, what diameter does the ball representing Jupiter need to be?
>
> $$\frac{11.2}{1} = \frac{x}{2 \text{ cm}}$$

Step 1: Cross-multiply.

$$\frac{11.2}{1} \diagdown\!\!\!\!\diagup \frac{x}{2}$$

$$11.2 \times 2 = x \times 1$$

Step 2: Multiply.

$$22.4 = x \times 1$$

Step 3: Isolate the variable by dividing both sides by 1.

$$x = \frac{22.4}{1}$$
$$x = 22.4 \text{ cm}$$

You will need to use a ball with a diameter of **22.4 cm** to represent Jupiter.

Percentages

A **percentage** is a ratio of a given number to 100.

> **Example:** What is 85 percent of 40?

Step 1: Rewrite the percentage by moving the decimal point two places to the left.

$$.85$$

Step 2: Multiply the decimal by the number you are calculating the percentage of.

$$0.85 \times 40 = 34$$

85% of 40 is **34**

Decimals

To **add** or **subtract decimals,** line up the digits vertically so that the decimal points line up. Then add or subtract the columns from right to left, carrying or borrowing numbers as necessary.

> **Example:** Add the following numbers: 3.1415 and 2.96.

Step 1: Line up the digits vertically so that the decimal points line up.

$$\begin{array}{r} 3.1415 \\ + \ 2.96 \\ \hline \end{array}$$

Step 2: Add the columns from right to left, carrying when necessary.

$$\begin{array}{r} 1\ 1 \\ 3.1415 \\ + \ 2.96 \\ \hline 6.1015 \end{array}$$

The sum is **6.1015**

Fractions

Numbers tell you how many; **fractions** tell you *how much of a whole.*

> **Example:** Your class has 24 plants. Your teacher instructs you to put 5 in a shady spot. What fraction does this represent?

Step 1: Write a fraction with the total number of parts in the whole as the denominator.

$$\frac{?}{24}$$

Step 2: Write the number of parts of the whole being represented as the numerator.

$$\frac{5}{24}$$

$\frac{5}{24}$ of the plants will be in the shade.

Reducing Fractions

It is usually best to express a fraction in simplest form. This is called *reducing* a fraction.

> **Example:** Reduce the fraction $\frac{30}{45}$ to its simplest form.

Step 1: Find the largest whole number that will divide evenly into both the numerator and denominator. This number is called the greatest common factor (GCF).

factors of the numerator 30: 1, 2, 3, 5, 6, 10, 15, 30

factors of the denominator 45: 1, 3, 5, 9, 15, 45

Step 2: Divide both the numerator and the denominator by the GCF, which in this case is 15.

$$\frac{30}{45} = \frac{30 \div 15}{45 \div 15} = \frac{2}{3}$$

$\frac{30}{45}$ reduced to its simplest form is $\frac{2}{3}$.

Adding and Subtracting Fractions

To **add** or **subtract fractions** that have the **same denominator,** simply add or subtract the numerators.

Examples:

$$\frac{3}{5} + \frac{1}{5} = ? \quad \text{and} \quad \frac{3}{4} - \frac{1}{4} = ?$$

Step 1: Add or subtract the numerators.

$$\frac{3}{5} + \frac{1}{5} = \frac{4}{} \quad \text{and} \quad \frac{3}{4} - \frac{1}{4} = \frac{2}{}$$

Step 2: Write the sum or difference over the denominator.

$$\frac{3}{5} + \frac{1}{5} = \frac{4}{5} \quad \text{and} \quad \frac{3}{4} - \frac{1}{4} = \frac{2}{4}$$

Step 3: If necessary, reduce the fraction to its simplest form.

$\frac{4}{5}$ cannot be reduced, and $\frac{2}{4} = \frac{1}{2}$

To **add** or **subtract fractions** that have **different denominators,** first find a common denominator (LCD).

Examples:

$$\frac{1}{2} + \frac{1}{6} = ? \quad \text{and} \quad \frac{3}{4} - \frac{2}{3} = ?$$

Step 1: Write the equivalent fractions with a common demominator.

$$\frac{3}{6} + \frac{1}{6} = ? \quad \text{and} \quad \frac{9}{12} - \frac{8}{12} = ?$$

Step 2: Add or subtract.

$$\frac{3}{6} + \frac{1}{6} = \frac{4}{6} \quad \text{and} \quad \frac{9}{12} - \frac{8}{12} = \frac{1}{12}$$

Step 3: If necessary, reduce the fraction to its simplest form.

$\frac{4}{6} = \frac{2}{3}$, and $\frac{1}{12}$ cannot be reduced

Multiplying Fractions

To **multiply fractions,** multiply the numerators and the denominators together, and then reduce the fraction to its simplest form.

Example:

$$\frac{5}{9} \times \frac{7}{10} = ?$$

Step 1: Multiply the numerators and denominators.

$$\frac{5}{9} \times \frac{7}{10} = \frac{5 \times 7}{9 \times 10} = \frac{35}{90}$$

Step 2: Reduce.

$$\frac{35}{90} = \frac{35 \div 5}{90 \div 5} = \frac{7}{18}$$

Dividing Fractions

To **divide fractions,** first rewrite the divisor (the number you divide *by*) upside down. This is called the reciprocal of the divisor. Then you can multiply and reduce if necessary.

Example:

$$\frac{5}{8} \div \frac{3}{2} = ?$$

Step 1: Rewrite the divisor as its reciprocal.

$$\frac{3}{2} \to \frac{2}{3}$$

Step 2: Multiply.

$$\frac{5}{8} \times \frac{2}{3} = \frac{5 \times 2}{8 \times 3} = \frac{10}{24}$$

Step 3: Reduce.

$$\frac{10}{24} = \frac{10 \div 2}{24 \div 2} = \frac{5}{12}$$

Scientific Notation

Scientific notation is a short way of representing very large and very small numbers without writing all of the place-holding zeros.

> **Example:** Write 653,000,000 in scientific notation.

Step 1: Write the number without the place-holding zeros.

653

Step 2: Place the decimal point after the first digit.

6.53

Step 3: Find the exponent by counting the number of places that you moved the decimal point.

6.53000000

The decimal point was moved eight places to the left. Therefore, the exponent of 10 is positive 8. Remember, if the decimal point had moved to the right, the exponent would be negative.

Step 4: Write the number in scientific notation.

$$\textbf{6.53} \times \textbf{10}^{\textbf{8}}$$

Area

Area is the number of square units needed to cover the surface of an object.

> **Formulas:**
> Area of a square = side × side
> Area of a rectangle = length × width
> Area of a triangle = $\frac{1}{2}$ base × height
> **Examples:** Find the areas.

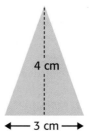

Triangle
Area = $\frac{1}{2}$ × base × height
Area = $\frac{1}{2}$ × 3 cm × 4 cm
Area = **6 cm²**

4 cm

3 cm

Rectangle
Area = length × width
Area = 6 cm × 3 cm
Area = **18 cm²**

3 cm

6 cm

Square
Area = side × side
Area = 3 cm × 3 cm
Area = **9 cm²**

3 cm

3 cm

Volume

Volume is the amount of space something occupies.

> **Formulas:**
> Volume of a cube = side × side × side
>
> Volume of a prism = area of base × height
>
> **Examples:** Find the volume of the solids.

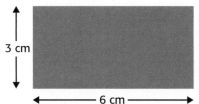

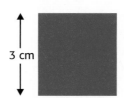

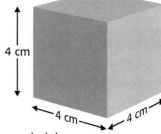

Cube
Volume = side × side × side
Volume = 4 cm × 4 cm × 4 cm
Volume = **64 cm³**

4 cm

4 cm

4 cm

3 cm

4 cm

5 cm

Prism
Volume = area of base × height
Volume = (area of triangle) × height
Volume = $\left(\frac{1}{2} \times 3 \text{ cm} \times 4 \text{ cm}\right) \times 5$ cm
Volume = 6 cm² × 5 cm
Volume = **30 cm³**

Periodic Table of the Elements

Each square on the table includes an element's name, chemical symbol, atomic number, and atomic mass.

Atomic number —————— 6
Chemical symbol —————— **C**
Element name —————— Carbon
Atomic mass —————— 12.0

The background color indicates the type of element. Carbon is a nonmetal.

The color of the chemical symbol indicates the physical state at room temperature. Carbon is a solid.

Background
Metals
Metalloids
Nonmetals

Chemical symbol
Solid
Liquid
Gas

Period 1

1
H
Hydrogen
1.0

Group 1	Group 2

Period 2

3	4
Li	**Be**
Lithium	Beryllium
6.9	9.0

Period 3

11	12
Na	**Mg**
Sodium	Magnesium
23.0	24.3

		Group 3	Group 4	Group 5	Group 6	Group 7	Group 8	Group 9

Period 4

19	20	21	22	23	24	25	26	27
K	**Ca**	**Sc**	**Ti**	**V**	**Cr**	**Mn**	**Fe**	**Co**
Potassium	Calcium	Scandium	Titanium	Vanadium	Chromium	Manganese	Iron	Cobalt
39.1	40.1	45.0	47.9	50.9	52.0	54.9	55.8	58.9

Period 5

37	38	39	40	41	42	43	44	45
Rb	**Sr**	**Y**	**Zr**	**Nb**	**Mo**	**Tc**	**Ru**	**Rh**
Rubidium	Strontium	Yttrium	Zirconium	Niobium	Molybdenum	Technetium	Ruthenium	Rhodium
85.5	87.6	88.9	91.2	92.9	95.9	(97.9)	101.1	102.9

Period 6

55	56	57	72	73	74	75	76	77
Cs	**Ba**	**La**	**Hf**	**Ta**	**W**	**Re**	**Os**	**Ir**
Cesium	Barium	Lanthanum	Hafnium	Tantalum	Tungsten	Rhenium	Osmium	Iridium
132.9	137.3	138.9	178.5	180.9	183.8	186.2	190.2	192.2

Period 7

87	88	89	104	105	106	107	108	109
Fr	**Ra**	**Ac**	**Rf**	**Db**	**Sg**	**Bh**	**Hs**	**Mt**
Francium	Radium	Actinium	Rutherfordium	Dubnium	Seaborgium	Bohrium	Hassium	Meitnerium
(223.0)	(226.0)	(227.0)	(261.1)	(262.1)	(263.1)	(262.1)	(265)	(266)

A row of elements is called a period.

A column of elements is called a group or family.

Lanthanides

58	59	60	61	62
Ce	**Pr**	**Nd**	**Pm**	**Sm**
Cerium	Praseodymium	Neodymium	Promethium	Samarium
140.1	140.9	144.2	(144.9)	150.4

Actinides

90	91	92	93	94
Th	**Pa**	**U**	**Np**	**Pu**
Thorium	Protactinium	Uranium	Neptunium	Plutonium
232.0	231.0	238.0	(237.0)	244.1

These elements are placed below the table to allow the table to be narrower.

This zigzag line reminds you where the metals, nonmetals, and metalloids are.

Group 18

| 2 |
| **He** |
| Helium |
| 4.0 |

Group 13	Group 14	Group 15	Group 16	Group 17
5	6	7	8	9	10
B	**C**	**N**	**O**	**F**	**Ne**
Boron	Carbon	Nitrogen	Oxygen	Fluorine	Neon
10.8	12.0	14.0	16.0	19.0	20.2
13	14	15	16	17	18
Al	**Si**	**P**	**S**	**Cl**	**Ar**
Aluminum	Silicon	Phosphorus	Sulfur	Chlorine	Argon
27.0	28.1	31.0	32.1	35.5	39.9

Group 10	Group 11	Group 12
28	29	30	31	32	33	34	35	36
Ni	**Cu**	**Zn**	**Ga**	**Ge**	**As**	**Se**	**Br**	**Kr**
Nickel	Copper	Zinc	Gallium	Germanium	Arsenic	Selenium	Bromine	Krypton
58.7	63.5	65.4	69.7	72.6	74.9	79.0	79.9	83.8
46	47	48	49	50	51	52	53	54
Pd	**Ag**	**Cd**	**In**	**Sn**	**Sb**	**Te**	**I**	**Xe**
Palladium	Silver	Cadmium	Indium	Tin	Antimony	Tellurium	Iodine	Xenon
106.4	107.9	112.4	114.8	118.7	121.8	127.6	126.9	131.3
78	79	80	81	82	83	84	85	86
Pt	**Au**	**Hg**	**Tl**	**Pb**	**Bi**	**Po**	**At**	**Rn**
Platinum	Gold	Mercury	Thallium	Lead	Bismuth	Polonium	Astatine	Radon
195.1	197.0	200.6	204.4	207.2	209.0	(209.0)	(210.0)	(222.0)
110	111	112
Uun	**Uuu**	**Uub**
Ununnilium	Unununium	Ununbium
(271)	(272)	(277)

The names and symbols of elements 110–112 are temporary. They are based on the atomic number of the element. The official name and symbol will be approved by an international committee of scientists.

63	64	65	66	67	68	69	70	71
Eu	**Gd**	**Tb**	**Dy**	**Ho**	**Er**	**Tm**	**Yb**	**Lu**
Europium	Gadolinium	Terbium	Dysprosium	Holmium	Erbium	Thulium	Ytterbium	Lutetium
152.0	157.3	158.9	162.5	164.9	167.3	168.9	173.0	175.0
95	96	97	98	99	100	101	102	103
Am	**Cm**	**Bk**	**Cf**	**Es**	**Fm**	**Md**	**No**	**Lr**
Americium	Curium	Berkelium	Californium	Einsteinium	Fermium	Mendelevium	Nobelium	Lawrencium
(243.1)	(247.1)	(247.1)	(251.1)	(252.1)	(257.1)	(258.1)	(259.1)	(262.1)

A number in parentheses is the mass number of the most stable isotope of that element.

Physical Science Refresher

Atoms and Elements

Every object in the universe is made up of particles of some kind of matter. **Matter** is anything that takes up space and has mass. All matter is made up of elements. An **element** is a substance that cannot be separated into simpler components by ordinary chemical means. This is because each element consists of only one kind of atom. An **atom** is the smallest unit of an element that has all of the properties of that element.

Atomic Structure

Atoms are made up of small particles called subatomic particles. The three major types of subatomic particles are **electrons, protons,** and **neutrons.** Electrons have a negative electrical charge, protons have a positive charge, and neutrons have no electrical charge. The protons and neutrons are packed close to one another to form the **nucleus.** The protons give the nucleus a positive charge. The electrons of an atom move in a region around the nucleus known as an **electron cloud.** The negatively charged electrons are attracted to the positively charged nucleus. An atom may have several energy levels in which electrons are located.

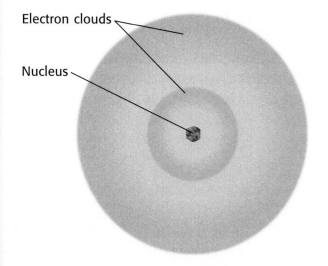

Electron clouds

Nucleus

Atomic Number

To help in the identification of elements, scientists have assigned an **atomic number** to each kind of atom. The atomic number is equal to the number of protons in the atom. Atoms with the same number of protons are all the same kind of element. In an uncharged, or electrically neutral, atom there are an equal number of protons and electrons. Therefore, the atomic number also equals the number of electrons in an uncharged atom. The number of neutrons, however, can vary for a given element. Atoms of the same element that have different numbers of neutrons are called **isotopes.**

Periodic Table of the Elements

In the periodic table, the elements are arranged from left to right in order of increasing atomic number. Each element in the table is in a separate box. Each element has one more electron and one more proton than the element to its left. Each horizontal row of the table is called a **period.** Changes in chemical properties across a period correspond to changes in the elements' electron arrangements. Each vertical column of the table, known as a **group,** lists elements with similar properties. The elements in a group have similar chemical properties because they have the same number of electrons in their outer energy level. For example, the elements helium, neon, argon, krypton, xenon, and radon all have similar properties and are known as the noble gases.

Molecules and Compounds

When the atoms of two or more elements are joined chemically, the resulting substance is called a **compound.** A compound is a new substance with properties different from those of the elements that compose it. For example, water (H_2O) is a compound formed when atoms of hydrogen (H) and oxygen (O) combine. The smallest complete unit of a compound that has all of the properties of that compound is called a **molecule.** A chemical formula indicates the elements in a compound. It also indicates the relative number of atoms of each element present. The chemical formula for water is H_2O, which indicates that each water molecule consists of two atoms of hydrogen and one atom of oxygen. The subscript number is used after the symbol for an element to indicate how many atoms of that element are in a single molecule of the compound.

Acids, Bases, and pH

An ion is an atom or group of atoms that has an electrical charge because it has lost or gained one or more electrons. When an acid, such as hydrochloric acid (HCl), is mixed with water, it separates into ions. An **acid** is a compound that produces hydrogen ions (H^+) in water. The hydrogen ions then combine with a water molecule to form a hydronium ion (H_3O^+). A **base,** on the other hand, is a substance that produces hydroxide ions (OH^-) in water.

To determine whether a solution is acidic or basic, scientists use pH. The **pH** is a measure of the hydronium ion concentration in a solution. The pH scale ranges from 0 to 14. The middle point, pH = 7, is neutral, neither acidic nor basic. Acids have a pH less than 7; bases have a pH greater than 7. The lower the number is, the more acidic the solution. The higher the number is, the more basic the solution.

Chemical Equations

A chemical reaction occurs when a chemical change takes place. (In a chemical change, new substances with new properties are formed.) A chemical equation is a useful way of describing a chemical reaction by means of chemical formulas. The equation indicates what substances react and what the products are. For example, when carbon and oxygen combine, they can form carbon dioxide. The equation for the reaction is as follows: $C + O_2 \rightarrow CO_2$.

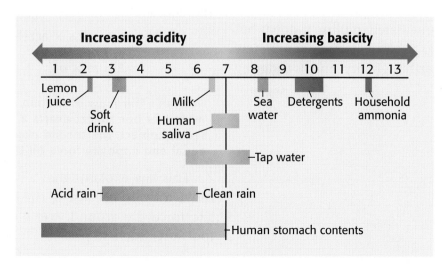

Physical Laws and Equations

Law of Conservation of Energy

The law of conservation of energy states that energy can be neither created nor destroyed.

The total amount of energy in a closed system is always the same. Energy can be changed from one form to another, but all the different forms of energy in a system always add up to the same total amount of energy, no matter how many energy conversions occur.

Law of Universal Gravitation

The law of universal gravitation states that all objects in the universe attract each other by a force called gravity. The size of the force depends on the masses of the objects and the distance between them.

The first part of the law explains why a bowling ball is much harder to lift than a table-tennis ball. Because the bowling ball has a much larger mass than the table-tennis ball, the amount of gravity between the Earth and the bowling ball is greater than the amount of gravity between the Earth and the table-tennis ball.

The second part of the law explains why a satellite can remain in orbit around the Earth. The satellite is carefully placed at a distance great enough to prevent the Earth's gravity from immediately pulling it down but small enough to prevent it from completely escaping the Earth's gravity and wandering off into space.

Newton's Laws of Motion

Newton's first law of motion states that an object at rest remains at rest and an object in motion remains in motion at constant speed and in a straight line unless acted on by an unbalanced force.

The first part of the law explains why a football will remain on a tee until it is kicked off or until a gust of wind blows it off.

The second part of the law explains why a bike's rider will continue moving forward after the bike tire runs into a crack in the sidewalk and the bike comes to an abrupt stop until gravity and the sidewalk stop the rider.

Newton's second law of motion states that the acceleration of an object depends on the mass of the object and the amount of force applied.

The first part of the law explains why the acceleration of a 4 kg bowling ball will be greater than the acceleration of a 6 kg bowling ball if the same force is applied to both.

The second part of the law explains why the acceleration of a bowling ball will be larger if a larger force is applied to it.

The relationship of acceleration (a) to mass (m) and force (F) can be expressed mathematically by the following equation:

$$\text{acceleration} = \frac{force}{mass} \quad \text{or} \quad a = \frac{F}{m}$$

This equation is often rearranged to the form:

$$\text{force} = \text{mass} \times \text{acceleration}$$
$$\text{or}$$
$$F = m \times a$$

Newton's third law of motion states that whenever one object exerts a force on a second object, the second object exerts an equal and opposite force on the first.

This law explains that a runner is able to move forward because of the equal and opposite force the ground exerts on the runner's foot after each step.

Useful Equations

Average speed

$$\text{Average speed} = \frac{\text{total distance}}{\text{total time}}$$

Example: A bicycle messenger traveled a distance of 136 km in 8 hours. What was the messenger's average speed?

$$\frac{136 \text{ km}}{8 \text{ h}} = 17 \text{ km/h}$$

The messenger's average speed was **17 km/h.**

Average acceleration

$$\text{Average acceleration} = \frac{\text{final velocity} - \text{starting velocity}}{\text{time it takes to change velocity}}$$

Example: Calculate the average acceleration of an Olympic 100 m dash sprinter who reaches a velocity of 15 m/s south at the finish line. The race was in a straight line and lasted 10 s.

$$\frac{15 \text{ m/s} - 0 \text{ m/s}}{10 \text{ s}} = 1.5 \text{ m/s/s}$$

The sprinter's average acceleration is **1.5 m/s/s south.**

Net force

Forces in the Same Direction

When forces are in the same direction, add the forces together to determine the net force.

Example: Calculate the net force on a stalled car that is being pushed by two people. One person is pushing with a force of 13 N northwest and the other person is pushing with a force of 8 N in the same direction.

$$13 \text{ N} + 8 \text{ N} = 21 \text{ N}$$

The net force is **21 N northwest.**

Forces in Opposite Directions

When forces are in opposite directions, subtract the smaller force from the larger force to determine the net force.

Net force (cont'd)

Example: Calculate the net force on a rope that is being pulled on each end. One person is pulling on one end of the rope with a force of 12 N south. Another person is pulling on the opposite end of the rope with a force of 7 N north.

$$12 \text{ N} - 7 \text{ N} = 5 \text{ N}$$

The net force is **5 N south.**

Density

$$\text{Density} = \frac{\text{Mass}}{\text{Volume}}$$

Example: Calculate the density of a sponge with a mass of 10 g and a volume of 40 mL.

$$\frac{10 \text{ g}}{40 \text{ mL}} = 0.25 \text{ g/mL}$$

The density of the sponge is **0.25 g/mL.**

Pressure

Pressure is the force exerted over a given area. The SI unit for pressure is the pascal, which is abbreviated Pa.

$$\text{Pressure} = \frac{\text{Force}}{\text{Area}}$$

Example: Calculate the pressure of the air in a soccer ball if the air exerts a force of 10 N over an area of 0.5 m^2.

$$\text{Pressure} = \frac{10 \text{ N}}{0.5 \text{ m}^2} = 20 \text{ N/m}^2 = 20 \text{ Pa}$$

The pressure of the air inside of the soccer ball is **20 Pa.**

Concentration

$$\text{Concentration} = \frac{\text{Mass of solute}}{\text{Volume of solvent}}$$

Example: Calculate the concentration of solution in which 10 g of sugar is dissolved in 125 mL of water.

$$\frac{10 \text{ g of sugar}}{125 \text{ mL of water}} = 0.08 \text{ g/mL}$$

The concentration of this solution is **0.08 g/mL.**

Properties of Common Minerals

Silicate Minerals

Mineral	Color	Luster	Streak	Hardness
Beryl	deep green, pink, white, bluish green, or light yellow	vitreous	none	7.5–8
Chlorite	green	vitreous to pearly	pale green	2–2.5
Garnet	green or red	vitreous	none	6.5–7.5
Hornblende (Amphibole)	dark green, brown, or black	vitreous or silky	none	5–6
Muscovite	colorless, gray, or brown	vitreous or pearly	white	2–2.5
Olivine	olive green	vitreous	none	6.5–7
Orthoclase	colorless, white, pink, or other colors	vitreous to pearly	white or none	6
Plagioclase	blue gray to white	vitreous	white	6
Quartz	colorless or white; any color when not pure	vitreous or waxy	white or none	7

Nonsilicate Minerals

Mineral	Color	Luster	Streak	Hardness
Native Elements				
Copper	copper-red	metallic	copper-red	2.5–3
Diamond	pale yellow or colorless	vitreous	none	10
Graphite	black to gray	submetallic	black	1–2
Carbonates				
Aragonite	colorless, white, or pale yellow	vitreous	white	3.5–4
Calcite	colorless or white to tan	vitreous	white	3
Halides				
Fluorite	light green, yellow, purple, bluish green, or other colors	vitreous	none	4
Halite	colorless or gray	vitreous	white	2.5–3
Oxides				
Hematite	reddish brown to black	metallic to earthy	red to red-brown	5.6–6.5
Magnetite	iron black	metallic	black	5–6
Sulfates				
Anhydrite	colorless, bluish, or violet	vitreous to pearly	white	3–3.5
Gypsum	white, pink, gray, or colorless	vitreous, pearly, or silky	white	1–2.5
Sulfides				
Galena	lead gray	metallic	lead gray to black	2.5
Pyrite	brassy yellow	metallic	greenish, brownish, or black	6–6.5

Density (g/cm³)	Cleavage, Fracture, Special Properties	Common Uses
2.6–2.8	1 cleavage direction; irregular fracture; some varieties fluoresce in ultraviolet light	gemstones, ore of the metal beryllium
2.6–3.3	1 cleavage direction; irregular fracture	
4.2	no cleavage; conchoidal to splintery fracture	gemstones, abrasives
3.2	2 cleavage directions; hackly to splintery fracture	
2.7–3	1 cleavage direction; irregular fracture	electrical insulation, wallpaper, fireproofing material, lubricant
3.2–3.3	no cleavage; conchoidal fracture	gemstones, casting
2.6	2 cleavage directions; irregular fracture	porcelain
2.6–2.7	2 cleavage directions; irregular fracture	ceramics
2.6	no cleavage; conchoidal fracture	gemstones, concrete, glass, porcelain, sandpaper, lenses
8.9	no cleavage; hackly fracture	wiring, brass, bronze, coins
3.5	4 cleavage directions; irregular to conchoidal fracture	gemstones, drilling
2.3	1 cleavage direction; irregular fracture	pencils, paints, lubricants, batteries
2.95	2 cleavage directions; irregular fracture; reacts with hydrochloric acid	minor source of barium
2.7	3 cleavage directions; irregular fracture; reacts with weak acid, double refraction	cements, soil conditioner, whitewash, construction materials
3.2	4 cleavage directions; irregular fracture; some varieties fluoresce or double refract	hydrochloric acid, steel, glass, fiberglass, pottery, enamel
2.2	3 cleavage directions; splintery to conchoidal fracture; salty taste	tanning hides, fertilizer, salting icy roads, food preservation
5.25	no cleavage; splintery fracture; magnetic when heated	iron ore for steel, gemstones, pigments
5.2	2 cleavage directions; splintery fracture; magnetic	iron ore
2.89–2.98	3 cleavage directions; conchoidal to splintery fracture	soil conditioner, sulfuric acid
2.2–2.4	3 cleavage directions; conchoidal to splintery fracture	plaster of Paris, wallboard, soil conditioner
7.4–7.6	3 cleavage directions; irregular fracture	batteries, paints
5	no cleavage; conchoidal to splintery fracture	dyes, inks, gemstones

Glossary

A

abiotic nonliving factors in the environment (306)

abrasion the grinding and wearing down of rock surfaces by other rock or sand particles (284)

absolute zero the lowest possible temperature (0 K, −273°C) (217)

abyssal (uh BIS uhl) **plain** the broad, flat portion of the deep-ocean basin (340)

acid precipitation precipitation that contains acids due to air pollution (116, 413)

active solar heating a solar-heating system consisting of solar collectors and a network of pipes that distributes energy from the sun throughout a building (233)

aerial photograph a photograph taken from the air (43)

air mass a large body of air that has the same temperature and moisture throughout (432)

air pressure the measure of the force with which air molecules are pushing on a surface (395)

alluvial (uh LOO vee uhl) **fan** fan-shaped deposits of sediment that form on dry land (257)

alluvium (uh LOO vee uhm) rock and soil deposited by streams (255)

altitude the height of an object above the Earth's surface (395)

anemometer (AN uh MAHM uht uhr) an instrument used to measure wind speed (443)

anticline a bowl-shaped fold in sedimentary rock layers (152)

aquifer (AHK wuh fuhr) a rock layer that stores and allows the flow of ground water (258)

arête (uh RAYT) a jagged ridge that forms between two or more cirques cutting into the same mountain (291)

artesian (ahr TEE zhuhn) **spring** a spring that forms when cracks occur naturally in the cap rock and the pressurized water in the aquifer flows through the cracks to the surface (260)

asthenosphere (as THEN uh SFIR) the partially molten layer of the upper mantle on which the tectonic plates of the lithosphere move (138)

astronomy the study of all physical objects beyond Earth (9)

atmosphere a mixture of gases that surrounds a planet, such as Earth (394)

atom the smallest particle into which an element can be divided and still retain all of the properties of that element (61)

azimuthal (AZ uh MOOTH uhl) **projection** a map projection that is made by transferring the contents of the globe onto a plane (42)

B

barometer an instrument used to measure air pressure (443)

beach an area of the shoreline made up of material deposited by waves (278)

benthic environment the ocean floor and all the organisms that live on or in it; also known as the bottom environment (345)

benthos organisms that live on or in the ocean floor (344)

bimetallic (BIE muh TAL ik) **strip** a strip made by stacking two different metals in a long thin strip; because the different metals expand at different rates when they get hot, a bimetallic strip can coil and uncoil with changes in temperature; bimetallic strips are used in devices such as thermostats (218)

biomass organic matter, such as plants, wood, and waste, that contains stored energy (124)

biome a large region characterized by a specific type of climate and certain types of plant and animal communities (460)

biosphere the part of the Earth where life exists (309)

biotic living factors in the environment (306)

breaker zone the near-shore area where waves first begin to tumble downward, or break (376)

C

caldera a circular depression that forms when a magma chamber empties and causes the ground above to sink (199)

calorie the amount of energy needed to change the temperature of 0.001 kg of water by 1°C; 1 calorie is equivalent to 4.184 J (226)

calorimeter (KAL uh RIM uht uhr) a device used to determine the specific heat capacity of a substance (226)

cardinal directions north, south, east, and west (35)

carnivore a consumer that eats animals (311)

carrying capacity the largest population that a given environment can support over a long period of time (317)

change of state the conversion of a substance from one physical form to another (229)

channel the path a stream follows (251)

chemical change a change that occurs when one or more substances are changed into entirely new substances with different properties; cannot be reversed using physical means (230)

cinder cone volcano a small, steeply sloped volcano that forms from moderately explosive eruptions of pyroclastic material (198)

cirque (suhrk) a bowl-like depression where glacial ice cuts back into mountain walls (291)

cirrus (SIR uhs) **clouds** thin, feathery white clouds found at high altitudes (429)

cleavage (KLEEV ij) the tendency of a mineral to break along flat, parallel surfaces (65)

climate the average weather conditions in a certain area over a long period of time (454)

cloud a collection of millions of tiny water droplets or ice crystals (428)

coal a solid fossil fuel formed underground from buried, decomposed plant material (112)

coevolution (KOH EV uh LOO shuhn) long-term changes that take place in two species because of their close interactions with one another (320)

combustion the burning of fuel; specifically, the process in which fuel combines with oxygen in a chemical change that produces thermal energy (234)

commensalism (kuh MEN suhl iz uhm) a symbiotic relationship in which one organism benefits and the other is unaffected (319)

community all of the populations of different species that live and interact in an area (308)

competition two or more species or individuals trying to use the same limited resource (317)

composite volcano a volcano made of alternating layers of lava and pyroclastic material; also called *stratovolcano* (198)

composition the makeup of a rock; describes either the minerals or elements present in it (85)

compound a pure substance composed of two or more elements that are chemically combined; forms when atoms of two or more different elements become chemically bonded (61)

compression stress that occurs when opposing forces apply pressure to a given material (151)

condensation the change of state from a gas to a liquid (337, 427)

conduction the transfer of thermal energy from one substance to another through direct contact; conduction can also occur within a substance (221, 401)

conductor a substance that conducts thermal energy well (222)

conic projection a map projection that is made by transferring the contents of the globe onto a cone (42)

consumer an organism that eats producers or other organisms for energy (311)

continental drift the theory that continents can drift apart from one another and that they have done so in the past (143)

continental margin the portion of the Earth's surface beneath the ocean that is made of continental crust (340)

continental rise the base of the continental slope (340)

continental shelf the flattest part of the continental margin (340)

continental slope the steepest part of the continental margin (340)

contour interval the difference in elevation between one contour line and the next (47)

contour lines lines that connect points of equal elevation (46)

convection the transfer of thermal energy by the movement of a liquid or a gas (222, 401)

convection current the circular motion of liquids or gases due to density differences that result from temperature differences (222)

convergent boundary the boundary between two colliding tectonic plates (148)

core the central, spherical part of the Earth below the mantle (137)

Coriolis (KOHR ee OH lis) **effect** the turning of moving objects, such as ocean currents or winds, by the Earth's rotation (368, 405)

crater a funnel-shaped pit around the central vent of a volcano (199)

creep the extremely slow movement of material downslope (297)

crest the highest point of a wave (374)

crevasse a large crack that forms where a glacier picks up speed or flows over a high point (289)

crust the thin, outermost layer of the Earth, or the uppermost part of the lithosphere (136)

crystal the solid, geometric form of a mineral produced by a repeating pattern of atoms (61)

cumulus (KYOO myoo luhs) **clouds** puffy, white clouds that tend to have flat bottoms (428)

D

deciduous (dee SIJ oo uhs) describes trees that have leaves that change color in autumn and fall off in winter (464)

decomposer an organism that gets energy by breaking down the remains of dead organisms and consuming or absorbing the nutrients (311)

deep current a streamlike movement of ocean water far below the surface (370)

deep-ocean basin the portion of the Earth's surface beneath the ocean that is made of oceanic crust (340)

deflation the lifting and removal of fine sediment by wind (283)

deformation the change in the shape of rock in response to stress (167)

delta a fan-shaped deposit of sediment at the mouth of a stream where the stream empties into a large body of water (256)

density the amount of matter in a given space; mass per unit volume (66)

deposition the process by which material is dropped or settles (255)

desalination the process of evaporating sea water so that the water and the salt separate (351)

dew point the temperature to which air must cool to be completely saturated (427)

discharge the volume of water transported by a stream in a given amount of time (251)

divergent boundary the boundary between two tectonic plates that are moving away from each other (149)

divide an area of higher ground that separates drainage basins (250)

drainage basin an area drained by a river system, including the main river and all of its tributaries (250)

dune a mound of wind-deposited sand (284)

E

ecology the study of the interactions between organisms and their environment (306)

ecosystem a community of organisms and their nonliving environment (10, 308)

elastic rebound the sudden return of elastically deformed rock to its undeformed shape (167)

element a pure substance that cannot be separated or broken down into simpler substances by ordinary physical or chemical means (60)

elevation the height of surface landforms above sea level; the height of an object above sea level (46, 458)

El Niño a periodic change in the location of warm and cool surface waters in the Pacific Ocean (373)

energy pyramid a diagram shaped like a triangle showing the loss of energy at each level of the food chain (313)

energy resource a natural resource that can be converted by humans into other forms of energy in order to do useful work (111)

epicenter the point on the Earth's surface directly above an earthquake's starting point (172)

equator an imaginary circle halfway between the poles that divides the Earth into the Northern and Southern Hemispheres (37)

erosion the removal and transport of material by wind, water, or ice (248)

evaporation the change from a liquid to a vapor (337)

evergreens trees that keep their leaves year-round (464)

external combustion engine a heat engine that burns fuel outside the engine, such as a steam engine (234)

extrusive (eks TROO siv) the type of igneous rock that forms when lava or pyroclastic material cools and solidifies on the Earth's surface (90)

F

fault a break in the Earth's crust along which blocks of the crust slide relative to one another; due to tectonic forces (153, 166)

fault block a block of the Earth's crust that moves relative to another block along a fault (153)

fault-block mountain a mountain that forms when faulting causes large blocks of the Earth's crust to drop down relative to other blocks (156)

felsic (FEL SIK) describes relatively light-colored, light-weight igneous rocks that are rich in silicon, aluminum, sodium, and potassium (88)

flood plain an area along a river formed from sediments deposited by floods (257)

focus the point inside the Earth where an earthquake begins (172)

fold a type of plastic deformation in rock layers that gives the layers a wavelike appearance (152)

folded mountain a mountain that forms when rock formations bend and fold due to stresses in the Earth's crust (155)

folding the bending of rock layers due to stress caused by movements in the Earth's crust (152)

foliated the texture of metamorphic rock in which the mineral grains are aligned like the pages of a book (98)

food chain a diagram that represents how the energy in food molecules flows from one organism to the next (312)

food web a complex diagram representing the many energy pathways in a real ecosystem (312)

footwall the fault block that is below a fault (153)

fossil fuel a nonrenewable energy resource that forms in the Earth's crust over millions of years from the buried remains of once-living organisms (111)

fracture the tendency of a mineral to break along curved or irregular surfaces (65)

front the boundary that forms between two different air masses (434)

G

gap hypothesis states that sections of active faults that have had relatively few earthquakes are likely to be the sites of strong earthquakes in the future (176)

gasohol a mixture of gasoline and alcohol that is burned as a fuel (124)

gems precious stones of natural origin; rare mineral crystals prized for their beauty and geometric form (71)

geology the study of the solid Earth (6)

geothermal energy energy resulting from the heating of the Earth's crust (125)

glacial drift all material carried and deposited by glaciers (292)

glacier an enormous mass of moving ice (287)

global warming a rise in average global temperatures (18, 402, 472)

gradient a measure of the change in elevation over a certain distance (251)

greenhouse effect the natural heating process of a planet, such as the Earth, by which gases in the atmosphere trap thermal energy (223, 402, 472)

ground water water that is stored in underground caverns or in porous rock below the Earth's surface (258)

H

habitat the environment where an organism lives (314)

hanging valley a small glacial valley that joins the deeper main valley (291)

hanging wall the fault block that is above a fault (153)

hardness the resistance of a mineral to being scratched (66)

heat the transfer of energy between objects that are at different temperatures; the amount of energy that is transferred between two objects that are at different temperatures; energy is always transferred from higher-temperature objects to lower-temperature objects until thermal equilibrium is reached (219)

heat engine a machine that uses heat to do work (234)

herbivore a consumer that eats plants (311)

horn a sharp pyramid-shaped peak that forms when three or more cirques erode a mountain (291)

host an organism on which a parasite lives (320)

hot spot a place on Earth's surface that sits directly above a rising column of magma called a mantle plume (203)

humidity the amount of water vapor or moisture in the air (425)

hurricane a large rotating tropical weather system with wind speeds equal to or greater than 119 km/h (439)

hydroelectric energy electricity produced by falling water (123)

hypothesis a possible explanation or answer to a question (14)

I

ice age a period during which ice collects in high latitudes and moves toward lower latitudes

iceberg a large piece of ice that breaks off an ice shelf and drifts into the ocean (288)

igneous rock rock that forms when magma, lava, or pyroclastic material cools and solidifies (84)

index contour a darker contour line that is usually every fifth line and is labeled by elevation (47)

inner core the solid, dense, spherical center of the Earth (139)

insulation a substance that reduces the transfer of thermal energy (232)

insulator a substance that does not conduct thermal energy well (222)

internal combustion engine a heat engine that burns fuel inside the engine, for example, an automobile engine (234)

intrusive (in TROO siv) the type of igneous rock that forms when magma cools and solidifies beneath Earth's surface (89)

isobars lines that connect points of equal air pressure (445)

J

jet streams narrow belts of high-speed winds that blow in the upper troposphere and the lower stratosphere over both the Northern and Southern Hemispheres (408)

K

karst topography areas where the effects of ground water are noticeable at the surface (262)

kilocalorie the unit of energy equal to 1,000 calories; the kilocalorie can also be referred to as the Calorie, which is the unit of energy listed on food labels (226)

L

landslide a sudden and rapid movement of a large amount of material downslope (295)

latitude the distance north or south from the equator; measured in degrees (37, 455)

lava magma that erupts onto the Earth's surface (84, 194)

lightning the large electrical discharge that occurs between two oppositely charged surfaces (437)

limiting factor a needed resource that is in limited supply (316)

lithosphere the outermost, rigid layer of the Earth that consists of the crust and the rigid, uppermost part of the mantle (138)

load the materials carried in a stream (252)

loess (LOH ESS) thick deposits of windblown, fine-grained sediments (286)

longitude the distance east or west from the prime meridian; measured in degrees (38)

longshore current the movement of water parallel to and near the shoreline (279)

luster the way the surface of a mineral reflects light (64)

M

mafic (MAYF ik) describes relatively dark-colored, heavy igneous rocks that are rich in iron, magnesium, and calcium (88)

magma the hot liquid that forms when rock partially or completely melts; may include mineral crystals (83, 194)

magnetic declination the angle of correction for the difference between geographic north and magnetic north (36)

magnetic reversal the process by which the Earth's north and south magnetic poles periodically change places (146)

mantle the layer of the Earth between the crust and the core (137)

map a model or representation of the Earth's surface (34)

mass the amount of matter that something is made of; its value does not change with the object's location (24)

mass movement the movement of any material downslope (294)

Mercator projection a map projection that results when the contents of the globe are transferred onto a cylinder (41)

mesosphere literally, the "middle sphere"—the rigid, lower part of the mantle between the asthenosphere and the outer core (139); *also* the coldest layer of the atmosphere (398)

metamorphic rock rock that forms when the texture or composition of preexisting rock changes due to heat or pressure (84)

meteorology the study of the entire atmosphere (8)

meter the basic unit of length in the SI system (23)

microclimate a small region with unique climatic characteristics (468)

mid-ocean ridge a long mountain chain that forms on the ocean floor where tectonic plates pull apart; usually extends along the center of ocean basins (145, 341)

mineral a naturally formed, inorganic solid with a crystalline structure (60)

model a representation of an object or system (19)

Moho a place within the Earth where the speed of seismic waves increases sharply; marks the boundary between the Earth's crust and mantle (181)

monocline a fold in sedimentary rock layers in which the layers are horizontal on both sides of the fold (152)

mudflow the rapid movement of a large mass of mud/rock and soil mixed with a large amount of water that flows downhill (296)

mutualism (MYOO choo uhl IZ uhm) a symbiotic relationship in which both organisms benefit (319)

N

natural gas a gaseous fossil fuel (112)

natural resource any natural substance, organism, or energy form that living things use (108)

neap tides tides with minimum daily tidal ranges that occur during the first and third quarters of the moon (382)

nekton (NEK TAHN) free-swimming organisms of the ocean (344)

niche an organism's way of life and its relationships with its abiotic and biotic environment (314)

nonfoliated the texture of metamorphic rock in which mineral grains show no alignment (98)

nonpoint-source pollution pollution that comes from many sources and that cannot be traced to specific sites (263, 354)

nonrenewable resource a natural resource that cannot be replaced or that can be replaced only over thousands or millions of years (109)

nonsilicate mineral a mineral that does not contain compounds of silicon and oxygen (63)

normal fault a fault in which the hanging wall moves down relative to the footwall (153)

nuclear energy the form of energy associated with changes in the nucleus of an atom; an alternative energy resource (118)

O

observation any use of the senses to gather information (14)

oceanography the study of the ocean (7)

ocean trench a deep trough in the deep-ocean basin that forms where one oceanic plate is forced underneath a continental plate or another oceanic plate (341)

omnivore a consumer that eats a variety of organisms (311)

ore a mineral deposit large enough and pure enough to be mined for a profit (70)

outer core the liquid layer of the Earth's core between the mesosphere and the inner core (139)

ozone a gas molecule that is made up of three oxygen atoms and that absorbs ultraviolet radiation from the sun (397)

P

parasite an organism that feeds on another living creature, usually without killing it (320)

parasitism (PAR uh SIET IZ uhm) a symbiotic association in which one organism benefits while the other is harmed (320)

passive solar heating a solar-heating system that relies on thick walls and large windows to use energy from the sun as a means of heating (233)

pelagic (pi LAJ ik) **environment** the entire volume of water in the ocean and the marine organisms that live above the ocean floor; also known as the water environment (347)

permeability (PUHR mee uh BIL uh tee) a rock's ability to let water pass through it (258)

petroleum an oily mixture of flammable organic compounds from which liquid fossil fuels and other products are separated; crude oil (111)

physical change a change that affects one or more physical properties of a substance; most physical changes are easy to undo (229)

plankton very small organisms floating at or near the ocean's surface that form the base of the oceans' food web (344)

plate tectonics the theory that the Earth's lithosphere is divided into tectonic plates that move around on top of the asthenosphere (147)

point-source pollution pollution that comes from one particular source area (263)

polar easterlies wind belts that extend from the poles to 60° latitude in both hemispheres (407)

polar zone the northernmost and southernmost climate zone (466)

population a group of individuals of the same species that live together in the same area at the same time (308)

porosity (poh RAHS uh tee) the amount of open space between individual rock particles (258)

precipitation water in liquid or solid form that moves from the atmosphere to the land and ocean (337, 430)

predator an organism that eats other organisms (318)

prevailing winds winds that blow mainly from one direction (457)

prey an organism that is eaten by another organism (318)

primary pollutants pollutants that are put directly into the air by human or natural activity (411)

prime meridian the line of longitude that passes through Greenwich, England; represents 0° longitude (38)

producer an organism that uses sunlight directly to make sugar (310)

psychrometer an instrument used to measure relative humidity (426)

P waves the fastest type of seismic wave; can travel through solids, liquids, and gases; also known as pressure waves and primary waves (170)

pyroclastic material magma and fragments of rock that are ejected into the atmosphere during a violent volcanic eruption (194)

R

radiation the transfer of energy through space as electromagnetic waves, such as visible light or infrared waves (223, 400)

reclamation the process of returning land to its original state after mining is completed (71)

recycling the use of used or discarded materials that have been reprocessed into new products (110)

reference point a fixed place on the Earth's surface used to describe direction and location (35)

relative humidity the amount of moisture the air contains compared with the maximum amount it can hold at a particular temperature (425)

relief the difference in elevation between the highest and lowest points of an area being mapped (47)

remote sensing gathering information about something without actually being nearby (43)

renewable resource a natural resource that can be used and replaced over a relatively short time (109)

reverse fault a fault in which the hanging wall moves up relative to the footwall (153)

rift a zone of thin, fractured lithosphere that forms between tectonic plates as they separate (202)

rift valley a valley that forms in a rift zone between mountains (341)

rock a naturally formed solid mass made of one or more minerals or noncrystalline materials (80)

rock cycle the continuous process by which one rock type changes into another rock type (82)

rock fall a group of loose rocks that fall down a steep slope (295)

S

salinity a measure of the amount of dissolved solids in a given amount of liquid (334)

saltation the movement of sand-sized particles by a skipping and bouncing action in the direction the wind is blowing (282)

scavenger an animal that feeds on the bodies of dead animals (311)

scientific method a series of steps that scientists use to answer questions and solve problems (13)

scrubber a device that attaches to smokestacks to remove some of the more harmful pollutants before they are released into the air (415)

sea-floor spreading the process by which new oceanic crust forms at mid-ocean ridges as tectonic plates are pulled away from each other (145)

seamount an individual mountain of volcanic material on the abyssal plain (341)

secondary pollutants pollutants that form from chemical reactions that occur when primary pollutants come into contact with other primary pollutants or with naturally occurring substances, such as water vapor (411)

sedimentary rock rock that forms when sediments are compacted and cemented together or when minerals crystallize out of oceans and lakes (84)

seismic (SIEZ mik) **gap** an area along a fault where relatively few earthquakes have occurred (176)

seismic waves waves of energy that travel through the Earth (170)

seismogram a tracing of earthquake motion created by a seismograph (172)

seismograph an instrument located at or near the surface of the Earth that records seismic waves (172)

seismology the study of earthquakes (166)

septic tank a large underground tank that collects and cleans waste water from a household (265)

severe weather weather that causes property damage and possible death (436)

sewage treatment plant a factory that cleans waste materials out of water that comes from sewers or drains (264)

shadow zone an area on the Earth's surface where no direct seismic waves from a particular earthquake can be detected (181)

shield volcano a large, gently sloped volcano that forms from repeated, nonexplosive eruptions of lava (198)

shoreline the boundary between land and a body of water (276)

silica a compound of silicon and oxygen atoms (194)

silicate mineral a mineral that is made mostly of silica, a combination of the elements silicon and oxygen (62)

smog a photochemical fog produced by the action of sunlight on air pollutants (117)

solar energy energy from the sun (119)

specific gravity the ratio of an object's density to the density of water (66)

specific heat capacity the amount of energy needed to change the temperature of 1 kg of a substance by 1°C; specific heat capacity is a characteristic property of a substance (224)

spring tides tides with maximum daily tidal ranges that occur during the new and full moons (382)

states of matter the physical forms in which a substance can exist (228)

station model a small circle showing the location of a weather station along with a set of symbols and numbers surrounding it that represent weather data (444)

storm surge a local rise in sea level near the shore that is caused by strong winds from a storm, such as a hurricane (379)

strata layers of sedimentary rock that form from the deposition of sediment (91)

stratification the layering of sedimentary rock (94)

stratified drift rock material that has been sorted and deposited in layers by water flowing from the melted ice of a glacier (292)

stratosphere the atmospheric layer above the troposphere (397)

stratus (STRAT uhs) **clouds** clouds that form in layers (428)

streak the color of a mineral in powdered form (65)

stress the amount of force per unit area placed on a given material (151)

strike-slip fault a fault in which the two fault blocks move past each other horizontally (154)

strip mining a process in which rock and soil are stripped from the Earth's surface to expose the underlying materials to be mined (115)

subduction zone the region where an oceanic plate sinks down into the asthenosphere at a convergent boundary, usually between continental and oceanic plates (148)

surf the area between the breaker zone and the shore (376)

surface current a streamlike movement of water that occurs at or near the surface of the ocean (367, 459)

S waves the second-fastest type of seismic wave; cannot travel through materials that are completely liquid; also known as shear waves and secondary waves (170)

swells rolling waves that move in a steady procession across the ocean (377)

symbiosis (SIM bie OH sis) a close, long-term association between two or more species (319)

syncline a trough-shaped fold in sedimentary rock layers (152)

T

tectonic plates huge pieces of the lithosphere that move around on top of the asthenosphere (140)

temperate zone the climate zone between the tropics and the polar zone (464)

temperature a measure of how hot (or cold) something is; specifically, a measure of the average kinetic energy of the particles in an object (25, 214)

tension stress that occurs when opposing forces act to stretch a given material (151)

texture the sizes, shapes, and arrangement of particles or grains that a rock is made of (86)

theory a unifying explanation for a broad range of hypotheses and observations that have been supported by testing (19)

thermal energy the total kinetic energy of the particles that make up an object (220)

thermal equilibrium the point at which two objects reach the same temperature; at thermal equilibrium, no net transfer of thermal energy occurs (220)

thermal expansion the increase in volume of a substance due to an increase in temperature (216)

thermal pollution the excessive heating of a body of water (237)

thermocline a layer of ocean water in which water temperature drops with increased depth faster than in other layers of the ocean (335)

thermometer a tool used to measure air temperature (442)

thermosphere the uppermost layer of the atmosphere (398)

thunder the sound that results from the rapid expansion of air along a lightning strike (437)

thunderstorms small, intense storm systems that produce strong winds, heavy rain, lightning and thunder (436)

tidal bore a body of water that rushes up through a narrow bay, estuary, or river channel during the rise of high tide, causing a very sudden tidal rise (383)

tidal range the difference between levels of ocean water at high tide and low tide (382)

tides daily movements of ocean water that change the level of the ocean's surface (380)

till unsorted rock material that is deposited directly by glacial ice when it melts (293)

topographic map a map that shows the surface features of the Earth's surface (46)

tornado a small, rotating column of air with high wind speeds and low central pressure that touches the ground (438)

trade winds the winds that blow from 30° latitude to the equator (406)

transform boundary the boundary between two tectonic plates that are sliding past each other horizontally (149)

tributary a small stream or river that flows into a larger one (250)

tropical zone the warm zone located around the equator (461)

troposphere (TROH poh SFIR) the lowest layer of the atmosphere (397)

trough (trahf) the lowest point of a wave (374)

true north the geographic North Pole (36)

tsunami a wave that forms when a large volume of ocean water is suddenly moved up or down (378)

U

upwelling a near-shore process in which cold, nutrient-rich water from the deep ocean rises to the surface to replace warm surface water that is blown farther out to sea by prevailing winds (373)

U-shaped valley a valley that forms when a glacier flows into and erodes a valley, changing the valley from its original V shape to a U shape (291)

V

vent a hole or crack in the Earth's crust through which magma rises to the surface (194)

volcano a mountain that forms when lava or pyroclastic material builds up around a volcanic vent (194)

volume the amount of space that something occupies or the amount of space that something contains (23)

W

water cycle the continuous movement of water from water sources into the air, onto land, into and over the ground, and back to the water sources (248, 337, 424)

water table an underground boundary where the zone of aeration and the zone of saturation meet (258)

wave height the vertical distance between a wave's crest and its trough (374)

wavelength the distance between one point on a wave and the corresponding point on an adjacent wave in a series of waves; for example, the distance between two adjacent crests or compressions (374)

wave period the time between the passage of two wave crests (or troughs) at a fixed point (375)

weather the condition of the atmosphere at a particular time and place (424, 454)

weather forecast a prediction of future weather conditions (442)

westerlies wind belts found in both the Northern and Southern Hemispheres between 30° and 60° latitude (407)

whitecap a white, foaming wave with a very steep crest that breaks in the open ocean before the wave gets close to the shore (377)

wind moving air (404)

wind energy energy in wind (122)

windsock an instrument used to measure wind direction (443)

wind vane an instrument used to measure wind direction (443)

Index

INDEX

Credits

Abbreviations used: (t) top, (c) center, (b) bottom, (l) left, (r) right, (bkgd) background

ILLUSTRATIONS

All illustrations, unless noted below, by Holt, Rinehart & Winston.

Table of Contents: Page ix(tl), Dan Stuckenschneider/Uhl Studios Inc; (br), Patrick Gnan; x(tr), Stephen Durke/Washington Artists; (bl), Mike Wepplo; xi(b), Will Nelson/Sweet Reps; xii(tl), Yuan Lee; (bl), Marty Roper/Planet Rep; xiiii(tl), Marty Roper/Planet Rep; (b), Dan Stuckenschneider/Uhl Studios Inc.

Chapter One Page 4(br), Barbara Hoopes-Ambler; 7(br), Craig Attebery/Jeff Lavaty; 9(b), David Schleinkofer/Mendola Ltd.; 10(tl), Robert Hynes; 12(b), Barbara Hoopes-Ambler; 14(all), 15(all), 16(tl), 16(cl), Carlyn Iverson; 16(b), 17(b), Christy Krames; 18(all), Dan Stuckenschneider/Uhl Studios Inc; 19(br), Stephen Durke/Washington Artists; 20(c), Jared Schneidman/Wilkinson Studios; 22(all), Stephen Durke/Washington Artists; 23(cl), MapQuest.com; 25(tr), Stephen Durke/Washington Artists; 26(cr), Christy Krames; 27(c), Dan Stuckenschneider/Uhl Studios Inc; 28(cr), Geoff Smith/Scott Hull; 29(cr), Sidney Jablonski; 30(c), Dan Stuckenschneider/Uhl Studios Inc.

Chapter Two Page 35(bl), John White/The Neis Group; 37(all), MapQuest.com; 38(tl), MapQuest.com; 39(all), MapQuest.com; 41(all), MapQuest.com; 42(all), MapQuest.com.

Chapter Three Page 60(bl), Gary Locke/Suzanne Craig; 61(c), Stephen Durke/Washington Artists; 68(bkgd), Dan Stuckenschneider/Uhl Studios Inc; 70(bl), Jared Schneidman/Wilkinson Studios; 72(all), Stephen Durke/Washington Artists.

Chapter Four Page 81(tr), Marty Roper/Planet Rep; 82(all), 83(all), Dan Stuckenschneider/Uhl Studios Inc; 84(c), The Mazer Corporation; 85(all), Sidney Jablonski; 87(all), Keith Locke; 88(l), Dan Stuckenschneider/Uhl Studios Inc; 89(b), Dan Stuckenschneider/Uhl Studios Inc; 90(bl), Geoff Smith/Scott Hull; 91(bl), The Mazer Corporation; 92(bl), Robert Hynes; 96(b), Dan Stuckenschneider/Uhl Studios Inc; 97(c), Stephen Durke/Washington Artists; 97(b), Dan Stuckenschneider/Uhl Studios Inc; 100(br), Sidney Jablonski; 102(bl), Stephen Durke/Washington Artists; 103(cr), Sidney Jablonski.

Chapter Five Page 106(tl), Dan Stuckenschneider/Uhl Studios Inc; 108(b), Dan Stuckenschneider/Uhl Studios Inc; 110(bl), Blake Thornton/Rita Marie; 113(bl), Dan Stuckenschneider/Uhl Studios Inc; 114(all), Dan Stuckenschneider/Uhl Studios Inc; 115(tr), MapQuest.com; 121(tr), John Huxtable; 125(br), Dan Stuckenschneider/Uhl Studios Inc; 126(cr), Dan Stuckenschneider/Uhl Studios Inc; 126(br), John Huxtable; 129(tr), Sidney Jablonski.

Unit Three Page 133(cr), Terry Kovalcik.

Chapter Six Page 136(b), Dan Stuckenschneider/Uhl Studios Inc; 137(br), Dan Stuckenschneider/Uhl Studios Inc; 138(all), Dan Stuckenschneider/Uhl Studios Inc; 139(b), Dan Stuckenschneider/Uhl Studios Inc; 140(t), Dan Stuckenschneider/Uhl Studios Inc; 141(c), Dan Stuckenschneider/Uhl Studios Inc; 142(cl), Dan Stuckenschneider/Uhl Studios Inc; 143(tr), Dan Stuckenschneider/Uhl Studios Inc; 143(cl), MapQuest.com; 143(bl), 143(br), Stephen Durke/Washington Artists; 144(all), MapQuest.com; 145(all), Dan Stuckenschneider/Uhl Studios Inc; 146(cl), Stephen Durke/Washington Artists; 146(cr), Dan Stuckenschneider/Uhl Studios Inc; 147(b), Dan Stuckenschneider/Uhl Studios Inc; 148(b), 149(b), Dan Stuckenschneider/Uhl Studios Inc; 152(all), Dan Stuckenschneider/Uhl Studios Inc; 153(tr), Marty Roper/Planet Rep; 153(cr), Dan Stuckenschneider/Uhl Studios Inc; 153(br), Dan Stuckenschneider/Uhl Studios Inc; 155(tr), Dan Stuckenschneider/Uhl Studios Inc; 156(t), Tony Morse; 156(b), Dan Stuckenschneider/Uhl Studios Inc; 158(all), Dan Stuckenschneider/Uhl Studios Inc; 159(cr), Marty Roper/Planet Rep.

Chapter Seven Page 164(tr), Tony Morse; 166(bl), MapQuest.com; 167(all), 168(all), Dan Stuckenschneider/Uhl Studios Inc; 169(all), Dan Stuckenschneider/Uhl Studios Inc; 170(all), Stephen Durke/Washington Artists; 171(tr), Sidney Jablonski; 171(cl), Stephen Durke/Washington Artists; 172(bl), Dan Stuckenschneider/Uhl Studios Inc; 173(tr), Sidney Jablonski; 175(b), MapQuest.com; 177(t), Jared Schneidman/Wilkinson Studios; 178(all), Dan Stuckenschneider/Uhl Studios Inc; 179(br), Marty Roper/Planet Rep; 181(all), Dan Stuckenschneider/Uhl Studios Inc; 182(all), Sidney Jablonski; 184(c), Stephen Durke/Washington Artists; 184(br), Sidney Jablonski; 186(br), Dan Stuckenschneider/Uhl Studios Inc; 187(cr), Sidney Jablonski.

Chapter Eight Page 194(tl), Dan Stuckenschneider/Uhl Studios Inc; 197(bl), Geoff Smith/Scott Hull; 198(all), Patrick Gnan; 199(tr), Dan Stuckenschneider/Uhl Studios Inc; 200(br), Dan Stuckenschneider/Uhl Studios Inc; 201(tr), Stephen Durke/Washington Artists; 201(br), MapQuest.com; 202(all), 203(all), 204(all), Dan Stuckenschneider/Uhl Studios Inc; 206(br), Dan Stuckenschneider/Uhl Studios Inc; 207(l), Patrick Gnan; 207(cr), Dan Stuckenschneider/Uhl Studios Inc; 209(tr), Ross Culbert & Lavery.

Chapter Nine Page 214(b), Charles Thomas; 215(all), Stephen Durke/Washington Artists; 216(b), Terry Guyer; 217(tr), Dave Joly; 218(all), Dan Stuckenschneider/Uhl Studios Inc; 220(all), Stephen Durke/Washington Artists/Preface Inc.; 221(all), Stephen Durke/Washington Artists/Preface Inc.; 222(bl), Mark Heine; 223(c), Jared Schneidman/Wilkinson Studios; (br), Geoff Smith/Scott Hull, Scott Hull Assoc.; 226(cr), Stephen Durke/Washington Artists; 228(all), Stephen Durke/Washington Artists; 229(b), Preface Inc.; 231(br), Dan Stuckenschneider/Uhl Studios Inc; 232(cr), Dan Stuckenschneider/Uhl Studios Inc; 233(b), Dan Stuckenschneider/Uhl Studios Inc; 234(all), Dan Stuckenschneider/Uhl Studios Inc; 236(c), Dan Stuckenschneider/Uhl Studios Inc; 237(c), Dan Stuckenschneider/Uhl Studios Inc; 238(c), Dave Joly; 240(br), Dan Stuckenschneider/Uhl Studios Inc; 241(cr), Preface Inc.; 243(all), Stephen Durke/Washington Artists.

Unit Four Page 245(tc), MapQuest.com

Chapter Ten: Page 249(bkgd), Mike Wepplo; 250(br), MapQuest.com; 252(all), Dan Stuckenschneider/Uhl Studios Inc; 255(b), Marty Roper/Planet Rep; 258(cl), Stephen Durke/Washington Artists; 258(bl), Geoff Smith/Scott Hull; 259(tl), MapQuest.com; 260(all), Stephen Durke/Washington Artists; 264(b), John Huxtable; 265(tl), John Huxtable; 265(b), Sidney Jablonski; 267(c), MapQuest.com; 268(c), Mike Wepplo; 271(tr), Sidney Jablonski.

Chapter Eleven Page 274(t), Paul DiMare; 278(bl), Dan Stuckenschneider/Uhl Studios Inc; 280(bkgd), 281(bkgd), Mike Wepplo; 281(tr), 282(cl), Keith Locke; 282(b), Dean Fleming; 284(bl), Geoff Smith/Scott Hull; 285(c), Dan Stuckenschneider/Uhl Studios Inc; 288(cr), Sidney Jablonski; 291(bkgd), Robert Hynes; 301(tr), Sidney Jablonski.

Chapter Twelve Page 305(all), David Beck; 306(b), Will Nelson/Sweet Reps; 307(all), Will Nelson/Sweet Reps; 308(b), John White/The Neis Group; 310(b), Will Nelson/Sweet Reps; 312(b), John White/The Neis Group; 313(b), Will Nelson/Sweet Reps; 315(br), Will Nelson/Sweet Reps; 316(bl), Blake Thornton/Rita Marie; 321(cr), Mike Wepplo; 322(cl), Will Nelson/Sweet Reps; 324(br), David Beck; 325(cr), Rob Schuster.

Chapter Thirteen Page 330(t), Rainey Kirk/The Neis Group; 332(all), Geoff Smith/Scott Hull; 333(all), MapQuest.com; 334(tl), Ross Culbert & Lavery; 335(tr), MapQuest.com; 335(b), Ross Culbert & Lavery; 337(bkgd), Mike Wepplo; 338(tl), Sidney Jablonski; 339(cl), Marty Roper/Planet Rep;340(b), 341(b), Dan Stuckenschneider/Uhl Studios Inc; 342(b), Dan Stuckenschneider/Uhl Studios Inc; 343(cr), Craig Attebery/Jeff Lavaty; (br), Ross Culbert & Lavery; 344(all), Yuan Lee; 345(all), 346(all), 347(all), Jared Schneidman/Wilkinson Studios; 352(all), Jared Schneidman/Wilkinson Studios; 355(br), Mark Heine; 358(br), Sidney Jablonski; 360(tr), MapQuest.com; 360(cl), Bill Mayer; 361(tr), Ross Culbert & Lavery.

Chapter Fourteen Page 364(t), John Huxtable; 364(bl), Tony Morse; 366(tr), Dean Fleming; 367(tr), Stephen Durke/Washington Artists; 367(bl), MapQuest.com; 368(all), MapQuest.com; 369(c), MapQuest.com; 370(all), Stephen Durke/Washington Artists; 371(all), Jared Schneidman/Wilkinson Studios; 372(all), MapQuest.com; 374(all), Jared Schneidman/Wilkinson Studios; 375(all), Jared Schneidman/Wilkinson Studios; 376(all), Dean Fleming; 378(cr), Dan Stuckenschneider/Uhl Studios Inc; 379(tr), MapQuest.com; 380(c), Marty Roper/Planet Rep; 381(all), 382(all), Sidney Jablonski; 384(c), Stephen Durke/Washington Artists/Sam Dudgeon/HRW Photo; (bl), Dean Fleming; 385(cr), Marty Roper/Planet Rep; 387(cr), Sidney Jablonski.

Unit Six Page 390(bl), John Huxtable; (br), Annie Bissett; 391(cl), Terry Kovalcik.

Chapter Fifteen Page 394(br), Sidney Jablonski; 395(br), 396(all), 397(cr), 398(all), Stephen Durke/Washington Artists; 400(b), 401(b), Dan Stuckenschneider/Uhl Studios Inc; 402(c), John Huxtable; 404(bl), 405(tr), 406(br), Stephen Durke/Washington Artists; 408(all), 409(all), Stephen Durke/Washington Artists; 411(b), John Huxtable; 415(br), John Huxtable; 417(cl), Stephen Durke/Washington Artists; 419(cr), The Mazer Corporation.

Chapter Sixteen Page 424(b), Robert Hynes; 426(bl), The Mazer Corporation; 429(b), Stephen Durke/Washington Artists; 430(tl), Stephen Durke/Washington Artists; 432(b), MapQuest.com; 434(all), 435(all), Stephen Durke/Washington Artists; 437(tl), 440(b), Paul DiMare; 442(tr), Dan McGeehan/Koralik Associates; 445(cr), MapQuest.com; 449(cr), MapQuest.com.

Chapter Seventeen Page 452(tr), John White/The Neis Group; 455(br), Stephen Durke/Washington Artists; 456(c), Craig Attebery/Jeff Lavaty; 457(tc), Stephen Durke/Washington Artists; 458(b), Dan Stuckenschneider/Uhl Studios Inc; 459(cr), MapQuest.com; 460(cl), Stephen Durke/Washington Artists; 460(b), MapQuest.com; 461(tr), Stephen Durke/Washington Artists; 461(c), MapQuest.com; 461(br), 462(tr), 463(tr), Annie Bissett; 464(tl), Stephen Durke/Washington Artists; 464(c), MapQuest.com; 464(bc), 465(all), 466(tl), Annie Bissett; 466(bl), Stephen Durke/Washington Artists; 467(t), MapQuest.com; 467(br), 468(cl), Annie Bissett; 469(tr), Marty Roper/Planet Rep; 469(bl), MapQuest.com; 470(all), Sidney Jablonski; 471(tl), Dan Stuckenschneider/Uhl Studios Inc; 471(br), MapQuest.com; 472(c), Marty Roper/Planet Rep; 474(cr), Stephen Durke/Washington Artists; 474(bl), Craig Attebery/Jeff Lavaty; 476(tr), Terry Kovalcik; 477(cr), Sidney Jablonski.

LabBook Page 480 (tl), Stephen Durke/Washington Artists; 487(tr), Mark Heine; 488(cl), Marty Roper/Planet Rep; 496(br), Mark Heine; 501(all), Mark Heine; 504(br), Mark Heine; 506(c), Dan Stuckenschneider/Uhl Studios Inc; 514(cl), Sidney Jablonski; 515(c), MapQuest.com; 516(b), MapQuest.com; 518(tl), Marty Roper/Planet Rep; (br), Ralph Garafola; 519(tr), Ralph Garafola; 522(br), Dave Joly; 525(t), Mark Heine; 527(tr), Mark Heine; 537(tr), Blake Thornton/Rita Marie; (br), Lori Anzalone; 538(cr), Dean Fleming; 539(cr), Sidney Jablonski; 541(cr), Geoff Smith/Scott Hull; 544(bc), Mark Heine; 545(b), Sidney Jablonski; 548(br), Mark Heine; 549(tr), Mark Heine; 551(tl), Mark Heine; 554(t), MapQuest.com; 556(tl), Dan McGeehan/Koralik Associates; (br), Mark Heine; 559(cr), Marty Roper/Planet Rep; 562(cr), MapQuest.com; (br), Sidney Jablonski; 563(tl), Sidney Jablonski; (tr), MapQuest.com; (cl), Sidney Jablonski; (cr), MapQuest.com.

Appendix Page 567(cl), Blake Thornton/Rita Marie; 570(t), Terry Guyer; 574(all), Mark Mille/Sharon Langley; 582, 583(all), Kristy Sprott; 584(bl), Stephen Durke/Washington Artists; 585(b), Bruce Burdick.

PHOTOGRAPHY

Cover and Title Page: (tl), Jack Dykinga/Tony Stone Images; (tr), Barry Rosenthal/FPG International; (bl), David Parker/Science Photo Library/Photo Researchers; (br), Geospace/Science Photo Library/Photo Researchers; owl (cover, spine, back, title page) Kim Taylor/Bruce Coleman.

Table of Contents: Page v(tr), E.R. Degginger/Color-Pic, Inc; (cr), K. Segerstrom/USGS; vi (tl), Jean Miele/Stock Market; vii(tr), Mike Husar/DRK (bl), Walter H. Hodge/Peter Arnold; ix(bl), Tom Bean/DRK Photo; xi (tr), Gay Bumgarner/Tony Stone Images; xii(tr), James B. Wood; xii (bl), TOMS/NASA; xix(br), William Manning/Stock Market.

Unit One Page 2(tr), Uwe Fink/University of Arizona, Department of Planetary Sciences, Lunar & Planetary Laboratory; (cl), Ed Reschke/Peter Arnold; (cl), T.A. Wiewandt/DRK Photo; (bl), National Air and Space Museum; (br), K. Segerstrom/USGS; 3(tl), Hulton Getty Images/Liaison International; (tr),